M. L.

STO

ACPL ITEM
DISCARDED

268 T17 v.81,
 1985-86
Tarbell's teachers' guide
 to...Intern.Bible Lessons
 for Christian teaching...

5003402

**DO NOT REMOVE
CARDS FROM POCKET**

ALLEN COUNTY PUBLIC LIBRARY

FORT WAYNE, INDIANA 46802

You may return this book to any agency, branch,
or bookmobile of the Allen County Public Library.

DEMCO

81st Annual Volume
September 1985—August 1986

TARBELL'S
Teacher's Guide
to the International Sunday School Lessons
Includes the RSV and KJV

Edited by WILLIAM P. BARKER

Fleming H. Revell Company
Old Tappan, New Jersey

This volume is based on The International Sunday School Lessons; the International Bible Lessons for Christian Teaching, copyright © 1970 by the Committee on the Uniform Series.

The text of the Revised Standard Version of the Bible and quotations therefrom are copyright 1946 and 1952 by the Division of Christian Education, National Council of Churches, and used by permission.

Unless otherwise identified biblical quotations in the material used by the author to illustrate the lesson are from the Revised Standard Version of the Bible.

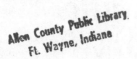
Allen County Public Library.
Ft. Wayne, Indiana

COPYRIGHT © 1985 BY FLEMING H. REVELL COMPANY
All rights reserved—no part of
this book may be reproduced in
any form without permission
in writing from the publisher.

Printed in the United States of America
ISSN: 0730-2622
ISBN: 0-8007-1420-2

CONTENTS

5003402

LIST OF LESSONS
SEPTEMBER–NOVEMBER 1985
THE LETTERS OF PAUL—PART II

5

JUNE–AUGUST 1986
JEREMIAH, EZEKIEL, AND DANIEL

A WORD TO THE TEACHER

"How can I teach a Sunday Church School class?" Have you ever asked this question?

Perhaps you have told yourself (or the minister or the Christian Education Committee or the Sunday-School Superintendent), "But I don't know enough about the Bible! I'm not that good a Christian."

All right, so you have never gone to theological seminary. And you have your share of human weaknesses.

But God delights in using those who are not so learned and not so strong to spread the Gospel. "God chose what is foolish in the world to shame the wise, God chose what is weak in the world to shame the strong" (1 Corinthians 1:27).

And God has chosen *you!*

Let's talk for a moment about your worries about not knowing the Bible. Start to read it. Study it not merely as lesson material for your class for next Sunday, but as God's message to you. Listen to the voice of the Spirit through the words of Scripture!

Don't look for gimmicks. Don't ask for shortcuts. Beware of those who offer neatly packaged tricks to make the Bible "easy." These almost always end by substituting human wisdom for God's Word. Paul warned, "We refuse to practice cunning or to tamper with God's word" (2 Corinthians 4:2).

Let's also talk about your commitment as a Christian. Are you dedicating yourself again to the Lord each day? Are you growing in your own faith?

In a church in London, a bronze tablet carries the words, "Here God laid His hands on William Booth." (William Booth was the valiant Christian who ministered to the helpless and hopeless in English slums and founded the Salvation Army.) One day, a man came into that church and stood a long time in front of that bronze tablet. The time came when the church was to be closed for the day, and the caretaker walked up to the man. The man begged for another minute. The caretaker impatiently stood aside. As he waited, he overheard the man praying. The man pleaded, "O God, do it again!" The man was William Booth.

God has laid His hands on you. Do you remember? Perhaps it was years ago. Perhaps it was recently. Pray. Pray daily. Pray, "O Lord, do it again!"

With the empowering Presence of the Risen Lord, you will be a master teacher! For—you are the Master's. You will have my prayers during this teaching year.

Your colleague in His ministry always,
William P. Barker

81st Annual Volume
September 1985—August 1986

TARBELL'S
Teacher's Guide
to the International Sunday School Lessons
Includes the RSV and KJV

SEPTEMBER, OCTOBER, NOVEMBER 1985

THE LETTERS OF PAUL—PART II

LESSON I—SEPTEMBER 1

CHRIST, THE FULNESS OF GOD

Background Scripture: Colossians 1; 2
Devotional Reading: Colossians 1:21–29

KING JAMES VERSION

COLOSSIANS 1 15 Who is the image of the invisible God, the firstborn of every creature:

16 For by him were all things created, that are in heaven, and that are in earth, visible and invisible, whether *they be* thrones, or dominions, or principalities, or powers: all things were created by him, and for him:

17 And he is before all things, and by him all things consist:

18 And he is the head of the body, the church: who is the beginning, the firstborn from the dead; that in all things he might have the preeminence.

19 For it pleased *the Father* that in him should all fulness dwell;

20 And, having made peace through the blood of his cross, by him to reconcile all things unto himself; by him, *I say,* whether *they be* things in earth, or things in heaven.

2 8 Beware lest any man spoil you through philosophy and vain deceit, after the tradition of men, after the rudiments of the world, and not after Christ.

9 For in him dwelleth all the fulness of the Godhead bodily.

10 And ye are complete in him, which is the head of all principality and power:

REVISED STANDARD VERSION

COLOSSIANS 1 15 He is the image of the invisible God, the first-born of all creation; 16 for in him all things were created, in heaven and on earth, visible and invisible, whether thrones or dominions or principalities or authorities—all things were created through him and for him. 17 He is before all things, and in him all things hold together. 18 He is the head of the body, the church; he is the beginning, the first-born from the dead, that in everything he might be pre-eminent. 19 For in him all the fulness of God was pleased to dwell, 20 and through him to reconcile to himself all things, whether on earth or in heaven, making peace by the blood of his cross.

2 8 See to it that no one makes a prey of you by philosophy and empty deceit, according to human tradition, according to the elemental spirits of the universe, and not according to Christ. 9 For in him the whole fulness of deity dwells bodily, 10 and you have come to fulness of life in him, who is the head of all rule and authority.

KEY VERSE: *He is the head of the body, the church; he is the beginning, the first-born from the dead, that in everything he might be pre-eminent.* Colossians 1:18.

HOME DAILY BIBLE READINGS

Aug.	26.	M.	*A Faithful, Loving Church.* Colossians 1:1–8.
Aug.	27.	T.	*Grounded in God's Will.* Colossians 1:9–14.
Aug.	28.	W.	*Christ the Image of God.* Colossians 1:15–23.
Aug.	29.	T.	*Christ the Hope of Glory.* Colossians 1:24–29.
Aug.	30.	F.	*Christ the Focus of Faith.* Colossians 2:1–7.
Aug.	31.	S.	*Christ the Giver of Life.* Colossians 2:8–15.
Sept.	1.	S.	*The Error of Excessive Ritualism.* Colossians 2:16–23.

BACKGROUND

Paul's letters make up the largest section of the New Testament. The letter to the Colossians is one of these pieces of correspondence. Paul, however, never wrote simply to pen "great literature." His writings were in response to a particular situation. The conditions in the Church at Colossae are a case in point.

Colossae was located in the midst of Greek thought and culture. Greek philosophy had a seductive quality about it. It had a certain sophistication and appeal. Greek intellectuals loved to discuss its ideas. Clever deductions were often made. In Colossae, some of these notions were seeping into the thinking and the teaching of Christian leaders. Many of these ideas eventually grew into what the Christian Church finally pronounced heresy.

For example, a type of thought known as Gnosticism taught that there were two entities, spirit and matter. Anything that is matter, however, was believed to be flawed and inherently evil. God, according to the Gnostics, would have nothing to do with impure material stuff. Therefore, anyone flirting with Gnostic ideas found themselves playing down the Incarnation (the Christian teaching that God was enfleshed in the human Jesus). Out of this thinking came the heresy called Docetism (Docetism comes from the Greek word *to seem*). These folks taught that Jesus only seemed to have a body. Docetism held that Jesus was merely a kind of phantom.

Many who tried to follow both the way of the Gnostics and the way of Christians also perverted the Apostles's teaching about who Christ was by denying Jesus' uniqueness and divinity. These heretics insisted that Jesus was merely one of a string of "emanations" between humans and God, perhaps the greatest, but in the long run simply another intermediary.

Paul saw at once that these false ideas undercut the claims of Jesus and His followers. If allowed to go unchallenged, Paul realized that Jesus would be reduced to the level of merely being one more fine teacher rather than the complete revelation of the fulness of God. The Gnostics and Docetists, Paul knew, had an attractive logic and certain superspiritual appeal. But he also knew that if allowed to prevail, such teachings would pervert the Gospel and destroy the Church!

NOTES ON THE PRINTED TEXT

If you were to start at the second chapter of Colossians, it would be obvious that Paul is responding to a heresy damaging to the Christian faith. News of the heresy has been brought to Paul by Epaphras, and Paul responds to the false teaching by writing to the Colossians. Although the first chapter initially appears to have nothing to say against the false teaching, in actuality, an important doctrinal section sets forth the preeminence and glory of Christ by adapting the words of an early Christian hymn.

He is the image of the invisible God, Paul insists. Jesus is not one of the "emanations" coming from God as the Gnostics taught. Rather, Christ is unique! He is the image of God. *Image* stands for the embodiment of God. Christ enables all persons to see and know God. Paul is convinced the Colossians will not find God in a world of vague visions or deep thoughts. God is met in the specific flesh and blood person of Jesus Christ.

He was *the first-born of all creation.* The Gnostics maintained Jesus was only one in a steady growing line of emanations descending from God to man. However, Paul stresses that Jesus is the most honored and favored Son of God and to Him belongs the highest honor in all creation. As Lord, He has no rival in creation.

In him all things were created. Paul shatters the Gnostic belief that the series of emanations, or angels as some insisted, simply included Jesus. Jesus created them,

Paul insists. In fact, *all things were created through him and for him.* He is the Agent through whom all came into being. He is the ultimate goal of creation. Jesus is the Creator, the Sustainer, and the End of all things. He is the glue that holds all things together.

As Lord and Ruler of all creation, Jesus is also *the head of the body, the church.* He stands over the community of believers. *He is the beginning.* Christ brought salvation to the redeemed community, the Church. The salvation the Colossians experience finds its roots, its very beginning, in Christ. He is *the first-born from the dead.* The Church (the earliest name for it was the Resurrection Community) has its foundations in Christ's Resurrection. His Resurrection established this community. It established this body. All this is done so that Christ *might be pre-eminent. For in him all fulness of God was pleased to dwell.* Writing against the Gnostic thought, Paul asserts the superiority and finality of the Christian belief centering in Christ. The Gnostics believed the various attributes of God were distributed among the various emanations. Paul flatly rejects that belief. No intermediaries can exist. God is seen in Jesus. God's love and care is demonstrated in Christ. God expressed His love for the Colossians through Jesus.

Through Jesus, God's purpose is seen. He is God's agent of reconciliation. All things *whether on earth or in heaven* are brought together in peace. No area of the universe is beyond His reach, nor is there any power or force beyond His control.

Paul pinpoints the false teaching at Colossae and attacks it. He warns against being taken in by philosophy which he labels empty deceit. Paul's warning literally calls on Christians to be on their guard lest they be kidnapped or carried off. The false teaching is *according to human tradition.* More serious, though, Paul warns against a belief in the *elemental spirits of the universe.* The false doctrine taught that these intermediary spirit beings controlled the planets and determined access to God. Again, Paul reiterates Christ's preeminence. In Christ, not in the intermediaries, is God's fulness seen. God is in Christ. He dwells in Jesus. Having Him, the believers have obtained fulness of life.

SUGGESTIONS TO TEACHERS

"What's a 'Unitarian'?" asked the college freshman.

"Why are you asking?" replied the chaplain.

"Well, some of the kids say that only Unitarianism makes sense."

The chaplain answered, "There are many fine people who are Unitarian, but your real question is 'Who is Jesus Christ?' "

"What do you mean?" stammered the student.

"Exactly what does Jesus mean to you? That's the central issue you must face."

This is what you as teacher must help your class to face during these next two lessons. You must guide your class presentation and discussion to focus on the person of Jesus Christ. Today, considering the ways that Christ is the "Fulness of God" suggested in Colossians 1 and 2, you will find more than enough material. Here are a few ideas. Remember that they are intended to help your class consider who Jesus Christ is.

1. *FORM OF THE FATHER.* Colossians 1:15 speaks of Christ being the "image of the invisible God." Perhaps a modern way of putting that would be to say that Jesus Christ is the photo of the Father. We can picture who God is and what God is like when we encounter Jesus.

2. *FOCUS OF THE FOUNDATION.* Paul writes of Jesus Christ being the "first-born of all creation" (and the one in whom "all things hold together" Colossians 1:15, 17). Paul insists that Jesus gives purpose, direction, and cohesion to every thing and event in the universe. Ask if your class agrees. If not Jesus Christ,

how else can all things hold together in one's personal life, or in a community?

3. *FOUNDER OF THE FAMILY.* Remind the class that Jesus Christ alone is the Head of the Church and the Foundation of the faith. Were it not for Jesus Christ, we would not be part of that family known as the Church. In fact, would we know much about God if the news of Jesus had not been passed on to us by His Church?

4. *FORERUNNER OF THE FUTURE.* As "the first-born from the dead," Jesus Christ assures us of a resurrection for the faithful in time to come. Your class may wish to ponder the fact that only Jesus Christ can grant assurance that God is able to cope with death. The Risen Lord is God's promise of resurrection for us.

5. *FULFILLER OF THE FAITH.* Press your class to think about the claims Paul makes for Jesus Christ: "In him, all the fulness of God was pleased to dwell" (Colossians 1:19). Paul (and Christian believers for centuries) insists that Jesus is more than the noblest leader, boldest prophet, greatest guru, or the best this or finest that. Have your class share candidly what each thinks of Jesus and why.

6. *FRIEND TO THE FALLEN.* Allow enough time in the lesson to let the class reflect on the claim that Jesus brings reconciliation. Read Colossians 1:20–23 and 2:13, 14 again. Where are areas in which reconciliation is needed in your community? In the personal lives of people in your church? How may you and your class members share Christ's reconciling love?

TOPIC FOR ADULTS
CHRIST, THE FULNESS OF GOD

Thousand Words About Jesus. Dr. George A. Buttrick, the scholarly minister at Madison Avenue Presbyterian Church for many years, once was asked to write a brief biography of Jesus for a magazine. The editors told Buttrick that the article had to be a thousand words and no longer. Buttrick acknowledged that he was greatly perplexed about what to include and what to leave out of the article. Knowing how much there was to tell about Jesus, it bothered him deeply to have to omit parts of the story about Him and to have to decide what parts were more important than others.

Suppose you were asked to write a 1,000-word article on Jesus. What would you say about Him? Who is He to you? Why?

He Sees You. L. Cardinal Suenens recounts a true story about a family whose home caught fire in the middle of the night. The parents woke their children and quickly let them out. The five-year-old, however, slipped away and ran back upstairs. It wasn't until they were outside that they saw him in a second-story window surrounded by smoke. The boy's father yelled, "Jump and I'll catch you!"

"But Daddy," the child protested, "I can't see you."

The father cried, "But I can see you and that's all that matters. Jump!"

We may say that we cannot see God. We may seem surrounded with problems and disillusionment. But God can see us. This we know through Jesus Christ. In the person of Jesus, God makes Himself known as One who sees and cares and saves!

Sound of Praise to Someone. Katherine Mansfield was a gifted writer who drifted into agnosticism. She recited all the reasons why she could not accept or trust God. One summer, however, she spent an afternoon in a lovely place in the Swiss Alps. Delighted at the experience, she wrote, "If only one could make some small grasshoppery sound of praise to someone—but to whom?"

Poor Kate Mansfield! She never took seriously the claim that Jesus is the One to whom she could make her "small grasshoppery sound of praise."

How about you? Have you learned personally that in Jesus all the fulness of God was present?

Questions for Pupils on the Next Lesson. 1. Who have been the most significant role models in your life? 2. In what ways are you aware that you are serving as a role model for others? 3. How does thinking of things worthy of praise help people experience the peace of God? 4. How does God's love provide security? 5. Is Paul's goal of seeking to be like Christ valid for us?

TOPIC FOR YOUTH
AN EXACT LIKENESS

Looking in Wrong Place. The German comedian, Karl Valentin, used to do a skit in Munich which always brought laughs.

The curtain goes up and reveals darkness; and in this darkness is a solitary circle of light thrown by a street lamp. Valentin, with his long-drawn and deeply worried face, walks around and around this circle of light, desperately looking for something.

"What have you lost?" a policeman asks who has entered the scene.

"The key to my house."

Upon which the policeman joins him in his search; and they find nothing; and after a while, he inquires, "Are you sure you lost it here?"

"No," says Valentin, and pointing to a dark corner of the stage: "Over there."

"Then why on earth are you looking for it here?"

"There is no light over there," says Valentin.

Perhaps this is the way it is with you in your search for God. You may be looking in the wrong place! You will find Him not in the harsh glare of pleasure, nor in the garish glow of success. God will be discovered in the shadows of the birth in the stable and the death on the Cross. In the person of Jesus Christ, we learn that here is the fulness of God dwelling with you.

No NIMBY Answer for God. The members of the Sierra Club have a word which they use for a person who is an unpaid organizer of an environmental group through protesting some unwanted intrusion into his community. This term is a *NIMBY. NIMBY* stands for "Not In My Back Yard."

A lot of people are religious NIMBY's. They think that God would not or could not come into their back yards. These folks imagine God to be distant and disinterested.

God came among us! Right into our own back yards. Yes, in the person of Jesus, all the fulness of God is known.

Atheist to Advocate. William Murray was raised an atheist by his mother, Madalyn Murray O'Hair. He was a key part in her noisy campaigns against Christianity. In 1963, as a Baltimore teenager, William Murray was the plaintiff of record in his mother's lawsuit that resulted in the United States Supreme Court decision banning group prayer and Bible reading in public schools. However, Murray says now that his life of atheism was "a life of misery."

"It left me with no sense of purpose, like a flea on a dog's back. Nothing made any difference, no matter what you did. There were no rules, no absolutes of right and wrong, no order in the universe, no meaning to life. I couldn't handle the negativism," Murray states. "I was in bad shape," he adds. "It nearly destroyed me."

The anti-God life, he said, was one of "constant conflict and inner chaos. It's a philosophy of dog-eat-dog, survival of the fittest. There's no universal moral code, no Ten Commandments. Everybody sets their own rules and tries to impose their own wills. That's what causes the conflict. It was sheer narcissism and self-gratification. The devout atheist is really playing God. You've got to have a lot of faith to believe there's nothing greater than yourself." For him, he said, it was increasingly "self-destructive. I drank heavily and took a lot of tranquilizers. The years I worked at the atheist center nearly destroyed me. By the time I left in 1977 I knew there was a God."

But his deeper conversion didn't come until 1980, he said, sparked initially by attending Alcoholics Anonymous meetings where prayer and dependence on a "higher power" are part of the program.

He said he was helped in his new outlook by numerous people but he credits studying the Bible "for at least 75 percent" of his change of heart. "This book was real to me. It turned me around.

"I came to know the God of the Trinity—God, Son, and Holy Spirit. I came to a personal relationship with Jesus Christ."

Questions for Pupils on the Next Lesson. 1. Who are your favorite role models, and why? 2. What are the marks of a mature person? 3. How can Jesus Christ enable you to grow to social, intellectual, spiritual, and emotional maturity? 4. How does a Christian handle anxiety? 5. How has your faith in Jesus Christ given you a closer relationship to God?

LESSON II—SEPTEMBER 8

CHRIST, OUR GUIDE TO MATURITY

Background Scripture: Philippians 3; 4
Devotional Reading: Philippians 4:10–13

KING JAMES VERSION

PHILIPPIANS 3 13 Brethren, I count not myself to have apprehended: but *this* one thing *I do*, forgetting those things which are behind, and reaching forth unto those things which are before,

14 I press toward the mark for the prize of the high calling of God in Christ Jesus.

15 Let us therefore, as many as be perfect, be thus minded: and if in any thing ye be otherwise minded, God shall reveal even this unto you.

16 Nevertheless, whereto we have already attained, let us walk by the same rule, let us mind the same thing.

17 Brethren, be followers together of me, and mark them which walk so as ye have us for an ensample.

18 (For many walk, of whom I have told you often, and now tell you even weeping, *that they are* the enemies of the cross of Christ:

19 Whose end *is* destruction, whose God *is their* belly, and *whose* glory *is* in their shame, who mind earthly things.)

20 For our conversation is in heaven; from whence also we look for the Saviour, the Lord Jesus Christ:

21 Who shall change our vile body, that it may be fashioned like unto his glorious body, according to the working whereby he is able even to subdue all things unto himself.

4 Therefore, my brethren dearly beloved and longed for, my joy and crown, so stand fast in the Lord, *my* dearly beloved.

4 Rejoice in the Lord alway: *and* again I say, Rejoice.

5 Let your moderation be known unto all men. The Lord *is* at hand.

6 Be careful for nothing; but in every thing by prayer and supplication with thanksgiving let your requests be made known unto God.

7 And the peace of God, which passeth all understanding, shall keep your hearts and minds through Christ Jesus.

8 Finally, brethren, whatsoever things are true, whatsoever things *are* honest, whatsoever things *are* just, whatsoever things *are* pure, whatsoever things *are* lovely, whatsoever things *are* of good report; if *there be* any virtue, and if *there be* any praise, think on these things.

9 Those things, which ye have both learned, and received, and heard, and seen in me, do: and the God of peace shall be with you.

REVISED STANDARD VERSION

PHILIPPIANS 3 13 Brethren, I do not consider that I have made it my own; but one thing I do, forgetting what lies behind and straining forward to what lies ahead, 14 I press on toward the goal for the prize of the upward call of God in Christ Jesus. 15 Let those of us who are mature be thus minded; and if in anything you are otherwise minded, God will reveal that also to you. 16 Only let us hold true to what we have attained.

17 Brethren, join in imitating me, and mark those who so live as you have an example in us. 18 For many, of whom I have often told you and now tell you even with tears, live as enemies of the cross of Christ. 19 Their end is destruction, their god is the belly, and they glory in their shame, with minds set on earthly things. 20 But our commonwealth is in heaven, and from it we await a Savior, the Lord Jesus Christ, 21 who will change our lowly body to be like his glorious body, by the power which enables him even to subject all thing to himself.

4 Therefore, my brethren, whom I love and long for, my joy and crown, stand firm thus in the Lord, my beloved.

4 Rejoice in the Lord always; again I will say, Rejoice. 5 Let all men know your forbearance. The Lord is at hand. 6 Have no anxiety about anything, but in everything by prayer and supplication with thanksgiving let your requests be made known to God. 7 And the peace of God, which passes all understanding, will keep your hearts and your minds in Christ Jesus.

8 Finally, brethren, whatever is true, whatever is honorable, whatever is just, whatever is pure, whatever is lovely, whatever is gracious, if there is any excellence, if there is anything worthy of praise, think about these things. 9 What you have learned and received and heard and seen in me, do; and the God of peace will be with you.

KEY VERSE: *Have no anxiety about anything, but in everything by prayer and supplication with thanksgiving let your requests be made known to God. And the*

19

peace of God, which passes all understanding, will keep your hearts and your minds in Christ Jesus. Philippians 4:6, 7.

HOME DAILY BIBLE READINGS

Sept. 2. M. Paul's Past Accomplishments. Philippians 3:1–6.
Sept. 3. T. Rejoice in the Lord. Philippians 3:7–11.
Sept. 4. W. Pressing Toward the Mark. Philippians 3:12–16.
Sept. 5. T. Remaining True. Philippians 3:17–22.
Sept. 6. F. Cooperating and Rejoicing. Philippians 4:1–7.
Sept. 7. S. Life's Focus and Strength. Philippians 4:8–13.
Sept. 8. S. A Mature Fellowship. Philippians 4:14–23.

BACKGROUND

Paul's letter to his Christian friends at Philippi is both a "thank-you" letter and a "love-note." Paul probably felt closer to the Philippian Church than any other. He had no clashes with them. He didn't have to help them resolve thorny problems. Instead, he was able to write an intimate letter as a dear friend.

Paul was touched by the generous gift of money the Philippians had sent him. He was in prison. He appreciated the money because it made it possible for him to buy a few little comforts which he otherwise never could have had in captivity. More important, he was grateful because the Philippian Christians' present of that purse represented their love, thoughts, prayers, and interest. The graciousness of those givers, Paul believed, reflected the grace of Christ, *the* Giver.

Not that Paul just had to have those minor luxuries which the gift permitted him to get. He makes it clear without belittling the gift or offending the givers that he has grown in his faith enough to have a sense of contentment in whatever circumstances he may find himself. Christ, Paul gently reminds the Philippians, is sufficient. With Jesus Christ, Paul has everything!

The gracious tone and kind words throughout the letter to the Christian Church members at Philippi make this epistle a masterpiece. Paul, however, sensitively urges his readers to keep on maturing in the faith. Without coming down on the Philippians harshly, he warns them about the legalistic mentality from certain Judaizers making the rounds of the churches. Paul reminds the Philippian Christians of his own Jewish background. He nudges them to realize that they as he have been privileged to leave behind the rule-keeping past in order to "gain Christ." Trying to get right with God by keeping rules is futile. Paul, out of personal experience, points his beloved associates in Philippi to trust in Christ, through whom God has made us right with Himself. Paul also joyfully testifies how Christ, the Guide to maturity, frees His followers from anxiety to a peace which steadies them in the worst of times and places!

NOTES ON THE PRINTED TEXT

In Philippians, Paul issues a warning against the Jewish propagandists and gently rebukes the perfectionists who are a part of the Philippian Church. However, he becomes quite severe when he addresses his comments to the sensualists and the materialists found in the church.

I press on toward the goal for the prize of the upward call of God in Christ Jesus. Many believers in the church were directing their efforts towards goals not worthy of their efforts. Paul suggests that a goal worthy of their strivings would be to try and be like Christ. To explain this, he plays on an athletic image. He compares life to a race. Just as a runner in a race directs his attention toward the finish line, so must a Christian in his life set his sights toward Christ. Press on in life's race so that at the end (of life), your name may be listed among the victors.

Let those of us who are mature be thus minded. Mature Christians are like seasoned athletes. They continue on and do not quit. Though discouraged and impatient, they remember to press on.

Brethren, join in imitating me, and mark those who so live as you have an example in us. Paul holds up his own life as an example to follow. He urges his brothers to in turn be examples to those around them. The Philippians must live, literally walk, as Christ calls them to do. Their conduct must reflect their commitment to Him. For any Philippian who might waver in his commitment, Paul summons him to look to Paul's life and conduct for an example. Paul tells them to turn away from the false teachers who are providing the wrong example. Paul makes this appeal tearfully since some Christians had shown themselves to be *enemies of the cross of Christ*. These Christians felt that being liberated from sin meant living as they chose and abandoning all principles. However, Paul reminds these people that their liberal conduct will only bring destruction to them. Excessive eating and drinking and sexual immorality by those *who glory in their shame* will result in their destruction. For these people have set their minds on things of the earth. Paul feels that their conduct has not refelected their call to live as Christ's people but rather as enemies of the cross.

But our commonwealth is in heaven. It must be remembered that the Philippians were living in a Roman colony or commonwealth. Though a Grecian city, Philippi was Roman in all other ways: in government, language, morals, and dress. However, Paul calls on the Philippians to reject this earthly, materialistic, sensual commonwealth and direct themselves to the heavenly community. The Jewish propagandists, the sensualists, and the materialists are wrong because they seek to tie religion to outward and material things. Christianity is a spiritual religion that frees people from slavery to things on earth. It makes them citizens of a heavenly colony. It assures them that they will be united with Christ in the future.

Therefore, my brethen . . . stand firm. Paul reminds the Philippians of their true allegiance. The dangers of false teaching are real to Christ's people. However, by holding fast to the true faith, they can emerge victors. Wear the victor's *crown* proudly, Paul exhorts.

Paul reiterates his plea to imitate him. *What you have learned and received and seen in me, do.* The Philippians had seen Paul's example when he lived among them. In spite of physical weakness, temptations, and persecution, his faith showed in his words and works. Paul calls the Philippians to remember his example. *And the God of peace will be with you.* God's peace is available to all. If they live as Christians are called to do, living a life worthy of praise, then they will experience God's peace.

SUGGESTIONS TO TEACHERS

A young man was being considered for an appointment to Naval Intelligence. He was a splendid physical specimen, having won letters in wrestling and awards in weightlifting. He was above average in intelligence, and had graduated near the top of his class in a leading southern university. However, when Navy people interviewed persons who had known him at home and at school, they kept hearing comments like, "He's got to grow up yet" and, "Still acts like a kid." Needless to say, these reports of the young man's immaturity kept him from a career with Naval Intelligence.

How does a person "grow up" emotionally and spiritually? This is the subject of today's lesson.

New Testament writers insist that Jesus Christ is our guide to maturity. You may wish to start the lesson discussion by asking people in your class to list the marks of a mature person. Or, you may suggest that they describe the most mature personality they each have known, and to tell why they feel this person is mature. Work the discussion around to comparing their lists with what Paul has to say on the subject in Philippians 3; 4. You will note that he suggests that Christ is our Guide to growing up in at least four ways.

1. *CLARIFIES OUR PURPOSE.* Throughout these chapters, we learn that Jesus Christ must be the center of our lives. When He is, we have a sense of direction. We are able to remain stable in a situation of instability.

Ask those in your class the blunt question: What are they living for? Where do they find meaning in their daily lives? A hobby? Sports? Activities? Job? Family? Remind them that these fail to confer the purpose to life which Jesus Christ promises.

2. *CONQUERS OUR PRIDE.* You may comment on the way in which Paul points out that he can not pat himself on the back for his own personal status or accomplishments which actually are better than others when he remembers Jesus Christ. Nor can any of us. Jesus pares our gigantic egos down to size. The mature person has a proper estimate of his or her own place and will not glorify himself or herself. The living Lord has conquered us. Paul states simply, "Christ Jesus has made me his own" (Philippians 3:12). Therefore, we boast not about ourselves but about His goodness and greatness!

3. *CONVEYS HIS POWER.* Consider the shaky setting for Paul's career. In fact, the Philippian letter was written while he was a prisoner with little hope of freedom. Paul, however, felt the steadying presence of the Risen Christ. Ask whether your people can truthfully state at the close of this past week, "Not that I complain of want; for I have learned, in whatever state I am, to be content. . . . I can do all things in him who strengthens me" (4:11, 13).

4. *COMMUNICATES HIS PERSONALITY.* Return to the list of personality traits of the mature person which you asked your class to prepare earlier. How do these square with Paul's list in Philippians 4:8? Aren't these the qualities of Jesus Christ Himself? Are your people learning to "think about *these* things"?

TOPIC FOR ADULTS
CHRIST, OUR GUIDE TO MATURITY

Maturity in the Face of Loss. Wilma Voth had married her husband, Carl, after her second year of college. She helped put Carl through college and Princeton Theological Seminary. When Carl was ordained and undertook pastoral responsibilities, Wilma worked closely with him. Together, they enjoyed a useful life. Carl's death came as a jolt. Only fifty-four, he had always been strong and active. Cancer took him in five months.

Wilma cried a great deal at first. Part of her weeping was for herself because she knew she'd have to move out of the house because it belonged to the church. She didn't know where to go or how to plan the future. "Friends are important," says Mrs. Voth, "but they soon tire of your story." The unresolved feelings of grief, anger, fear, guilt, and depression brought her suffering.

Wilma Voth, daughter of Mennonite wheat-farming people in Kansas, discovered for herself that Christ is the Guide to maturity. She returned to school and received her degree nearly thirty-three years after leaving college, then went on to take a Master's in Social Work. Later, working with cancer patients and their families in the Vassar Brothers Hospital in Poughkeepsie, New York, Wilma Voth saw an opportunity to minister in Christ's name. Remembering her own hurt and anxiety as a widow, and also realizing the maturity Christ brings, she organized a widows' support group. She searched the hospital's medical records during the previous two years and located women who had lost husbands. From that first widows' mutual support group, three others have been established.

Christ guides us to mature ways of handling the worst of our problems, as Mrs. Voth learned in person!

Being Like the Real Thing. Sir Alec Guinness, the great actor, is a devout Christian and active church member. Although a nominal Anglican, he was for many years "anti-clerical, agnostic certainly, if not atheistic." But he found himself being drawn back to the Church. The moment of his conversion, however, came while he was filming one night in the middle of France. He was dressed as a priest. He had changed into his priest costume about a mile and half from the small mountaintop village where the filming was taking place. He had been told to report at 10 P.M., but when he got there he was informed he'd not be needed for several hours.

"So I turned and started to walk away. It was getting dark and suddenly I heard footsteps behind me. There I was in this cassock and it was a small boy, age seven to eight, and he pattered along. He must have seen I was not a familiar figure. I mean, I wasn't his local priest. But he took my hand and held my hand all the way down, prattling away. I didn't dare answer him in case my appalling French frightened him.

"Suddenly, with a 'Bonsoir, mon pere,' he disappeared into a hedge. Sweet little kid. And I thought, my God . . . I changed my attitude at that very moment because, I thought, a religion that can provide whoever is wearing that particular robe with (an air of comforting security) so that a kid in the night knows that he's a perfectly safe person to run up and take his hand to prattle with, has got more to it than I had credited it."

That night in the French village Alec Guinness turned his life over to Jesus Christ, his personal Guide for maturity.

Restless and Immature. Jack London, the author of fifty-two books and many short stories, lived a life of adventure and apparent success. He became an expert seaman, shipping aboard a seal-hunting vessel in the North Atlantic, Later, in 1897, he joined the gold rush to the Yukon. After his first triumph in print, *The Call of the Wild,* he was acclaimed a major cultural figure. A series of books and stories followed. Jack London became wealthy. His writings earned him more than a million dollars. He covered the Russo-Japanese War as a correspondent, sailed his own boat to the South Pacific, won great recognition. At the same time, London suffered terrible, black moods of depression and self-destruction, frequently driving him to drink to a point of collapse. He even tried to commit suicide at least once. He married, divorced, remarried, separated. Although he had two lovely daughters, status, fame, money, and accomplishments of every kind, he could not find the key to mature living. He died at the age of forty, in debt, in California, in 1916.

Without Jesus Christ to guide us to maturity, we seem to find ourselves restless and driven. Our fame and fortunes do not seem to be able to help us to cope or to grow. Jesus Christ is our true Guide to mature living.

Questions for Pupils on the Next Lesson. 1. Why do we sometimes seek a greater unity to resolve the contradictory forces in our lives? 2. Do you long to make some worthwhile contribution somewhere? 3. Why is there a desire among so many for a reconciliation among warring intercultural groups? 4. What is Paul's notion of God's unfolding purpose in Christ in Ephesians? 5. What does Paul mean when he speaks of Christian believers as the "temple"?

TOPIC FOR YOUTH
PATTERN FOR MATURITY

Most Courageous Athlete. Andre Thornton experienced a tragedy in 1977. His wife, Gert, and four-year-old daughter, Theresa, were killed in an accident while he was driving the family's van in the mountainous areas of western Pennsylvania.

The Thornton family was on the way to the player's home in Phoenixville after the 1977 season. It was raining and the forecast indicated snow, sleet, and freezing rain.

Thornton said he kept the van at slow speeds, praying he would reach a safer road. But a gust of wind rocked the van and it hit an icy patch, sending the vehicle into a skid and lurching to the right toward a guardrail.

He did everything he could to stop the skid, but the van smashed into the rail and overturned.

"It was the worst imaginable nightmare. In the midst of total darkness, I was searching for those most precious to me—I was enveloped in darkness and the only sound was the wind, howling as if someone had turned on the soundtrack of a horror movie."

Andre Thornton overcame the tragedy by remembering his faith in Christ. Thornton's pattern for Christian maturity, grounded in Christ, enabled him to survive the loss of Gert and Theresa. He devoted himself to spreading God's Word and found the strength to cope.

The following year, Thornton hit thirty-three home runs and drove in 105 the next year. He was chosen the Cleveland Indians' Man of the Year.

In November 1978 he remarried. He said he knew people would think remarrying so soon was unusual, but he thought his son needed a mother.

In 1979, Thornton hit twenty-six home runs, drove in ninety-three, was named winner of the ninth Roberto Clemente Award. In 1982, the Cleveland first baseman was honored by the Philadelphia Sports Writers Association with its coveted award for the "Most Courageous Athlete."

Andre Thornton has learned personally that Christ gives a person courage in the face of the worst adversity and tragedy.

Strength to Save. An outstanding Christian from India a generation ago was Sundar Singh. He tirelessly roamed northern India and the borders of Tibet and China to announce the Good News of the God who acted in Jesus Christ.

On one memorable session, he was crossing the passes through the range of mountains in Tibet. A heavy snowstorm and penetrating cold descended. Singh was joined by a stranger, a Tibetan. The two struggled along through the intense cold. Finally, it became doubtful that they would be able to survive to make it to the next village. They struggled on, but both were disturbed that they would sink in numbness and freeze to death.

Then they noticed a man lying in the snow about thirty feet below the path. Singh asked the Tibetan to help him go to the man. The Tibetan refused and trudged on, in spite of Singh's pleas. Finally Singh edged himself down the steep, treacherous slope to where the victim was lying. The other was unconscious and had obviously slipped and fallen. With a new superhuman effort, Sundar Singh managed to roll, push, and drag the man up to the path, then to hoist the other on his shoulders. Along the perilous path, Singh slipped and staggered, with the heavy unconscious form on his back.

Sometime later, he came upon something in the snow by the path. It turned out to be a body, the body of his Tibetan companion, frozen to death. Sundar Singh, however, found himself more alive than ever. Warmed by the extra exertion and the friction of the living body on his back and shoulders, he had been kept alive. Gradually, the man on his back came to. Together, they both reached the safety of the village, thankful to be alive.

God did not come to criticize when we fall from the path. Nor to sympathize. He came to seek us, serve us, save us in the person of Jesus Christ.

We, in turn, are sent to one another when we slip down the slope.

Fresh Bearings. An astronomer who is studying a star must continuously keep reaiming his telescope. Otherwise, the earth's turning will put the star he's watching out of range. At each part of our lives, we must get fresh bearings on Jesus Christ. Otherwise, the changing situations we find ourselves in will put Him out of focus and soon out of sight. Are you carefully and continuously reaiming your life toward Christ?

Questions for Pupils on the Next Lesson. 1. What is meant in the New Testament by the term, "The Body of Christ"? 2. How is your congregation and your denomination part of the universal Church? 3. Can you be a Christian and keep growing in Christ apart from other Christians? 4. What is the purpose God has in mind for the Church, according to Ephesians?

LESSON III—SEPTEMBER 15

HOW THE BODY OF CHRIST IS FORMED

Background Scripture: Ephesians 1; 2
Devotional Reading: Ephesians 1:11–23

KING JAMES VERSION

EPHESIANS 1 3 Blessed *be* the God and Father of our Lord Jesus Christ, who hath blessed us with all spiritual blessings in heavenly *places* in Christ:

4 According as he hath chosen us in him before the foundation of the world, that we should be holy and without blame before him in love:

5 Having predestinated us unto the adoption of children by Jesus Christ to himself, according to the good pleasure of his will,

6 To the praise of the glory of his grace, wherein he hath made us accepted in the beloved:

7 In whom we have redemption through his blood, the forgiveness of sins, according to the riches of his grace;

8 Wherein he hath abounded toward us in all wisdom and prudence;

9 Having made known unto us the mystery of his will, according to his good pleasure which he hath purposed in himself:

10 That in the dispensation of the fulness of times he might gather together in one all things in Christ, both which are in heaven, and which are on earth; *even* in him:

2 8 For by grace are ye saved through faith; and that not of yourselves: *it is* the gift of God:

9 Not of works, lest any man should boast.

10 For we are his workmanship, created in Christ Jesus unto good works, which God hath before ordained that we should walk in them.

11 Wherefore remember, that ye *being* in time past Gentiles in the flesh, who are called Uncircumcision by that which is called the Circumcision in the flesh made by hands;

12 That at that time ye were without Christ, being aliens from the commonwealth of Israel, and strangers from the covenants of promise, having no hope, and without God in the world:

13 But now, in Christ Jesus, ye who sometimes were far off are made nigh by the blood of Christ.

14 For he is our peace, who hath made both one, and hath broken down the middle wall of partition *between us;*

15 Having abolished in his flesh the enmity, *even* the law of commandments *contained* in ordinances; for to make in himself of twain one new man, *so* making peace;

16 And that he might reconcile both unto God in one body by the cross, having slain the enmity thereby.

REVISED STANDARD VERSION

EPHESIANS 1 3 Blessed be the God and Father of our Lord Jesus Christ, who has blessed us in Christ with every spiritual blessing in the heavenly places, 4 even as he chose us in him before the foundation of the world, that we should be holy and blameless before him. 5 He destined us in love to be his sons through Jesus Christ, according to the purpose of his will, 6 to the praise of his glorious grace which he freely bestowed on us in the Beloved. 7 In him we have redemption through his blood, the forgiveness of our trespasses, according to the riches of his grace 8 which he lavished upon us. 9 For he has made known to us in all wisdom and insight the mystery of his will, according to his purpose which he set forth in Christ 10 as a plan for the fulness of time, to unite all things in him, things in heaven and things on earth.

2 8 For by grace you have been saved through faith; and this is not your own doing, it is the gift of God—9 not because of works, lest any man should boast. 10 For we are his workmanship, created in Christ Jesus for good works, which God prepared beforehand, that we should walk in them.

11 Therefore remember that at one time you Gentiles in the flesh, called the uncircumcision by what is called the circumcision, which is made in the flesh by hands—12 remember that you were at that time separated from Christ, alienated from the commonwealth of Israel, and strangers to the covenants of promise, having no hope and without God in the world. 13 But now in Christ Jesus you who once were far off have been brought near in the blood of Christ. 14 For he is our peace, who has made us both one, and has broken down the dividing wall of hostility, 15 by abolishing in his flesh the law of commandments and ordinances, that he might create in himself one new man in place of the two, so making peace, 16 and might reconcile us both to God in one body through the cross, thereby bringing the hostility to an end.

KEY VERSE: For by grace you have been saved through faith; and this is not your own doing, it is the gift of God. Ephesians 2:8.

HOME DAILY BIBLE READINGS

Sept.   9.   M.   *Chosen for a Purpose.* Ephesians 1:1–6.
Sept.   10.   T.   *Our Riches in Christ.* Ephesians 1:7–14.
Sept.   11.   W.   *The Hope of Our Calling.* Ephesians 1:15–23.
Sept.   12.   T.   *Life Apart From God.* Ephesians 2:1–5.
Sept.   13.   F.   *Saved by Grace.* Ephesians 2:6–10.
Sept.   14.   S.   *Christ the Reconciler.* Ephesians 2:11–16.
Sept.   15.   S.   *The Fellowship of the Church.* Ephesians 2:17–22.

BACKGROUND

Some Christians maintain that Paul's letter to the Ephesians was his finest epistle. John Calvin, for example, called Ephesians his favorite among Paul's writings.

Certain scholars have wondered whether Paul actually wrote this letter because the writer does not seem to know his readers personally, as in the other epistles. However, Paul apparently sent this epistle as a sort of circular letter to a string of Gentile congregations in Asia Minor. Paul had Tychicus, his close friend and associate, carry it as he visited these churches. Paul was anxious that these small struggling congregations catch a broader vision of themselves as Christ's Church.

Paul undoubtedly dictated this great epistle from his prison cell after a lot of reflection on God's dreams for the community of Christ's people. The theme of Ephesians, therefore, is that God has a destiny not only for the Christians in the city of Ephesus but for His Church everywhere as the "Body of Christ."

By this, Paul means that the Church as the community of Christ's people has been brought into being as the society in history which embodies God's eternal purpose. The Church, Paul insists, is the community called into existence by the Creator who has made clear in Jesus Christ that He wills unity throughout all of His creation. The Church is the people of God; the Church knows God's secret blueprint, so to speak, for the universe! The Church exists to bring to pass that master plan of God disclosed in Jesus Christ.

What a different idea from the one so commonplace among us. "Oh, I joined a Baptist church back home when I was a kid, but I'm into Transcendental Meditation and aerobics these days," burbled a woman sales engineer to an interviewer, as if the Church is merely one of a number of diversions or affiliations one may choose. Haven't you heard people-express this notion of involving themselves with the Church when and where and how it may suit them? Imagine how Paul would have reacted to such talk! More important, consider what your calling is as Christ's. Further, consider what the calling of other Christians is meant to be as part of Christ's Body.

NOTES ON THE PRINTED TEXT

Blessed be the God and Father of our Lord Jesus Christ. After this brief salutation, Paul shifts to a sustained thanksgiving for the spiritual blessings found through Jesus Christ. The wideness of God's love was shown to men in the form of Christ through whom God gave *every spiritual blessing in the heavenly places.* Our talents, our experiences, and our material blessings all come from God. He *chose us* on which to bestow His gifts. The gifts were not given as a second thought or passing fancy. God intentionally selected His people with the purpose *that we should be holy and blameless before him.* God intended for us to be dedicated to Him and to be without sin.

It is Paul's conviction that God is in total control of this world. God has chosen us to be His children *according to the purpose of his will*. As if anticipating the Westminster Shorter Catechism which asks, "What is man's chief end?" Paul answers that man's chief end is to glorify God. Christ's people are created to be in *praise of his glorious grace* and to offer thanksgiving to Him for His grace in Jesus, *the beloved*, through their words and works.

In him we have redemption. By God's grace, a grace that is *lavished upon us*, we are saved. Paul reminds us that we have been forgiven *of our trespasses* through Christ's death and *his blood*. It is in Christ that we, through our *wisdom and insight*, become aware of God's purpose which is to *unite all things in him*. We are all forgiven and made one in Christ. Jesus breaks down the dividing walls between Greek and Jew and brings them both to God.

Through God's grace, the redeemed have a position in the household of God which is shared equally by Jewish and Gentile believers, explains Paul. *By grace you have been saved*. Salvation comes as a *gift of God*. Reminding the Ephesians again of their purpose, Paul writes, *we are . . . created in Christ Jesus for good works*.

However, the ultimate purpose of God is to create a great circle of friends. The body of Christ is formed when all divisions are dropped, and Jew and Gentile are brought together in one worshiping Church. Paul urges the Gentiles to remember the time in their past when they were *separated* or *alienated* or *far off* from Christ and had *no hope*. *But now* you are *in Christ*, Paul says. You *have been brought near in the blood of Christ*.

In the great Temple of Jerusalem, there was a wall that separated the Courts of the Gentiles and the Courts of the Israelites. On the wall was an inscription which listed the penalty of death for any Gentile who passed beyond the wall. Paul states with a very real image that through Christ, Gentiles and Jews are now both one for Christ *broke down the dividing wall of hostility*. Through Christ, a *new man* is created from these two once divided groups. The two are reconciled *through the cross* to make peace and bring hostilities to an end.

SUGGESTIONS TO TEACHERS

Suppose you were to ask each person in your class the question, "What is the Church?" What do you think you'd hear? (You may find it useful to toss this question to them as a lesson starter!) "The Church is where we go on Sunday?" "The building at the corner of Third and Main?" "Our congregation?"

As teacher, you must move the thinking of those in your class to a deeper understanding of the Church. Get them to consider the Church as more than a piece of real estate, or a religious club, but the Body of Christ. In fact, you will be studying the Church as Christ's Body for the next three lessons.

Today's subject is how the Church as Christ's Body comes to exist. The scriptural material from Ephesians 1; 2 will offer rich insights. Some of these will be useful to examine:

1. *SILENCE TO SELECT*. What a cosmic claim the Bible makes: ". . . he chose us in him before the foundation of the world" (Ephesians 1:4). Imagine the significance of this statement! Even in the silent nothingness, before creation of this planet, God had in mind to bring us into being as part of His divine scheme! We, the Body of Christ, have been selected to be part of the process of new creation through Jesus Christ!

2. *SCUM TO SONS*. Ephesians 1:5 insists that we nobodies have been "destined . . . in love to be his sons (and daughters) through Jesus Christ." Ask your class members to tell what they think this notion of destiny should mean to them as Christians. Do they sense their destiny to be God's own?

3. *SINNERS TO SAINTS.* Take note of the many references to the new standing we have as forgiven people because of Jesus Christ. Check the original meaning of the word *redemption* (a term used to describe payment made to free a slave
or release a captive). The Church, Christ's Body, comes into being through
Christ's mercy freeing us from slavery and captivity!

4. *SENSELESS TO SIGNIFICANT.* Throughout the Scripture in this lesson,
the idea recurs that we, the Body of Christ, are people who've been given "the
mystery of his will." Once we had no sense or wisdom. Through God's astonishing
act in Christ, however, we have been selected to know the most significant piece
of wisdom in the universe! We know God's "Master plan." And that is reconciliation! Take lots of minutes in this lesson to talk together about this point.

5. *SOLITUDE TO SPLENDOR.* God has not left us in isolation. In Christ, He
brings us into community. Here is an appropriate time to emphasize that Christians are never loners. We are meant to stand in close relationship with the Lord
and with each other.

6. *STRANGERS TO CITIZENS.* Raised to life by the Resurrected Lord, we in
the Church are aware that we one-time nobodies have had dignity and responsibility conferred upon us. Reflect on the notion of your congregation being "fellow
citizens with the saints and members of the household of God" (Ephesians 2:19).
What does this kind of citizenship entail?

TOPIC FOR ADULTS
HOW THE BODY OF CHRIST IS FORMED

Rebirth of a Cathedral in E-Flat. The magnificent York Minster (the Cathedral
of St. Peter in York, England) showed alarming signs of collapse a few years ago.
Although the great edifice had stood since the twelfth century, the sinking water
table under the foundations and the death-watch beetle in the timbers seemed to
spell the end. Through heroic efforts, a restoration program was begun in 1967
and finally completed recently. Huge steel rods and concrete casings deep below
the great tower averted the threat of disaster. New wood and special chemical
treatment of old wood continued the restoration process. One day, curious workmen asked the organist what note their drills were making as they bored through
the stone to install the big reinforcing rods. The organist told them it was E-Flat.
Intrigued by the workmen's question, the organist decided to compose a special
piece of music to celebrate the rebirth of the lovely old cathedral. When the
building was rededicated, he played the specially-written sonata. Remembering
the drills' sound, he called the piece, "The Rebirth of a Cathedral in E-Flat."

Christ is the Restorer of decaying lives and decaying institutions. He restores
that institution known as the Church. His presence and power bring new hope
and vitality to your congregation. In fact, through Him, your church continually
is reformed. Are you asking Him to bring a restoration program in the Church,
starting with you? You will find that new harmony and hope results. You can
write your own sonatas about the rebirth of your church!

United by a Secret Bond. "One of Doctor Schweitzer's most important con-
cepts is that of the Fellowship of Those Who Bear the Mark of Pain. I and my
men have found this Fellowship wherever we have gone. Who are its members?
Doctor Schweitzer believes the members are those who have learned by experience what physical pain and bodily anguish mean. These people, all over the
world, are united by a secret bond. He who has been delivered from pain must
not think he is now free, at liberty to continue his life and forget his sickness. He
is a man whose eyes are opened. He now has a duty to help others in their battles
with pain and anguish. He must help to bring to others the deliverance which he
himself knows."—Thomas A. Dooley, M.D., *The Edge of Tomorrow.*

A Parable. An official church board was examining a candidate for church membership, and it went like this:

Board Chairman: "What part of the Bible do you like best?"

Candidate (brightly): "I like the New Testament best!"

Board Chairman: "What book in the New Testament?"

Candidate: "The Book of Parables, sir."

Chairman: "Would you kindly relate one of these parables to this group?"

Candidate (quite uncertain, bluffed along as follows): "Once upon a time, a man went down from Jerusalem to Jericho, and fell among thieves; and the thorns grew up and choked him; however, he went on and met the Queen of Sheba, and she gave him a thousand talents of gold and silver, and a hundred changes of raiment. So he got in his chariot and drove furiously, and when he was driving along under a tree, his hair caught in a limb and left him hanging there. He hung there many days and many nights, and ravens brought him food to eat and water to drink. One night while he was hanging in the tree asleep, his wife, Delilah, came along and cut off his hair, and he dropped, falling on the stony ground. And it began to rain, and it rained forty days and forty nights, so he hid in a cave. When it quit raining, he went on and met a man who said, "Come in and take supper with me," but he said, "I can't come for I have married a wife!" So the man went out into the highways and byways and compelled him to come in. He then went on to Jerusalem and saw Queen Jezebel sitting high up in a window, and she also saw him. He laughed and said, "Throw her down out of there!" They threw her down seventy times seven, and the fragments they picked up was twelve baskets full."

The members of the Board marveled at this man's great knowledge of the Scriptures and voted unanimously to receive him into membership!

Laugh if you wish. But ask yourself if church membership is not too easy in your church. How is the Body of Christ formed among you and your friends?

Questions for Pupils on the Next Lesson. 1. Why is unity and harmony among church members essential for growth of the Church? 2. What special gifts has Christ given you as part of the Body of Christ? 3. Why are these gifts given to you? 4. How does the Church continue growing in every way?

TOPIC FOR YOUTH
MEMBERS OF CHRIST'S BODY

From Street Gang to Pastor. "It's a long way from the tenement streets of New York City to a small, central Indiana town.

"And it's a completely different world from a young street gang war lord to that of a Presbyterian minister.

"Yet that's precisely the route traveled by Walter Ungerer, pastor of the First Presbyterian Church in Kokomo, Indiana.

"As a young boy, Ungerer grew up in the Bedford-Stuyvesant/Park Slope area of Brooklyn, a high-crime area.

"He lived with his family in a three-room-and-bath cold water flat.

" 'My family life was a very, very fine, wholesome life,' he noted. 'My mother and father were good people.

" 'You discover very early that you're poor. My father was unemployed, but very industrious. He would do anything that was legal for us to survive.

" 'He got up at 5 A.M. and went out with his junk cart. He'd pick up rags, newspapers and cardboard and old junk he could find to sell to a junk dealer. Then he'd buy cereal or bread or milk, bring it home for us to eat, and then go back out for more junk.'

"As a street-wise teen-ager in Brooklyn, Ungerer became a member of the Bengals, a street gang in Brooklyn.

" 'I joined the gang for several reasons,' he explained. 'It was a big thing to be in the Bengals, because they were important. I wanted to be important. I wanted to be somebody. There was a sense of security in numbers. Life was pretty rough.'

"Ungerer said the turning point in his life came unexpectedly, after an aborted gang fight. 'The other gang didn't show,' he added.

"Ten to fifteen gang members came upon a group of Presbyterians conducting an open-air meeting. 'About forty feet away, we decided to conduct our meeting, and we were shouting, 'Hallelujah, Amen, Praise the Lord.' "

" 'A young man came over to us and tried to quiet us down. We roughed him up—but then he got up and started to preach. For some reason his voice carried over our noise to my ears. The essence of what he said was that no matter what circumstances we find ourselves in, God loves us and is willing to forgive our sins. All of us are going to die and have to account for our lives before Him. Jesus came to die for people like all of us. That's when I went home. I wrestled with God that night.'

"That night the young gang leader reached under his bed, and even though he had trouble reading, picked out a few phrases and words from the fourth chapter of the book of James.

"It was the beginning of the end of gang life.

"He sought out the Presbyterians after that meeting and they began to disciple him. 'They taught me to change my circumstances,' he said.

"And change he did. The Presbyterian church sent Ungerer to school two years later at Northeastern Bible Institute in New Jersey, where he learned to read and write.

"After graduation he attended Nyack College in New York and then New Brunswick Theological Seminary and Princeton Theological Seminary. He is now a candidate for a Doctor of Ministries degree (thesis stage) from Princeton.

"He was called to the Kokomo pastorate in 1977 after he had served churches in New York and Ohio.

"How does Ungerer feel about his experiences? 'Christ and the church were there when I needed them most in a very desperate and debilitating situation. I couldn't have accomplished such a radical change on my own, but it was made in me by the Living Christ,' he said."—This article is based on a story by Julie McClure in the *Kokomo* (Indiana) *Tribune* and is reprinted from *Trailmarker*, the paper of the Synod of Lincoln Trails. *Presbyterian Outlook*, 512 W. Main Street, Richmond, Va., January 24, 1983.

The Greatest Thing. "Someone once asked the Reverend Lyman Beecher what he considered the greatest thing a human being could be or do. Without any hesitancy whatever the famous preacher replied:

" 'The greatest thing is, not that one shall be a scientist, important as that is; nor that one shall be a statesman, vastly important as that is; nor even that one shall be a theologian, immeasurably important as that is. The greatest thing of all,' he said, 'is for one human being to bring another to Christ Jesus, the Saviour.' "

Quaint Relic. The frigate, U.S.S. Constitution, is a Man-of-War launched in 1797. Her forty-four guns brought her undying fame and the nickname, "Old Ironsides" from engagements in the West Indies and the War of 1812. Today, she lies in Boston Navy Yard, carefully preserved for visitors.

We so often look upon the Church in the same way: A quaint relic of the past, a sort of living museum of antiquarian interest, resplendent with glories of another age, but hopelessly out-dated and useless for today's battles. We will look to something else for these times.

So often church members try to keep the Church as such a monument. Just as the *Constitution* will never be taken out for battle and at most leaves the berth in Boston harbor once a year—under tugs—to be turned around so her timbers will weather on the other side, so church members try to keep the Church for their own interest and comfort.

Questions for Pupils on the Next Lesson. 1. Do you sometimes feel that you do not quite "fit in" with any group and wish you had a group which really supported you? 2. Do you think that you don't count for much in the organizations your belong to? 3. Do you have any special gifts which God has given you? If so, what are they? 4. What are the special God-given gifts meant to be used for? 5. How do you respond to the New Testament claim that your gifts are essential for the Church?

LESSON IV—SEPTEMBER 22

HOW THE BODY OF CHRIST GROWS

Background Scripture: Ephesians 4:1–16
Devotional Reading: 2 Corinthians 9:6–15

KING JAMES VERSION

EPHESIANS 4 1 Therefore, the prisoner of the Lord, beseech you that ye walk worthy of the vocation wherewith ye are called.

2 With all lowliness and meekness, with long suffering, forbearing one another in love;

3 Endeavoring to keep the unity of the Spirit in the bond of peace.

4 *There is* one body, and one Spirit, even as ye are called in one hope of your calling;

5 One Lord, one faith, one baptism,

6 One God and father of all, who *is* above all, and through all, and in you all.

7 But unto every one of us is given grace according to the measure of the gift of Christ.

11 And he gave some, apostles; and some, prophets; and some, evangelists; and some, pastors and teachers;

12 For the perfecting of the saints, for the work of the ministry, for the edifying of the body of Christ:

13 Till we all come in the unity of the faith, and of the knowledge of the Son of God, unto a perfect man, unto the measure of the stature of the fulness of Christ:

14 That we *henceforth* be no more children, tossed to and fro, and carried about with every wind of doctrine, by the sleight of men, *and* cunning craftiness, whereby they lie in wait to deceive;

15 But speaking the truth in love, may grow up into him in all things, which is the head, *even* Christ:

16 From whom the whole body fitly joined together and compacted by that which every joint supplieth, according to the effectual working in the measure of every part, maketh increase of the body unto the edifying of itself in love.

REVISED STANDARD VERSION

EPHESIANS 4 1 therefore, a prisoner for the Lord, beg you to lead a life worthy of the calling to which you have been called, 2 with all lowliness and meekness, with patience, forbearing one another in love, 3 eager to maintain the unity of the Spirit in the bond of peace. 4 There is one body and one Spirit, just as you were called to the one hope that belongs to your call, 5 one Lord, one faith, one baptism, 6 one God and Father of us all, who is above all and through all and in all. 7 But grace was given to each of us according to the measure of Christ's gift.

11 And his gifts were that some should be apostles, some prophets, some evangelists, some pastors and teachers, 12 to equip the saints, for the work of ministry, for building up the body of Christ, 13 until we all attain to the unity of the faith and of the knowledge of the Son of God, to mature manhood, to the measure of the stature of the fulness of Christ; 14 so that we may no longer be children, tossed to and fro and carried about with every wind of doctrine, by the cunning of men, by their craftiness in deceitful wiles. 15 Rather, speaking the truth in love, we are to grow up in every way into him who is the head, into Christ, 16 from whom the whole body, joined and knit together by every joint with which it is supplied, when each part is working properly, makes bodily growth and upbuilds itself in love.

KEY VERSE: *Speaking the truth in love, we are to grow up in every way into him who is the head, into Christ.* Ephesians 4:15.

HOME DAILY BIBLE READINGS

Sept. 16. M. *The Mystery of the Gospel.* Ephesians 3:1–6.
Sept. 17. T. *Paul's Calling and Hope.* Ephesians 3:7–21.
Sept. 18. W. *A Life That Is Worthy.* Ephesians 4:1–6.
Sept. 19. T. *Gifts for the Church.* Ephesians 4:7–16.
Sept. 20. F. *Gifts That Differ.* 1 Corinthians 12:4–11.
Sept. 21. S. *All Gifts Are Necessary.* 1 Corinthians 12:12–26.
Sept. 22. S. *Christian Humility.* Romans 12:3–8.

BACKGROUND

What does a Brazilian Pentecostal have in common with a Ugandan Anglican, or a Canadian Baptist share with a Korean Presbyterian? Not much, you may say. After all, each speaks a different language, each comes from a different culture, each represents a different race, each has a different nationality.

Paul faced a similar situation in his day. He knew that Christians were from a variety of backgrounds. A believer in Judea had a completely different background and outlook, a different language and customs from a believer in Greece. Christians in Asia Minor wondered what ties they could possibly have with Christians elsewhere.

Furthermore, each collection of believers seemed to acquire its own pecking order. The all-too-human tendency to rank people in a list of importance showed up in Christian gatherings. "I'm a prophet," one would say, "therefore I'm more significant than others." "You don't teach or preach or evangelize," someone else would say, "therefore you're not as important."

After giving a magnificent overview of God's purpose in human history in what we now call the first three chapters of the Epistle to the Ephesians, Paul turns to practical matters. Topping the list of these practical matters was the matter of how the Church, Christ's Body, is a living organism in which each member is related to each other member.

In fact, Paul boldly uses the analogy of a human body to get across his point. This is not the only place Paul takes up this idea. He also talks of the organic connection of all Christians in terms of a human body in Romans 12 and 1 Corinthians 12.

The idea Paul wants us to understand and live by is that each Christian—not merely some but *each* Christian—shares a life of being connected to the lives of all other Christians. Just as a thumb is useless and lifeless apart from the human organism to which it belongs, an individual Christian believer has no usefulness or vitality unless joined to the body of believers. That Brazilian Pentecostal, that Ugandan Anglican and that Canadian Baptist and that Koren Presbyterian and you and I are linked as much as separate fingers are coupled together in a hand which belongs to a live body!

Furthermore, Ephesians stresses that you and I need each of them and they need us. Every Christian belongs to the same body, and every Christian has a calling to help the entire body carry out its task. The Living Christ, of course, is the One who infuses us all, with all our diversity, with life!

NOTES ON THE PRINTED TEXT

In his letter to the Ephesians, Paul writes about the Christian way of life. He describes the unity of believers through the Spirit and the enjoyment of the Spirit's gifts to the Church. The first three chapters are doctrine. Now Paul speaks in practical terms by telling the Ephesians how to promote the unity of the church.

Paul, the prisoner, begs the Ephesians to *lead a life worthy of the calling of the Lord.* Paul exhorts the Ephesians to conduct themselves as Christ has called them to do. Their lives must be expressive of their commitment to God. They can show their love for one another by being humble and meek. *With all lowliness and meekness* and *with patience,* the Ephesians can build unity within the Church. Paul urges the Ephesians to develop these qualities. Humility is better than blatant pride or bragging. The Ephesians are to be patient, literally long tempered. They must endeavor to deal with one another *in love,* the greatest of virtues. The Church is full of people who are annoying and have faults, but the Christian must act toward all in love, thus preventing any disruption of unity in the Church.

The Christian must be *eager to maintain the unity of the Spirit* in the *bond of peace.* Spare no effort to keep peace. Be on guard to watch for anything that can cause dissension and threaten the unity of the Church.

Paul offers a model of unity. *There is one body:* the Church. Though from different backgrounds and classes, the believers became one through Christ and the Church. There is *one Spirit* that unifies all peoples: Jew and Greek, male and female, slave and freeman. There is one Spirit who calls them all to their *one hope* in Jesus. There is *one Lord,* Jesus Christ. There is *one faith.* Life can be committed to one person only: Jesus Christ. That commitment is expressed and confessed in *one baptism,* a practice symbolizing the joining of the community of believers. Paul affirms there is *one God and Father* of all the believers.

While Paul has spoken of unity, it is not uniformity. God's grace gives certain gifts to each individual. *Grace was given to each of us according to the measure of Christ's gift.* Each person is given special gifts to use for the common good. Some gifts can be used to build up the Church. Other gifts can be used to provide leadership.

And his gifts were that some should be apostles. The apostles were the original recipients of the Spirit and the founders of the Church. There are *prophets* who speak God's Word. There are *evangelists* who share the Gospel as missionaries to the nonbelievers. Other people have special gifts to be *pastors or teachers.* These people work with a particular church instructing the congregation about Christ, giving insights into Christian conduct, and providing care and counseling.

The gifts are given to all these different individuals to *equip the saints, for the work of the ministry* and *for building up the body of Christ.* Gifts are given so that God's people, the saints, are equipped and prepared for service. The believers are to serve the community and one another. In addition, the gifts are to to be used to build up the Body of Christ by adding and integrating new members to the Church and preventing any dissensions from dividing the Church. It continues to be a responsiblity of believers now.

Until we attain the unity of faith, the Church must continuously work toward all in faith and a *knowledge of the Son of God.* Another of the goals is to reach maturity. Through mature and total love, obedience, and loyalty, we can be unified in the *fulness of Christ so that we may no longer be children.* Believers, like young children, are attracted to false doctrines by cunning and crafty individuals. However, the believer is to grow in unity through Christ and the Church. The believer is to become part of the Body and work as one, just as the parts of a human body grow and work together. And, Paul ends, the Body works best *in love.*

SUGGESTIONS TO TEACHERS

Some of the leaders in a congregation in Nebraska got the notion that church growth meant lots of new members. They took out newspaper advertisements. They blitzed the community with leaflets. They hired a famous revivalist for a week of special meetings. They paid for expensive materials outlining a campaign for, "Surefire Shortcuts to Successful Sunday Services." But nothing much happened. Eight months later, the same leaders asked themselves, "What's wrong with us?"

Your class also has people in it who think that growth in the church means playing the numbers game. Coupled with this notion is the idea that gimmicks and gadgets will make the church grow.

Today's lesson is designed with these folks in mind. The New Testament's ideas on how Christ's Body grows will probably run counter to some of the opinions of persons like those in that Nebraska congregation.

1. *COMMISSIONED BY CALLING.* Taking your start from Ephesians 4, point out that those in the Church must recognize that they have been "called" to be Christ's. Here is a good opportunity to talk about what the "call" of a Christian is. Remind your people that Christ's "call" comes to every Christian, not only to preachers. Help your class to identify the meaning of Christ's call in the lives of each member.

2. *CHARACTERIZED BY CARING.* Insist that the class investigate the verse (Ephesians 4:2) describing the way members of the church are intended to act toward one another. Ask specifically what it means to live "with all lowliness and meekness, with patience, forbearing one another in love."

3. *COMMITTED TO COMPLETENESS.* Stress the way Ephesians calls for a recognition of *one* body, *one* Spirit, *one* Lord, *one* faith, *one* baptism, *one* God. Allow some time in the lesson to talk over the way the Church seems to have so many divisions and what your congregation and denomination could do to bring the Body of Christ together as one.

4. *CONSCIOUS OF GIFTS.* Devote a sizable chunk of your lesson on the portion in Ephesians 4 which discusses "gifts." Note the diversity of the gifts of the Spirit. Point out that these gifts are given to equip the people in the Church to carry out Christ's ministry. The gifts are not for private enjoyment, but must be shared. Have your class members help each other ascertain what the gift of each member in the class is, perhaps by having each person put name and gift or gifts of the others in the class on a slip of paper, then sharing them with each other.

5. *CONNECTED BY CHRIST.* Place before your people the concept of the "Body of Christ" in which each Christian is joined to all others as the many parts of the body. As with a human body, every part is needed because it has a vital function. Furthermore, apart from the body, no part can survive or is useful.

6. *CONTINUING IN COMMUNITY.* In the face of the tendency to think of ourselves as a collection of individuals who may gather with other Christians when we feel like it, the New Testament insists that we must consciously join ourselves to fellowship. The Body of Christ grows when we grow closer to Christ and closer to each other.

TOPIC FOR ADULTS
HOW THE BODY OF CHRIST GROWS

We Can All Play Music. "One of the most poignant stories about Plymouth Church belongs to Ann and Bud Turnbull, whose lives have been defined in great part by the fact that they have a handicapped child. Both teach special education at Kansas University and have a strong desire to educate people to the realities of life for the handicapped.

"Ann had decided to tell their six-year-old daughter that her older brother was mentally retarded. She explained that retardation means that someone's brain is damaged so that he learns more slowly than other people.

" 'I don't know anyone like that,' her daughter replied.

" 'Yes, you do,' said Ann. 'Jay is mentally retarded.'

"They talked about the fact that Jay would always learn more slowly than most children, and then Amy asked how her own brain and her little sister's brain worked.

" 'They work fast,' Ann told her.

"Then Amy thought for a while and said, 'Mommy, is that like my record player? There's that button on the side, and if you push it one way, the record goes slowly and if you push it another way, the record goes fast. It plays music on both speeds. Jay might be slow and Kate and I might be fast, but, Mommy, all three of us still play music.'

"Ann Turnbull finds her child's wonderfully knowing analogy the perfect description for Plymouth Church. 'We can all play music at Plymouth. We can be different and yet included.' "—Christina Doudna, *Quote*, February 1, 1983.

Spectators or Participants? "Too many people find no sense of excitement or joy of God's presence in a public worship service. A recent Gallup poll of 'the unchurched' revealed that a majority of these people felt the Church had 'lost the real spiritual part of religion' (*see* "Unchurched Americans Say Church is Not Spiritual Enough," *A.D. Magazine*, September 1978). John Updike makes the same observation in his novel, *A Month of Sundays*, when one of his characters says that 'most churches are like the Coca-Cola billboard. They promote thirst without quenching it.'

"Part of the problem is the way we modern Christians approach public worship. Too often we go as spectators ready to be entertained rather than to worship. As the Danish philosopher Soren Kierkegaard noted, we are not the audience in worship. We are the actors: 'In the most earnest sense,' he writes, 'God is the critical theater-goer, who looks on to see how the lines are spoken and how they are listened to . . . hence, the listener is the actor, who in all truth acts before God.'

"A church service has to be judged by more than the flow of the liturgy. Congregation and worship leader together make the difference between a good worship service and a poor service. Do we come with a sense of expectancy? Do we believe God deals with us in a time of worship? Do we sing and pray and act our faith with all our heart, mind, and strength?"—Ronald G. Stegall.

What Kind of Church Member Are You? "A lot of Christians are like wheelbarrows—Not good unless pushed. Some are like canoes—they need to be paddled. Some are like kites—if you don't keep a string on them they fly away. Some are like footballs—you can't tell which way they'll bounce next. Some are like balloons—full of air and ready to blow up. Some are like trailers—they have to be pulled. Some are like neon lights—they keep going on and off. And, we would like to add, some are like a good watch; open face, pure gold, quietly busy and full of good works.

"Which are you?"—Author unknown.

Questions for Pupils on the Next Lesson. 1. What do you think should be expected of members of a Christian congregation? 2. Are you conscious of your life being transformed because of being a Christian? If so, in what ways? If not, why not? 3. What does the phrase about grieving the Holy Spirit mean? 4. In what groups have you experienced a loving community? 5. How can the Church support you better in your attempt to conform more to Christ?

TOPIC FOR YOUTH
GIFTS FOR GROWING IN CHRIST'S BODY

Names or Numbers? A census taker asked a woman at one house where he called, how many children she had. "Well," she said, "there's Willie and Henry and Martha and . . . ." Then the census taker broke in with, "Oh, never mind the names, give me numbers." The interruption and the tone of it roused the mother's indignation. "They haven't got numbers," she said, "they all have names." That census man had got so obsessed with numbers that he seemed to have forgotten that mothers do not number; they name.

God does not remember you as a number. Nor does the Lord regard you as part of a huge number. You are assured through Jesus Christ that you are never a statistic with God. In fact, you are unique. You are special. You have been given exceptional gifts by the Lord to be shared with the others in Christ's community. Are you aware of these gifts?

Get Involved! Flip Wilson, in one of his funny skits, was once asked what religion he belonged to. Flip replied, "I'm a Jehovah's Bystander."

"Jehovah's Bystander?" replied the other. "Never heard of that. What do you mean?"

"Well," replied Flip, "they asked me to be a witness, but I didn't want to get involved."

Is this the way you sometimes think or act? Remember you have been given gifts for growing in Christ's Body and helping others to grow as Christians!

Sprinkler Christians. Why are some church people called, "Sprinklers"?

Because they go to church only to be sprinkled with water, rice, or ashes!

Is this the level of your or your family's commitment to Christ? Are you a Christian only to be "hatched, matched, and dispatched"—when you're baptized, married, or buried?

Share your gifts from the Lord with that family of His people by consciously being part of His Church!

Questions for Pupils on the Next Lesson. 1. What would you state if you were asked what should be expected of every church member? 2. What do you think the Lord expects of you as a church member? 3. In what ways has your life been transformed by Christ? 4. How has the Church been a support group for you? 5. How is your congregation mirroring the ways God has acted on behalf of His people in Jesus Christ?

LESSON V—SEPTEMBER 29

HOW THE BODY OF CHRIST LIVES IN THE WORLD

Background Scripture: Ephesians 4:17–5:20
Devotional Reading: Ephesians 5:3–20

KING JAMES VERSION

EPHESIANS 4   17 This I say therefore, and testify in the Lord, that ye henceforth walk not as other Gentiles walk, in the vanity of their mind,

18 Having the understanding darkened, being alienated from the life of God through the ignorance that is in them, because of the blindness of their heart:

19 Who being past feeling have given themselves over unto lasciviousness, to work all uncleanness with greediness.

20 But ye have not so learned Christ;

21 If so be that ye have heard him, and have been taught by him, as the truth is in Jesus:

22 That ye put off concerning the former conversation the old man, which is corrupt according to the deceitful lusts;

23 And be renewed in the spirit of your mind;

24 And that ye put on the new man, which after God is created in righteousness and true holiness.

25 Wherefore putting away lying, speak every man truth with his neighbour: for we are members one of another.

26 Be ye angry, and sin not: let not the sun go down upon your wrath:

27 Neither give place to the devil.

28 Let him that stole steal no more: but rather let him labour, working with *his* hands the thing which is good, that he may have to give to him that needeth.

29 Let no corrupt communication proceed out of your mouth, but that which is good to the use of edifying, that it may minister grace unto the hearers.

30 And grieve not the holy Spirit of God, whereby ye are sealed unto the day of redemption.

31 Let all bitterness, and wrath, and anger, and clamour, and evil speaking, be put away from you, with all malice:

32 And be ye kind one to another, tenderhearted, forgiving one another, even as God for Christ's sake hath forgiven you.

5 Be ye therefore followers of God, as dear children;

2 And walk in love, as Christ also hath loved us, and hath given himself for us an offering and a sacrifice to God for a sweetsmelling savour.

REVISED STANDARD VERSION

EPHESIANS 4   17 Now this I affirm and testify in the Lord, that you must no longer live as the Gentiles do, in the futility of their minds; 18 they are darkened in their understanding, alienated from the life of God because of the ignorance that is in them, due to their hardness of heart; 19 they have become callous and have given themselves up to licentiousness, greedy to practice every kind of uncleanness. 20 You did not so learn Christ!—21 assuming that you have heard about him and were taught in him, as the truth is in Jesus. 22 Put off your old nature which belongs to your former manner of life and is corrupt through deceitful lusts, 23 and be renewed in the spirit of your minds, 24 and put on the new nature, created after the likeness of God in true righteousness and holiness.

25 Therefore, putting away falsehood, let every one speak the truth with his neighbor, for we are members one of another. 26 Be angry but do not sin; do not let the sun go down on your anger, 27 and give no opportunity to the devil. 28 Let the thief no longer steal, but rather let him labor, doing honest work with his hands, so that he may be able to give to those in need. 29 Let no evil talk come out of your mouths, but only such as is good for edifying, as fits the occasion, that it may impart grace to those who hear. 30 And do not grieve the Holy Spirit of God, in whom you were sealed for the day of redemption. 31 Let all bitterness and wrath and anger and clamor and slander be put away from you, with all malice, 32 and be kind to one another, tenderhearted, forgiving one another, as God in Christ forgave you.

5 Therefore be imitators of God, as beloved children. 2 And walk in love, as Christ loved us and gave himself up for us, a fragrant offering and sacrifice to God.

KEY VERSE: *Put on the new nature, created after the likeness of God in true righteousness and holiness.* Ephesians 4:24.

HOME DAILY BIBLE READINGS

Sept.	*23.*	*M.*	*Renewed in the Spirit.* Ephesians 4:17–24.
Sept.	*24.*	*T.*	*Imitators of God.* Ephesians 4:25—5:2.
Sept.	*25.*	*W.*	*Children of Light.* Ephesians 5:3–20.
Sept.	*26.*	*T.*	*The Christian's Resources.* Ephesians 6:10–17.
Sept.	*27.*	*F.*	*The New Nature in Christ.* Colossians 3:5–11.
Sept.	*28.*	*S.*	*Love Is the Context.* Colossians 3:12–17.
Sept.	*29.*	*S.*	*How to Do Good.* Romans 12:9–21.

BACKGROUND

Paul has charged his Christian readers in Ephesians 4:1–17 to work to promote the unity of the Church so that the Church as a living organism may grow the way God intends it to grow. In Ephesians 4:17—5:20 (the material in today's lesson), the Apostle Paul gives another charge. This section calls for believers to make a complete break from their old pagan ways.

Paul appeals to these recent converts from paganism to recall not only who they were but now whose they are. He emphasizes that they belong to Jesus Christ. They have been transformed from the futile, destructive existence of being separated from God, through Christ's deliverance. Therefore, Paul insists, they can no longer continue with practices which will inevitably drag them back into futile destructive existences.

It must have been truly hard for these new Christians to cut themselves away from the ways of the pagan world. After all, Ephesus and the other cities in that part of the world were renowned for their brothels, bars, and casinos. Most of their neighbors asked them, "Why do you bother with chastity and sexual purity? What's wrong with trampling on others to get what I want? What's the point of living if you don't assert yourself?" Some in the Church found themselves listening to these comments from pagan associates and slipping into the lifestyle of a typical greedy, immoral, pleasure-loving Gentile.

"Put off your old nature . . . and put on the new nature, created after the likeness of God," Paul pleads with his readers (Ephesians 4:22–24). He follows up with specific lists of six vices typifying the old nature of the Christ-less person and six virtues typifying the new nature of the Christ-filled person. Practices such as lying, anger, stealing, malicious gossip, and filthy talk have no place among members of Christ's community. Instead, members of the Body of Christ actively show kindness and consciously remember their identity constantly as Christ's people.

NOTES ON THE PRINTED TEXT

Paul continues discussing the matter of conduct for the Ephesians. Since a Christian's life is a new life in Christ, a Christian must make a complete break from the old way of life. Paul appeals to the Ephesians to let their conduct reflect their commitment to Christ. *You must no longer live as the Gentiles do.* The Jews followed the Ten Commandments and the Law of Moses which set forth a high standard of conduct. However, the Gentiles had no such standards. Their behavior, particularly in sexual matters, was very casual. Paul insists that Christians must behave in a moral manner.

The Ephesians are not to live *in the futility of their minds.* Rather than see life as pointless and meaningless, they are challenged to realize life's meaning and purpose which is given to them through Jesus Christ. The unbelievers are *darkened in their understanding.* They can make no moral distinctions between right and wrong, good and evil, and righteous and unrighteous. These unbelievers are also *alienated from the life of God* because of their ignorance of God. They have no new life because they do not know God through Christ. They are victims of alienation in need of reconciliation through Christ. However, their ignorance is due to their *hardness of heart.* It is a deliberate rejection of Christ. *They have given themselves up to licentiousness.* Deliberately and greedily they have given themselves over to immoral behavior that practices *every kind of uncleanness.* Biblically, the word *greedily* means with a ruthless appetite. The unbelievers have a ruthless appetite for sexual sins.

You did not so learn Christ! Paul reminds the Ephesians that they accepted a new life that taught something far different than immoral behavior. They learned the truth in Jesus. They learned of Him and the conduct appropriate to a disciple of Jesus. Just as they changed from old clothes to new clothes after baptism, Paul urges them to *put off your old nature* and *be renewed.* Cast off the old manner of life with all its lusts. *Put on the new nature created after the likeness of God.* The change in their lives must be total. Christ, not lusts, must now rule the believer's life. Through the desires, attitudes, values, and actions of the Christian, God's likeness must be seen. Above all, the new nature is seen in *true righteousness and holiness.* Believers are different from others since God rules their hearts.

Paul has urged Christians to abandon all immoral practices associated with the old nature. He then advocates some conduct that will express the new nature.

Therefore, putting away falsehood, let everyone speak the truth. Lying must be replaced by the truth. *Be angry but do not sin.* If there is anger, it must be free from sin. The anger must be directed at what is evil or harmful to others. *Do not let the sun go down on your anger.* Anger must not be fostered or kept. *Let the thief no longer steal.* Stealing must cease. Honest work must be done. The needs of others must be supplied. Instead of evil, cynical, or depressing talk, there should be talk which brings hope and encouragement. *Do not grieve the Holy Spirit of God.* Do not sadden God's Spirit with *bitterness, wrath, anger, clamor,* or *malice.* The new nature demands kindness, tenderheartedness, and forgiveness from the Christian. The believer is summoned to be a mini-Christ who forgives as God in Christ forgave. The Ephesians and all believers are summoned to be *imitators of God,* by conducting themselves in self-sacrificing love molded after the love shown to them through Jesus Christ.

SUGGESTIONS TO TEACHERS

Recently, a survey was made of how Americans view those of different races. The study reported some surprising answers. Church people, it showed, were about as prejudiced toward others as nonchurch folk.

Should Christians reflect the values of the culture? Or are Christians "different"?

The topic of this lesson for this Sunday examines these important questions.

As the teacher, you may be tempted to scold the class members for not showing the world how Christ has transformed them. This may help you work out some of your frustrations, but it's not the most productive way to present this lesson. Instead, try to introduce your people to the challenges of the Ephesians passage.

1. *NEW NATURE.* The key word throughout the scriptural material in this lesson is *new.* Jesus Christ makes all things—including us—*new!* We are to shuck off our old nature of preoccupation with our own selfish interests, and "put on the new nature" (4:24) as a new creation by God through Jesus Christ. As Christians, we are intended to be in "the likeness of God." What exactly do your people think this means? Ask if being a Christian has really made any difference in the thinking and doing of each person in the class.

2. *NEW RELATIONSHIPS.* Take note of the way in which the new nature inevitably means new relationships within the Christian community. Christians, Ephesians states, handle practical, daily issues differently from pagans. Have your

class look at the specifics: these include speaking openly and honestly with others; handling angry feelings in constructive instead of destructive ways; showing a concern for others by working and sharing instead of taking; building up the community in conversation instead of slandering others.

3. *NEW MOTIVE.* Obviously, no person can show kindness very long without a deep inner motive. Ephesians insists that we can be forgiving and gracious toward others only as we realize "God in Christ forgave you" and "Christ loved us and gave himself up for us" (4:32; 5:2). It is easy to gloss over these verses as pious fringe. Point your class to Jesus Christ's goodness to us as the reason for all our good acts.

4. *NEW MORALITY.* The new morality is not the Playboy philosophy. That's the old, dreary pagan world's morality. The new morality is a life mirroring the concern of Jesus Christ. Ephesians has excellent practical advice in regard to morality. Be careful that "no one deceive you with empty words" (5:6), trying to convince you in the name of art or psychology or learning that you should please yourself. Christians firmly reject hedonism and sexual permissiveness.

5. *NEW MISSION.* Have your class think about the task given it to battle darkness in all its forms by bringing light. Think of some of the kinds of darkness which paralyze others, as ignorance, prejudice, anxiety, violence. Christians are called to bring the light of the Gospel. Are your people doing this?

TOPIC FOR ADULTS
BEING CHRIST'S BODY IN THE WORLD

Armed With the Memory. Sir Francis Drake, whose English ships made England a world naval power, is regarded as the greatest English seaman by the British. Grateful for his leadership and desirous of perpetuating his influence, the British have designated the Royal Naval Barracks at Portsmouth, England, "H.M.S. DRAKE." By naming the place after Drake where all future navy officers live, Great Britain has hoped that there will always be British seamen armed with memory and association of that great naval hero.

We who are members of Christ's Body, the Church, likewise consider ourselves armed with Christ's name and stirred by our associations with Him as the Risen, Living Lord. We are equipped as the Church not to remain "in the barracks" so to speak but to sally forth boldly into the world! We are to continue what Christ started!

To Be Present. "To be present is to be vulnerable, to be able to be hurt, to be willing to be spent—but it is also to be awake, alive, and engaged actively in the immediate assignment that has been laid upon us.

"I believe that in the period that lies ahead, there is no deeper challenge in our personal, spiritual, and social witness all over the globe than this issue of learning to be present where we are in our personal relationships and making our witness and effort to rouse men and women to dare to be present to each other. The issue of peace and war, the issue of racial tensions, the issue of an educational breakthrough, the issue of our responsibility to contribute to the quickening of the relationships of the great world religions—all come down in the end to this daring to be present where we are.

"There is One who, on the road out of Jerusalem to the little town of Emmaus, taught his companions of the road and of the table what it was to be present. 'Did not our hearts burn within us while he talked with us by the way?' That same quickening presence still walks by our side. That same presence kindles our meetings for worship and reveals to us our failure to be truly present with our families, our friends, and our brothers in the world. It is there in his presence when we are given again the gift of tears, that we are once more joined to all the living, that hope is restored to us, and that we are re-baptized into the sacredness of the gift of life and of the gift of being set down here among our fellow humans who, in the depth of their being, long to be truly present to each other."—Douglas V. Steere, *Together in Solitude*, Crossroad, 1983.

Significant Sign. A sign in front of a church building states: "This congregation exists to do three things: to introduce Jesus Christ to those who do not know Him and love Him (that is evangelism); secondly, to deepen the faith and commitment of those who already know Him (that is Christian education and nurture); and thirdly, to demonstrate Christ's way of love in service to the world (that is our social commitment to a needy world)."

Could this sign be placed in front of your church? Is this how you and those in your local congregation live as Christ's Body in the world?

Questions for Pupils on the Next Lesson. 1. Why was the church at Corinth split into squabbling factions? 2. Who were some of the personalities involved in the church quarrel in Corinth? 3. How did Paul try to handle the Corinthian church problems? 4. What is the foundation for a Church unity? 5. How should the church in your community go about healing church conflict?

TOPIC FOR YOUTH
BEING CHRIST'S BODY IN THE WORLD

Murky Image. George Gallup was commissioned to make a careful study of Americans' religious beliefs recently. His Gallup poll used scientifically validated gathering tools and interviewed a sizeable cross section for a reliable sampling of opinion. Gallup's findings were interesting.

Eighty-seven percent of all those Americans interviewed claim that Jesus has influenced their lives. Eighty-one percent reported that they considered themselves Christians. Seventy-eight percent stated that they regarded Jesus as somehow divine. Obviously, Jesus is overwhelmingly viewed in a favorable light. However, the image of the Jesus we admire is murky. Although nearly nine out of ten say they've been influenced by Jesus as a moral and ethical teacher, and nearly eight out of ten insist Jesus is in some varying way to be considered divine, about four out of ten could not name any of the four Gospels. About six out of ten did not know that Jesus gave the Sermon on the Mount. And two out of ten didn't know what Easter stood for!

The question which emerges from this Gallup poll is how does the Body of Christ live in the world? Are Christians aware of their calling? Do believers understand who Jesus Christ is? Are they informing themselves and growing in their understanding of their mission?

Sealed-Up Sect. Several years ago, in the town of Benson, Arizona, all the members of a sect called Full Gospel, Inc., suddenly vanished. Their neighbors were surprised because the members of the group had seemed to be normal persons when they settled in Benson a few months earlier and built a small stucco church. But one day, all the homes of the members of the Full Gospel, Inc., were shut and silent, and their cars stood in their driveways.

When the husband of one of the sect's members complained to the county attorney that his wife and four children had disappeared, the sheriff was called to investigate.

After careful searching, sheriff's deputies discovered that the entire group had literally gone underground. Inside the closets of several members' houses, cunningly concealed trapdoors led to passages excavated below. Huddled in various underground chambers beneath the houses were the members of Full Gospel, Inc. They refused to emerge, saying that there would soon be a devastation on earth destroying one-third of all the people. (This was in August, 1960.)

Is this how the Body of Christ should live in the world? Look again at the early Church described in the New Testament. Underground? No way! These Church members boldly confronted the culture and the society they were in. And they won!

Likewise, we as the Body of Christ are sent out into the world, not to adopt the ways of the world, but to share Christ's ways with the world.

Restore the Luster. "I keep a little sign on my desk as a daily reminder. It reads: 'Don't Lose the Luster.'

"But try as we will, occasionally we do lose some of the luster in our lives, in our jobs, and in our attitudes. So it's important to know how to restore the luster. When our silver or brass gets a bit tarnished, we get the polish off the shelf and do a bit of rubbing. We restore the luster.

"We can restore the luster in our lives by pausing early in the day to pray, meditate, and to seek God's will and guidance. If we're too busy to pray, we're too busy.

"We can restore the luster in our lives by counting our blessings, and by taking time to name them one by one. An attitude of gratitude rids our lives of the film of frustration, and rust of resentment, and the varnish of vanity. When we gratefully count our blessings, we add to the world's happiness; we multiply good will and harmony.

"We can restore the luster in our lives—and in the lives of others—by looking for the best in everyone and by seeking the Christ spirit in every person we meet. When we seek the Christ in others we truly put into practice the Golden Rule.

"We can restore the luster in our lives by forgetting ourselves in loving service to others. When we generously give ourselves away, we discover that life takes on a new sparkle, a joyful radiance, and a beautiful luster.

"Don't lose the luster. But if you do, get busy and restore it!"—William Arthur Ward, *Quote*, November 1, 1982.

Questions for Pupils on the Next Lesson. 1. Why are Church fights always so destructive and hurtful? 2. What caused the church fights in Corinth? 3. What did Paul do to try to bring healing to that church? 4. How can Christians deal with conflict and handle disagreements in a congregation? 5. What is the basis for our unity in a church?

LESSON VI—OCTOBER 6

A DIVIDED CHURCH

Background Scripture: 1 Corinthians 1:10–4:21
Devotional Reading: 1 Corinthians 4:1–5

KING JAMES VERSION

1 CORINTHIANS 1 10 Now I beseech you, brethren, by the name of our Lord Jesus Christ, that ye all speak the same thing, and *that* there be no divisions among you; but *that* ye be perfectly joined together in the same mind and in the same judgment.

11 For it hath been declared unto me of you, my brethren, by them *which are of the house* of Chloe, that there are contentions among you.

12 Now this I say, that every one of you saith, I am of Paul; and I of Apollos; and I of Cephas; and I of Christ.

13 Is Christ divided? was Paul crucified for you? or were ye baptized in the name of Paul?

14 I thank God that I baptized none of you, but Crispus and Gaius;

15 Lest any should say that I had baptized in mine own name.

3 5 Who then is Paul, and who *is* Apollos, but ministers by whom ye believed, even as the Lord gave to every man?

6 I have planted, Apollos watered; but God gave the increase.

7 So then neither is he that planteth any thing, neither he that watereth; but God that giveth the increase.

8 Now he that planteth and he that watereth are one: and every man shall receive his own reward according to his own labour.

9 For we are labourers together with God: ye are God's husbandry, *ye are* God's building.

10 According to the grace of God which is given unto me, as a wise master-builder, I have laid the foundation, and another buildeth thereon. But let every man take heed how he buildeth thereupon.

11 For other foundation can no man lay than that is laid, which is Jesus Christ.

12 Now if any man build upon this foundation gold, silver, precious stones, wood, hay, stubble;

13 Every man's work shall be made manifest: for the day shall declare it, because it shall be revealed by fire; and the fire shall try every man's work of what sort it is.

14 If any man's work abide which he hath built thereupon, he shall receive a reward.

15 If any man's work shall be burned, he shall suffer loss: but he himself shall be saved; yet so as by fire.

REVISED STANDARD VERSION

1 CORINTHIANS 1 10 I appeal to you, brethren, by the name of our Lord Jesus Christ, that all of you agree that there be no dissensions among you, but that you be united in the same mind and the same judgment. 11 For it has been reported to me by Chloe's people that there is quarreling among you, my brethren. 12 What I mean is that each one of you says, "I belong to Paul," or "I belong to Apollos," or "I belong to Cephas," or "I belong to Christ." 13 Is Christ divided? Was Paul crucified for you? Or were you baptized in the name of Paul? 14 I am thankful that I baptized none of you except Crispus and Gaius; 15 lest any one should say that you were baptized in my name.

3 5 What then is Apollos? What is Paul? Servants through whom you believed, as the Lord assigned to each. 6 I planted, Apollos watered, but God gave the growth. 7 So neither he who plants nor he who waters is anything, but only God who gives the growth. 8 He who plants and he who waters are equal, and each shall receive his wages according to his labor. 9 For we are God's fellow workers; you are God's field, God's building.

10 According to the grace of God given to me, like a skilled master builder I laid a foundation, and another man is building upon it. Let each man take care how he builds upon it. 11 For no other foundation can any one lay than that which is laid, which is Jesus Christ. 12 Now if any one builds on the foundation with gold, silver, precious stones, wood, hay, straw—13 each man's work will become manifest; for the Day will disclose it, because it will be revealed with fire, and the fire will test what sort of work each one has done. 14 If the work which any man has built on the foundation survives, he will receive a reward. 15 If any man's work is burned up, he will suffer loss, though he himself will be saved, but only as through fire.

KEY VERSE: No other foundation can any one lay than that which is laid, which is Jesus Christ. 1 Corinthians 3:11.

HOME DAILY BIBLE READINGS

Sept.	30.	M.	*Avoid Party Spirit.* 1 Corinthians 1:10–17.
Oct.	1.	T.	*The Wisdom and Power of God.* 1 Corinthians 1:18–31.
Oct.	2.	W.	*Paul's One Aim.* 1 Corinthians 2:1–9.
Oct.	3.	T.	*God's Spirit Reveals God's Thoughts.* 1 Corinthians 2:10–16.
Oct.	4.	F.	*Co-Workers With God.* 1 Corinthians 3:1–9.
Oct.	5.	S.	*Take Care How You Build.* 1 Corinthians 3:10–17.
Oct.	6.	S.	*Leaving Judgment to God.* 1 Corinthians 4:1–5.

BACKGROUND

Sometimes, we have an idealized notion of the early Church. We carry the idea that every Christian in the first century glowed with pure love, and that every congregation radiated perfect harmony.

A quick reading of today's Background Scripture will debunk these ideas. The New Testament Church had problems. Christians then were often no more paragons of virtue than we are. They sometimes disagreed. In fact, they sometimes squabbled. On occasion, the Church was divided into quarreling factions. Personality cults appeared. Although church members said they were loyal to Jesus Christ and committed to exhibiting His grace, they did not always show either love or unity.

Sound familiar? Before you shrug and say, "Well, that's human nature!" consider both the causes and the cure, as discussed in 1 Corinthians 1:10–4:21.

The Christian congregation at Corinth was Paul's "problem church." The members were raw recruits to Christ. Nearly all of them had come directly from a raunchy, free-wheeling paganism. And Corinth's paganism shocked even the easygoing Romans, who tolerated nearly every form of vice and viciousness. "Go Corinthian" was the way people in those times called the lifestyle of a person who threw over all restraint and indulged in immorality.

The Corinthian cluster of Christians soon developed a unique set of problems. It split into rival groups. Various leaders popped up, each insisting on being first. Some of the church members continued to cling to their old forms of immoral living. Other church members smiled and ignored the immorality practiced by fellow church members. Worship turned into a shambles. Some members made drunken gluttons of themselves at church gatherings while others, especially poor, working-class Christians, went hungry.

The Corinthian correspondence in our New Testament was the Apostle Paul's attempt to help the church folk in that city to resolve their problems. Chief among those problems, according to Paul, was their failure to appreciate that the Church is Christ's, not their own. Jesus Christ is the basis of the Church's life. Human leaders ultimately matter little. "No other foundation can any one lay," Paul writes, "than that which is laid, which is Jesus Christ!" (1 Corinthians 3:11).

NOTES ON THE PRINTED TEXT

After initial greetings, Paul moves right to the major emphasis. He is concerned about the unity of the Corinthian church. Chloe's slaves have reported the *dissensions* and the *quarrelings* in the church to Paul. *I appeal to you . . . that all of you agree that you be united in the same mind and the judgment.* It is an appeal for unity of purpose. A split in loyalties to Paul, to Apollos, or to Peter (Cephas) was the cause of the dissension. There is nothing conclusively known about this Christ faction of which Paul speaks. However, Paul argues that these divisions give preeminence to the teachers and not to Christ. *Is Christ divided?* Though the community is divided, Christ cannot be divided. Not one of the three teachers can occupy His position. It was Christ's death that brought salvation. *Was Paul crucified? Were you baptized in the name of Paul?* Paul uses himself to show that he is not criticizing any one teacher's supporters more than his own. Believers were baptized in the name of Christ. They were not baptized in Paul's name. In fact, Paul claims that he baptized none of the Corinthians except Crispus, Gaius, and Stephanas.

Paul's final argument is that the apostles are not competing against one another. Rather, they are fellow workers. *What then is Apollos? What is Paul?* They are servants of God *through whom you believe.* Using agricultural imagery Paul reminds the Corinthians that he planted the Gospel, and *Apollos watered* it. Though Paul planted the Gospel, his co-worker Apollos cared and tended the young church. *But God gave the growth,* Paul affirms. It is God's power that brought about growth. It was not because of Paul or Apollos. *He who plants and he who waters are equal.* We are fellow workmen for God. The Corinthians, Paul summarizes, *are God's field, God's building.*

With the mentioning of *building,* Paul changes images. He pictures himself as a master builder. God commissioned him to lay a foundation. The foundation was Jesus Christ. Now, another man is building upon this foundation. However, Paul is concerned about the quality of the work that others lay on his foundation. Thus, he warns, *let each man take care of how he builds upon it.* For the only foundation that can be laid is Jesus Christ. If a foundation other than Jesus Christ is used by the teachers, the true quality of these materials will be shown at judgment. Paul is thinking of the work of the teachers. *Gold, silver, precious stones, wood, hay, straw* are not good building materials. On Judgment Day, *fire will test what sort of work each one has done.* In this statement, Paul is using the Old Testament conception of fire as an element of purification. Fire burns away any impurities and leaves behind only the pure, tempered material. Paul is certain that the wrong type of teaching will be destroyed. *If any man's work is burned up, he will suffer loss, though he himself will be saved.* However, if the work is truly built on the foundation of Christ, it will survive, and the man will be rewarded.

SUGGESTIONS TO TEACHERS

There is a hoary joke in which the question is asked: What happens when two Scots meet? Answer: They start the First Presbyterian Church—and the Second Presbyterian Church.

Sadly, the Church has been broken into squabbling factions. (It took the American Presbyterians 122 years to reunite after the tragic split of the Civil War.) One of the problems for Christians in every century is how to let Christ's reconciling mercy bring healing to the Body of Christ. Today's lesson offers you as teacher and member of Christ's Church the opportunity of working to end the destructive divisiveness.

1. *FALLACY OF FACTIONS.* Steep yourself and your class in the scriptural material from 1 Corinthians for this week. Call attention to the claim in this section that dissension means, in effect, dividing Christ. Make it clear to your class that quarrels among church members not only destroy the relationship between persons but also with Christ. A divided church is a broken church. Church disputes permit only a partial Presence of Christ.

2. *FOOLISHNESS OF GOD.* Examine 1 Corinthians 1:18–25 with your people. Why is Christ always absurd to the "wise"? Talk over together what is *wisdom* by the world's standards and *wisdom* by God's standards. Why must Christians constantly be confronted by the Cross in order to avoid the foolishness which leads to a divided church?

3. *FOLLY OF PRIDE.* The Apostle Paul tells the squabbling Corinthian Church that no one in that group has any right to consider himself or herself outstanding ("... not many of you were wise ... powerful [or] of noble birth"). No

person can "boast in the presence of God" (1 Corinthians 1:29). Church fights, like human quarrels, start with a sense of boasting on someone's part. The truly wise Christian realizes that the only cause to boast is Christ's. Pride is seen for the foolishness it is.

4. *FOOD FOR FELLOW WORKERS.* Paul and Apollos and the other early Christian leaders would not let themselves be preeminent. They were builders. They were building a "living Temple"—Christ's Church made up of humans transformed by Christ. 1 Corinthians 3:5–17 provides a significant picture of us, the Church, as "God's Temple." Is His Presence sensed through the life of your class? Or your congregation? Of your denomination?

5. *FATHER IN THE FAITH.* The old Apostle Paul, writing to the Corinthians, considers himself not merely their "guide" but their spiritual father. This is an opportunity for your class members to reflect on who were the "fathers" and "mothers" in Christ. Who brought the meaning of the Gospel to you? How are you and your people being such "parents" in the Lord to others? Are you united as Christ's "family" as a starting point?

TOPIC FOR ADULTS
A DIVIDED CHURCH

T-Shirt Theology. A visitor to California reported seeing an unusual number of people wearing T-shirts with inscriptions on them. Some T-shirts carried obscene messages. Some advertised some product. But the T-shirt message which caught the eye of the visitor was the one which announced in bold letters: "HOW CAN I FLY LIKE AN EAGLE WHEN I HAVE TO WORK WITH TURKEYS?"

Come to think of it, this is the way we often feel about the people in our church. How can we reach the heights of spirituality when we have to associate with such hypocrites?

Be careful! That attitude is at the root of every division within Christ's Church! Whenever any of us assumes that the others are "turkeys" or speaks disparagingly of other Christians, we are breaking the community into eagles versus turkeys, me versus them.

Christ means for us to live together in love!

One or Two Can Do It. "Even one or two spiritually strong individuals (who may by no means be 'leader types' psychologically) can have a quite fantastic effect if they really put themselves at the disposal of God. It is not only that they may move mountains of local prejudice and suspicion. Even if they don't shift the mountains an inch, they very often inspire their children, and their friends, and their friends' children to greater things. . . . You should not be, and you will not be, alone for long. Nothing is more certain than that God intends his people to work in groups, in fellowships, together. All over the place, cutting across the whole messy entanglements of denominational barriers, there are springing up informal groups of Christians, clerical and lay together, who really care about God's world. . . . And these groups are genuine manifestations of God's church. . . ."—Mark Gibbs and T. Ralph Morton, *God's Frozen People*, Philadelphia: Westminster Press, 1965.

Root of Schism. "I believe that the root of almost every schism and heresy from which the Church of God has suffered has been the effort of man to earn rather than to receive his salvation and that the reason that preaching is commonly so ineffective is that it calls on men oftener to work for God than to behold God working for them."—John Ruskin.

Questions for Pupils on the Next Lesson. 1. What were some of the behavior problems in the church at Corinth to which Paul had to respond? 2. Why does sexual immorality weaken the Church? 3. What does it mean when the Bible says that our bodies are the "temple of God"? 4. How can the Church offer greater support for those wanting to live a wholesome life? 5. Is every adult Christian a model for others?

TOPIC FOR YOUTH
OVERCOMING DIVISIONS WITHIN

Ruined by His Own Scheme. Divisions in the Church are often caused by jealousy among church members. Almost invariably, such jealousy brings grief to everyone. It brings to mind the story of the king's staff in Burma one time many years ago. Members of the king's entourage were often deeply jealous of one another. Sometimes they plotted against each other.

One time, the royal potter grew envious of the man who washed the king's elephant. The jealousy led the potter to hatch a scheme to ruin the washerman. The potter persuaded the king to order the washerman to scrub the elephant, which was black in color, until it was completely white. The washerman stated that he would have to have a container large enough to contain the elephant. Thereupon, the king commanded the potter to make a pot big enough to accommodate the elephant. The potter fashioned such an enormous container. However, as soon as the elephant stepped into the huge clay bowl, it caused the container to break into pieces. The king ordered the potter to make another great bowl for the elephant. Again, the weight of the elephant broke the vessel. The potter tried crafting many more pots big enough to hold the elephant, but each time the bowl crumbled. The potter was finally ruined. His jealousy backfired!

Envy in a church group also has destructive effects. Our envy can lead us to devise ways to put ourselves ahead and to belittle others. Such jealousy ends by hurting us as well as the other!

Support System. In a Prisoner-of-War Camp in Vietnam, Captain James Stockdale was kept in solitary confinement for long periods. He was often tortured. Stockdale, however, relates that even while he was being beaten by his cruel captors, he could hear other prisoners tapping out the supportive message, "God bless you, Jim Stockdale."

This is what we, the members of the Christian community, are meant to do. Instead of allowing ourselves to be divided, we with Christ's help tap our encouraging and supportive messages to one another. We pray for God's blessing on each other instead of allowing ourselves to be separated from one another.

Where Are Your Hurting? A disciple said to his revered rabbi, "Rabbi, I love you."

The rabbi replied, "Do you know where I am hurting?"

The disciple admitted he did not.

Then, said the rabbi, "How can you love me if you do not know what gives me pain?"

When we know what gives pain to one another within Christ's community, we will show love to each other. Then—and only then—we will overcome divisions within Christ's Church!

Questions for Pupils on the Next Lesson. 1. What were the behavior problems upsetting the Christians in Corinth, according to 1 Corinthians 5:11? 2. Does sexual immorality really weaken a Christian community? 3. Isn't sex strictly a personal matter between two people, or does our sexual behavior also affect others? 4. What does the Bible mean when it calls our bodies the "temple of God"?

LESSON VII—OCTOBER 13

IMMORALITY WEAKENS THE BODY OF CHRIST

Background Scripture: 1 Corinthians 5; 6
Devotional Reading: 1 Corinthians 6:1–8

KING JAMES VERSION

1 CORINTHIANS 6 9 Know ye not that the unrighteous shall not inherit the kingdom of God? Be not deceived: neither fornicators, nor idolaters, nor adulterers, nor effeminate, nor abusers of themselves with mankind,

10 Nor thieves, nor covetous, nor drunkards, nor revilers, nor extortioners, shall inherit the kingdom of God.

11 And such were some of you: but ye are washed, but ye are sanctified, but ye are justified in the name of the Lord Jesus, and by the Spirit of our God.

12 All things are lawful unto me, but all things are not expedient: all things are lawful for me, but I will not be brought under the power of any.

13 Meats for the belly, and the belly for meats: but God shall destroy both it and them. Now the body *is* not for fornication, but for the Lord; and the Lord for the body.

14 And God hath both raised up the Lord, and will also raise up us by his own power.

15 Know ye not that your bodies are the members of Christ? shall I then take the members of Christ, and make *them* the members of a harlot? God forbid.

16 What? know ye not that he which is joined to a harlot is one body? for two, saith he, shall be one flesh.

17 But he that is joined unto the Lord is one spirit.

18 Flee fornication. Every sin that a man doeth is without the body; but he that committeth fornication sinneth against his own body.

19 What? know ye not that your body is the temple of the Holy Ghost *which is* in you, which ye have of God, and ye are not your own?

20 For ye are bought with a price: therefore glorify God in your body, and in your spirit, which are God's.

REVISED STANDARD VERSION

1 CORINTHIANS 6 9 Do you not know that the unrighteous will not inherit the kingdom of God? Do not be deceived; neither the immoral, nor idolaters, nor adulterers, nor sexual perverts, 10 nor thieves, nor the greedy, nor drunkards, nor revilers, nor robbers will inherit the kingdom of God. 11 And such were some of you. But you were washed, you were sanctified, you were justified in the name of the Lord Jesus Christ and in the Spirit of our God.

12 "All things are lawful for me," but not all things are helpful. "All things are lawful for me," but I will not be enslaved by anything. 13 "Food is meant for the stomach and the stomach for food"—and God will destroy both one and the other. The body is not meant for immorality, but for the Lord, and the Lord for the body. 14 And God raised the Lord and will also raise us up by his power. 15 Do you not know that your bodies are members of Christ? Shall I therefore take the members of Christ and make them members of a prostitute? Never! 16 Do you not know that he who joins himself to a prostitute becomes one body with her? For, as it is written, "The two shall become one flesh." 17 But he who is united to the Lord becomes one spirit with him. 18 Shun immorality. Every other sin which a man commits is outside the body; but the immoral man sins against his own body. 19 Do you not know that your body is a temple of the Holy Spirit within you, which you have from God? You are not your own; 20 you were bought with a price. So glorify God in your body.

KEY VERSE: *You were washed, you were sanctified, you were justified in the name of the Lord Jesus Christ and in the Spirit of our God.* 1 Corinthians 6:11.

HOME DAILY BIBLE READINGS

Oct.	7.	M.	*Sex Is God's Idea.* Genesis 2:21–25.
Oct.	8.	T.	*Sex and the Way of Wisdom.* Proverbs 6:20–32.
Oct.	9.	W.	*Immorality in the Church.* 1 Corinthians 5:1–13.
Oct.	10.	T.	*Christian Freedom and Responsibility.* 1 Corinthians 6:9–20.
Oct.	11.	F.	*Christian Marriage.* 1 Corinthians 7:1–11.
Oct.	12.	S.	*The Christian's Life Situation.* 1 Corinthians 7:12–24.
Oct.	13.	S.	*Christ Forgives Sexual Sin.* John 8:3–11.

BACKGROUND

A few years ago, social scientists dubbed the sexual revolution of permissiveness and hedonism "the New Morality." Actually, it was as old as the oldest parts of the Bible. The acts and attitudes labelled "the New Morality" in Cambridge and Kalamazoo were old stuff in Corinth. Proof? Merely look at Paul's letters to the Corinthians in the New Testament.

The ancient Mediterranean world was not exactly puritanical, but was tolerant toward vice in all its dreary, sordid forms. Only the Jews and Christians refused to indulge in the sexual circus and held to a strict practice of sex only between a husband and his wife. The Greeks and Romans, and nearly everyone else, laughed at the people of the Bible. After all, the pagans reasoned, life consists of merely gratifying one's desires, and the appetite for sex like the appetite for food should be satisfied in whatever pleasurable way one wishes.

This notion permeated the culture of the first century. In the city of Corinth, however, it had become an article of faith and a way of life for most. Corinth had the reputation of being the cesspool for vice in the Roman world. A wealthy port, strategically located on the busiest isthmus of the Mediterranean, it attracted all the flotsam of the world. Its prostitutes and porno-centers peddled every known form of vice.

Imagine trying to organize a church in this kind of setting! But Paul did just that. And imagine trying to be Christians in such an environment! Some succeeded. Others, however, found themselves being sucked downward into the prevailing Corinthian culture. "Why not? It's my body. And if I gratify my craving for sex, it's like food for my stomach—doing what comes naturally," some church people were saying. Worse, one of the church leaders was regularly sleeping with his stepmother.

One of the purposes of Paul's writing to the young church in Corinth was to remind the new Christians who they were. "You were washed, you were sanctified, you were justified in the name of the Lord Jesus Christ and in the Spirit of our God," Paul pleads (1 Corinthians 6:11).

NOTES ON THE PRINTED TEXT

Another consideration in the Corinthian correspondence is the matter of discipline. Sexual immorality next occupies Paul's attention. *Do you not know that the unrighteous will not inherit the kingdom of God?* Paul is greatly concerned with the immorality in the church. The licentious habits of the pagans are being reflected in the Corinth Church. Paul reminds the church that Christians must be righteous. The lives of the believers must be different from the lives of the unrighteous. Believers inherit the Kingdom of God, while the *immoral, idolaters, homosexuals, thieves, greedy, drunkards, revilers, and robbers* will not. However, Paul reminds the Corinthians that *some* of the church's numbers were originally drawn from the ranks of this list.

But you were washed, Paul says. The Corinthians were baptized and cleansed of their sins. They were set apart from the others in Corinth. They were to be distinguishable from other Corinthians by their righteous acts. This is the meaning of *sanctified.* And, their sins have been forgiven. Literally they have been *justified in the name of the Lord Jesus Christ.* Washed, sanctified, and justified. What a marvelous definition of the people of the Church!

Some believers felt that being a Christian gave them unrestricted freedom. They could live as they pleased without any responsibility and still be secure in the belief that God would forgive them. Paul debates this belief with them. *"All things are lawful for me,"* argue those who believe they can do as they please. Paul simply replies, *but not all things are helpful.* He reminds them of the danger of being slaves to their passions. He raises the issue of food. He quotes the Epicureans in the Corinth church who believed that *food is meant for the stomach and the stomach for food.* Paul believes in their conviction that food is meant to supply the stomach's hunger. Excesses in eating are as immoral as excesses in sex. Paul squelches the belief by some that the body was made for sexual liberty when he declares *the body is not meant for immorality.* The body is meant for the Lord. Within the Church, all *bodies are members of Christ.* All bodies are part of Christ. Therefore, sexual immorality among some weakens the body of Christ. Sex within marriage is a union of love. Sex outside marriage is a physical act that separates individuals from the body of Christ. *Do you not know that he who joins himself to a prostitute becomes one body with her?* The two become one! And, Paul asks, should he *take the members of Christ and make them members of a prostitute?* Never! Believers cannot give themselves over to physical desires. They must give themselves to God. *He who is united to the Lord becomes one spirit with him.*

So prevalent was sexual immorality in Corinth that Paul's counsel is to flee from it. *Shun immorality.* His total horror of sexual immorality causes him to overlook other sins that people commit against their bodies. Paul believes that sexual immorality is a sin against God, against the other person involved, and against one's own body.

Again, Paul asks rhetorically, *Do you not know that your body is a temple of the Holy Spirit?* Christians' bodies are the Temples of God. The Holy Spirit dwells in them. We are to glorify God in our bodies because we were bought *with a price.* Christ paid our ransom. Our redemption was paid for on the Cross. Having been redeemed by Christ, we are to serve, glorify, and praise God in our bodies.

SUGGESTIONS TO TEACHERS

Everyone has heard stories of ministers running off with organists, or the church officer having an affair with a Sunday-School teacher. Robert Burns wrote a biting description of such scandalous behavior in his poem "Holy Willie," in which a sanctimonious elder, William Fisher, brings a bad name to his parish. Burns and others become cynical and disillusioned about the Church after seeing Fisher and other "Holy Willies." Immorality weakens the Church!

Your lesson this Sunday explores this important point. Using the Corinthian congregation as a case study, you will assist your class to reflect on how immorality weakens the Body of Christ in every setting, from Corinth to Kalamazoo.

1. *LEVITY OF LIBERTINES.* Start by pointing out that the Corinthian Christians not only practiced immoral acts but, worse, countenanced them. In fact, they laughed and boasted of what went on in their church. You don't have to strain to note the parallels between then and now. Suggest ways in which Church people still excuse their immoral behavior.

2. *LEAVEN OF LICENTIOUSNESS.* The problem, of course, is that instead of the Church pervading the society, the society pervades the Church. And society laughs at morality. Immoral acts and thoughts among church members are like an infection spreading throughout an organism. Have your class members bring up examples from their own experience of how destructive immorality is to a congregation.

3. *LAMENTATION OF LORD'S FOLK.* Take careful note of the way in which Paul insists that vigorous action must be taken when immorality appears in a church. Church people, although regretful, must nonetheless be resolute in taking a firm stand in the face of sinful carryings-on. Discuss the place of Church discipline within a Church family.

4. *LOSSES OF LEGALISM.* The New Testament consistently urges Christians

to resolve disagreements among themselves without going to the civil courts. Paul insists that every congregation should be able to handle squabbles between members without recourse to the law. The reason: a win-lose adversarial relationship among Christians always ends as a lose-lose situation for the entire Christian community. What does this mean in an era where litigation seems to be on the rise, even among Christians and congregations?

5. *LAW OF LOVE.* Stress to your class that Christians always respect others, and that necessarily means sexual purity. Such purity may fly in the face of popular slogans and attitudes, such as in Corinth or contemporary culture. Emphasize also how Christians are responsible to Christ and to each other. The verse, "You are not your own; you were bought with a price," should be thoroughly chewed and digested by your class in this lesson.

TOPIC FOR ADULTS
IMMORALITY WEAKENS THE BODY OF CHRIST

Pro Big 7. "I'm pro Big 7! By that I mean, when I hear the 'pro-lifers' and the 'pro-choicers' come down hard on the real issue at hand, I'll know of their sincerity.

"Adulterous behavior is the most rampant social plague in Western society today. As a community-minded pastor who does a significant amount of counseling, I know it is illicit sex and the current philosophy in favor of philandering that are at the root of error on the part of both 'pros.'

"And let not our good churches escape the critique; our hypocrisy is related to the seventh of the Big Ten as we debate these and other lifestyle issues without relating them to the Lord's clear directives about mismanagement of the sexual side of our lives. Homosexuality is also illicit sex based in a promiscuous philandering philosophy. Being 'fair' to all sorts of 'lifestyles' seems to drive church persons from the simple proscription, 'Thou shalt not commit adultery.' Jesus was clear that any sex (even including mental) outside of marriage is adulterous.

"Married husbands and wives make the positive choice—and then *have* the choices by their responsible relationship. This nuclear family is the stable foundation of all society. The personal, irresponsible, greedy, 'me first' of those who chose to reject the simple proscription by God is evident in their minds as they make political, social, and religious issues of their anti-Big Ten way of life. Our job, as interpreters of God's Word, is to preach to the dry bones of this sin and pray God to bring the new life of adherence to His Way for all. Now when you start taking issue like that, the wrestling you will be doing with your community will be more than a football game."—Lee H. Poole, *Monday Morning*, April 18, 1983.

Wrecks the Orchestra. The concert A for all musicians today stands at 440 cycles per second. This is standard pitch everywhere. Any singer or instrumentalist who varies from that standard will sing or play off-key. Moreover, if any performer persists in deviating from that standard pitch, he will wreck the performance of the entire group.

There are no variations in what the concert A is. It is fixed. Every musician must conform to it. Likewise, there are no variations on the norms of sexual behavior expected of Christians. In fact, any church member who decides to flout that standard will not only live out of tune with the rest but will ruin the performance of the entire church!

Don't wreck the orchestra by trying to perform to the wrong pitch!

Shame on the Name. Mark Maharg is a deeply committed Christian and a busy lay leader in church circles in Pennsylvania. Someone asked him what the origin of his unusual name was. Mr. Maharg explained how his name came into being.

Originally, he stated, the family lived in Scotland. At one time, several generations ago, the name was *Graham*. One of Mr. Maharg's ancestors, however,
brought dishonor to the Graham clan by a shameful act. It was decreed that
henceforth that branch of the Grahams was not worthy to carry the name but
would be required to spell the name backwards. Therefore, instead of *Graham*
Mark Maharg's distant ancestor was forced to reverse the letters to *Maharg*. Although the original cause for the name change has long been forgotten, the effects of the act have affected the family for years and years.

In the same way, any dishonorable act on the part of any member of Christ's
family brings shame and long-lasting effects on others. Immorality is never purely
a personal matter, but affects the entire Church!

Questions for Pupils on the Next Lesson. 1. How would you describe the culture surrounding the church at Corinth? 2. How does a Christian remain faithful
to Christ when in a conflict with the culture? 3. Is a Christian free to do whatever
he or she pleases because the Gospel frees us from trying to save ourselves
through keeping rules? 4. Exactly what does it mean when Christians are ex-
horted to do everything "to God's glory"?

TOPIC FOR YOUTH
GOD'S PLAN FOR OUR BODIES

Games With Others. Akbar the Great, the famous Mogul ruler in India, built a
magnificent palace for himself not far from Agra in northern India. He used the
place for sixteen years. An absolute ruler, he gratified all his whims. One part of
the huge palace has a great parchesi board laid out in beautiful shades of thousands and thousands of pieces of marble. This huge parchesi board used young
girls as the pieces on the board. Akbar indulged himself by using these women as
his playthings.

God's plan for our bodies is directly opposite from this Mogul emperor. Instead
of treating others as toys for our own amusement, including our sexual amusement, we remember that we live responsibly before God with each other. Our
very bodies belong to God, not to ourselves. Therefore, we never play immoral
games. We treat our own lives and others' as "temples of God."

Tethered for Our Own Safety. A visitor to a famous farm in England where
racing horses were raised was startled to notice that several of the magnificent
animals had weights fastened to one of their legs. The visitor asked the trainer
why the weights were on these horses.

"I must do that for their own safety and well-being," explained the trainer, an
experienced horsewoman. "If I let them run free," she continued, "those horses
have a tendency to jump fences and injure themselves permanently. Unless they
are controlled, they could damage themselves badly and be of no use to the
owner."

You may think, "Why can't I do as I please? Why all these restrictions on my
sexual feelings? It's my body, isn't it? So why can't I use it to enjoy myself any
way any time I feel like it?"

For your own well-being, the Lord puts restraints on you and every Christian.
We are not allowed to jump the fences and do as we please. God knows that we
may hurt ourselves. He also knows that the damage from "doing as I please" can
result in not carrying out the plans intended by Him, our Owner!

Parody on Vows. Former President Jimmy Carter has a deep commitment to
Christian marriage. Unknown to many, the ex-President also has a good sense of
humor. Remembering how his speech writers often rewrote his manuscripts,
Jimmy Carter sent his former speech writer Rick Hertzberg a tongue-in-cheek
copy of the wedding service when Hertzberg married Michele Slung. Mr. Carter

edited the vows in the marriage service as if it were a speech Hertzberg had written. For example, Carter circled, "till death do us part" and wrote, "Too morbid—do you want to alienate every sick person in America?" When he got to, "I, Rick, take you, Michele, to be my lawful wedded wife," the former President deleted "wife" and inserted "partner," warning, "Do not use sexist expressions."

Next to, "For better, for worse, for richer, for poorer," Carter wrote, "Polarizing—how about the middle ground?"

There is, of course, no "middle ground" when it comes to commitments to each other as husband and wife, as both the ex-President and his speech writer know.

Questions for Pupils on the Next Lesson. 1. Is the Church always able to fit in with the ideas of society or is it ever in conflict with culture? 2. What is the situation of the Church in the culture where you live: is it ever criticized by some who don't like its standards? 3. What do you find is shaping your beliefs and values? 4. How is it possible to remain faithful to Christ in the face of a hostile culture? 5. How can a Christian cherish Christian freedom without offending or hurting others?

LESSON VIII—OCTOBER 20

THE CHURCH IN CONFLICT WITH CULTURE

Background Scripture: 1 Corinthians 8:1—11:1
Devotional Reading: 1 Corinthians 9:15–23

KING JAMES VERSION

1 CORINTHIANS 10 6 Now these things were our examples, to the intent we should not lust after evil things, as they also lusted.

7 Neither be ye idolaters, as *were* some of them; as it is written, The people sat down to eat and drink, and rose up to play.

8 Neither let us commit fornication, as some of them committed, and fell in one day three and twenty thousand.

9 Neither let us tempt Christ, as some of them also tempted, and were destroyed of serpents.

10 Neither murmur ye, as some of them also murmured, and were destroyed of the destroyer.

11 Now all these things happened unto them for ensamples: and they are written for our admonition, upon whom the ends of the world are come.

12 Wherefore let him that thinketh he standeth take heed lest he fall.

13 There hath no temptation taken you but such as is common to man: but God *is* faithful, who will not suffer you to be tempted above that ye are able; but will with the temptation also make a way to escape, that ye may be able to bear *it*.

14 Wherefore, my dearly beloved, flee from idolatry.

31 Whether therefore ye eat, or drink, or whatsoever ye do, do all to the glory of God.

11 Be ye followers of me, even as I also *am* of Christ.

REVISED STANDARD VERSION

1 CORINTHIANS 10 6 Now these things are warnings for us, not to desire evil as they did. 7 Do not be idolaters as some of them were; as it is written, "The people sat down to eat and drink and rose up to dance." 8 We must not indulge in immorality as some of them did, and twenty-three thousand fell in a single day. 9 We must not put the Lord to the test, as some of them did and were destroyed by serpents; 10 nor grumble, as some of them did and were destroyed by the Destroyer. 11 Now these things happened to them as a warning, but they were written down for our instruction, upon whom the end of the ages has come. 12 Therefore let any one who thinks that he stands take heed lest he fall. 13 No temptation has overtaken you that is not common to man. God is faithful, and he will not let you be tempted beyond your strength, but with the temptation will also provide the way of escape, that you may be able to endure it.

14 Therefore, my beloved, shun the worship of idols.

31 So, whether you eat or drink, or whatever you do, do all to the glory of God.

11 Be imitators of me, as I am of Christ.

KEY VERSE: *Whether you eat or drink, or whatever you do, do all to the glory of God.* 1 Corinthians 10:31.

HOME DAILY BIBLE READINGS

Oct. 14. M. *My Right and My Neighbor's Good.* 1 Corinthians 8:1–13.
Oct. 15. T. *Supporting God's Servants.* 1 Corinthians 9:1–15.
Oct. 16. W. *Paul's Great Concern.* 1 Corinthians 9:19–23.
Oct. 17. T. *God Can Be Trusted.* 1 Corinthians 10:1–13.
Oct. 18. F. *A Worthy Motive.* 1 Corinthians 10:23—11:1.
Oct. 19. S. *Jesus and Religious Custom.* Luke 6:1–11.
Oct. 20. S. *What Harms Persons.* Mark 7:14–23.

BACKGROUND

Everyone has seen or heard of the little lizardlike creature called a chameleon. Because of a series of pigment-releasing cells under its skin, this small reptile can camouflage itself by taking on the color of various shades of earth or foliage. It manages to blend in with its surroundings so well that it escapes detection.

Christian churches easily take up the protective coloration of the culture around them. Sometimes, it is difficult to tell whether Christ or the culture is most influential in the lives of certain congregations.

Paul wrestled with this problem also. His congregation in Corinth seemed to be composed of a lot of chameleon-believers. Paul, dismayed at the way so many of these Corinthian Christians willingly took on the ways of the Corinthian culture, tried to point out that the Church almost always finds itself in conflict with culture.

We can appreciate the pressures the Corinthian church people faced. Picture what it must have been like. A pagan lifestyle was the accepted way to live. In fact, if one was not a sexual swinger, he or she was sneered at for being stupid, silly, or stuck-up. Towering over the great metropolis of Corinth was an acropolis on which stood a magnificent temple dedicated to Aphrodite, the goddess of erotic pleasure. Over 1,000 prostitutes, male as well as female, were kept near those so-called sacred premises to service devotees to the cult. In short, the culture of Corinth catered to pleasure and self-indulgence in every form. "Anything goes!" might have been the official motto of Corinth. In the face of such cultural values and practices, it was difficult to preserve one's identity as a Christian and maintain one's loyalty to Jesus Christ. A Christian was daily pressured to "go along." After all, everyone else seemed to do as he pleased!

In the face of such surroundings, Christians must remember, "Whatever you do, do all to the glory of God" (1 Corinthians 10:31).

NOTES ON THE PRINTED TEXT

An overriding concern of Paul is the immoral pagan culture that surrounds and threatens the Corinthian church. Paul knows the strength of temptation. He understands that no one is immune or secure from temptation. Therefore, he urges the Corinthians not to repeat the sins of the children of Israel who dabbled with the culture of their surrounding neighbors. He supports this with illustrations from the Old Testament.

Now these things are warnings for us not to desire evil as they did. Paul recalls the Israelites' lust for the fleshpots of Egypt (Numbers 11:4–34). He shares his fear of worshiping idols by recalling the story of the golden calf (Exodus 32:6) *when the people sat down to eat and drink and rose up to dance.* The meal celebrating the creation of the idol turned into a drunken orgy. Paul again speaks against immorality. *We must not indulge in immorality as some of them did.* He mentions the Israelites' seduction by the Moabite women and the resulting destruction (Numbers 25:1–9). In addition Paul writes, *we must not put the Lord to the test ... nor grumble.* Paul urges the Corinthians not to tempt God. He pictures the Israelites who tempted God and challenged God to provide food for them but were punished by poisonous snakes (Numbers 21:5–9). He also tells the Corinthians not to complain and murmur as Israel did during its wanderings. *Now these things happened as a warning.* Paul recalled these terrible events as a warning for the Corinthians. They are examples recorded for the Corinthians' instruction.

Therefore let anyone who thinks he stands take heed lest he fall. Paul warns the Corinthian church that temptations can overpower even the most confident and secure individual. Self-defense begins with the understanding that no one is immune to temptation. Moreover, he tells them that the temptations they have withstood have not been exceptional. *No temptation has overtaken you that is not common to man.* Worse temptations can and will follow, Paul promises. However, Paul also promises that God will provide the strength to remain faithful through these temptations. *God is faithful, and he will not let you be tempted be-*

yond your strength. God will also provide the way to endure the temptation. Paul knows that people will suffer temptations, but he is confident that God will give them the strength to endure the temptations. Through examples from the history of Israel, Paul has shown that God's chosen people were not immune to temptation. In particular, they were not immune to the worship of idols. Paul sums up his argument in one appeal. Run from idol worship! *Therefore, my beloved, shun the worship of idols.*

In his conclusion, Paul declares *whether you eat or drink, or whatever you do, do all to the glory of God.* Food offered to idols was the subject that occasioned this entire discussion (*see* 8:1 on). Paul argues that there is nothing wrong in eating food sacrificed to idols except where there was an idol feast in the pagan temple (10:21). However, out of love for a weaker brother who could not forget the old associations, a Christian should not let his freedom become a stumbling block to others (8:9). Christian freedom should not be an offense to a neighbor. *Give no offense to Jews or to Greeks or to the church of God.* Paul reminds the Corinthians that in his work as an apostle, he constantly has had to give up rights in the interests of others (9:1–23). So it is not surprising that he closes by presenting himself as a model for his church to imitate. *Be imitators of me, as I am of Christ.*

SUGGESTIONS TO TEACHERS

A vacationing family was driving through rural Lancaster County, Pennsylvania, and encountered Amish people driving horses and buggies and plowing with mule teams. "Why don't the Amish people use cars and tractors like everyone else, Daddy?" asked one of the children. The father was hard put to offer a good answer. Later, it occurred to him that these people didn't want to go along with current culture. Still later, it began to stir questions within his mind of how easily he and other Christians went along with present-day culture. Although he didn't sell his car and buy a horse, he became more sensitive to the ways in which the Church is in conflict with society.

This is what you as the teacher are to be about today. You are to help those in your class to become more aware that the Christian Church is almost never on the same course as the society around it. The scriptural material from 1 Corinthians offers splendid examples.

1. *HOW MUCH YOU KNOW OR HOW MUCH YOU LOVE?*   Take enough time in your lesson to explore the difference between *knowledge* according to the world and according to the Lord. There are "wise guys" at times within the Christian fellowship whose worldly knowledge will lead them to think that their smartness is superb. Remind your folks that it's caring, not knowing, that counts most in Christ's family.

2. *HOW MUCH YOU PLEASE YOURSELF OR HOW MUCH YOU HEED CHRIST?* Here is where you must lead your people to a deeper understanding of what freedom means for Christians. Although Christ frees us from rules, this does not mean we can do as we please. Rules, No; responsibility, *Yes!*

3. *HOW MUCH YOU GO ALONG WITH CULTURE AND HOW MUCH YOU STAND UP AS CHRIST'S?* Refer to the pressures and temptations facing Christians in ancient Corinth. Paul and other seasoned leaders knew, however, that the Church would be in conflict with ideas on sexual behavior, to name the most obvious. Have your class indicate what the areas of greatest conflict are between the Church and the world around us today.

4. *HOW MUCH IS LAWFUL AND HOW MUCH IS HELPFUL?* The problem over eating meat offered to idols may seem silly to us, but it was a real one to Corinthian church people. The topic you will talk about with your class is not the

butcher shops in Corinth but whether a Christian glorifies himself or God. Which comes first; your rights or the other's needs? This is the real issue in the meat-to-idols matter in 1 Corinthians. Where do those in your class find it most difficult to sort out whether personal rights or another's need is most important?

TOPIC FOR ADULTS
THE CHURCH IN CONFLICT WITH CULTURE

Dangers of Conformity. "The story is told of a man who had a canary which sang sweetly. When summer came, the man thought it was a pity to keep the canary indoors in its safe and accustomed surroundings, so he hung its cage out in a tree in his yard.

"Now, it happened that this tree was frequented by sparrows. Before long the canary's song lost much of its sweetness and by the end of summer it couldn't sing like a canary at all. All it could do was twitter, twitter, twitter, like an English sparrow. It had spent the summer in bad company and it had become like them, losing its gift."—*Sunshine Magazine,* Litchfield, IL, April, 1983.

Worship and Work. "In the '60's and '70's many theologians emphasized that the true 'life situation' of Christians was in the world. As far as coming in for worship was concerned, it was said that 'we are inside only for the sake of those outside.' . . . This appealed to the pragmatic, utilitarian, secularized American church in particular, a church that was never sure about the value of corporate worship. After all, what good does all that singing and praying do anyone?

"It gave such a heavy emphasis to God's action outside the church and in secular diakonia, that it implicitly cast doubt on the importance of leitourgia—prayer, preaching, sacraments. . . .

"I fear that after two decades of this thinking the church finds itself losing its identity, its integrity and coherence in its marriage with the world. The world has become the transformer of the church rather than that which is being transformed. The church which has let the world set the agenda has now forgotten why it came to the meeting.

"The only way the church will remain distinctive and lively in this world is through close attention to her identity-forming liturgies and rites. The term *anonymous Christian* is a theological non-sequitur. How can there be disciples who are unidentified with the Master or are indistinguishable from those who are not disciples? How is there a Messiah without a messianic community?"—William H. Willimon, *The Service of God: How Worship and Ethics Are Related,* Nashville: Abingdon, 1983.

Peace Umbrella. "During the Nazi occupation of Paris, a husky storm trooper stepped into a subway car and tripped headlong over the umbrella of a little old lady sitting next to the door. After picking himself up, the bruised Nazi launched a tirade of abuse, then bolted from the car at the next station.

"When he was gone, the passengers burst into spontaneous applause for the elderly woman. 'I know it isn't much,' she said, graciously accepting the compliments, 'but he's the sixth one I've brought down today.'

"Salute the lady. She was no political bureaucrat, she occupied no official seat of power, made no policy, held no gun, conferred with no ambassador—but she had her say. Her umbrella was her shepherd's rod to beat off wild, roaming scavengers in high boots. She made her statement. She took her stand. She did what she could with what she had. She may have inspired millions of the French to carry umbrellas even on dry days."—Wayne M. Hoffman, *A.D.,* June, 1983.

Questions for Pupils on the Next Lesson. 1. How would you define a true Church leader? 2. Is there such a person as a "perfect" leader? 3. How do you distinguish between strength and weakness in leadership? 4. In what ways do you find yourself thrust into leadership as a Christian? 5. Can God use anyone as a leader?

TOPIC FOR YOUTH
SEARCHING FOR GOD'S WAY

Monday Morning Ministry. " 'No doubt the most difficult decision I must face in my job,' he said, 'is whether to shut down my plant now or keep losing money in the hope that I can turn things around. I've got some good people who have been with us for over thirty years and I owe it to them to try to keep things going.' He looked at his feet and sighed. 'But if I hang on too long, I'll lose every penny I own, and then who will take care of my family?'

"We were gathered in a tight circle of six at a weekend retreat dealing with the ministry of the laity in the world. Early in the program we had gathered participants into small groups in order to begin thinking about their worldly ministries. Each person was asked to respond to three questions: In what way are you spending the greatest amount of your waking time? What are the problems or decisions you are dealing with in that 'occupation'? How do you see your faith relating to those problems or decisions?

"I asked him about that third question. 'Vince,' I said, 'in what way do you see your faith relating to the big decision you have to make?'

" 'I've never really thought about it until tonight,' he replied. 'I guess I have to say that I really don't see any connection.' "—William E. Diehl, *A.D.*, July–August 1982.

Listening to the Bystanders. We often try to do what the culture around us calls us to do. We forget to search for God's Way. Listening only to the crowd will cause us to miss God's Way. We will be like the man and his son described in an old story. The father and son were on their way to market with their donkey. At first, the man sat on the animal and the boy walked alongside. Then they heard people saying, "How terrible! Look at that strong man riding on the donkey and that poor little boy having to walk." So the father got off and put the boy on the donkey. They continued further, but heard other people saying, "Look at that lazy boy, sitting there on that donkey and making his poor father walk." At this, the father got back on the donkey and they both rode. However, they saw people pointing at them and heard them say, "What cruel people, both of them sitting on one donkey." So they both got off and walked alongside of the donkey. They had not gone much farther when they heard some bystanders laughing and stating: "How silly! A healthy donkey with no one on its back, and those two people walking!" Embarrassed, the man and his boy picked up the donkey and started to carry it. They never did get to the market!

Bring on the Christians. Red Smith, the sportswriter, once was invited to lunch in New York at a restaurant called the Roman Forum. The restaurant had recently been redecorated in a classical motif. Red Smith glanced around at the place and commented to the owner, "This is more Roman than Rome itself. All you need are a few lions and some Christians."

The restaurant owner paused for a minute, then answered, "Lions I can get."

Questions for Pupils on the Next Lesson. 1. What are the qualities a true Church leader should have? 2. Who are some genuine Christian leaders that you personally have known? 3. Have you ever thought of yourself as a leader? 4. What leadership style should you as a leader have? 5. How should adults handle their authority?

LESSON IX—OCTOBER 27

WHO ARE TRUE CHURCH LEADERS?

Background Scripture: 2 Corinthians 3; 4; 11; Titus 1:5–9
Devotional Reading: 2 Corinthians 5:6–15

KING JAMES VERSION

2 CORINTHIANS 4 THEREFORE, seeing we have this ministry, as we have received mercy, we faint not;

2 But have renounced the hidden things of dishonesty, not walking in craftiness, nor handling the word of God deceitfully; but, by manifestation of the truth, commending ourselves to every man's conscience in the sight of God.

3 But if our gospel be hid, it is hid to them that are lost:

4 In whom the god of this world hath blinded the minds of them which believe not, lest the light of the glorious gospel of Christ, who is the image of God, should shine unto them.

5 For we preach not ourselves, but Christ Jesus the Lord; and ourselves your servants for Jesus' sake.

6 For God, who commanded the light to shine out of darkness, hath shined in our hearts, to give the light of the knowledge of the glory of God in the face of Jesus Christ.

7 But we have this treasure in earthen vessels, that the excellency of the power may be of God, and not of us.

8 We are troubled on every side, yet not distressed; we are perplexed, but not in despair;

9 Persecuted, but not forsaken; cast down, but not destroyed;

10 Always bearing about in the body the dying of the Lord Jesus, that the life also of Jesus might be made manifest in our body.

11 For we which live are alway delivered unto death for Jesus' sake, that the life also of Jesus might be made manifest in our mortal flesh.

12 So then death worketh in us, but life in you.

REVISED STANDARD VERSION

2 CORINTHIANS 4 Therefore, having this ministry by the mercy of God, we do not lose heart. 2 We have renounced disgraceful, underhanded ways; we refuse to practice cunning or to tamper with God's word, but by the open statement of the truth we would commend ourselves to every man's conscience in the sight of God. 3 And even if our gospel is veiled, it is veiled only to those who are perishing. 4 In their case the god of this world has blinded the minds of the unbelievers, to keep them from seeing the light of the gospel of the glory of Christ, who is the likeness of God. 5 For what we preach is not ourselves, but Jesus Christ as Lord, with ourselves as your servants for Jesus' sake. 6 For it is the God who said, "Let light shine out of darkness," who has shone in our hearts to give the light of the knowledge of the glory of God in the face of Christ.

7 But we have this treasure in earthen vessels, to show that the transcendent power belongs to God and not to us. 8 We are afflicted in every way, but not crushed; perplexed, but not driven to despair; 9 persecuted, but not forsaken; struck down, but not destroyed; 10 always carrying in the body the death of Jesus, so that the life of Jesus may also be manifested in our bodies. 11 For while we live we are always being given up to death for Jesus' sake, so that the life of Jesus may be manifested in our mortal flesh. 12 So death is at work in us, but life in you.

KEY VERSE: *For what we preach is not ourselves, but Jesus Christ as Lord, with ourselves as your servants.* 2 Corinthians 4:5.

HOME DAILY BIBLE READINGS

Oct. 21. M. *Paul's Qualifications.* 2 Corinthians 3:1–6.
Oct. 22. T. *Mirrors of God's Glory.* 2 Corinthians 3:7–18.
Oct. 23. W. *Integrity.* 2 Corinthians 4:1–6.
Oct. 24. T. *Courage and Hope.* 2 Corinthians 4:7–18.
Oct. 25. F. *Paul's Concern for His Children.* 2 Corinthians 11:1–15.
Oct. 26. S. *Endurance.* 2 Corinthians 11:21–32.
Oct. 27. S. *Leadership Qualities in the Church.* Titus 1:5–9.

BACKGROUND

Three lay leaders of a congregation, in which two pastors in a row had caused problems and left scars in that church, approached a neighboring minister respected for his wisdom and integrity. The trio of lay leaders related the dismal facts of how their two previous pastors had not been true Christian leaders. "What do we do to make sure we won't get taken again?" they asked the wise neighboring minister.

This is the kind of situation which Paul the Apostle had to address in some of his writings. In Corinth and elsewhere, he discovered that some leaders were frankly preying on the Christians. Paul called these preachers "peddlers of God's word" (2 Corinthians 2:17). What a perfect description of people reducing the Gospel to a product to be sold for their own gain!

The longest topic in 2 Corinthians is the section from 4:1 to 6:13 on the ministry. In this portion (part of which covers today's lesson), Paul deals with what it means to be a true minister. Prior to chapter 4, Paul has written about the commission of a true pastor and the meaning of the New Covenant which a true minister preaches. Beginning at chapter 4, Paul writes about what a true church leader should be and do.

You may think that this is a section for professional leaders only. You may be tempted to slide over this part of 2 Corinthians as "shoptalk" among pastors and advice to seminary students. Remember, however, that Paul was writing for lay persons. You can not skip this portion. It answers the question asked by the three leaders who wanted to know how they could choose a genuine Christian leader and not be duped by a "peddler."

Paul gives clear guidelines on how a true church leader is a faithful servant who consistently proclaims Jesus Christ as Lord. He adds that every preacher may be compared to a cheap crock holding a magnificent collection of jewelry. It is the message, the priceless treasure of the News of Jesus Christ, not the human messenger, which is important.

NOTES ON THE PRINTED TEXT

Second Corinthians is the most personal of Paul's letters. In this unit, Paul discusses the nature of Christian ministry, particularly his own. *Having this ministry . . . we do not lose heart.* The "we" refers to Paul and to his fellow workers in the church in Corinth. They have a task to perform for Christ. It must be done in all conscientiousness and faithfulness. Though there will be troubles and the temptation to quit, Paul reminds his fellow workers that they cannot lose heart. They must press onward.

Thinking of his earlier correspondence concerning the "false apostles" with whom he and the Corinthians dealt (*see* 2:17; 11:5, 13), Paul reminds them that *we have renounced disgraceful, underhanded ways.* Paul has been honest with them. He is not guilty of shameful hidden things. He has not been cunning or crafty. His preaching to the Corinthians has been the truthful and straightforward Word of God. His words and actions have been commendable and his integrity unquestionable. He knows that ultimately all are judged for their words and their works *in the sight of God.*

Paul is wise enough to know that not everyone who hears the Gospel will believe in it. This is not his fault nor the preacher's fault. The Gospel is often hidden or veiled to those *who are perishing* because of their rejection of the Gospel. *In their case . . . the god of this world has blinded the minds of unbelievers.* The gods of wealth or power still keep people from seeing the light of Christ. *For what we preach is not ourselves, but Jesus Christ as Lord.* Paul denies preaching about himself as he was accused of doing in 3:1. Paul preaches Christ. He is a servant of

God and of the Church. It is God's light that shines from him so that others might have knowledge and thereby give glory to God.

Paul preaches the *glory of God,* not the glory of Paul. The glory belongs entirely to God, not to Paul. God's glory is a precious treasure stored in human beings. *We have this treasure in earthen vessels.* Earthen vessels are fragile. People's bodies are like earthen vessels. They are weak, fragile, and humble. God's glory is contained in such bodies. However, God's spirit inhabits such people in order to show God's power. Paul reminds the Corinthians that this incomparable power comes from God and does not have its origin in people. *The transcendent power belongs to God and not to us.*

We are afflicted . . . but not crushed; persecuted, but not forsaken; struck down, but not destroyed. Though the ministry of a Christian will seem tough, it will never be hopeless. Paul is certain that God will be with His ministers.

Paul endures his suffering *for Jesus' sake, so that the life of Jesus may be manifested in our mortal flesh.* However, Paul also accepts the sufferings for the Corinthians' sake. *Death is at work in us, but life in you.* Christ's ministers suffer for others. As Christ suffered on the Cross, so too, a Christian must suffer. This willingness to suffer for others is part of the Gospel of Jesus Christ.

SUGGESTIONS TO TEACHERS

The Church, like every other organization, has leaders. It always has.

What makes a person a leader in the Church? Appointment? Election? Ordination? Obviously, there is more to it than laying on hands or taking a vote. Why are certain people selected? What personal qualities are needed for church leaders? This, dear Teacher, is the substance of the lesson for today.

Look over the scriptural material for this lesson. You will find a treasure trove of ideas on Christian leadership.

1. *SENSIBLE SELFHOOD.* The credentials for leadership in the Church quickly turn out to be different from the business world or the army. A church leader must not promote himself. A church leader doesn't care about getting credit or recognition. The only testimonials a church leader desires are in the form of changed lives. (This is also true of Sunday-School teachers!) It will be interesting for your class to look at the "boasting passage" in 2 Corinthians 11, where Paul points out that as a leader he has more to brag about than anyone, but refuses to play that game. Leaders in the Church remain humble!

2. *SIMPLE SUFFICIENCY.* A leader recognizes that his or her strength comes from God, not from himself or herself. All qualifications for leadership are gifts of the Spirit, and not found in human codes.

3. *STRAIGHTFORWARD STATEMENT.* Christian leaders renounce human cleverness and maneuvering. They tell the Good News of Jesus Christ as plainly as possible. They can also acknowledge their own fraility, foibles, and fallibility. Do those in your class recognize people in your church as leaders because they point others to Christ?

4. *SPIRITUAL STAMINA.* Church leaders persevere. They do not lose heart. They can "take it." Internal and external problems don't make genuine church leaders give up. Remind your class members that as leaders in the Church they, too, must learn spiritual stamina!

5. *SOUND STEWARD.* Titus 1:5–9 offers a good summary of the traits and lifestyle desirable for Church leaders. Before looking at the leadership profile in Titus, however, you may wish to have your class prepare its own list of leadership qualities. It may be desirable to ask the class members to carry copies of that list during the coming week and examine it each day. "How are class members doing as leaders?" may well be part of next week's lesson also.

TOPIC FOR ADULTS
WHO ARE TRUE CHURCH LEADERS?

Stop the Music. Dr. William Matz of Moravian Seminary tells of being at Tanglewood one summer to hear the music. Seiji Ozawa, the conductor of the Boston Symphony, was rehearsing the orchestra one Saturday morning. Bill Matz sat and enjoyed the rehearsal. He was puzzled, however, when a little man got up from the audience and walked up to the platform and whispered something to Ozawa, and even more puzzled that the great Ozawa would stop the rehearsal to let this little man interrupt him. This happened another time, and still a third time. Why, thought Dr. Matz, would Ozawa permit this member of the audience to break into his conducting like that? Later, Matz found out who the little man who got up out of a seat in the audience was. It was the composer of the piece. Ozawa humbly wanted to learn the way the master intended the piece to be performed. Great and famous though Seiji Ozawa is, he is a disciple or a learner when it comes to music.

A true church leader is like the conductor of a symphony. He orchestrates. He helps everyone to bring the beauty and meaning of the music to others. But the leader in Christian circles also humbly heeds the counsel of the Composer or Author, the Lord!

Bring Up the Regiment! In the Civil War battle of Corinth, a certain regiment of Wisconsin infantry was under fire for the first time. They were ordered to advance and hold a certain ridge. Their color sergeant was a fresh young college boy named Jerome Davis, later to become a great Congregational missionary to Japan. Sergeant Davis marched ahead with his flag as ordered until he was on the ridge. Crouching behind a stump, he looked back. The regiment was not there. Far down the slope he saw their line, ragged and wavering and threatening to break as the enemy bullets whined about them and a few men fell. But Sergeant Davis held his ground. In a few minutes, an orderly came crawling forward on his stomach. When near enough he shouted in a lull in the firing, "Davis, bring back the colors." Davis shouted back, "The colors are where they belong! Bring up the regiment!" This they did, helping win the battle.

The banner of the Son of God is carried by the true leaders of the Church. Sometimes, we want to pull the colors back. Instead, let us bring up the regiment! Let's go forward as we see our leaders carrying the Gospel!

How About the Grownups? " 'Daddy, I want to ask you a question,' said little Bobby after his first day in Sunday school. 'Yes, Bobby, what it it?' 'The teacher was reading the Bible to us, all about the children of Israel building the temple, the children of Israel crossing the Red Sea, the children of Israel making sacrifices. Didn't the grownups do anything?' "—*Pulpit Helps,* Volume 8, Number 10, July, 1983.

Questions for Pupils on the Next Lesson. 1. What were the heretical teachings confronting the Church in New Testament times? 2. Is the world basically evil or good? 3. How is an effective church leader effectively nourished spiritually? 4. How are you sometimes confused by the conflicting ideas of religious speakers, especially on television, today? 5. What should the Church do when false teachers present themselves?

TOPIC FOR YOUTH
ME, A LEADER?

Forward With the Work! Ashleigh Brilliant, author of *Pot-Shots,* captions one of his delightful cartoons with the words: "The Great Work Must Go Forward—as soon as we all find someone else to do it."

God means for His work to advance. In you, He calls a person to help do it! Have you sensed that God intends you to take responsibility as a leader?

The Point Is You Are Chosen! President Harry Truman is supposed to have said, "There are at least three million men in the United States better qualified than I am to be President of the United States. But that is not the point. The point is that I was elected President of the United States!" There may be a room, a church, or a hall full of persons better qualified than we are.

The point is that you are a leader. You have been chosen by Christ to serve.

Refuse Not This Holy Vocation. John Knox, the great Scottish reformer, had no notion of being a leader in the Church as he grew up. Others, however, saw in him possibilities for leadership. One of these was a pastor named the Reverend John Rough. Although many, including Rough, had told Knox that he should consider leadership responsibilities in the church, Knox refused. One Sunday, Rough preached on the election of ministers: "What power the congregation, however small, had over any man in whom they supposed and espied the gifts of God to be; and how dangerous it was to refuse, and not to hear the voice of such as desired to be instructed." It must have been quite a long sermon, with several "heads" to the argument. But the tension and silence must have grown as the preacher reached the climax: and called upon Knox, who was taken completely by surprise.

"Brother, be not offended that I speak to you what I have in charge, even from all those present, which is this: In the name of God, and of His Son Jesus Christ, and in the name of those that presently call you by my mouth, I charge you, that ye refuse not this holy vocation."

Knox accepted his "call" as a leader, and spearheaded the advance of Christ's cause in Scotland.

Questions for Pupils on the Next Lesson. 1. Who are some false teachers in the Church that you have heard about? 2. What is a heresy? 3. What were some of the false teachings confronting Christians in New Testament times? 4. How can a leader remain true to Christ? 5. What do you do when you think you are receiving conflicting signals from parents, teachers, ministers, peers, and society?

LESSON X—NOVEMBER 3

CONFRONTING FALSE TEACHERS

Background Scripture: 1 Timothy 1; 4; Titus 2:1–5
Devotional Reading: 1 Timothy 1:12–17

KING JAMES VERSION

1 TIMOTHY 4 Now the Spirit speaketh expressly, that in the latter times some shall depart from the faith, giving heed to seducing spirits, and doctrines of devils;

2 Speaking lies in hypocrisy; having their conscience seared with a hot iron;

3 Forbidding to marry, *and commanding* to abstain from meats, which God hath created to be received with thanksgiving of them which believe and know the truth.

4 For every creature of God *is* good, and nothing to be refused, if it be received with thanksgiving:

5 For it is sanctified by the word of God and prayer.

6 If thou put the brethren in remembrance of these things, thou shalt be a good minister of Jesus Christ, nourished up in the words of faith and of good doctrine, whereunto thou hast attained.

7 But refuse profane and old wives' fables, and exercise thyself *rather* unto godliness.

8 For bodily exercise profiteth little: but godliness is profitable unto all things, having promise of the life that now is, and of that which is to come.

9 This *is* a faithful saying, and worthy of all acceptation.

10 For therefore we both labour and suffer reproach, because we trust in the living God, who is the Saviour of all men, specially of those that believe.

11 These things command and teach.

12 Let no man despise thy youth; but be thou an example of the believers, in word, in conversation, in charity, in spirit, in faith, in purity.

13 Till I come, give attendance to reading, to exhortation, to doctrine.

14 Neglect not the gift that is in thee, which was given thee by prophecy, with the laying on of the hands of the presbytery.

15 Meditate upon these things; give thyself wholly to them; that thy profiting may appear to all.

16 Take heed unto thyself, and unto the doctrine; continue in them: for in doing this thou shalt both save thyself, and them that hear thee.

REVISED STANDARD VERSION

1 TIMOTHY 4 Now the Spirit expressly says that in later times some will depart from the faith by giving heed to deceitful spirits and doctrines of demons, 2 through the pretensions of liars whose consciences are seared, 3 who forbid marriage and enjoin abstinence from foods which God created to be received with thanksgiving by those who believe and know the truth. 4 For everything created by God is good, and nothing is to be rejected if it is received with thanksgiving; 5 for then it is consecrated by the word of God and prayer.

6 If you put these instructions before the brethren, you will be a good minister of Christ Jesus, nourished on the words of the faith and of the good doctrine which you have followed. 7 Have nothing to do with godless and silly myths. Train yourself in godliness; 8 for while bodily training is of some value, godliness is of value in every way, as it holds promise for the present life and also for the life to come. 9 The saying is sure and worthy of full acceptance. 10 For to this end we toil and strive, because we have our hope set on the living God, who is the Savior of all men, especially of those who believe.

11 Command and teach these things. 12 Let no one despise your youth, but set the believers an example in speech and conduct, in love, in faith, in purity. 13 Till I come, attend to the public reading of scripture, to preaching, to teaching. 14 Do not neglect the gift you have, which was given you by prophetic utterance when the elders laid their hands upon you. 15 Practice these duties, devote yourself to them, so that all may see your progress. 16 Take heed to yourself and to your teaching; hold to that, for by so doing you will save both yourself and your hearers.

KEY VERSE: *Take heed to yourself and to your teaching; hold to that, for by so doing you will save both yourself and your hearers.* 1 Timothy 4:16.

HOME DAILY BIBLE READINGS

Oct.	28.	M.	*Need for Sound Doctrine.* 1 Timothy 1:1–11.
Oct.	29.	T.	*Mercy for the Sinner.* 1 Timothy 1:12–20.
Oct.	30.	W.	*Pray for All Men.* 1 Timothy 2:1–7.
Oct.	31.	T.	*Responsibility of Older Christians.* Titus 2:1–5.
Nov.	1.	F.	*God's Creation Is Good.* 1 Timothy 4:1–5.
Nov.	2.	S.	*Nourished in Faith and Doctrine.* 1 Timothy 4:6–10.
Nov.	3.	S.	*An Example of Believers.* 1 Timothy 4:11–16.

BACKGROUND

By the time Paul wrote 1 Timothy, the Church had spread from the area near Jerusalem to the far corners of the Mediterranean world. With the growth of the Christian movement came organization and leaders. Paul's later letters indicate this. In fact, 1 Timothy and Titus gave us a picture of a church with a structure and titles. Elders are mentioned in 1 Timothy 5:1, 17–19 and Titus 1:5–7. Bishops or superintendants or overseers are discussed in 1 Timothy 3:1–7 and Titus 1:7–18. Deacons are described in 1 Timothy 3:3–18. Apparently some of these, particularly some elders, were paid salaries, according to 1 Timothy 5:17, 18. There is also indication that widows were recognized as belonging to some organized body or order in 1 Timothy 5:2–16.

Undoubtedly, many if not most of these persons were committed Christians and competent leaders. Unfortunately, others were not. This was the problem in the Church then as now.

One of the biggest difficulties was that some of these leaders held and taught opinions which went against the Gospel. We call such leaders, "Heretics." At the time Paul wrote to Timothy and Titus, these false teachers threatened the future of the Church with a variety of notions which ran contrary to God's Good News in Jesus Christ.

1) a love of useless speculation and pointless controversy;
2) an arrogant pride in human intellectualism;
3) a tendency to rigid legalism and asceticism on one hand or sexual permissiveness and immorality on the other.

Many scholars deduce that many of these false teachers were caught up in the philosophy known as Gnosticism, and that others were obsessed with imposing the Jewish rules on all Christians. Leaders and teachers taking either of these systems seriously invariably perverted the meaning of God's mighty saving act in Jesus Christ.

Paul wrote to his helpers, Timothy and Titus, warning them of the dangers of such false teachers and their teachings and instructing them to confront such persons who were spreading confusion. Above all, Paul urged his young helpers to be models of Christian teaching in their own personal lives—a lesson we all can take to heart!

NOTES ON THE PRINTED TEXT

Today begins a four week study in the "Pastoral Epistles," letters written to individuals by their pastor Paul. In this letter, Paul writes to Timothy, his authorized representative in Ephesus, who is in need of help and encouragement in overseeing the work there.

In 1 Timothy, the apostle admonishes Timothy to deal decisively with certain teachers who have perverted notions of the Law and the Gospel. *Now the Spirit expressly says that in the later times some will depart from the faith by giving heed to deceitful spirits and doctrines of demons.* Paul sees the Church threatened by heresy that could seduce Christians from their faith. The teachings have a demonic origin, and its teachers lure believers away from the true faith through deceit and lies. They pervert the faith so badly that they have had their consciences branded by their own hypocrisy. They can no longer differentiate truth from error. Although Paul never gives a detailed explanation of the false teaching, he does warn against tendencies which forbid marriage and the eating of certain foods. The heresy taught that the physical world was evil and should be despised. This false teaching was symbolized by the renunciation of marriage and the abstinence from certain foods such as meat and wine. However, Paul vigorously affirms the goodness of God's world. *Everything created by God is good and nothing is to be rejected. Those who believe and know the truth* should enjoy life not renounce it. Twice he affirms that life should be *received with thanksgiving.* Thanksgiving literally means giving thanks to God in prayer.

In contrast to those who depart from the faith, Timothy must give himself to godliness and to profitable Christian service.

Paul urges Timothy to *have nothing to do with godless and silly myths.* They are nothing more than silly old wives' tales. Instead of absurd chatter, Timothy must *be nourished on the words of faith and of good doctrine.* Timothy must keep himself spiritually fit just as any athlete must keep himself fit for a contest. Paul bids Timothy to give himself to piety for this holds value and promise in every way.

To this end we toil and strive because we have our hope set on the living God. Continuing his athletic analogy, Paul reminds Timothy that all training and conditioning is for life, now in the present and life to come. Paul advises his young protégé to *command and teach these things.* Moreover, realizing the difficulty a young man has with such responsibility, Paul pleads with Timothy to *let no one despise your youth.* Rather, win the respect and confidence of all people by setting *an example in speech and conduct, in love, in faith, in purity.*

Paul also encourages the young minister to *attend to the public reading of scripture, to preaching, to teaching.* Timothy is also told not to neglect the preaching and teaching to which he was ordained. *Devote yourself* and *practice* diligently these duties: the reading, the preaching, and the teaching. Stick to your work and take care of yourself spiritually, Paul urges, so that *you will save both yourself and your hearers.*

SUGGESTIONS TO TEACHERS

Last week, you examined leaders and leadership in the Church. You probably became aware that there are also bad Church leaders. Unfortunately, some of these faulty leaders are teachers!

This gets down to where you, a teacher, are. And it may shake you to realize that false teachers in the Church have done great harm. This lesson may have the effect of reminding you again what an important calling you have as a teacher!

Your class is fortunate in having you as its teacher. You are trying to do a responsible job in presenting the lesson material each week. But you and your class should remember that you all are also encountering plenty of other "teachers." Unfortunately, some of these who claim to be instructing in the faith are charlatans.

How can you pick out the phonies? What are the distinguishing features of a true teacher? How does the Church handle the false teachers?

1. *RIGHT ESTIMATE OF YOURSELF.* The Apostle Paul offers sound advice to all Christians, including teachers, when he states that Christ came to save sinners and that Paul admits he is "the foremost of sinners" (1 Timothy 1:12). A teacher who is genuine will be humble enough to label himself "sinner." (By the way, do you?)

2. *RIGHT EMPHASIS ON CHRIST.* A genuine teacher stresses the Gospel. A bogus one strays into speculation, myths, genealogies, legalism. Christian teachers care more for Christian doctrine than their personal theories.

3. *RIGHT ENGAGEMENT IN LIFE.* Have your class examine the number of references to living a disciplined life in today's scriptural material. Paul, the writer, insists young Timothy consider himself called as a soldier to active duty, or chosen as an athlete for tough contests ("Train yourself in godliness"—1 Timothy 4:7). Discuss in your class what it means to be a disciplined Christian church member today.

4. *RIGHT EXPECTATION OF OPPOSITION.* The Bible takes evil seriously. Today's Scripture readings (especially 1 Timothy 4) warn Christians not to take a casual attitude toward false teachers or others bringing discord and destruction within the Church. It would be useful to reflect on the messages of some of the radio and television preachers and the emphases of some of the popular religious writers. Are all of them always true teachers?

5. *RIGHT ENCOURAGEMENT OF LEADERS.* The class should talk over Titus 2:1–5. In the light of the fact that every Christian is meant to be a leader and teacher of others, what do these words suggest to those in your class?

TOPIC FOR ADULTS
CONFRONTING FALSE TEACHERS

Testing the Teachers. "How can we separate true from false prophets? On which side of the line would you place Reverend Ike or the Maharishi? Who really speaks for God? How can you tell if your own imaginative aspect of personality is functioning correctly? If all the *Peanuts* cartoon characters are looking at cloud formations, and three of them see wonderful aesthetic shapes, and delight to call them out, whereas Charlie Brown only sees 'a ducky and a fishy,' who is to say which one is right?

". . . within the canon there is sometimes great difficulty in knowing who speaks for God. For a while, Jeremiah is not sure whether Hananiah's prediction of success against Nebuchadnezzar is a more accurate word than his own. It is only later, under futher leading of the Spirit, that his own insight is reaffirmed (cf. Jeremiah 28:10–13). In Acts, the church is not quite sure of Paul; Paul is not sure of John Mark; Peter trusts his vision of unclean animals and then later denies the import of it. Therefore, the canon has within it God's people who are struggling to find out what is valid and what is not—the same question that we in modern times have to face. John generalizes, but he may be saying all that can be said so far as criteria of truth are concerned: 'Test the spirits to see whether they are of God' (1 John 4:1).

"A possible test that is often used, consciously or unconsciously, is the stamp of approval of the Christian community. When the church ordains a candidate for the ministry, it says in effect that the person's prime vision is authentic. The church is willing to be exposed to the message that he or she brings."—From *Religious Imagination,* by Robert D. Young. Copyright © 1979 The Westminster Press. Used by permission.

"Only I Am Qualified." Sometimes we are so intent on our right to do as we please, we become intense individualists and forget the Church. False teachers do this sometimes. There was an early Congregationalist minister named John Smyth who became so convinced of his right of individualism that he objected to reading anyone else's translation of Scripture but his own, which he made afresh for each reading from the original languages. Then he objected to using anyone else's hymnbook. He insisted that each person had to compose and sing his or her own hymns, though fortunately stipulating that each sing one at a time. Finally, Smyth decided that no one was qualified to baptize him. So his congregation was

treated to the unedifying spectacle of the Reverend John Smyth baptizing himself!

Confronting False Teaching in San Antonio. In September, 1983, a fifteen-year-old boy name Domingo Ibarra looked out the window toward his neighbors' house in San Antonio's South Side. Domingo insists that he saw the image of the Virgin Mary on the side of the Gutierrez's small frame house. Domingo told his mother and others. Soon, hundreds of people began collecting each night in the street in front of the Gutierrez house to see the "miracle." Many clutched rosaries and prayed and wept. The large noisy crowds, however, quickly made life miserable for residents of the neighborhood. Homeowners Angie and Candalaria Gutierrez said the image was not Virgin Mary, but rather the reflection made by a neighbor's porch light bouncing off the bumper of a 1975 Chevrolet parked nearby. When the crowds increased, Gutierrez and the neighbors finally decided to take the matters into their own hands by installing two powerful floodlights to blot out the reflection. Members of the crowd cried and yelled for the lights to be extinguished. Six policemen stood by for several nights. Finally, after the lights were left on for many nights, the crowds began to thin and disperse. The only ones not happy with the floodlights seemed to be Domingo and his mother, who continued to insist that the reflection was a miraculous appearance of the Virgin Mary.

Questions for Pupils on the Next Lesson. 1. Why do people only with temporal aims find themselves empty and disappointed when they finally succeed? 2. Why must the person of faith continually refocus on the most important aims in life? 3. Does God continually provide good things? 4. Do generosity and sharing have any reward? 5. Where is real security for your life?

TOPIC FOR YOUTH
WHAT AM I WORTH?

Heinz Kramp's Vision of Worth. "In our darkness we have looked for a trace of light in the sky, a beacon, or even one brave soul out in the storm with a lantern. Last week I found one, at the base of Pasture Fence Mountain, near Wildcat Hollow in Albermarle County, Virginia.

"On this mountain, as the prophet said in our Old Testament lesson for Easter Sunday, the Lord of Hosts has 'swallow(ed) up that veil that shrouds all the peoples, the pall thrown over all the nations' (Isaiah 25:6, 7). Here I have heard 'shouts of deliverance in the camp of the victors!' (Psalms 118:15). Here the message of Resurrection has been heard anew.

"Innisfree Village, at the base of the mountain, is growing out of the vision of its founder, German-born Heinz Kramp.

"Innisfree has come from Heinz's concern for the mentally retarded and brain-damaged persons 'who fall through the cracks in our society.' At Innisfree, a beautiful, environmentally non-retarding place, Heinz and volunteers are building a community where they and the handicapped are co-workers in a gentle, affirming society. Together they bake bread for sale and for their own use, make wooden furniture for their houses and other wooden products for sale, weave beautiful garments, care for a few farm animals and work in their gardens. The volunteers come for a minimum of a year for room and board and a small monthly stipend. The handicapped villagers are accepted on probation and pay tuition that covers only about two-thirds of their expenses. Heinz must raise additional funds. There is a waiting list both for volunteers and villagers. Such long-term care facilities are rare in this country, even though it costs twice as much to maintain someone in a state facility.

"One of the residents, whose face is so badly deformed she would likely have had a miserable existence 'outside,' laughed with great pleasure as she told us of the joy she feels, working in the shop and weavery. Her brightly colored, attractive paintings hang in the dining room for all to admire. She is accepted, loved, and feels worthy.

"If Heinz can have a vision and build on it, others can too. We, as those 'others,' in whatever way we feel called, must dream 'impossible' dreams and act upon them, not waiting for someone else to lead the way."—Patricia M. Churchman, *Presbyterian Outlook*, 512 W. Main Street, Richmond, Va., April 5, 1982.

Right Sense of Worth. Some persons have an exaggerated sense of their own worth and can never be wrong. Often, these are false teachers. Always, however, they are difficult to deal with.

George Patton, the World War II general, was such a person. It is recorded that he once accepted an invitation to dine at a press camp in Africa. The wine was served in canteen cups. Patton poured cream into his cup, as if it had been filled with coffee. The correspondents stared as the general stirred the sugar, cream and red wine.

"That's wine, sir, not coffee," he was warned.

General Patton, who could never, never be wrong, replied, "I know, I like my wine this way."

And he drank it.

Destructive, Deadly Teachings. A true teacher and leader values human life and does all he or she can to strengthen life. In the light of this, it is difficult to square the teachings of the leader of a Wilmot, Indiana, sect named Hobart Freeman who reportedly instructs the members of his Faith Assembly to shun doctors. Unfortunately, according to careful research by the Fort Wayne *News-Sentinel,* fifty-two people, including twenty-eight babies and seven other children, have died because of refusal to receive medical attention. Freeman also allegedly tells his followers that he does not expect to die and that those who turn from his teaching will go to hell.

God, however, insists that you and everyone has great worth. Furthermore he wants you and others to appreciate that worth by caring for your bodies in the most responsible ways.

Questions for Pupils on the Next Lesson. 1. How can faith bring a sense of contentment? 2. Does your personal faith help give you a vision of where you want to go in life? 3. Have you ever experienced a letdown after getting something you wanted? 4. How do you set priorities in life? 5. Why is it so important to have an aim in life?

LESSON XI—NOVEMBER 10

KEEPING LIFE'S PRIORITIES STRAIGHT

Background Scripture: 1 Timothy 6:6–21
Devotional Reading: 1 Timothy 4:11–16

KING JAMES VERSION

1 TIMOTHY 6 6 But godliness with contentment is great gain.

7 For we brought nothing into *this* world, *and it is* certain we can carry nothing out.

8 And having food and raiment, let us be therewith content.

9 But they that will be rich fall into temptation and a snare, and *into* many foolish and hurtful lusts, which drown men in destruction and perdition.

10 For the love of money is the root of all evil: which while some coveted after, they have erred from the faith, and pierced themselves through with many sorrows.

11 But thou, O man of God, flee these things; and follow after righteousness, godliness, faith, love, patience, meekness.

12 Fight the good fight of faith, lay hold on eternal life, whereunto thou art also called, and hast professed a good profession before many witnesses.

13 I give thee charge in the sight of God, who quickeneth all things, and *before* Christ Jesus, who before Pontius Pilate witnessed a good confession;

14 That thou keep *this* commandment without spot, unrebukable, until the appearing of our Lord Jesus Christ:

15 Which in his times he shall shew, *who is* the blessed and only Potentate, the King of kings, and Lord of lords;

16 Who only hath immortality, dwelling in the light which no man can approach unto; whom no man hath seen, nor can see: to whom *be* honour and power everlasting. Amen.

17 Charge them that are rich in this world, that they be not high-minded, nor trust in uncertain riches, but in the living God, who giveth us richly all things to enjoy;

18 That they do good, that they be rich in good works, ready to distribute, willing to communicate;

19 Laying up in store for themselves a good foundation against the time to come, that they may lay hold on eternal life.

REVISED STANDARD VERSION

1 TIMOTHY 6 6 There is great gain in godliness with contentment; 7 for we brought nothing into the world, and we cannot take anything out of the world; 8 but if we have food and clothing, with these we shall be content. 9 But those who desire to be rich fall into temptation, into a snare, into many senseless and hurtful desires that plunge men into ruin and destruction. 10 For the love of money is the root of all evils; it is through this craving that some have wandered away from the faith and pierced their hearts with many pangs.

11 But as for you, man of God, shun all this; aim at righteousness, godliness, faith, love, steadfastness, gentleness. 12 Fight the good fight of the faith; take hold of the eternal life to which you were called when you made the good confession in the presence of many witnesses. 13 In the presence of God who gives life to all things, and of Christ Jesus who in his testimony before Pontius Pilate made the good confession, 14 I charge you to keep the commandment unstained and free from reproach until the appearing of our Lord Jesus Christ; 15 and this will be made manifest at the proper time by the blessed and only Sovereign, the King of kings and Lord of lords, 16 who alone has immortality and dwells in unapproachable light, whom no man has ever seen or can see. To him be honor and eternal dominion. Amen.

17 As for the rich in this world, charge them not to be haughty, nor to set their hopes on uncertain riches but on God who richly furnishes us with everything to enjoy. 18 They are to do good, to be rich in good deeds, liberal and generous, 19 thus laying up for themselves a good foundation for the future, so that they may take hold of the life which is life indeed.

KEY VERSE: Aim at righteousness, godliness, faith, love, steadfastness, gentleness. 1 Timothy 6:11.

HOME DAILY BIBLE READINGS

Nov. 4. M. *Provide for the Family.* 1 Timothy 5:1–8.
Nov. 5. T. *Advice Concerning Widows.* 1 Timothy 5:9–16.
Nov. 6. W. *Honor Church Leaders.* 1 Timothy 5:17–24.

Nov.	7.	T.	*"A Model of Good Deeds."* Titus 2:7–15.
Nov.	8.	F.	*Teach Sound Words.* 1 Timothy 6:1–8.
Nov.	9.	S.	*Seek Life, Not Riches.* 1 Timothy 6:9–13.
Nov.	10.	S.	*How to Be Rich.* 1 Timothy 6:14–21.

BACKGROUND

Paul had a special affection for Timothy. He called him "my true child in the faith" (1 Timothy 1:2). The old apostle frequently recalled his first visit to Lystra when he met the young Timothy and Lois and Eunice, Timothy's mother and grandmother. Paul's courage must have inspired the boy. Probably there was more than a touch of hero worship on the part of young Timothy. When Paul returned to Lystra on his second missionary journey, he found that the boy Timothy had already become a respected young leader in the little congregation of new converts. Paul, who had no son, and Timothy, whose father was a pagan Greek with little interest in him, "adopted" each other. Paul subsequently referred to Timothy as his "son" (1 Corinthians 4:17; Philippians 2:20–22). When Paul set out again from Lystra, he took Timothy along.

Paul faced intense personal opposition. He also had to contend with conflict and questions threatening to rip apart his recently-organized churches. Paul often learned that opponents followed up his efforts to welcome pagan Gentiles into the new life in Christ by undercutting his efforts and his message with false teachings. Furthermore, the apostle had constantly to shore up shaky believers fresh from the raw, greedy immoral paganism of the Greek-Roman world. Since Paul could not be everywhere at once, he dispatched helpers such as Timothy to the trouble spots. Later, when Paul was imprisoned and unable to visit any of the torn churches in person, he had to depend almost completely on a handful of faithful associates like Timothy.

Paul laid heavy responsibilities on the young man Timothy. Although still unsure of himself in many ways because of his youth and inexperience, Timothy found himself having to cope with church problems that would have tested the wisdom and patience of the most seasoned pastor. When Paul wrote the personal letter we know as 1 Timothy, Timothy was undoubtedly at Ephesus trying to provide leadership in that great capital. Obviously, Timothy felt intimidated and insecure. The young minister keenly sensed all the pressures of trying to carry out his assignment in such a hostile setting.

Paul wrote his "son" reminding him of the sense of contentment his faith should bring. Throughout the letter, Paul firmly urges his beloved young associate to focus constantly on the most important aims and follow them.

NOTES ON THE PRINTED TEXT

In closing his letter to Timothy, Paul warns against covetousness and challenges him to wage a good fight for truth.

The false teachers, whom Paul opposes, deceive for their own financial gain (vs. 5). However, Paul insists that wealth is unnecessary. *For we brought nothing into the world, and we cannot take anything out of the world.* Since we bring nothing into the world or take it out, the pursuit of wealth is unessential for the Christian, argues Paul. To a Christian, contentment through faith in God is of far greater value than monetary wealth. For all we really need for our bodily existence are the basics of food and clothing. The desire to be wealthy is characterized as a *snare* or a trap. This temptation is to be avoided by a Christian for it plunges (literally drowns) *men into ruin and destruction.*

For the love of money is the root of all evils quotes Paul from a proverb. Paul says it is the false teachers' craving for money that has led some to *wander from the faith and pierced their hearts with many pangs.* Paul realized that those with only temporal aims will find themselves empty and disappointed when they accumulate wealth. All they will experience is sorrow.

However, the Christian's life is one of focusing on the most important aims and following them. *Aim at righteousness, godliness, faith, love, steadfastness, gentleness.* Speaking directly to Timothy and to us, Paul is listing what should be pursued and what should be avoided. Paul knows it will be a difficult struggle achieving these ends. He exhorts Timothy and the Church to *fight the good fight of the faith.* Using athletic imagery, Paul coaches all Christians to hold onto the prize of eternal life. Life is a long distance marathon begun at baptism when the Christian confesses "Jesus is Lord." Through this confession he pledges his lifelong loyalty to Christ. We, too, must ask ourselves if we have fought a good fight or if we have wandered from our faith and experienced the many pangs that pierce hearts.

In the presence of God and *Jesus Christ,* Paul charges Timothy to *keep the commandment unstained and free from reproach.* The commandment Timothy is to keep unspotted is to be faithful. Against the vast body of false teaching, Timothy's faith must be shared intact and unaltered *until the appearing of our Lord Jesus Christ* which *will be made manifest at the proper time.* The very mention of Christ's coming causes Paul to lapse into song that perhaps contained the lines of a familiar hymn in Timothy's church or of an ancient creed. The words ring of Christ's Lordship.

> *The King of kings and Lord of lords, who alone has*
> *immortality and dwells in unapproachable light, whom*
> *no man has ever seen or can see. To him be honor and*
> *eternal dominion. Amen.*

Before closing, Paul again returns to the subject of wealth. He urges the rich *not to be haughty, nor to set their hopes on uncertain riches.* They are to fight the temptation towards pride, arrogance, and the belief that their ultimate hope rests on their wealth. Instead, he reminds them that it is God who gives all good things. The rich have a special responsibility to use their wealth *to do good.* Their generosity and sharing will be rewarded in the future. For the goals and actions that Christians pursue have consequences now and in the life to come.

SUGGESTIONS TO TEACHERS

A young man considering entering the ministry came to talk to his minister. The prospective pastor made it clear to the older man that he would have to continue his current interests and activities. These included owning expensive sports cars, and spending two days each week to ski in the winter and surf in the summer. The young man's questions dealt mostly with how quickly he could expect to get a "big, well-paying church," and what the retirement benefits were for clergy. The older minister tried gently to suggest that the youth's priorities were skewed, and that he had best not think about becoming a Christian pastor.

This week's lesson deals with keeping life's priorities straight. Every person in your class needs help in establishing what comes first, second, and third. Paul's letter to Timothy will be helpful to you and the class in sorting out and ranking what is important and what's not in the light of the Gospel. Using the scriptural material, try putting your lesson together by posing the questions most people ask (like the young would-be ministerial student).

1. *WHAT ABOUT AMBITION?* You may find it additionally challenging to your class to ask it to make two columns, one listing the society's ideas of what are top priorities for life and the other column listing what 1 Timothy 6 suggests. Under the question of "What about Ambition?" the world says your ambition

must center on making money and acquiring possessions. What are the ambitions of a Christian, according to Scripture?

2. *WHAT ABOUT SECURITY?* Money is a "must" for everyone, but money also brings dangers. Point out the dangers of greed. A priority which places security at the top of the list will mean corrosion and ultimate destruction of one's personality.

3. *WHAT ABOUT STATUS AND RECOGNITION?* Paul advises Timothy to "make the good confession" (1 Timothy 6:14), that is, to concern himself primarily with serving Jesus Christ. Talk with your people candidly about what signs of status-seeking are to be found in your community. Ask why so many persons seem to be obsessed with being recognized—even in the Church. Remind your people that Christians find sufficient recognition and standing simply by being Christ's.

4. *WHAT ABOUT PERSONAL PLANS?* "Guard what is entrusted to you," Paul admonishes (1 Timothy 6:20). He intends Timothy and us to remember we are on duty, exactly as a soldier has been inducted and given an assignment. Our personal plans take second place to those of the Commander!

5. *WHAT ABOUT WORLDLY WISDOM?* There are always "know-it-all's" who parade their own learning or delight in intellectual games. Paul tells his readers to "avoid godless chatter and contradictions of what is falsely called knowledge" (1 Timothy 6:20). Remind your class that Christians aren't called to have answers for everything but to witness to God's Good News.

TOPIC FOR ADULTS
KEEPING LIFE'S PRIORITIES STRAIGHT

Flyer or Pilot? I have a friend who is an expert pilot. In fact, he teaches instrument flying at times and serves as an examiner for the F.A.A. on occasion. I once asked him how he started flying. He told me that he'd had a longing to know the freedom and fun of flying for a long time, but finally, after the war, decided to act upon his interest. He sought out the best flight instructor he could find, an old-timer named Frank Vaneck. Frank Vaneck was obviously dubious about taking on my friend and sensed that here was another Sunday afternoon aeronautic enthusiast. Frank had seen enough people who liked the glamor of fooling around with airplanes, to impress friends or to fulfill ego drives or to find a new hobby. So Frank put a question to my friend. The question startled my friend, because it was not the answer he was expecting. My friend, bubbling with enthusiasm for being in the air, had looked for some encouragement and appreciation. Instead Frank asked bluntly, "Are you just a flyer or do you want to learn to be a pilot?"

At first, Frank's question seemed chilling and rude. But Frank was serious. Just another flyer, a person who got enough quick instruction to fly in an airplane on weekends, or a learner at becoming a pilot? Thirty-five years later, my friend knows what Frank was talking about, for there's a difference between being a flyer and a pilot. My friend, along with Frank Vaneck himself, knowing what they know, still call themselves learners!

Just as Frank Vaneck has seen too many people with romantic notions of being weekend flyboys soaring into the wild blue yonder and indulging in the glamor of some hangar talk, so the Lord isn't interested in having followers who won't get their priorities straight. Dabbler or disciple? Flyer or pilot? Loafer or learner? Keep your priorities clearly in mind if you hope to soar and grow!

The Thief in the Church. "The thief in your church is Indifference. It steals the congregation, saps the enthusiasm of the members, kidnaps the members of Sunday School, steals the life of the services, robs the choir of its joy of serving, and takes the pleasure out of giving of both time and money to the work of the Lord.

"Indifference keeps the usher from being faithful to his post of duty, makes the

Sunday-School teacher 'just as soon stay home,' robs the Christian of his zeal.

"Indifference binds the tongues of many in the congregation, keeping them from singing and enjoying the service. It steals the ears of others, closing out the words of help and wisdom that would free them from the chains with which they are most surely bound. It closes eyes to the needs of others; and purses are held firmly shut, and clutched by the hand of indifference.

"Indifference keeps souls from the altar of surrender. It blinds sinners to their need of Christ; and blinds Christians to the value of the sinner's soul. It lurks around the corner ready to capture the new convert, enticing him with every attraction the world can offer.

"Indifference causes its victims to shirk their responsibilities, but he never rests. He ceaselessly endeavors to steal from the Church the very principles of its foundation.

"Indifference is a thief and a robber. Drive him from your place of worship!"—*Pulpit Helps,* Vol. 8, No. 10, July 1983.

A Matter of Values. CDF, Children's Defense Fund, says: "We support a strong national defense, but we believe we cannot have a secure nation if our children are sick, our graduates cannot read, and our families are divided by economic devastation." Here are some ways they suggest to find the needed money.

"1. Build nine fewer of the proposed one hundred B-1 bombers at $250 million each. This would finance Medicaid for all pregnant women and children living below the poverty level.

"2. Build one less of the 240 MX missiles at $110 million each. This would pay for child welfare services needed to ensure permanent families for the approximately 500,000 children now under foster care.

"It's a matter of values. And it goes without saying that values have a lot to do with the reality and depth of Christian commitment."

Questions for Pupils on the Next Lesson. 1. What persons in your family do you remember as having helped you in learning and growing in the Christian faith? 2. What have been some of the special times in your life when God was real to you? 3. How does your faith help you to face hardships? 4. What is the purpose of Scripture, according to 1 Timothy 2? 5. What are you personally doing to help in the religious training of children?

TOPIC FOR YOUTH
FIRST THINGS FIRST

Examples of Parents. The parents of Abraham Lincoln, Mr. and Mrs. Thomas Lincoln, were influential to a greater degree than most people imagine in shaping their son's antislavery views. For Lincoln's parents, it was a matter of putting priorities in order. And it was not easy. Six months before Abraham Lincoln's birth in 1809, the Lincolns moved to the Kentucky community where he was born. They affiliated with the South Fork Baptist Church. They found the minister, William Whitman, a staunch foe to slavery. When controversy over slavery forced the congregation to disband, the Lincolns joined the Little Mount Antislavery Baptist Church. A few years later, as Abraham Lincoln related in 1860, the Lincoln family moved from Kentucky to Indiana, "partly on account of slavery." In Indiana, the Lincolns attended the Pigeon Creek Baptist Church, whose minister, the Reverend Adam Shoemaker, was well-known for his strong antislavery sermons. These early childhood influences undoubtedly helped shape Abraham Lincoln's later decision to emancipate all slaves. It happened, however, because his parents put first things first in spite of the cost.

What's Your Purpose? A few years ago, the Bell Laboratories came up with a fascinating invention. It was a box slightly smaller than an ordinary bread box.

When a certain button was pushed, the machinery started inside. The lid of the box would quietly open, then a hand would come up and slowly reach over the side of the box and shut off the mechanism. The hand would then go back into the box and the lid would close. The silly but interesting device had no useful purpose but was only a toy which merely turned itself off.

Some people seem to be like that. They never let themselves get any useful purpose in life and merely exist to turn themselves off.

Through Jesus Christ, however, God has plans for you to be helpful and productive. Put the Lord first, and discover for yourself that you are meant to be more than a worthless machine closing the lid on life.

First Things First. Dean Crisp started out to be a baseball player. Although a bonus shortstop and outfielder with the Minnesota Twins organization, he felt something was missing. Dean Crisp is also an avid Christian and active Methodist. He returned to his home in North Carolina and enrolled at college. He signed on as a police cadet out of interest in law enforcement sparked by an instructor at West Carolina University. Dean Crisp's volunteer work took him, a white man, to the Hillcrest, an all-black housing project outside of Asheville. The first winter, he told skeptical youngsters in Hillcrest that he would take them to camp the following summer. That led Dean Crisp to help the Fraternal Order of Police to develop a camp that works with 500 poor children each year. Dean Crisp also took the boys on softball trips and often brought home a group for the weekend. Fortunately, Dean's wife also believes in helping others. Dean has been sneered at as a "nigger lover" by some whites. After over five years of serving in Hillcrest, Dean has brought change. Years ago, Asheville police refused to go to the project alone but only in pairs of police cars. Today, Dean is warmly greeted by everyone. In 1983, the Institute of Public Service passed out the institute's annual Jefferson Awards to celebrities, including Kirk Douglas, Helen Hayes, and Paul Volcker. One of those who also received a Jefferson Award was a young white police officer nobody outside of Asheville or Hillcrest had heard of—Dean Crisp. But Dean Crisp, the man with his priorities in the right order because of his Christian commitment, was perhaps the most outstanding celebrity of all that day!

Questions for Pupils on the Next Lesson. 1. Who in your family has influenced you the most in your growth as a Christian? How? Why? 2. When were the times in your life when God seemed most real to you? 3. Where do you turn for guidance in life? 4. Why does God allow us to face times of hardship? 5. Why is Scripture so important for us, according to 2 Timothy?

LESSON XII—NOVEMBER 17

THINGS WORTH REMEMBERING

Background Scripture: 2 Timothy
Devotional Reading: 2 Timothy 2:20–26

KING JAMES VERSION

2 TIMOTHY 1   PAUL, an apostle of Jesus Christ by the will of God, according to the promise of life which is in Christ Jesus,

2 To Timothy, *my* dearly beloved son: Grace, mercy, *and* peace, from God the Father and Christ Jesus our Lord.

3 I thank God, whom I serve from *my* forefathers with pure conscience, that without ceasing I have remembrance of thee in my prayers night and day;

4 Greatly desiring to see thee, being mindful of thy tears, that I may be filled with joy;

5 When I call to remembrance the unfeigned faith that is in thee, which dwelt first in thy grandmother Lois, and thy mother Eunice; and I am persuaded that in thee also.

6 Wherefore I put thee in remembrance, that thou stir up the gift of God, which is in thee by the putting on of my hands.

7 For God hath not given us the spirit of fear; but of power, and of love, and of a sound mind.

3.   10 But thou hast fully known my doctrine, manner of life, purpose, faith, long suffering, charity, patience,

11 Persecutions, afflictions, which came unto me at Antioch, at Iconium, at Lystra; what persecutions I endured: but out of *them* all the Lord delivered me.

12 Yea, and all that will live godly in Christ Jesus shall suffer persecution.

13 But evil men and seducers shall wax worse and worse, deceiving, and being deceived.

14 But continue thou in the things which thou hast learned and hast been assured of, knowing of whom thou hast learned *them;*

15 And that from a child thou hast known the holy scriptures, which are able to make thee wise unto salvation through faith which is in Christ Jesus.

16 All scripture *is* given by inspiration of God, and *is* profitable for doctrine, for reproof, for correction, for instruction in righteousness:

17 That the man of God may be perfect, thoroughly furnished unto all good works.

REVISED STANDARD VERSION

2 TIMOTHY 1   Paul, an apostle of Christ Jesus by the will of God according to the promise of the life which is in Christ Jesus.

2 To Timothy, my beloved child: Grace, mercy, and peace from God the Father and Christ Jesus our Lord.

3 I thank God whom I serve with a clear conscience, as did my fathers, when I remember you constantly in my prayers. 4 As I remember your tears, I long night and day to see you, that I may be filled with joy. 5 I am reminded of your sincere faith, a faith that dwelt first in your grandmother, Lois and your mother Eunice and now, I am sure, dwells in you. 6 Hence I remind you to rekindle the gift of God that is within you through the laying on of my hands; 7 for God did not give us a spirit of timidity but a spirit of power and love and self-control.

3.   10 Now you have observed my teaching, my conduct, my aim in life, my faith, my patience, my love, my steadfastness, 11 my persecutions, my sufferings, what befell me at Antioch, at Iconium, and at Lystra, what persecutions I endured; yet from them all the Lord rescued me. 12 Indeed all who desire to live a godly life in Christ Jesus will be persecuted, 13 while evil men and impostors will go on from bad to worse, deceivers and deceived. 14 But as for you, continue in what you have learned and have firmly believed, knowing from whom you learned it 15 and how from childhood you have been acquainted with the sacred writings which are able to instruct you for salvation through faith in Christ Jesus. 16 All scripture is inspired by God and profitable for teaching, for reproof, for correction, and for training in righteousness, 17 that the man of God may be complete, equipped for every good work.

KEY VERSE: I remind you to rekindle the gift of God that is within you through the laying on of my hands. 2 Timothy 1:6.

HOME DAILY BIBLE READINGS

Nov.   11.   M.   *A Sincere and Unfeigned Faith.* 2 Timothy 1:1–7.
Nov.   12.   T.   *The Surety of Belief.* 2 Timothy 1:8–14.
Nov.   13.   W.   *"Remember Jesus Christ."* 2 Timothy 2:1–13.

Nov. 14. T.   *A Workman, Approved and Unashamed.* 2 Timothy 2:14, 15, 20–26.
Nov. 15. F.   *Times of Stress and Peril.* 2 Timothy 3:1–9.
Nov. 16. S.   *The Purpose of Scripture.* 2 Timothy 3:10–17.
Nov. 17. S.   *"Preach the Word."* 2 Timothy 4:1–13.

BACKGROUND

The little letter in our New Testament we call 2 Timothy is the most personal of all of Paul's correspondence known to us. Every line shows Paul's feelings. When Paul wrote this epistle, he was no longer the hard-charging warrior for Christ, rushing throughout Asia Minor and Greece to establish and bolster Christian congregations. He was old. He was in prison. He was condemned to die. He was almost deserted. He was suffering from cold and illness from being chained in a damp cell in Rome. In spite of the loneliness, pain, and dreariness Paul was enduring, his letter does not show any hint of self-pity. Paul realized his days were numbered, but he displays no depression or anger. Rather, the old missionary quietly reflects on his long, active career as a Christian and shares some of what that pilgrimage in the faith has come to mean to him with his beloved "son" Timothy.

The immediate purpose for writing to Timothy was to ask him to come for a final visit. Paul wanted to have the joy of seeing Timothy as a father would be anxious to have his son join him to share memories and dreams.

There was also another purpose to this letter we call 2 Timothy. Paul realized that Timothy was sensitive and timid. He knew that Timothy felt acutely inadequate to the task he had been given. And what an assignment! What leader could have felt equal to the assignment of superintending the church in mighty Ephesus! That congregation seemed to be besieged on every side. From within, the Ephesus church was threatened by false leaders who belittled Timothy, exalted themselves and promulgated corruptions of the Christian faith. From without, harsh persecution by Roman authorities promoting the emperor cult of Nero menaced the church. Surrounding Timothy and the faithful in Ephesus was a cruel, sensuous pagan culture which tried to drag everyone to degrading depths. Paul wrote to strengthen and encourage Timothy. He did this by reminding Timothy of his heritage, his calling, his gifts. Most of all, Paul tried to put new resolve in Timothy by helping him to remember that Jesus Christ may be trusted to be sufficient for meeting the worst of hardships and persecution.

NOTES ON THE PRINTED TEXT

FROM: *Paul, an apostle*
TO: *Timothy, my beloved child*

In brief, memo fashion, Paul begins this short, urgent letter to Timothy. Timothy is Paul's designated representative overseeing the Ephesian church. Languishing in prison and aware of his ultimate and nearing end, Paul thanks God for Timothy. Paul recalls the close relationship between himself and this young minister. He remembers Timothy's *sincere faith* that was learned from his grandmother Lois and his mother Eunice, and he longs to see Timothy. He keeps him in his prayers.

Aware of his own approaching death, Paul is concerned about the dangers of false teaching. He urges Timothy to *rekindle the gift of God.* He wants Timothy to fan the faith into a white, hot fire. Just as a good breath of air on hot coals can rekindle a dying fire, so must Timothy rekindle the gift of God in himself and in his church. Timothy's faith and zeal must burn hot! God did not give him *a spirit of timidity but a spirit of power and love.* No mousey timidness or cowardliness for Timothy! God gives power. The Greek word for power is *dynamis* from which our word *dynamite* is derived. Timothy's faith must be like dynamite—bold and explosive. Yet, this dynamism must be tempered with loving warmth for others. There must be *self-control* and self-discipline or, as the good Presbyterian expression states it, "Ardor and order!"

Aware that soon he will be executed, Paul reminds Timothy of the years they served together. However, overriding this memory is his concern that Timothy remain alert to those who oppose the faith or who teach falsely. *You have observed my teachings, my conduct, my aim in life, my faith, my patience, my love, my steadfastness.* Timothy must remember what he has learned from Paul: his teachings, his leadership, his church management and organization. Paul also points out the hardships that a Christian can expect. He holds up his own persecutions and sufferings as an example. *Indeed all who desire to live a godly life in Christ Jesus will be persecuted* but will be rewarded with the promised salvation. However, for the imposters and false teachers who seek to deceive, there will be no salvation.

But as for you, continue in what you have learned and have firmly believed. Timothy has learned well from Paul. He is to remember his responsibility as a church leader. Paul urges him to continue his study of the Scriptures to learn of God's redeeming work in Christ. Unlike the words of the false teachers, Timothy is to rely on the Word of God for his teaching and preaching. *Scripture is inspired by God and profitable for teaching.* Only through the Scriptures can a Christian learn of Christ. Only through these inspired words can an individual attain full maturity in Christ. For with the Scriptures at his side, Timothy is equipped with the best and needs no other books or writings.

SUGGESTIONS TO TEACHERS

A woman recently paid $125 for a course of eight lessons on improving her memory. She had wanted to be able to bring to mind the names of business clients more readily and to recall appointments more easily. After the eight weeks' instruction, complete with tricks to sharpen memory skills, the woman concluded, "I guess you remember what you want to remember."

The Scriptures tend to agree with the woman's observation. In fact, Paul in 2 Timothy suggests there are things worth remembering. These are the basis for your lesson. Try to find your own things worth remembering in the Scripture for this lesson. Here are some pointers:

1. *REMEMBER TO GIVE THANKS.* Two Timothy 1:3 opens (like most of Paul's letters) with a ringing expression of thanksgiving. Why is it so important for Christians to remember to give thanks?

2. *REMEMBER TO PRAY FOR OTHERS.* Paul constantly mentions that he prays for his friends. Devote some time in this lesson on the purpose and plan of praying for others. Intercessory prayer calls for discipline and love.

3. *REMEMBER TO SHARE THE FAITH.* Two Timothy 1:8 tells of Paul recalling his missionary assignment even when he is suffering. Point out to your class that each Christian must always remember he or she is called to be a faith-sharer, no matter what the setting or circumstances.

4. *REMEMBER TO ENCOURAGE OTHERS.* Thoreau commented how many of his neighbors seemed to live existences of "quiet desperation." It's also true of people around you and those in your class. It's even true of Christians. How helpful a simple word of encouragement often proves to be! Paul encouraged Timothy. How can your class encourage other believers the best?

5. *REMEMBER TO REKINDLE THE GIFT OF GOD IN YOU.* Paul admonishes young Timothy not to grow lazy in his Christian living. Timothy is urged to "rekindle the gift" (2 Timothy 1:6). Emphasize to your class that Christians today

must do the same through daily devotions. Take time in this lesson to talk about ways of "rekindling God's gift" in each person.

6. *REMEMBER TO STAND FIRM IN THE FAITH.* There will be diversions, temptations, and discouragement, Paul warns. Two Timothy 2:1–7 offers help to us who find our faith wavering.

7. *REMEMBER TO LIVE AS A NEW PERSON.* Help your class to learn to practice the memory feat of recalling who they are—each day. And who are they? Christ's! He has given each believer new life. Therefore, remember that as Christ's new person to practice kindness and gentleness. (*See* especially 2 Timothy 2:8, 11–16 for remembering Christ and the new life He brings.)

8. *REMEMBER TO LEARN SCRIPTURE.* Look at 2 Timothy 3:15, 16, where Paul calls Timothy's attention to Scripture he has learned as a child. Take plenty of time in the class period to discuss the need for remembering the Bible.

TOPIC FOR ADULTS
THINGS WORTH REMEMBERING

Remembering to Care. God has made Himself known through Jesus Christ, and discloses Himself by the Holy Spirit through Scripture. Sometimes, God makes His presence felt deeply when one human personality reaches out to another in answer to human need.

Richard Wawro is a twenty-eight-year-old artist who lives in Edinburgh, Scotland. He was born with cataracts inside both eyes. At three weeks of age, he had four operations on his eyes to allow some light to penetrate; even now he is almost blind. At the age of three years, he was diagnosed as hopelessly retarded; presently he has an I.Q. of thirty. During his early years, he displayed many autistic behaviors. He did not speak aloud until he was eleven. And, early on, the family doctor advised his parents to put Richard in a home and forget about him. And yet, today this young, retarded Scotsman, who has had no formal training as an artist, is being compared to van Gogh. For in spite of the advice of their doctor (and I would NOT recommend this action to every parent of a retarded child), his parents' love for Richard made them refuse to institutionalize Richard and they continued their search to find ways to open up life to their severely retarded son.

Art critics and psychologists all over the world say that the paintings of this young man exhibit a remarkable sense of detail, color, light, and depth, in spite of the fact that he is almost blind and presses his glasses against the paper to draw; that he has an I.Q. of thirty, but has a phenomenal memory for details; and that he can neither read nor write. It is clear that none of this would have ever happened had not it been for the love of his parents.

Copies of Nothing. Dwight L. Morrow, once our ambassador to Mexico, was a very absent-minded man. One day he stood for half an hour by the side of his stenographer in perfect silence; then he said suddenly, "And make three copies, please."

How often we Christians act like that! We think it's enough to think about something. Or we speak about what a fine thing such-and-such would be if something were done about it, or imagine if only someone would do something about a certain problem. We mistakenly suppose something is done if we've thought about it or talked about it.

As Christ's people, we must remember to do!

The Son of Tears. "Patricius, a pagan living in the fourth century in North Africa, married a seventeen-year-old Christian by the name of Monica. Patricius was a wicked man and the son he and Monica had followed his example. Monica's pain was almost unbearable as she watched her son read everything and then try everything. But even though she suffered as she saw the direction her son was going, Monica never ceased to pray for his conversion. She was comforted by the prayer and prophecy of an elderly bishop: 'Go thy way and God bless thee, for it is not possible for the son of these tears to perish.'

"Monica has gone down in history as a faithful, praying mother. Her son was Augustine.

"As a young man Augustine turned away from his mother's Christianity for Manichaeanism, a pagan religion that rejected what it considered the objectionable commandments of Christianity. Its followers considered God as being both evil and good. They believed that the evil half of God dominated most men; there was no choice in the matter for the man. Young Augustine liked the philosophy because it gave him an excuse for his sinful ways.

"But Augustline slowly discovered that even though there was a force tempting him to sin, he himself was granting the permission. He discovered his free will. Later in his Confessions he wrote: 'And just this was my incurable sin that I thought myself not to be a sinner. What raised me into light was that I knew as well that I had a free will, as I knew that I lived.' "—Wayne E. Warner, *Quote,* December 15, 1982.

Questions for Pupils on the Next Lesson. 1. Was the early Christian Church made up of people of one social class or several classes? 2. What is the reason why Paul wrote the lovely little letter to Philemon? 3. Why does the New Testament insist that members of the Christian community are accountable to one another? 4. What, in your opinion, is your status before God? 5. What motivates Christians to work for justice in society?

TOPIC FOR YOUTH
THINGS WORTH REMEMBERING

Remembering Caesar and Shakespeare. What sense of history do you have? Do you have some idea of who lived when? Whom do you remember? Why?

Many leaders in our nation are worried because young people don't have a sense of wanting to remember important parts of our heritage. For example, in a university classroom in California, a student asked his English professor in a class discussion on Shakespeare's plays, "Did Julius Caesar resent Shakespeare's portrayal of him?" (Obviously the young man did not remember that the Roman leader, Julius Caesar, died some 1,500 years before the great English bard!) It has been said that the trouble with the younger generation is that it has not read the minutes of the last meeting.

This is particularly apt when it comes to understanding our faith. Scripture and knowledge of the Christian story is important for us in order for us to know who we are and for what we're here.

Human Chain. In Abergrave, Wales, a chain of eighty-five men pulled two explorers to safety from a flooded underground Welsh cave where they had been trapped for three days. The two men had been imprisoned deep inside a cavern under the mountains. A sudden rainstorm sent down tons of water and blocked all exits from the cave. Deep-sea divers plunged through the stream to reach the explorers. Then a human chain was formed through the swift underground water.

This is like the way each of us has been influenced by, helped by others. Our family, our church, our teachers, and others have been part of the human chain bringing us to the hope we enjoy and the standing we have as Christians!

Forgot to Remember. Edinburgh Castle in Scotland was supposed to be impregnable. Perched atop a towering rock, the mighty fortification could be approached only by a steep ramp from one side. It was assumed that no one could scale the precipitous sides. Therefore, the cannons were ranged and watch was kept toward the front ramp. This was the weakest point of defense. The strong areas were the near-perpendicular cliffs around the rest of the mighty citadel. Ironically, this is where the castle was entered and captured, not the weak area around the ramp and gate.

With us Christians, we are most frequently overcome in our areas where we think we are strongest. We become aware of our weaknesses and take steps to guard these. But we forget our strong sides, assuming we don't need to take heed in these realms. The things worth remembering in life are those which we think we can forget!

Questions for Pupils on the Next Lesson. 1. How would you describe the little church which met in Philemon's house? 2. What were some of the different kinds of social classes meeting together in that church? 3. Who was Onesimus? Who was Philemon? 4. How do Christians go about working for justice in society? 5. Do you long to be part of a "family" group?

LESSON XIII—NOVEMBER 24

ONE IN CHRIST JESUS

Background Scripture: Philemon; Galatians 3:23–29; 1 Corinthians 12:12, 13
Devotional Reading: Galatians 4:1–7

KING JAMES VERSION

PHILEMON Paul, a prisoner of Jesus Christ, and Timothy *our* brother, unto Philemon our dearly beloved, and fellow labourer,

2 And it *our* beloved Apphia and Archippus our fellow soldier, and to the church in thy house:

3 Grace to you, and peace, from God our Father and the Lord Jesus Christ.

8 Wherefore, though I might be much bold in Christ to enjoin thee that which is convenient,

9 Yet for love's sake I rather beseech *thee,* being such a one as Paul the aged, and now also a prisoner of Jesus Christ.

10 I beseech thee for my son Onesimus, whom I have begotten in my bonds:

11 Which in time past was to thee unprofitable, but now profitable to thee and to me:

12 Whom I have sent again: thou therefore receive him, that is, mine own bowels:

13 Whom I would have retained with me, that in thy stead he might have ministered unto me in the bonds of the gospel:

14 But without thy mind would I do nothing; that thy benefit should not be as it were of necessity, but willingly.

15 For perhaps he therefore departed for a season, that thou shouldest receive him for ever;

16 Not now as a servant, but above a servant, a brother beloved, specially to me, but how much more unto thee, both in the flesh, and in the Lord?

17 If thou count me therefore a partner, receive him as myself.

18 If he hath wronged thee, or oweth *thee* aught, put that on mine account;

19 I Paul have written *it* with mine own hand, I will repay *it:* albeit I do not say to thee how thou owest unto me even thine own self besides.

20 Yea, brother, let me have joy of thee in the Lord: refresh my bowels in the Lord.

REVISED STANDARD VERSION

PHILEMON Paul, a prisoner for Christ Jesus, and Timothy our brother,

To Philemon our beloved fellow worker 2 and Apphia our sister and Archippus our fellow soldier, and the church in your house:

3 Grace to you and peace from God our Father and the Lord Jesus Christ.

8 Accordingly, though I am bold enough in Christ to command you to do what is required, 9 yet for love's sake I prefer to appeal to you—I, Paul, an ambassador and now a prisoner also for Christ Jesus—10 I appeal to you for my child, Onesimus, whose father I have become in my imprisonment. 11 (Formerly he was useless to you, but now he is indeed useful to you and to me.) 12 I am sending him back to you, sending my very heart. 13 I would have been glad to keep him with me, in order that he might serve me on your behalf during my imprisonment for the gospel; 14 but I preferred to do nothing without your consent in order that your goodness might not be by compulsion but of your own free will.

15 Perhaps this is why he was parted from you for a while, that you might have him back for ever, 16 no longer as a slave but more than a slave, as a beloved brother, especially to me but how much more to you, both in the flesh and in the Lord. 17 So if you consider me your partner, receive him as you would receive me. 18 If he has wronged you at all, or owes you anything, charge that to my account. 19 I, Paul, write this with my own hand, I will repay it—to say nothing of your owing me even your own self. 20 Yes, brother, I want some benefit from you in the Lord. Refresh my heart in Christ.

KEY VERSE: By one Spirit we were all baptized into one body—Jews or Gentiles, slaves or free—and all were made to drink of one Spirit. 1 Corinthians 12:13.

HOME DAILY BIBLE READINGS

Nov.	18.	M.	*Heirs With Christ Jesus.* Romans 8:9–17.
Nov.	19.	T.	*"One Body and One Spirit."* Ephesians 4:1–7.
Nov.	20.	W.	*Prayer for Unity.* John 17:20–26.
Nov.	21.	T.	*Members of His Body.* 1 Corinthians 12:12–21.
Nov.	22.	F.	*An Appeal in Love.* Philemon 1–14.

Nov. 23. *S.*   *Brothers in the Lord.* Philemon 15-25.
Nov. 24. *S.*   *"One in Christ Jesus."* Galatians 3:23-29.

BACKGROUND

Sometimes reading parts of the New Testament seems to be like listening to one person speaking in a telephone conversation. You hear only one part of the conversation, and you wonder what all is going on. A hasty first reading of Philemon may be something like catching a portion of the story, causing you to wish you could understand everything that has gone on.

Philemon was one of Paul's dearest friends. He was a convert to the Good News of Jesus Christ. We don't know details about his conversion or his background. Paul apparently inspired Philemon to share his faith. Philemon became the leader of a house church. Paul stayed in Philemon's home and became a beloved member of the household.

Philemon, like many in the Greek world, owned a slave. The slave was named Onesimus. One of the estimated sixty million slaves in the Roman Empire at that time, Onesimus did what many slaves tried to do. He robbed his master and took off.

Somehow, Onesimus got to Rome. Incredibly, he linked up with Paul. We don't know how this happened, whether by accident or by intention on Onesimus's part. The fugitive thief and runaway found himself freed from the slavery of the soul through his assocation with Paul in Rome. He became a devout Christian.

Paul quickly came to appreciate Onesimus. He also would have liked to have had Onesimus remain with him. He realized that he was both legally and morally obliged to have Onesimus return to Philemon. Paul also knew that Philemon could choose to carry out harsh punishment on Onesimus. But he also knew that Philemon and Onesimus had both turned over their lives to Jesus Christ as their Lord. That made them members of one family.

Out of his great affection for both Philemon and Onesimus, Paul sent a letter to accompany the returning slave. That letter we call the Epistle to Philemon. In it, Paul delicately appreciates Philemon's rights but gently urges him to welcome Onesimus back to his household not as a slave but as a Christian brother. After all, Paul insists, they are all one in Jesus Christ!

NOTES ON THE PRINTED TEXT

This personal, tender letter was written from a Roman cell block by Paul. He was writing to Philemon, his wife Apphia, and their son Archippus. He was also writing to an entire church that met in the home of Philemon. Included in this church's numbers were slaves.

This short letter shows how the early Christians dealt with the issue of slavery. Instead of trying to abolish it, the Church sought to improve relations between masters and slaves. Liberation was to come through Christian love, a love shared by all.

Paul is writing this letter to urge Philemon to receive back with leniency the runaway slave, Onesimus. Paul expects the whole house church to support his return. He asks this in *love* though he knows that he could *command* Philemon *to do what is required.* Paul is *an ambassador for Christ Jesus.* His authority to command rests on the apostleship that he received directly from Jesus. He could command, but he does not.

Paul does not write as an authoritarian dictator. He writes as a loving, caring parent. He *appeals* for his *child,* Onesimus, to whom he has become a father while in prison. With deep heartfelt regrets, Paul is sending Onesimus back to

Philemon. Onesimus has become a Christian and is now living up to his name—which means "useful." So useful is Onesimus that Paul confesses *I would have been glad to keep him with me, in order that he might serve me on your behalf during my imprisonment for the gospel.* However, Paul prefers to let Philemon respond to Christian love as his faith would dictate him to do by accepting Onesimus and freeing him from slavery. He goes on to suggest that *perhaps this was why he was parted* from Philemon for a while, so that Onesimus could return as *more than a slave, as a beloved brother.*

Secure in the reception Paul knows awaits Onesimus, he has encouraged Onesimus to return to Philemon. *If you consider me your partner, receive him as you would receive me.* Paul emphasizes that all of the members of the Christian community are one and are accountable to each other for their actions. *If he owes you anything, charge that to my account, I will repay it.* Out of courteousness, Paul offers to repay any debts incurred by Philemon because of Onesimus's departure.

Knowing he will not be held accountable, Paul reminds Philemon that Philemon owes his own life to Paul, and Paul now *wants some benefit. Refresh my heart in Christ,* appeals Paul, by welcoming Onesimus back to the house church as a free man.

SUGGESTIONS TO TEACHERS

A team of young Japanese Christians was visiting church groups on the West Coast. When they came to one affluent suburban congregation in California, the minister was surprised that few people bothered to attend the reception and hear the reports by the Christians from Japan. He asked a group of people working on the church bazaar the following day why none of them had come out to meet the visting Japanese church people. "Oh, Reverend Jackson, we have nothing in common with those people," answered the president of the women's guild.

Nothing in common with others who belong to Jesus Christ? Not according to the New Testament! Here is where your lesson catches fire for this Sunday. Look seriously at the background Scripture for this lesson, and take note of the way Christians everywhere share a oneness in Christ.

1. *DIVERSITY ACKNOWLEDGED.* The little book (actually a letter) of Philemon makes a beautiful case of how believers are one in Jesus Christ. Paul, the writer, is in prison and is old and poor. He apparently has nothing in common with Philemon who is wealthy, or with Timothy, who is young, or with Onesimus, who is a slave. Yet he insists that they all share a oneness because of their common life in Christ. Have your people acknowledge the diversity found within your class. Or within your congregation. What do you really have in common? Your faith in Christ!

2. *DESCRIPTIONS OFFERED.* What does it mean to be one in Christ? Paul gives examples. List these from the Scripture in this lesson: "fellow worker"; "sister" and "brother"; "fellow soldier"; members of the "church in your house." How can these terms be applied to your church or to your class?

3. *DESTINY DISCLOSED.* Paul uses an interesting figure in Galatians 3:25, when he points out that Christians are no longer like children under the "tutor" of the Law but are welcomed as grown-up members of God's family circle. Here is the time to talk about what God has in mind for each of your class members. God wants them to grow up and associate with Him. With this maturity, your people will see that they share a kinship with other members of God's family everywhere.

4. *DISTINCTIONS REMOVED.* Make sure your class takes a long, hard look at Galatians 3:28. Emphasize that there never can be a "But we have nothing in common with them" when it comes to associating with other Christians.

Whether from Japan or Jersey, whether rich or poor, whether male or female, whether young or old, whether whatever, in Christ we all are one!

5. *DEFINITION GIVEN.* Save enough time in your lesson to study 1 Corinthians 12:12, 13, with its reference to Christians being many members of one body. Ask what it means to be part of Christ's "body," the Church? Can a part survive or be useful if severed from the rest of the body? Tell your class that each Christian has his or her purpose in life defined by being in relationship with Christ and other Christians.

TOPIC FOR ADULTS
ONE IN JESUS CHRIST

"Gung Ho Christians." Gung Ho came to us from American Marines in the South Pacific during WWII. *Gung* is the Chinese word for work, and *Ho* is the word for harmony. What a perfect description for the way we Christians are one in Christ Jesus! We work together in harmony! Each of our congregations should be *Gung Ho* churches filled with *Gung Ho* Christians.

The Perfect Church. "I think that I shall never see a church that's all it ought to be. A church whose members never stray beyond the straight and narrow way; a church that has no empty pews whose pastor never has the blues; a church whose elders always seek, and none is proud, and all are meek; where gossips never peddle lies, or make complaints, or criticize; where all are always sweet and kind, and all to others' faults are blind; such perfect churches there may be, but none of them are known to me; but still, we'll work, and pray, and plan, to make our own the best we can."—Author unknown.

Mistaken Differences. Sometimes, we forget our oneness in Christ Jesus and emphasize the differences. Other times, we note the wrong things which may be different among Christians, thinking that these insignificant differences should keep us apart. We are something like the little five-year-old boy who was playing with the small daughter of new neighbors. They had been wading in the lake, and finally decided the only way to keep their clothes dry was to take them off.

As they were going back into the water, the little boy looked the little girl over. "Gosh!" he remarked. "I didn't know there was *that* much difference between Lutherans and Methodists."

Questions for Pupils on the Next Lesson. 1. What was the Angel Gabriel's message to Mary? 2. How did Mary respond to that message? 3. How do you as a Christian respond to challenges which involve uncertainty and risk? 4. What opportunities has God given you to do something of significance? 5. Do you think that better days will ever come?

TOPIC FOR YOUTH
ONE IN CHRIST JESUS

Getting into the Picture. Several years ago, experts restored the famous painting, *The Night Watch,* by the Dutch painter Rembrandt. The magnificent painting had hung for years in Amsterdam without proper protection and acquired a heavy layer of dust and grime. As the restorers painstakingly cleaned the masterpiece, they were astonished to find figures emerging in the shadows which had been hidden by the accumulation of dirt. These long-obscured figures added greatly to the beauty and majesty of the great work of art.

In Christ Jesus, we are brought into the picture, so to speak, of God's great design. We belong in the collection of figures belonging to Christ Jesus. Sometimes, we forget or find that our presence is overlooked. Christ, however, is also the Restorer. He brings us back into the picture!

Spirit of Unity. When the movie *Gandhi* was conceived by Sir Richard Attenborough, everyone said it would be impossible to produce or sell. Indeed, when filming began in India, it appeared hopeless. With 250 Indian and British crew members present on the filming locations, there was friction. But then the spirit of Gandhi himself began to take hold. The great holy man's serenity, his creed that everyone is needed and important, and his concern for others began to affect camera crews, prop men, make-up assistants, actors, sound technicians—everyone. The large international crew making the movie parted the firmest of friends. Martin Sheen, the actor playing a hardbitten newsman, was so affected by the experience that he gave his entire salary to charity in India, mostly to Mother Teresa. Even Attenborough himself acknowledged that he moved from atheism to faith.

How much more Jesus Christ welds a group of people into a closely-cooperating team. In fact, the closer persons are to Him, the closer they are to each other. The more they know Christ Jesus, the more they know harmony within themselves and with others!

Supplying the Wants of the Saints. "It is a prosperous, mainline denomination church in a Pennsylvania town. Many who attend it really know Christ personally; quite a few go because it is the only church in town. A large portion of the church's money is making money through investments on the stock market, although there are also the attendant losses.

"It has a sister church in Pittsburgh. Same denomination. Given the amount of correspondence between these congregations, you might have called them extremely distant cousins. The city church was struggling. The people were poor, the building inadequate, the possibility of a bank loan out of sight.

"These churches knew of each other, but not having the same ethnic background and being so far apart, they did not exchange many insights.

"One day someone got to thinking and said to the rest of the trustees of the town chuch: 'I know some of the folks over at the city church. Why don't we lend them some money?'

"Eyes widened, then narrowed. 'What money?' everyone wanted to know.

" 'Some of our investment portfolio.' The atmosphere turned decidedly chilly.

"Then he suggested, 'Well, how about if we lend it to them at half the interest of a bank and for a longer period? After all, they're our brothers.'

"Apparently not many had considered such a financial arrangement, and no one had considered the sibling relationship in Christ.

"They went ahead and did it. It was not exactly Paul's idea of equality of resources, but it was much better than acting like they were not responsible for fellow Christians forty-five miles away."—Reprinted from *Adult Teacher's Guide,* © 1979 David C. Cook Publishing Co., Elgin, IL 60120. Used by permission.

Questions for Pupils on the Next Lesson. 1. Why had the Old Testament people hoped for a Deliverer as promised by the prophets? 2. What did the Angel Gabriel tell Mary? 3. How did Mary respond to Gabriel's announcement? 4. How do you handle uncertainty and risk? 5. How do you react when you remember how scary the future looks?

DECEMBER 1985, JANUARY, FEBRUARY 1986

ADVENT: TO YOU A SAVIOR (4 SESSIONS)

LESSON I—DECEMBER 1

THE ANNOUNCEMENT

Background Scripture: Isaiah 9:1–7; Luke 1:26–56
Devotional Reading: Luke 1:46–56

KING JAMES VERSION

LUKE 1   26 And in the sixth month the angel Gabriel was sent from God unto a city of Galilee, named Nazareth,

27 To a virgin espoused to a man whose name was Joseph, of the house of David; and the virgin's name *was* Mary.

28 And the angel came in unto her, and said, Hail, *thou that art* highly favoured, the Lord *is* with thee: blessed *art* thou among women.

29 And when she saw *him*, she was troubled at his saying, and cast in her mind what manner of salutation this should be.

30 And the angel said unto her, Fear not, Mary: for thou hast found favour with God.

31 And, behold, thou shalt conceive in thy womb, and bring forth a son, and shalt call his name JESUS.

32 He shall be great, and shall be called the Son of the Highest; and the Lord God shall give unto him the throne of his father David:

33 And he shall reign over the house of Jacob for ever; and of his kingdom there shall be no end.

34 Then said Mary unto the angel, How shall this be, seeing I know not a man?

35 And the angel answered and said unto her, The Holy Ghost shall come upon thee, and the power of the Highest shall overshadow thee: therefore also that holy thing which shall be born of thee shall be called the Son of God.

36 And, behold, thy cousin Elisabeth, she hath also conceived a son in her old age; and this is the sixth month with her, who was called barren.

37 For with God nothing shall be impossible.

38 And Mary said, Behold the handmaid of the Lord; be it unto me according to thy word. And the angel departed from her.

REVISED STANDARD VERSION

LUKE 1   26 In the sixth month the angel Gabriel was sent from God to a city of Galilee named Nazareth, 27 to a virgin betrothed to a man whose name was Joseph, of the house of David; and the virgin's name was Mary. 28 And he came to her and said, "Hail, O favored one, the Lord is with you!" 29 But she was greatly troubled at the saying, and considered in her mind what sort of greeting this might be. 30 And the angel said to her, "Do not be afraid, Mary, for you have found favor with God. 31 And behold, you will conceive in your womb and bear a son, and you shall call his name Jesus.

32 He will be great, and will be called the
Son of the Most High;
and the Lord God will give to him the
throne of his father David,

33 and he will reign over the house of Jacob
for ever;
and of his kingdom there will be no end."

34 And Mary said to the angel, "How can this be, since I have no husband?"

35 And the angel said to her,

"The Holy Spirit will come upon you,
and the power of the Most High will overshadow you;
therefore the child to be born will be
called holy,
the Son of God.

36 And behold, your kinswoman Elizabeth in her old age has also conceived a son; and this is the sixth month with her who was called barren. 37 For with God nothing will be impossible." 38 And Mary said, "Behold I am the handmaid of the Lord; let it be to me according to your word." And the angel departed from her.

KEY VERSE: He will be great, and will be called the Son of the Most High. Luke 1:32.

HOME DAILY BIBLE READINGS

Nov.   25.   M.   *To Us a Child Is Born.* Isaiah 9:2–7.
Nov.   26.   T.   *John Is Promised.* Luke 1:5–17.
Nov.   27.   W.   *Zechariah Is Struck Dumb.* Luke 1:18–25.
Nov.   28.   T.   *The Announcement to Mary.* Luke 1:26–38.
Nov.   29.   F.   *Mary Visits Elizabeth.* Luke 1:39–45.
Nov.   30.   S.   *Mary's Song of Praise.* Luke 1:46–56.
Dec.   1.   S.   *Zechariah's Song of Praise.* Luke 1:67–79.

BACKGROUND

ADVENT. The term itself comes from the Latin word for *coming.* It refers, of course, to the coming of the Savior. For the next four lessons, this course will focus on the Coming of Jesus in the form of a baby in Bethlehem and the significance of that Coming of God among us for us today.

Jesus' Coming was the fulfillment of God's promise to the Old Testament community for a Messiah. However, His Coming has significance not only for the Jewish people but for all people in all ages.

For the first three of these lessons on Advent, we will draw upon Luke's Gospel. These lessons will include the announcement to Mary, the birth of Jesus, and the visit by the shepherds. The fourth lesson will be based on Matthew's report of the visit of the wise men from the East. Additional Background Scriptures from Isaiah and Micah underline the longing for a Messiah and confidence in God's continuing action.

Today's lesson, discussing the Announcement of Jesus' Coming to Mary, poignantly describes the deep hopes of the Jewish people for the long-promised Deliverer. It is almost impossible for us to understand how profound and widespread this hope was at the time of Jesus' Coming. Mary certainly shared these longings. She had been raised to pray for the Messiah's Coming. She had certainly heard the synagogue leaders and her elders express their desire and expectation that some day God would send the long-promised One.

Imagine Mary's feelings when she learned that she was to be the mother of this promised Messiah! What a frightening prospect for a young woman! Remember, too, that Mary was still unmarried. How did she feel about being told that she would conceive a child before being married to Joseph?

We Protestants are often uneasy about talking very much about Mary the Mother of Jesus because of reacting to Roman Catholic dogma or piety over Mary. However, because we may not recite the rosary does not mean we ignore this remarkable personality. Mary responded to the angel's announcement about her wonderful conception as a sign of God's power with trust and obedience. We may give thanks for her faithfulness, and renew our commitment to trust and obey.

NOTES ON THE PRINTED TEXT

The Prophet Isaiah wrote during a time of turmoil and uncertainty. His little nation of Judah was threatened by the terrible Assyrians. Isaiah knew that the Lord is the God of all nations and all history. To his dismay, however, the prophet also knew that his beloved Judah refused to take God seriously. In fact, Judah seemed to flaunt God by permitting social injustice. Many of its kings could not bring themselves to set an example or to act decisively for righteousness. It was against this background that Isaiah spoke to his ruler, King Ahaz, and his countrymen. Isaiah solemnly warned that a day of reckoning would come. Chapters 1 through 8 record Isaiah's pleas to Judah to return to God and warnings of doom if she does not repent.

Isaiah 9:1–7 shifts from warnings of doom to a promise of God's ultimate deliverance. God will provide the ideal king! Like a trumpet note of hope after somber strains of a death march, this great passage sings of a ruler who will bring victory to God's people and institute a new era of justice and peace!

... and his name will be called Wonderful Counselor. This is the first of the series of titles that the promised Deliverer is given. (Note that there should not be any comma between Wonderful and Counselor.) The Messiah will be the fount of great wisdom and be "Wonderful in His Purpose."

... Mighty God, Everlasting Father. In addition, the Coming Deliverer sent by God will have great might, and will be a caring Parent-Ruler forever. The Messiah will combine the attributes of both power and love.

... Prince of Peace. The Hebrew word for "peace" is *shalom.* It means more than merely the absence of war, *Shalom* always refers to the condition of harmony between God and humans, and between humans and humans. *Shalom* means wholeness and well-being.

Jesus is the fulfillment of each of these titles. Looking back at this great passage in Isaiah, those affected by Jesus' Coming were inspired to use these words about the ideal ruler as an excellent description of who Jesus is.

The Announcement of the long-promised Deliverer to Mary was made by the same announcement-bearer, Gabriel, who had announced the birth of John the Baptist. Note that there is no description of the Angel Gabriel. No feathered wings, no halo, no flowing white robe are mentioned. The emphasis is on the message, not the messenger. In fact, the word *angel* is simply the term for a messenger.

SUGGESTIONS TO TEACHERS

Everybody in your class has heard the Christmas story before. You may ask how you can teach four lessons on material that everyone already knows. But ask yourself: Do the people in your class *really* know the Christmas story? (Do you?) A mishmash of biblical facts and popular sentiment is what most know. Your task is to separate Santa, Rudolph, the littlest shepherd, and the pious fluff from the momentous announcement of God's Coming among us.

Look at the scriptural material in this lesson as if you are reading it for the first time. You will find startling new insights into the meaning of Advent!

1. *ANCIENT'S MESSAGE.* The Old Testament Prophet Isaiah promised a Deliverer. Ponder with your class what hope that meant for the people of that time. Also consider together what a hopeful message it is for us to know that God has not abandoned us but has come as Deliverer in the person of Jesus Christ!

2. *ANGELIC MESSENGER.* Part of the significance of the Christmas story is the unexpected intervention of God into human history. The angel surprised Mary with the astonishing announcement that the Almighty would visit in person. Have your class understand the meaning of the word and doctrine of *Incarnation.*

3. *ASTONISHED MAIDEN.* Some Protestants are reluctant to pay much attention to Mary, the Mother of Jesus. Without accepting Roman Catholic dogmas about Mary, however, it is possible to reflect appreciatively on this outstanding woman. Why did God choose Mary? Why not a famous empress instead of this unknown village girl? This can lead your class to think about why God selected any of us! God seems to delight in picking out people like Mary—and those in your class—for His work.

4. *ABLE MAKER.* "For with God nothing is impossible" (Luke 1:37) is a phrase which must be examined and discussed. God is able! This verse is a special Word to doubters and scoffers of Jesus as God's only Son. People sometimes get hung up on the genetic impossibility of a virgin birth, thereby missing the deeper

truth in the Christmas story. That deeper truth is that God came to us in human form.

5. *ADORING MAGNIFICAT.* You and your class should take some minutes to ponder the glorious words of the hymn (called the *Magnificat* because the first word in the Latin version of this song opens with this word). Part of Christmas is reflecting quietly and singing joyfully because of what God has done. Perhaps you may even want to close this lesson with some time to enjoy and praise.

TOPIC FOR ADULTS
THE ANNOUNCEMENT

Gospel Affirms God's Friendliness to Man. " 'Is the universe friendly?'

"An inquisitive man whose name I can't recall asked that question. He wondered, as most of us do, whether the universe is for or against us.

"Astonomers see nothing but planets, stars and lesser satellites in the void of dark, cold, unfriendly space. A Russian cosmonaut who circled the Earth reported that he didn't see God anywhere out there.

"Blaise Pascal, a French mathematician and philosopher, was frightened by the 'eternal silence of the fathomless vastness.' Sigmund Freud used the word *helplessness* to describe human feelings of finiteness in the face of the universe.

"Our Earth also seems unfriendly. We have extremes of hot and cold, flood and drought, earthquake and tornado, dangerous insects and animals, poisonous plants, and man's inhumanity to man. Nature is careful of the species but not of the individual. Death is the end of all living individuals.

"Nature's alleged unfriendliness has rubbed off on human beings. People have exploited the resource of Mother Nature unmercifully. There's no need to go into details about our ecological dilemma. Suffice it to say we have little regard for Albert Schweitzer's 'reverence for life'—as well as for Mother Nature.

"Those who don't believe in God have plenty of evidence to support their view—if we falsely assume it's possible to believe in God only when we're in Heaven.

"Isn't the Gospel simply the affirmation of the friendliness of God and life and the universe? The Good News is that God is for and not against us, and since this is God's world, it, too, must be for rather than against us. Jesus called God the Father who notices the fall of a sparrow, cares for the flowers of the fields, numbers the hair on our heads and knows us by our names."—Joseph Mohr, *The Morning Call/Weekender,* Allentown, PA, February 21, 1981. Reprint from Call-Chronicle Newspapers, Allentown, Pa.

Step Out of the Frame. A missionary's son came to the United States to attend college. He missed his family and kept a picture of his father over his desk. A few weeks before Christmas, a faculty member dropped by to ask what the student would like for Christmas. The young man was silent for several moments, then said softly, "I want my father to step out of that frame."

Throughout history, human beings have had that same sense of longing about God. If only He would disclose Himself.

The wondrous announcement is that God has stepped out of the frame. The hope of the prophets has been fulfilled! The longing of the Jewish people and, indeed, all people, has been met. God has come among us in the birth of the baby named Jesus!

Any Announcement? An international group of scientists is urging governments not to abandon efforts to communicate with other civilizations in space, if any exist.

Sixty-nine prominent scientists and academicians, in a letter published recently in *Science* magazine, said that humans have the capacity to communicate through radio signals with civilizations thousands of light years away.

They called for a concerted, worldwide effort to locate possible civilizations in outer space by listening for their radio signals.

Without such an effort, the decades-long debate over whether there is other intelligent life is likely to remain unsolved, they said.

The scientists, including astronomers, engineers, biologists, physicians, philosophers, anthropologists, and computer experts from many countries, said they were unanimous in their conviction that the only significant test of the existence of extraterrestrial intelligence is an experimental one.

"Using current radioastronomical technology, it is possible for us to receive signals from civilizations no more advanced than we are over a distance of at least many thousands of light years," said the letter.

This Season of the Announcement of the Angel to Mary is the Good News that our planet has already been visited from beyond. God has communicated with us directly! Moreover, the Creator Himself has come in human form! Out of the silent and distant spaciousness of eternity, the Lord Almighty has announced Himself as present with us!

Questions for Pupils on the Next Lesson. 1. What does the name *Jesus* mean in the original language? 2. How would you describe Joseph? 3. Where in the Bible is the prophecy about Bethlehem being the birthplace of the Messiah? 4. Why did Joseph go to Bethlehem to pay his taxes and be enrolled? 5. How do you cope with feelings of emptiness and helplessness?

TOPIC FOR YOUTH
A PROMISE RETOLD

Wonder-filled Announcement. "Children are more disappointed than children were eighty years ago when they learn that Santa is not real"—*Psychology Today.*

However, the survey's authors, Benjamin, Langley, and Hall, go on to report that though modern school children feel "cheated" or "sorry" more than twice as often as their 1896 counterparts (45% to 22%) to find out about Santa, they are less likely to ascribe supernatural powers to St. Nick. The wonder and awe has diminished.

"Perhaps today's children, raised with Wonder Woman, Spiderman, Batman, and the Bionic Woman, find Santa Claus a bit lackluster as a mythological figure," conclude the authors.

In today's world of advanced technology and computerized living, have you lost the wonder of the Christmas story? Does Christmas bring on feelings of sorrow or diappointment or a feeling of being cheated? Have the superheroes and mythological figures of today blotted out the awe of Christmas for you? Are you like those children?

Look at the Gospels of Matthew and Luke. "To you is born a Savior, who is Christ the Lord!" I can't think of anything more wondrous, awesome, or majestic than the thought conveyed in these simple lines of Scripture. Here is the wondrous news that God Himself has come into the world to be with us. (Immanuel, God with us!) Frosty, Scrooge, and the Grinch are all fine but seem quite lacking in light of the News that our Savior is born!

God cared enough about us to come to us. Here is our hope and our future. There is nothing lackluster or mythological about this event. The wonder and the birth still stand giving cause to celebrate joyfully again this season. Let that wonder work on you. Jesus is born and lives!—J.B. Barker.

Ancient Prayer Fulfilled. "A Deliverer! Lord, bring one to us!" This hope was a feature of Judaism for generations. This longing was repeatedly voiced in the

Amadiah benediction: "Blessed art Thou, O Lord our God and the God of our fathers, God of Abraham, God of Isaac, and God of Jacob, the great, mighty, and revered God, the most revered God, who bestowest loving kindnesses and possesseth all things, who rememberest the pious deeds of the Patriarchs, and in love wilt bring a redeemer to their children's children for thy name's sake." Christmas for Christians is the celebration of the fulfillment of this prophecy and hope. John the Apostle unmistakably confirms the realization of this hope when he says, "The Word became flesh and dwelt among us." John saw in Christ the Incarnate God. The chief cause for rejoicing at Christmas should be that God has become the Known God.

Bah Humbug for Postal Worker. A Hollywood, Florida, Post Office worker named Lou Giacobazzi became so fed up with the pressures and extra work of the Christmas season in December, 1980, that he put on a big button with the words *BAH HUMBUG* printed on it. His supervisor told him to remove the pin. Giacobazzi refused. The supervisor said that the badge reflected poorly on the Postal Service. Giacobazzi stated that he had worn the badge each Christmas season for six years. The supervisor was adamant. Giacobazzi was fired. Some of the patrons at the Hollywood Post Office were outraged at the firing. "We think that *Bah Humbug* represents the feelings of many people working with the public during the frantic holiday season," stated Rose Hicks, the office manager of a business across the street from the Post Office.

Is this the announcement that you are sharing this season? Is "Bah Humbug" the most you can say about Christmas?

Jesus Christ, the promised Deliverer, is born! This is the badge to sport this season and every day!

Questions for Pupils on the Next Lesson. 1. What was the angel's message to Mary about her pregnancy? 2. What kind of a man was Joseph? 3. What does the name *Jesus* mean? 4. Why did Joseph and Mary travel from Nazareth to Bethlehem? 5. Does God identify with people who sometimes feel helpless?

LESSON II—DECEMBER 8

THE BIRTH OF JESUS

Background Scripture: Isaiah 11:1–9; Micah 5:2; Matthew 1:18–25; Luke 2:1–7
Devotional Reading: Isaiah 11:1–9

KING JAMES VERSION

MATTHEW 1 18 Now the birth of Jesus Christ was on this wise: When as his mother Mary was espoused to Joseph, before they came together, she was found with child of the Holy Ghost.

19 Then Joseph her husband, being a just *man*, and not willing to make her a publick example, was minded to put her away privily.

20 But while he thought on these things, behold, the angel of the Lord appeared unto him in a dream, saying, Joseph, thou son of David, fear not to take unto thee Mary thy wife: for that which is conceived in her is of the Holy Ghost.

21 And she shall bring forth a son, and thou shalt call his name JESUS: for he shall save his people from their sins.

22 Now all this was done, that it might be fulfilled which was spoken of the Lord by the prophet, saying,

23 Behold, a virgin shall be with child, and shall bring forth a son, and they shall call his name Emmanuel, which being interpreted is, God with us.

24 Then Joseph being raised from sleep did as the angel of the Lord had bidden him, and took unto him his wife:

25 And knew her not till she had brought forth her firstborn son: and he called his name JESUS.

LUKE 2 AND it came to pass in those days, that there went out a decree from Cæsar Augustus, that all the world should be taxed.

2 (*And* this taxing was first made when Cyrenius was governor of Syria.)

3 And all went to be taxed, every one into his own city.

4 And Joseph also went up from Galilee, out of the city of Nazareth, into Judea, unto the city of David, which is called Bethlehem; (because he was of the house and lineage of David:)

5 To be taxed with Mary his espoused wife, being great with child.

6 And so it was, that, while they were there, the days were accomplished that she should be delivered.

7 And she brought forth her firstborn son, and wrapped him in swaddling clothes, and laid him in a manger; because there was no room for them in the inn.

REVISED STANDARD VERSION

MATTHEW 1 18 Now the birth of Jesus Christ took place in this way. When his mother Mary had been betrothed to Joseph, before they came together she was found to be with child of the Holy Spirit; 19 and her husband Joseph, being a just man and unwilling to put her to shame, resolved to divorce her quietly. 20 But as he considered this, behold, an angel of the Lord appeared to him in a dream, saying, "Joseph, son of David, do not fear to take Mary your wife, for that which is conceived in her is of the Holy Spirit; 21 she will bear a son, and you shall call his name Jesus, for he will save his people from their sins." 22 All this took place to fulfil what the Lord had spoken by the prophet:

23 "Behold, a virgin shall conceive
and bear a son,
and his name shall be called
Emmanuel"

(which means, God with us). 24 When Joseph woke from sleep, he did as the angel of the Lord commanded him; he took his wife, 25 but knew her not until she had borne a son; and he called his name Jesus.

LUKE 2 In those days a decree went out from Caesar Augustus that all the world should be enrolled. 2 This was the first enrollment, when Quirinius was governor of Syria. 3 And all went to be enrolled, each to his own city. 4 And Joseph also went up from Galilee, from the city of Nazareth, to Judea, to the city of David, which is called Bethlehem, because he was of the house and lineage of David, 5 to be enrolled with Mary, his betrothed, who was with child. 6 And while they were there, the time came for her to be delivered. 7 And she gave birth to her first-born son and wrapped him in swaddling cloths, and laid him in a manger, because there was no place for them in the inn.

KEY VERSE: You shall call his name Jesus, for he will save his people from their sins. Matthew 1:21.

HOME DAILY BIBLE READINGS

Dec.	2.	M.	*The Messianic King.* Isaiah 11:1–9.
Dec.	3.	T.	*The Deliverer From Bethlehem.* Micah 5:2–4.
Dec.	4.	W.	*Preparing the Way of the Lord.* Isaiah 40:1–11.
Dec.	5.	T.	*The Lord's Messenger.* Malachi 3:1–4, 42.
Dec.	6.	F.	*The Eternal Word.* John 1:1–5.
Dec.	7.	S.	*Born in a Stable.* Luke 2:1–7.
Dec.	8.	S.	*The Birth of Jesus.* Matthew 1:18–25.

BACKGROUND

Every time you write a letter or put a date on a check, you are recognizing that the birth of Jesus is the pivotal event in human history. Everything that has ever happened is reckoned in terms of either prior to Jesus' Coming or after, B.C. or A.D.

The Gospel writers knew this, although at the time they wrote, everyone measured time by the reigns of the Roman emperors. What a turnaround! Today we set dates for the Caesars by the date of the birth of a baby to an obscure Jewish woman in a stable in an insignificant town located in a distant province!

Look at the main characters in the great drama of the birth of Jesus. Mary and Joseph were betrothed. This meant that they were more than engaged. Betrothal was a bond that could not be dissolved except by proceedings like going through a divorce. Mary's pregnancy by the miraculous intervention of the Holy Spirit, shocked and hurt Joseph. Obviously, Joseph was a deeply religious Jew. He was also an honorable man. He didn't want to cause his betrothed additional disgrace or hurt, so he planned to sever the betrothal with as little fuss as possible. At this point, the Lord directly intervened. To Joseph's great credit, he listened to the whispers of God's messenger and accepted Mary's story. Like Mary, Joseph heard that the unborn baby was to be named *Jesus.*

Jesus signifies "Yahweh's salvation." Names were immensely important to the Jewish people, and the name of the baby Mary was carrying conveyed a powerful message! God had cosmic plans for Mary's holy child.

The journey to Bethlehem from Nazareth would have taken three days. For a woman in the last days of pregnancy, it must have been uncomfortable and frightening. Yet they had to make the long and difficult journey. Mary and Joseph also knew what it was to be pushed around by governmental bureaucracy and treated like insignificant cyphers.

The stable in Bethlehem was actually a hillside cave where animals could huddle in bad weather. It's easy to imagine Mary and Joseph's relief when the special Baby arrived safely in such miserable surroundings. Part of the irony of the story of the birth of our Savior is the fact that He was born to a plain village girl in the most humble setting imaginable! God truly came among the lowliest of us humans in the lowliest of locations!

NOTES ON THE PRINTED TEXT

When his mother Mary had been betrothed to Joseph, before they came together, she was found to be with child of the Holy Spirit. In New Testament times, the betrothal established a permanent contract between the man and the woman prior to their marriage. This contract was almost irrevocable. The woman, if she was being married for the first time, was under the jurisdiction of her intended husband for one year. The couple did not live together, and normally the woman remained a virgin throughout the betrothal period. Infidelity during this premarriage period ranked with adultery. The betrothed husband could demand the penalty of death by stoning against his fiancée if she was caught in an adulterous act during betrothal (Deuteronomy 22:23, 24).

Mary was betrothed to Joseph. However, before the two came together or literally consummated their marriage, Mary was found to be with child. Rather than disgrace Mary and *being a just man,* Joseph *resolved to divorce her quietly.*

But an angel of the Lord appeared to him in a dream. God would not let Joseph divorce Mary. In the dream, Joseph understood that God wanted him to accept Mary as his wife. The unborn child was Holy. His name, when born, was to be Jesus. It meant "God's salvation." It was an appropriate name for it was promised that this child would *save his people from their sins.* So Joseph, being a man of integrity, compassion, and, above all, faith, took Mary as his wife.

In this account, Matthew puts the birth of Jesus into a theological perspective. Matthew was so sure of God's salvation through Jesus that he could see the fulfillment of the prophecy of Isaiah (7:14). The hopes of the Jews regarding a Messiah were fulfilled in the birth of this child. *Emmanuel,* "God with us," was a reminder that God would be with His people to save them from their sins.

In Luke's account, he tells us that Joseph was of *the house and lineage of David.* He had a family and a tribal tie to David, Israel's greatest king. A decree had gone out from the Roman Emperor Caesar Augustus when Quirinius was governor of Syria. The decree called for a census to be taken. Joseph had to register for the census in his hometown. So Joseph took *Mary his betrothed, who was with child,* from Nazareth to Bethlehem.

Arriving in Bethlehem, the poor couple had to settle for a stable since the rooms in the inn were filled. That night, Mary delivered her own child, named Him Jesus, and laid Him in the feed trough of the animals. It is strange that the One who would become the "Bread of Life" for human beings was laid in the feed box of the animals.

In his account, Luke puts the birth of Jesus into a historical perspective. He tells us that Jesus was born on a definite date in history, at a definite place, and in a definite time. Luke was certain that God had acted in a specific backwater village, to a specific peasant girl, and during a specific ruler's reign.

SUGGESTIONS TO TEACHERS

When some distinguished scholars were asked to submit lists of the most important events in history, they remembered such milestones as the discovery of America and the invention of the steam engine. The birth of Jesus, however, was found in fifteenth place.

You may be interested in having your class try its hand at formulating such a list. Where would the birth of Jesus Christ fall in the composite list which your class might prepare? And why?

The writers of the scriptural material in today's lesson leave no doubt what their idea would be. Here are some of the reasons why the Birth of Jesus Christ would take first place.

1. *INAUGURATION OF ERA OF HARMONY.* Isaiah presents a magnificent description of the Messiah. He will be filled with the Spirit; He will have wisdom; He will judge fairly (Isaiah 11:1–5). Isaiah goes on to give a beautiful vision of the new era of harmony even in nature which the Messiah's Coming will bring (11:6–9). Take some time in your lesson to talk about the harmonious relationships which Jesus' birth makes possible. Is your church a good example of the harmony Christ's birth brings?

2. *IMPORTANCE OF THE APPARENTLY UNIMPORTANT.* Talk about Bethlehem for a while. Remind your people how minor and insignificant the town was. Yet this place became the location of the birth of the Savior! Do your people sometimes think that their town, or their place of origin, or their jobs are

relatively unimportant? Take a cue from Micah. Because of Bethlehem, each place and each person has a purpose with the Lord.

3. *INTERVENTION OF THE ALMIGHTY.* Use enough of this lesson time to get your people acquainted with Joseph in the Christmas story. It is easy to understand why he was unwilling to go through with marriage after learning that Mary was pregnant. In fact, his reluctance was overcome only when God directly intervened. Here is a parable of what Christmas is all about: God intervenes in human affairs! Remind your class that God is not a distant, disinterested deity, but the Lord of all human life!

4. *INTERRUPTION OF HISTORY.* You and your class should notice that Luke's account of the birth of Jesus is peppered with historical references. Luke, the careful researcher, wants his readers to know that the birth of Jesus is not myth or fable, but historical fact. The birth of Jesus can be fixed with dates of contemporaries such as King Herod, Caesar Augustus, and Governor Quirinius. The event of Jesus' arrival is the most momentous event in the annals of time! All human records henceforth have been dated in relation to that birth: B.C. or A.D.! How are your class members living—in an A.D. era or as if Jesus had never been born?

TOPIC FOR ADULTS
THE BIRTH OF JESUS

"In Its Small Person All Our Tribal History." "Rejoice! A Prince Is Born!" the headlines bannered. The blasts of cannon salutes and the popping of champagne bottles' corks, the billowing of multicolored flags, the peals of hundreds of churches' bells, and the sweet voiced churchmen's prayers to the roaring crowd's choruses of "Rule Britannia," all heralded the birth of a new prince, the twenty-second Prince of Wales. The *London Times* headlined one story with "In Its Small Person All Our Tribal History."

It is quite a contrast to the birth of another Prince halfway around the world. An angel, later joined by others, sang in great joy. But the sounds of a barn, the shuffling and munching of the animals, the sweet hushing of a mother trying to calm a baby's cries, and the nervous breathing and comments of a first-time father were all that were heard. No headlines, no cannonades, no roaring crowds and yet in this small Person was all our tribal history!

God has come to this world in the person of Jesus, the Prince of Peace. God has entered our history. God has touched each of us through this birth of a baby in Bethlehem. As a citizen of this planet, you can rejoice! You can hope! You can believe! "For to you is born this day in the city of David a Savior, who is Christ the Lord!" (Luke 2:11).—J.B. Barker.

A Shoot From the Stump. " 'A shoot shall sprout from the stump of Jesse, and from his roots a bud shall blossom. The spirit of the Lord shall rest upon him . . .' (Isaiah 11:1, 2).

"These words from last night's liturgy have stayed with me during the day. Our salvation comes from something small, tender, and vulnerable, something hardly noticeable. God, who is the Creator of the Universe, comes to us in smallness, weakness, and hiddenness.

"I find this a hopeful message. Somehow, I keep expecting loud and impressive events to convince me and others of God's saving power; but over and over again, I am reminded that spectacles, power plays, and big events are the ways of the world. Our temptation is to be distracted by them and made blind to the 'shoot that shall sprout from the stump.'

"When I have no eyes for the small signs of God's presence—the smile of a baby, the carefree play of children, the words of encouragement and gestures of love offered by friends—I will always remain tempted to despair.

"The small child of Bethlehem, the unknown young man of Nazareth, the rejected preacher, the naked man on the cross, he asks for my full attention. The work of our salvation takes place in the midst of a world that continues to shout, scream, and overwhelm us with its claims and promises. But the promise is hidden in the shoot that sprouts from the stump, a shoot that hardly anyone notices."— Henri Nouwen, *Gracias: A Latin American Journal.* Copyright © 1983 Henri J.M. Nouwen. Reprinted by permission of Harper & Row, Publishers, Inc.

Turned Away—Almost. The story is told of a famous actress for whom a benefit performance was to be given at a large theater. The actress herself came to the theater but there were no unsold seats. When they were about to turn her away she exclaimed, "But I am the actress!" At this, they arranged to let her stand in the wings and watch the performance being given in her honor. Is this not how we often treat Him? Many generations have passed into silence, praying and longing to know what we know. The Word has become flesh and we have seen His glory—a glory lighting up the pages of nineteeen centuries of otherwise tragic history.

"God has become known. And in response we have a debt to honor and serve Him. To worship Jesus as God is worshiped, to trust Him as God is trusted, and to owe Him what we owe God alone—this," says James Denney, "is the essence of Christianity." We cannot do better at Christmas than to judge ourselves by this definition and commit our lives to fulfilling its implications.

Questions for Pupils on the Next Lesson. 1. What exactly did the shepherds hear announced to them? 2. Why do you feel a sense of joy and peace in the message of Christmas? 3. Why did the shepherds want to tell others about the birth at Bethlehem? 4. Have you ever felt like singing to express special hopes and ideas? If so, when? Have you ever felt such an urge when remembering Christmas?

TOPIC FOR YOUTH
THE BIRTH OF JESUS

God's Calligraphy. "I remember seeing a film on the human misery and devastation brought by the bomb on Hiroshima. Among all the scenes of terror and despair, emerged one image of a man quietly writing a word in calligraphy. All his attention was directed to writing that one word. That image made this gruesome film a hopeful film. Isn't that what God is doing? Writing his Word in the midst of our dark world?"—Henri Nouwen, *Gracias: A Latin American Journal.* Copyright © 1983 Henri J.M. Nouwen. Reprinted by permission of Harper & Row, Publishers, Inc.

Let's Make Room. " 'There is no room,' the innkeeper tells them. To this travel-worn young couple from the North Country this announcement comes as a shock because they knew that the time had come for the birth of their first child.

"... 'There is no room'—and the click of that shutting door was to echo down the next two thousand years as the audible sign of man's most persistent folly and deepest tragedy—his rejection of God. Clicking shut—until he is crushed in the slamming door of man's ultimate rejection on Calvary.

"There is no basis, you see, for us to make of Christmas, as Bernhard Iddings Bell said, 'an orgy of sentimentality beside a cute little manger in a romantic barn beneath an angel-studded sky.' God comes to man, and the words sound, 'There is no room.' The door clicks shut, and he is relegated to a patch of straw in a little stall next to the dung heap. 'His only human worshipers are a few dazed yokels and three star-mad astrologers. . . . Adore the babe of Bethlehem, for in him God so loves the world . . . but we can also weep before the manger that man should greet God with such contempt.' "—Dennis F. Nyberg, *Advent—A Calendar of Devotion,* 1967 © Abingdon.

One of Us. "It had been snowing for twenty-four hours. Knowing that it had been a hard winter, I filled the bird feeder with an extra supply of feed that morning. Since the feeder was sheltered, it held the only food not hidden by the snow. A short while later a small bird appeared in the yard, obviously weak, hungry, and cold. Searching for food, he pecked at the snow. How helpless I felt, I wanted to go out and point to the feeder; but had I opened the door to throw out more food, he would have flown away.

"Then I realized that only if I were another bird could I indicate to him where he could find food. Only if I were another bird could I fly with him, identify myself with his hunger and cold and let him know that I understood and cared.

"Our God, looking at man, knew that he must become one of us in order that we might know his love for us; in order that we might know his forgiveness; in order that we might point above our heads to the source of nourishment and eternal life. The Word, his Word, became flesh! God was in Christ, reconciling the world to himself."—Betty E. Stone, *The Pulpit* Copyright 1963 Christian Century Foundation, December 1963.

Questions for Pupils on the Next Lesson. 1. Why did the shepherds feel so happy when they heard the announcement of the Birth? 2. What did these shepherds do after they heard the news? 3. Why is the announcement of Jesus' birth such a source of joy and hope? 4. Exactly what does the phrase mean, ". . . on earth peace among those with whom He is pleased"? 5. Is Christmas a sacred or a secular celebration to you?

LESSON III—DECEMBER 15

THE JOYFUL NEWS

Background Scripture: Luke 2:8–20
Devotional Reading: Luke 1:67–80

KING JAMES VERSION

LUKE 2 8 And there were in the same country shepherds abiding in the field, keeping watch over their flock by night.

9 And, lo, the angel of the Lord came upon them, and the glory of the Lord shone round about them; and they were sore afraid.

10 And the angel said unto them, Fear not: for, behold, I bring you good tidings of great joy, which shall be to all people.

11 For unto you is born this day in the city of David a Saviour, which is Christ the Lord.

12 And this *shall be* a sign unto you; Ye shall find the babe wrapped in swaddling clothes, lying in a manger.

13 And suddenly there was with the angel a multitude of the heavenly host praising God, and saying,

14 Glory to God in the highest, and on earth peace, good will toward men.

15 And it came to pass, as the angels were gone away from them into heaven, the shepherds said one to another, Let us now go even unto Bethlehem, and see this thing which is come to pass, which the Lord hath made known unto us.

16 And they came with haste, and found Mary and Joseph, and the babe lying in a manger.

17 And when they had seen *it*, they made known abroad the saying which was told them concerning this child.

18 And all they that heard *it* wondered at those things which were told them by the shepherds.

19 But Mary kept all these things, and pondered *them* in her heart.

20 And the shepherds returned, glorifying and praising God for all the things that they had heard and seen, as it was told unto them.

REVISED STANDARD VERSION

LUKE 2 8 And in that region there were shepherds out in the field, keeping watch over their flock by night. 9 And an angel of the Lord appeared to them, and the glory of the Lord shone around them, and they were filled with fear. 10 And the angel said to them, "Be not afraid; for behold, I bring you good news of a great joy which will come to all the people; 11 for to you is born this day in the city of David a Savior, who is Christ the Lord. 12 And this will be a sign for you: you will find a babe wrapped in swaddling cloths and lying in a manger." 13 And suddenly there was with the angel a multitude of the heavenly host praising God and saying,

14 "Glory to God in the highest,
    and on earth peace among men with
        whom he is pleased!"

15 When the angels went away from them into heaven, the shepherds said to one another, "Let us go over to Bethlehem and see this thing that has happened, which the Lord has made known to us." 16 And they went with haste, and found Mary and Joseph, and the babe lying in a manger. 17 And when they saw it they made known the saying which had been told them concerning this child; 18 and all who heard it wondered at what the shepherds told them. 19 But Mary kept all these things, pondering them in her heart. 20 And the shepherds returned, glorifying and praising God for all they had heard and seen, as it had been told them.

KEY VERSE: I bring you good news of a great joy which will come to all the people. Luke 2:10.

HOME DAILY BIBLE READINGS

Dec.	9.	M.	*Glory to God in the Highest.* Luke 2:8–14.
Dec.	10.	T.	*The Visit of the Shepherds.* Luke 2:15–20.
Dec.	11.	W.	*A Song of Praise.* Psalms 145:1–9.
Dec.	12.	T.	*Praise to the Creator and Sustainer.* Psalms 147:1–11.
Dec.	13.	F.	*Let Everything Praise the Lord!* Psalm 150.
Dec.	14.	S.	*Jesus in the Temple.* Luke 2:41–52.
Dec.	15.	S.	*When the Time Had Fully Come.* Galatians 4:1–7.

BACKGROUND

Think how a Madison Avenue public-relations firm would publicize the joyful news of Jesus' birth. Special gilt-edged announcements to the American President, the Prime Ministers, Premiers, Kings, Queens, and other important political leaders, movers and shakers in governmental circles. A three-hour television extravaganza, complete with mass rallies in the stadiums in every big city, parades, the Goodyear blimp blinking the message, newspaper headlines, billboards and radio spots, interviews with famous entertainers, statements by well-known TV evangelists.

Instead of the world hype one would expect, God announced the joyful news to an unexpected audience—a few scruffy shepherds. *Shepherds:* A sampling of the roughest least-respectable people. Shepherds, in those times, had the social standing that, say, used-car salesmen and carnival roustabouts have in our society. The Lord saw fit to select the least-liked and loneliest people of all to be the first to hear the joyful News which is for "all the people" (Luke 2:10). Note that the news was and is not just for some of the people, *but all.* And that word *all* included even shepherds. It also includes *each* of us.

NOTES ON THE PRINTED TEXT

In the Messiah's ministry, God revealed His message to the poor and the outcasts. It really began at Jesus' birth. The angels' song came to *shepherds out in the field, keeping watch over their flock by night.* Shepherds were not held in high regard. Their job made it impossible for them to keep many of the hundreds of laws that governed the ancient Israelites' lives. They were unable to obey the strict law of cleanliness. They could not keep the appointed hours of prayer. Most shepherds were suspected of supplementing their meager income by smuggling. They seemed unable to keep God's laws; so, they were outcasts.

But, *an angel of the Lord appeared to them* saying, *"Be not afraid."* The usual fireside banter of these wandering shepherds was interrupted by an angel. Immediately, they recognized that God was speaking to them. Instinctively, they were frightened by this unexpected Presence before them. Calming their fears, the angel made a joyous announcement.

To you is born this day in the city of David a Savior, who is Christ the Lord. To the humble, lowly outcasts, the message of the Good News was first shared. *Savior* is a term given to God, the One who brings salvation. Christ the Lord implies the long-expected Messiah. Israel's hope is now born. God's annointed One is come!

The angel even offers proof of this holy birth. In Bethlehem the shepherds will find a *babe wrapped in swaddling cloths and lying in a manger.*

With the angel's announcement that the day of salvation has come upon them *this day,* heaven proclaims the glory of God and the peace that this birth brings to earth. God's peace will reconcile all sinful people to Him.

The amazed shepherds hurriedly journeyed to Bethlehem, searched, and found Mary, Joseph, and the babe. They poured out to the parents and to others all that they had seen and heard. Most were astonished since it must have seemed like another of the shepherds' tales. *All who heard it wondered at what the shepherds told them.* But not Mary. Prepared by the angel's announcement nine months earlier, Mary treasured the events and thought about them.

However, the shepherds had to return to tending their flocks out in the field, but they left the stable *glorifying and praising God* for all that they had heard and seen.

SUGGESTIONS TO TEACHERS

A newspaper was started a few years ago which promised to print only good news. After several issues, the paper went out of business. The reasons: not enough good news and not enough interest by readers.

The announcement of the birth of Jesus was the best piece of news anyone had ever heard. And it still is. Why? Well, ask some of those who first heard it. Here are the shepherds on the hillside near Bethlehem. Let them tell their story.

This, basically, is what you are doing in today's lesson. Make those shepherds as real to your people as the folks down the street.

1. *UNSUSPECTING NOBODIES.* Start by pointing out that the shepherds were as ordinary folks as anyone can find. They were not well-known. No one even knows their names. In fact, as shepherds they were looked down upon by people who prided themselves on wealth or position. Yet it was to the shepherds that the news of Jesus' birth was first announced. Why the shepherds? Ask your people to think about God's interesting way of picking out the ordinary people, the shepherds in the world, to give joyful news. Also remind your class members that the shepherds were in the midst of an ordinary night's work when the news came. They were not in a pious mood. Nor were the shepherds at worship. God brought them the joyful news of Jesus where they were. So also with your class members.

2. *UNEXPECTED NEWS.* The shepherds were frightened. This is the opening for you to lead a helpful discussion on fear. The people in your class, like those shepherds, know fear. Everyone has an assortment of anxieties. Some are silly and insignificant fears, like being afraid of bats. Others are just as real but are more serious, such as being afraid of losing your job or facing a cancer operation. The joyful news of Jesus' birth was the antidote to the shepherds' fears, and is also God's way of allaying our worst fears! Have your class members relate some of their deepest fears and the way Jesus Christ enables them to handle these fears.

3. *UNHEARD-OF KNOWLEDGE.* The shepherds saw for themselves what was told them about the birth in Bethlehem. The joyful news was not a second-hand report but a firsthand experience. They *knew* personally about the joyful news in the Bethlehem manger. Encourage your class members to do as the shepherds did, that is, to investigate in person what has been reported. Get personally acquainted with Jesus! Discover how this person is truly the best news ever!

4. *UNHESITATING NEIGHBORLINESS.* After going to the manger to see the joyful event for themselves, the shepherds went back to work and "made known the saying which had been told them concerning this child" (Luke 2:17). Tell your students that they, too, will respond to the news of Jesus' birth by sharing the joyful Word with neighbors. Every participant in the manger story is also a missionary!

TOPIC FOR ADULTS
GOOD NEWS OF GREAT JOY

Truth! "As we think of the baby in the manger to whom this Christmas Day the worship of a world is offered, let us remember that his childhood tells us something of the eternal truth of God. It is this which gives Christmas its significance. (Our) belief depends for its value primarily upon its truth. If it is a beautiful fiction, its power is gone. The claim of the Christian Gospel is not chiefly that it is uplifting or comforting but that it is true."—William Temple, *Religious Experience,* London: James Clarke & Co. Ltd., 1958.

A Real Live Jesus! "The excitement reminds me of what happened in a Nativity play last Christmas in a church back at home. The children were dressed for the annual performance in their fancy clothes, with stars and angels and a pretty baby doll laid in a crib. And suddenly the minister said, 'I have a surprise for you,' and she brought into the church her own newborn son and placed him in the crib. And Mary and the angels and the shepherds stopped acting their parts and stood on tiptoe with excitement to peer into the crib to see this new baby in their midst. And the diminutive Joseph was heard to exclaim, 'We've got a real live Jesus!' And as if on cue the baby let out a cry.

"We are like those children on tiptoe with expectancy because of what has happened to us. We have seen the reality of Jesus in our midst. . . . And this Assembly itself will be an event, a happening of the Word of God among us."—Pauline Webb, World Council of Churches meeting, quoted in *Presbyterian Survey*, October 1983.

The Lah-Lah Is Born. A Jewish woman described how she felt left out of Christmas celebrations at her school when she was a girl. One year, it was too much. She broke down and cried and cried. Her parents could not understand. She felt she could not tell them what was bothering her. They were at the point of calling the doctor when she broke down and confessed the guilt and envy of wanting to sing the Christmas carols. The parents talked with her about the problems of not living in the Jewish ghetto and residing in a Gentile neighborhood. Finally, the girl's father relented and told her to sing the Christmas carols but not to say Jesus' name. The girl, delighted with this permission, joyfully returned to school at Christmas time. Decades later, she says she still feels left out, but that she sings the carols anyway. "You might recognize me if you heard me," she states. "I'm the one who sings, "Lah lah, the lah lah is born!'"

Although this woman wants to retain her Jewish identity, yet participate in the joy of the Coming of Israel's Lord, her words, "Lah lah, the lah lah is born," are what some Christians may as well be singing!

It's more than a "lah lah" who has come. It's Jesus! A Savior is born! This Good News is for *everyone*—for shepherds and for Jewish schoolgirls!

Questions for Pupils on the Next Lesson. 1. Exactly who were the "Wise Men" who came to the manger at Bethlehem? 2. What was King Herod's reaction when he heard about the Wise Men? 3. Why would these Wise Men have come to the manger? 4. How would you characterize King Herod? 5. To what lengths would you go to find what you are seeking in life?

TOPIC FOR YOUTH
GOOD NEWS FOR EVERYONE

Tell the Good News for Everyone! Gutsy old General William Booth, the founder of the Salvation Army, was joyfully occupied with showing and telling the Good News of Jesus Christ to everyone, especially the outsiders and lower classes. One time, Booth was embarking on a ship in England for a visit to America. As Booth walked up the gangplank, the Salvation Army bands were playing on the dock. Some stuffy passenger sniffed that this public display of Booth's faith was unseemly for a Christian movement. Booth laughed and replied, "My friend, if I thought I could win one more to Christ by doing a handstand and beating a tambourine with my feet, I would do it!"

That kind of approach to the Coming of Jesus Christ is what the shepherds had when they left the manger. Do you? If not, why not?

Einstein's Friend. During the time when the great Albert Einstein worked in Princeton, New Jersey, a little girl often arrived home from school thirty or forty minutes late. Her mother, worried about what she was doing, asked her why she took so long coming home.

"Oh, I stop on the way to see my friend, Mr. Einstein," answered the little girl.

"Einstein? *The* Dr. Einstein?, how can he be your friend?" asked the astonished mother. "Why, he is probably the greatest thinker in the world, so what could he have in common with you?"

"Oh," replied the girl, "We have lots of things to talk about. Besides, he likes the gumdrops I share with him."

Truly great persons will be able to find common bonds with humble, little people. The Good News of Jesus' birth is that God insists on associating with us!

Good News for Orientals. "It is still difficult for Western Christians to understand how foreign the Gospel message is to most Chinese. Writing the Chinese word for *God* is like drawing a strong tree. This illustrates a way of thinking about God as the Great Emperor, the one who dwells in a supernatural realm, always removed from earthly cares. It is a challenge for Chinese people to conceive of God becoming a human.

The Good News for Chinese as well as Westerners is that God, the Great Emperor of the universe, chooses not to dwell in supernatural isolation from us humans, but to share our cares by becoming like one of us. In Jesus' birth, God came for Orientals, too!

Questions for Pupils on the Next Lesson. 1. Exactly who were the "Wise Men" who came to Bethlehem to worship? 2. Why did they make the long trip to Bethlehem? 3. What was King Herod like? 4. Why did he react as he did to the news of the birth of the Baby in Bethlehem? 5. What do you do when you are threatened by competition?

LESSON IV—DECEMBER 22

THE VISITORS FROM AFAR

Background Scripture: Matthew 2
Devotional Reading: Matthew 2:13–18

KING JAMES VERSION

MATTHEW 2 Now when Jesus was born in Bethlehem of Judea in the days of Herod the king, behold, there came wise men from the east to Jerusalem.

2 Saying, Where is he that is born King of the Jews? for we have seen his star in the east, and are come to worship him.

3 When Herod the king had heard *these things,* he was troubled, and all Jerusalem with him.

4 And when he had gathered all the chief priests and scribes of the people together, he demanded of them where Christ should be born.

5 And they said unto him, In Bethlehem of Judea: for thus it is written by the prophet.

6 And thou Bethlehem, *in* the land of Juda, art not the least among the princes of Juda: for out of thee shall come a Governor, that shall rule my people Israel.

7 Then Herod, when he had privily called the wise men, inquired of them diligently what time the star appeared.

8 And he sent them to Bethlehem, and said, Go and search diligently for the young child; and when ye have found *him,* bring me word again, that I may come and worship him also.

9 When they had heard the king, they departed; and, lo, the star, which they saw in the east, went before them, till it came and stood over where the young child was.

10 When they saw the star, they rejoiced with exceeding great joy.

11 And when they were come into the house, they saw the young child with Mary, his mother, and fell down, and worshipped him: and when they had opened their treasures, they presented unto him gifts; gold, and frankincense, and myrrh.

12 And being warned of God in a dream that they should not return to Herod, they departed into their own country another way.

REVISED STANDARD VERSION

MATTHEW 2 Now when Jesus was born in Bethlehem of Judea in the days of Herod the king, behold, wise men from the East came to Jerusalem, saying, 2 "Where is he who has been born king of the Jews? For we have seen his star in the East, and have come to worship him." 3 When Herod the king heard this, he was troubled, and all Jerusalem with him; 4 and assembling all the chief priests and scribes of the people, he inquired of them where the Christ was to be born. 5 They told him, "In Bethlehem of Judea; for so it is written by the prophet:

6 'And you, O Bethlehem, in the land of
   Judah,
are by no means least among the rulers
   of Judah;
for from you shall come a ruler
who will govern my people Israel.' "

7 Then Herod summoned the wise men secretly and ascertained from them what time the star appeared; 8 and he sent them to Bethlehem, saying, "Go and search diligently for the child, and when you have found him bring me word, that I too may come and worship him." 9 When they had heard the king they went their way; and lo, the star which they had seen in the East went before them, till it came to rest over the place where the child was. 10 When they saw the star, they rejoiced exceedingly with great joy; 11 and going into the house they saw the child with Mary his mother, and they fell down and worshiped him. Then, opening their treasures, they offered him gifts, gold and frankincense and myrrh. 12 And being warned in a dream not to return to Herod, they departed to their own country by another way.

KEY VERSE: *When they saw the star, they rejoiced exceedingly with great joy.* Matthew 2:10.

HOME DAILY BIBLE READINGS

Dec. 16. M. *The Wise Men Seek Jesus.* Matthew 2:1–6.
Dec. 17. T. *The Wise Men Worship Jesus.* Matthew 2:7–12.
Dec. 18. W. *The Flight Into Egypt.* Matthew 2:13–18.
Dec. 19. T. *From Egypt to Nazareth.* Matthew 2:19–23.
Dec. 20. F. *All Live in Christ.* 1 Corinthians 15:21–28.

Dec. 21. S. *Arise, Shine; Your Light Has Come.* Isaiah 60:1–5.
Dec. 22. S. *The True Light.* John 1:9–18.

BACKGROUND

The Old Testament prophets stated that the promised Messiah would be Deliverer for all people. They assured their hearers and readers that the coming Savior would come for more than the Jewish nation. The promised One would be for
all people, "a light to the nations" (Isaiah 42:6; 49:6). Furthermore, these spokesmen for the Lord assured, "Kings shall see and arise; princes and they shall pros-
trate themselves" (Isaiah 49:7).

Matthew was steeped in Jewish lore and tradition. He remembered all the
hopes and promises passed down through the centuries. When Jesus came,
Matthew the writer with such a sense of Jewishness saw Jesus as the culmination
of all the Jewish prophets' dreams. Matthew's account of Jesus' Coming reflects
this powerful awareness of Jewishness. Matthew took pains to point out details
about Jesus' birth, career, and death which seemed to confirm that Jesus was in
every way the promised Deliverer.

The story of the visitors from the East was one of those details of Jesus' life that
only Matthew put into his Gospel account. None of the other Gospel writers
mention these visitors.

Who were they? They were *Magi*. Strictly speaking, they were more than
merely "wise men." They were professional scholars. Although some translators
call them astrologers or magicians, they were the research scientists of the day. If
their studies seemed to have included what appears to be astrology and magic
according to our notions of scientific research, it should be remembered that in
those times the *magi* were deeply respected as the learned caste. Originally *magi*
were from Persia, but in the first century *magi* were found studying and teaching
in various places.

No one knows how many *magi* came to the manger. Although tradition places
them as three in number, there could have been two or four or more.

The main point that Matthew wants to establish is that the birth of Jesus was of
importance not only to Jews but to all nationalities. The visit at the manger by
these Persian Ph.D.-types symbolized the way Jesus' Coming fulfills the Old Testament hopes of a Savior for every type of person everywhere!

NOTES ON THE PRINTED TEXT

Matthew, unlike Luke, offers no description of Jesus' birth. However, like
Luke, he does date Jesus' birth to *the days of Herod the king.* And like Luke,
Matthew clarifies the significance of the birth. The birth, acknowledged by repre-
sentatives of the non-Jewish world, provokes only hostility on the part of the
Jews.

Wise Men from the East came to Jerusalem. The *Magi* were probably kings or
priests from Media, Persia, or Arabia. They were keen astrologers who watched a
star in the East. Like many in the ancient world, they believed the star heralded
the birth of a great man. Believing the star heralded the birth of a Jewish king,
they traveled to Jerusalem. However, they did not know where to find the new
king. Being of high social rank themselves, they went to King Herod. They asked,
Where is he who has been born king of the Jews?

They did not receive an immediate answer. Herod and the Jewish leaders were
unaware of the birth, and Herod was troubled and all of Jerusalem with him by
the wise men's inquiry.

Herod consulted *the chief priests and scribes of the people.* Together they announced that, as had been prophesied by Micah, the Lord's Anointed was to be

born in Bethlehem of Judea where King David, the greatest king of Israel, had been born.

Herod, threatened by this report of the birth of a King of the Jews, secretly met with the *Magi*. In order to determine the child's age, he questioned them as to when the star first appeared. He also pretended to be interested in worshiping the child and asked that they bring him word when they found the child. It was probably Herod who sent murderers along who slaughtered all the male infants in Bethlehem.

And lo, the star which they had seen in the East went before them, till it came to rest over the place where the child was. Matthew laid out Jesus' credentials. The Wise Men's coming was unique, but the birth was even more miraculous because it was a star that enabled the Wise Men to find the babe and worship Him.

They fell down and worshiped him . . . they offered him gifts. The Wise Men's worship included gifts of gold, frankincense, and myrrh, which were common offerings in the ancient East for a monarch. However, even more, gift giving in the ancient world symbolized submission and allegiance. By giving gifts to the child the Messiahship of the babe was affirmed.

Being warned in a dream not to return to Herod, the Wise Men departed to their own country in the East by another way. However, the coming of these visitors from afar pointed to the Coming of the Messiah for all people, Jews and non-Jews, alike.

SUGGESTIONS TO TEACHERS

Today, let's try to get behind the cute Christmas pageant-picture of the *Magi*. We've all seen too many Wise Men trios with costume jewelry crowns, paste-on cotton beards, oversized bathrobes, and cardboard camels. We don't have to debunk the story of the Wise Men, but we do have to understand who the *Magi* were and why they came to worship at the manger. We then can set clues about what their visit means to us.

1. *WHO IS WISE?* Open this lesson by asking who are the wise men and women in these days? Why have your people selected these as examples of wisdom? The scriptural material tells that these visitors from afar, although among the most learned scholars of their era, were truly wise because they sought the Savior. Wisdom truly starts at the manger, in other words. The really wise man or woman acknowledges Jesus Christ as Lord, and kneels before Him. Are your class members able to affirm this kind of wisdom?

2. *WHERE IS HE?* The *Magi* wanted to meet Jesus in person. They asked directions from others, "Where is he who has been born king of the Jews?" (Matthew 2:2). People are asking how to meet Jesus today. How do you guide someone to a personal encounter with the Lord? This part of your lesson is particularly important, because at least some of your class will need specific help on pointing others to a relationship with Jesus Christ. As teacher, you can be of immense assistance in enabling folks in the class to be able to answer the questions wise people are asking in these times: "Where is He?"

3. *WHICH KING?* Turn the discussion next to the subject of Herod. Admittedly this ruler was cruel and crazy, jealous and jittery. But he was also one of the most powerful people in his time. Strangely, however, no one at that time thought that people would come to remember this mighty monarch because of a baby born in Bethlehem. Herod could not abide any competition.

He tried to be sole ruler. Jesus also demands complete allegiance. Which king do we choose? Herod, representing power and security and wealth, continues to claim he is in control. Help your class members to be aware of this king's claims. Remind them that only Jesus is worthy of their worship.

4. *WHAT OFFERING?* The visitors from afar brought gifts of gold, frankincense, and myrrh. The background notes indicate how valuable these presents were. The *Magi* were grateful. Therefore, they gave their best. They shared their treasures. In this season of giving, discuss in this lesson what true Christian giving is. Christians want to share their most cherished possessions, especially their money, if they have been made aware of God's gift! Stewardship starts at the manger!

TOPIC FOR ADULTS
STAR IN THE EAST

God's Son in the Service. Someone has told a story of World War II. It was at the time when a service star hung in the windows of millions of American homes to show that a son from that home was in the service. A little boy and his father were out walking one night. Only one star was visible in the sky. The little boy said, "Daddy, God must have a son in the service." The little lad that night was touching all unconsciously upon the heart of Christmas. The star of Bethlehem told of a Father who loved and who gave His Son to taste the bitterness of the Cross and the grave.

Gift of the Magi. The Wise Men gave the best they had. Their gifts of gold, frankincense, and myrrh represented sacrifice. Real giving means personal sacrifice. The writer O. Henry knew this. Remembering the gift of the Wise Men, he wrote a short story called, "The Gift of the Magi." In the story, a poor couple struggling desperately to make ends meet lived in a tiny, wretched apartment in a slum. They were so poor they could afford no frills. Their proudest possessions were Jim's gold watch, a family heirloom, and Della's beautiful brown hair. When Christmas came, the couple had no money to buy each other presents worthy of the love each had for the other. Without telling Della, Jim sold his watch the day before Christmas and used the money to buy a gorgeous set of combs for Della to use to fix her lovely long tresses. And without letting Jim know, Della went out the afternoon before Christmas, sold her hair to a wigmaker, then took the proceeds to purchase a good watch fob for Jim! In spite of the irony and impracticality of Jim and Della, they showed a sacrificial love for each other. Their reckless giving might be seen as foolish in some ways, but it exemplifies the Christmas giving of God Himself. It echoes the gift-bringing of the Wise Men at the Manger.

Real devotion to Jesus Christ calls for sacrifice! Have you given more than in token ways to Him?

Don't Cut Off the Buttons! Halford Luccock once reflected on a clothing drive in which someone had given some old worn coats—but had cut off all the buttons. The gift was cheap to start with, but became practically useless after the buttons had been removed.

The real gift is not necessarily expensive, but chosen with care and is given in love. This is the way God gave. He didn't look for ways to hold back. He gave "buttons and all."

In your living and giving to others, don't cut off the buttons. Learn the generosity of Jesus!

Questions for Pupils on the Next Lesson. 1. What is meant by the phrase, "The Kingdom of God"? 2. What is at the core of Jesus' ethical teachings? 3. How did Jesus summarize the will of God? 4. Why does our understanding of God determine the way we live? 5. What is the basis for the big decisions in your life?

TOPIC FOR YOUTH
RESPONDING TO GOOD NEWS

Devoted Give Guru Twenty-Fourth, Twenty-Fifth Luxury Autos for Birthday.
In Rajneeshpuram, Oregon, in 1982, devotees of Bhagwan Shree Rajneesh wanted
to give the guru something special on his fifty-first birthday, so they picked out
just the thing: His twenty-fourth and twenty-fifth Rolls-Royces. Ma Prem Sheela,
a spokeswoman for his commune-ranch in central Oregon, said the guru from
India will celebrate his birthday with live-in disciples and a few who have traveled for the fete. Singing and dancing are planned for the occasion, which she
called a *darshan.* The word is Sanskrit for " 'sitting in the presence of the master,'
which is quite a happy occasion for us," she said.

In 1980, the disciples moved onto the 100 square-mile ranch and incorporated
their own city. The ranch is owned by a foundation associated with the guru.

Sheela said the Rolls-Royces actually belong to the Rajneesh Investment Corporation. The guru drives at least one of them every day. Commune leaders said
recently that they give him the cars to repay him for the love he gives them and
the world.

Jesus does not want luxury automobiles as gifts from us. Rather, He wants our
commitment to serve others in His name. He deserves more than the costliest car.
All of the Rolls-Royces in the world are not good enough presents for Jesus Christ.
He must have our best: ourselves!

A Matter of Seeking. The Wise Men from the East persisted in seeking the Savior. They journeyed. They watched. They asked where to find the promised One.
They kept on in their search until they reached the manger.

It's like finding dinosaurs. A few years ago, an amateur fossil collector named
Bill Walker discovered parts of the skeleton of a new species of dinosaur. The
skeleton revealed a monster that ate flesh and had huge claws a foot long. Experts
on both sides of the Atlantic hailed the exciting find in a clay pit in Surrey, a
county southwest of London.

How did Bill Walker, a fifty-five-year-old heating contractor from London,
make such a momentous discovery? It's all a matter of persisting and looking,
Walker insists. "Bits of dinosaurs are lying all over the place, but your average
person walks straight over them," says Walker, who hunts fossils in his spare
time.

Evidence of Jesus' presence are everywhere, but many ignore them. Start again
with the manger. Join the procession of wise men and women who have persisted
on the journey of faith until they have come to the wondrous event at Bethlehem,
then rejoiced at having discovered the Savior!

Seek! Persist in the search until you learn that Jesus Christ is truly the greatest
discovery in your life!

Find the Road to Bethlehem. "By this time, many will be well along on the
road to Christmas, but one wonders, 'How far are we along on the road to Bethlehem?' for it is only at Bethlehem where we see what Christmas is all about.

"Many in their annual pilgrimage will follow the road to Christmas who will
not follow the road to Bethlehem. The tiring, often joyless shopper's road to
Christmas leaves many too exhausted to go on the road to Bethlehem to discover
the joy of Jesus Christ, who is God's great gift to all of us.

"Sometimes the noise and the tension from the road to Christmas diverts us
from finding the road to Bethlehem. The situation is like the country boy a number of years ago whose father gave him money to go into town to see the circus.
Arriving at the city's outskirts, he joined the crowd moving toward the downtown
section where people of all ages were lining the sidewalks in a festive mood. Presently, down the middle of the main thoroughfare came a contingent of mounted

uniformed policemen. Behind them was a brass band, followed by a group of elephants and other circus animals. Then came the clowns, the acrobat, and the remaining circus performers, all stepping to the music of the drum corps.

"As the procession ended, the crowds began to hustle away. The boy took to the road and wended his way homeward. Upon his arrival, he handed his father the money that he had been given. His father exclaimed: 'What? Didn't you see the circus?' To which the elated son replied: 'Yes, I saw the circus, but I didn't have to pay. It was free. It wasn't even at the Fairgrounds; it came right down the Main Street.'

"Many at Christmas time mistake the parade for the main attraction; it is so easy to get lost in the trivial, the trite, and the trappings and to miss the actual main event of Christmas. It is so easy to get only part of the message and think you have the real thing."—William G. Rusch, *Synod of the Trinity Newsletter,* December 1979.

Questions for Pupils on the Next Lesson. 1. What does Jesus mean by "the Kingdom of God"? 2. How would you sum up Jesus' teachings about what God's will is? 3. How did Jesus summarize God's will? 4. On what do you base your important decisions in life? 5. Why is humble confession of sin an important first step in right living?

LESSON V—DECEMBER 29

THE REIGN OF GOD

Background Scripture: Mark 4:26–32; Matthew 22:34–40; Luke 18:9–14
Devotional Reading: Mark 4:26–32

KING JAMES VERSION

MARK 4   26 And he said, So is the kingdom of God, as if a man should cast seed into the ground;

27 And should sleep, and rise night and day, and the seed should spring and grow up, he knoweth not how.

28 For the earth bringeth forth fruit of herself; first the blade, then the ear, after that the full corn in the ear.

29 But when the fruit is brought forth, immediately he putteth in the sickle, because the harvest is come.

MATTHEW 22   34 But when the Pharisees had heard that he had put the Sadducees to silence, they were gathered together.

35 Then one of them, *which was* a lawyer, asked *him a question*, tempting him, and saying,

36 Master, which *is* the great commandment in the law?

37 Jesus said unto him, Thou shalt love the Lord thy God with all thy heart, and with all thy soul, and with all thy mind.

38 This is the first and great commandment.

39 And the second *is* like unto it, Thou shalt love thy neighbour as thyself.

40 On these two commandments hang all the law and the prophets.

LUKE 18   9 And he spake this parable unto certain which trusted in themselves that they were righteous, and despised others:

10 Two men went up into the temple to pray; the one a Pharisee, and the other a publican.

11 The Pharisee stood and prayed thus with himself, God, I thank thee, that I am not as other men *are*, extortioners, unjust, adulterers, or even as this publican.

12 I fast twice in the week, I give tithes of all that I possess.

13 And the publican, standing afar off, would not lift up so much as *his* eyes unto heaven, but smote upon his breast, saying, God be merciful to me a sinner.

14 I tell you, this man went down to his house justified *rather* than the other: for every one that exalteth himself shall be abased; and he that humbleth himself shall be exalted.

REVISED STANDARD VERSION

MARK 4   26 And he said, "The kingdom of God is as if a man should scatter seed upon the ground, 27 and should sleep and rise night and day, and the seed should sprout and grow, he knows not how. 28 The earth produces of itself, first the blade, then the ear, then the full grain in the ear. 29 But when the grain is ripe, at once he puts in the sickle, because the harvest has come."

MATTHEW 22   34 But when the Pharisees heard that he had silenced the Sadducees, they came together. 35 And one of them, a lawyer, asked him a question, to test him. 36 "Teacher, which is the great commandment in the law?" 37 And he said to him, "You shall love the Lord your God with all your heart, and with all your soul, and with all your mind. 38 This is the great and first commandment. 39 And a second is like it, You shall love your neighbor as yourself. 40 On these two commandments depend all the law and the prophets."

LUKE 18   9 He also told this parable to some who trusted in themselves that they were righteous and despised others: 10 "Two men went up into the temple to pray, one a Pharisee and the other a tax collector. 11 The Pharisee stood and prayed thus with himself, 'God, I thank thee that I am not like other men, extortioners, unjust, adulterers, or even like this tax collector. 12 I fast twice a week, I give tithes of all that I get.' 13 But the tax collector, standing far off, would not even lift up his eyes to heaven, but beat his breast, saying, 'God, be merciful to me a sinner!' 14 I tell you, this man went down to his house justified rather than the other; for every one who exalts himself will be humbled, but he who humbles himself will be exalted."

KEY VERSE: The time is fulfilled, and the kingdom of God is at hand; repent, and believe in the gospel. Mark 1:15.

HOME DAILY BIBLE READINGS

Dec. 23. M. *Love, the Heart of the Law.* Deuteronomy 6:4–9.
Dec. 24. T. *Holiness of Behavior.* Leviticus 19:17, 18.
Dec. 25. W. *What Does the Law Require?* Micah 6:6–8.
Dec. 26. T. *The Parable of the Self-Growing Seed.* Mark 4:26–32.
Dec. 27. F. *The Greatest Commandment.* Matthew 22:34–40.
Dec. 28. S. *The Pharisee and the Tax Collector.* Luke 18:9–14.
Dec. 29. S. *Hearing and Doing.* James 1:22–27.

BACKGROUND

Throughout the early 1940s, every person in the Allied nations and in occupied Europe was hoping for the war with the Axis powers to draw to a close. Everyone also understood that this would happen only after the Allies landed on the continent and conquered the evil empires of Hitler and Mussolini. Finally, in the spring of 1944, the Allies had built up enough resources of men and supplies to plan an invasion. General Eisenhower had his staff examine maps of the European coastline, tide charts, meteorological studies, weather forecasts, movements of German troops, transportation arrangements in England, shipping problems across the channel, and every other facet of an invasion. At last, everything was ready. The date was carefully selected: June 6, 1944. D-Day! The time had come! The great armada moved. The invasion was on! Victory for the Allies was assured, although much savage fighting was still to be done.

The writers of the New Testament had the same kind of a sense of the timing in the world history about Jesus' Coming. "The time is fulfilled!" Jesus announced, according to Mark (1:15). The great moment has arrived! The hour of God's invasion into human history is at hand! Everything beforehand has been a build-up for this great occasion! The time for God's Coming truly has been fulfilled! The waiting is over. The time everyone has been waiting for has finally come!

Jesus added, "The Kingdom of God is at hand!" (Mark 1:15). The reign of God has now begun. God has laid claim on all of life. He insists that His realm include every person, every community, every institution, every nation, everything! This mighty "invasion" of God into human affairs comes through Jesus the King! Jesus Christ is God's "D-Day." Victory is assured for God's reign, Jesus makes clear.

The Kingdom of the reign of God established by the Messiah or King Jesus is the background for all of Jesus' teachings. His words must be listened to in the light of the staggering claim of the Kingdom's coming through Him. The new era Jesus brings calls for new lives. New lives must have new teaching. The following series of lessons on Principles of Christian Living are part of the new lifestyle required for new people living in a new age!

NOTES ON THE PRINTED TEXT

"Nothing ever seems to be happening in the church," one frustrated member snapped to her new pastor. Jesus knew such attitudes. *The Kingdom of God is like . . . seed sown on the ground.* Jesus envisioned the activity of the Kingdom like the growing of a seed. A farmer sowed the seed. Following the sowing was a period of what seemed to be inactivity, but the farmer was patient and confident. The seed germinated, sprouted, and gradually grew. *First the blade, then the ear, then the full grain in the ear.* Though the process was slow, it was sure and unstoppable. The farmer did not know how it grew. He knew only that God gave it growth. And the farmer was confident that the harvest would come. It began with a small seed but the results at harvest would be great.

The teachings of Jesus have at their core God's Kingdom. When speaking of the Kingdom, Jesus did not mean an area of land or a political domain. Jesus thought of the Kingdom as a condition of heart, mind, and will where God was

Lord of all. Do not be fretful for results of the Kingdom. It is coming. But it comes at God's time. The challenge for Christians is to live in a loving relation to God and to one another. Jesus summarized this challenge to the Pharisees who wanted to test Him.

One of them, a lawyer, asked him a question. *Teacher, which is the greatest commandment in the law?* A favorite method of Jewish teaching was summarizing the Law. They liked to reduce the Law to its minimum. Jesus summarizes the will of God by using two commands. *You shall love the Lord your God with all your heart, and with all your soul, and with all your mind* (Deuteronomy 6:4–9). Heart, soul, and mind emphasize how totally a person needs to be involved with God.

Of equal importance is the Second Commandment. *You shall love your neighbor as yourself.* This comes from Leviticus 19:18. The Kingdom of God challenges Christians to love one another as well. Love for God, for a neighbor, and for oneself must be the basis for all decisions. These two are the most important commandments. Together they provide a resumé of all the Law and the prophets.

Jesus' challenge is made in another parable. Jesus *told this parable to some who trusted in themselves that they were righteous.* (There may even be some spiritual descendants of the Pharisees in your class!) These people are dedicated and guided by the full observance of the Law. The Pharisee stood and carefully recited his own achievements to God. He has scrupulously kept the commandments of the Law. Pompously, he announced to God how different he was from the tax collector. In contrast, the tax collector adopted a pose of humility, afraid to look even at God. He emphasized his own sinfulness, by beating his breast as an act of penitence. He confessed his sins. *God be merciful to me a sinner.* Some translations read "the sinner!" He claimed to be the number one sinner in the world. Jesus concluded the parable with the declaration that it was the tax collector rather than the Pharisee who departed justified.

The immediate points are that humble confession of sin and dependence on God are the essential first steps toward righteous living. However, Jesus summarizes the real gulf between Himself and His critics. For the Pharisees, the Kingdom was a reward to be earned. For Jesus, the Kingdom was God's gift. The presence of this gift demanded repentance. "The time is fulfilled, and the Kingdom of God is at hand; repent, and believe in the gospel."

SUGGESTIONS TO TEACHERS

You are aware that Jesus opened His ministry with the announcement that the Kingdom of God is at hand. However, you and your class may not be sure what the Kingdom is or what it means. Therefore, the next nine lessons are geared to helping people like you and those in your class to understand that the Kingdom is both promise and challenge. The promise is that you and other Christians will be empowered individually and collectively to do God's will. The challenge is for you and all others who hear of the Good News to live in loving relationship to God and to each other, and to reach out in self-giving service to those in need.

Jesus' teachings about the abundant life form a large part of the Gospel records. These teachings offer guidance to disciples to grow in understanding, attitudes, and convictions which will mean fruitful service. These next nine lessons will look at the implications of Jesus' teachings for principled, practical Christian living. Today's lesson and the three following lessons will examine the principles of Christian living.

But back to the Kingdom of God that Jesus spoke of introducing. What exactly is that Kingdom? The lesson for today centers on that subject and presents the

Kingdom in terms of the Reign of God! The Reign of God—this means we are citizens of His realm.

Look at the Scripture for today's lesson for guidelines on how we as subjects of the reigning God are to live. Here are a few of the many notions which you will notice.

1. *TRUST.* Start with the pair of parables in Mark. In one, the seed grows silently. In the other, the tiniest seed produces the greatest bush. God's realm is like these. Just as a seed germinates quietly, so God's reign comes. Not much seems to be happening with a seed and it apparently is not growing after it is planted. So also with God's realm. Like the mustard seed, it may seem to many people to be so insignificant that it may be ignored. Discuss with your class the impatience we often feel with the Lord. Do your class members sometimes get the idea that God isn't doing much. Remind them of the parables' messages in Mark 4. Trust God to bring about what He has begun!

2. *LOVE.* Dwell long enough on Matthew 22:34–40 to have your people get the point that God's realm means caring for both God and others. Point out that the two go together in the Kingdom of God.

3. *HUMILITY.* Move on to the parable of the Pharisee and the Publican in Luke 18. Remind your class members that the story of the two men at prayer had particular bite to Jesus' hearers because everyone assumed the Pharisee (like the pious, self-righteous church member) was the person whose prayers would bring blessings. Instead, in the story it is the humble man (who happened to be one of the most despicable of persons!) who became right with God. Take time to talk together how hard it is to have genuine humility, especially before God.

TOPIC FOR ADULTS
DOING GOD'S WILL

California Going Fast, Take the Money and Run—So Says Guru. "Earthquakes, disastrous weather, nuclear war, and volcanoes will level San Francisco, Los Angeles, New York, Bombay, and Tokyo during the next fifteen years," said Bhagwan Shree Rajneesh, leader of a red-garbed sect. The predictions of doom prompted many of Rajneesh's California followers to make plans to leave the Golden State for safer areas before the expected disasters were to begin in 1984.

"California is going to go under," said Swami Anand Salam, director of the Deepta Rajneesh Meditation Center in Berkeley. "This is not something you can try to figure out. It's not logical. Bhagwan said he would like us to leave and we want to do what he wants us to do."

"No ordinary Noah's arks are going to save humanity," wrote Rajneesh.

Contrast this attitude to that of Jesus and His followers in the New Testament. Christ's people do not cut and run. They know God's Kingdom has been inaugurated through Jesus Christ. Therefore, they look with hope toward the future. They stand and serve!

Stand Next to the King! Plutarch, the ancient Greek writer in his *Life of Lycurgus,* once told the story of a wrestler in one of the ancient Olympic games. The wrestler had struggled valiantly against a particularly powerful competitor, and finally with immense difficulty threw and pinned his opponent. Gasping and bleeding, the winner staggered to the edge of the ring to receive the laurel wreath. One of the spectators called to him, "And now, Sir Lacedaemonian, what did you get out of your victory?" A logical question. After all, a bruised, weary body in exchange for a few leaves didn't make much sense. The fighter's answer silenced the critic. "I shall fight next to the king," he replied, referring to the custom in which the victor of the Olympic match got to stand beside the ruler in the next battle. The reward was being with the king. And that was reward enough.

Interval Time. "There still remains for our consideration what is after all the central phrase in St. Mark's summary of the announcement with which our Lord began his public ministry: 'The reign of God is at hand.' The more usual English rendering is 'Kingdom of God,' but the other is better because it suggests as it should an administration rather than a realm, and a time rather than a place. In the early decades of the present century there was keen debate among New Testament scholars whether Jesus thought of this reign as being already inaugurated with his advent or as about to be inaugurated in the very near future. But if we take the New Testament teaching as a whole, it may be said that there is something like an even balance between the note of fulfillment, as of a new age that has already dawned, and the note of expectation, as of a consummation that is still to be awaited. Christians knew themselves to be living in the new age, but they knew also that the old age had not yet passed away, so that they were living in both ages at once. God, writes St. Paul, had indeed 'delivered us from the dominion of darkness and transferred us to the kingdom of the Son of his love'; yet he has much to say also of the havoc that the powers of darkness are still working in the world and even within the Christian community. Christ has decisively defeated these powers, so that they are now 'under his feet,' but they still carry on their guerilla warfare among men; so that, as it has been so felicitously expressed by Dr. Oscar Cullmann in his much-quoted simile, men are now living in the interval between the decisive battle and Victory Day."—John Baillie, excerpted from *The Sense of the Presence of God.* Copyright © 1962 F. Jewel Baillie. Reprinted with the permission of Charles Scribner's Sons.

Questions for Pupils on the Next Lesson. 1. Why is the dignity and welfare of human beings so important to God? 2. How did Jesus regard the Sabbath? 3. Was Jesus concerned mostly about spiritual matters? 4. Do you always sense your own value and dignity as a person? 5. In the midst of the stresses pulling you apart, do you think that wholeness is a possibility?

TOPIC FOR YOUTH
WHERE'S YOUR LOYALTY?

"Best Experience of My Life." Missionary John Haspels said that his two weeks in the summer of 1983 as a hostage of Sudanese rebels fostered a relationship with natives that he and his co-workers had sought for years. "For me personally, it was the best experience of my life." During three years of work in the Boma area of southern Sudan, Haspels and his colleagues had been unable to establish close relations with local residents, he said. "But during the first week of our captivity, we were able to develop relations with the local people on a much deeper level than before," he reported. Haspels, thirty-six, said local people concerned about him and four other hostages came to the rebels' encampment and spent hours drinking tea and talking.

The rebels, who said they were fighting to free black, Christian southern Sudan from the domination of Arab Moslems in the north, had threatened to kill the hostages unless their demands were met. Haspels said that after he was taken hostage, he noticed every opportunity to escape and got a knot in his stomach when the chances weren't seized. But as the hostages read Scriptures, a theme surfaced, he said. One of the Bible passages, for instance, said: "Rest in the Lord, Wait patiently for Him to act."

"Finally we realized what God was really wanting of us was to not try to escape but to wait on Him to deliver us," Haspels said. The group's one attempt at escape failed. The hostages were freed safely during an aerial raid by the Sudanese army.

John Haspels learned that loyalty to God means serving Him wherever and whenever opportunity presents itself, even as a hostage. Remembering that loyalty to the Lord means every experience can be used for good.

Forgotten Purpose. Lucy is in the outfield in a baseball game. She is calling in to Charlie Brown and says, "Hey, Manager! Ask your catcher if he still loves me!" Charlie Brown, on the pitcher's mound, interrupts his pitching and says to his catcher, "She wants to know if you still love her." Then, Charlie turns and calls out to Lucy, "He says, 'No!' " Then, Lucy wants to know why not, so dutiful Charlie Brown asks the catcher, "She wants to know why not . . .?" He relays the information to Lucy: "He says there are so many reasons he can't remember them!"

This upsets Lucy, and she responds, "Really? That's very depressing." Finally, Charlie Brown is so exasperated with her that he cries out, "Do you mind if we get on with the game?" Lucy's pathetic response is, "What game? What game?" "The baseball game!" shouts the frustrated Charlie, to which Lucy replied, "Oh, that's right . . . I was wondering why I was standing out here!"

Are you wondering why you're here? Have you forgotten the purpose for your life? It's to carry out your loyalty to Jesus Christ! You are a citizen of His realm, and your reason for living is to live as a member of the Kingdom!

Anti-Christmas Celebration. Members of the Truth Tabernacle Church in Burlington, North Carolina, a few years ago decided to show their disgust at the way Christmas had been commercialized. They made a stuffed figure in a red suit, hung a white beard on it, and hung it from a tree in a nearby grove. Then they burned the Santa Claus in effigy. It was, they claimed, their way of protesting the commercialism of the season.

Perhaps you also are weary of the way Christmas is commercialized. Although burning a dummy Santa may not be the most effective way of getting your point across, you can show your desire to live out the true meaning of Christ's birth. You can demonstrate your loyalty to Jesus Christ by living as a person who is certain Jesus has brought about a new time and a new administration—God's Kingdom! Live as a "Kingdom Kid," under Christ's rule!

Questions for Pupils on the Next Lesson. 1. When do you feel as if you don't have much worth? 2. Does your faith in Jesus Christ give you any sense of personal dignity? 3. Was Jesus more interested in spirit than He was in body? 4. What did Jesus teach that takes precedence over rules and regulations? 5. Why is the welfare of human beings so precious in God's sight?

LESSON VI—JANUARY 5

THE WORTH OF EVERY PERSON

Background Scripture: Matthew 10:28–31; Mark 2:23—3:6
Devotional Reading: Luke 13:10–17

KING JAMES VERSION

MATTHEW 10 28 And fear not them which kill the body, but are not able to kill the soul: but rather fear him which is able to destroy both soul and body in hell.

29 Are not two sparrows sold for a farthing? and one of them shall not fall on the ground without your Father.

30 But the very hairs of your head are all numbered.

31 Fear ye not therefore, ye are of more value than many sparrows.

MARK 2 23 And it came to pass, that he went through the corn fields on the sabbath day; and his disciples began, as they went, to pluck the ears of corn.

24 And the Pharisees said unto him, Behold, why do they on the sabbath day that which is not lawful?

25 And he said unto them, Have ye never read what David did, when he had need, and was an hungered, he, and they that were with him?

26 How he went into the house of God in the days of Abiathar the high priest, and did eat the shewbread, which is not lawful to eat but for the priests, and gave also to them which were with him?

27 And he said unto them, The sabbath was made for man, and not man for the sabbath:

28 Therefore the Son of man is Lord also of the sabbath.

3 And he entered again into the synagogue; and there was a man there which had a withered hand.

2 And they watched him, whether he would heal him on the sabbath day; that they might accuse him.

3 And he saith unto the man which had the withered hand, Stand forth.

4 And he saith unto them, Is it lawful to do good on the sabbath days, or to do evil? to save life, or to kill? But they held their peace.

5 And when he had looked round about on them with anger, being grieved for the hardness of their hearts, he saith unto the man, Stretch forth thine hand. And he stretched *it* out: and his hand was restored whole as the other.

6 And Pharisees went forth, and straightway took counsel with the Herodians against him, how they might destroy him.

REVISED STANDARD VERSION

MATTHEW 10 28 And do not fear those who kill the body but cannot kill the soul; rather fear him who can destroy both soul and body in hell. 29 Are not two sparrows sold for a penny? And not one of them will fall to the ground without your Father's will. 30 But even the hairs of your head are all numbered. 31 Fear not, therefore; you are of more value than many sparrows.

MARK 2 23 One sabbath he was going through the grainfields; and as they made their way his disciples began to pluck ears of grain. 24 And the Pharisees said to him, "Look, why are they doing what is not lawful on the sabbath?" 25 And he said to them, "Have you never read what David did, when he was in need and was hungry, he and those who were with him; 26 how he entered the house of God, when Abiathar was high priest, and ate the bread of the Presence, which it is not lawful for any but the priests to eat, and also gave it to those who were with him?" 27 And he said to them, "The sabbath was made for man, not man for the sabbath; 28 so the Son of man is lord even of the sabbath."

3 Again he entered the synagogue, and a man was there who had a withered hand. 2 And they watched him, to see whether he would heal him on the sabbath, so that they might accuse him. 3 And he said to the man who had the withered hand, "Come here." 4 And he said to them, "Is it lawful on the sabbath to do good or to do harm, to save life or to kill?" But they were silent. 5 And he looked around at them with anger, grieved at their hardness of heart, and said to the man, "Stretch out your hand." He stretched it out, and his hand was restored. 6 The Pharisees went out, and immediately held counsel with the Herodians against him, how to destroy him.

KEY VERSE: *Fear not, therefore; you are of more value than many sparrows.* Matthew 10:31.

HOME DAILY BIBLE READINGS

Dec.	30.	M.	*The Sabbath Made for Man.* Mark 2:23–28.
Dec.	31.	T.	*Lawful Deeds on the Sabbath.* Mark 3:1–6.
Jan.	1.	W.	*More Value Than Sparrows.* Matthew 10:25–33.
Jan.	2.	T.	*Concern on the Sabbath.* Luke 14:1–6.
Jan.	3.	F.	*All Persons Have Worth.* Mark 10:13–16.
Jan.	4.	S.	*The Value of Persons.* Matthew 6:25–33.
Jan.	5.	S.	*Jesus Demonstrates Compassion.* John 5:1–9.

BACKGROUND

Human life was cheap in the ancient world. Slavery was accepted. Some scholars estimate that as many as two out of every three persons in Rome were slaves. Prisoners of war and captive populations were routinely sold as chattel to the highest bidders, branded, and used as the owners wished.

Violence and cruelty were accepted. The bloody brutality of the Roman arenas attracted throngs, watching humans fighting to the death against other humans or animals.

Babies, children, and women had little value to most of those living in those times. Unwanted infants were routinely drowned or abandoned to perish in the Greek and Roman cities. With few exceptions, women were relegated to the degrading roles of either males' playthings or work-animals. The sick and helpless were ignored by all except their families. Filthy coughing victims of nearly every imaginable disease crowded the narrow streets, begging for handouts. Most people passed them by.

In Greek culture, which the Romans eagerly adopted, pity was a sign of weakness. Any person showing compassion toward other humans was sneered at. The gods and goddesses in the various religions were apathetic in the face of human misery, and this attitude was emulated by the thinkers and movers in the ancient Mediterranean world.

You can imagine the sense of despair most people had. Slaves and serfs and the "scum" of society—the bulk of the population—lived and died without hope. No wonder the news of Jesus was so eagerly welcomed by the great numbers of the underclass in the Roman world! The sense of worth and dignity given each man and woman by Jesus meant a life with meaning! It was among the slaves and have-nots that the Gospel won the greatest numbers of new Christians.

Jesus confers worth to each person. Jesus makes us human. Jesus cares about each as if he or she is the only one. To the sick, suffering, lonely, and despairing of every age in every place, Jesus Christ's Coming means Good News!

NOTES ON THE PRINTED TEXT

The fear of men and of persecution should not keep the disciples from proclaiming the Kingdom of God. *Rather, fear him who can destroy both soul and body in hell.* The disciples should fear only God. It is worse to disobey God, than to be put to death as martyrs.

Are not two sparrows sold for a penny? Jesus asks. Sparrows were common birds sold very cheaply in the markets. They were used for food by the poor. Even though they are insignificant, their death did not go unnoticed by God. *Not one of them will fall to the ground without your Father's will.* The personal worth of the disciples is far greater than a sparrow Jesus says. So how much more will God be concerned with them? Why, *even the hairs of your head are all numbered. Fear not, therefore; you are of more value than many sparrows.* Every person's dignity and welfare is precious in God's sight.

The particular teaching of Jesus was borne out during a controversy that arose one Sabbath. The Sabbath was holy. The Law of Moses mandated that no work be done. Traditions and definitions were developed and expounded by the Pharisees defining exactly what constituted work. Harvesting of grain was classified as work. The disciples, *as they made their way through grain fields, began to pluck the ears of grain.* They were hungry. However, the Pharisees saw the action of picking the grain and rubbing off the chaff as literally reaping and threshing. This constituted work and was not permitted on the Sabbath.

Jesus responded with a counter-question. *Have you never read what David did, when he was in need and was hungry?* Referring to David's eating of the shewbread (the fresh bread continually kept on the altar of the temple as an offering to God, in 1 Samuel 21:1–6), Jesus reminded the legalists that even the great David himself occasionally infringed on the Law. Human need and necessity had prior claim over ritual law.

The Sabbath was made for man, not man for the Sabbath. Jesus views the Sabbath as a gift of God, not a meaningless ritual or burden. People are important and precious in God's sight. Traditions must take into account the importance of personhood. *Again he entered the synagogue . . . and they watched him . . . so that they might accuse him.*

The controversy over this teaching was not over. The Pharisees were intent on discrediting Jesus. Bringing to them a man with a withered hand, Jesus asked, *Is it lawful on the sabbath to do good or to do harm, to save life or to kill?* Their silence indicated their dilemma. It was good to save a life, but Jesus' question to them lifted the controversy to a new level. To heal would save a life. However, to heal on the Sabbath was work and against the Law. Jesus was concerned with the body as well as the spirit. He was concerned with the value and worth of the person. Mercy and love always took priority over rules and regulations.

The seething, hostile, resentful Pharisees showed their *hardness of heart.* Their inability to see the worth of every person and their legalist attitudes angered and grieved Jesus.

Jesus then restores the use of the man's hand. Jesus demonstrates the steadfast love of God, but the healing and controversy only made the Pharisees more bitter. *They immediately held counsel with the Herodians against him, how to destroy him.*

SUGGESTIONS TO TEACHERS

In the spring of 1983, a computer called Robot Redford delivered the commencement address at a leading college. Hailing the event as another milestone in microchip technology, two bright graduate students meeting with incoming freshmen at another institution solemnly stated that human intelligence and personality had little value.

As a thinking person, you have already reflected on the fact that humans are accorded little dignity or worth. Many in your class feel that they don't count for much. The lesson for this Sunday, therefore, has particular meaning.

1. *SPARROW'S VALUE.* Have your students study the passage about the sparrows' worth in Matthew 10:28–31. Remind them that the point of Jesus' comment is that even these puny little birds are known by the Father. If a common sparrow is known by the Lord, how much more we humans are remembered! Get the class members to disclose when and where they are made to feel of little value. Have the persons in your class also comment on the way our culture dehumanizes people, including them. Get back to the passage about the sparrows, and suggest that your class members consider their own worth in a new light as members of the realm of God.

2. *SABBATH VIEWPOINT.* The episode of the disciples plucking and eating grains of barley as they walked through a field may not strike anyone in your class

as wrong. Point out, however, that to Jesus' critics, this act constituted a sin since it was defying the Sabbath rules against work (picking the barley was harvesting, technically speaking). Jesus emphasized that the Sabbath rules take a back seat to human need. This was Jesus' way of stressing the worth of every person. Are there occasions in which we place tradition or regulations ahead of people?

3. *SYNAGOGUE VENTURE.* Take your class into the synagogue on the Sabbath Day when Jesus healed the man with the withered hand (Mark 3:1–6). Use your imagination to set the scene. Note description of Jesus' reaction at the bystanders: "he looked around at them with anger, grieved at their hardness of heart" (verse 5). Jesus insisted that actively doing good to another human being takes precedence over *every* regulation. Be sure to point out to the class that the authorities were so incensed that they began to plot to destroy Jesus. Jesus suffered and died in order to confer worth to each individual. There was a cost to be paid before every person be given value! And that cost was a Cross!

TOPIC FOR ADULTS
PERSONS ARE IMPORTANT

To Kiss Frogs. "Once upon a time . . . there was a frog. But he wasn't really a frog, but a handsome prince who merely looked and felt like a frog because a wicked witch had cast a spell on him, and only the kiss of a beautiful maiden could save him. But nobody wanted to kiss this frog, so there he sat . . . an unkissed prince in frog form.

"Then, one day, along came a beautiful maiden who gave this frog a great big smack. CRASH. . . . BOOM. . . . ZAP! There he was . . . a handsome dashing prince. And you know the rest . . . they lived happily ever after.

"So what has this to do with the Church? Its mission is to kiss frogs—of course!

"Surely you know this isn't about frogs at all, but about people . . . people who have within themselves the beauty and Godliness with which God created them. But too often this inner Godliness is stifled and frustrated for lack of a loving person . . . or a loving community . . . which will use the liberating power of love by which that inner beauty can be set free to express itself.

"The saving and liberating nature of God is to love the unloved (and unloveable) . . . to 'kiss the frog' in each of us, and set us free to be our true self; to give us the courage to come out from beyond the defenses we think we need for protection in an unloving and threatening world.

"All about us are people who are hungering within for some assurance of love and caring for others. How many of us might indeed be unlovely 'frogs' were it not for the love and caring others have given us?"—St. Paul's Episcopal Church, Des Moines, Iowa.

Rejected by Humans. A deformed baby born to a surrogate mother a couple of years ago was rejected by both the mother who carried the child and the father who conceived him through artificial insemination. The baby was born in Lansing, Michigan, with microcephaly, a condition in which the head is smaller than normal and may indicate mental retardation. Neither the woman who was impregnated for a fee of $10,000 nor the man whose sperm allegedly was used want the deformed boy. The case raises many legal questions about surrogate parenthood. It also raised the deeper question of God's acceptance of the deformed and the unlovely.

The Gospel means that God's Kingdom includes microcephalic babies. The love of Jesus Christ extends to everyone. Through Jesus Christ, *every* person is regarded as one with value and importance!

Robots at the Console. A one-armed robot developed by Professor Ichiro Kato of Waseda University in Tokyo, Japan, posed with human counterpart at the keyboard of an electronic organ. Kato claims the robot can play the organ with its five fingers as skillfully as a human. He said the robot, named WAM-7, has fourteen joints made of carbon fiber and seven degrees of freedom in its fingers; that it can strike keys ten times a second in motions controlled by a microcomputer, and can also perform cross-finger piano techniques by crossing its index finger or its middle finger over its thumb. Kato said he plans to build an organ-playing robot complete with head and body. Robot organists, however, are never going to replace a human at the console. In spite of the ingenuity of Professor Kato and others, WAM-7 and its successors will not be able to interpret Braham's *Requiem* nor play for a worship service at your church. Humans may be replaced in certain mechanical tasks, but they will always be needed in the creative work which God allocates to men and women!

Questions for Pupils on the Next Lesson. 1. Do wrong attitudes inevitably breed wrong actions? 2. Is it possible to live in a right relationship with God without being at peace with others? 3. Why did Jesus insist on more than ritual cleanness? 4. What happens when human traditions replace God's Commandments? 5. Which do you think is more important: inner condition or outward appearance?

TOPIC FOR YOUTH
HOW IMPORTANT IS EVERYONE?

What Worth Is a Person? English words are fascinating. Often, they have a meaning now which is completely different from when they were first used. Take the word *salary*. You may think that the word *salary* has to do with money. It does now. But the root of the word has to do with salt! It goes back to the time when salt was the most precious and important substance for a person's needs. A person's value, in fact, was measured by how much he or she was worth in salt. (We still use the expression, "Worth his salt.") From this humble idea of valuing a person by salt grew the use of the word *salary*.

But Christians remember that they cannot measure any other person in terms of salt or anything. Each human life is of immeasurable worth. Why? Because of Jesus Christ. He died for all. Not for just some, but for every person. In the light of Jesus Christ, we now see each other as unique and valued by God. Because each person has such worth for God, each person also now has worth for us.

Computers Aren't the Last Word. "Consider the computer that books a coach flight to Des Moines. Just because a gadget can splendidly perform some feat that taxes human intelligence, it does not mean that the mechanism acts intelligently.

"It is the very speed and accuracy of computers that makes us suspect that they display no intelligence.

"Human thinking is essentially at will: creative and free—and for that very reason very much subject to being bizarre, wayward and wrong. Human intelligence may choose to follow rules, follow them grumpily or invent quite new rules. 'What if parallel lines meet?' asks the creative geometer who invents a new mathematics.

"Computers lack a sense of humor and our assorted neuroses. If intelligent behavior is the aim of college education, computers flunk the entrance exam.

"Being intelligent is not at all like doing something instantaneously or memorizing the passenger list to Des Moines. Rather, being intelligent comprises a great messy set of peformances from calculating to giggling. One can't specify exactly how many items are in the set, and there seem to be surprising but essential links between the oddest clusters of behavior. Kekule's dream about a snake led to his invention of organic chemistry; Kepler's Christian piety caused him to discover the proper orbits of the solar system.

"Human beings not only do intelligent things, they also enjoy exercise of the mind. No computer so far conceived could be programmed to enjoy its performances. Would that joy were a performance! We would then program either humans or computers for happiness. It would be a great boon to psychiatrists.

"But enjoyment is not a performance. Performances (like addition) take time and can be done well or ill. But it makes no sense to ask whether I do my enjoying well or I bungle it. You can ask how long I spent yesterday doing math, but never how long I spent being happy.

"The fact that humans can and do enjoy intelligent behavior is the secret of higher education. Real academic performance is the activity of an aware and intelligent person who has engaged wit, soul and mind in a task."—Ennis O'Brien, *New York Times* editorial, Sunday, August 28, 1983. Copyright © 1983 by The New York Times Company. Reprinted by permission.

Questions for Pupils on the Next Lesson. 1. Why was Jesus so concerned about inner motives rather than outward appearances? 2. Can a person be in a right relationship with God and not be at peace with others? 3. Do wrong attitudes always produce wrong actions? 4. What happens when human traditions replace God's Commandments?

LESSON VII—JANUARY 12

THE INWARDNESS OF MORALITY

Background Scripture: Mark 7:1–23; Matthew 5:21–30
Devotional Reading: Matthew 5:13–16

KING JAMES VERSION

MARK 7 Then came together unto him the Pharisees, and certain of the scribes, which came from Jerusalem.

2 And when they saw some of his disciples eat bread with defiled, that is to say, with unwashen, hands, they found fault.

3 For the Pharisees, and all the Jews, except they wash *their* hands oft, eat not, holding the tradition of the elders.

4 And *when they come* from the market, except they wash, they eat not. And many other things there be, which they have received to hold, *as* the washing of cups, and pots, brazen vessels, and of tables.

5 Then the Pharisees and scribes asked him, Why walk not thy disciples according to the tradition of the elders, but eat bread with unwashen hands?

14 And when he had called all the people *unto him*, he said unto them, Hearken unto me every one *of you*, and understand:

15 There is nothing from without a man, that entering into him can defile him: but the things which come out of him, those are they that defile the man.

16 If any man have ears to hear, let him hear.

17 And when he was entered into the house from the people, his disciples asked him concerning the parable.

18 And he saith unto them, Are ye so without understanding also? Do ye not perceive, that whatsoever thing from without entereth into the man, *it* cannot defile him;

19 Because it entereth not into his heart, but into the belly, and goeth out into the draught, purging all meats?

20 And he said, That which cometh out of the man, that defileth the man.

21 For from within, out of the heart of men, proceed evil thoughts, adulteries, fornications, murders,

22 Thefts, covetousness, wickedness, deceit, lasciviousness, an evil eye, blasphemy, pride, foolishness:

23 All these evil things come from within, and defile the man.

MATTHEW 5 21 Ye have heard that it was said by them of old time, Thou shalt not kill; and whosoever shall kill shall be in danger of the judgment:

22 But I say unto you, That whosoever is angry with his brother without a cause shall be in danger of the judgment: and whosoever shall say to his brother, Raca, shall be in danger of the council: but whosoever shall say, Thou fool, shall be in danger of hell fire.

REVISED STANDARD VERSION

MARK 7 Now when the Pharisees gathered together to him, with some of the scribes, who had come from Jerusalem, 2 they saw that some of his disciples ate with hands defiled, that is, unwashed. 3 (For the Pharisees, and all the Jews, do not eat unless they wash their hands, observing the tradition of the elders; 4 and when they come from the market place, they do not eat unless they purify themselves; and there are many other traditions which they observe, the washing of cups and pots and vessels of bronze.) 5 And the Pharisees and the scribes asked him, "Why do your disciples not live according to the tradition of the elders, but eat with hands defiled?"

14 And he called the people to him again, and said to them, "Hear me, all of you, and understand: 15 there is nothing outside a man which by going into him can defile him; but the things which come out of a man are what defile him." 17 And when he had entered the house, and left the people, his disciples asked him about the parable. 18 And he said to them, "Then are you also without understanding? Do you not see that whatever goes into a man from outside cannot defile him, 19 since it enters, not his heart but his stomach, and so passes on?" (Thus he declared all foods clean.) 20 And he said, "What comes out of a man is what defiles a man. 21 For from within, out of the heart of man, come evil thoughts, fornication, theft, murder, adultery, 22 coveting, wickedness, deceit, licentiousness, envy, slander, pride, foolishness. 23 All these evil things come from within, and they defile a man."

MATTHEW 5 21 "You have heard that it was said to the men of old, 'You shall not kill; and whoever kills shall be liable to judgment.' 22 But I say to you that every one who is angry with his brother shall be liable to judgment; whoever insults his brother shall be liable to the council, and whoever says, 'You fool!' shall be liable to the hell of fire."

KEY VERSE: Create in me a clean heart, O God, and put a new and right spirit within me. Psalms 51:10.

HOME DAILY BIBLE READINGS

Jan.	6.	M.	*Life's Alternatives.* Proverbs 11:23–28.
Jan.	7.	T.	*Choice Can Overcome Circumstances.* Proverbs 13:12–21.
Jan.	8.	W.	*A Happy Disposition.* Proverbs 15:13–17.
Jan.	9.	T.	*Spiritual Values.* Proverbs 16:1–5.
Jan.	10.	F.	*Actions and Reactions.* Jeremiah 6:16–21.
Jan.	11.	S.	*The Day of the Lord.* Isaiah 2:12–22.
Jan.	12.	S.	*Getting What We Deserve.* Proverbs 22:9–12.

BACKGROUND

A young engineer left a mainline congregation to join a small sect with strict rules. "I want to know exactly how to be a good Christian and my new church tells me," he stated. When asked what they told him in his new church that made him a good Christian, he promptly answered, "No drinking, no smoking, no cards, no dancing, only Christian literature and books, no Sunday movies or sports, prayer meeting every Wednesday, and 10 percent of my gross income to the church."

There is, of course, nothing wrong with any of these practices. Furthermore, every Christian must show some discipline in being faithful to Christ. The problem with the young engineer and his list is that he and his sect overlook the inwardness of morality. They are most concerned with the outward forms.

This approach of being concerned mostly with the outward forms of moral living was the way of the scribes and Pharisees in Jesus' time. Nothing evil, mind you, about these people. They were trying to be as devout as they possibly could be. Their problem, however, was that they put all emphasis on the outward action and neglected the inward attitude. Being religious, for them, meant scrupulously observing 613 rules of Jewish tradition. These superreligious people worked strenuously to keep those 613 regulations.

Their problem was that they overlooked the inner person. They forgot that evil actions arise out of the thoughts and character of the inner self.

Depth psychology in recent times confirms what Jesus taught long ago, namely that ritual cleanness and rule-keeping are meaningless unless accompanied by a change in heart.

Jesus demanded a radical change of attitude and direction. "Repent!" He insisted. To *repent* means to reorient life completely, literally "to turn." He knew His hearers—and He knows us—better than they knew themselves. A person's values shape his or her acts. And those values are shaped by the person's orientation toward God. God has come to us in Jesus Christ, making us in a right relationship with Him. Right with Him, we now have the right orientation toward ourselves, toward others, and toward life! We can practice moral living in the right way because we are right from within!

NOTES ON THE PRINTED TEXT

Cleanliness was connected with holiness. Israel, according to Jewish tradition, had to reject any uncleanliness, or God would turn His face from her. The nation's survival, it was taught, depended on purity in every form. Consequently, Jewish Law had strict and detailed regulations about cleanliness and uncleanliness. This was particularly true in regard to eating.

Before a man could eat, he had to wash his hands in a certain way. He had to take at least a quarter of a log of water (a measure equal to one and a half eggshells). He had to hold his hand with the fingertips up and pour the water over them until it ran down to the wrists. Then he had to cleanse the palm of each hand with the fist of the other. Finally, he had to hold the hands with the fingertips pointing down and pour water on them from the wrists down so that the water ran off at the fingertips. This was not a matter of hygiene but a matter of ritual. Even if the hands were spotless, this ritual had to be followed. To do so was to please God, while to fail to do so was to sin. This kind of ritualism became rigid legalism. Religion became an external matter. No matter what was in a person's heart or thoughts, he was considered good if he followed the rituals correctly. Few were able to adhere to such traditions.

It was some of the strict followers of these rigid traditions who met with Jesus. The local Pharisees and some scribes from Jerusalem noticed *that some of the disciples ate with hands defiled, that is, unwashed.* These elders noted that the former fishermen among the disciples had not observed *the tradition of the elders* that governed the cleansing of cups, pots, and utensils. Since the disciples did *not live according to the tradition,* the Pharisees asked Jesus why the disciples were eating with *hands defiled.*

Jesus squarely responds to the Pharisees but also addresses his comments to the people whom He has called to listen. *There is nothing outside a man which by going into him can defile him.* Nothing outward can defile a person. The only defilement of any importance comes from within, Jesus explains. What enters from the outside enters *not the heart* but the stomach and then passes on. *But, the things which come out of a man are what defile him.*

Patiently explaining this statement, Jesus leads the listeners to understand that it is the inner self that must be cleansed. *From within, out of the heart of man, come evil thoughts.* Wrong attitudes come from inside and breed only wrong actions. From man's heart comes *fornication, theft, murder, adultery, and coveting.* Sexual immorality was forbidden in the Seventh Commandment, and the Eighth, Sixth, and Tenth Commandments prohibited other evils originating in the heart. An *evil eye* refers to jealousy. *Slander* is a form of murder since it is character assassination. *Pride and foolishness* are also evil attitudes from within that can produce evil actions. *All these come from within, and . . . defile a man* says Jesus.

Jesus' intention is to show that ritual cleanliness of the outside of the body was meaningless unless accompanied by a change of heart from within. Human traditions must not replace God's Commandments.

You have heard that it was said to the men of old, you shall not kill. Matthew records other instances of Jesus expanding and superseding the old tradition of Moses. The Sixth Commandment read not to kill. In explanation, Jesus expanded this law to include the cause of murder that came from within: anger and insult. These emotional responses arise from the inner character of a person. Morality, a principle of Christian living, begins inside a person.

SUGGESTIONS TO TEACHERS

In Pakistan, strong-man ruler, General Mohammad Zia ul-Haq, has vowed to bring about what he calls the *Islamization* of society in his country. This means a rigorous enforcement of Moslem Law. Drinking alcoholic beverages, for example, is punished by eighty lashes. Many other offenses are also enforced with flogging. It is legal in Pakistan now to stone to death a person convicted of adultery, and to cut off the right hand for stealing. There is no public dancing or nightlife. Women are now confined mostly to home and kitchen, and must wear clothing covering most of their bodies. General Zia states that his objective is to set his nation "straight on the path of righteousness." His harsh laws have also meant political parties have been squashed, leaders arrested, civil liberties suspended, and democracy abolished. Zia's brand of morality is intended to restructure

Pakistani society so "there will be no returning to any other system," he states.

The people of Pakistan, however, are learning that morality is not merely an outward matter of behavior. Civil unrest and public protests against the laws enforcing Zia's puritanism are testing the Zia regime.

Jesus, long before Mohammed and Zia and other zealous spokesmen for moral living, emphasized the inwardness of morality. Look at the scriptural references in today's lesson. He stresses inner attitude as much as outward act.

1. *RITUALS OR RIGHTEOUSNESS.* Clean hands or clean hearts? The showdown between Jesus and His adversaries revolved on the inwardness versus the outwardness of moral living. Call attention to the way Jesus insisted that those living trustingly and obediently before God had to move beyond mere ritual. What does this mean to believers in these times?

2. *TRADITIONS OR TRUTH.* Take enough time to interpret the section of Mark 7:9–13 in which Jesus denounces sanctimonious leaders for practicing what was called *Corban.* See the Background for comments on what *Corban* was. Jesus excoriated those who twisted the law to suit their own wishes. However, do we not sometimes try to excuse ourselves in our Christian living—in effect manipulating Christ's demands to our desires?

3. *EXTERIOR OR INTERIOR.* Jesus had strong words on what defiled a person. The real source of defilement was not something from outside, such as a certain food or drink (although these can harm one), but the inner thoughts or the will of a person.

4. *REVENGE OR RECONCILIATION.* Devote plenty of time on Jesus' definition of violence and hurt (Matthew 5:21ff). Anger, insults, and denunciation can be as destructive as the most lethal weapon or assault! Murder comes from what lies within a person.

5. *LUST OR LOVE.* Likewise, spend sufficient part of the lesson in discussing Jesus' comments on sexual morality. Rules on sex must go deeper than giving boundaries for the physical act of intercourse, according to Jesus. Sexual morality means a respect for and a caring for the other.

TOPIC FOR ADULTS
THE INWARDNESS OF MORALITY

Honest Abe. Abraham Lincoln understood the inwardness of morality. Not only as the sixteenth President but also as a practicing attorney, he showed moral character. Throughout his days as a lawyer in Illinois, Lincoln always had a partner. Usually, Lincoln would ride through the circuit handling legal cases while his partner stayed in Springfield to look after the office. In most cases, the suit or legal matter was resolved on the spot and the fee paid to Lincoln before he returned to the office. Abe Lincoln always carefully divided the money before putting it in his billfold. He would wrap his partner's half in a piece of paper and write the partner's name and the case. In this way, if anything happened to Lincoln, his partner would get the money without question. No wonder Lincoln acquired the title, "Honest Abe."

Inner Morality Key to Survival. "The U.S. Navy pilot was sick and weak in a North Vietnamese prison in the fall of 1965. His untreated, smashed left knee would fuse so straight it could never be fixed, and the torture sessions were about to begin. As the highest ranking American prisoner in the Vietnam war and a constant irritant to his captors, James B. Stockdale suffered months without treatment of his injured shoulder, back, and smashed left leg. He still cannot bend his leg at the knee. He encountered several times the torturer dubbed 'Pig Eye,' an expert in applying excruciating pain with rope bindings and rods. He cut and bruised himself intentionally so he would be unsuitable for propaganda display.

" 'History abounds with examples of extortion, of people manipulating other people through the imposition of feelings of fear and guilt,' Stockdale said in his course description for Stanford, where he serves as a Senior Fellow of the Hoover Institution. 'Though sometimes done in an easily recognized, explicit, and illegal way, the process is usually more subtle, more insidious, and within the law.

" 'Those who are in hierarchies—be they academic, business, governmental, military, or other—are frequently in positions in which people are trying to manipulate them, to get moral leverage on them by methods which are not easily recognized by the victims.'

"As an example, he cites his wife Sybil's struggle to organize the League of Families of American Prisoners and Missing in Southeast Asia in 1967 and 1968 despite subtle pressure and opposition from the U.S. government.

"He recalled his own decision to resign in 1980 as president of the South Carolina military academy, The Citadel, after only one year in the job that had persuaded him to leave the Navy before he needed to.

"The school's board would not let him upgrade the academic program and curb traditional hazing. Compromise, he had learned already, would not get him what he wanted.

" 'Most people have to knuckle under to the organization, to "big daddy"—as someone put it, "cooperate to graduate," ' Stockdale said. 'This process can become a quagmire if you let it become one. You can become compromised by so many little steps that seem insignificant, and before you know it you have passed the point of no return.' "—From article by Jan Mathews, *Morning Call*, January 27, 1983. Reprint from Call-Chronicle Newspapers, Allentown, Pa.

Sleepless Morality. Our morality must be built on values held and supported from within by each believer. It must mean more than rule-keeping. This kind of morality also means more than feelings. Sometimes we are like the person who once wrote to the Internal Revenue Service:

"Dear Sirs: I am a distraught taxpayer who cheated on my income tax and cannot sleep. I enclose my check for $50. Sincerely yours." Attached to this note was a P.S. saying, "If I am still unable to sleep, I will send you the balance."

Questions for Pupils on the Next Lesson. 1. For what do you think God holds us accountable? 2. What are the actions commended in the parable in Matthew 25:31–46? 3. Where, according to this parable, is Christ to be found? 4. Is the teaching of this parable about the future life or the present life? 5. What responsibilities do Christians have to those in need?

TOPIC FOR YOUTH
ARE YOUR VALUES SHOWING?

The Problem Is Within. They that go down in the sea for old ships sometimes come up with treasure troves, but rarely the ship itself. So when a British salvage operation raised the *Mary Rose*—King Henry VIII's joy when it sailed in 1511, his despair when it sank in 1545—archeologists hit a gold mine.

"It's a perfect time capsule," said Andrew Fielding, an assistant director of the expedition. Most of the ship's oak frame and starboard hull was intact, preserved by the mud and silt of Portsmouth harbor. It sank there with some 700 men, 91 cannons and the stuff of life aboard a Tudor man-of-war: a chess board; dice; breech-loading and muzzle-loading guns; leather jerkins; food; 4,000 arrows; long-bows; a complete barber surgeon's chest. In all, about 17,000 artifacts have been retrieved from the wreck since it was found in 1970.

Mary Rose was sailing to meet the French when she went down in full view of King Henry; historians believe an unsecured cannon careened through her side.

Imagine! The mighty *Mary Rose* sank not because of the enemy without but because of a loose cannon within. Isn't this the way it is with our lives also? The real trouble is inside, not outside us. Unless we are strongly secured by a set of Christian values, our thoughts and acts may be like a loose cannon. Many lives have been sunk by lack of interior constraints and ideals. Make sure your commitment to Christ means goals and ideals which avert destruction.

Imprint of His Values. Your values invariably show. A Glasgow baker named Peter McGhee, however, didn't think that his values (or lack of them) would leave such an imprint. It seems that McGhee's stone oven needed repairs. Peter McGhee didn't want to spend money to put the oven right. He noticed an old graveyard nearby. One night, he went over the wall and collected some old gravestones lying about. He figured that nobody would ever know that he stole the stones for his oven. The new oven looked fine. But the loaves all came out with the reverse of the legend, "Sacred to the Memory of Effie Coutts" imprinted on the bottoms! Pete's values showed up!

More Than Respectability. Jesus demands a morality which is more than merely being respectable. Every generation has to learn this. For example, in Victorian England, playing the piano on Sunday was considered terribly wicked. However, few people questioned child labor in which little tykes of six and seven were sent into coal mines or forced to work twelve-hour factory shifts six days a week. Our morality must be from within, and must result in concern for others!

Questions for Pupils on the Next Lesson. 1. Are we accountable to God both for what we do and for what we neglect to do? 2. According to the parable in Matthew 25:31–46, what is every Christian expected to do? 3. Do you agree with the words in the parable that in serving the unfortunate we serve Christ Himself? 4. Is this parable about the present or about the future life? 5. What standards does God use to judge us?

LESSON VIII—JANUARY 19

THE CONCERN FOR OTHERS

Background Scripture: Matthew 25:31–46
Devotional Reading: Matthew 18:10–14

KING JAMES VERSION

MATTHEW 25   31 When the Son of man shall come in his glory, and all the holy angels with him, then shall he sit upon the throne of his glory:

32 And before him shall be gathered all nations: and he shall separate them one from another, as a shepherd divideth *his* sheep from the goats:

33 And he shall set the sheep on his right hand, but the goats on the left.

34 Then shall the King say unto them on his right hand, Come, ye blessed of my Father, inherit the kingdom prepared for you from the foundation of the world:

35 For I was an hungered, and ye gave me meat: I was thirsty, and ye gave me drink; I was a stranger, and ye took me in:

36 Naked, and ye clothed me: I was sick, and ye visited me: I was in prison, and ye came unto me.

37 Then shall the righteous answer him, saying, Lord, when saw we thee an hungered, and fed *thee?* or thirsty, and gave *thee* drink?

38 When saw we thee a stranger, and took *thee* in? or naked, and clothed *thee?*

39 Or when saw we thee sick, or in prison, and came unto thee?

40 And the King shall answer and say unto them, Verily I say unto you, Inasmuch as ye have done *it* unto one of the least of these my brethren, ye have done *it* unto me.

41 Then shall he say also unto them on the left hand, Depart from me, ye cursed, into everlasting fire, prepared for the devil and his angels:

42 For I was an hungered, and ye gave me no meat: I was thirsty, and ye gave me no drink:

43 I was a stranger, and ye took me not in: naked, and ye clothed me not: sick, and in prison, and ye visited me not.

44 Then shall they also answer him, saying, Lord, when saw we thee an hungered, or athirst, or a stranger, or naked, or sick, or in prison, and did not minister unto thee?

45 Then shall he answer them, saying, Verily I say unto you, Inasmuch as ye did *it* not to one of the least of these, ye did *it* not to me.

46 And these shall go away into everlasting punishment: but the righteous into life eternal.

REVISED STANDARD VERSION

MATTHEW 25   31 "When the Son of man comes in his glory, and all the angels with him, then he will sit on his glorious throne. 32 Before him will be gathered all the nations, and he will separate them one from another as a shepherd separates the sheep from the goats, 33 and he will place the sheep at his right hand, but the goats at the left. 34 Then the King will say to those at his right hand, 'Come, O blessed of my Father, inherit the kingdom prepared for you from the foundation of the world; 35 for I was hungry and you gave me food, I was thirsty and you gave me drink, I was a stranger and you welcomed me, 36 I was naked and you clothed me, I was sick and you visited me, I was in prison and you came to me.' 37 Then the righteous will answer him, 'Lord, when did we see thee hungry and feed thee, or thirsty and give thee drink? 38 And when did we see thee a stranger and welcome thee, or naked and clothe thee? 39 And when did we see thee sick or in prison and visit thee?' 40 And the King will answer them, 'Truly, I say to you, as you did it to one of the least of these my brethren, you did it to me.' 41 Then he will say to those at his left hand, 'Depart from me, you cursed, into the eternal fire prepared for the devil and his angels; 42 for I was hungry and you gave me no food, I was thirsty and you gave me no drink, 43 I was a stranger and you did not welcome me, naked and you did not clothe me, sick and in prison and you did not visit me.' 44 Then they also will answer, 'Lord, when did we see thee hungry or thirsty or a stranger or naked or sick or in prison, and did not minister to thee?' 45 Then he will answer them, 'Truly, I say to you, as you did it not to one of the least of these, you did it not to me.' 46 And they will go away into eternal punishment, but the righteous into eternal life."

KEY VERSE: *As you did it to one of the least of these my brethren, you did it to me.* Matthew 25:40.

HOME DAILY BIBLE READINGS

Jan.	13.	M.	*Joy in God's Forgiveness.* Psalms 103:1–12.
Jan	14.	T.	*Acting and Talking Go Together.* James 1:22–26.
Jan.	15.	W.	*Partiality Not Recommended.* James 2:1–7.
Jan.	16.	T.	*Words Will Not Provide Shelter.* James 2:14–26.
Jan.	17.	F.	*Forgiving Often.* Matthew 18:21–35.
Jan.	18.	S.	*All Have Sinned.* Luke 18:9–14.
Jan.	19.	S.	*Forgiveness for Our Brothers.* Luke 19:1–10.

BACKGROUND

Jesus was the Master Teacher. He frequently got the points of His teaching across through parables. His parables are quick "picture stories." Each illustrates an important facet of His teachings. Jesus did not intend these picture stories to be used as allegories (that is, where every detail is to be interpreted symbolically). Nor did He relate them as literal descriptions of the hereafter. He used parables as a way of communicating a vital point in His teaching.

Keep this in mind when studying the parable of the Last Judgment in Matthew 25:31–46. Remember also that it is the final in a series of parables in the section of Matthew 24:42 through 25:46 on the general theme of being watchful. "Watch therefore!" is the note throughout this part of Matthew. Jesus is aware in this section of Matthew's Gospel that time is running out for Him on earth. He warns His hearers that the end is coming. When He reappears, will they be ready? Through the string of parables, including the Thief in the Night (Matthew 24:42–44), the Faithful or Wicked Servant (24:45–51), the Wise and Foolish Bridesmaids (25:1–13), the Talents entrusted to the three servants (25:14–30), and, finally, the Last Judgment (25:31–46), Jesus asks the question in a variety of ways: "Will you be ready when you will be surprised by the Coming of the Lord?"

Jesus throws in several startling details in these parables. The first is that the basis of God's judgment is practical service to the least, the last, and the lost of the world. Second, everyone is accountable to God both for what he or she does and also for what he or she neglects to do. Third, in showing simple acts of service to the hurting persons around us, we are serving Christ. Likewise, in refusing to serve these people, we refuse to serve Christ. Fourth, those who were commended in the parable were not aware of doing anything praiseworthy and were astonished that they were singled out for recognition.

NOTES ON THE PRINTED TEXT

The Kingdom of God is the heart of the Gospel. It challenges all who hear of it to live in loving relation with God and with one another by reaching out in self-giving service to those in need. No other teaching of Jesus so dramatically expresses this challenge.

The parable He tells describing the Last Judgment surprises the Jews. They expected to be judged by whether or not they had kept the Law. If they kept the regulations and observed the Ten Commandments, they felt they would enter the Kingdom. They also expected preferential treatment because they were God's chosen. However, through this parable, Jesus leads them to realize that this future depends on their reactions to the needs of others.

Gathering all the nations, the Son of man *will separate them one from another as a shepherd separates the sheep from the goats.* Mixed flocks of goats and sheep are common, but in the evening, they are separated from each other. The more valuable sheep are placed in a position of honor *at his right hand.*

The blessed are welcomed into the Kingdom. They are considered children of

God. However, the surprise to Jesus' listeners is that the blessed are welcomed because they have served. By relieving human suffering and showing compassion, they have done God's work. *For I was thirsty . . . a stranger . . . naked . . . sick . . . in prison . . . and you came to me.* The faithful (the righteous) who had done this were surprised. They had not been aware that in their self-giving service to others they had been serving the Son of man.

The King answered them, *Truly, I say to you, as you did it to one of the least of these my brethen, you did it to me.* Jesus disclosed His interest in the needy and the suffering. In serving the unfortunate, we serve Him, the Christ. However, in refusing to serve others, we refuse to serve Christ. The sin Jesus condemns is the failure to see the opportunity to serve. Judgment of this failure is severe.

Depart from me, you cursed, into the eternal fire prepared for the devil. The unsympathetic and calloused sinners who are guilty of neglect of the needy and the suffering are banished. These guilty ones attempt a defense of their actions. *Lord, when did we see thee hungry or thirsty or a stranger or naked or sick or in prison, and did not minister to thee?* If they had recognized Him, they insist, they would have gladly served Him. However, they did not know that Jesus had identified so completely with the needy and suffering people. *Truly, I say to you, as you did it not to one of the least of these, you did it not to me.* They failed to minister to their King and their Lord by failing to serve their needy fellow people. Those who have been callous are sent *away to eternal punishment, but the righteous into eternal life.*

This parable addresses the future, but it also concerns the present. We are held accountable to God for what we do and for what we neglect to do. The actions commended in this parable are simple acts of service. The sin condemned is the failure to serve others in need.

SUGGESTIONS TO TEACHERS

Margaret Mitchell whose novel, *Gone With the Wind,* was a sensational best-seller in 1936, shared many qualities with Scarlet O'Hara, her famous fictional character. A neurotic and immature egoist, Margaret Mitchell never grew or wrote after publishing *Gone With the Wind,* her sole accomplishment. One biographer stated that the self-centered Mitchell could never "endure a conversation of which she was not the subject."

We all like to talk about ourselves. Jesus counters this form of selfishness by a call for concern for others. In fact, He insists that as citizens of His Kingdom, the reign of God, we understand that concern for others is a cardinal principle of Christian living.

This is the heart of the lesson for this week. Reread the well-known passage in Matthew 25:31–46, and develop your lesson around these points:

1. *SENTENCE WITH SURPRISE.* In the parable of the Last Judgment, everyone is astonished at who is welcomed and who is not—and *why!* Many who assumed that they were "saved" are surprised to find they are rejected, and vice-versa. Your class should be given time to ponder the meaning of the parable. Do not turn it into an allegory. Let the element of the unexpected sink in.

2. *SERVICE WITH SUPPLIES.* Call attention to the way judgment is administered. It is on whether a concern for others has been shown. And emphasize the way that concern is shown—through a practical, down-to-earth attending to the needs of others. A concern for others means food, water, medicines, warm clothing, personal attention. Ask whether our inclination to delegate caring to the "experts" or to leave it up to the agencies or government is consistent with Jesus' parable.

3. *SOLICITUDE OR DEMISE.* Jesus' parable (and other teachings on the principles of Christian living) have a "do this—or else!" ring to them. "Serve and care, or perish!" Those who do not have concern for others separate themselves from God. And this means spiritual death.

4. *SAVIOR IN DISGUISE.* Have your class people remark on the way Jesus travels incognito. In the parable, the people do not recognize that they have given or withheld the cup of cold water to the Lord Himself. Jesus is found in the person of the one in need! Allow sufficient time in your lesson to reflect in detail who the needy are in your community. Where do your people think they would find Jesus in the world today?

TOPIC FOR ADULTS
WAYS CHRISTIANS SERVE

Christ's Nominations. " 'Inasmuch as you did it to one of the least of these my brethren, you did it to me.' No more beautiful words have ever been spoken, nor have any others given us clearer direction as to what we are to do with ourselves in our passage through the world. They tell us that only in our service of our needy human brethren can our loving gratitude to God find outlet in action. God has, as it were, nominated these as his proxy, and what I would fain have given to him had he needed it, I must now give to them. It will be remembered that when in 1925 George Bernard Shaw was offered the Nobel Prize of some £8,000 in recognition of his literary eminence, he replied at once that while gratefully accepting the compliment he had no need of the money and would like it to be applied rather for the encouragement of other and younger writers who had not yet made their name and did need the money badly. It was as if he had said, 'Inasmuch as you give it to the least of these my literary brethren, you give it to me.' He nominated a definite class as his proxy, and Jesus did no less; but his nominations were (a) those who lack food or drink, (b) those who are insufficiently clad, (c) strangers (or, as we might say today, displaced persons and refugees), (d) those who are sick (and there is no more authentically and originally Christian way of employing our time than going to see people when they are sick), (e) those who are in prison (and for us that would include the inmates of concentration camps). Elsewhere he adds (f) little children—'Whosoever receives one such little child in my name, receives me.' Nor does he allow any distinction between what is thus done to him the Son and what is done to God the Father: 'He who recieves me receives him who sent me.' "—John Baillie, excerpted from *The Sense of the Presence of God.* Copyright © 1962 F. Jewel Baillie. Reprinted with the permission of Charles Scribner's Sons.

Sign on the Wall. General William Booth, the founder of the movement extending Christ's concern to the slum-dwellers of England which grew into the world-famous Salvation Army, kept a sign on the wall of his small, spartan office. The words of this sign read:

SOME WANT TO LIVE AND WORK WITHIN
THE SOUND OF CHAPEL BELL:
I WANT TO RUN A RESCUE SHIP WITHIN A YARD OF HELL.

What better way of describing the response every Christian should have to Christ's call for concern to others!

What inscription would you choose to emblazon on the wall of your office?

Suffer the Little Children. Rep. George Miller, Chairman of the House Select Committee on Children, Youth, and Families, states: The ranks of the poor have grown so that now more than one in every five children in the nation lives in poverty ($9,862 or less in 1982 for a family of four). Among blacks, one of every two children lives in poverty: among Hispanics, one of every three. Approximately 12.5 million children (one in every five) live with their mothers only. The increase is due to a rise in divorce and out-of-wedlock births. The number of babies born outside of marriage has more than quadrupled since 1950, when 142,000 such babies were born. In 1980, almost one in five births was to an unmarried woman. There were 666,000 such births that year. There are 5.87 million families in the U.S. headed by a female. Almost 50% of all black families are headed by a woman. Nearly 8.5% of black children live with neither parent. More than 20% of all children live in other than a two-parent family.

These facts come from the first report of his committee, "U.S. Children and Their Families: Current Conditions and Recent Trends," which was compiled by Child Trends Inc., a nonprofit research organization.

Questions for Pupils on the Next Lesson. 1. Is there any limit to the number of times a person must forgive another? 2. Why did Jesus put so much emphasis on forgiving others? 3. Why do so many people tend to harbor grudges? 4. Is forgiveness a sign of weakness and revenge a sign of strength? 5. What often happens when nations set out to take revenge on one another?

TOPIC FOR YOUTH
HOW ABOUT OTHERS?

How God Comes to Us. "God comes to us in the hungry man we do not have to feed, comes to us in the lonely man we do not have to comfort, comes to us in all the desperate human need of people everywhere that we are always free to turn our backs upon. It means that God puts Himself at our mercy not only in the sense of the suffering that we can cause Him by our blindness and coldness and cruelty, but the suffering that we can cause Him simply by suffering ourselves."—Frederick Buechner, *The Hungering Dark,* Seabury Press, 1969.

Impact of Christ. Maude Royden, a great English woman preacher, recently related how in 1928 she was told of the dreadful sufferings of the wounded Chinese soldiers who had been brought back from some battle between the then powerful war lords, laid out on the station platform and left there throughout a cruelly cold autumn night. Many of them were found dead in the morning. The others were removed to hospitals. She asked eagerly who took pity on them at last, and was told that it was a philanthropic Buddhist society. She supposed her interlocutor read her feelings in her face, for he said: "You wish it had been a Christian society?" and she admitted that she did. He said, "You needn't mind— it is only the impact of Christian teaching on Chinese life that has created a Buddhist philanthropic society at all."

No One Cared. "Yesterday was an old man's birthday. He was ninety-one. He awakened earlier than usual, bathed, shaved and put on his best clothes. Surely they would come today, he thought. He didn't take his daily walk to the gas station to visit with the oldtimers of the community, because he wanted to be right there when they came. He sat on the front porch with a clear view of the road so he could see them coming. Surely they would come today. He decided to skip his noon nap because he wanted to be up when they came. He has six children. Two of his daughters and their married children live within four miles. They hadn't been to see him for such a long time. But today was his birthday. Surely they would come today. At suppertime he refused to cut the cake and asked that the ice cream be left in the freezer. He wanted to wait and have dessert with them when they came. About 9 o'clock he went to his room and got ready for bed. His last words before turning out the lights were, 'promise to wake me up when they come.' It was his birthday and he was ninety-one." (A Heavy-Hearted Observer)

Questions for Pupils on the Next Lesson. 1. How many times must you forgive someone who has hurt you? 2. Why does Jesus put such stress on forgiving others? 3. What happens when you harbor a grudge? 4. Is revenge a sign of strength and forgiveness a sign of weakness? 5. Why is it so hard to forgive someone who has really hurt you?

LESSON IX—JANUARY 26

BE FORGIVING

Background Scripture: Matthew 18:21–35; John 8:2–11
Devotional Reading: Psalms 85:1–7

KING JAMES VERSION

MATTHEW 18 21 Then came Peter to him, and said, Lord, how oft shall my brother sin against me, and I forgive him? till seven times?

22 Jesus saith unto him, I say not unto thee, Until seven times: but, Until seventy times seven.

23 Therefore is the kingdom of heaven likened unto a certain king, which would take account of his servants.

24 And when he had begun to reckon, one was brought unto him, which owed him ten thousand talents.

25 But forasmuch as he had not to pay, his lord commanded him to be sold, and his wife, and children, and all that he had, and payment to be made.

26 The servant therefore fell down, and worshipped him, saying, Lord, have patience with me, and I will pay thee all.

27 Then the lord of that servant was moved with compassion, and loosed him, and forgave him the debt.

28 But the same servant went out, and found one of his fellowservants, which owed him a hundred pence: and he laid hands on him, and took *him* by the throat, saying, Pay me that thou owest.

29 And his fellowservant fell down at his feet, and besought him, saying, Have patience with me, and I will pay thee all.

30 And he would not: but went and cast him into prison, till he should pay the debt.

31 So when his fellowservants saw what was done, they were very sorry, and came and told unto their lord all that was done.

32 Then his lord, after that he had called him, said unto him, O thou wicked servant, I forgave thee all that debt, because thou desiredst me:

33 Shouldest not thou also have had compassion on thy fellowservant, even as I had pity on thee?

34 And his lord was wroth, and delivered him to the tormentors, till he should pay all that was due unto him.

35 So likewise shall my heavenly Father do also unto you, if ye from your hearts forgive not every one his brother their trespasses.

REVISED STANDARD VERSION

MATTHEW 18 21 Then Peter came up and said to him, "Lord, how often shall my brother sin against me, and I forgive him? As many as seven times?" 22 Jesus said to him, "I do not say to you seven times, but seventy times seven.

23 "Therefore the kingdom of heaven may be compared to a king who wished to settle accounts with his servants. 24 When he began the reckoning, one was brought to him who owed him ten thousand talents; 25 and as he could not pay, his lord ordered him to be sold, with his wife and children and all that he had, and payment to be made. 26 So the servant fell on his knees, imploring him, 'Lord, have patience with me, and I will pay you everything.' 27 And out of pity for him the lord of that servant released him and forgave him the debt. 28 But that same servant, as he went out, came upon one of his fellow servants who owed him a hundred denarii; and seizing him by the throat he said, 'Pay what you owe.' 29 So his fellow servant fell down and besought him, 'Have patience with me, and I will pay you.' 30 He refused and went and put him in prison till he should pay the debt. 31 When his fellow servants saw what had taken place, they were greatly distressed, and they went and reported to their lord all that had taken place. 32 Then his lord summoned him and said to him, 'You wicked servant! I forgave you all that debt because you besought me; 33 and should not you have had mercy on your fellow servant, as I had mercy on you?' 34 And in anger his lord delivered him to the jailers, till he should pay all his debt. 35 So also my heavenly Father will do to every one of you, if you do not forgive your brother from your heart."

KEY VERSE: *Judge not, and you will not be judged; condemn not, and you will not be condemned; forgive, and you will be forgiven. Luke 6:37.*

HOME DAILY BIBLE READINGS

Jan.	20.	M.	*Speaking Truth in Love.* Ephesians 4:25–32.
Jan.	21.	T.	*Putting on Compassion.* Colossians 3:12–17.
Jan.	22.	W.	*Love More Than Sinners Do.* Luke 6:32–38.
Jan.	23.	T.	*The Heart Speaks Through the Mouth.* Luke 5:39–49.
Jan.	24.	F.	*Learning to Forgive.* Matthew 18:21–35.
Jan.	25.	S.	*Ministering to Others.* 2 Corinthians 2:5–17.
Jan.	26.	S.	*Be Good Stewards.* Luke 12:41–48.

BACKGROUND

A Jewish rabbi was addressing a church Singles' Group. He was gracious and learned. His presentation on Judaism was well-received. During the question-answer session afterward, he was asked how he, a Jew, would define Christianity. He smiled and said, "With us in Judaism, everything is orthopraxis, that is, correct action. With you in Christianity, everything is orthodoxy, that is, correct doctrines."

How would you have responded to this rabbi's statement?

The next five lessons should clarify your thinking on this topic. For us Christians, it is both orthodoxy and orthopraxis! This unit of five sessions will focus on Jesus' practical directions for His disciples. The daily doing and details of a disciplined living will be emphasized. Jesus, who was also called "rabbi," did not deal in hazy generalities or pious feelings. He gave specific guidance on how His followers show their response to Him.

Running throughout everything that Jesus ever said is the note of forgiveness. Just as the British Navy's ropes, lines, and hawsers are woven with a red strand through them, Jesus' teachings carry the blood-colored strand of mercy.

Jesus, of course, was not the only person to teach forgiveness. However, He was the only person to live forgiveness. That blood-red strand of mercy in His teachings was woven into them by His own example. He forgave! Reflecting on the meaning of the Cross and Resurrection after those events, all of His followers comprehended the extraordinary fact of divine grace. Through Jesus, Matthew, Mark, Luke, and a host of others realized the miracle of God's unmerited mercy in their lives!

Later, writing their accounts of the meaning of Jesus Christ in their own experience as well as for others, these authors recalled the heavy stress Jesus laid on being forgiving. God had not condemned them, but accepted them. Forgiven by God through Jesus Christ, they knew that they had to practice forgiveness in daily living!

In today's lesson, Peter is the central character. He smugly assumes that he was exemplary because he was willing to "forgive" another seven times. After all, even the rabbis taught that four times was enough. Peter privately congratulated himself for being so magnanimous.

Jesus responded to this disciple in the kindergarten stage of learning the meaning of grace. Jesus told Peter that forgiveness had no limits. "Seventy times seven" means that the mathematics of mercy are beyond human calculation. The parable of the Unforgiving Servant lights up the significance of receiving and granting forgiveness.

NOTES ON THE PRINTED TEXT

Only Matthew records this long sermon of Jesus' to the disciples. In it Jesus gives the disciples some directions. His chief concern is the mutual and unlimited forgiveness that must be demonstrated by the disciples at all times. Jesus' words are triggered by a question from Peter.

Lord, how often shall my brother sin against me, and I forgive him? As many as seven times? For Peter, forgiveness had its limits. The rabbis had taught that a man should forgive a maximum of four times. Peter attempts to exceed the Jewish regulations by offering seven pardons, but it still is not enough. *Jesus said to him, I do not say to you seven times, but seventy times seven.* Jesus insisted that there must be no limits to forgiveness. This was part of the challenge issued with the Coming of the Kingdom of God. He reiterates this challenge with yet another teaching on forgiveness.

Jesus told of *a king who wished to settle accounts with his servants.* In rabbinic parables, a king often stood for God. In Jesus' parable, one servant was brought to the king because he owed him an incredible amount of money. The amount owed was almost ten million dollars. The servant admitted that he could not pay his debts. So the king ordered the servant and his wife and children to be sold so that the debt could be paid. Of course, selling the servant and his family into slavery would realize only a tiny fraction of the debt since the debt was beyond all imagination.

The servant pleaded for mercy. Adopting an attitude of submissiveness and subservience, he pleaded, *Lord, have patience with me, and I will repay you everything.* The use of this particular verb *to have patience* is used in reference to God's patiently giving more opportunities for repentance. The servant's plea for more time to pay is one that he cannot possibly hope to fulfill.

However, the king was more than patient. *Out of pity for him the lord of that servant released him and forgave him the debt.* The king canceled the debt and released the servant of his loan.

The servant promptly proved heartless towards a fellow servant who owed him only twenty dollars. The fellow servant *fell down and besought him, "have patience with me, and I will pay you,"* but the heartless servant refused to grant the request he himself had just used. He had the debtor thrown into prison. There, the freedom to work, earn money, and eventually pay off his debt was denied him.

The attitude of the servant is astonishing and inconsistent considering the forgiveness he has recently received. The unforgiving servant's failure to forgive others indicated his own unworthiness to receive forgiveness from others. After receiving forgiveness, it was his duty to forgive.

He is told exactly this by a furious king. The distressed, literally grieving, friends of the imprisoned servant reported to the king all that had taken place. The angry lord summoned the unforgiving servant. *Should not you have had mercy on your fellow servant as I had mercy on you?*

Jesus was teaching the vital importance of learning to forgive others. The duty of the servant to forgive was linked directly to the forgiveness given him. "I had mercy, so you must have mercy, too."

Jesus teaches that those who receive God's pardon must show the same forgiving attitude toward others.

SUGGESTIONS TO TEACHERS

In sports parlance, a grudge match is an event in which two contestants are trying to avenge previous grievances or losses. The participants in a grudge match are not playing because of love of the game but primarily to get even.

Most people turn the game of life into a dreary grudge match. Ask your class members for personal anecdotes from their own experiences of persons they've known about or heard about who have used most of their energies to seeking revenge or to thinking themselves slighted or offended.

Jesus' directions for His disciples, the basis for the next five lessons, rule out the vengeful attitude and call for forgiveness. Today's lesson calls for a thorough study of forgiving others.

1. *MATHEMATICS OF MERCY.* "How many times must I forgive?" Look at Matthew 18:21, 22, where Peter tries to reduce forgiveness to a matter of arithmetic. Peter assumes that he is being magnanimous by going far beyond the required number of times of forgiving another. Seven times was being truly generous. Jesus' reply, of course, means that there can be no limit to the times a disciple of His will forgive another. *"Seventy times seven!"* You may even want to try to introduce some role playing at this point in your lesson, and have members of the class act out Peter's part by using their own words. Be sure that Jesus' stern demand of mercy without measure is understood.

2. *PARABLE OF PATIENCE.* Move on to an investigation of the Parable of the Unforgiving Servant (Matthew 18:23–35). This vivid vignette or picture story may also be a subject for impromptu play-acting on the part of some in your class. Allow plenty of time to talk over the way the servant failed to take his cue from the merciful king. Stress to the class that God's graciousness toward us is the reason and motive for our forgiveness of others. Likewise, remind the class that failure to extend forgiveness is to lose it for yourself!

3. *SOCIETY OF SINNERS.* The story in John 8:2–11 about Jesus and the woman caught in adultery offers another view of Jesus and His forgiveness. Help your people to comprehend that no one may dare presume that he or she can condemn someone else. Jesus' comment, "Let him who is without sin cast the first stone" (John 8:7) makes clear that we are a society of sinners. Each of us needs God's mercy! Therefore, Be Forgiving!

TOPIC FOR ADULTS
BE FORGIVING

Symbol of Forgiveness. A survivor of the nuclear holocaust who was a junior high-school student in Hiroshima on August 6, 1945 and is now a reporter, wrote: "My father was never found. I don't know where he died. . . . My mother went through the suffering of a typical hibakusha for two months. When she died, she was only skin and bones. . . . As I stood in the charred ruins that once had been our house, I saw a mound of white ashes where my father's bookcase used to stand. . . . The dead totaled 140,000 at the end of 1945 and reached 200,000 at the end of 1950. . . . It is so simple to blame the United States. . . . But had Japan possessed the same bomb, she would have used it. This is war. . . . Repay malice with malice and you get trapped in a vicious circle."

Christians in both Japan and America sensed the need to break the vicious circle of hurt and hate. Malice could not be allowed to supplant forgiveness.

In January, 1946, Dr. John MacLean of Richmond, Virginia, preached a sermon expressing sorrow over Hiroshima and Nagasaki and suggested Christians make gifts as a tangible expression of the desire for reconciliation. Japanese Christians' highest priority was a new university. Japan's international Christian University came into existence in 1952. Since that time, this institution has been a living, growing symbol of Christ's forgiveness not only within Japan but to the entire world.

A Check for the "Enemy's" Missions. Forgiveness must be more than feelings. Forgiveness must be demonstrated—especially toward the enemy. This kind of mercy was shown in the dark days of 1941. War had engulfed Europe. Britain and Germany were enemies. All German funds were frozen in Germany, and German churches were unable to send a single pfennig to support their Protestant mission work around the world. Then a miracle of forgiveness occurred. A Scotsman whose country was deeply involved in the war sent a generous check to the Edinburgh headquarters of the Scottish mission work, stipulating that the check was to be used wherever *German* missions were in peril of being closed for lack of funds. This act of forgiveness caught the attention of other Christians. As a result, many others contributed to a project expressly set up for "orphan missions," or missionary outposts of German Christians, so that not one mission station stopped work because of lack of funds. Here was forgiveness toward the "enemy" in action!

See Christ's Life in You. Rabindranath Tagore, the Bengali poet and literary critic, had a profound effect on literary and cultural life in India. A practicing Hindu, he also spent much of his time teaching and meditating at a school he founded. In 1913, Tagore won the Nobel prize for literature. Tagore was frequently asked to address audiences on the subject of religion. Although Hindu, he had a deep respect for the person of Jesus and Christian teachings on forgiveness. Once someone asked why he could not become Christian. The Indian writer replied, "On that day when we see Christ living *His* life in you, we Hindus will flock to your Christ."

Christ's life was essentially a life of forgiveness. When others see us forgiving, they will encounter the vision of Jesus Christ that brings life. Forgive that His forgiveness may be known!

Questions for Pupils on the Next Lesson. 1. What is the starting point for all Christian ethics? 2. Is it all right to have an appreciation of yourself as well as others? 3. What are the limits of concern you show to others? 4. How do you try to express your love for God in practical terms? 5. According to Jesus' definition, who is your neighbor?

TOPIC FOR YOUTH
WHY SHOULD I FORGIVE?

Healing for a Broken Land. Some of the most remarkable instances of transformation through forgiveness have been occurring in Northern Ireland. Although the world press has concentrated on reporting violence and atrocities that have taken a dreadful toll in lives and injuries over the past years, Christian prison visitors are reporting increased receptivity to the Gospel on the part of inmates, according to Prison Fellowship.

It is estimated that dozens of imprisoned terrorists have become Christians in recent years. That number includes both IRA and Protestant hardline inmates. Present at a symposium in 1983 were two inmates from Maggilligan Prison. One had been an IRA terrorist who had been sentenced to ten years for his activities. He had participated during his imprisonment in the well-publicized blanket and "dirty" protest and spent fifty-five days on a hunger strike in 1981. He told the symposium of his conversion and appeared there with a converted Protestant inmate. Asked how the two would have responded to each other if they had met prior to their conversion, Lian, the former IRA member, replied that they would have attempted to shoot each other.

Prison Fellowship of Northern Ireland also sponsored a meeting in Downpatrick, where St. Patrick is thought to be buried. Those who attended one meeting witnessed a memorable demonstration of Christian reconciliation when a Protestant Christian mother, whose daughter had been shot last year by a terrorist, embraced the former terrorist who had become a Christian. "Only Christ can heal our broken land," she said as she clasped the young man's hand.

Cost of Vengeance. "Why Should I Forgive?" some may ask. One answer is to ask that person to consider the alternative. Vengeance costs. Vengeance destroys. Only forgiveness builds and creates. Any way except forgiveness brings ruin. For example, consider this true story of ballplayer John McGraw. In May, 1894, the legendary John McGraw, then with the Baltimore Orioles, got into a fight with Boston's third baseman. Soon both teams were battling, and the warfare spread to the stands, which were promptly set on fire. The entire ballpark burned to the ground, along with 170 other Boston buildings. The memories of that incident were so bitter that when the New York Giants—with McGraw managing—won the National League title in 1904, McGraw refused to play in the World Series against the American League champion Boston Red Sox.

Pilgrimage of Reconciliation. A few years ago the head of the Taize Ecumenical Community told a gathering of "pilgrims" in New York that in the midst of political and international conflict "the gaps are getting wider, the divisions are increasing in the human family. One of the consequences of this is that throughout the world, there is more and more discouragement, crippling discouragement, the temptation par excellence of our time," said Brother Roger Schutz, the Swissborn Protestant monk who founded the monastic community in France forty years ago. His address was delivered to an audience overflowing the aisles of St. Patrick's Cathedral in New York. Some 4,000 Christians from Protestant and Catholic churches all over the New York metropolitan area converged there in a Pilgrimage of Reconciliation. Noting the sharp political and theological divisions within the Christian faith, the gray-haired, sixty-five-year-old monk proposed a "necessary precondition" to reconciliation, namely: "getting out of the habit of thinking that there always has to be an opponent, someone who is right and someone who is wrong." Rather than engage in fruitless confrontations," Brother Roger urged the crowd to "set out toward one another, making a pilgrimage to a place of worship where you can pray together, with or without words."

Questions for Pupils on the Next Lesson. 1. Is it all right to have an appreciation for yourself as well as others? 2. Are there risks involved in caring for others? 3. Are there limits to the concern you should show for others? 4. According to Luke 10, who is your neighbor? 5. In an increasingly pluralistic society, what is involved in loving other people?

LESSON X—FEBRUARY 2

LOVE YOUR NEIGHBOR

Background Scripture: Luke 10:25–37
Devotional Reading: James 2:8–13

KING JAMES VERSION

LUKE 10   25 And, behold, a certain lawyer stood up, and tempted him, saying Master, what shall I do to inherit eternal life?

26 He said unto him, What is written in the law? how readest thou?

27 And he answering said, Thou shalt love the Lord thy God with all thy heart, and with all thy soul, and with all thy strength, and with all thy mind; and thy neighbour as thyself.

28 And he said unto him, Thou hast answered right: this do, and thou shalt live.

29 But he, willing to justify himself, said unto Jesus, And who is my neighbour?

30 And Jesus answering said, A certain *man* went down from Jerusalem to Jericho, and fell among thieves, which stripped him of his raiment, and wounded *him*, and departed, leaving *him* half dead.

31 And by chance there came down a certain priest that way; and when he saw him, he passed by on the other side.

32 And likewise a Levite, when he was at the place, came and looked *on him*, and passed by on the other side.

33 But a certain Samaritan, as he journeyed, came where he was; and when he saw him, he had compassion *on him*,

34 And went to *him*, and bound up his wounds, pouring in oil and wine, and set him on his own beast, and brought him to an inn, and took care of him.

35 And on the morrow when he departed, he took out two pence, and gave *them* to the host, and said unto him, Take care of him: and whatsoever thou spendest more, when I come again, I will repay thee.

36 Which now of these three, thinkest thou, was neighbour unto him that fell among the thieves?

37 And he said, He that showed mercy on him. Then said Jesus unto him, Go, and do thou likewise.

REVISED STANDARD VERSION

LUKE 10   25 And behold, a lawyer stood up to put him to the test, saying, "Teacher, what shall I do to inherit eternal life?" 26 He said to him, "What is written in the law? How do you read?" 27 And he answered, "You shall love the Lord your God with all your heart, and with all your soul, and with all your strength, and with all your mind; and your neighbor as yourself." 28 And he said to him, "You have answered right; do this, and you will live."

29 But he, desiring to justify himself, said to Jesus, "And who is my neighbor?" 30 Jesus replied, "A man was going down from Jerusalem to Jericho, and he fell among robbers, who stripped him and beat him, and departed, leaving him half dead. 31 Now by chance a priest was going down that road; and when he saw him he passed by on the other side. 32 So likewise a Levite, when he came to the place and saw him, passed by on the other side. 33 But a Samaritan, as he journeyed, came to where he was; and when he saw him, he had compassion, 34 and went to him and bound up his wounds, pouring on oil and wine; then he set him on his own beast and brought him to an inn, and took care of him. 35 And the next day he took out two denarii and gave them to the innkeeper, saying, 'Take care of him; and whatever more you spend, I will repay you when I come back.' 36 Which of these three, do you think, proved neighbor to the man who fell among the robbers?" 37 He said, "The one who showed mercy on him." And Jesus said to him, "Go and do likewise."

KEY VERSE: *You shall love the Lord your God with all your heart, and with all your soul, and with all your strength, and with all your mind; and your neighbor as yourself.* Luke 10:27.

HOME DAILY BIBLE READINGS

Jan.   31.   F.   *Accept One Another.* Romans 15:1–3.
Feb.   1.   S.   *Love Your Brother.* 1 John 3:13–18.
Feb.   2.   S.   *Mercy Triumphs Over Judgment.* James 2:8–17.

BACKGROUND

Love your neighbor. Nobody can quarrel with this idea. Doesn't every religious leader worth his salt say this? Why spend an entire session on this ho-hum subject with which everyone agrees?

Jesus, as usual, lifted what seemed to be a commonplace idea to astonishing heights. However, He does not spin lofty theories. Jesus' teachings offer new insights on the definition of neighbor and also on obligation to neighbor.

The interview with the lawyer should have ended with this skilled debater either making Jesus look like a dunce or forcing Jesus to compliment him on his piety. The lawyer "stood up to put Jesus to the test" (Luke 10:25). When he found that he could not best Jesus in the thrust-and-parry of a verbal duel he tried to pin Jesus by demanding a definition of *neighbor.* He was startled when Jesus related the unforgettable parable of the three travelers coming upon the helpless victim on the Jericho road.

For all of Jesus' hearers, *neighbor* meant merely a fellow Jew. Neighborliness stopped with one's next-of-kin. In fact, the Pharisees and other ultra-religious folks made certain that they didn't defile themselves by associating with any heathen non-Jews. In those times, one could always identify the religion of another person by glancing at the clothing. The tassels on the robe, like an identity card, stated who the other was. If the other was a Jew, he was a neighbor. But anyone else was suspect. After all, the temple authorities had laid down strict rules about associating with unclean outsiders.

One of the sidelights of Jesus' parable is that the victim on the notoriously dangerous Jericho road had been stripped. He had no robe, no tassels. The man could not be identified as a "neighbor." Furthermore, he was unconscious and could not speak. For all that any passerby could tell, he could have been a pagan Gentile. Part of the reasoning of the priest and the Levite to pass by on the other side of the naked, unconscious body in the road was that they could not risk polluting themselves by associating with a possible unclean non-Jew.

Jesus' point is, of course, that *anyone* in need is the lawyer's neighbor.

Furthermore, loving one's neighbor means *doing* for that person in need!

NOTES ON THE PRINTED TEXT

In the previous lesson, Peter wished to place limits on forgiveness. In today's lesson, there is an individual who wishes to place limits on his concern. The teaching begins with a question dealing with eternal life. The religious official asks a question of one he considers to be an unofficial teacher. He is testing Jesus to see whether Jesus can answer correctly. It is a typical question that would be asked by the pupils of a rabbi. *What shall I do to inherit eternal life?* Jesus, however, replies by directing the lawyer to the Old Testament. *What is written in the law?* The lawyer replies by reciting Deuteronomy 6:5 and Leviticus 19:18. *You shall love the Lord your God with all your heart, and with all your strength, and with all your mind; and you shall love your neighbor as yourself.* Having heard the lawyer respond to the very heart of Jewish religion, Jesus simply calls the lawyer to practice what he preaches. *You have answered right; do this and you will live.*

Having been made the fool, the lawyer continues to press Jesus. *Desiring to justify himself,* he wants to set limits on loving one's neighbor. By asking, *Who is my neighbor?* the lawyer implies that there are persons who do not warrant love.

Jesus responds with a parable. *A man was going down from Jerusalem to Jeri-*

cho. Jericho is seventeen miles east of Jerusalem in the Jordan valley. The twisting, narrow road runs through rocky, wilderness country cut with ravines. It is an area ideally suited for thieves. Not surprisingly, the lone traveler of Jesus' parable was attacked, stripped, beaten, robbed, and left to die from exposure in the hot sun. Even though the road was lonely, *by chance, a priest was going down that road.* Returning to Jericho after services at the Temple in Jerusalem and unwilling to defile himself or, perhaps, suspicious of an ambush by robbers, *he passed by on the other side.* By coincidence, *a Levite* also came long. Levites were Temple officials responsible for the liturgies in the Temple and for policing the Temple. They were a privileged group in Jewish society and part of the religious class. Lukan language implies that the Levite actually went up to the mugging victim to look at him. However, he, too, then *passed by on the other side.*

Jesus contrasts the first two travelers by speaking of a Samaritan. *Samaritan* was a dirty word. It was a vulgar epithet. Samaritans were despised and hated by the Jews. They were considered heretics. Relations were bad between the Jewish and Samaritan communities. However, the Samaritan *came to where he was; and when he saw him, he had compassion.* Using the simple emergency first aid skills of the ancient world, the Samaritan poured oil and wine on the wounds and then bound the wounds with bandages. The Samaritan mounted the man on his own animal and took him to an inn to care for him.

Having to resume his journey the next day, the Samaritan took steps to provide additional care for the injured man. He made an advanced payment for three weeks to the innkeeper with a promise of additional monies if required!

The lawyer is drawn into the story by being asked to offer the verdict. *Which of these three, do you think, proved neighbor to the man who fell among robbers?* The lawyer's question has been deliberately altered from, "Who is my neighbor?" to "Who was neighbor?" thus making a neighbor a state of being, a relationship.

Priggishly, the lawyer answered, *The one who showed mercy.* Even after hearing the parable, the lawyer still refused to say that foul word *Samaritan.*

Anyone needing aid or mercy is a neighbor. Any considerations, be they national or racial, are irrelevant. Aiding the needy takes precedence over religious scruples and self interests.

All that remains is to fulfill Jesus' command to *go and do likewise.* The Samaritan's love is an example to all of us. Christian ethics begin with a love of God. Love is then to be shown to others. Helping a neighbor is an expression of love for God. We must be prepared to be a neighbor to all.

SUGGESTIONS TO TEACHERS

"Love your neighbor." Perhaps you put these words in the same category as innocuous slogans like respecting the flag and supporting motherhood. As a teacher, you may feel little challenge to address this subject.

Spend a few minutes studying the scriptural passage. Get inside the thinking of the lawyer meeting Jesus. Ponder the details of Jesus' definition of *neighbor* and also Jesus' idea of loving the neighbor. You will begin to see that Jesus puts a radical new twist to the notion of neighbor-love.

1. *KEY QUESTIONS.* Kick off your lesson by noting the questions asked by the lawyer, "What shall I do to inherit eternal life?" and "Who is my neighbor?" Put these questions to your class. How do the members of the class answer them? How did Jesus? Point out that there is a connection between eternal life and love of neighbor.

2. *COSMIC CONCERN.* Be sure that your class understands the way Jesus defines *neighbor.* A neighbor, according to Him, is *anyone* in need. It does not matter who the other person is. In fact, part of the meaning of the Parable of the

Good Samaritan is that no one knew who the victim was on the side of the road. Since the person had been stripped of his clothing, his identity marks had been removed. No one could tell if he was friend or foe, rich or poor, Jew or Gentile. Everyone in Jesus' time would have excused the priest and Levite from seeing the victim as a neighbor because a neighbor was only a fellow Jew. Work your class discussion around to considering who "neighbors" are in our times, according to Jesus' definition. What about the victims whom we do not know personally in famine-torn areas of Africa? How about the street people in American cities?

3. *CARING COLLEAGUE.* One of the details that shocked Jesus' hearers was the fact that the hero of the story was, of all people, a Samaritan! To Jesus' associates, there was no such thing as a "good" Samaritan. Yet Jesus deliberately chooses to show that a despised outsider can demonstrate a love for neighbor that the self-righteous religious folk overlook. Take plenty of time to think about the reasons why the priest and the Levite passed by the man on the Jericho road. Were they going to church meetings? Were they unwilling to get involved? Didn't they want to get their hands dirty, handling a bloody, battered mugging victim? Did they think the man was dead and not want to contaminate themselves ritually? All three people on the road realized that loving a neighbor meant suffering an interruption. Are your class members able to accept interruptions as the cost of loving neighbors?

4. *CRUCIAL COMMAND.* Strike hard on the closing words, "Go and do likewise!" (10:37). Neighbor love is *doing* for the other person!

TOPIC FOR ADULTS
WHO IS MY NEIGHBOR?

Tasting the New Life. "Newark State Hospital, located some fifty miles east of Rochester, N.Y., is a tolerable institution for the mentally retarded. At least it was when I spent time there as a volunteer.

"I worked in a pilot program for eight blind, deaf, and retarded children. Prior to our program, these children existed without undue attention. (For that matter, without undue anything—who had time for excesses?) They were fed regularly, diapered frequently and bathed occasionally. To prevent them from running around and injuring themselves, they were, by the law of necessity, kept in their cribs day and night. Life for them was, as far as they knew, adequate. All the requirements were met.

"After a few weeks in our program, however, we noticed a change in our kids. We discovered that all of our charges were not as severely incapacitated as supposed. In fact, most possessed partial vision and several had only impaired hearing. One even seemed to have normal intelligence.

"Because we had been able to work with them specifically, attend to them individually and love them personally, they began to grow, emerging from their stifling cocoons. It didn't take any stupendous miracle for them to grow. It didn't even take our professional instruction to help bring them out. All it took was for us to care for each of them, day and night. Our kids eventually learned to run and prance around the ward.

"Our love for them had given them new life. We realized then how truly inadequate was their "adequate" existence in their cribs. What was formerly sufficient, satisfying all the requirements of life, had been exposed as woefully restrictive and incomplete. Our love had released them from the conformity to mere sufficiency; we had introduced them to the wonders without.

" 'And the blind shall see, the deaf shall hear.'

"Our kids prospered because they experienced our rather simple kind of love. We, too, prosper; we, too, emerge forth; we, too, see and hear and believe and realize new life—the redeemed life of spirit and truth—whenever we experience Christ's rather simple kind of love. It is not the great miracles or the incredible signs that induce faith, nor does it take our acknowledgment of the wise reasonableness of the Gospel for faith to be produced in our souls. No, it only takes the experience of Christ's concern, compassion, dedication. Christ came that we might live the redeemed life, that we might truly worship, that we, too, might run that race of faith.

"Tasting this new life, then, we realize how bland our former existence has been, even if our former life met the requirements of the moral code, even if our life was ethically responsible. It was still incomplete, still inadequate, still lacking—as when my kids spent their days and nights confined, by the law of necessity, to their cribs.

"The law proscribes, but the spirit of Christ's love prescribes. By his divine prescription we are healed and the way of life seems wondrously clear."—Robert J. Andrews, *Presbyterian Outlook*, 512 W. Main Street, Richmond, Va., March 8, 1982.

Settler Theology or Pioneer Theology? In Settler theology, the Christian is the settler. Her concern is to stay out of the sheriff's way. He tends a small garden. Her motto is Safey First. To him the courthouse is a symbol of security, order, and happiness.

In Pioneer theology the Christian is a pioneer. She is a person of risk and daring, hungry for adventure, new life. He is tough, rides hard, and knows how to handle himself through trials and danger. She enjoys the challenge of the trail. He dies with his boots on.

Man's Kindness Is Returned. A Dover, New Hampshire, variety store owner who erased unpaid charge accounts from his books to stimulate business has received money from people who read news reports about him. Ernest T.J. Peters, owner of E.J.'s Variety store, said he has received letters containing cash.

"God bless you," one of the letter writers said. "It was so good to see good news and love and forgiveness on the front-page amidst the reports of war, trouble and man's inhumanity to man." Postmarked Scranton, Pennsylvania, the letter continued: "I am sending you $20 to express in my own way the joy you gave me by your act of love. I owe you much more. May you prosper greatly. With respect and appreciation. A Scrantonian."

Peters, who said he canceled customers' debts hoping to lure back customers who might be staying away from his struggling store because of unpaid bills, said he gives the money to the Rochester Child Development Center in Rochester, New Hampshire, which he says has "performed miracles" for his nineteen-year-old son, Scott, who was brain-damaged at birth.

"I accept it graciously from the people," he said of the gifts. "I feel that people gave this to me to do what I wanted."

Kindness is loving your neighbor. Neighborliness such as Ernest Peters's kind evokes neighborly love from others! Christ means for us to find each other as neighbors, and show kindness.

Questions for Pupils on the Next Lesson. 1. How are your basic commitments to the Lord best shown? 2. What are the dangers of possessions, according to Jesus? 3. Exactly what does it mean to seek God's Kingdom? 4. What is the proper use of possessions? 5. On what do you base your decisions on how you spend your money and time?

TOPIC FOR YOUTH
YOU MEAN I HAVE TO LOVE?

Record Knockout. "Do you mean I have to love?" Jesus emphatically answers *yes.* Otherwise, your anger will eventually defeat you. You will be something like the fighter named Bigboy Blalock who managed to knock himself out in a prize-fight. It happened like this: Back in the early 1930s, C.D. "Bigboy" Blalock of Louisiana State University—a six-foot, six-inch giant of a boxer—was taking on a stocky fellow from Mississippi State. In the second round, Bigboy let loose a roundhouse. The Mississippi man stepped in, and his head caught Bigboy's arm inside the elbow. With the opponent's head acting as a lever, Bigboy's arm whipped around in almost full circle, connecting with haymaker force on Bigboy's own chin. He staggered, grabbed the rope, walked almost all the way around the ring, and fell flat for the count—the only prizefighter who ever knocked himself out with a right to his own jaw.

Your actions toward another always have reactions toward yourself. Love the other and you receive love. Hurt another and you hurt yourself! Whatever kind of a roundhouse you try to deliver toward another, whether the word or blow of anger, or whether the act of love and word of peace, it will come back to hurt or heal you!

Tips for Rude People. The former editor of the humor magazine, *National Lampoon,* is a young satirist and author named P.J. O'Rourke. O'Rourke has been visiting campuses speaking on "Modern Manners: Etiquette for Very Rude People." His lectures present amusing comments on behavior at food fights and other social gatherings, and on dressing "weird." He also claims to give tips on "how to get a meaningful relationship to mean less."

Although O'Rourke's snide remarks bring laughs, his speeches do not promote manners or relationships. Contrast his words to Jesus, compare O'Rourke's advice to the Lord's. Jesus sends us to our neighbor in love. Jesus calls us to take each other seriously. We may laugh at our foibles, but we treat each other with gentleness and good manners. These, after all, are simply love in action.

Sentence Sermons. "The test of our progress is not whether we add more to the abundance of those who have more; it is whether we provide enough for those who have too little."—Franklin D. Roosevelt in his second inaugural speech in 1937.

"The person who pursues revenge should dig two graves."— Anonyomous

Questions for Pupils on the Next Lesson. 1. Is success measured primarily in terms of wealth? 2. What guidelines do you follow in the way you spend your money and use your time? 3. Have you set any priorities for your life? If so, what are they? 4. Why did Jesus warn His followers about accumulating possessions?

LESSON XI—FEBRUARY 9

USE POSSESSIONS WISELY

Background Scripture: Matthew 6:19–21; Luke 12:13–21, 27–34
Devotional Reading: Luke 16:19–31

KING JAMES VERSION

LUKE 12 13 And one of the company said unto him, Master, speak to my brother, that he divide the inheritance with me.

14 And he said unto him, Man, who made me a judge or a divider over you?

15 And he said unto them, Take heed, and beware of covetousness: for a man's life consisteth not in the abundance of the things which he possesseth.

16 And he spake a parable unto them, saying, The ground of a certain rich man brought forth plentifully:

17 And he thought within himself, saying, What shall I do, because I have no room where to bestow my fruits?

18 And he said, This will I do: I will pull down my barns, and build greater; and there will I bestow all my fruits and my goods.

19 And I will say to my soul, Soul, thou hast much goods laid up for many years; take thine ease, eat, drink, *and* be merry.

20 But God said unto him, *Thou* fool, this night thy soul shall be required of thee: then whose shall those things be, which thou hast provided?

21 So *is* he that layeth up treasure for himself, and is not rich toward God.

27 Consider the lilies how they grow: they toil not, they spin not; and yet I say unto you, that Solomon in all his glory was not arrayed like one of these.

28 If then God so clothe the grass, which is to day in the field, and tomorrow is cast into the oven; how much more *will he clothe* you, O ye of little faith?

29 And seek not ye what ye shall eat, or what ye shall drink, neither be ye of doubtful mind.

30 For all these things do the nations of the world seek after: and your Father knoweth that ye have need of these things.

31 But rather seek ye the kingdom of God; and all these things shall be added unto you.

32 Fear not, little flock; for it is your Father's good pleasure to give you the kingdom.

33 Sell that ye have, and give alms; provide yourselves bags which wax not old, a treasure in the heavens that faileth not, where no thief approacheth, neither moth corrupteth.

34 For where your treasure is, there will your heart be also.

REVISED STANDARD VERSION

LUKE 12 13 One of the multitude said to him, "Teacher, bid my brother divide the inheritance with me." 14 But he said to him, "Man, who made me a judge or divider over you?" 15 And he said to them, "Take heed, and beware of all covetousness; for a man's life does not consist in the abundance of his possessions." 16 And he told them a parable, saying, "The land of a rich man brought forth plentifully; 17 and he thought to himself, 'What shall I do, for I have nowhere to store my crops?' 18 And he said, 'I will do this: I will pull down my barns, and build larger ones; and there I will store all my grains and my goods. 19 And I will say to my soul, Soul, you have ample goods laid up for many years; take your ease, eat, drink, be merry.' 20 But God said to him, 'Fool! This night your soul is required of you; and the things you have prepared, whose will they be?' 21 So is he who lays up treasure for himself, and is not rich toward God."

27 "Consider the lilies, how they grow; they neither toil nor spin; yet I tell you, even Solomon in all his glory was not arrayed like one of these. 28 But if God so clothes the grass which is alive in the field today and tomorrow is thrown into the oven, how much more will he clothe you, O men of little faith? 29 And do not seek what you are to eat and what you are to drink, nor be of anxious mind. 30 For all the nations of the world seek these things; and your Father knows that you need them. 31 Instead, seek his kingdom, and these things shall be yours as well.

32 "Fear not, little flock, for it is your Father's good pleasure to give you the kingdom. 33 Sell your possessions, and give alms; provide yourselves with purses that do not grow old, with a treasure in the heavens that does not fail, where no thief approaches and no moth destroys. 34 For where your treasure is, there will your heart be also."

KEY VERSE: Take heed, and beware of all covetousness; for a man's life does not consist in the abundance of his possessions. Luke 12:15.

HOME DAILY BIBLE READINGS

Feb.	3.	M.	*Treasures in Heaven.* Matthew 6:19–21, 25–32.
Feb.	4.	T.	*Good News for the Poor.* Luke 4:16–21.
Feb.	5.	W.	*The Rich Fool.* Luke 12:13–21.
Feb.	6.	T.	*Seek God's Kingdom.* Luke 12:27–34.
Feb.	7.	F.	*Sow Generously.* 2 Corinthians 9:6–15.
Feb.	8.	S.	*Be Generous and Willing to Share.* Leviticus 25:17, 35–38.
Feb.	9.	S.	*Giving and Receiving.* Acts 20:32–35; Hebrews 13:1–5.

BACKGROUND

Most of Jesus' disciples and hearers were poor people. They had few possessions. Some were fishermen—hard-working men like Peter and Andrew, James and John. All lived in a cash-poor economy. All paid oppressively heavy taxes. All came from the peasant classes. Except for an occasional Zacchaeus (who disposed of much of his wealth) or the nameless "rich, young ruler" (who couldn't bear to part with his wealth), Jesus' audiences were made up of people with little money and few worldly goods. His twelve disciples certainly owned little except a few tools or implements and articles of clothing.

Jesus knew that they often thought about money, security, success, and material comfort. He also knew that their culture put great emphasis on these. It seemed obvious to everyone that the rich man was to be envied. In fact, it appeared that God was rewarding the rich person. Some even reasoned that wealth was a sign of God's favor.

Don't ever think that Jesus dealt only with ethereal "spiritual" matters. He talked often about money. In fact, some New Testament scholars declare that almost one out of four verses in the Gospel has to do with possessions.

The reason? Jesus knew the human situation better than any other teacher before or since. He understood that our sense of anxiety and insecurity in life will never be cured by accumulating money and possessions.

Furthermore, Jesus realized the dangers of centering one's life on money and possessions. Living to become rich and successful means pronouncing one's own doom.

To illustrate, Jesus related a parable in which the main character is a fantastically successful man of the world. Jesus' listeners must have heard the details with wide eyes and gaping jaws. Then Jesus inserted the hooker; He stated God called this man of means a fool! With few swift phrases, Jesus points up the folly of the man's life!

We think that we're here to make a living; Jesus insists we're here to make a life!

NOTES ON THE PRINTED TEXT

The request for a ruling on an inheritance becomes the occasion for this direction for the disciples and the crowd concerning material possessions. Like the parable of the Good Samaritan, this parable is an example story. It is an illustration drawn from reality which in effect says: "Go and do (or do not do) likewise."

Teacher, bid my brother divide the inheritance with me. Jesus is called upon to intervene in a dispute. An elder brother has refused to share a portion of his father's inheritance. Jewish Law was specific. The elder son was to receive two-thirds of the inheritance and a younger son one-third. The younger boy is unhappy about this. Such disputes that arose concerning inheritances were settled by appealing to a rabbi. However, Jesus refused. He was opposed to the covetous desire that underlaid the request.

Jesus urges the disciples to guard against greed. The real life of a person is not dependent on the abundance of his possessions. In fact, this greed directs the individual to the wrong things in life instead of what really matters, which is being "rich towards God."

Jesus tells a parable showing the futility of avarice. *The land of a certain rich man brought forth plentifully.* The rich man's estate had yielded so well that he discovered that he did not have enough permanent storage facilities for all the grain. *He thought to himself . . . what shall I do?* The rich man's soliloquy showed his greed and lack of concern for those around him. Notice, for instance, the heavy use of "I" and "my." The rich man's solution was to tear down the existing barns and build bigger ones.

Having solved his problem of storing his wealth, the rich man relaxed and selfishly enjoyed life. *Soul, you have ample goods laid up for many years; take your ease, eat, drink, be merry.*

Such an attitude angered God. God addressed the rich man personally. *Fool! This very night your soul is required of you.* That very night the rich man's life was taken from him. Though he had prepared for his own comfort, he had not prepared for his ultimate destiny. *The things you have prepared, whose will they be?* Now his possessions were of no value to him. His life could not be measured in terms of his possessions or the accumulation of his wealth. In God's eyes, the rich man was poor. Seeking God's Kingdom or being "rich toward God" should have been the man's only foundation for living.

Disciples are not to be anxiously concerned about earthly possessioins. God will supply them with food (vs. 22–24). *Do not seek what you are to eat and what you are to drink, nor be of anxious mind. Your Father knows what you need.* God will clothe them. If God gives to the flowers an appearance far beyond that of Solomon, can He not be trusted to clothe His disciples? *Consider the lilies . . . even Solomon in all his glory was not arrayed like one of these.*

Instead, seek his kingdom. Be a seeker of the Kingdom, not a seeker of material things. Instead of laying up treasure on earth, *sell your possessions, and give alms.* Proper use of possessions must include serving the needs of others. True disciples of Jesus have a special ministry to the poor and the oppressed. *Provide yourselves with purses that do not grow old.* Instead of materialistic treasures, the disciples are to lay up imperishable treasures in heaven by doing for others. These treasures cannot be stolen by a thief nor attacked by a moth. Trusting in this treasure yields God's blessings. *For where your treasure is, there will your heart be.* If the disciples seek the heavenly treasure, their affections are directed in the right manner. If they are bent on building up a store of earthly treasures, their hearts are not directed toward God. Disciples who continue to hold onto their wealth are not seeking the Kingdom of God.

SUGGESTIONS TO TEACHERS

Many people have amassed fortunes. It seems significant, however, that we remember mostly those who shared their wealth. There were others in the nineteenth and early twentieth century who made a lot of money, but the ones who endowed universities or established foundations are the names which have endured. It almost seems that history bears out what Jesus taught!

This brings us to today's Sunday-School lesson on the wise use of possessions. We who possess so much realize that we are always in danger of finding that our possessions possess us. We need to learn Jesus' directions for disciples on the place of money and priorities.

1. *PERISHING VS. PERMANENT.* We have the notion that if we acquire enough things that we will have security. We think (mistakenly) that we can buy permanence in the midst of change. Jesus brusquely dismisses these ideas as nonsense. We live a transient existence here on earth. Everything we think we own

will perish. To get these points across, ask your class to state what each person thinks is lasting and valuable. Then inquire how many years that will remain. Jesus warns that all earthly treasures are temporary! Ask the class to state what each believes "treasures in heaven" may be (Matthew 6:20).

2. *PLACE FOR THE HEART.* Jesus insists that where one's treasure is, there his or her heart will also be (Matthew 6:21). If this be the case, does this mean that the hearts of your class members are fixed on a sporty automobile, a fancy wardrobe, a growing stock portfolio, a vacation cottage, or what? You may have each person take the "checkbook test" by listing on what each spends his or her money not required for food or housing. This is an indicator of where one's heart may be!

3. *PERIL OF GREED.* Look at Luke's record of Jesus' words on greed, especially the Parable of the Rich Fool. Ask whether this man would be called a fool in our society. Have your class put the parable in a contemporary setting by rewriting its details to fit our culture's ideas of a successful person.

4. *PRIORITIES IN LIFE.* Budget enough time in your lesson to allow your people to do some priority-setting in the light of Jesus' words about seeking first the Kingdom (Luke 12:32). What is most important in life to each and why? Perhaps a pencil and paper for each to create a personal list would give this exercise more meaning.

5. *PLACE OF POSSESSIONS.* The Luke passage also makes clear that the real purpose of possessions is to be able to share with others. The hoarder worries about holding on to what he thinks he owns. The citizen of God's reign hangs loose with possessions. God's person can part with possessions to help others. That person also will not be a worrier. In fact, putting God's realm first is the best antidote to anxiety! Therefore, use possessions wisely.

TOPIC FOR ADULTS
SHARE YOUR POSSESSIONS

The Little Church That Wanted a Steeple. "Once upon a time a preacher was called to a tiny country church. In the nave there was a tower that went up into the sky—and suddenly stopped. It looked like the workmen had just stopped, because there was no steeple and it was quite obvious that there should be one. Everyone thought that there should be one. The committee that called the new preacher said to him: 'One thing we want you to do is to start a fund-raising drive to build a steeple.'

"Everyone was excited when, in the very first sermon, the minister announced he would begin a campaign to raise money to build a steeple. And he did. There were bake sales, rummage sales, pledge drives and even guest speakers. Soon the money was raised.

"On the Sunday that the meeting was to follow morning worship, Mrs. Smith stood up during the time for pastoral concerns. She told about her son Jimmy, who was very sick with a disease of the bone. He could be cured if he could have the proper treatment, but it was expensive. Needless to say, they didn't vote for a steeple that day; instead, the congregation saved Jimmy's life with their steeple fund.

"The money for the steeple was raised again with barbeque suppers, handicraft sales, and more pledge drives. The day before the congregational meeting to vote on the steeple a refugee family arrived in town without a penny. This time the steeple fund went to help a family establish a home that was safe and free.

"Through the years the steeple fund was raised five more times altogether. One year it provided money to build a mission in Africa. Still another time it was used to help several families who were out of work. Another time it went to help a family that had been burned out. After a long pastorate the minister died, and the steeple still had not been built. He hadn't kept his promise to the people that he would help them raise money for a steeple.

"But he hadn't failed in his calling. He had nurtured a church of people who cared for and loved one another."—M. Gray Clark.

Prevented from Entering the Front Door. We used to have a neighbor named Harold who collected things. Originally, Harold sold most of the things he gathered. He would then use the proceeds to buy and sell more articles. At first, Harold claimed that he was in the antiques business, and attended auctions, yard sales, and flea markets to purchase old furniture for resale. Gradually, Harold branched out into other areas. He bought collections of old glassware. He acquired cartons of phonograph records. He discovered and acquired boxes and boxes of back issues of the *National Geographic* and *Life.* He shopped for old postcards. He collected sets of dishes. He contracted with a second hand store to take all their old chairs. He obtained rolls of odd-lot carpet and linoleum. He picked up shipments of paint and roofing materials from fire sales and bankruptcy sales. Ostensibly, Harold got this enormous hoard to sell. In spite of Harold's bargain prices, however, he didn't sell very much. He enjoyed gathering and talking about his purchases. Eventually, Harold's treasure trove of "you-name-it, I-have-it" overflowed his basement, his living room, dining room, bedrooms, and kitchen. Even the bathtub in the bathroom was filled with stacks of aluminum cookware and some picture frames. Harold's living space was reduced to a small area in a downstairs hallway in which he put a cot for sleeping. Finally, his mass of possessions spilled onto the front porch, blocking the door. (The back door had long since been barricaded by a huge pile of wooden chairs and tables.) Harold was forced to enter and leave his house by a window! He had allowed his possessions literally to take over his life, blocking him from entering his own home and preventing him from living in comfort!

This World in Arms. "Every gun that is made, every warship launched, every rocket fired signifies, in the final sense, a theft from those who are hungry and are not fed, those who are cold and are not clothed. This world in arms is not spending money alone. It is spending the sweat of its (society's) laborers, the genius of its scientists, the hopes of its children. . . . This is not a way of life at all, in any true sense. Under a cloud of war, it is humanity hanging from a cross of iron."—Dwight D. Eisenhower

Questions for Pupils on the Next Lesson. 1. Exactly what does it mean to be a peacemaker? 2. What are the implications for you and your church in Jesus' command to love your enemies? 3. Why do people ignore Jesus' instruction to refrain from striking back at those who hurt us? 4. What are the areas of greatest conflict in the nation and world today? 5. How is your church working to bring reconciliation?

TOPIC FOR YOUTH
HOW DO YOU MEASURE SUCCESS?

What Price for Success? Jim Hall is the administrator-director of Ghost Ranch, a church-related retreat and conference center in northeastern New Mexico. In the spring of 1983, a fire destroyed the headquarters building. A replacement was estimated to cost $425,000. Jim Hall and the devoted people at Ghost Ranch worked hard to try to collect funds to rebuild, but money was hard to come by. The ministry of Ghost Ranch has been run on faith and has never exactly had what you would call enough dollars to do all it would like to do. Then, in the fall of 1983, Ghost Ranch had an opportunity to make some big money. A major film maker was producing a "big budget" movie in New Mexico. The movie people had already looked over Ghost Ranch and decided it would be ideal for the site of the filming. Shooting schedules were set up and plans made to move in actors, staff, and crew. Finally, Jim Hall was approached and asked for permission to use the facilities of his conference center. He was told that there would be the prospect of a donation to the building program as well as a fat fee for using Ghost Ranch as a film location. Jim asked about the story line of the film. When he learned that it was a "third world war and we win," Jim reported, "I said I felt the notion that any one could win a third world war was a disservice to humanity and given our church's stand and concern for peacemaking and peacekeeping, I didn't think we wanted to be a part of it. I did agree to read the script; no redeeming features, lots of violence, youthful heroes, war glorified, so in spite of pressures from Governor's office to 'keep those millions in New Mexico,' and the prospect of 'very generous' gifts to the building program, I still said *no*. Parted amicably, door open to show the ranch for films that would be in keeping."

Wealth as a Wall. "Wealth acts as a wall more invincible by far than the famous walls of Jericho: We set ourselves apart, we make ourselves untouchable, and our wall is soundproof so that we cannot hear the cries of the poor and oppresed. Apartheid is not just a political system in an African country; apartheid is a certain way of thinking, feeling and living without being conscious of what is happening around us. There is a way of doing theology in which the poor and economically exploited are never seen or heard—and that is apartheid theology. . . .

"Money and violence go together: Those who make money their God are bound to make 'security' their state ideology and armaments a political priority."—Dorothee Solle, World Council of Churches meeting, quoted in *Presbyterian Survey,* October 1983.

A New Perspective on Shoes and Life. Father LaSalle and Father Kleinsorge were two German Jesuit priests at Hiroshima the morning of August 6, 1945. Miraculously spared from death when the blast came, they fled for their lives when fire swept the stricken city. A young Japanese theological student accompanied them. Picking their way through the clutter of survivors—many horribly mutilated and burned—and corpses, the debris and ruins, they were carrying their most important belongings. Father Kleinsorge had brought Mission records and deposits and his missal. The theological student, who was wearing slippers had carried with him a bundle of clothes, in which he had packed two pairs of leather shoes. When he sat down with the others, he found that the bundle had broken open and a couple of shoes had fallen out, and now he had only two lefts. He retraced his steps and found one right. When he rejoined the priests, he said, "It's funny, but things don't matter any more. Yesterday, my shoes were my most important possessions. Today, I don't care. One pair is enough."

Questions for Pupils on the Next Lesson. 1. Why is our immediate reaction to strike back when we are wronged or hurt? 2. Is it possible to love everyone, even enemies? 3. What does it mean to be a peacemaker? 4. Is there conflict and tension in your community or school? If so, what should Christians do about it?

LESSON XII—FEBRUARY 16

MAKE PEACE

Background Scripture: Matthew 5:9, 38–48; Luke 6:27–36
Devotional Reading: Leviticus 26:3–6

KING JAMES VERSION

MATTHEW 5 9 Blessed *are* the peace-makers: for they shall be called the children of God.

38 Ye have heard that it hath been said, An eye for an eye, and a tooth for a tooth:

39 But I say unto you, That ye resist not evil: but whosoever shall smite thee on thy right cheek, turn to him the other also.

40 And if any man will sue thee at the law, and take away thy coat, let him have *thy* cloak also.

41 And whosoever shall compel thee to go a mile, go with him twain.

42 Give to him that asketh thee, and from him that would borrow of thee turn not thou away.

43 Ye have heard that it hath been said, Thou shalt love thy neighbour, and hate thine enemy.

44 But I say unto you, Love your enemies, bless them that curse you, do good to them that hate you, and pray for them which despitefully use you, and persecute you;

45 That ye may be the children of your Father which is in heaven: for he maketh his sun to rise on the evil and on the good, and sendeth rain on the just and on the unjust.

46 For if ye love them which love you, what reward have ye? do not even the publicans the same?

47 And if ye salute your brethren only, what do ye more *than others?* do not even the publicans so?

48 Be ye therefore perfect, even as your Father which is in heaven is perfect.

LUKE 6 31 And as ye would that men should do to you, do ye also to them likewise.

34 And if ye lend *to them* of whom ye hope to receive, what thank have ye? for sinners also lend to sinners, to receive as much again.

35 But love ye your enemies, and do good, and lend, hoping for nothing again; and your reward shall be great, and ye shall be the children of the Highest: for he is kind unto the unthank-ful and *to* the evil.

36 Be ye therefore merciful, as your Father also is merciful.

REVISED STANDARD VERSION

MATTHEW 5 9 "Blessed are the peace-makers, for they shall be called sons of God.

38 "You have heard that it was said, 'An eye for an eye and a tooth for a tooth.' 39 But I say to you, Do not resist one who is evil. But if any one strikes you on the right cheek, turn to him the other also; 40 and if any one would sue you and take your coat, let him have your cloak as well; 41 and if any one forces you to go one mile, go with him two miles. 42 Give to him who begs from you, and do not refuse him who would borrow from you.

43 "You have heard that it was said, 'You shall love your neighbor and hate your enemy.' 44 But I say to you, Love your enemies and pray for those who persecute you, 45 so that you may be sons of your Father who is in heaven; for he makes his sun rise on the evil and on the good, and sends rain on the just and on the unjust. 46 For if you love those who love you, what reward have you? Do not even the tax collectors do the same? 47 And if you salute only your brethren, what more are you doing than others? Do not even the Gentiles do the same? 48 You, there-fore, must be perfect, as your heavenly Father is perfect."

LUKE 6 31 "And as you wish that men would do to you, do so to them.

34 "And if you lend to those from whom you hope to receive, what credit is that to you? Even sinners lend to sinners, to receive as much again. 35 But love your enemies, and do good, and lend, expecting nothing in return, and your reward will be great, and you will be sons of the Most High; for he is kind to the ungrateful and the selfish. 36 Be merciful, even as your Father is merciful."

KEY VERSE: Blessed are the peacemakers, for they shall be called sons of God. Matthew 5:9.

HOME DAILY BIBLE READINGS

Feb.	10.	M.	*Blessed Are the Peacemakers.* Matthew 5:9, 38–43.
Feb.	11.	T.	*Love Your Enemy.* Matthew 5:44–48.
Feb.	12.	W.	*Do Good to Others.* Luke 6:27–31.
Feb.	13.	T.	*Be Merciful.* Luke 6:32–36.
Feb.	14.	F.	*Love Must Be Sincere.* Romans 12:9–18.
Feb.	15.	S.	*Keep Peace.* Romans 14:13–19.
Feb.	16.	S.	*Things Which God Hates.* Proverbs 6:12–19.

BACKGROUND

Jesus was the Messiah. As Messiah, He was the long-awaited "Prince of Peace" promised in Isaiah 9:6. He fulfilled the prophecies of Isaiah 57:18, 19 and 60:17 that an age would come in which humans would be reconciled to God and would know *shalom.* The Kingdom of God, inaugurated by Jesus, means peace or *shalom.*

In the Hebrew, the word *shalom* signifies well-being, health, a harmony between all of the created order and the Creator. *Shalom* meant a new sense of the unity and wholeness everywhere in the universe which had been broken by humans. *Shalom* was interpreted to mean a return to good relationships between humans and the Lord, and among humans themselves. The word also implied a sense of harmony within the individual's personal life. Most of all, however, the Hebrew term for *peace* reflected the deep longing for a world in which humans lived as members of God's family, treating each other with the same help and sensitivity that God shows all persons.

Jesus indicated that the reign of God which He was introducing would be an era of *shalom.* Furthermore, Jesus made clear that those responding to His call to citizenship in the Kingdom of God were to be enrolled as active workers in his own "peace movement." Specifically, every one carrying Christ's name of "Christian" must be about Christ's work of making peace.

Jesus laid down startling examples of what it means for His followers to extend God's realm by peacemaking. In fact, He shocked His hearers by making such tough demands. Formerly, the Old Testament Law had put limits on vengeance and laid down rules for proper punishments. This was a giant step forward. Jesus, however, insisted on more than human justice. He appealed to God's norms. Jesus pointed out that God does not think of "rights" or "restitution." Love has no limits. Therefore, the person or community belonging to the Lord does not answer violence with violence, and suffers insults and indignities. Most of all, however, Christ's people actively promote peace in all their relationships with each other and with the world.

NOTES ON THE PRINTED TEXT

Peacemaking is another active discipline Jesus directs His disciples to practice. *Blessed are the peacemakers.* Literally, Jesus is saying that those who seek peace are happy. The term *peacemaker* was rarely used in the Greek language. When used, it normally applied to emperors. It referred to those who worked to bring about peace, God's *shalom.* God's peace means more than just living in the absence of war and practicing nonresistance. God's peace is a reconciling peace where all relationships are in harmony, whether they be the relationships of husband and wife, people, family, community, church, or nations. *For they shall be called sons of God.* Those who actively seek peace will become objects of God's love, care, and special attention. These people have the distinction of being acknowledged and adopted by Him as sons. Peacemakers are God's children.

Later, Jesus gives some guidelines for making peace. *You have heard that it was said, an eye for an eye and a tooth for a tooth.* The Law of Moses permitted retaliation. (*See* Exodus 21:24; Deuteronomy 19:21 or Leviticus 24:20). The Law limited revenge to an exact compensation for an injury. However, Jesus tells the disciples that they must not live asserting the rights of retaliation. A new attitude must surpass this legal code. Instead, *if anyone strikes you on the right cheek, turn to him the other also.* Jesus is not speaking of an act of physical violence but of an insulting slap on the face. Rather than retaliate, He says, let the person insult you again. Jesus gives another example. *If anyone would sue you and take your coat, let him have your cloak as well.* If someone claims your long, close-fitting undergarment, surrender the outer garment as well. *If anyone forces you to go one mile, go with him two miles.* The government or military could forcibly compel citizens to perform services such as carrying luggage or equipment (or a cross, as with Simon of Cyrene). If anyone demands a mile of you, go the extra mile. The appropriate behavior for a disciple is to go beyond what was demanded.

Give to him who begs . . . and do not refuse him who would borrow. Disciples are not to be selfish or miserly regarding money. They are to be generous to all who are in need for God's reconciling peace is to be shared by all.

God's peace is born out of love. Jesus insists that the disciples are to love everyone, including enemies. Reversing the established idea of loving a neighbor and hating an enemy, Jesus says, *Love your enemies and pray for those who persecute you.* The love Jesus calls for is a love which shows itself in actions. Praying for the persecutor is one such action. Disciples must act toward others in this manner because God acts toward His people in this manner. God's love is generously shared with all people, *the evil and . . . the good, the just and . . . the unjust.*

The usual Jewish greeting was *Shalom* meaning "Peace be to you." This salutation must be more than a simple greeting. The greeting must truly express the desire for the peace and well-being of all people. Therefore, the disciples' attitude *must be perfect* like God's. They must imitate God in all ways.

Luke records similar instructions for the disciples to love in order to make peace. *And as you wish that men would do to you, do so to them.* This is how the disciples are to act regardless of how others act towards them. They must love. They are to love their enemies and do good to them, even lending to them and expecting nothing in return. As in Matthew, love is expressed by the disciples because this is the way God loves them. He loves and is kind to the ungrateful and the selfish. Peace is made by being *merciful, even as your Father is merciful.*

SUGGESTIONS TO TEACHERS

When President Reagan named a cruise missile "The Peacemaker," some cheered him while others chided him on his choice of a name for a particularly destructive weapon.

To the writers of the New Testament, a peacemaker was what every disciple is called to be. Peacemaking also goes far deeper than working to prevent war. Peacemakers, in the reign of God, strive to bring about the harmony which God intends to have in every part of His realm.

Your lesson, therefore, is more than a polemic for or against the peace movement. It goes to the heart of the Gospel.

1. *GOD'S HAPPY HEIRS.* Do your homework on the meaning of the words in the Beatitude, "Blessed are the Peacemakers . . ." and remind your class that the Greek words here mean, "How superbly happy are those who work to bring about God's *shalom.*" Peacemakers know a deep joy! Furthermore, they know that they are related directly to God and can call themselves His children! Discuss why peacemakers may have such a sense of happiness and closeness to the Lord. Ask whether the lack of joy and kinship to God may not be caused by a failure to be a peacemaker.

2. *GIVER'S HABITUAL HARMONY.* Tell your class about the old rules of reprisal and revenge (and the attitude which still dominates many persons' thinking). Christian disciples, however, do not concern themselves with getting even. The words *my rights* are not on their tongues. Instead of the ancient eye-for-an-eye, tooth-for-a-tooth code of behavior, Jesus' people seek reconciliation with others. Discuss in detail what it means to try to be reconcilers on the level of personal relationships and also in the area of group relationships. How many Christians are peacemakers in the realms of labor-management disputes or international tensions?

3. *GRACIOUSNESS' HEAVENLY HINT.* God's goodness has no limits. He cares without distinction. Furthermore, Jesus reminds His hearers, even sinners will share with other sinners. There's nothing noble about helping a friend merely for the sake of sentiment or of being repaid sometime. Peacemaking means actively working to mend the quarrel with the enemy! Talk for a time with your class who the "enemies" are for the members of your group. What may those in the class do to be peacemakers with those enemies?

4. *GRATITUDE'S HIGH HEALING.* Being a peacemaker brings harmony and healing in society. It also brings harmony and healing within the life of a believer. "Your reward will be great. You will be called sons of the Most High," Jesus promises (Luke 5:35, 36). What greater promise than this!

TOPIC FOR ADULTS
CALLED TO MAKE PEACE

The Star Thrower. One morning, a naturalist walked down to a beach. It was before the sun came up. In the predawn darkness, he noticed a group of professional shell gatherers at work. He saw that they were collecting starfish, plunging them into a pail of boiling water to clean them and placing them on a pile of other marine specimens to be sold. The naturalist felt a sense of sadness that so many beautiful starfish were being collected and brutally killed.

As he looked at the scene, he noticed that the approaching light of the new day was creating a gorgeous rainbow beyond where the shell gatherers were working. He studied the beauty of the rainbow and saw that a figure was moving in the colors of the light spectrum. He studied the figure and observed the person picking up objects and throwing them out to the ocean.

As the naturalist approached the figure hurling the objects from the beach into the water, he became aware that the person was picking up live starfish and returning them to the safety of the sea by throwing them as far as possible. He asked the other why he was doing this.

Stretching out his hands in pity and love, the star thrower replied that some of those starfish might have a chance of surviving if the offshore pull was powerful enough.

The naturalist walked over to where the star thrower was busily picking up starfish and returning them to the sea. He began to throw back living starfish with the other. Both people were now part of the rainbow! The naturalist mused that The Thrower knew what they were trying to do, namely to save life!

God calls us to be "star throwers"—to stand in the rainbow and to save life!

Box Score on Wars. The Center for Defense Information is a think tank in Washington that keeps a tally on the wars, rebellions, and other violent uprisings going on in the world. Its latest report reminds us of some things we're inclined to forget. Between 1980 and 1984 six new wars have started while only two have ended—with over 4 million people engaged in combat. Forty-five of the world's 164 nations were involved in these wars and even the CDI can merely estimate that the number of people killed ranges from 1 million to 5 million. About 500,-

000 foreign combat troops are now involved. There are ten conflicts in the Middle East-Persian Gulf, ten more in Asia and Africa, seven in Latin America, and three in Europe. Five are conventional wars and thirty-five are internal guerrilla struggles.

The United States and the Soviet Union and its satellites are the major suppliers of military arms to thirteen nations now at war, and in 1981, the forty-five nations involved in forty conflicts spent over $528 billion on their armed forces.

According to the CDI, between 1 million and 4 million have died in Cambodia since 1970. In east Timor, it has been 100,000–250,000 since 1975. In Afghanistan, 100,000 since 1978. In the conflict between Iran and Iraq, 80,000–100,000 since 1980. In Lebanon, nobody knows.

These, of course, are only rough estimates, and cannot take into account the suffering of families or the loss of property, but they may remind us of the madness and cost of violence in a world where half the human race is going to bed hungry every night.

Peacemaking Starts at Home. Janice and Virgil Everhart of Central City, Kentucky, could not make peace in their home. Janice moved out of the house in early 1983. Virgil got angry. Finally, he decided on his own idea of a property settlement. Taking a chain saw, Virgil Everhart began cutting their house in half. By the end of one day, he had cut through most of the flooring, although he had run into problems with nails and wiring. Everhart even insisted on getting a cutting torch and dividing the bathtub in two. Everhart reported that he would live in his half of the house.

Virgil Everhart's "solution" to discord, of course, resolved nothing. In fact, soon after his chain saw job on the house, he received a summons for a court hearing. He kept insisting, however, that his notion of a property settlement would bring peace.

Peacemaking is more than dividing territories or properties and keeping to oneself. Peacemaking is building closer relationships. Peacemaking is actively working for reconciliation—starting under your own roof!

Questions for Pupils on the Next Lesson. 1. Does bearing a cross mean a willingness even to die for others? 2. Why were the disciples of Jesus ashamed when Jesus found them arguing who was the greatest among them? 3. What were Jesus' standards for measuring greatness? 4. How do the society's ideas of success differ from Jesus' teachings about success? 5. Why is a life commitment to Jesus which calls for personal sacrifice not always attractive to people?

TOPIC FOR YOUTH
ASKING THE IMPOSSIBLE?

Time to Rethink the Game. "The arms race is awesome and the church is pussyfooting. If we can kill the enemy six times in what we call 'overkill' and the enemy suddenly can overkill eight times—our mentality at the moment is to raise the overkill ten times. And here is an illustration that graphically motivates rethinking—

"A football game is about to be played—and the stadium is full. Before the kickoff—the announcer states that underneath the field is a heavy charge of explosives that will destroy everyone present. The first team to score will detonate the explosives. The gates are locked—no one can escape. This would require a rethinking of the whole game. So the world must rethink or the survivors will envy the dead."—Albert Winn.

A Tale of Peacemaking. While in Vietnam, Jim Wetherald and a few U.S. servicemen swam ashore to see a Buddhist shrine near a group of small grass huts.

Coming ashore they attracted an enormous number of children—healthy, curious children just like the ones back home.

As the men walked ashore, some of the children splashed water, some threw sand pebbles. While his friends looked on, Jim gestured for the sand throwing to stop. Just like at home, more sand followed.

Frustrated, Jim grabbed the hands of several of the children . . . and began singing, "Old MacDonald Had a Farm" and dancing in a circle. More and more children stopped throwing sand and joined the circle. Whenever sand was thrown, the dancing and singing would stop and one young boy would run over to the sand thrower and reprimand him.

When the men left, a young boy pressed a very small white stone into Jim's hand, a "peace stone" that Jim still cherishes.

Moving in the Circles of Peace. St. Andrew Presbyterian Church in Boulder, Colorado, met the call to peacemaking with a peacemaker's response. With members working together to grow toward greater love and clearer vision, this congregation of less than 400 members has involved itself in all the contexts of peacemaking.

In worship, at adult Bible classes, and through individual study aided by their peacemaking library, St. Andrew's members are growing in the spirit of Jesus Christ, who is the perfect Peacemaker.

Lay leaders in the church planned and led a conflict resolution retreat that helped open windows through which families could see strengths behind every-day stress.

Members serve on a "Peace Team" which presents aspects of peacemaking to other churches in their area. Some have joined the Boulder Presbytery Peace Fellowship, and others are in the Boulder Presbytery Peacemaking Task Force.

The pastor and the members of the congregation led in the development of a "fresh air" program which brought inner-city youngsters from Kansas City into the homes of Coloradoans. They are involved in a ministry to prisoners in the Boulder County Justice Center. They have gleaned fields to enable those in need to receive the often wasted, surplus food.

St. Andrew members have a vital concern for what is happening around the world. The session has endorsed the bilateral nuclear freeze, and one person at-tended the World Council of Churches' Meeting on Nuclear Weapons and Dis-armament.

St. Andrew Presbyterian Church is not a unique congregation. It is representa-tive of the hundreds of Presbyterian Churches committed to responding to God's call to do peacemaking in the name of Jesus Christ.

Questions for Pupils on the Next Lesson. 1. What does Jesus say about success? How does this differ from what the society around us says? 2. Why do some peo-ple think that humility is a sign of weakness? 3. What are the Christian norms for being a truly great person? 4. Why do many people shy away from Jesus' call to sacrifice for others? 5. To whom or to what is your main commitment in life?

LESSON XIII—FEBRUARY 23

BEAR YOUR CROSS

Background Scripture: Mark 8:34, 35; 9:33–37; 10:35–45
Devotional Reading: Hebrews 12:1, 2

KING JAMES VERSION

MARK 9   33 And he came to Capernaum: and being in the house he asked them, What was it that ye disputed among yourselves by the way?

34 But they held their peace: for by the way they had disputed among themselves, who *should be* the greatest.

35 And he sat down, and called the twelve, and saith unto them, If any man desire to be first, *the same* shall be last of all, and servant of all.

36 And he took a child, and set him in the midst of them: and when he had taken him in his arms, he said unto them,

37 Whosoever shall receive one of such children in my name, receiveth me; and whosoever shall receive me, receiveth not me, but him that sent me.

10   35 And James and John, the sons of Zebedee, come unto him, saying, Master, we would that thou shouldest do for us whatsoever we shall desire.

36 And he said unto them, What would ye that I should do for you?

37 They said unto him, Grant unto us that we may sit, one on thy right hand and the other on thy left hand, in thy glory.

38 But Jesus said unto them, Ye know not what ye ask: can ye drink of the cup that I drink of? and be baptized with the baptism that I am baptized with?

39 And they said unto him, We can. And Jesus said unto them, Ye shall indeed drink of the cup that I drink of; and with the baptism that I am baptized withal shall ye be baptized:

40 But to sit on my right hand and on my left hand is not mine to give; but *it shall be given to them* for whom it is prepared.

41 And when the ten heard *it*, they began to be much displeased with James and John.

42 But Jesus called them *to him*, and saith unto them, Ye know that they which are accounted to rule over the Gentiles exercise lordship over them; and their great ones exercise authority upon them.

43 But so shall it not be among you: but whosoever will be great among you, shall be your minister:

44 And whosoever of you will be the chiefest, shall be servant of all.

45 For even the Son of man came not to be ministered unto, but to minister, and to give his life a ransom for many.

REVISED STANDARD VERSION

MARK 9   33 And they came to Capernaum; and when he was in the house he asked them, "What were you discussing on the way?" 34 But they were silent; for on the way they had discussed with one another who was the greatest. 35 And he sat down and called the twelve; and he said to them, "If any one would be first, he must be last of all and servant of all." 36 And he took a child, and put him in the midst of them; and taking him in his arms, he said to them, 37 "Whoever receives one such child in my name receives me; and whoever receives me, receives not me but him who sent me."

10   35 And James and John, the sons of Zebedee, came forward to him, and said to him, "Teacher, we want you to do for us whatever we ask of you." 36 And he said to them, "What do you want me to do for you?" 37 And they said to him, "Grant us to sit, one at your right hand and one at your left, in your glory." 38 But Jesus said to them, "You do not know what you are asking. Are you able to drink the cup that I drink, or to be baptized with the baptism with which I am baptized?" 39 And they said to him, "We are able." And Jesus said to them, "The cup that I drink you will drink; and with the baptism with which I am baptized, you will be baptized; 40 but to sit at my right hand or at my left is not mine to grant, but it is for those for whom it has been prepared." 41 And when the ten heard it, they began to be indignant at James and John. 42 And Jesus called them to him and said to them, "You know that those who are supposed to rule over the Gentiles lord it over them, and their great men exercise authority over them. 43 But it shall not be so among you; but whoever would be great among you must be your servant, 44 and whoever would be first among you must be slave of all. 45 For the Son of man also came not to be served but to serve, and to give his life as a ransom for many."

KEY VERSE: If any man would come after me, let him deny himself and take up his cross and follow me. Mark 8:34.

HOME DAILY BIBLE READINGS

Feb.	17.	M.	*The World Versus the Soul.* Mark 8:34–38.
Feb.	18.	T.	*Who Is the Greatest?* Mark 9:33–37.
Feb.	19.	W.	*The Great Must Become as a Servant.* Mark 10:35–45.
Feb.	20.	T.	*Don't Be Ashamed of God.* Luke 9:23–26; Matthew 10:37, 38.
Feb.	21.	F.	*Take Up Your Cross.* Matthew 16:24–28.
Feb.	22.	S.	*The Cost of Discipleship.* Luke 14:26–35.
Feb.	23.	S.	*Acknowledge God.* Matthew 10:32–39.

BACKGROUND

No one in our culture can ever quite appreciate the sense of horror that people in Jesus' time felt toward a cross. Without exception. Jews and Romans alike regarded death by crucifixion as the most disgraceful as well as the most painful way that a person could die.

Rome would never execute a citizen by nailing him to a cross but reserved this form of tortuous death for slaves and despised foreigners. The Roman armies put down revolts and punished criminals in the provinces by crucifying thousands of offenders. In Galilee, a hotbed of unrest, crosses bearing the writhing, gasping victims were a common sight. The gruesome instruments were also constant reminders of the loathsome Roman overlords. Crosses were indescribably offensive to patriotic Jews.

Jews also remembered the ancient curse in Deuteronomy: ". . . a hanged man is accursed by God" (Deuteronomy 21:23). No self-respecting Jew wanted to fall into disrepute by having anything to do with a cross.

Imagine, therefore, the shock when Jesus called His followers to take up their crosses and follow Him! To the strict Jews, this was blasphemous. In fact, Jesus' own death by being crucified brought Him into disrepute with many Jews. They could not square the idea of the promised Messiah dying in such a disgraceful way.

Others, however, understood the Crucifixion of Jesus as the most vivid demonstration of His love and power. The Cross for them became the symbol of Jesus Christ's love and His power. These Christians adopted this shameful object of a Cross as their own sign of obedience to Jesus.

They recalled Jesus' own words about cross-bearing. They realized that following Jesus meant a willingness to suffer for others and even to die. Greatness in Christ's Kingdom, they learned, comes not from avoiding service and sacrifice but from accepting them!

NOTES ON THE PRINTED TEXT

Former Green Bay Packers' Coach, Vince Lombardi, once said, "If you're not number one, you're not worth much." The disciples thought the same way. Along the way to Capernaum, they had been discussing *with one another who was the greatest.* Jesus questions them about this when they arrive at Capernaum. However, they are silent, being ashamed and embarrassed by His understanding of the situation. Gathering the disciples around Him, Jesus sits down. *If any one would be first, he must be last of all and servant of all.* Jesus points out that true greatness means humble service. Desire for preeminence should be abandoned. Being number one is not the goal. True worth comes through lowly, humble, footwashing servanthood.

And he took a child saying to them *whoever receives one such child in my name receives me; and whoever receives me, receives not me but him who sent me.* Whoever identifies with this child, who seems insignificant, and serves him is receiving Jesus and ultimately God Himself. Whoever has the same trusting humility as the child who came to Jesus when called and demonstrates the same unconcern for status will be received by the Father.

The teaching in Capernaum was lost on James and John. Later, as they were on the way to Jerusalem, the two schemers approached Jesus with a demand. *We want you to do for us whatever we ask of you.* Questioning the two impulsive fishermen as to their request, He is told to *Grant to us to sit, one at your right hand and one at your left, in your glory.* They had witnessed the glory of Jesus at the Transfiguration. They believe He is the Messiah, but they wrongly assume that Jesus is a Messiah who will march on Jerusalem, kick out the Romans, reinstate David's monarchy, and live happily ever after. They want to be with Jesus in this victory as His top aides, with number one and two positions in the Kingdom.

You do not know what you are asking, Jesus replies. Realizing their blindness to His earlier teaching, He knows that James and John still think in terms of being served instead of serving.

Are you able to drink the cup that I drink, or to be baptized with the baptism with which I am baptized? In the Old Testament, *cup* could mean joy and salvation, or, as Jesus uses the word, suffering (Isaiah 51:17, 22). *Baptism* (as in Psalms 42:7 and 69:2; and Isaiah 43:2) meant martyrdom. Following Jesus requires a willingness to die. Jesus is asking if James and John are able to share His coming death on the cross that He had announced three separate times before. Still missing the point and still locked into dreams of being number one, James and John announce *we are able.*

Soberly, Jesus announces that they will suffer for they will drink the cup that He will soon drink and, likewise, be baptized as He shortly must be baptized. *But to sit at my right hand or at my left is not mine to grant.* This is God's prerogative.

Hearing this discussion between James, John, and Jesus, the other disciples are indignant and resentful. They feel that they, too, should have an equal chance at the best positions in the Kingdom.

Patiently Jesus calls the group together to help them all come to a new understanding of greatness. Normally great men exercise power and authority over others. *But it shall not be so among you,* He sternly says. *Whoever would be great among you must be a servant and whoever would be first among you must be a slave of all.* The words Jesus used are jarring. The disciples must act like slaves because the Kingdom involves serving.

In conclusion, Jesus drills home the meaning of His life and His coming death. *The Son of man came not to be served but to serve, and to give His life as a ransom for many.* In just a few short days following this discussion at a place called the Skull, Jesus, the Suffering Servant, acted out these very words on the Cross.

SUGGESTIONS TO TEACHERS

This lesson could well be taught each week. All of us are kindergartners in Jesus' School of the Cross. As we approach the season commemorating Jesus' Resurrection, we must not glide over the meaning of the Crucifixion. We Protestants sometimes shout, "Hooray, Jesus rose!" without appreciating the significance of His death—or His call for cross-bearing.

Teachers like yourself must regularly remind Sunday-School classes that Christians must bear their crosses. This is not easy to get across. People don't always like to hear of grim duty. Sacrifice does not come easily. It's no fun to suffer, especially for others who don't seem worth suffering for. Part of your cross-bearing as a teacher is to put up with people in your class who may not welcome a lesson on bearing a cross.

1. *CALL TO CROSS-BEARING.* Let the words of Jesus speak for themselves. After all, Scripture has its own authority. You need not apologize for Jesus' stern call to self-denial. If the people in your class want to question or quarrel with the message of cross-bearing, remember that they are arguing not with you but with the Lord! Have the folks in the class reread Mark 8 and react to the message. Those hoarding their lives selfishly lose everything, whereas those giving themselves away lavishly in acts of generous service will discover a richer, deeper form of living! Ask your people what sacrifices they have had to make as Christians so far in their lives.

2. *GOAL OF GREATNESS.* Working with Mark 9:33–37, consider Jesus' definition of greatness. You and the class will quickly note how different His idea is from society's idea of greatness. To sharpen the contrast, have your students report what they think the present-day culture's notions of being a "great person" are. Most of these will have to do with power over others. Christians, however, don't struggle to gain mastery over others. Nor do Christians strive to be first in anything except service. Using the two lists of ideas of greatness, the world's and Jesus', let your class members give examples of people they've know who exemplify greatness according to Jesus.

3. *CUP OF CRUCIFIXION.* Plan your lesson to allow plenty of discussion time of Mark 10:35–45. Try to bring out the James and John in each of us, the desire for places of honor, recognition, status. The James and John in us yells out to be served and yammers to lord it over others. Lead your people into a deeper consciousness of what the "Cup" means in this passage. To drink with Jesus means accepting responsibilities to suffer for others. Consider specific ways in which Christians must be willing to make sacrifices in these days. How much are your class members hurting on behalf of others?

TOPIC FOR ADULTS
BEAR YOUR CROSS

A Religion Without a Cross or Commitment. Pollster George Gallup recently made a scientific survey of Americans' religious interests and practices. His findings are astonishing. He calculated that 57 percent indicates 102 million Americans lately have become more concerned with religion, as found in interviews with a representative 1,029 adults (eighteen or older) of 178.5 million Americans in that category.

"It means that people are turning to religion much more than they have in the last several years," Gallup said. "Indeed, the majority say they are more reliant on God. We find that six in ten say they are more interested in religion than they were five years ago."

In his survey, Gallup said he found that four out of ten adults recently have taken part in one or more of ten religious activities besides formal worship services. The various indicators, Gallup said, are "That there's a very definite upsurge in religious interest and involvement. Of course, we have to acknowledge that this does not necessarily point to deep commitment and informed commitment."

While people are increasingly involved with religion . . . only 12 percent have a "really deep, informed commitment."

What Gallup suggests, in other words, is that in spite of the upswing of interest in religion, only a handful are committed to bearing a cross. What about you?

Stunted Lives. We cannot live only for ourselves. We stunt, dwarf our growth.

We end up as runts. The Japanese have perfected the practice of growing dwarf trees—cramping the roots in a small pot so the tree never grows larger than a houseplant. We must send our roots throughout the world—not be confined in a small area—else we dwarf ourselves. Or as a Church, we stunt our growth and be a mere decorative curiosity instead of a useful, beautiful tree with sturdy branches offering shade and fruit. We must live for others. And that means bearing our crosses!

Willing to Go to a Cross? One Saturday night in September several decades ago, thousands of people gathered on Madison Street, Chicago, attracted by what appeared to be a man climbing up the spire of a church to the cross at the very top. The strange play of light and shadows gave the appearance of a moving figure. It was difficult to determine exactly what was moving there on the steeple. The rumor spread that a man was going up to the cross, probably to leap to death. For two hours the crowd watched. Police and newspaper reporters rushed to the scene.

On Sunday morning, Charles Goff, pastor of the First Methodist Church of Chicago, reported what had happened the night before, concluding with these words:

"We have crosses on churches all over the world. I'm afraid they are not looked at very often. Here we have one, the highest of all, but actually seen by a relatively small number. Why? We now know that crowds gather when they think a man is on the cross. That makes the symbol come alive. But there are few who are willing to go to a cross. There was One once who did, and His Cross has become the world's most moving symbol."

Questions for Pupils on the Next Lesson. 1. What should belief in the Resurrection of Jesus Christ mean to a Christian for his or her own life? 2. Where can you find any evidence of hope in these times? 3. Why do so many people have misgivings and fears about the future—both in this world and the next? 4. How can your church show that the Resurrection of Jesus Christ means hope in the midst of difficult circumstances? 5. How does the Resurrection of Jesus enable us to think about life after death?

TOPIC FOR YOUTH
HOW CAN I BE GREAT?

Hollow Cross With a Rubber Wheel. Jim Miller quit his job at the Energy Research and Development Co. in Indianapolis a few years ago, built a twelve-foot wooden cross with a rubber wheel on the end, and set off to wander around the country. The cross is hollow and serves as Miller's suitcase for a tent and his clothes. Miller shoulders the beam, and allows the end of the cross to roll along behind him on the little rubber wheel. Miller, however, makes no particular point of pointing to Jesus Christ and His Cross. When asked what Miller's message is, a young man says it's "Slow down. Get off the clock."

Without wanting to appear critical of Jim Miller, the question persists, "Is this what Christ's Cross is all about?" Is towing a hollow cross-shaped suitcase with a rubber wheel to carry the strain what Jesus means about cross-bearing? Is the message of Jesus regarding suffering and sacrificing in His name to be reduced to trite sayings about slowing down and getting off the clock?

No. The road to greatness is not hiking out on Route 30 with a twelve-foot beam in tow. It is in following the Crucified One up the Calvary of personal service to others each day.

The Fitness Fad. Fitness is a business that is notably prospering and likely to get considerably bigger. Imprecisely defined but including at least the gyms, equipment, clothing, foods, and vitamins for staying healthy, the fitness market will reach $35 billion this year, up from $30 billion just two years ago. This is bigger than the combined sales of Coca-Cola, Procter & Gamble, and Kodak. The industry first began blooming in the mid 70s, when the young and affluent discovered tennis. Soon thereafter came jogging, aerobics, and other fitness fads. No one would criticize anyone for taking care of his or her body. That is a Christian obligation. But obligation becomes obsession with some. Salvation through exercise emerges as a new religion. For many Americans, the cult of fitness is a form of idol worship. The key to greatness in the minds of millions lies in developing and maintaining a perfect human body.

What about your spiritual fitness? Are you as disciplined and committed in building your Christian life as you are in polishing your racquet-ball skills? Do you realize that Christ's standard of greatness has nothing to do with your physique or fitness but with your faith and your faithfulness?

Hoarded Life, Wasted Life. In Bethlehem, a man got hold of a bushel basket full of priceless fragments of Dead Sea Scrolls. Instead of selling them or getting them into safe keeping of others' hands, he buried the basket during the Arab-Israeli troubles. A few years later, when he dug it up, he found only a worthless, gluey pulp. The pieces were completely ruined. No one knows the loss to the world of this precious basketful of Scroll fragments.

When we hoard ourselves, we "lose our lives." We are meant to put ourselves into circulation and spend ourselves for others. This is the clue to greatness.

Questions for Pupils on the Next Lesson. 1. Do you sometimes wonder what will happen to you after you die? 2. Why do so many young people have so little hope for the future? 3. What does the News of the Resurrection of Jesus Christ mean to you? 4. How can the hope which comes from Jesus' Resurrection help you to accept difficult times? 5. Can a person trust God with complete confidence?

MARCH, APRIL, MAY 1986

THE CHRISTIAN HOPE

LESSON I—MARCH 2

A LIVING, CONFIDENT HOPE

Background Scripture: 1 Peter 1:1—2:10
Devotional Reading: 2 Corinthians 5:1–9

KING JAMES VERSION	REVISED STANDARD VERSION

KING JAMES VERSION

1 PETER 1 3 Blessed *be* the God and Father of our Lord Jesus Christ, which according to his abundant mercy hath begotten us again unto a lively hope by the resurrection of Jesus Christ from the dead,

4 To an inheritance incorruptible, and undefiled, and that fadeth not away, reserved in heaven for you,

5 Who are kept by the power of God through faith unto salvation ready to be revealed in the last time.

6 Wherein ye greatly rejoice, though now for a season, if need be, ye are in heaviness through manifold temptations:

7 That the trial of your faith, being much more precious than of gold that perisheth, though it be tried with fire, might be found unto praise and honour and glory at the appearing of Jesus Christ:

8 Whom having not seen, ye love; in whom, though now ye see *him* not, yet believing, ye rejoice with joy unspeakable and full of glory:

9 Receiving the end of your faith, *even* the salvation of *your* souls.

13 Wherefore gird up the loins of your mind, be sober, and hope to the end for the grace that is to be brought unto you at the revelation of Jesus Christ;

14 As obedient children, not fashioning yourselves according to the former lusts in your ignorance:

15 But as he which hath called you is holy, so be ye holy in all manner of conversation;

16 Because it is written, Be ye holy; for I am holy.

17 And if ye call on the Father, who without respect of persons judgeth according to every man's work, pass the time of your sojourning *here* in fear:

18 Forasmuch as ye know that ye were not redeemed with corruptible things, *as* silver and gold, from your vain conversation *received* by tradition from your fathers;

19 But with the precious blood of Christ, as of a lamb without blemish and without spot:

20 Who verily was foreordained before the foundation of the world, but was manifest in these last times for you,

REVISED STANDARD VERSION

1 PETER 1 3 Blessed be the God and Father of our Lord Jesus Christ! By his great mercy we have been born anew to a living hope through the resurrection of Jesus Christ from the dead, 4 and to an inheritance which is imperishable, undefiled, and unfading, kept in heaven for you, 5 who by God's power are guarded through faith for a salvation ready to be revealed in the last time. 6 In this you rejoice, though now for a little while you may have to suffer various trials, 7 so that the genuineness of your faith, more precious than gold which though perishable is tested by fire, may redound to praise and glory and honor at the revelation of Jesus Christ. 8 Without having seen him you love him; though you do not now see him you believe in him and rejoice with unutterable and exalted joy. 9 As the outcome of your faith you obtain the salvation of your souls.

13 Therefore gird up your minds, be sober, set your hope fully upon the grace that is coming to you at the revelation of Jesus Christ. 14 As obedient children, do not be conformed to the passions of your former ignorance, 15 but as he who called you is holy, be holy yourselves in all your conduct; 16 since it is written, "You shall be holy, for I am holy." 17 And if you invoke as Father him who judges each one impartially according to his deeds, conduct yourselves with fear throughout the time of your exile. 18 You know that you were ransomed from the futile ways inherited from your fathers, not with perishable things such as silver or gold, 19 but with the precious blood of Christ, like that of a lamb without blemish or spot. 20 He was destined before the foundation of the world but was made manifest at the end of the times for your sake. 21 Through him you have confidence in God, who raised him from the dead and gave him glory, so that your faith and hope are in God.

KING JAMES VERSION

21 Who by him do believe in God, that raised him up from the dead, and gave him glory; that your faith and hope might be in God.

KEY VERSE: Blessed be the God and Father of our Lord Jesus Christ! By his great mercy we have been born anew to a living hope through the resurrection of Jesus Christ from the dead. 1 Peter 1:3.

HOME DAILY BIBLE READINGS

Feb. 24. M.   *A Hope That Lives.* 1 Peter 1:3–9.
Feb. 25. T.   *A Call to Right Living.* 1 Peter 1:13–17.
Feb. 26. W. *Confidence in God Through Christ.* 1 Peter 1:18–25.
Feb. 27. T.   *Hope in Christ, the Chosen Stone.* 1 Peter 2:4–10.
Feb. 28. F.   *Hope in God.* Psalms 146:3–10.
Mar.   1. S.   *The Hope of Sharing God's Glory.* Romans 5:1–11.
Mar.   2. S.   *Living With Hope.* Romans 8:31–39.

BACKGROUND

Two high-school sophomores watched the 1983 ABC film, *The Day After*, depicting a nuclear strike on Lawrence, Kansas, and then took their own lives with overdoses of drugs. Their brief farewell note stated that they were convinced there was no hope for the future.

Hope is not widespread in many circles. In fact, Christians are the only persons who speak much of hope in these days. Why? Because of the God who acted in the life, death, and Resurrection of Jesus Christ, and who continues to act in the world.

The next seven lessons explore the theme of Christian hope. These lessons are based on that body of literature in the New Testament called the General Epistles, including selections from 1 Peter and 2 Peter, the Letters of John, and Jude.

Why were these letters written? Basically, to offer encouragement and hope. The Christians receiving these epistles were living in situations similar to ours today. They also faced issues parallel to those confronting the Church today. The circumstances in those times included controversy over truth and heresy, anxiety over the future, and the threat of persecution and danger.

One Peter was written to impart a sense of hope because of Jesus Christ to scattered groups of Christian believers in the northern part of what is now Asia Minor. These church people were enduring persecution. Most were Gentile converts. Few had any background knowledge of Scriptures. Consequently, many were surprised when the "fiery ordeal" came upon them. They struggled to understand the meaning of their sufferings as Christ's people. Many felt a sense of despair.

The writer of 1 Peter did not resort to pep talks or try to cheer up his readers with glib assurances that "everything would be all right." Rather, he pointed to Jesus. He recalled the meaning of what God has done through Jesus Christ. Jesus Christ, this writer asserted, is Good News. Jesus Christ brings hopes in the midst of hopelessness! In the light of the Good News of Jesus Christ, 1 Peter's author affirms that his readers and hearers have a basis for genuine hope. Moreover, these same readers and hearers—both then and now—may endure sufferings, realizing that these may be used to test their faith, because the readers and hearers will ultimately receive their reward for remaining faithful.

NOTES ON THE PRINTED TEXT

Today begins a series on the Catholic Epistles. Since *catholic* denotes universality, these letters are addressed to the whole or the universal Church, not to any single congregation. First Peter, for example, was addressed to a group of churches in Asia Minor. What better way to begin a study of Christian hope than by beginning with First Peter, the Epistle of Hope.

Peter opens by praising God. *Blessed be the God and Father of our Lord Jesus Christ!* No aloof deity for Peter. Peter knows God personally through His Son Jesus. (Through our Lord, we Christians have this same personal bond that Peter does through our Lord.) Peter thanks God because *by his great mercy we have been born anew to a living hope through the resurrection of Jesus Christ.* Peter reminds his readers that they cannot obtain their own salvation. It is a great and merciful gift. His reference to rebirth describes the experience of Christian baptism. Christian baptism, when regarded as a baptism for the forgiveness of sins, involves the Cross. It implies the participation of the Christian in the death and Resurrection of Christ. So Peter can insist that God's people are renewed and given a living hope through Christ's Resurrection from the dead. Belief in Jesus' Resurrection should give Christians confidence in their own resurrection. Peter does not simply encourage his readers to believe this but insists that they have a living hope!

Peter expounds further on the living hope. He describes it as *an inheritance.* Since Christians are God's children and His heirs, they share in His inheritance. Peter has in mind God's grace which is freely and mercifully given by God. It does not need to be earned. This God given grace cannot be destroyed, polluted, or made to decay. It *is imperishable, undefiled, and unfading.* Moreover, God's children can have a living, confident hope in this grace for God is keeping it safe. It is *kept in heaven.* They can be joyful for this grace is assured by God's power. *In this you rejoice.*

Having reviewed Christ's suffering and death and the confidence it instills, Peter subtly draws attention to the possible persecution his readers would face. *In a little while you may have to suffer various trials.* He assures them that in all situations they are *guarded through faith for a salvation* by *God's power.* Their hope is not misplaced. They can be confident of God's protection even in the severest trials and afflictions. These trials will serve to demonstrate the reader's genuine faith which is far more precious than gold. As gold is refined by fire, so too, God's people are purified by the flames. The more successfully their faith endures the trials, the greater the *praise, glory,* and *honor* will be at the *revelation* or Coming of Jesus Christ.

While some of Peter's readers may have known Jesus, most did not. Yet, *without having seen him* (as Peter had), *you love him.* Christians must love Jesus even if they have not really seen Him. Even though they cannot see Him now, they are to believe *in him and rejoice with unutterable and exalted joy.* As a result of their faith in Christ, they will be full of joy. They can be full of this inexpressible joy for soon they will reach the goal of their faith: salvation. *As the outcome of your faith you obtain the salvation of your souls.*

Following his exposition of salvation, Peter pleads for holiness. Having a confident hope encourages Christians to live a holy life. He outlines a pattern of behavior. *Gird up your minds.* To gird one's loins involved pulling up and tightening the long, wide outer garment so that it would not cause the wearer to stumble at work. Likewise, Peter tells the Christians to be prepared and pulled together spiritually and mentally to be ready to meet the Lord.

He also urges his readers to *be sober.* Biblically, sobriety refers to clarity of mind. Peter is urging steadfast faithfulness.

Set your hope fully upon the grace that is coming. No halfhearted faith for Peter! Without any hesitation or reservation, Christians are to set their hopes on God's grace which is seen at the Coming of Christ in glory.

Peter demands obedience to God as contrasted with those who are *conformed to the passions* of their *former ignorance.* His readers must totally break from the sensual lustful lives of their past. They lived these lives in ignorance, unaware of Christ and His demands. In place of ignorance, he challenges his followers to holiness. *Be holy yourselves in all your conduct.* God demands this! God calls them to be holy as He is holy. Peter cites Leviticus 19:2. Therefore, all of their conduct must be above reproach. Their moral integrity must be unblemished.

If you invoke as Father him who judges each one impartially according to his deeds, conduct yourselves with fear. From Peter's viewpoint, if his readers address God as Father, they would be wise if they have respect of His judgment and shape their behavior accordingly. God is kind and forgiving, but, when necessary, He punishes the disobedient. They must not be complacent about grace. God must be held in awe and feared.

Peter focuses on the motive for their conduct. They were *ransomed by the precious blood of Christ.* The price for their redemption was not *silver or gold* but the blameless and stainless Lamb of God, Jesus. Through this sacrifice, their salvation is assured. This salvation has been available from the very beginning of the world.

Through him you have confidence in God, who raised him from the dead and gave him glory, so that your faith and hope are in God. Again, Peter reminds his readers that they have a living confident hope in Christ. He is the guarantee of their faith and hope in God *through His resurrection from the dead and His entrance to glory.*

SUGGESTIONS TO TEACHERS

A group of tourists was looking at the ruins of the Colosseum at Rome. The guide explained how early Christians were sometimes herded into the ring to be mauled and torn to death by hungry lions. Seeing the actual place and reflecting on the grisly facts, one of the party remarked, "Golly, pretty hopeless odds." Her partner, who knew her history, answered, "Yes, but they weren't without hope."

No, the early Christians seemed to have hope in spite of all the odds being against them. Today's lesson reflects that living, confident hope, and the next series of studies will focus on the hope that sustained these believers.

Remember that the lesson material from the Scriptures for this lesson comes from 1 Peter, written at a time when the outlook looked hopeless for the Church. Several important points emerge from this passage.

1. *PROMISE FOR THE FUTURE.* Some people today think that there is nothing to hope for in the future. It's hopeless, they sigh. One Peter was written in days when many felt the same way. Peter, however, insists that Christians have been "born anew to a living hope through the Resurrection of Jesus Christ." Make it clear to your class that Christians' hope rests on God's act, not humans' attitude. God's act of bringing back Jesus Christ from the dead is the divine demonstration of God's willingness and ability to deal with any kind of hopeless situation! Through Jesus Christ, God assures us that there will never be a condition or situation which is totally hopeless. The Risen Christ means hope!

2. *PROCESS OF REFINING.* One Peter was written when many Christians were tempted to think all was hopeless because of persecution. In 1 Peter 1:6-9, these wavering believers are told that their suffering should be thought of in terms of the refining process for precious metals in which the impurities are burned off. How does this notion of suffering seem to you and your class?

3. *PURCHASED FROM FUTILITY.* Take a little time in your lesson to ponder the alternative to hope. We call that state of trying to exist without hope "a feeling of futility" or "hopelessness." Point out examples from the daily newspaper of how widespread this attitude is. One Peter 1:18, however, insists that Jesus

Christ has "ransomed" us from "futile ways." Have your students reflect on exactly what is meant to be bought from the slavery of futility. And have your people offer examples of "futile ways" they encounter in the workaday world.

4. *PRIESTHOOD FOR THE FATHER.* Allow sufficient time in your lesson for the important notion of 1 Peter that every believer is called to the priesthood. Remind your class, however, that this does not mean merely that every Christian can go directly to the Lord without going through some human intermediary. It means that each believer is called and appointed to "declare the wonderful deeds" of Christ who brings hope! Discuss in your class what this idea of priesthood of all believers should impel each Christian to be and to do.

TOPIC FOR ADULTS
A LIVING, CONFIDENT HOPE

Hope for a Prisoner of Castro. "Armando Valladares was a twenty-three-year-old minor bureaucrat in Cuba's Ministry of Communications when the police arrested him in December 1960. The charge: 'counterrevolutionary activity' because he had publicly criticized Fidel Castro's increasing dependence on the Soviet Union. Although he had supported Castro's 1959 overthrow of Dictator Fulgencio Batista, Valladares was, after a two-hour trial, sentenced to thirty years' imprisonment. During his confinement, Valladares began to record images and thoughts on the torn-off margins of Castro's official newspaper, Granma.

" 'For a long time I worked in agricultural camps and marble quarries. It was exhausting. We were victims of the constant blows of the officers responsible for the work squads. A few years later, I was taken to the Boniato prison in Oriente province. All the doors and windows were steel-shuttered. That period was one of the worst. But I felt myself neither alone nor abandoned because God was with me inside that jail. The greater the hatred my jailers directed at me, the more my heart brimmed over with Christian love and faith. I never felt hatred for my jailers, and even today, with the detachment of time, I offer prayers for them that they might repent. Once I succeeded in getting hold of a small Bible, but the soldiers ultimately found it and furiously tore it to shreds.' "—*Time*, August 15, 1983. Copyright 1983 Time Inc. All rights reserved. Reprinted by permission from TIME.

Grace Pilgrimage. John Claypool, now co-pastor of Second Baptist Church, Lubbock, Texas, tells how, through various struggles, including a divorce and remarriage, his eyes have been opened to see God and himself in a new way, which gave him a living, confident hope.

Vocationally, he moved from seeing himself as a person who had to *be* something to one who had to *do* something. That could be misunderstood. What Claypool means is "the challenge to move from 'I am' to 'I can' to 'I will.' " He thought he had to be the prestigious person, judged and justified by his works that supported that status. But his eyes were opened to see that this is not what matters with God at all, and that accepting himself had to lead to action.

"My earliest images of God, as well as of myself—not surprisingly—were decidedly negative. God was the Great Killjoy, the enemy of all happiness, the One to whom one finally 'surrendered' and thereafter lived a life of drabness and sacrifice. . . . The love of such a One must be earned, of course, by strenuous effort. Obviously I was as mistaken about God as I was about myself, and an exciting new dimension of my grace pilgrimage has been that I see God differently and am learning to relate to Transcendence in light of this new vision.

"My perception of God has changed as much as my sense of self. I now see God as joy and generosity. For example, I can imagine that long ago, finding aliveness so joyful a reality, God said, 'This is too good to keep to myself. I want others to feel some of this ecstasy. I know what I shall do: I shall create—not to *receive* anything *for* myself, but to *give* something of myself.' Thus, Creation was an act of bottomless sharing! . . .

"From these visions, it follows that a relationship with such a God becomes one of trust and discernment, rather than placation and manipulation. Thus, my prayer life is another area that has undergone a significant transformation. Before my encounter with grace, prayer was largely a matter of making my requests known to God, trying to enlist God's aid, using God as a means to attain the ends that I had in mind. Prayer was just another effort in the process of acquisition. As I became more and more reconciled to the goodness and wisdom and mystery of God, however, the focus shifted and, with it, even the way I go about prayer. Now I have become a means for the attaining of God's ends, rather than the other way around. I attempt to empty myself and silence myself sufficiently so that what God wants to give and say can be received and heard."—John R. Claypool, *Opening Blind Eyes*, Nashville: Abingdon, 1983.

Hope in Spite of Death. "Death, indeed, is not the result of a whim but is to define what is human. Astonishingly, then, in concept, death is not simply evil any more than winter is evil in the passing of the year. Death is not a reality designed to call humans to refuse the enjoyment of living. Death, the definer, gives meaning to life and history. It is an instrument that helps provide meaning for daily existence."—Martin Marty, *A Cry of Absence*, New York: Harper & Row, 1983.

Questions for Pupils on the Next Lesson. 1. Should Christians expect that their faith in Jesus Christ should mean they will not have to expect much suffering? 2. Have you ever had to suffer for your faith? 3. Why may a Christian rejoice when suffering for living his or her faith? 4. Who are some Christians you have heard of who have been willing to do right even when it involved suffering? 5. Why may present suffering bring future rewards?

TOPIC FOR YOUTH
BE CONFIDENT!

Gotta Have Something to Hope For! A newspaper reporter interviewed numbers of young people on welfare and discovered that many of them bought the daily lottery ticket. Although the ticket cost one dollar and the men and women had little cash to spend, they lined up each morning to buy what each hoped to be his or her "lucky winner." The odds against winning, of course, were hopelessly stacked against them. Nevertheless, they considered the daily lottery ticket a "must." As one young mother, struggling to support herself and her two small children on food stamps, welfare, and handouts stated, "I gotta have something to hope for. How can I live otherwise?"

How would you answer this woman? Would you assure her that Christ offers a living, confident hope that no gambling scheme or human endeavor can offer?

Set Free the Angel. The great Italian artist, Michelangelo, once saw in a builder's yard a chunk of worthless marble waiting to be discarded. Michelangelo said to the builder, "Take it to the studio! There's an angel in there and I can set it free!"

Be confident! Although you may give up hope for yourself, God has not. You may see only a worthless chunk, and think you are only fit to be thrown on the discard pile.

Through Jesus Christ, God has come to bring you hope for yourself and your future! He brings a beautiful angel out of what may appear to be useless material.

Let Him free the angel in you!

The Ebb and Flow of God's Presence With Us. "It is true there is an Ebb and Flow, but the sea remains the same. You are the sea. Although I experience many ups and downs in my emotions and often feel great shifts and changes in my inner life, you remain the same. Your sameness is not the sameness of a rock, but the sameness of a faithful lover. Out of your love I came to life, by your love I am sustained, and to your love I am always called back. There are days of sadness and days of joy; there are feelings of guilt and feelings of gratitude; there are moments of failure and moments of success, but all of them are embraced by your unwavering love.

"My only real temptation is to doubt in your love, to think of myself as beyond the reach of your love, to remove myself from the healing radiance of your love. To do these things is to move into the darkness of despair.

"O Lord, sea of Love and goodness, let me not fear too much the storms and winds of my daily life, and let me know that there is Ebb and Flow, but the sea remains the sea. Amen."—Vincent van Gogh, *The Redeeming Love of God.*

Questions for Pupils on the Next Lesson. 1. Have you ever felt rejected by others when you refused to be led into wrongdoing? 2. Why is it so difficult to stand by your beliefs if you know you may have to suffer as a consequence? 3. Do you think that any good can come from suffering? If so, why? 4. Are you willing to suffer for any cause? If so, what? If not, why not? 5. Have you ever experienced joy because of suffering for something you believed in?

LESSON II—MARCH 9

A HOPE WORTH SUFFERING FOR

Background Scripture: 1 Peter 2:11—5:14
Devotional Reading: 1 Peter 2:21-25

KING JAMES VERSION

1 PETER 3 13 And who *is* he that will harm you, if ye be followers of that which is good?

14 But and if ye suffer for righteousness' sake, happy *are ye:* and be not afraid of their terror, neither be troubled;

15 But sanctify the Lord God in your hearts: and *be* ready always to *give* an answer to every man that asketh you a reason of the hope that is in you, with meekness and fear:

16 Having a good conscience; that, whereas they speak evil of you, as of evil doers, they may be ashamed that falsely accuse your good conversation in Christ.

17 For *it is* better, if the will of God be so, that ye suffer for well doing, than for evil doing.

4 12 Beloved, think it not strange concerning the fiery trial which is to try you, as though some strange thing happened unto you:

13 But rejoice, inasmuch as ye are partakers of Christ's sufferings; that, when his glory shall be revealed, ye may be glad also with exceeding joy.

14 If ye be reproached for the name of Christ, happy *are ye;* for the Spirit of glory and of God resteth upon you: on their part he is evil spoken of, but on your part he is glorified.

15 But let none of you suffer as a murderer, or *as* a thief, or *as* an evildoer, or as a busybody in other men's matters.

16 Yet if *any man suffer* as a Christian, let him not be ashamed; but let him glorify God on this behalf.

17 For the time *is come* that judgment must begin at the house of God: and if *it* first *begin* at us, what shall the end *be* of them that obey not the gospel of God?

18 And if the righteous scarcely be saved, where shall the ungodly and the sinner appear?

19 Wherefore, let them that suffer according to the will of God commit the keeping of their souls *to him* in well doing, as unto a faithful Creator.

REVISED STANDARD VERSION

1 PETER 3 13 Now who is there to harm you if you are zealous for what is right? 14 But even if you do suffer for righteousness' sake, you will be blessed. Have no fear of them, nor be troubled, 15 but in your hearts reverence Christ as Lord. Always be prepared to make a defense to any one who calls you to account for the hope that is in you, yet do it with gentleness and reverence; 16 and keep your conscience clear, so that, when you are abused, those who revile your good behavior in Christ may be put to shame. 17 For it is better to suffer for doing right, if that should be God's will, than for doing wrong.

4 12 Beloved, do not be surprised at the fiery ordeal which comes upon you to prove you, as though something strange were happening to you. 13 But rejoice in so far as you share Christ's sufferings, that you may also rejoice and be glad when his glory is revealed. 14 If you are reproached for the name of Christ, you are blessed, because the spirit of glory and of God rests upon you. 15 But let none of you suffer as a murderer, or a thief, or a wrong-doer, or a mischief-maker; 16 yet if one suffers as a Christian, let him not be ashamed, but under that name let him glorify God. 17 For the time has come for judgment to begin with the household of God; and if it begins with us, what will be the end of those who do not obey the gospel of God? 18 And

"If the righteous man is scarcely saved,
where will the impious and sinner appear?"

19 Therefore let those who suffer according to God's will do right and entrust their souls to a faithful Creator.

KEY VERSE: *Rejoice in so far as you share Christ's sufferings, that you may also rejoice and be glad when his glory is revealed.* 1 Peter 4:13.

HOME DAILY BIBLE READINGS

Mar.	3.	M.	*Living Stones of the Holy Nation.* 1 Peter 2:1–10.
Mar.	4.	T.	*Respect Authority.* 1 Peter 2:13–17.
Mar.	5.	W.	*Christ, the Suffering Servant.* 1 Peter 2:18–25.
Mar.	6.	T.	*Suffering for Right.* 1 Peter 3:8–17.

Mar.	7.	F.	*Physical Suffering Changes Lives.* 1 Peter 4:1–11.
Mar.	8.	S.	*Sharing Christ's Suffering.* 1 Peter 4:12–19.
Mar.	9.	S.	*God's Care, a Sure Defense.* 1 Peter 5:1–11.

BACKGROUND

"What oxygen is for the lungs, such is hope for the meaning of life," Emil Brunner preached. Christian believers in northern Asia Minor gasped for some wisp of hope. Some had been executed for their faith. Others rotted in prisons. The survivors lived in daily dread of arrest and torture. They asked whether it was worth it to cling to their trust in Jesus Christ and to live responsibly as His people.

The beautiful little letter we know as 1 Peter answers these plaintive questions with a mighty, *Yes!* Through Jesus Christ, 1 Peter emphasizes, we have a hope worth suffering for!

The first letter of Peter as part of the New Testament literature known as the General Epistles lays special stress on the theme of hope. Other letters in this grouping have different emphases. The Epistle of James, for example, stresses works along with faith. John speaks out on behalf of love. Jude puts great weight on the need for a pure faith. One Peter, however, while touching on many important Christian doctrines offers a message of hope as its principal theme.

And how those scattered little congregations of Christians needed words of hope! Up until the time of the Emperor Nero, the Roman authorities had been reasonably tolerant of Christians. The Roman system put all religions in one of two categories: *religiones licitae* or permitted religions, and *religiones illicitae* or prohibited religions. The government didn't bother anyone practicing a permitted religion. But a person practicing an illicit religion was treated as harshly as a burglar or even a murderer. For a time, Judaism was a permitted religion. The Romans, not knowing the difference between Jews and Christians, lumped Christianity in with Judaism, and didn't bother Christians. Nero changed that drastically. Needing a scapegoat for the disastrous fire in Rome in A.D. 64, Nero began a savage and systematic crackdown against Christians. Christianity became a *religiones illicitae,* and every Christian automatically became a criminal.

The writer of 1 Peter tells his readers to be prepared to suffer for their faith, because their faith is to be toughened just as metal is tempered by fire. In fact, suffering should be expected by Christians. In so doing, believers are being fellow sharers of Christ's sufferings. Peter's epistle also insists that Christians must remain loyal citizens and show the charges against them as false. Even under persecution, Christians are to demonstrate through their citizenship that they are persons who have been transformed by Jesus Christ.

NOTES ON THE PRINTED TEXT

Peter wrote this letter late in his life. Paul has been taken to Rome as a prisoner. James has been martyred. There is a growing opposition to Christians. So Peter prepares his readers for persecution. Right conduct brings suffering, but it also brings divine vindication just as it did for Christ, the crucified and exalted Lord.

Who is there to harm you if you are zealous for what is right? There can be no real danger for a Christian if he behaves correctly. A Christian must be devoted to what is good. Peter has in mind the zealots, a fanatical band of guerrilla fighters who pledged to drive out the Romans. Peter urges the Christians to have this same zealous commitment for good that was exhibited by these Jewish fanatics.

But even if you do suffer . . . you will be blessed. Peter continues his reassurances since he knows that Christians must be prepared to suffer for their faith.

Although suspicious authorities might carry out threats of persecution on blameless Christians, the Christians must remember that their suffering would be for Christ's sake. *Have no fear of them.* Do not be frightened or troubled by these authorities. *But in your hearts reverence Christ as Lord.* Find the courage to face suffering in faith. The heart was believed to be the seat of faith. If Christians were attacked by government authorities, they should testify openly and give an account of their Christian hope to them. This should be done in *gentleness and reverence.* Moreover, Peter urges each to *keep your conscience clear.* Hide nothing. Treat the authorities with respect. In this way, *those who revile your good behavior . . . may be put to shame* whether or not *you are abused.* The believers should be confident and open in their conduct. Even though Rome was not tolerant about religious matters, there was a good chance that nothing bad would happen to them if they were blameless. It is the perfect opportunity to share the Gospel. If they do suffer for good, it leads to blessedness. *For it is better to suffer for doing right, if that should be God's will, than for doing wrong.*

Beloved, do not be surprised at the fiery ordeal. Later, Peter reinforces the theme of suffering. Peter pleads for his followers not to be shocked by illtreatment. The ordeal of persecution is like the refining of metal. As a piece of metal is tempered by the flames of a refiner's fire, so will the believer's faith be tested by persecution. Instead of being upset, the believers are urged to rejoice for they are sharing in the sufferings of Christ. Their joy is all the greater when they share real joy at the glorious Coming of Christ at the End. *Rejoice . . . as you share Christ's sufferings, that you may also rejoice . . . when his glory is revealed.*

If you are reproached for the name of Christ, you are blessed. Peter further assures his readers of their blessedness if they are insulted, reviled, or disgraced for Christ's sake. They are blessed *because the spirit of glory and of God rests upon them.* Christians who share Christ's sufferings also share in His glory.

However, the blessedness does not extend to those suffering just punishments for crimes committed. *Let none of you suffer as a murderer . . . thief . . . wrongdoer, or a mischiefmaker.* But, *if one suffers as a Christian let him not be ashamed.* If a believer suffers because he is a Christian, he should feel no disgrace because he is glorifying God!

Peter asserts that the slander and persecution the Christians are enduring is a sign that the Last Judgment has begun. It has begun *with the household of God,* the Church. As hard as it is, the judgment of those persecuting the Church (*those who do not obey the gospel*) will be worse. The reference to Proverbs 11:31 indicates a far harsher punishment for the sinful opponents of the Church.

Therefore, let those who suffer . . . do right, and entrust their souls to a faithful Creator. Drawing the theme of suffering to a close, Peter calls Christians to confidently entrust their lives to God. He is the faithful Creator. He is the Giver and Taker of life. He is the hope for which suffering is made worthwhile.

SUGGESTIONS TO TEACHERS

Open this lesson by asking if anyone in the class has ever been called upon to suffer for his or her faith. If anyone indicates, *Yes,* ask in what way. Chances are nobody has really known much hurting because of being a Christian. It may be helpful to point out that fellow Christians in many other places today are suffering. And it can be useful to remind the class that we enjoy the fruits of the Gospel in our time only because many Christians before us did suffer for the sake of Good News of Jesus Christ. There is also the possibility that those in your class may find themselves forced to accept pain and sacrifice because of their commitment to the Lord.

This brings up the question, "How can a person face suffering for as apparently a flimsy a matter as faith?" Here is where 1 Peter offers great insights. A series of key ideas come from today's biblical material.

1. *SERVANT.* Every believer, Peter insists, is a servant as Christ was a servant. That means a Christian does not fret to have his or her own way and push to get his or her "rights." Peter offers a series of examples of how a Christian's servant ways must be put into action—in the realm of citizenship (2:13–17), of daily work (2:18), and marriage (3:1–7). Obviously, each of these can be the subject of an entire lesson. The key idea to keep before your class, however, is that the Christian like his or her servant Lord must take up the role of servant. And that means suffering!

2. *SUFFERER.* Face this idea head-on. Serving costs. Serving means some hurting. Recall that Jesus suffered, and His people have no right to think that they will be exempt from abuse or hurts. Discuss as a class the way religious people sometimes think that they should not have to suffer.

3. *SANITY.* Look at 1 Peter 4:1–11, noting that Christ's example and power enable a believer to remain stable and sober in the face of pressures to participate in destructive behavior. Examine Peter's list of how the Gentile world behaves. Notice that these practices are the antithesis of Christ's own lifestyle. As such, they are signs of insanity, since only He was truly sane and stable.

4. *SERENITY.* In the face of any fiery ordeals, Jesus brings calm. Go over the words in 1 Peter 4:12–19, with the plea that suffering should be for the sake of Christ, not for wrongdoing.

5. *SHEPHERD.* The fifth chaper of 1 Peter was written not only for early church leaders but for every person in your class. Consider who the "flock of God" may be that each in your class must tend—or could tend!

TOPIC FOR ADULTS
A HOPE WORTH SUFFERING FOR

Liverpool Leader's Testimony. Alfred Stocks serves as the City Manager of the large English city of Liverpool. He faces immense pressures and near-impossible challenges. Liverpool is experiencing the throes of massive urban change. The population is declining. The old industries have left or are leaving. Massive unemployment and a shrinking tax base cause serious financial problems. Once respectable neighborhoods are declining. Urban decay spreads through hundreds of acres of aging buildings and empty lots on the Mersey waterfront. Racial tensions flared into several nights of riots and fire-bombings a few summers ago. Restless youth, unable to find work, are drifting into street crime. Marxist leaders have been playing on the pent-up anger of the jobless, deepening divisions between races and classes. It means hope is in short measure for most civic leaders and government officials. Alfred Stocks, however, is a Christian. He has hope. Stocks also understands the meaning of suffering because he feels the pain of his fellow citizens and because he has to accept the hurts inflicted by angry critics. But Alfred Stocks maintains his hope. He comments, "Before I get there in the morning, Jesus Christ is already in the office and there to meet me when I open the door." Stocks therefore goes to work with hope.

Glass Shines Better When Broken. "The more I think about the meaning of living and acting in the name of Christ, the more I realize that what I have to offer to others is not my intelligence, skill, power, influence, or connections, but my own human brokenness through which the love of God can manifest itself. The celebrant in Leonard Bernstein's Mass says: 'Glass shines brighter when it's broken. . . . I never noticed that.' This, to me, is what ministry and mission are all about. Ministry is entering with our human brokenness into communion with others and speaking a word of hope. This hope is not based on any power to solve the problems of those with whom we live, but on the love of God, which becomes visible when we let go of our fears of being out of control and enter into His presence in a shared confession of weakness.

"This is a hard vocation. It goes against the grain of our need for self-affirmation, self-fulfillment, and self-realization. It is a call to true humility. I, therefore, think that for those who are pulled away from their familiar surroundings and brought into a strange land where they feel again like babies, the Lord offers a unique chance not only for personal conversion but also for an authentic ministry."—Henri Nouwen, *Gracias: A Latin American Journal* by Henri J.M. Nouwen. Copyright © 1983 by Henri J.M. Nouwen. Reprinted by permission of Harper & Row, Publishers, Inc.

Hope Through Christ's Pardon. Watergate figure Jeb Stuart Magruder confessed at his sentencing that he had lost his "ethical compass."

Magruder was deputy director of then-President Richard Nixon's 1972 re-election campaign. He served seven months in prison after pleading guilty to conspiracy, admitting he helped plan the Watergate burglary and lied to a grand jury investigating the case and at trial.

He said he had considered becoming a minister when first out of college, but decided against it. Even after experiencing a rekindled religious feeling in 1973, he said, "It took me a long time . . . to realize that I wanted to be in the organized ministry."

After Magruder's release from prison in 1975, he worked in Colorado with a Christian service group for teenagers. In 1978, he entered Princeton Theological Seminary, graduating in 1981.

In 1983, Jeb Magruder was ordained as a pastor. The month before, President Reagan denied him a pardon, while granting one to Watergate burglar Eugenio R. Martinez.

Dismissing the rejection, Magruder said last month, "My pardon was through Jesus Christ."

Questions for Pupils on the Next Lesson. 1. Why do some people doubt the promise of God? 2. Why does God seem to delay fulfilling His divine promise for the world? 3. How do you react when your dreams for the future are slow in being fulfilled? 4. Have you ever felt the need to be rescued from difficult circumstances? 5. Do you sincerely feel that your life is part of a divine plan for the world?

TOPIC FOR YOUTH
WORTH THE COST!

Happiest Religion. C. S. Lewis, the great English Christian writer, was once asked, "Which of the religions of the world gives its followers the greatest happiness?"

Lewis, without hesitation, replied, "Why, the religion of oneself, of course!"

We sometimes mistakenly imagine that Christian faith means constant pleasure and ease. We even tend to lose hope when things do not go the way we want and we experience setbacks. We resist serving others. We cater to our own whims. We want to do what pleases ourselves. Our religion of "self" is what will bring us happiness, we are convinced.

The truth of the matter is that the happiness cult brings us despair instead of hope. We may be able to avoid pain and suffering, especially pain and suffering on behalf of others, but we will not realize the hope that Christ brings those who stand with Him by standing with others!

Loneliness and Hopelessness. The loneliest people are usually the people with least hope. With the loneliest people in America today, according to recent studies, tending to be under the age of twenty-five, that means a high preponderance of young men and women with little hope for themselves or the future. Studies suggest that loneliness is not an illness, but is more like hunger. Although painful, loneliness is a signal of unmet needs. Just as hunger signals the body's need for nourishment, loneliness warns that needs of hopefulness are not being met.

Only the Lord can meet those needs. And through Jesus Christ, He offers you friendship—and hope!

Charity Under Suffering. "Hell is where no one has anything in common with anybody else except the fact that they all hate one another and cannot get away from one another and from themselves.

"And yet the world, with all its wars, is not yet hell. And history, however terrible, has another and deeper meaning. For it is not the evil of history that is its significance, and it is not by the evil of our time that our time can be understood. In the furnace of war and hatred, the City of those who love one another is drawn and fused together in the heroism of charity under suffering, while the city of those who hate everything is scattered and dispersed, and its citizens are cast out in every direction, like sparks, smoke, and flame."—Thomas Merton, *Blaze of Recognition: Through the Year With Thomas Merton,* New York: Doubleday & Co., 1983.

Questions for Pupils on the Next Lesson. 1. Do you sometimes find it difficult to wait for what you want? How do you handle these times? 2. In the light of your scientific understanding of the creation process, do you sometimes have problems accepting God's control of the universe? 3. Are you ever concerned that we humans now have the power to destroy the earth? 4. In the light of your experience, do you sometimes wonder who is in control of the world?

LESSON III—MARCH 16

A HOPE WORTH WAITING FOR

Background Scripture: 2 Peter
Devotional Reading: 2 Peter 1:3–11

KING JAMES VERSION

2 PETER 3 THIS second epistle, beloved, I now write unto you; in *both* which I stir up your pure minds by way of remembrance:

2 That ye may be mindful of the words which were spoken before by the holy prophets, and of the commandment of us the apostles of the Lord and Saviour:

3 Knowing this first, that there shall come in the last days scoffers, walking after their own lusts,

4 And saying, Where is the promise of his coming? for since the fathers fell asleep, all things continue as *they were* from the beginning of the creation.

5 For this they willingly are ignorant of, that by the word of God the heavens were of old, and the earth standing out of the water and in the water:

6 Whereby the world that then was, being overflowed with water, perished:

7 But the heavens and the earth, which are now, by the same word are kept in store, reserved unto fire against the day of judgment and perdition of ungodly men.

8 But, beloved, be not ignorant of this one thing, that one day *is* with the Lord as a thousand years, and a thousand years as one day.

9 The Lord is not slack concerning his promise, as some men count slackness; but is longsuffering to us-ward, not willing that any should perish, but that all should come to repentance.

10 But the day of the Lord will come as a thief in the night; in the which the heavens shall pass away with a great noise, and the elements shall melt with fervent heat, the earth also and the works that are therein shall be burned up.

11 *Seeing* then *that* all these things shall be dissolved, what manner *of persons* ought ye to be in *all* holy conversation and godliness,

12 Looking for and hasting unto the coming of the day of God, wherein the heavens being on fire shall be dissolved, and the elements shall melt with fervent heat?

13 Nevertheless we, according to his promise, look for new heavens and a new earth, wherein dwelleth righteousness.

REVISED STANDARD VERSION

2 PETER 3 This is now the second letter that I have written to you, beloved, and in both of them I have aroused your sincere mind by way of reminder; 2 that you should remember the predictions of the holy prophets and the commandment of the Lord and Savior through your apostles. 3 First of all you must understand this, that scoffers will come in the last days with scoffing, following their own passions 4 and saying, "Where is the promise of his coming? For ever since the fathers fell asleep, all things have continued as they were from the beginning of creation." 5 They deliberately ignore this fact, that by the word of God heavens existed long ago, and an earth formed out of water and by means of water, 6 through which the world that then existed was deluged with water and perished. 7 But by the same word the heavens and earth that now exist have been stored up for fire, being kept until the day of judgment and destruction of ungodly men.

8 But do not ignore this one fact, beloved, that with the Lord one day is as a thousand years, and a thousand years as one day. 9 The Lord is not slow about his promise as some count slowness, but is forbearing toward you, not wishing that any should perish, but that all should reach repentance. 10 But the day of the Lord will come like a thief, and then the heavens will pass away with a loud noise, and the elements will be dissolved with fire, and the earth and the works that are upon it will be burned up.

11 Since all these things are thus to be dissolved, what sort of persons ought you to be in lives of holiness and godliness, 12 waiting for and hastening the coming of the day of God, because of which the heavens will be kindled and dissolved, and the elements will melt with fire! 13 But according to his promise we wait for new heavens and a new earth in which righteousness dwells.

KEY BIBLE VERSE: *The Lord is not slow about his promise as some count slowness, but is forbearing toward you, not wishing that any should perish, but that all should reach repentance. 2 Peter 3:9.*

HOME DAILY BIBLE READINGS

BACKGROUND

The second letter from Peter was written with two purposes in mind. First, the writer wanted to encourage Christians whose faith was weakening because Christ's Second Coming seemed to be so slow. Second, the author of 2 Peter wanted to warn his readers about false teachers.

Nearly every Christian living in the first century A.D. expected Jesus to return to earth soon. When this did not occur within their lifetimes, many began to ask, "Why?" Persecution and hardships made life terribly difficult for many believers. The delay of the Second Coming of Jesus Christ seemed to diminish these Christians' sense of hope even more. "How can we keep holding on to our faith when things seem to be getting worse and Christ still has not come?" they were thinking.

The writer of the brief letter we call 2 Peter tried to answer their question, to offer some insights into why Christ's coming again seemed to be so slow. He explains the delay in Jesus Christ's Second Coming is because God wants to show His kindness and patience to all, so that "all should reach repentance" (2 Peter 3:9). This author has a beautiful vision of the Almighty as the One who does not want to see anyone destroyed and who wants everyone to repent and turn from their sins.

The false teachers in the time this letter was written were undermining the faith of many and spreading immoral practices. We forget that most of the Christian believers of that time came out of a pagan Roman background and lived in a licentious environment where sexual purity was practically unknown except among the Jews and Christians. So-called leaders and teachers priding themselves on their learning in religious matters wandered throughout the cities. They were spiritual fakes, of course, but they found eager audiences. They often caused newer and immature Christians to slip back into the destructive practices of pagan cults and the "anything goes" immorality of the Greek-speaking first-century Mediterranean world.

The writer of 2 Peter denounced these phony religious teachers for prompting immoral ways and for their greed. He does not speak gently, but bluntly warns them that they will be dealt with harshly when God's judgment comes. At the same time, he promises that the faithful will be rescued.

NOTES ON THE PRINTED TEXT

This is now the second letter that I have written you. Referring to his first letter to the exiles (First Peter), the author emphasizes that the purpose of both letters is the same. *In both of them I have aroused your sincere mind by way of reminder.* Peter aroused the "sincere mind" in First Peter by writing about avoiding immorality and living a blameless, holy life with the blessed inheritance as a goal. Peter asked Christians to remember this and encourages them to *remember the predictions of the holy prophets . . . the commandment of the Lord* given by the *apostles.* Instructions for living and conduct have been given through the Old Testament prophets, Christ, and the apostles.

Most first century Christians to whom Peter is writing believed the Lord would come again in their lifetime. Many were perplexed or anxious at the delay in His arrival. Some became skeptical. Peter points out that there will be those who doubt the promise of God. *First of all ... scoffers will come.* Mockers will arise who only follow *their own passions* without any regard for the coming judgment. These disappointed people will reject and abandon the Christian hope and give themselves over to their lusts. Peter warns that these mockers will also try to seduce devoted Christians from their faith with enticing ways. *Where is the promise of his coming? For ever since the fathers fell asleep, all things have continued as they were.* The skeptics point out that the first Christians ("the fathers") have died ("fallen asleep"), but there is still no visible sign of the End. Life continues on as if nothing has happened.

Peter answers this attitude of the skeptics by saying *they deliberately ignore this fact ... the world that then existed was deluged with water and perished.* He reminds his readers that God created the world by His Word. God controls the heavens and the earth. Far from allowing the world to continue unaltered from the beginning, He has already destroyed it once before at the Flood and will destroy it again at the appropriate time. The *ungodly* scoffers will be held accountable at the coming judgment when the world is again destroyed, this time through *fire.*

Having dealt with the skeptics, Peter turns his attention to the faithful who are anxious over the delay in the Coming of the Lord. *Do not ignore this ... beloved ... that with the Lord one day is a thousand years.* God's perspective of time is vastly different from men's. Because of this, they must wait patiently and expectantly for His coming in His own time.

Peter adds another thought. *The Lord is not slow ... but is forbearing ... not wishing that any should perish.* The Lord is not negligent or inactive. Rather, the Lord is generous. Christians should be thankful because God has delayed fulfilling the divine promise in order to allow all persons the opportunity to repent and be saved.

But the day of the Lord will come. The day will come unexpectedly *like a thief* striking without warning. No one should feel secure. Finding his basis for such a statement in the Old Testament prophecy, Peter describes a fiery, cosmic catastrophe. The Refiner's fire will expose and burn away all that is wicked. Each Christian's true character will be exposed at this judgment.

Knowing that the day of the Lord will come, Christians must live holy and godly lives. They must strive to live as God's expectant people both morally and spiritually. Their faithful living will hasten *the coming of the day of God.*

For the faithful, judgment will not lead to destruction and death but to newness of life! *According to his promise we wait for new heavens and a new earth in which righteousness dwells.* In the new world, the righteous will dwell and the wicked will be cast off. Confident that God's promise will be fulfilled, Christians can wait with hope.

SUGGESTIONS TO TEACHERS

The two men met at a seminary class reunion. They hadn't seen each other for twenty years. "What church are you serving now, Al?" the first asked. "Nowhere. I'm working in a shoe store," Al replied.

"But, Al, you were so involved when you graduated from seminary. All those civil rights marches and causes you worked for. What happened?"

Al sighed, "Guess I just burned out. As a matter of fact, I don't even attend church anymore."

His classmate expressed surprise.

"Look," Al continued. "I worked hard for all the right causes back in the 1960s.

But for what? Nothing has really changed. Don't give me all the old God-talk. Nothing is ever going to change."

Al, the seminarian who had once worked for noble ideals, had quit on everything—even quit on God. He had no hope for the present or the future. His life had shrunk to putting in enough hours as a shoe clerk to pay his bills. Twenty years earlier, Al had a song and wings. He praised God and he soared. Somehow, however, Al never understood that the Gospel offers a hope worth waiting for, such as described in 2 Peter 3:13.

1. *REPLY TO SCOFFERS.* To those who insist that nothing ever changes and therefore there is no hope for the future, as Al charged, 2 Peter offers a ringing challenge. God changes things. The future has possibilities. God who raised up Christ alive can raise up openings for us for tomorrow!

2. *RELIANCE ON SCHEDULE.* In the times when 2 Peter was written as well as now, some people grow impatient with God. God, however, is never slow about His promise. He has His own sense of timing. Sometimes, our sense of timing is not synchronized with His. As the text reminds us, with the Lord "one day is as a thousand years" (2 Peter 3:8).

3. *RECOGNITION ON THE SURPRISE.* God is never slow. He is always forbearing. He presents His goodness to us constantly—and in ways we don't always expect. Be prepared, tell your class, for God's offering hope in surprising ways. Have the class members reminisce and recount examples from their own lives when God surprised them with His own gift of new hope.

4. *READINESS FOR SERVICE.* God gives His gift of hope not only to bolster believers but to busy them in serving others. Two Peter describes the purpose of God's offering Christians hope so that they will live "lives of holiness and godliness" (2 Peter 3:11).

TOPIC FOR ADULTS
A HOPE WORTH WAITING FOR

Vision of Hope. Emily Dickinson lived all of her days in Amherst, Massachusetts, a quiet village. She never traveled far. Her life to most of us today would seem oppressively restricted. Yet she became a universal woman who could reveal the dimensions of eternity. She wrote:

> I never saw a Moor—
> I never saw the Sea—
> Yet know I how the Heather looks
> And what a billow be.

> I never spoke with God
> Nor visited in Heaven—
> Yet certain am I of the spot
> As if the Checks were given—

Cynical Beatitude. "Blessed are those that nought expect, for they shall not be disappointed," wrote "Peter Pindar," the pen name for a cynical satirist named John Wolcot (1738–1819). Wolcot delighted in writing savage essays, revealing an absence of Christian hope and defaming every well-known person in his early nineteenth-century London. Wolcot's "beatitude" may well be a motto for many living in these times, who live without expecting anything. The New Testament, in contrast, offers a hope worth waiting for: "The Lord is not slow about his promise as some count slowness, but is forbearing toward you, not wishing that any should perish, but that all should reach repentance" (2 Peter 3:9).

A Speaking Silence. "There are certain voices which we never hear save when everything is silent. They reach us as a revelation of the stillness. Sometimes on a summer afternoon one gets away from city or from town, and climbs up the grassy hillside till all the noise of human life is lost, and it is often then that there breaks upon the ear a certain indistinguishable murmur as of the moving of innumerable wings. Travellers tell us that there are rivers flowing beneath the streets of the ancient city of Shechem. During the hours of the day you cannot hear them, for the noise of the narrow streets and the bazaars. But evening comes, and the clamor dies away, and the dews of kindly sleep rest on the city; and then quite audibly, in the hush of night, you may hear the music of the buried streams. There are many voices like those hidden waters. You never can hear them save when things are still. There are whisperings of conscience in the bosom which a very little stir can easily drown. There are tidings from the eternal Spirit who is not far away from any one of us; tidings that will come and go unnoticed, unless we have won the grace of being still."—George Herbert Morrison (1866–1928) in his sermon "The Ministry of Silence."

Questions for Pupils on the Next Lesson. 1. How do you feel when your lifestyle corresponds to your professed beliefs? How do you feel when your lifestyle does not conform to your beliefs? Why? 2. Why do so many people in our transient society often yearn for a deeper sense of belonging? How can the Christian faith offer them help? 3. What does it mean, "to abide in Christ"? 4. How do you anticipate the future, with eagerness or with anxiety, or with a mixture of both? Why?

TOPIC FOR YOUTH
WORTH THE WAIT!

Hopeful Rebuilding in Spite of Defeats. Christians continue to hope regardless of how dark everything looks. Christian believers have a hope worth waiting for.

Here is a man in war-torn Central America who exemplifies this type of hope.

Kwan Pack Sung has fled two revolutions and one war. Now he lives in El Salvador! Sung has been in El Salvador for thirty-two years. He expected to settle in permanently, as the owner of a Chinese restaurant in a backwater country of Latin America. Speaking of the war there, he says, "We couldn't have imagined this in our worst dreams."

In 1937, he had left his native China to escape the war with Japan. "I made the mistake of going to Vietnam," he said, "and at the end of World War II we were caught between the French and the Viet Minh guerrillas." By 1947, the conflict was escalating and the Sung family was caught between two hostile forces.

When the guerrillas put a bomb in the building where he worked, the family decided it was time to leave. Sung took the family back to China. They arrived just in time for the revolution. "In 1949, we left again for Vietnam and then El Salvador. Finally, we thought, we had found a place to settle and raise a family."

He opened the China House Restaurant in San Miguel. They reared five children there. Four of his children now work in San Francisco and one continues to work in the restaurant. Battle weary as he is, Sung says that, despite the war, he will not move again.

Now Sung patiently studies English grammar as troop transports rumble past his restaurant and helicopters descend a few hundred yards away. He says, "When the tourists come back, I want to be able to say, 'Good Morning' to them in English."

Word of Hope. Sometimes a word that there is a hope worth waiting for is desperately needed by a person. Jackie Robinson, the great ball player, once needed that kind of a word.

Robinson was the first black man to play in major-league baseball. When

Branch Rickey brought him to big-league ball, all the other club owners had voted against letting him play because of his color. Most of the men on his team were opposed to having him on their roster and hoped he would fail. Opponents took every opportunity possible to make him angry and unwelcome. The first year in spring training, Jackie Robinson was playing in a game with the old Brooklyn Dodgers. He was feeling the pressures. Because he was trying so desperately to succeed, he was not doing well. He felt it was becoming hopeless for him or any black athlete to play in the major leagues.

In this particular game he managed to get on base on a walk, took second on a wild pitch, and came up out of his slide running for third as the ball again was thrown away. The other team still didn't seem to have control of the ball when he reached third, so the coach there waved him in. He ran as fast and slid as hard as he could, but through the dust and commotion he saw the umpire's arm go up and heard his voice bellow, "You're out!" A hurricane of boos came from the stands (directed at Robinson) as he made the long, painful walk back to the dugout. The bench jockeys, on the opponent's bench as well as on his own bench, were riding him hard. So were the loudmouths in the stands.

He said he did the best he could to block out everything. He isolated himself in the corner of the dugout and kept his face a stoic mask as best he could. But then he looked across the diamond and saw a little white boy standing up and shouting at the top of his lungs. "Attaboy, Jackie! Nice try, Jackie!"

Jackie Robinson later often recalled that unknown white kid's word of encouragement. It was almost like God's word of hope, a personal message that he had been waiting for to help him persevere. When he was ready to quit, the cry of hope from an anonymous youngster turned the tide for this great black athlete. He stayed with the game, and opened the way for other minority players to follow.

Have you considered that you may be the unknown young person who may offer a word from the Lord that there is a hope worth waiting for?

Only One Year to Live. "A while ago a woman's doctor sadly shook his head and told her that he had done all he could and that she only had a year to live. Somehow the story came to the attention of a reporter who saw it from the human interest point of view. He knew that people all across the country were facing verdicts like that every day. So he interviewed the woman and wrote up her story in the form of a question: Since I only have one year to live, how shall I live it? The account appeared in papers everywhere, and replies began to come in with advice.

"Those who were sensual advised her to live every minute for her own pleasure and gratification. Those who were community minded advised her to forget herself and live for others. Some counseled her to cast off all restraint and indulge herself in her life-long fantasies or wishes. Others felt she would spend the year best if she traveled to distant and exotic places. There were those who sensibly advised her to accept the facts and calmly live just one day at a time, and find satisfaction in it. She did not lack for good spiritual advice either. She was counseled to be sure of her soul's salvation by a personal faith in the Lord Jesus Christ. Of the various kinds of advice given her, we do not know which she chose, nor any more details as to the outcome of her story. But the thought her story raises is a rather sobering one, isn't it?

"What would you tell a person who knew he had only one year to live? In fact what would you think and do if you had only a year to live? That's a hard subject to face. No one cares to think about his own death. Many people can't face it. But regardless of how you react to the fact, death is a reality which cannot be escaped. 'It is appointed unto man once to die,' the Bible says. The sensible thing to do is to be ready because the Bible also says, 'after this the judgment,'

"You probably have said: 'Not now, some other time'—when you were face to face with your sinfulness and need for salvation. OK, what 'other time' do you have in mind? Would you be willing to say a year from now, 'I'm going to get right with God'? That might be OK if you are sure you are going to be alive a year from now, but are you sure? Six months from now? Sure you'll be alive then? One month? Sure you'll be alive then?

"You say, 'Not now'—God says, 'Now.' 'NOW is the accepted time; Behold now is the day of salvation.' "—*Highway Evangelist*, Route 25, Trip 8.

Questions for Pupils on the Next Lesson. 1. If your activities are a measure of what you believe is imporant in life, what do your activities say about your faith? 2. Do a person's goals in life influence their actions? 3. Why is it sometimes difficult to do what is expected of you? 4. What exactly does it mean to "abide in Christ?" 5. What kind of a relationship do you have with Jesus Christ—close, casual, none whatsoever, or what? How do you know?

LESSON IV—MARCH 23

A HOPE LEADING TO ACTION

Background Scripture: 1 John 1—3
Devotional Reading: 1 John 3:11–18

KING JAMES VERSION

1 JOHN 2 MY little children, these things write I unto you, that ye sin not. And if any man sin, we have an advocate with the Father, Jesus Christ the righteous:

2 And he is the propitiation for our sins: and not for ours only, but also for *the sins of* the whole world.

3 And hereby we do know that we know him, if we keep his commandments.

4 He that saith, I know him, and keepeth not his commandments, is a liar, and the truth is not in him.

5 But whoso keepeth his word, in him verily is the love of God perfected: hereby know we that we are in him.

6 He that saith he abideth in him ought himself also so to walk, even as he walked.

28 And now, little children, abide in him; that, when he shall appear, we may have confidence, and not be ashamed before him at his coming.

29 If ye know that he is righteous, ye know that every one that doeth righteousness is born of him.

3 BEHOLD, what manner of love the father hath bestowed upon us, that we should be called the sons of God: therefore the world knoweth us not, because it knew him not.

2 Beloved, now are we the sons of God, and it doth not yet appear what we shall be: but we know that, when he shall appear, we shall be like him; for we shall see him as he is.

3 And every man that hath this hope in him purifieth himself, even as he is pure.

REVISED STANDARD VERSION

1 JOHN 2 My little children, I am writing this to you so that you may not sin; but if any one does sin, we have an advocate with the Father, Jesus Christ the righteous; 2 and he is the expiation for our sins, and not for ours only but also for the sins of the whole world. 3 And by this we may be sure that we know him, if we keep his commandments. 4 He who says "I know him" but disobeys his commandments is a liar, and the truth is not in him; 5 but whoever keeps his word, in him truly love for God is perfected. By this we may be sure that we are in him: 6 he who says he abides in him ought to walk in the same way in which he walked.

28 And now, little children, abide in him, so that when he appears we may have confidence and not shrink from him in shame at his coming. 29 If you know that he is righteous, you may be sure that every one who does right is born of him.

3 See what love the Father has given us, that we should be called children of God; and so we are. The reason why the world does not know us is that it did not know him. 2 Beloved, we are God's children now; it does not yet appear what we shall be, but we know that when he appears we shall be like him, for we shall see him as he is. 3 And every one who thus hopes in him purifies himself as he is pure.

KEY VERSE: *Abide in him, so that when he appears we may have confidence and not shrink from him in shame at his coming.* 1 John 2:28.

HOME DAILY BIBLE READINGS

Mar.	17.	M.	*We Declare Him Unto You.* 1 John 1:1–5.
Mar.	18.	T.	*Walking in the Light.* 1 John 1:6–10.
Mar.	19.	W.	*Striving to Keep His Commandments.* 1 John 2:1–6.
Mar.	20.	T.	*A Message for All Ages.* 1 John 2:12–14.
Mar.	21.	F.	*Warning Against Apostasy.* 1 John 2:18–23.
Mar.	22.	S.	*Abiding in Christ.* 1 John 2:24–29.
Mar.	23.	S.	*The Test of Sonship.* 1 John 3:1–12.

BACKGROUND

How do you know that you are a Christian? How do others know you are a Christian? How would *you* answer these questions?

The writer of the First Letter of John hits his readers with these questions as he tries to deepen their spiritual life. John's letter has two purposes: to encourage others to live in fellowship with God and with Jesus Christ, and to warn them against false teachers whose ideas undermine this fellowship. The author states that his readers will know they are Christians when they live in fellowship with God and with Jesus Christ. He further announces that fellowship with God and Jesus must lead to fellowship with others, and that this love of others is the way others will know they are Christians. Love for the Lord and love for others in response to God's love for them: this is the key to Christian living.

The false teaching which John was battling was Gnosticism. Basically, Gnosticism was the error being promoted by many that God had not truly become human in Jesus. The notion behind this dangerous doctrine was that the physical world was completely evil, and God would never have contact with evil, material stuff such as a human body. Such a doctrine, of course, denied the Incarnation.

On a more practical level, this teaching led many to think that to be saved was to be set free from any material or physical concerns in the world. Some Gnostic ideas filtering into the Church taught that Christians could forget matters of moral living and compassion for others.

The First Letter of John vigorously opposed these ideas. He exposed them for the dangerous threat they were. He insisted that no one could live in sin and claim to be "spiritual" or a "child of God." John realized clearly that Gnostic notions, even when couched in Christian terms, cut believers off from fellowship with God and fellowship with others. And without such fellowship, Christians had no hope.

NOTES ON THE PRINTED TEXT

Even though the three letters of John are classified as Catholic Epistles, none of them is intended for the universal Church. Each is local in its references. After hearing of the spread of false doctrine, John wrote these letters to churches particularly close to his heart. *My little children,* a warm, tender, endearing greeting, shows that the old apostle is adopting a fatherly approach. *I am writing you so that you may not sin.* John's purpose in writing is to prevent sin by warning his young, easily influenced converts. Knowing that no one is sinless, John continues by reminding the Christians that *we have an advocate with the Father. Advocate* is a legal term, literally meaning "pleader." The advocate was a person who took the side of one individual in a lawsuit and pleaded in his or her favor. John affirms that *Jesus Christ the righteous* is such an advocate for them. Christ pleads for them and through His intercession, they are forgiven of their sins. Jesus Christ, the Righteous, provides them with access to God. *He is the expiation for our sins, and not for ours only but also for the sins of the whole world.* Biblically, *expiation* refers to the covering or wiping away of sins. John is reminding his readers that Christ wiped away or blotted out not only their sins, but the sins of the whole world through His death and Resurrection.

By this we may be sure that we know him, if we keep his commandments. John is responding to the false doctrine of Gnosticism. Gnostics claimed that by mystical contemplation they were able to gain special illumination and higher knowledge which they could use to rise to true fellowship with God. John rejects this notion of special knowledge. Christians know God if they keep His commandments. The hope in Christ is the basis of faith. Faith is expressed in actions such as keeping the Commandments. Gnostics believed salvation came through a secret knowledge that freed them from moral standards and enabled them to live as they desired. Countering this belief, John writes, *He who says "I know him" but disobeys his commandments is a liar and the truth is not in him.* True knowledge of God is never intellectual. True knowledge of God is demonstrated in the daily actions of life itself. *Whoever keeps his word, in him truly love for God is perfected. Perfected* implies the growing or maturing a child does as he moves toward adulthood. Whoever lives by God's commandments and shows His love in daily actions is an individual who demonstrates a mature understanding of God. John adds a simple test to prove his point. *He who says he abides in him ought to walk in the same way in which he walked.* The best test of keeping the Commandments is to live as Jesus lived. Imitate Christ, John writes. Abide in Christ by walking in His ways.

John adds another thought. Abiding in God brings righteousness and readiness for the Coming of the Lord. *And now, little children, abide in him, so that when he appears we may have confidence and not shrink from him in shame at his coming.* Alluding to the judgment that will occur at Christ's Coming, John pleads for righteous living. Faithfulness enables believers to stand confidently as they await His Coming.

If you know that he is righteous, you may be sure that everyone who does right is born of him. Since John's readers know Him, they abide with Him always. In fact, all Christians born of Him, are with Him always and are His children. Being born of a loving God makes Christians His children. John has to call attention to this belief. *See what love the Father has given us, that we should be called children of God.* He tells them that because of their relationship with Christ, they should know themselves to be God's children. *And so we are,* John affirms. For Christians see God's Fatherly love through Christ. Jesus reveals God. So if the world does not know Christ, it does not know God.

We know that when he appears we shall be like him, for we shall see him as he is. The Coming will be in the future at an undisclosed time. However, as *God's children,* Christians can be confident of a continued fellowship with Christ. In the meantime, the expectation of His Coming has a purifying power. *Everyone who thus hopes in him purifies himself as he is pure.* Because of their hope, Christians are motivated to follow Christ's righteous example.

SUGGESTIONS TO TEACHERS

Palm Sunday's lesson continues the theme of the hope that Christians have through Jesus Christ. Because of Him, believers can hope, no matter how bleak the circumstances may be. After all, the Crucifixion was the bleakest set of circumstances imaginable. But God took the death of Jesus and turned it into triumph!

With the events of Holy Week in mind, put together your lesson from 1 John 1—3 so that the Hope-Bringer, Jesus Christ, will be stressed. At the same time, emphasize that the hope Christ brings must lead to action! He brings us from darkness to light, from death to life in order to have us live forgivingly and creatively with others.

1. *CHRIST, OUR ADVOCATE.* Christians must regularly look at what Jesus means. We easily take Him for granted. Or we fall into the habit of speaking of His meaning in terms of clichés. This lesson offers us the opportunity to consider who Jesus Christ is for us as our *advocate.* Notice how this word is used in 1 John 2:1, 2. The writer states that Jesus pleads our cause and intercedes for us. What a hope-inspiring idea! We are never forsaken. We are never without hope. We have Him looking after our interests!

2. *COMPANIONSHIP OUR AWARD.* As teacher, you will have to make clear that God gives His gift of hope in Christ to those who are obedient to Him. Admittedly, obedience is not a popular idea. However, explain to your class that knowing Jesus Christ means keeping His commandments (*see* 1 John 1:3–6), and obeying Him means the privilege of His companionship.

3. *CARING OUR ACTIVITY.* Allow sufficient time in your class period to go over the "New Commandment" Jesus Christ gives His followers (1 John 2:7, 8). Discuss why this is so new. Get below the superficial understanding of the word *love* so that your class will comprehend the idea of Christ's kind of love, based on the Greek word *Agape.*

4. *CONFIDENCE OUR ATTITUDE.* Throughout this section of Scripture, the writer maintains that Christians can hope in the worst of situations. On this Palm Sunday, look ahead with your class to the events of Maundy Thursday and Good Friday. Remind your class that the Crucifixion of Jesus Christ was the most hopeless period for humankind. However, God acted! Because of God's mighty act of deliverance of raising up Christ on Easter, 1 John shouts exultantly that believers also "have passed out of death into life" (3:14). Christians have confidence in God; therefore they have hope which impels them to act!

TOPIC FOR ADULTS
A HOPE LEADING TO ACTION

Eternal Life. Zane Grey once wrote a Western which came to a surprising climax. It was about an Eastern society girl, called "Majesty" by her friends, who went out West. Majesty fell in love with a tall, lanky, fast-drawing cowboy, and in a reckless moment married him. He was a rough man of courage, of principle, but he had a way of getting into trouble.

As the story goes, he got into trouble south of the border, was accused of killing a Mexican, and was condemned to death by an unjust court. He was sentenced to take what was called, "The Walk of Death." At sunrise he was to start walking down the main street of the shabby little town. At some place in the walk, he knew not where, gunfire would greet him from around some corner, and he would die.

The morning came. As the sun peeked over the distant mountain he calmly rolled a cigarette, lit it, then slowly began to walk. Often he would pause, looking at some building, expecting death to burst upon him. On he walked, but still no gunfire. He was almost at the end of the short street. Only one more corner, and that must be it. Then as he sauntered past the scrubby building out stepped— Majesty! "It is I, Majesty, your wife." Unknown to him she had been able to pay off the authorities and he was free.

Do you know why I think of this at Easter? I am taking that walk, and so are you. I know not when death will step out to claim me, but I know something else. I know Someone who loves me, and whom I love, who has paid it all—for me. Because He did, the last step in life is not death, but life—Eternal Life. Because He lives, I, too, shall live!

May you have a closer walk with Him!

Success and Failure. "My successes are not my own. The way to them was prepared by others. The fruit of my labors is not my own, for I am preparing the way for the achievements of another. Nor are my failures my own. They may spring from the failure of another, but they are also compensated for by another's achievement. Therefore, the meaning of my life is not to be looked for merely in the sum total of my own achievements. It is seen only in the complete integration of my achievements and failures with the achievements and failures of my own generation, my own society and time."—Thomas Merton, *Blaze of Recognition: Through the Year with Thomas Merton,* New York, Doubleday & Co. 1983.

What Makes a Live Church?
"LIVE CHURCHES always have a parking problem;
... dead churches don't.

"LIVE CHURCHES are constantly changing their methods;
. . . dead ones don't have to.
"LIVE CHURCHES have lots of noisy kids;
. . . dead churches are quiet.
"LIVE CHURCHES' expenses always exceed their income;
. . . dead churches take in more than they ever dream of spending.
"LIVE CHURCHES are constantly improving and plan for the future;
. . . dead churches worship their past.
"LIVE CHURCHES grow so fast you forget people's names;
. . . in dead churches you've known everyone's name for years.
"LIVE CHURCHES move out in faith;
. . . dead churches operate totally by sight.
"LIVE CHURCHES support missions heavily;
. . . dead churches keep it all at home.
"LIVE CHURCHES are filled with tithers;
. . . dead churches are filled with tippers.
"LIVE CHURCHES dream great dreams for God;
. . . dead churches relive nightmares,
"LIVE CHURCHES have the fresh wind of love blowing;
. . . dead churches are stale with bickering.
"LIVE CHURCHES don't have 'can't' in their vocabulary;
. . . dead churches have nothing but.
"LIVE CHURCHES EVANGELIZE! Dead churches fossilize."

Christ crucified and raised alive brings hope, and the hope He brings always leads to action in a congregation. The hope of the Living Lord makes a live Church!

Questions for Pupils on the Next Lesson. 1. What is our assurance of our union with God? 2. If we have an assurance of union with God, how may we face the unknown furture? 3. Do you feel a sense of acceptance in life or do you often fear rejection? 4. Do you sometimes have problems relating to others because you lack a sense of self-worth? 5. Do you sometimes wrestle with the issue of what will happen to you after death?

TOPIC FOR YOUTH
LIVE YOUR FAITH

Habitat for Humanity. " 'If you lend money to any of my people with you who is poor, you shall not be to him as a creditor, and you shall not exact interest from him.' Exodus 22:25.

"Habitat for Humanity sells cheap, well-built homes to the poor at biblical rates: no profit, no interest. The sales pitch is irresistible. For $700 down and a maximum of $60 a month, the downtrodden can buy a small piece of the system.

"Millard Fuller, a forty-seven-year-old former millionaire, past commune leader, current radical lawyer, and constant religious critic, began the non-profit corporation dedicated completely to building houses for the poor.

"Qualification for the program is the inability to obtain a conventional loan.

"Construction work is done primarily by volunteers, college and church youth groups who spend a week or two and then leave.

"The houses are frame only. Brick is too expensive, and would require skilled labor. Except for the plumbing and electricity, the houses are built by people more at ease with books than hammers.

"There are Habitat offices in thirty-three cities throughout the United States, and fourteen offices overseas in Zaire, Kenya, Guatemala, Peru, and other nations.

" 'The poor need capital, not charity,' is a slogan that is found hanging in many of the Habitat offices, usually located in a neighborhood on the wrong side of town. They operate without strings on private donations only. Their aim is to eliminate substandard housing completely.

" 'They can do things a lot easier. They don't have all the red tape and government regulations to cover,' said an unnamed envious community-development director who does the same thing with federal funds that are bound by volumes of rules.

" 'And of course, they do it all at a much lesser cost,' he admitted.

"Habitat encourages, if possible, the early payment of the twenty-year mortgages it lets, to allow the money to circulate faster at a less devalued rate.

"In 1966, Millard Fuller turned his back on the fortune he had made in an Alabama mail-order business, to devote his life to Christ and the poor.

"The pride that people who formerly lived in slums and who now own their own home gives Fuller a sense of optimism.

"He says, 'Instead of sitting around bemoaning the bigness of the problem, you roll up your sleeves and do what you can.' "—Jim Galloway, *Quote*, November 1, 1983.

Feel the Weight and Play the Part. An American businessman traveled to Oberammergau, Germany, to view the famous Passion Play. The Easter season drama enthralled him. In rapt attention, the businessman watched the events leading up to a dramatic crucifixion of Jesus Christ.

After the play, he made his way backstage to meet Mr. Anton Lang, who played the part of Christ. After taking a picture of the actor, the man noticed a large, wooden cross resting in the corner. It was the same cross Mr. Lang carried in the play. "Here," the businessman said to his wife. "You take the camera. When I lift the cross on my shoulder, snap the picture."

Before the actor could speak, the businessman stooped to lift the prop onto his shoulder. He was amazed that the cross would not budge! It was made of heavy oak beams and could be moved only with great difficulty. Panting from strain and frustration, he turned to Mr. Lang and said, "Why, I thought it would be light. I thought the cross was hollow. Why do you carry a cross so heavy?"

The actor replied, "Sir, if I didn't feel the weight of the Cross, I could not play this part."

Questions for Pupils on the Next Lesson. 1. Do you do what is expected of you out of fear of being punished or out of personal belief that what you are doing is right? 2. Do you sometimes fear that you cannot measure up to other's standards and sincerely want a change in your life? 3. What assurance do you have that God is truly your friend? 4. What do the Scriptures mean by stating that God gave us eternal life through Jesus Christ?

LESSON V—MARCH 30

A HOPE FOCUSED ON JESUS

Background Scripture: 1 John 4; 5.
Devotional Reading: 1 John 4:1–6

KING JAMES VERSION

1 JOHN 4 13 Hereby know we that we dwell in him, and he in us, because he hath given us of his Spirit.

14 And we have seen and do testify that the Father sent the Son *to be* the Saviour of the world.

15 Whosoever shall confess that Jesus is the Son of God, God dwelleth in him, and he in God.

16 And we have known and believed the love that God hath to us. God is love; and he that dwelleth in love dwelleth in God, and God in him.

17 Herein is our love made perfect, that we may have boldness in the day of judgment: because as he is, so are we in this world.

5 Whosoever believeth that Jesus is the Christ is born of God: and every one that loveth him that begat loveth him also that is begotten of him.

2 By this we know that we love the children of God, when we love God, and keep his commandments.

3 For this is the love of God, that we keep his commandments: and his commandments are not grievous.

4 For whatsoever is born of God overcometh the world: and this is the victory that overcometh the world, *even* our faith.

5 Who is he that overcometh the world, but he that believeth that Jesus is the Son of God?

6 This is he that came by water and blood, *even* Jesus Christ; not by water only, but by water and blood. And it is the Spirit that beareth witness, because the Spirit is truth.

7 For there are three that bear record in heaven, the Father, the Word, and the Holy Ghost: and these three are one.

8 And there are three that bear witness in earth, the spirit, and the water, and the blood: and these three agree in one.

9 If we receive the witness of men, the witness of God is greater: for this is the witness of God which he hath testified of his Son.

10 He that believeth on the Son of God hath the witness in himself: he that believeth not God hath made him a liar; because he believeth not the record that God gave of his Son.

11 And this is the record, that God hath given to us eternal life, and this life is in his Son.

12 He that hath the Son hath life; *and* he that hath not the Son of God hath not life.

REVISED STANDARD VERSION

1 John 4 13 By this we know that we abide in him and he in us, because he has given us of his own Spirit. 14 And we have seen and testify that the Father has sent his Son as the Savior of the world. 15 Whoever confesses that Jesus is the Son of God, God abides in him, and he in God. 16 So we know and believe the love God has for us. God is love, and he who abides in love abides in God, and God abides in him. 17 In this is love perfected with us, that we may have confidence for the day of judgment, because as he is so are we in this world.

5 Every one who believes that Jesus is the Christ is a child of God, and every one who loves the parent loves the child. 2 By this we know that we love the children of God, when we love God and obey his commandments. 3 For this is the love of God, that we keep his commandments. And his commandments are not burdensome. 4 For whatever is born of God overcomes the world; and this is the victory that overcomes the world, our faith. 5 Who is it that overcomes the world but he who believes that Jesus is the Son of God?

6 This is he who came by water and blood, Jesus Christ, not with the water only but with the water and the blood. 7 And the Spirit is the witness, because the Spirit is the truth. 8 There are three witnesses, the Spirit, the water, and the blood; and these three agree. 9 If we receive the testimony of men, the testimony of God is greater; for this is the testimony of God that he has borne witness to his Son. 10 He who believes in the Son of God has the testimony in himself. He who does not believe God, has made him a liar, because he has not believed in the testimony that God has borne to his Son. 11 And this is the testimony, that God gave us eternal life, and this life is in his Son. 12 He who has the Son has life; he who has not the son of God has not life.

KEY VERSE: This is the testimony, that God gave us eternal life, and this life is in his Son. 1 John 5:11.

HOME DAILY BIBLE READINGS

Mar.	24.	M.	*God's Promise, Our Hope.* Hebrews 6:13–20.
Mar.	25.	T.	*Choosing the Good Part.* Luke 10:38–42.
Mar.	26.	W.	*Jesus and the Father Are One.* 1 John 14:8–14.
Mar.	27.	T.	*Testing the Spirit.* 1 John 4:1–6.
Mar.	28.	F.	*An Exhortation to Love.* 1 John 4:7–16.
Mar.	29.	S.	*God's Love Inspires Confidence.* 1 John 4:17–28.
Mar.	30.	S.	*Blessed Assurance.* 1 John 5:1–12.

BACKGROUND

From time to time, forceful personalities appear with interesting and attractive messages. Often, their arguments seem logical. These teachers persuade many to their own way of thinking. Some cults in our time have grown because of such alluring ideas and convincing leaders.

This was the situation when the First Letter of John was written. Certain leaders from within the Christian Church thought they were improving on traditional doctrine by introducing novel arguments. These leaders were not setting out to oppose the faith. Rather, they insisted they were making it respectable and relevant. In particular, these teachers were determined to incorporate the popular philosophical thinking of their time into Christian beliefs. The problem was that the popular philosophy among the intellectuals was Gnosticism, the notion that only "spirit" was good and anything material was evil. These would-be teachers in the Church insisted upon squeezing the Gospel into a Gnostic mold. What resulted was a denial of the centrality of Jesus Christ.

The writer of our First Letter of John was not fighting against a pernicious power from outside the Church. He was struggling against influential teachers who once were inside the Church. He knew that their ideas sounded impressive to many still within the Church. John also realized that these false teachers were seducing some to forsake the faith in Jesus as truly completely divine and truly completely human. For example, in 1 John 5:6, the writer emphasizes that Jesus "came by water and blood." He refutes the Gnostic churchmen who said that the divine Christ came by water (that is, at the baptism of Jesus) but denied that He came by blood (in other words, by the Cross) because they insisted the divine part of Jesus left the human Jesus before His crucifixion! John states that such efforts to spiritualize the person of Jesus undercut the central facts and acts of our faith, namely that Jesus Christ who truly is human as well as truly divine suffered and died on the Cross and was raised from death!

John knew from personal experience that all hope focuses on Jesus. He calls on his readers to keep their eyes fixed on the God-Man, and not be diverted by intriguing intellectual theories about spirituality.

NOTES ON THE PRINTED TEXT

One of the characteristics of John's writing is the repetition of themes. In this lesson, he returns to the theme of love. As John outlines the basis of hope, notice the repetition of terms and ideas from last week's lesson.

We know that we abide in him and he in us, because he has given us of his own Spirit. Love for one another proves that God abides in His people (*see* 4:7–12). His presence with us is also shown through His gift of the Spirit. Through the presence of the Spirit and an awareness of God's abiding love, Christians have the assurance of a union with God.

The theme of God's abiding presence is shown when Christians confess or witness to Jesus' Sonship. *We ... testify that the Father has sent his Son as the Savior of the world. Whoever confesses that Jesus is the Son of God....* John recites the confessions of the early Church. Jesus is the Son of God and the Savior of the world. As Christians confess and witness that Jesus is Lord, *God abides in* them and they *in God.*

John then draws together the themes. *So we know and believe the love God has for us. God is love, and he who abides in love abides in God, and God abides in him.* God is defined as love. He is the love Christians see in Jesus. God acted in love when He sent His Son (14) into the world. Whoever confesses Jesus abides in God (15). Whoever loves abides in God (16).

This abiding love of God instills *confidence* in the believers so they need not fear *the day of judgment.* The reason for the confidence is that Christians are God's children. Love has reached its perfection in them. Perfect love drives out fear. Because Christians have assurance of union with God, they need not be anxious about judgment. Christians simply trust in the life and love of God. *We may have confidence ... because as he is so are we in this world.* Christians are like God since they abide in God and love one another. Likeness to Christ is based on His status as God's Son. Christians are like Him so they will not be judged harshly.

In chapter five, John continues the theme of love but approaches it in a different manner. *Every one who believes that Jesus is the Christ is a child of God.* Citing the old adage, "Love the parent and love the child," John states that the love of God and the love of others go together. *Every one who loves the parent loves the child.* Every Christian is a child of God and loves His Father. Because of this love of God as a Father, a Christian will love God's other children as well. *By this we know that we love the children of God, when we love God.* However, the love of God also requires believers *to obey his commandments.* Christians have further assurance of union with God when they manifest love toward other believers and obey God's commandments. John refutes the false teachers who claimed to love God, but put no emphasis on keeping the Commandments.

His commandments are not burdensome, John affirms. John encourages his readers reminding them that they have God's power and can overcome the world. Their *faith* and belief that *Jesus is the Son of God* gives them *the victory.* Victory is achieved through the Christians' faith that Jesus is the Son of God.

One aspect of the false teaching that John is combating stressed that Christ did not actually suffer but only appeared to suffer. John presents a bodily Christ, One who was no phantom. *He ... came ... with the water and blood.* John refers to Christ's baptism and Crucifixion which were real occurrences. Another aspect of the false teaching stressed that special knowledge led to salvation. John reaffirms that it is Christ the Son who brings eternal life not special knowledge bestowed on a few.

And the Spirit is the witness because the Spirit is the truth. The Spirit has revealed Jesus as God's Son through His birth, baptism, ministry, death, and Resurrection. The Spirit affirms Jesus as God's Son. However, the Spirit is not the only witness. *There are three witnesses, the Spirit, the water, and the blood. The water* is the sacrament of baptism and *the blood* is the sacrament of the Lord's Supper. Jewish Law held that the agreement of three witnesses was conclusive. *The Spirit, the water, and the blood; and these three agree* that Christ is God's Son. Men also testify, John writes. However, *the testimony of God is greater.* God testifies through the Son. *He who believes in the Son of God has the testimony in himself.* Knowledge of Jesus can be received and retained. When it is not believed, that person makes God a *liar.* Faith must be internalized. Faith must be personal. Christians must do more than know about Jesus. Jesus must be known personally. If this occurs, Jesus abides in each of the believers. John stresses it is Jesus' life, the witness of the Spirit, and God's own testimony that affirm Jesus as God's Son.

The reward of faith is eternal life. *This is the testimony, that God gave us eternal life.* God's gift to us through Jesus Christ is eternal life. However, it is only those who respond in faith to Jesus that have eternal life. *He who has the Son has life; he who has not the Son has not life.*

SUGGESTIONS TO TEACHERS

Several years ago, a submarine had a mechanical failure and could not surface. The craft sank to the bottom. A rescue bell and divers worked feverishly to try to save the trapped crew. As the air supply diminished and the rescuers still had not been able to devise a method to extricate the men inside the doomed sub, divers heard a message being tapped in Morse code by one of the submarine's crewmen: "Is there any hope?"

That is the messaage on the minds of many persons today. Some in your class are privately asking if there is any hope. After looking at the evening news or reading the morning paper, you must sometimes wonder, too.

Easter is God's mighty *YES!* to that question. The Resurrection of Jesus Christ means hope! Basing your lesson on 1 John 4, 5, develop your lesson on the Good News of a hope focused on Jesus.

1. *TRIUMPH OF TRUTH.* Jesus is alive! Emphasize to your class that Jesus IS alive, not was once alive, or is simply reported by some to be alive. Easter means the Risen, Living Lord! Furthermore, because God raised Jesus up alive, "we might live through him" (1 John 4:9). Death is not the final word. Nor is despair. The Resurrected Christ in your midst means *life!*

2. *TALE OF TENDERNESS.* The Resurrection is also God's mercy in action. He has loved us so much that He would not leave us. He brought back Jesus to us, in spite of what we humans did to Him. Take enough time in your lesson to talk about how each person needs to receive love. Point out that God initiates love. Ask how the grace—the undeserved love—of God has been experienced in the lives of those in the class.

3. *TESTIMONY OF TRUST.* Have those in your class work on understanding the meaning of the verse, "He who believes in the Son of God has the testimony in himself" (1 John 5:9). Help them to home in on the notion that proofs of God's hope in the world are not needed when one trusts in the Living Christ. The presence of the Risen One is proof enough! The knowledge that Jesus Christ lives is all the evidence for hope that anyone needs!

4. *TRAITS OF TRANSCENDENCE.* Jesus is more than another human leader. He is certainly more than another deceased human leader. This Easter lesson should be a time for you and your class to ponder the meaning of the personality of Jesus Christ. Lift Him out of the pages of the past by helping your class to meet Him as today's Savior. Perhaps a brief exercise with paper and pencils where each draws or writes some diagram or set of sentences to try to put in graphic form who Jesus is (not was).

5. *TOUCHSTONE OF TEACHING.* The letters of John stress love for others as the mark of authentic discipleship. Unless a person shows care for others in specific ways, words and feelings are empty. Do not overlook this essential point in your lesson presentation. With all of the joy of the Easter message through music, preaching, and celebrating, Christians must exhibit love!

TOPIC FOR ADULTS
A HOPE FOCUSED ON JESUS

Surrender to the Person. A minister has related how a member of the Jewish faith became interested in Christianity. After attending the services at the church where he ministered, the Jew sought out the minister. After several conferences no really definite progress seemed to be made, and the Jew came one evening saying flatly: "Tonight I decide one way or the other. When I walk out the door, I will either have decided to become a Christian or will close the door on Christianity forever." During the conversation that followed, the inquirer seemed to be little convinced until the minister declared, "Christianity is not simply the acceptance of a set of ideals and teachings—it is surrender to a person." The idea almost startled the Jew, who exclaimed, "That appeals to me!" Before the appointment was over, the Jew had decided to become a Christian and to join the church.

Hope of Eternal Life in a P.O.W. Camp. When Singapore fell to the Japanese in 1942, Mrs. Rogers Mulvaney, a Canadian, was working there for the Red Cross. Along with more than four thousand other civilians she was locked in Changi jail which had been built to accommodate four hundred and fifty prisoners. They suffered four years of crowding and hunger, loneliness and isolation, with no news of families and home.

As the first Easter approached, Mrs. Mulvaney went to the guards and asked if they might be allowed to sing hymns in the courtyard on Easter morning. At first they were refused, but were finally given permission to sing for five minutes. In the presence of one guard they sang for five precious minutes, praising God for Christ's Resurrection, the only hope to which they could cling. Then silently they marched back. But as Mrs. Mulvaney entered the passageway, the guard stepped up, reached under his brown shirt, drew out a tiny orchid, and placing it in her hand softly spoke, "Christ *did* rise." Then with a smart military about-face, he was gone. But Mrs. Mulvaney stood there, eyes filled with tears, knowing that she and the others need never feel forsaken again. To know this is to know eternal life now!

We Know How the Story Ends. "Hearses become 'Funeral Coaches,' graves become 'Burial Estates,' and funeral wreaths become 'Floral Offerings.' The funeral industry, with the public's support and encouragement, has worked hard at turning the cold hand of death into a warm, or at least benign, touch. It doesn't work. Despite all the verbal veneers, eventually we realize that the friend or family member is not just sleeping on the innerspring mattress of his or her coffin. They will not wake up. They are dead.

"Ezekiel, Martha, and Mary all knew that death was real and final. All the greater, therefore, their amazement at the sight of the resurrection. Death had been redefined, which is quite different from our attempts to soften its blow by redescribing it. We try to make death different by inventing new names for it. Paul says that death is different because, for the Christian, life is different. It is life in Christ which changes the definition of death.

"As the Lenten clock ticks closer to its conclusion, a certain sense of intensity builds. The shadow of a cross falls across our worship. No mortician has yet thought of an acceptable and easier word for crucifixion. We survive the devastating words of Christ's impending death because we live on this side of the resurrection. We have read the last chapter of the book. We know how the story ends. The reality of his crucifixion and death are no less, but we live in the confidence of those for whom death has been redefined by his life."—George M. Conn, Jr., *Presbyterian Outlook*, 512 W. Main Street, Richmond, Va., March 30, 1981.

Questions for Pupils on the Next Lesson. 1. When do you think a person reaches spiritual and emotional maturity? 2. What is the support community for you in which you can find help in living your values and beliefs? 3. How do you resolve the struggle between tolerance of and tacit approval of rival beliefs? 4. How do you handle situations where others try to undermine your faith in Jesus Christ? 5. Where is it the most difficult for you to adhere to the truth of God centered on Jesus Christ?

TOPIC FOR YOUTH
JESUS, YOUR HOPE

He That Lives. "Emperor Numerianus, who succeeded to the throne of Rome when his father was killed in A.D. 283 during a campaign against Persia, led his army on a retreat of 1,500 miles. During the eight months of this long journey, Numerianus was never seen by his men. His aides announced that this was because the emperor was suffering from an eye defect. However, suspicious army officers forced their way into the emperor's tent. They discovered that he had died months ago and had been reduced to a mere skeleton by the desert heat.

"Perhaps some of you feel that Easter is the same. Maybe some of you feel that the disciples announced that Jesus was alive in an effort to perpetuate His memory, His life, and His teachings. Perhaps some of you even feel that Easter is a rip-off, a big hoax. Instead of retreating into obscurity, the disciples made one final campaign. They convinced others into believing that Jesus was alive when anyone with a suspicious nature would have checked and discovered that perhaps a skeleton or body was hidden somewhere.

"Never imagine for a minute that the resurrection of Jesus was a hoax pulled off by loyal aides. Even a disbelieving look at the Gospels should make this clear. None of the followers ever expected to see Jesus alive again. And yet, the disciples discovered the Risen Lord. The announcements of Easter stand! HE IS RISEN! 'I am He that lives, and was dead; and behold, I am alive for evermore.' "—J. B. Barker.

Victorious Christ Brings You Victory. Michelangelo has a great work entitled, *The Risen Christ.* The cross is present in his painting, but Christ is not nailed to it in the agony of death. He is standing with the cross beside Him, His right arm around it. He is victorious. This is the ultimate spirit of Christianity.

The note of victory, confidence, calm strength, joy, and gladness ought to characterize the Christian.

Insistent Message. "One of the most meaningful observances of Easter in which I ever took part was two years ago on the Greek Island of Naxos. On Easter Eve the whole island community gathered in the square outside the main Orthodox Church—there was no room for most of us inside. Through the loudspeakers we heard the chanting of the liturgy as priest and people inside the church made their preparatory devotions. Then just before midnight priest and choir came out on to the church steps and the bells began to ring for another Easter Day. At once all hell broke out; candles were lit, fireworks were set off, people cheered, shouted greetings, kissed each other; bicycle bells and car horns were sounded and the ships in the harbour hooted on their sirens; and amid and through all this cacophony there came the insistent sound of the chant priest and choir—CHRISTOS aneste! Christ is risen!

"We celebrate Easter in a world that is full of all sorts of cacophonies—of quarrelling voices and violent altercations, of the bangs of things much more lethal than Greek fireworks, of people sounding off about everything under the sun. But in the midst of that world the Church proclaims the insistent message of Easter—Christ is risen! It is in *that* world among *that* confusion and noise and dispeace that God is at work and Christ is alive in his risen power."—W. B. Johnston, "Easter Meditation," *Life and Work,* April, 1980.

Questions for Pupils on the Next Lesson. 1. Do you sometimes find yourself confused by the many causes vying for your allegiance? How do you handle these times? 2. Do you feel guilty because your actions do not always match what you say you believe? 3. Do you sometimes find you are swayed by people who present their beliefs forcefully? 4. Are there any clear, reliable standards for evaluating claims of truth? 5. Do you ever encounter persons who actively oppose the truth that God's Son came in the flesh?

LESSON VI—APRIL 6

A HOPE BUILT ON TRUTH

Background Scripture: 2 John and 3 John
Devotional Reading: 1 John 5:13–21

KING JAMES VERSION

2 JOHN The elder unto the elect lady and her children, whom I love in the truth; and not I only, but also all they that have known the truth;

2 For the truth's sake, which dwelleth in us, and shall be with us for ever.

3 Grace be with you, mercy, *and* peace, from God the Father, and from the Lord Jesus Christ, the Son of the Father, in truth and love.

4 I rejoiced greatly that I found of thy children walking in truth, as we have received a commandment from the Father.

5 And now I beseech thee, lady, not as though I wrote a new commandment unto thee, but that which we had from the beginning, that we love one another.

6 And this is love, that we walk after his commandments. This is the commandment, That, as ye have heard from the beginning, ye should walk in it.

7 For many deceivers are entered into the world, who confess not that Jesus Christ is come in the flesh. This is a deceiver and an antichrist.

8 Look to yourselves, that we lose not those things which we have wrought, but that we receive a full reward.

9 Whosoever transgresseth, and abideth not in the doctrine of Christ, hath not God. He that abideth in the doctrine of Christ, he hath both the Father and the Son.

10 If there come any unto you, and bring not this doctrine, receive him not into *your* house, neither bid him God speed:

11 For he that biddeth him God speed is partaker of his evil deeds.

3 JOHN 2 Beloved, I wish above all things that thou mayest prosper and be in health, even as thy soul prospereth.

3 For I rejoiced greatly, when the brethren came and testified of the truth that is in thee, even as thou walkest in the truth.

4 I have no greater joy than to hear that my children walk in truth.

REVISED STANDARD VERSION

2 JOHN The elder to the elect lady and her children, whom I love in the truth, and not only I but also all who know the truth, 2 because of the truth which abides in us and will be with us for ever:

3 Grace, mercy, and peace will be with us, from God the Father and from Jesus Christ the Father's Son, in truth and love.

4 I rejoiced greatly to find some of your children following the truth, just as we have been commanded by the Father. 5 And now I beg you, lady, not as though I were writing you a new commandment, but the one we have had from the beginning, that we love one another. 6 And this is love, that we follow his commandments; this is the commandment, as you have heard from the beginning, that you follow love. 7 For many deceivers have gone out into the world, men who will not acknowledge the coming of Jesus Christ in the flesh; such a one is the deceiver and the antichrist. 8 Look to yourselves, that you may not lose what you have worked for, but may win a full reward. 9 Any one who goes ahead and does not abide in the doctrine of Christ does not have God; he who abides in the doctrine has both the Father and the Son. 10 If any one comes to you and does not bring this doctrine, do not receive him into the house or give him any greeting; 11 for he who greets him shares his wicked work.

3 JOHN 2 Beloved, I pray that all may go well with you and that you may be in health; I know that it is well with your soul. 3 For I greatly rejoiced when some of the brethren arrived and testified to the truth of your life, as indeed you do follow the truth. 4 No greater joy can I have than this, to hear that my children follow the truth.

KEY VERSE: *No greater joy can I have than this, to hear that my children follow the truth.* 3 John 4.

HOME DAILY BIBLE READINGS

Mar.	31.	M.	*Walk in the Truth.* 2 John 1–6.
Apr.	1.	T.	*Beware of Deceivers.* 2 John 6–13.
Apr.	2.	W.	*Jesus' Instructions to Believers.* Mark 13:5–11.
Apr.	3.	T.	*What Makes Us Free?* John 8:31–38.

Apr.	4.	F.	*Support Fellow Believers.* 3 John 1–8.
Apr.	5.	S.	*Do Not Be Haughty Towards Others.* 3 John 9–14.
Apr.	6.	S.	*The Haughty Will Be Judged.* James 2:8–13.

BACKGROUND

The three beautiful literary gems known as 1 John, 2 John, and 3 John in our New Testament, have usually been called letters or epistles. In a sense, 1 John was more of a sermon or a theological treatise than a letter. Two John and 3 John are more truly letters intended for specific readers. What we call the second letter of John was addressed to "the elect lady and her children," and the third letter was intended for "the beloved Gaius."

We are not certain who the "elect lady" was, except that it was probably a pet name for a congregation and its members. And we cannot be sure of Gaius's identity except that he was a respected church leader. We can be certain that John the writer was the same author of the first letter of John and the Gospel of John.

The main reason for John's writing to the "elect lady and her children" and to "beloved Gaius" was his continuing concern for the harm certain false teachers were causing. These leaders were spreading poisonous errors. John, who called himself "the elder" because of his age and long experience as a Christian, pleads with his readers to build their hope on the truth that is found in God's love expressed in Jesus Christ.

In addition, we catch a glimpse of life in the early Church. Apparently it was the practice for teachers to wander from one congregation to another. Some of these teachers were sincere, godly people. Others, however, were fakes. John urges his readers to turn away those who were false teachers.

In 3 John, we see that a leader named Diotrephes in the church has been arrogantly refusing hospitality to genuine Christian teachers. John feels upset by Diotrephes's dictatorial ways. By contrast, John mentions another leader, Demetrius, who apparently is a leader of a group of wandering committed Christian preachers who will soon be visiting Gaius's congregation.

These little letters give us a peek into conditions in first century churches. They also reveal the state of flux of the organization of the Church, in which there were apostles, the witnesses to the Risen Lord, prophets or wandering preachers and teachers, and elders or officials of the Christian community.

NOTES ON THE PRINTED TEXT

FROM: The elder John
  TO: The elect lady and her children
        (The "elect lady" is a local church and "her children" are the church members.)

John uses the word *truth* five times in the four opening verses of Second John. John uses the word *truth* in reference to Jesus. The truth is the Good News of Christ. For John the Christian life and hope are centered in this truth of God's. He is writing to Christians with whom he has had close affections. He describes them as children *whom I love in the truth* and *who know the truth.*

After the customary expression of thanksgiving, John commends these children for their fidelity to (Christ) the truth. *I rejoiced greatly to find some of your children following the truth as we have been commanded by the Father.* All who know God's truth are to live according to that truth. John is happy that some are living in love by following the truth, but he is concerned that some are not. *I beg you, lady . . . that we love one another.* He comes to the purpose of his letter by begging them to love. All who live according to God's truth are to love one another. He is not writing *a new commandment*. It is an old commandment, one which they *have had from the beginning*. In order that they understand his intentions, John defines love for them: *This is love, that we follow his commandments*.

John also stresses the importance of holding to the doctrine that Christ is the incarnate Son of God. He warns them about those who do not hold to this doctrine and yet pose as Christian teachers. *For many deceivers . . . men who will not acknowledge the coming of Jesus Christ in the flesh; such a one is a deceiver and the antichrist*. Many who do not believe in Christ try to deceive others about the truth. Christians should guard against those who oppose the truth that God's Son came in the flesh. The false teachers deny Christ's bodily existence and claim that He only "appeared" to be here. These people are liars and deceivers. Christians must follow the truth in order that they do *not lose what they have worked for but may win a full reward*. Living in love and holding to the truth brings salvation. Those people who *abide in the doctrine of Christ* have *both the Father and the Son*. Those who do not, do not have God. John urges his children to not even greet or receive into their house these itinerant, roving false teachers *for he who greets him shares his wicked work*.

Third John is addressed to Gaius. Gaius was John's close friend and is addressed as *beloved*. John praises Gaius for the *truth* of his life. Numerous reports have been passed along by other brethren testifying to his following the truth. No better compliment can be written to any believer than that which John pays to Gaius when he says *no greater joy can I have than this, to hear that my children follow the truth*.

SUGGESTIONS TO TEACHERS

Some church people used to refer to the Sunday after Easter as "Low Sunday." After the "high" of the Resurrection celebration, with big crowds and special music, the week after seemed to be a dismal comedown.

There was no such slump among early Christians. The Sunday following the appearance of the Risen Lord, and, indeed, *every* Sunday after that brought a renewal of hope. Each Sunday was an occasion to celebrate! Sunday, the first day of the week, became the day for gathering to worship the Living Christ who rose from death on the first day. Every such Sunday was regarded as a mini-Easter!

That's the mood you and your class can have for this April 6, 1986. A mini-Easter! A renewal of hope built on the truth of the Resurrection!

The writer of our 2 John and 3 John offers such a positive message for this post-Easter lesson. Develop your lesson around some of the themes emerging from a careful reading of these epistles, including:

1. *COMPLETENESS OF THE COMMANDMENT*. The emphasis on *Love* in the letters of John may seem like tired themes. Beginning with the flower children in the 1960s the word *love* has been used excessively. It seems that everyone from social scientists to psychedelic songsters urges *love*. However, most of these are guilty of plagarism; they have stolen the notion from the New Testament! Furthermore, these advocates of *love* omit the key to love—God's love through Jesus Christ! "We love because he first loved us" (1 John 4:19). His command to us to love is in actuality an insistence that we share the same graciousness to others that He shares with us, in Jesus Christ. Moreover, your class needs to remember that such a sharing of graciousness in the Spirit of Christ means hope both for us and for others.

2. *DANGERS FROM DECEIVERS*. Even in the earliest days of the Christian community, there were those who tried to exploit others or pervert the truth. Such people are around today as well. Some even try to pretend that they are teaching or acting in the name of the Gospel. In your class today, it would be

helpful to discuss how these deceivers may be identified. Two John offers constructive comments about deceivers not acknowledging the biblical understanding of Jesus Christ, but substituting their own notions of who He was and is.

3. *DIRECTION OF DOCTRINE.* How may errors in Christian teaching be targeted? And how may these "deceivers" be shown up? Two John 9, 10 pointedly reminds us that all our religious beliefs must square with Jesus Christ. Jesus Christ is the beginning and the end of spiritual truth. Unless our doctrines all center on Jesus, they are suspect! He is not merely a clue to truth; Jesus is the truth!

4. *CONCLUSIVENESS OF CHRIST.* This lesson stresses the finality of Jesus Christ. To make it more than simply an academic discussion of theology, work in the kind of personal testimony that 2 and 3 John offer. Jesus Christ is a personal companion. Have your class members probe their memories to recall instances of where the Living Lord's companionship was known in their own lives. Remind your people that His friendship continues. Furthermore, Jesus promises to be The Companion in every situation!

TOPIC FOR ADULTS
A HOPE BUILT ON TRUTH

Standard Meter. All length measurements rely on a standard and unvarying unit of measuring length known as a meter. There is one way of defining a meter which is accepted by everyone. This is the true meter.

For many decades, all length measurements were based on the meter as defined by the distance between two scratches on a platinum-iridium bar stored in a vault at the International Bureau of Weights and Measures at Sèvres, near Paris. Since 1960, length measurements have been based on a more accurate and more readily available standard—the wavelength of orange light emitted by the gas krypton 86. Under the new system, one meter is defined as the distance traveled by light through a vacuum in one-299,792,458th of a second.

Jesus is the norm. Everyone and everything in life is measured in terms of Him. He called Himself the Way, the Truth, and the Life, insists we examine our goals and acts and values and thoughts in the light of whether or not these conform to Him. When we base our lives on Him as the truth, we discover we are building with hope.

Who Made the Difference? A few years ago, in 1983, *Esquire* magazine celebrated its fiftieth anniversary. The anniversary issue asked fifty different leading writers to select the person in the past fifty years who has made the most difference in the world, and headed the article, "Fifty Who Made the Difference."

Saul Bellow picked Franklin D. Roosevelt. Truman Capote picked Katharine Hepburn. David Halberstam picked Martin Luther King, Jr. Alistair Cooke picked Duke Ellington. Marilyn French picked Betty Friedan. William F. Buckley, Jr., picked Henry Luce. Ken Kesey picked Jack Kerouac. Tom Wolfe picked Robert Noyce, the developer of the computer chip. Sara Davidson picked Dr. John Rock, the developer of the birth-control pill.

If someone asked you which person had made a difference in the past fifty years in the world as you see it, whom would you pick?

Would Jesus Christ ever be listed as one who has made a difference to you or to the world?

Faith Resting on the Promise to a Crook. Newspaper columnist Garry Wills continues to be a Christian, to the surprise of many of his colleagues. Wills was interviewed by an editor of a leading magazine, and said, "I read the New Testament every day, since I am a Christian." When the editor asked Wills why he still believes, he gave this eloquent reply: " 'Today we two shall be in Paradise.' Only one man, I believe, could keep that promise, made to his fellow crook while they were being executed. How can I tell that? As I would gauge the size of a vessel that has passed, by the turbulence of wake it left behind. . . . By a consonance of mysteries, each incomplete in itself but the correlate of others—myself one of those mysteries; and you another; and He another (the darkest). . . . By prayer. By listening for a promise from my fellow crook."

Questions for Pupils on the Next Lesson. 1. How do you stand up to those who try deliberately to deny God's truth? 2. How should a Christian act toward those who doubt and deny God's truth? 3. Will God give you enough to withstand *any* danger? 4. Do you sometimes struggle with how to relate to others who differ with you in beliefs and values? 5. Why do we find it difficult to live with ambiguity in our lives?

TOPIC FOR YOUTH
BUILD ON THE TRUTH

Sing It Again. A woman who rarely attended worship stopped before the minister at the door of the church and asked shrilly, "Why is it when I come to church you're always singing "Christ the Lord Is Risen Today"?

Obviously, she only attended on Easter Sundays. But she could serve to remind us that every Sunday is a kind of Easter. We celebrate the Resurrection of Jesus Christ each week. When we proclaim Him the Living Lord, we build on truth. And we have hope!

Building on the Truth of Brother Christ's Will. There was a time in Scotland when a Catholic queen tried to stamp out the rising Protestant growth. Attendance at Protestant church services was outlawed. A little Scottish girl on her way late one Sunday to a secret service was stopped by a soldier. Asked where she was going at that hour, she could not bring herself to lie, and she said, "My elder brother has died and I am going to my Father's house to see what he has left me in his last will and testament." Going to church should be for us that exciting adventure of claiming the promise God has given us in Christ.

She was building on the truth!

Are you?

Reason for Climbing. A world-famous mountaineer was asked his reasons for scaling the highest peaks. "Do you climb the mountain because 'it's there'?" inquired his interviewer.

"No," answered the climber. "I climb because at the peak of the mountain is where all the lines converge."

The same thing is true of the hill of Calvary, where Jesus Christ died. At the Cross is where all the lines converge. He is the Truth. He is the only One on which to build a life in which there is adventure and fulfillment.

Questions for Pupils on the Next Lesson. 1. Have you sometimes found it difficult to know that God has called you? 2. How can a Christian stand up for the faith when others are putting it down? 3. Are there people you know personally who deny God's truth? 4. Do you find yourself sometimes questioning your parents' beliefs? 5. Are you sometimes afraid you won't be able to hold on to your beliefs under pressures?

LESSON VII—APRIL 13

A HOPE WORTH GUARDING

Background Scripture: Jude
Devotional Reading: John 10:22–30

KING JAMES VERSION

JUDE Jude the servant of Jesus Christ, and brother of James, to them that are sanctified by God the Father, and preserved in Jesus Christ, *and* called:

2 Mercy unto you, and peace, and love, be multiplied.

3 Beloved, when I gave all diligence to write unto you of the common salvation, it was needful for me to write unto you, and exhort *you* that ye should earnestly contend for the faith which was once delivered unto the saints.

4 For there are certain men crept in unawares, who were before of old ordained to this condemnation, ungodly men, turning the grace of our God into lasciviousness, and denying the only Lord God, and our Lord Jesus Christ.

17 But, beloved, remember ye the words which were spoken before of the apostles of our Lord Jesus Christ;

18 How that they told you there should be mockers in the last time, who should walk after their own ungodly lusts.

19 These be they who separate themselves, sensual, having not the Spirit.

20 But ye, beloved, building up yourselves on your most holy faith, praying in the Holy Ghost,

21 Keep yourselves in the love of God, looking for the mercy of our Lord Jesus Christ unto eternal life.

22 And of some have compassion, making a difference:

23 And others save with fear, pulling *them* out of the fire; hating even the garment spotted by the flesh.

24 Now unto him that is able to keep you from falling, and to present *you* faultless before the presence of his glory with exceeding joy,

25 To the only wise God our Saviour, *be* glory and majesty, dominion and power, both now and ever. Amen.

REVISED STANDARD VERSION

JUDE Jude, a servant of Jesus Christ and brother of James,

To those who are called, beloved in God the Father and kept for Jesus Christ:

2 May mercy, peace, and love be multiplied to you.

3 Beloved, being very eager to write to you of our common salvation, I found it necessary to write appealing to you to contend for the faith which was once for all delivered to the saints. 4 For admission has been secretly gained by some who long ago were designated for this condemnation, ungodly persons who pervert the grace of our God into licentiousness and deny our only Master and Lord, Jesus Christ.

17 But you must remember, beloved, the predictions of the apostles of our Lord Jesus Christ; 18 they said to you, "In the last time there will be scoffers, following their own ungodly passions." 19 It is these who set up divisions, worldly people, devoid of the Spirit. 20 But you, beloved, build yourselves up on your most holy faith; pray in the Holy Spirit; 21 keep yourselves in the love of God; wait for the mercy of our Lord Jesus Christ unto eternal life. 22 And convince some, who doubt; 23 save some, by snatching them out of the fire; on some have mercy with fear, hating even the garment spotted by the flesh.

24 Now to him who is able to keep you from falling and to present you without blemish before the presence of his glory with rejoicing, 25 to the only God, our Savior through Jesus Christ our Lord, be glory, majesty, dominion, and authority, before all time and now and for ever. Amen.

KEY VERSE: *Now to him who is able to keep you from falling and to present you without blemish before the presence of his glory with rejoicing, to the only God, our Savior through Jesus Christ our Lord, be glory, majesty, dominion, and authority, before all time and now and for ever. Amen. Jude 24, 25.*

HOME DAILY BIBLE READINGS

Apr.	7.	M.	*Warning Against False Teachers.* Jude 1–9.
Apr.	8.	T.	*False Teachers Described.* Jude 10–15.
Apr.	9.	W.	*Be Not Deceived.* 1 Thessalonians 2:1–12.
Apr.	10.	T.	*Compare Teaching and Deeds.* Titus 1:10–16.

Apr. 11. F.   *Christ Is the Foundation for Faith.* Acts 4:7-13.
Apr. 12. S.   *Christ Is Sufficient.* Colossians 2:8-15.
Apr. 13. S.   *Guard Your Testimony Against Error.* Jude 17-25.

BACKGROUND

Tradition insists that Jude, author of the short letter near the end of our New Testament, was the Jude who was the brother of Jesus and James. Thomas Hardy, the English writer, wrote a novel with the title, *Jude the Obscure,* and the author of this letter and the letter itself both are obscure as far as most Christians are concerned. Before dismissing Jude as unimportant, however, Christians should read the brief epistle bearing his name. Jude will appear to have a relevance. His book should not be pushed aside as "obscure."

James Moffatt described the letter of Jude as "a fiery cross to rouse the churches" in the way that ancient Scottish chieftains used to send around a fiery cross through Highland glens to rally their clans for battle. Jude was determined to arouse Christian congregations to be alert to mortal dangers confronting them. Jude was not so much one meticulously expounding the faith as one shouting that the enemy was coming. Jude was a watchman, not a detached theologian.

In particular, Jude was warning against leaders who were immoral and heretical. In his time, as we have noticed in studies in other letters, certain clever charlatans were traveling among Christian churches, claiming to be inspired by God, but spreading their own dubious ideas. Unfortunately, many of these false teachers won a hearing. Some of them also made a comfortable living by sponging on others while spreading their wise-sounding ideas. What disturbed Jude most deeply, however, was the immoral lifestyle of many of these religious phonies who were claiming to be Christian prophets. Jude saw them cynically claiming to be above all restraints. He knew that their arguments were pious nonsense when they stated that since Christ forgave everything they could do as they pleased. Jude warned that turning God's grace into a license for immorality was the height of godlessness.

Determined to have Christians guard their hope carefully, Jude uses military terms. "Fight on for the faith which once and for all God has given to his people" (Jude 3, *Good News* translation).

NOTES ON THE PRINTED TEXT

Short in length but strong in purpose, Jude memorializes a struggle of the first century Church against the Gnostic teachers. It reminds Christians to be on their guard. They are never safe because corruption will always threaten to destroy them until the day of Christ's Coming.

Jude, a servant of Jesus Christ and brother of James, literally sees himself as a slave of Jesus Christ. Jude is most likely the brother of Jesus and James. He is humble enough to claim only his servant relationship to Jesus, but he does claim a relationship to James, the leader of the Jerusalem church. His letter is addressed *to those who are called beloved in God the Father and kept for Jesus Christ.* The readers are those who have responded to God's call. These people are preserved by God's love in Christ. Jude implies that God loves and keeps all those who have responded to His call. Because of Jude's conviction that God keeps these responders, he writes the prayer: *May mercy, peace, and love be multiplied to you.*

While preparing a longer letter about their *common salvation* (perhaps a letter about their salvation through Christ), Jude has received word of the false teaching. With a sense of urgency, he immediately writes this letter *appealing* to his readers *to contend for the faith.* Jude urges them to fight for the faith that had been entrusted to them. Christians must be ready at all times to contend for their faith.

For admission has been secretly gained by some ... ungodly persons who pervert the grace of our God into licentiousness and deny our only Master and Lord, Jesus Christ. False teachers have crept in and seduced the believers. These teachers were the Gnostics. They believed that since they were saved by grace, they did not need to concern themselves with being lawful. This is what Jude is referring to when he claims that these teachers have perverted the grace of God. The Greek word *gnosis* from which the name Gnostics comes, means superior knowledge. The Gnostics believed they were superior beings with superior knowledge exempt from moral laws. They believed that they were free to live as they pleased. Early Christians confessed Jesus as Master and Lord and accepted His law for living. However, the false teachers denied Christ by their sexual licentiousness and their indecent voluptuous living.

Those who *delivered* the faith *to the saints* (verse 3) also warned of the false teaching of these scoffers. *You must remember ... the predictions of the apostles ... they said ... in the last time there will be scoffers, following their own ungodly passions.* Jude reminds Christians that these mockers are devoid of spiritual life and cause schisms within the Church. *It is these who set up divisions, worldly people, devoid of the Spirit.* The Gnostics divided people into three classes. The first class possessed the required knowledge for salvation. The second class could earn their salvation by hard work and study. However, the third class could never hope for salvation. Jude refutes this belief. All people can receive the Holy Spirit. It is the Gnostics who through their worldly knowledge and intellectual arrogance demonstrate a true lack of God's Spirit.

Christians have a hope worth guarding. *Build yourselves up on your most holy faith.* Using the terminology of a construction worker, Jude urges the believers to let their house be built up through their faith. Complete the structure by building on the foundation of Christ. *Pray in the Holy Spirit.* When Jude mentions prayer he means that his readers should seek and follow the Spirit. The Holy Spirit enables Christians to withstand those who deny God's truth. *Keep yourselves in the love of God.* Jude urges the believers to love. This love is a defense against despair or defeat. It is God's love which is love that will not let go. *Wait for the mercy of our Lord Jesus Christ unto eternal life.* Wait patiently and without fear for Jesus Christ. He will come in mercy and with the gift of eternal life. Christians today are to wait actively for the completion of their redemption. This is the hope worth guarding.

Convince some who doubt. Teach, and preach to those who are caught up in their false intellectual knowledge. Make every effort to *snatch them out of the fire* of judgment. *Have mercy with fear, hating even the garment spotted by the flesh.* Christians are to act with mercy and caution toward those who doubt and deny God's truth. They are not to condone their sins. For these non-Christians must repent and be baptized. They must put on the unsoiled, unspotted, clean garments that will symbolize new life.

Jude closes with a long benediction and doxology encouraging his beloved to guard their hope. Christians can be confident that God will enable them to withstand any danger. *Now to him who is able to keep you from falling and to present you without blemish before the presence of his glory with rejoicing, to the only God our Savior through Jesus Christ our Lord, be glory, majesty, dominion, and authority, before all time and now and for ever. Amen.*

SUGGESTIONS TO TEACHERS

"I used to have hope that what I was doing in life was worthwhile and would help to make the world better," said the civic leader. She had served for many years in her community in P.T.A., helping organize Meals on Wheels, as a hospital volunteer, and a precinct worker for her political party. Now she described herself as "jaded and disillusioned." In short, she had lost hope.

How does a person maintain a sense of hope?

This is the question you are working with in today's lesson. It is a question which may not surface among church people immediately because it is not fitting to admit (publically, at least) to feeling jaded and disillusioned. But many folks in church work find their supply of hope running very low.

The point of the lesson for this Sunday is that hope must be based on a personal trust in Jesus Christ, but that this sense of trust must be carefully guarded. Hope is not something a believer has like brown eyes or a soprano voice. Brown eyes and a soprano voice remain and cannot be taken away. Hope can be snatched or can be allowed to be stolen by small degrees. Hope needs to be protected from the enemies bent on destroying it. The little piece of writing called Jude makes this point.

1. *FAITH DELIVERED.* Hope rests on trust in Jesus Christ. Jude emphasizes that the content of faith is summed up in Jesus, and "was once for all delivered to the saints" (Jude 3). Our hope is secure. It is based on the fact of God's act in Jesus Christ, not on some ephemeral idea or on human speculation. Encourage your class to consider what this "once for all" dimension of the Gospel is. Further, help your class to understand more deeply how the life, death, Resurrection and exaltation of Jesus Christ is the indispensable factor in faith, and therefore for hope.

2. *FAITH DENIED.* Faith is not something that flows automatically to a believer. It can be denied. Faith may be squelched by self-indulgent living, "licentiousness" (Jude 4). Jude offers examples from history which may be found in Scripture, such as the disobedient Israelites in the desert or the people in ancient Sodom and Gomorrah. Your lesson should point to the need for believers to live carefully and responsibly, avoiding evil and immoral ways. Jude warns that carelessness and ungodliness will "pervert the grace of God into licentiousness and deny our only Master and Lord, Jesus Christ" (Jude 4).

3. *FAITH DOCUMENTED.* Jude offers a rather complete catalogue of examples of persons who failed to guard the hope God gives by neglecting their faith. Essentially, these were all "scoffers, following their own ungodly passions . . . who set up divisions, worldly people, devoid of the Spirit" (Jude 18, 19). It would be helpful to have your class members prepare its own list of ways to guard hope by helping faith to flourish. Also, it could be profitable to have the class make another list of dangers or threats to faith.

4. *FAITH DIVULGED.* Jude closes with a ringing missionary challenge. Faith in Jesus Christ must be shared! "And convince some who doubt; save some" (Jude, 22, 23). Allow enough time to talk over the Why and the How of faith-sharing in everyday life by members of the class.

TOPIC FOR ADULTS
A HOPE WORTH GUARDING

Believing Hope. The Right Reverend James Pike had a meteoric career as an attorney then as a cleric. Before he was fifty, he had risen to become one of the leading bishops and religious leaders in the United States. Then his life seemed to come unravelled. In an article in an old *LOOK* magazine, he described how he had lost "believing hope" and chronicled the subtle change in his thinking from living by Christian hope to no hope. Pike cut himself away from the church he had served for over twenty-five years. He dabbled in the occult. He lost a son through suicide. He divorced his wife and faced domestic problems. In spite of his brilliance and gifts, Pike could not bring himself to guard the hope he had once had. He perished tragically one day when he foolishly tried to drive a small rental car into a remote desert area of the Jordan Valley without proper equipment or provisions or maps on an ill-planned quest for truth through archaeological exploration.

Even bishops can forget to guard their hope in Jesus Christ. So can ordinary church members. Any of us can forget that we have a living hope, a hope worth guarding carefully each day in spite of the pressures and strains of life.

Obedient Belief. The German Lutheran theologian Dietrich Bonhoeffer, killed by the Nazis, once wrote that the Christian must always remember two statements that are equally true about faith, even though they may appear to be contradictory. The first of these is that only the one who believes is obedient. The second is that only the one who is obedient believes.

The first statement is partly what the Easter message makes clear. Only those who know that in Christ sin and death have been overcome can have the freedom and power to begin life of radical obedience to the will of God. Faith grounded in the Resurrection makes real obedience possible.

Remembering the Old Kentucky Home. Stephen Collins Foster wrote the song "My Old Kentucky Home," yet never once visited Kentucky! Foster was from Pittsburgh. Although he never saw any beloved old Kentucky home, he made the place real to many others who never had seen it either. He enabled many to carry a cherished picture of such a pleasant home "far away" yet very real.

Jesus assures us that in His Father's House are many rooms and that He has gone to prepare a place for us. We have never seen that mansion, but we cling to the promise that there is a home for us with the Lord. We can guard the hope that, although we have not yet been there in person, we have a hope worth guarding!

Questions for Pupils on the Next Lesson. 1. Do you think that you are capable and open to receiving new truths and insights for living? 2. Do you ever wish that you could have new meaning for your life which will give fuller meaning in your family relationships? 3. Has the Holy Spirit ever brought you a sense of spiritual insight and understanding? 4. Do you sometimes have difficulty in relating to the spiritual dimension in your life?

TOPIC FOR YOUTH
HOLD TO THE TRUTH

On the Edge of D. O. R. Before becoming a jet pilot in the Navy, a recruit is sent to Naval Aviation Officer Candidate School. Officer Candidate School is a grueling thirteen weeks of training which is designed to weed out those unfit for the physical and psychological demands of a naval officer. During these thirteen weeks, many candidates find themselves on the edge of D. O. R. ("Dropping Out on Request"). Those who saw the film *An Officer and a Gentleman* will remember the tension between Sgt. Foley, the mean, tough drill instructor, played capably by Louis Gossett, Jr., and the recruits, in which the sergeant appears to delight in brutally pushing his recruits into D. O. R. Only great determination on the part of the young recruits to stand up to the nerve-straining tests enables them to keep alive their hopes of becoming officers and fliers.

We Christians are constantly pressured to the point of D. O. R. by the forces opposed to God. Tough and mean people, and tough and mean circumstances try to force us to drop out of God's community and forsake our calling. Only a determined attempt to guard our dreams and carry out our resolve will bring the Helper, the Holy Spirit, to our side. We have a hope worth guarding!

Following the Cross. "Following the cross does not mean copying the suffering of Jesus, it is not the reconstruction of the cross. That would be presumption. But it certainly means enduring the suffering which befalls me in my inexchangeable situation—in conformity with the suffering of Christ. Anyone who wants to go with Jesus must deny himself and take on himself not the cross of Jesus nor just any kind of cross, but his cross, his own cross; then he must follow Jesus."—Hans Kung, *On Being a Christian* New York: Doubleday, 1976.

Any Hope? Cicero, the great Roman orator, was filled with grief when his daughter Tullia died. Lighting a taper at her tomb, Cicero knelt and raised his voice, in a combination lament and question, "Is this the quenching of your life, O my daughter?"

How would you have answered the great Senator? What words of hope do you guard for yourself and for others?

Questions for Pupils on the Next Lesson. 1. Are you curious about the reports of supernatural experiences of others? 2. Why do you feel anxious when you are confronted with situations for which there is not a rational explanation? 3. Does your faith give you support and encouragement in exploring new ideas and experiences? 4. What is your idea of the kind of future which the Lord means for you to have? 5. Do you ever wish that you had a deeper spiritual dimension in your life?

THE PERSON AND WORK OF THE HOLY SPIRIT

LESSON VIII—APRIL 20

THE HOLY SPIRIT AND JESUS' BIRTH

Background Scripture: Luke 1:5–56; 2:21–40
Devotional Reading: Luke 1:8–17

KING JAMES VERSION

LUKE 1   35 And the angel answered and said unto her, The Holy Ghost shall come upon thee, and the power of the Highest shall overshadow thee: therefore also that holy thing which shall be born of thee shall be called the Son of God.

36 And, behold, thy cousin Elisabeth, she hath also conceived a son in her old age; and this is the sixth month with her, who was called barren.

37 For with God nothing shall be impossible.

38 And Mary said, Behold the handmaid of the Lord; be it unto me according to thy word. And the angel departed from her.

39 And Mary arose in those days, and went into the hill country with haste, into a city of Juda;

40 And entered into the house of Zacharias, and saluted Elisabeth.

41 And it came to pass, that, when Elisabeth heard the salutation of Mary, the babe leaped in her womb; and Elisabeth was filled with the Holy Ghost:

42 And she spake out with a loud voice, and said, Blessed *art* thou among women, and blessed *is* the fruit of thy womb.

2   25 And, behold, there was a man in Jerusalem, whose name *was* Simeon; and the same man *was* just and devout, waiting for the consolation of Israel: and the Holy Ghost was upon him.

26 And it was revealed unto him by the Holy Ghost, that he should not see death, before he had seen the Lord's Christ.

27 And he came by the Spirit into the temple: and when the parents brought in the child Jesus, to do for him after the custom of the law,

28 Then took he him up in his arms, and blessed God, and said,

29 Lord, now lettest thou thy servant depart in peace, according to thy word:

30 For mine eyes have seen thy salvation,

31 Which thou has prepared before the face of all people;

32 A light to lighten the Gentiles, and the glory of thy people Israel.

REVISED STANDARD VERSION

LUKE 1   35 And the angel said to her,
"The Holy Spirit will come upon you, and the power of the Most High will overshadow you;
therefore the child to be born will be called holy,
the Son of God.

36 And behold, your kinswoman Elizabeth in her old age has also conceived a son; and this is the sixth month with her who was called barren. 37 For with God nothing will be impossible." 38 And Mary said, "Behold, I am the handmaid of the Lord; let it be to me according to your word." And the angel departed from her.

39 In those days Mary arose and went with haste into the hill country, to a city of Judah, 40 and she entered the house of Zechariah and greeted Elizabeth. 41 And when Elizabeth heard the greeting of Mary, the babe leaped in her womb; and Elizabeth was filled with the Holy Spirit 42 and she exclaimed with a loud cry, "Blessed are you among women, and blessed is the fruit of your womb!"

2   25 Now there was a man in Jerusalem, whose name was Simeon, and this man was righteous and devout, looking for the consolation of Israel, and the Holy Spirit was upon him. 26 And it had been revealed to him by the Holy Spirit that he should not see death before he had seen the Lord's Christ. 27 And inspired by the Spirit he came into the temple; and when the parents brought in the child Jesus, to do for him according to the custom of the law, 28 he took him up in his arms and blessed God and said,

29 "Lord, now lettest thou thy servant depart in peace,
according to they word;
30 for mine eyes have seen thy salvation
31 which thou hast prepared in the presence of all peoples,
32 a light for revelation to the Gentiles, and for glory to thy people Israel."

KEY VERSE: The angel said to her, "The Holy Spirit will come upon you, and the power of the Most High will overshadow you; therefore the child to be born will be called holy, The Son of God." Luke 1:35.

HOME DAILY BIBLE READINGS

BACKGROUND

Throughout the Old Testament and the New Testament, the Spirit of God or the Holy Spirit signifies God in action. The Hebrew word *ruach* and the Greek word *pneuma* for "spirit" have the imagery of "air in motion." Both words mean "wind" or "breath" as well as "spirit." The Revised Standard Version of Genesis 1:2, for example, states that "the Spirit (*ruach*) of God was moving over the face of the waters, while the New English Bible translates this verse as "a mighty wind" sweeping over the waters. And in John 3:8, Jesus tells Nicodemus, "The wind (*pneuma*) blows where it wills . . . so it is with everyone born of the Spirit (*pneuma*)."

The New Testament adds much more. This section of our Bible states that God was present and in action in Jesus the Christ as nowhere else. The New Testament writers announced that from the very beginning, Jesus' life and ministry were "anointed by the Spirit," "led by the Spirit," "full of the Spirit." Luke, the author of the Book of the Acts, for instance, quotes Peter's sermon: "How God anointed Jesus of Nazareth with the Holy Spirit and with power; how he went about doing good and healing all that were oppressed by the devil, for God was with him" (Acts 10:38).

The next six studies are designed to help you and your class gain a clearer picture of the role of the Holy Spirit in Jesus' life and also in the life of the Christian community. You will notice that great emphasis is put on the dynamic power released by the Spirit and also on the way people relate to God and others when they live by the Spirit.

The first three lessons have the subtitle, "The Holy Spirit Active in Jesus." The second set of three lessons carry the subtitle, "The Holy Spirit Active in the Church." Today's lesson and the following two lessons deal with the role of the Holy Spirit in Jesus' birth, in His calling, and in His ministry.

Luke stresses the activity of the Holy Spirit throughout his Gospel account, starting with the Christmas story. In the opening verse of Acts, he states that in his first volume (the Gospel according to Luke), "I have dealt with all that Jesus began to do and teach." Luke understands that all that Jesus did and taught was the Spirit's doing, or God in action!

NOTES ON THE PRINTED TEXT

Today's lesson is based upon information that can only have been supplied by Mary herself. *The Holy Spirit will come upon you and the power of the Most High will overshadow you.* Luke boldly asserts that the Holy Spirit, the power of God, is God's agent in the new creation. As God's Spirit created life for the Prophet Ezekiel in the valley of the dry bones, so, too, will God's powerful presence rest on Mary. She will bear a child who *will be called the Son of God.* The title indicates that there will be something special and unique about the child. He will have a unity with God because He is to be born of the Spirit. Jesus is to be born of Mary by the power of the Holy Spirit.

The angel offers a sign to confirm the announcement. Mary's cousin *Elizabeth in her old age has also conceived a son and this is the sixth month with her who has been called barren.* God intervened in Elizabeth's advanced years and enabled her to have a baby. Elizabeth interpreted her pregnancy as an act of God. The angel explains to Mary how barren Elizabeth became pregnant. *For with God nothing will be impossible.* Mary humbly acknowledges God's will. She agrees to be His servant. *Behold, I am the handmaiden of the Lord; let it be to me according to your word.*

Frightened, seeking comfort and support but obeying the angel's command, Mary goes to visit Elizabeth and receives the promised sign. Like many of the priests, Zechariah lived outside Jerusalem *in a city of Judah* in the *hill country.* As Mary enters Zechariah's house, she greets Elizabeth. Even before Elizabeth can respond to Mary, *the babe leaped* in Elizabeth's womb. As a physician, Luke knows that an emotional experience can cause a movement of the fetus. However, Elizabeth sees this movement as a confirmation of the Holy Spirit and as a connection between the two pregnancies. The Holy Spirit was revealing to Elizabeth that Mary's child was the Lord. Inspired by the Holy Spirit (literally *filled with the Holy Spirit*), Elizabeth joyfully proclaims that Mary is truly unique. *Blessed are you . . . and blessed is the fruit of your womb!*

Shortly after Jesus' birth, the Holy Spirit is evidenced again. This time it is in the great temple in Jerusalem. Three specific acts of the Spirit are connected with an aged but pious Jew named Simeon. Simeon was part of the pious minority who refused violence but waited for deliverance from the hated Romans and the oppression of the High Priests. This *righteous and devout man* was *looking for the consolation of Israel.* Simeon was waiting for the Messiah. *The Holy Spirit was upon him* assuring him that he would live to see the Messiah. *It had been revealed to him by the Holy Spirit that he should not see death before he had seen the Lord's Christ.* Moved by the inspiration of the Spirit, Simeon is in the Temple at the right moment when Mary and Joseph arrive to present their first child to the Lord. He recognizes the child. *And inspired by the Spirit he came into the temple . . . he took him up in his arms.*

Having seen the fulfillment of God's promise in this child, Simeon offers a prophetic prayer. Simeon is ready to die. By the power of the Holy Spirit, Simeon understands and announces the universal significance of Jesus' life. Salvation has been *prepared in the presence of all peoples.* The true significance of the child in his arms, Simeon says, is that He will be *a light for revelation to the Gentiles, and a glory to thy people.* Like Simeon, those who respond to the Holy Spirit receive spiritual insight and understanding and a sense of joy that must be shared with all people.

SUGGESTIONS TO TEACHERS

William Temple was a beloved Archbishop of Canterbury. He was also an astute theologian and profound thinker. Temple said that belief in the Holy Spirit is the most neglected doctrine in the Church in our times.

Some have associated words about the Holy Spirit with the charismatic movement and have assumed that the Spirit is the monopoly of a few enthusiasts. These lessons are designed to help us understand that the Holy Spirit was active in the person and work of Jesus and continues to be active in our lives. Today's lesson points to the activity of the Spirit in the Coming of Jesus. At first, it may look like a replay of the Christmas story. Remember, however, the emphasis is on the presence and power of the Holy Spirit in the lives of the principal characters of the familiar Christmas story.

1. *SPIRIT AND THE PROMISED PREDECESSOR.* Take careful note of the way in which John the Baptist's arrival was the work of the Holy Spirit. Luke, the doctor-writer, stresses the astonishing details of John's birth. The Spirit surprises

Elizabeth and Zechariah, John's parents. Allow enough time to have your class contemplate the surprises the Holy Spirit continues to bring in the lives of each believer! What are some of the astonishing ways in which the Spirit has brought new life and new hope into lives of those seated in your classroom? Also think together what it means in the Scriptures when it says that a person is "filled with the Holy Spirit." Are those in your class conscious of a divine power filling their lives?

2. *SPIRIT AND THE GODLY GIRL.* The angel-messenger Gabriel announces to Mary that the Holy Spirit will make it possible for her to bring forth a baby. Luke, a physician and careful researcher, was convinced that Mary's pregnancy was unique because of the work of the Holy Spirit. The report of the Virgin Birth was not a crude myth like the stories of the Greek gods and goddesses. Rather, Luke concludes reverently that Jesus' Coming to our world was made possible from the initial stages by the activity of the Spirit. Ponder with your class the sense of mystery that Jesus' birth story in Luke produces.

3. *SPIRIT AND THE CARING COUSIN.* Next, look at the story of Elizabeth. How easily we overlook this woman and the important role she played in the life of Mary. The Spirit operates in and through caring people. The Spirit uses folks like Elizabeth to minister to people like Mary who may be experiencing times of anxiety and hurt. Ask if the Spirit is allowed to use each member of the class for caring.

4. *SPIRIT AND A SERIOUS SEEKER.* Finally, turn the spotlight on Simeon. Let your imagination roam a bit as you think about the details of his meeting the Babe. Simeon had sought. And he had waited. Most of all, Simeon had trusted. Simeon was rewarded by his faith in the Spirit. The Spirit brought Simeon to the Temple and allowed him to cradle the infant Savior in his arms. Point out that the Spirit is constantly at work. He gives all serious seekers a glimpse of the Promised One!

TOPIC FOR ADULTS
THE HOLY SPIRIT AND JESUS' BIRTH

Find the Key! Fifty-six years ago, a group of thirty-eight World War I veterans set aside a bottle of cognac to go to the man who outlived the rest. They called themselves the Last Man's Club, and they all lived in Tacoma, Washington. For safe keeping, they put the bottle of 1917 vintage into a safe-deposit box in the Puget Sound National Bank. Each year since 1937, the group held a banquet, and sometimes the bottle would be taken from the vault to grace the table. The last time the bottle was brought out was several years ago. It was promptly locked up again—and the key was misplaced. Since that time, the four surviving members cannot remember what happened to the key. The cause for celebrating is there, but for the life of them they cannot find the key to get at it.

This is the way it is with the meaning of the Holy Spirit in our lives. We know the presence of the Spirit is a reason for celebration in our lives, but we can't seem to find the key to appreciating the Spirit in person. The report is that Jesus Christ brings Good News, but it seems to be locked up.

The coming of the Spirit unlocks the reality of the power of God in our midst. That same Spirit came among us in the Coming of Christ, and is promised to us today.

Attempt to Manipulate the Holy Spirit. In 1958, a series of earthquakes and volcanic eruptions rocked the Azores. The islands' inhabitants were frightened and thought they would have to resort to desperate measures to protect themselves. They marched to the cathedral and carefully removed the Espiritu Santo (the "Holy Spirit"), a large silver crown with a dove on the top. Carrying the

Espiritu Santo, the procession solemnly filed to the tip of the main island to the lighthouse and hoped this gesture would avert disaster.

Sometimes, people have the notion they can manipulate the Holy Spirit or use the Spirit for their own ends. Although the people of the Azores at least recognized the place of the Holy Spirit in their lives, they mistakenly held a magical idea of the work of the Spirit. If they had known their Bible, they would have realized the Spirit had been present at Jesus' birth and continues to dwell among us. They would not have regarded the Spirit as encased in a silver shrine or confined to sacred cathedrals but actively at work everywhere.

The Marks of the Holy Spirit. "There are some people who talk upon this subject excitedly, losing their heads and all sense of proportion, impatiently brushing aside the other facts and wonders of the faith as the mere small dust of the balance, in a way that seems to me ungrateful and unreal. Yet, open the Testament, and there, too, when men speak about the Holy Spirit, they are carried out of themselves. Obviously they are striving to express the inexpressible: something that breaks through language, that will not describe, what a man can only very dimly understand until he has had some experience of it for himself.

"And that something is not an intellectual doctrine. What those men are trying to get across to us is the depths of their spiritual experience. They are telling us that in Jesus Christ they have entered into a communion with God so real and near that they can only say a power that is not their power, but that works in and through them, has come upon them, mastered them, transformed them, used them in their weakness, in ways that are unbelievable and yet are true for His own glorious divine ends. How can you put that into language? As Luther said, 'When we speak about Jesus Christ, we are really babies talking brokenly in quarter words.' And here the beach shelves so steeply that, by taking only a step or two from the margin, I for one am swept away on mighty currents out into the infinite depths of that wonderful grace of God, blinded, bewildered, lost."— Arthur John Gossip.

Questions for Pupils on the Next Lesson. 1. Have you ever sensed a new direction for your life as a result of great spiritual experiences? 2. Why is carrying out the role of a servant as a Christian such a meaningful model for one's life and vocation? 3. How can adults respond to human needs in creating ways in the midst of changing times? 4. To whom do those around you go for support in times of crises, such as loss of a job, illness, divorce? 5. What is the symbolic meaning of the details of Jesus' baptism?

TOPIC FOR YOUTH
BORN OF THE SPIRIT

Afraid to Turn It On. A man in the Orient found himself suddenly fabulously rich. He ordered a custom-built Rolls Royce. The costly automobile was finally delivered. Everyone admired it. The owner, however, had it carefully pushed from place to place in the town. A friend finally asked him, "Is there no power in your handsome car?"

"Of course there is power in it," replied the wealthy owner, "but I am afraid to turn it on."

There is a marvelous power available to us. But many of us are afraid to use it. We therefore continue to feel weak and fearful. Why don't we turn on the power of the Holy Spirit in our lives? By an act of faith and repentance, let us be born of the Spirit. Even as the Spirit brought life to the world through Jesus, so He brings us power and hope now!

Weird Visions. In the fall of 1983, a sixteen-year-old orphan boy named Miguel Angel Poblete attracted attention in his native country of Chile in South America by claiming to talk to the Virgin Mary. Miguel Angel would collapse on the ground in apparent trances, then wander through the crowds in a glazed state, insisting he was talking to the Virgin Mary. Assistants followed the boy around with a microphone and loudspeaker. The messages beamed to the throngs by the boy were admonitions to "the people of Russia to come closer to God," "to men to stop dressing like women." Superstitious people, often numbering several thousands, flocked to the hilltop where Miguel Angel claimed to be contacted by the mother of Jesus. The Roman Catholic Church leaders in the area have ordered the faithful to stay away and say that the purported sightings of Mary "have no basis of credibility." The Archbishop denounces the gatherings, calling them "highly harmful to the true image of the Church."

Miguel Angel admits that the Virgin Mary first contacted him in 1983 when he was about to get high by sniffing glue with friends.

Our faith has no need for spurious spirituality dealing with visions of the Virgin Mary. This is weird—and harmful—nonsense. Miguel Angel's "talking" with Mary is completely foreign to the New Testament's account of the Spirit's visitation of the Virgin Mary. Look again at the words in Luke. There is no razzle-dazzle stuff or spooky scenario. Rather, an announcement quietly and simply that the Holy Spirit is active in Mary's offspring. Let's remember to keep it that way and not be swayed by dramatic reports of sightings and voices.

Administrative Agent. We have to learn to lean on the Holy Spirit.

Many of us do not, partly perhaps because we have not understood who the Spirit is. Here is Samuel Chadwick's definition of the Holy Spirit.

"The Holy Spirit is the active, administrative Agent of the glorified Son. He is the Paraclete, the Deputy, the acting Representative of the ascended Christ. His mission is to glorify Christ by perpetuating his character, establishing his Kingdom, and accomplishing his redeeming purpose in the world. The church is the body of Christ, and the Spirit is the Spirit of Christ. He calls and distributes, controls and guides, inspires and strengthens."—Samuel Chadwick, *The Way to Pentecost,* Hodder & Stoughton, London, 1932.

Is the Spirit the active administrative Agent for your life?

Questions for Pupils on the Next Lesson. 1. Do you ever feel need for encouragement and guidance when you probe beneath the surface meaning of life? 2. Are you willing to work for justice even when you must challenge prevailing attitudes and practices? 3. Are you always aware of the consequences of your choices? 4. What persons have challenged you most to become active in a good cause or a great undertaking? 5. Have you ever felt challenged by Jesus Christ? If so, how? If not, why not?

LESSON IX—APRIL 27

THE HOLY SPIRIT AND JESUS' CALLING

Background Scripture: Luke 3:15–22; 4:1–30
Devotional Reading: Luke 4:1–13

KING JAMES VERSION

LUKE 3 15 And as the people were in expectation, and all men mused in their hearts of John, whether he were the Christ, or not;

16 John answered, saying unto *them* all, I indeed baptize you with water; but one mightier than I cometh, the latchet of whose shoes I am not worthy to unloose: he shall baptize you with the Holy Ghost and with fire.

17 Whose fan *is* in his hand, and he will thoroughly purge his floor, and will gather the wheat into his garner; but the chaff he will burn with fire unquenchable.

21 Now when all the people were baptized, it came to pass, that Jesus also being baptized, and praying, the heaven was opened,

22 And the Holy Ghost descended in a bodily shape like a dove upon him, and a voice came from heaven, which said, Thou art my beloved Son; in thee I am well pleased.

4 16 And he came to Nazareth, where he had been brought up: and, as his custom was, he went into the synagogue on the sabbath day, and stood up for to read.

17 And there was delivered unto him the book of the prophet Esaias. And when he had opened the book, he found the place where it was written,

18 The Spirit of the Lord *is* upon me, because he hath anointed me to preach the gospel to the poor; he hath sent me to heal the brokenhearted, to preach deliverance to the captives, and recovering of sight to the blind, to set at liberty them that are bruised,

19 To preach the acceptable year of the Lord.

REVISED STANDARD VERSION

LUKE 3 15 As the people were in expectation, and all men questioned in their hearts concerning John, whether perhaps he were the Christ, 16 John answered them all, "I baptize you with water; but he who is mightier than I is coming, the thong of whose sandals I am not worthy to untie; he will baptize you with the Holy Spirit and with fire. 17 His winnowing fork is in his hand, to clear his threshing floor, and to gather the wheat into his granary, but the chaff he will burn with unquenchable fire."

21 Now when all the people were baptized, and when Jesus also had been baptized and was praying, the heaven was opened, 22 and the Holy Spirit descended upon him in bodily form, as a dove, and a voice came from heaven, "Thou art my beloved son; with thee I am well pleased."

4 16 And he came to Nazareth, where he had been brought up; and he went to the synagogue, as his custom was, on the sabbath day. And he stood up to read; 17 and there was given to him the book of the prophet Isaiah. He opened the book and found the place where it was written, 18 "The Spirit of the Lord is upon me,

because he has anointed me to preach good news to the poor.
He has sent me to proclaim release to the captives
and recovering of sight to the blind,
to set at liberty those who are oppressed,
19 to proclaim the acceptable year of the Lord."

KEY VERSE: The Spirit of the Lord is upon me, because he has anointed me to preach good news to the poor. He has sent me to proclaim release to the captives and recovering of sight to the blind, to set at liberty those who are oppressed, to proclaim the acceptable year of the Lord. Luke 4:18, 19.

HOME DAILY BIBLE READINGS

Apr.	21.	M.	*The Spirit Comes Upon Jesus.* Luke 3:15–22.
Apr.	22.	T.	*Jesus Is Tempted by the Devil.* Luke 4:1–13.
Apr.	23.	W.	*Jesus Defines His Ministry.* Luke 4:14–21.
Apr.	24.	T.	*Jesus Prophesies His Rejection.* Luke 4:22–30.
Apr.	25.	F.	*Jesus As the Bread of God.* John 6:32–40.
Apr.	26.	S.	*Jesus, the Light of the World.* John 8:12–19.
Apr.	27.	S.	*Jesus Was Sent From God.* John 8:25–30.

BACKGROUND

We use the word *spirit* in several ways. We sometimes speak of someone being "in good spirits" or tell a friend to "keep your spirits up." In this case, the word *spirit* means something like morale.

Or, we may hear patriotic speakers advising us to have the "spirit of 1776" or the "spirit of the Pilgrim fathers" or the "spirit of our pioneers." We have heard sermons extolling the "spirit of Luther" or the "spirit of the Reformation" or the "spirit" of a certain creed. Used in these ways, *spirit* means the fine qualities of a person or group, or the essential characteristics of a leader or a movement.

All these references to *spirit* have to do with the inner temperament of a human being. They refer to the attributes of a person or a group. *Spirit* in these uses has to do with the best within a human.

Holy Spirit is different. When we speak of the Holy Spirit, we refer to One who is *holy*, or belongs solely to God. *Holy* Spirit refers to the wholly Other. Holy Spirit does not spring out of the created world or our human thinking. God is the *Holy*. Belief in the Holy Spirit is belief in the Spirit of God, not in the spirit of humanity, not in good or evil spirits, not in some divine spark within a person. The Holy Spirit is the sheer power and presence of God in action in the world, completely unrelated to any human understanding of spirit within the world.

John the Baptist understood this. Jesus understood this. So did Luke, who wrote the Gospel material in today's lesson.

John the Baptizer recognized in Jesus the One who would baptize followers with the power of the Holy Spirit. When Jesus was baptized, the Holy Spirit descended and a voice from heaven confirmed Jesus' unique relationship to God. Jesus claimed the power of the Holy Spirit when He began His ministry. His first sermon opened with the quotation from the Prophet Isaiah, "The Spirit of the Lord is upon me because he has anointed me. . . ." The Spirit strengthened Jesus during His temptation in the wilderness. The Holy Spirit empowered Jesus for His ministry of liberation and reconciliation. Throughout Jesus' life, God was in action. The *Holy* Spirit—not merely a human spirit—was powerfully at work!

NOTES ON THE PRINTED TEXT

The witness of John the Baptist moves swiftly in Luke's third chapter. The nature of John's mission, the emphasis of his message, culminates with the crucial question of his being the Messiah and his prophecy of the Coming of the Messiah.

The people were in expectation, Luke records. John was a great and powerful revival preacher. Not only did he preach the need of repentance but he offered hope. He was to "prepare the way of the Lord," and the multitudes responded to this. They awaited expectantly God's salvation in *the Christ,* God's Anointed One, the Messiah. Some of the people *questioned in their hearts* whether John was the Messiah. John's reply was that a mightier One was coming *whose sandals I am not worthy to untie.* John was saying that he was unworthy to even be the Messiah's slave and do the menial, degrading work of removing the Master's sandals. John distinguished himself in two other ways from the Messiah. John only preached judgment. The Messiah will execute it. John baptized *with water.* The Messiah will *baptize . . . with the Holy Spirit and fire.* John recognized in Jesus the One who would baptize followers with the power of the Holy Spirit. Luke mentioned the Holy Spirit as a sign of redemption. Luke was looking ahead anticipating Pentecost. The image of fire denoted judgment. This theme of judgment continued when Luke tells of a farmer who used his winnowing fork to separate the wheat from the chaff. The wheat was kept in the granary but the chaff was destroyed. John pictured the Messiah's judgment as one which would destroy that which is evil and save that which is good.

John baptized to wash away and cleanse the individual of the pollution and stain of sin. Baptism symbolized a new birth. *All the people were baptized* including Jesus. Following baptism, while in prayer, *heaven was opened. And the Holy Spirit descended upon him in bodily form as a dove, and a voice came from heaven, "Thou art my beloved Son; with thee I am well pleased."* At Jesus' baptism, the Holy Spirit descended upon Him, and a voice from heaven confirmed Jesus' unique relationship to God. The dove did not symbolize the Holy Spirit. It was the Holy Spirit. The voice confirmed Jesus' uniqueness and Sonship. Moreover, Luke recorded that the Holy Spirit was with Jesus during the time of temptation in the wilderness.

Jesus brings God's message first of all to the people of His home town, *Nazareth, where he had been brought up.* Synagogue attendance was expected of every devout Jew. Since it was the *Sabbath Day,* He went to the synagogue. As a visiting rabbi, He was allowed to read. Each week a segment was read from the Law and from one of the prophets. In this way, over a three year cycle, all the books would be covered. *There was given to him the book of the prophet Isaiah.* He opened the book (a scroll) and read. Jesus read the opening of Isaiah 61. The speaker in Isaiah, with whom Jesus identified Himself, was the servant of the Lord. From the beginning, Jesus' ministry was a fulfillment of the servant role described in the Book of Isaiah. *The Spirit of the Lord is upon me.* When He began His ministry, Jesus openly claimed the power of the Holy Spirit. As the suffering servant of God, Jesus saw Himself called upon to make known the Good News of God's intervention into His people's lives. *He has anointed me to preach good news to the poor.* To those people in need of God's help the most, Jesus promised forgiveness and redemption through His message. *He has sent me . . . to the captives, to the blind, to those who are oppressed.* The Holy Spirit empowered Jesus for a ministry of liberation and reconciliation, and Jesus was anointed *to proclaim the acceptable year of the Lord.* Salvation has arrived, Jesus is saying. A new era of salvation has begun. This is the year of the Lord's favor.

SUGGESTIONS TO TEACHERS

Why was Jesus so different from all others? One reason is that He was led by the Holy Spirit in everything He did during His ministry. Luke underlines this fact in his Gospel account.

You will be teaching a lesson on this Sunday which illuminates the way the Holy Spirit activated Jesus' sense of His unique and divine mission. You should first reflect on the fact that apart from the Holy Spirit and His work the call and ministry of Jesus cannot be understood. You will find several important aspects of Jesus' own calling take new meaning once you remember the place of the Spirit in His career.

1. *COMPARISON TO CHRIST.* Open your lesson by noting the way John the Baptist contrasts himself to Jesus. John insists that Jesus is so superior that comparisons are impossible. John maintains that he merely baptizes with water whereas Jesus will baptize with the Holy Spirit. Have your class examine the words of John in Luke 3:15–17. Ask what makes Jesus stand out so much above all other teachers and religious leaders.

2. *CONFIRMATION OF HIS CALLING.* The Holy Spirit's coming upon Jesus at the time of His baptism was understood to be a sense of divine confirmation of His call. Jesus realized His unique mission. The Spirit substantiated that He was called as no one ever had been called before or would be called again. Do not move on to other parts of the lesson until your class grasps the meaning of the words, "Thou art my beloved Son; with thee I am well pleased" (Luke 3:22).

3. *CONTINUATION OF HIS COMMITMENT.* Next, work for a time with the

account of Jesus' temptations. Testing, trials, and temptations followed the deeply spiritual time of Jesus' call. The same also happens to us! A call or a moving religious experience does not shield us from "wilderness experiences" in our lives, where we struggle against devilish temptations. Open up the discussion of times when people in your class were confronted with appealing choices which were not God's will. Impress upon those in your class that it is only when we, like Jesus, are "full of the Holy Spirit" (Luke 4:1) that we can survive in the "wilderness" of temptation.

4. *COMPLETION OF THE QUEST.* Examine the episode where Jesus preached His first sermon in His home town, particularly studying the meaning of His text from Isaiah 61 (*see* Luke 4:16–21). Have your class tell what these words from the prophet meant to Jesus, to His hearers, and what they mean to us. Particularly make certain that the class comprehends Jesus' remark about Isaiah's words being fulfilled through Jesus' ministry!

5. *CONFRONTATION BY THE CARPENTER.* Jesus confronted His hearers that day in the Nazareth synagogue. He continues to confront people. Have His words produced any reaction in your people? If so, what? If not, why not? Jesus is so filled with the Holy Spirit that people can never be neutral about Him. They will find themselves either rejecting or rejoicing! Which is it for your class members?

TOPIC FOR ADULTS
THE HOLY SPIRIT AND JESUS' CALLING

His Whole Life, His Whole Soul. . . . Music for Louis Armstrong was a lifelong compulsion to reach people, to amuse and excite them, to touch them and be touched by them. Music took him from an impoverished boyhood in New Orleans to fifty years of touring the world, until his shining trumpet and wide grin became universal emblems of good will and good times tonight.

A New Orleans musician, Danny Barker, recalls a night in Armstrong's dressing room. A rabbi, a blind man, two nuns, a hustler, an ex-con, and a few kids and cops surrounded Armstrong, who sat laughing and talking to them all. "Always a word of encouragement, see. . . . All the diverse people . . . and everybody's looking, got their eyes dead on him, just like they were looking at a diamond." That sweet cheerfulness was Armstrong's music, and every note always rang true.

"My whole life, my whole soul, my whole spirit is to blooow that hooorn," Louis Armstrong told a doctor a few months before he died in 1971. No he wouldn't cancel an upcoming date at the Waldorf-Astoria. "The people are waiting for me," he said, "I got to do it, Doc. I got to do it."

For Jesus, His whole life, His whole soul, His whole spirit was to carry out the calling by the Spirit. He would not cancel His trip to Jerusalem which led to Calvary. He had to do it! The Spirit of the Lord was upon Him, from the time of His calling.

Surprising Call. Sometimes the Holy Spirit surprises us by calling us. Just as the Spirit operated in Jesus' call at the time of His baptism, the Spirit also operates in our lives. The Spirit's call, however, frequently comes in unexpected times and places. Take the case of Wilfred Grenfell.

Grenfell was a young medical student in London. Although there was nothing evil in his life there was nothing specifically Christian. He had been out visiting an out-patient in the Shadwell district. On the way home, he turned out of curiosity into a big tent where, as it happened, a mission was being conducted by Moody and Sankey. "It was so new to me," he said, "that when a tedious prayer-bore began with a long oration, I started to leave. Suddenly the leader, whom I learned afterwards was D. L. Moody, called out to the audience, 'Let us sing a hymn while our brother finishes his prayer.' His practicability interested me and I stayed the service out. When eventually I left, it was with a determination either to make religion a real effort to do as I thought Christ would do in my place as a doctor, or frankly to abandon it." So the turning point in Grenfell's career was a chance visit to an evangelistic mission and a most unconventional remark by D. L. Moody.

Wilfred Grenfell, later Sir Wilfred Grenfell, went on to become a mission doctor on the desolate coasts of Labrador whose Christian service became a legend inspiring millions.

The Push to Start You. C. S. Lewis describes the call of the Holy Spirit in the lives of Christians in a letter. It reads:

"To Mrs. G.   The only (possibly, not necessarily) unfavourable symptom is that you are just a trifle too excited.

"It is quite right that you should feel that 'something terrific' has happened to you. . . . Accept these sensations with thankfulness as birthday cards from God, but remember that they are only greetings, not the real gift. I mean that it is not the sensations that are the real thing. The real thing is the gift of the Holy Spirit which can't usually be—perhaps not ever—exerienced as a sensation or emotion. The sensations are merely the response of your nervous system. Don't depend on them. Otherwise when they go and you are once more emotionally flat (as you certainly will be quite soon), you might think that the real thing had gone, too. But it won't. It will be there when you can't feel it. May even be most operative when you can feel it least.

"Don't imagine it is all 'going to be an exciting adventure from now on.' It won't. Excitement, of whatever sort, never lasts. This is the push to start you off on your first bicycle: You'll be left to lots of dogged pedalling later on. And no need to feel depressed about it either. It will be good for your spiritual leg muscles. So enjoy the push while it lasts, but enjoy it as a treat, not as something normal."—From *Letters of C. S. Lewis,* copyright © 1966 by W. H. Lewis and Executors of C. S. Lewis. Reprinted by permission of Harcourt Brace Jovanovich, Inc.

Questions for Pupils on the Next Lesson. 1. How do you react when you are confronted with competing claims to power and authority? 2. Why are you sometimes afraid to take a stand for what you believe? 3. Where do you turn to find guidance to discover your purpose for living? 4. Do you use times of solitude to help you find strength to deal with everyday problems? 5. How can you remain positive in the midst of those who are negative about life?

TOPIC FOR YOUTH
CALLED BY THE SPIRIT

Unexpected Calling by the Spirit. The last thing a fifteen-year-old boy named Charles Spurgeon expected was for the Holy Spirit to give him a sense of calling that Sunday morning. It was a New Year's day. The snow had fallen heavily. He set off that New Year's morning for church. There was such a blizzard of snow that he was not able to reach the church which he was in the habit of attending. "When I could go no farther," he said, "I turned down a court and came to a little Primitive Methodist Chapel." It was by chance he entered it at all. The preacher who was to have conducted the service never got there for he too was held up by the weather, and quickly one of the office-bearers had to be brought forward to conduct the service with a congregation of perhaps fifteen people. "The man," said Spurgeon, "was really stupid. His text was, 'Look unto me and be ye saved all the ends of the earth,' and he kept repeating it because he had nothing else to say." Something about young Spurgeon caught the impromptu preacher's eye. "Young man," he said suddenly, "you look very miserable; and you will always be miserable—miserable in life and miserable in death—if you do not obey my text." Then suddenly he literally shouted, "Young man, look to Jesus! Look, look, look!" "And," said Spurgeon, "I did and then and there the cloud was gone, the darkness had rolled away, and that moment I saw the sun!"

Charles H. Spurgeon, surprised at the Spirit's call to him through that bumbling lay preacher, became a Christian. And what a Christian! Spurgeon's preaching as a minister in London touched the lives of millions! The Spirit who called Jesus Christ and called Charles Spurgeon also whispers His call to you.

Invaded by the Spirit. Over nineteen hundred years ago, there lived upon this earth a Man who gave up His life freely and willingly in order that we might know the redemptive love of God. Through His death, a way of deeper fellowship with God was opened to all persons. "He that hath seen me hath seen the Father," He said. Ever afterward, those who have served Him have found God as a Living Presence in their own lives. And having found God, neither persecution, nor distress, nor peril, nor sword, nor height, nor depth, nor anything else in the world has been able to separate them from the love of God which is in Jesus Christ.

Over and over again, people have found through Jesus an experience of God so powerful that it sets their whole life afire. They find themselves invaded to the depths of their being by God's presence, and they understand why Pascal wrote, in the center of his greatest experience of God, the single word: "Fire."

More Than Pep Talk or Illusion. Farmer (plowing with one mule): "Giddap, Pete! Giddap, Barney! Giddap, Johnny! Giddap, Tom!"

Stranger: "How many names does that mule have, anyway?"

Farmer: "Only one. His name is Pete, but he don't know his own strength, so I put blinders on him, yell a lot of names at him, and he thinks three other mules are helping him."

The operation of the Holy Spirit is more than pep talks or illusions, such as the old farmer's mule experienced. The Spirit's calling is a gentle, insistent persuasion that Power and Presence are upon you, and that the Lord has plans for you to serve! Are you personally aware of the Holy Spirit's calling in *your* life?

Questions for Pupils on the Next Lesson. 1. How do you react when authorities do not conform to your expectations? 2. What happens when you are confronted with conflicting viewpoints in making a decision about what position to take? 3. Why do you find yourself scared to take a stand for what is right? 4. What is meant to be your purpose in living? 5. What was the secret of Jesus' authority and power?

LESSON X—MAY 4

THE HOLY SPIRIT IN JESUS' MINISTRY

Background Scripture: Matthew 12:22–32; Luke 11:5–13
Devotional Reading: John 3:3–15

KING JAMES VERSION

MATTHEW 12   22 Then was brought unto him one possessed with a devil, blind, and dumb: and he healed him, insomuch that the blind and dumb both spake and saw.

23 And all the people were amazed, and said, Is not this the son of David?'

24 But when the Pharisees heard *it*, they said, This *fellow* doth not cast out devils, but by Beelzebub the prince of the devils.

25 And Jesus knew their thoughts, and said unto them, Every kingdom divided against itself is brought to desolation; and every city or house divided against itself shall not stand:

26 And if Satan cast out Satan, he is divided against himself; how shall then his kingdom stand?

27 And if I by Beelzebub cast out devils, by whom do your children cast *them* out? therefore they shall be your judges.

28 But if I cast out devils by the Spirit of God, then the kingdom of God is come unto you.

LUKE 11   5 And he said unto them, Which of you shall have a friend, and shall go unto him at midnight, and say unto him, Friend, lend me three loaves;

6 For a friend of mine in his journey is come to me, and I have nothing to put before him?

7 And he from within shall answer and say, Trouble me not: the door is now shut, and my children are with me in bed; I cannot rise and give thee.

8 I say unto you, though he will not rise and give him, because he is his friend, yet because of his importunity he will rise and give him as many as he needeth.

9 And I say unto you, Ask, and it shall be given you; seek, and ye shall find; knock, and it shall be opened unto you.

10 For every one that asketh receiveth; and he that seeketh findeth; and to him that knocketh it shall be opened.

11 If a son shall ask bread of any of you that is a father, will he give him a stone? or if *he ask* a fish, will he for a fish give him a serpent?

12 Or if he shall ask an egg, will he offer him a scorpion?

13 If ye then, being evil, know how to give good gifts unto your children: how much more shall *your* heavenly Father give the Holy Spirit to them that ask him?

REVISED STANDARD VERSION

MATTHEW 12   22 Then a blind and dumb demoniac was brought to him, and he healed him, so that the dumb man spoke and saw. 23 And all the people were amazed, and said, "Can this be the Son of David?" 24 But when the Pharisees heard it they said, "It is only by Beelzebul, the prince of demons, that this man casts out demons." 25 Knowing their thoughts, he said to them, "Every kingdom divided against itself is laid waste, and no city or house divided against itself will stand; 26 and if Satan casts out Satan, he is divided against himself; how then will his kingdom stand? 27 And if I cast out demons by Beelzebul, by whom do your sons cast them out? Therefore they shall be your judges. 28 But if it is by the Spirit of God that I cast out demons, then the kingdom of God has come upon you.

LUKE 11   5 And he said to them, "Which of you who has a friend will go to him at midnight and say to him, 'Friend, lend me three loaves; 6 for a friend of mine has arrived on a journey, and I have nothing to set before him; 7 and he will answer from within, 'Do not bother me; the door is now shut, and my children are with me in bed; I cannot get up and give you anything'? 8 I tell you, though he will not get up and give him anything because he is his friend, yet because of his importunity he will rise and give him whatever he needs. 9 And I tell you, Ask, and it will be given you; seek, and you will find; knock, and it will be opened to you. 10 For every one who asks receives, and he who seeks finds, and to him who knocks it will be opened. 11 What father among you, if his son asks for a fish, will instead of a fish give him a serpent; 12 or if he asks for an egg, will give him a scorpion? 13 If you then, who are evil, know how to give good gifts to your children, how much more will the heavenly Father give the Holy Spirit to those who ask him!"

KEY VERSE: If you then, who are evil, know how to give good gifts to your children, how much more will the heavenly Father give the Holy Spirit to those who ask him! Luke 11:13.

HOME DAILY BIBLE READINGS

Apr.	28.	M.	*Christ's Mission in Prophecy.* Isaiah 42:1–9.
Apr.	29.	T.	*How to Meet Opposition.* Matthew 7:1–12.
Apr.	30.	W.	*The Blessing of Trial.* James 1:12–21.
May	1.	T.	*Avoiding the Unforgivable Sin.* 2 Thessalonians 1:5–12.
May	2.	F.	*The Value of Confidence.* James 1:2–8.
May	3.	S.	*Getting What We Ask For.* 1 John 3:19–24.
May	4.	S.	*Sources of Jesus' Power.* Matthew 12:22–32.

BACKGROUND

Even the harshest of Jesus' critics recognized that Jesus had power. After all, they personally witnessed the way He healed apparently hopelessly ill people. Some of these critics were present when Jesus enabled a pathetic man who was both blind and dumb to see and speak. How could they dismiss Jesus as a "crank" or "fake" when they saw Jesus' power so dramatically at work?

When these critics tried to accuse Jesus of being in league with the prince of demons, Jesus quickly refuted them. He pointed out that it was hardly possible for the power of the evil one to be at work to destroy the work of the evil one. Jesus then went on to remind His hearers that the Holy Spirit was actively at work in His ministry: ". . . it is by the Spirit of God that I cast out demons" (Matthew 12:28). Jesus asserted then and always that the Holy Spirit gave Him His power and authority.

By challenging the authority behind that power, the critics were challenging the Holy Spirit or God in action. These critics, although professing to be the religious leaders of the nation, were actually blaspheming! They were denying the authority of God. They insisted on committing the unpardonable; they placed their own authority above the Lord's. They elevated themselves to the place where God's grace could have no meaning for their lives.

The conflict between Jesus and His Pharisee critics sharpened on this point of how a person is related to the Spirit and how one recognizes the work of God in the world. The critics insisted that Jesus was not activated by the Spirit. Jesus, on the other hand, viewed His ability to heal by the Spirit as a sign of the dawning of the Kingdom of God.

In Luke 11, Jesus promised that the Spirit empowering His ministry also would empower His followers. He told them to pray for the gift of the Spirit. The parable of the friend at midnight and the sayings about a parent offering fish and eggs instead of snakes and scorpions are examples of teaching by contrast, not by comparisons. God is not grudging or reluctant! He freely and willingly answers our requests for the Holy Spirit to continue Jesus' ministry!

NOTES ON THE PRINTED TEXT

In the time of Jesus, people believed in demons. They believed that the air was so full of them that it was not possible to insert the point of a needle into the air without touching one. Some believed that there were seven and a half million of them! The universal belief was that the demons were invisible powers bent on injuring people. They were responsible for mental illness and all physical diseases. The ruler of these demons was Beelzebub.

Then a blind and dumb demoniac was brought to him, and he healed him. Jesus' exorcisms are closely connected with His message of the dawning Kingdom of God. They are not the works of a human wonder-worker, but acts of the Spirit. The Holy Spirit gave power and authority to the ministry of Jesus.

The crowd of people is amazed. *Can this be the Son of David?* "Son of David" was a popular title for the Messiah, and the crowds present at this healing question whether Jesus is the long expected Messiah. However, the Pharisees argue, *"It is only by Beelzebub, the prince of demons, that this man casts out demons."* The Pharisees challenge the authority behind Jesus' power. They say that Jesus can control demons in people because He is possessed by Beelzebub who controls all the demons. He is not sent from God but from the devil!

Jesus shows that this charge is nonsense. *Every kingdom divided against itself is laid waste ... no city or house divided against itself will stand.* Internal strife leads to doom. Continuing His argument, Jesus questions *if Satan casts out Satan, he is divided against himself; how then can his kingdom stand?* If Satan is in Him and He is driving out other of Satan's helpers, then the kingdom is divided and therefore doomed.

Then, turning the argument against the Pharisees, Jesus asks, *If I cast out demons by Beelzebub, by whom do your sons cast them out?* How do the Jewish exorcists cast out demons unless they operate by God's power? To judge Him is to judge them. The conflict between Jesus and the Pharisees focuses on how one is related to God and how one recognizes the work of God in the world. *But if it is by the Spirit of God that I cast out demons then the kingdom of God has come upon you.* In this claim, Jesus implies that the Spirit of God is empowering Him to cast out demons. Jesus views His ability to heal by the power of the Spirit as a sign of the dawning of the Kingdom.

Jesus' teaching in Luke 11 concerning prayer and the gift of the Holy Spirit is a teaching by contrast rather than comparison. There are two units of instruction. The first is the humorous story set in a Palestinian village at midnight. In the parable, a person unexpectedly arrives at the home of a friend. The host needs food to feed his guest. Since oriental hospitality is a community affair, the host hurriedly goes to his neighbor to ask for bread and whatever else he needs to serve his guest. For a villager to refuse his requests for help would be unthinkable. It would be an insult. Jesus asks, "Can you imagine going to a friend with a sacred request to help entertain your guest and being offered a silly excuse about the kids being asleep?" The listeners know the communal responsibility for the guest and would say, "We cannot imagine such a thing." Jesus assures His listeners, *ask, and it will be given ... seek, and you will find ... knock and it will be opened to you.* He drives home this assurance in the statements that follow.

His listeners can ask confidently of God knowing that He will respond even better than a father. For as the second part of the instruction points out, what good father would not grant good gifts to the son who seeks him out and asks of him? So, says Jesus, is God, the Father in heaven more eager to share the gift of the Holy Spirit with those who ask. *How much more will the heavenly Father give the Holy Spirit to those who ask Him?*

SUGGESTIONS TO TEACHERS

A Sunday-School child trying to draw a picture of the Trinity crayoned a large bearded figure labelled "God" and a slightly smaller bearded figure identified as "The Son." Hovering off to one side was a third figure, also bearded, but wearing a pair of feathery wings, which the ten-year-old stated was the Holy Spirit.

Some in your class may not depict the Trinity in quite such a crude or graphic way, but nevertheless have a blurry notion of three deities with the Holy Spirit as a sort of hazy also-ran. Probably not very many are sure of the relationship of the Holy Spirit to Jesus Christ.

This lesson is not meant to be an exercise in theological hairsplitting. It is to help your class members be more effective disciples of Jesus. You as teacher can assist them in becoming better Christians by giving them a clearer understanding of the power of the Spirit at work through Jesus. You and your class won't be discussing abstract issues. You will be reading and talking over New Testament Gospel accounts which depict the ways the Holy Spirit operated in Jesus' ministry.

1. *DEPOSES THE DEMONS.* Start by having the class play "You Are There!" with the story in Matthew 12:22–32 about the dumb and blind man who was brought to Jesus. Encourage the folks in your class to put themselves in the place of the spectators, the Pharisees, and, of course, the unfortunate person who could not speak or see. Most of all, help them to grow more deeply aware of the extraordinary power at work through Jesus. This "spiritual power" of course is the Spirit. And the Spirit empowers Jesus to conquer the most destructive powers in the world—savage powers which oppose God. Don't be put off with the way the New Testament writers refer to these terrible powers as "demons." This was the common way of speaking of all illnesses and emotional disorders. The main point is that the Spirit's power is mightier than any of these demonic powers.

2. *DELINEATES OUR DUTY.* The Matthew account also warns about the sin against the Holy Spirit. Some of your class may think that this is saying nasty "cuss" words about the Lord. Others may imagine it's an unforgivable private crime. Instead of wasting a lot of valuable lesson time on the sin against the Holy Spirit, guide the discussion to ways in which your church and your people may work *for* and *with* the Spirit. In fact, the point of all these references about the Holy Spirit is that your class members are meant to act cooperatively with the Spirit! The Spirit, furthermore, shows believers in Jesus Christ ways whereby they may serve Him. He outlines our responsibilities.

3. *DESCRIBES THE DEITY.* Finally, turn to the passage in Luke 11:5–13. The point of this little parable is the generosity of God. God gives! If a neighbor or a parent can give good things to those who ask, "How much more will the heavenly Father give the Holy Spirit to those who ask Him?" Remind your students that the Spirit is not a private luxury for a few elite Christians, but the empowering Presence who draws near to anyone who asks!

TOPIC FOR ADULTS
THE HOLY SPIRIT IN JESUS' MINISTRY

The Holy Spirit in Our Ministry. A living faith always is a working faith. The results we receive for our labors usually are in proportion to what we are willing to give of ourselves in ministry, as used by the Holy Spirit.

Rabindranath Tagore, in *Gitanjali*, writes: "I had gone abegging from door to door in the village, when thy golden chariot appeared in the distance like a gorgeous dream and I wondered who was this King of all kings.

"My hopes rose high and methought my evil days were at an end, and I stood waiting for alms to be given unasked and for wealth scattered on all sides in the dust.

"Thy chariot stopped where I stood. Thy glance fell on me and thou camest down with a smile. I felt that the luck of my luck had come at last. Then, of a sudden, thou didst hold out thy right hand and say, 'What hast thou to give me?'

"Ah, what a kingly jest was it to open thy palm to a beggar to beg! I was confused and stood undecided, and then from my wallet I slowly took out the least little grain of corn and gave it to thee.

"But how great my surprise when, at the day's end, I emptied my bag on the floor to find a least little grain of gold among the poor heap. I bitterly wept and wished that I had had the heart to give thee my all."

So the Spirit uses what we give in our ministering to others.

"Veni Creator Spiritus." So many Christians fail to rely upon the power of the Holy Spirit in their lives. Christians should pray for Pentecost to take place in 1986 with all of the consequences that will follow.

Dr. Willem Visser't Hooft has emphasized that to pray for the Holy Spirit is risky business. When he addressed the Nineteenth General Council of the World Alliance of Reformed Churches in 1964, he stated: "To pray *Veni Creator Spiritus* cannot possibly be taken to signify: 'Let's have a little bit of Holy Spirit; just enough to put some more energy into our often sleepy ecclesiastical institutions.' It can only mean: 'Come, Thou living God, Thou living Christ, and Thou Creator Spirit, Giver of Life, and transform us altogether, so that we may be truly converted, radically changed.'"

With the world suffering as it is in 1986, we need a fresh Pentecost to empower us to undertake the mission and the ministry to which Lord Jesus has called us.

Strange Will. Harry Golden has a story about an old uncle of the very wealthy philanthropist, Frederic R. Mann. The old man did not let his nephew give him very much and was satisfied with just enough to live simply as he had always done. When the old uncle died, he left a will with all kinds of bequests to charities, institutions, schools, synagogues, friends. Everyone was astounded for no one knew that the old man had any personal fortune. Had he lost his mind at the end of his life? But it was all made clear and reasonable in the last paragraph of the will which read: "All these bequests I am turning over to my beloved nephew, Frederic R. Mann, who will supply the money in my name."

Yet, in a strange way, is that not exactly what the Christian is always doing? He makes *promises* that he cannot fulfill himself, but he turns it all over to his Heavenly Father to make good the promises. We cannot give another relief from pain, but God can and we promise it. We cannot give another meaning for his life, but God can and we make the offer in His name. We cannot give anyone eternal life, but in the name of Jesus Christ, we announce His victory over death which He won for all of us. Perhaps this is the chief joy of the Christian life. We who are so poor and helpless are commissioned by the great God to distribute the unspeakable gifts in His name. The Spirit uses us in this way to continue Christ's ministry.

Questions for Pupils on the Next Lesson. 1. Why do you think the Church often seems powerless? 2. What are some of the channels through which the Holy Spirit led the earliest Christians? 3. Do you someimes feel powerless and incapable of making a difference in the world? 4. Have you learned to find meaning in prayer, fasting, and worship? 5. Does your church offer single adults a sense of belonging, empowerment, and fulfillment?

TOPIC FOR YOUTH
EMPOWERED BY THE SPIRIT

Definition of the Spirit. Winston Churchill once observed that Russia remains "a riddle wrapped in a mystery inside an enigma." Some young people in the Church would say that this is the way they feel about the Holy Spirit.

However, other young people have learned personally that the Holy Spirit is no spooky secret, but the sense of the Presence and Power of the Lord in their midst. They have learned that the Spirit who energized Jesus in His ministry also energizes them as they move out to minister in His name today!

Empowered to Snare. Eva Braverman, a fifteen-year-old Chicago girl, won $75,000 in the Juvenile Diabetes Foundation Raffle. She walked up to the stage amid applause from the several thousand people who held the $100 raffle tickets. Eva's father had bought tickets for each member of the family in order to help the Diabetes Foundation. Eva's stepsister, Stephanie Berger, fourteen, was diagnosed as a diabetic when she was seven, and suffers from the dread disorder. When Eva reached the stage, however, she did not accept the $75,000. Instead, she admitted tearfully that she was very nervous but said that she loved her stepsister and therefore wanted to give the money back to the Foundation so it could be used for research to help diabetics like Stephanie. "I just thought it was the right thing to do," reported Eva, "I mean it, it's important."

This is the way the Spirit empowers people to serve others. It's the way the Spirit empowered Jesus to minister. Have you asked and allowed the Spirit to direct you to minister to other people?

Empowered by the Spirit, Therefore Lent to Be Spent. "No more saints? With LeChambron, Albert Schweitzer, Mother Teresa, and who knows who else? No more suffering for and with the suffering Christ? Outstanding saints and martyrs have always been in short supply. But silent Christian witnesses, those who yearn and pray for others, nameless helpers who in so many ways complete Christ's sufferings—these have always thought of themselves as lent to be spent."—Hugh T. Kerr. *Theology Today,* July, 1980.

Questions for Pupils on the Next Lesson. 1. Why do you think the Church sometimes seems dead? 2. What did the Holy Spirit do for early Christians on Pentecost? 3. How may we know the power of the Holy Spirit in our lives? 4. Does the Holy Spirit still enable people to respond positively to the risks and adventures of new undertakings? 5. Are you looking for meaningful avenues of service?

LESSON XI—MAY 11

PROMISE AND POWER OF THE HOLY SPIRIT

Background Scripture: Acts 1:4–8; 2:1–21; 13:1–12
Devotional Reading: John 16:12–15

KING JAMES VERSION

ACTS 1   4 And, being assembled together with *them,* commanded them that they should not depart from Jerusalem, but wait for the promise of the Father, which, *saith he,* ye have heard of me.

5 For John truly baptized with water; but ye shall be baptized with the Holy Ghost not many days hence.

6 When they therefore were come together, they asked of him, saying, Lord, wilt thou at this time restore again the kingdom to Israel?

7 And he said unto them, It is not for you to know the times or the seasons, which the Father hath put in his own power.

8 But ye shall receive power, after that the Holy Ghost is come upon you: and ye shall be witnesses unto me both in Jerusalem, and in all Judea, and in Samaria, and unto the uttermost part of the earth.

2 And when the day of Pentecost was fully come, they were all with one accord in one place.

2 And suddenly there came a sound from heaven as of a rushing mighty wind, and it filled all the house where they were sitting.

3 And there appeared unto them cloven tongues like as of fire, and it sat upon each of them.

4 And they were all filled with the Holy Ghost, and began to speak with other tongues, as the Spirit gave them utterance.

13 NOW there were in the church that was at Antioch certain prophets and teachers; as Barnabas, and Simeon that was called Niger, and Lucius of Cyrene Manaen, which had been brought up with Herod the tetrarch, and Saul.

2 As they ministered to the Lord, and fasted, the Holy Ghost said, Separate me Barnabas and Saul for the work whereunto I have called them.

3 And when they had fasted and prayed, and laid *their* hands on them, they sent *them* away.

4 So they, being sent forth by the Holy Ghost, departed unto Seleucia; and from thence they sailed to Cyprus.

5 And when they were at Salamis, they preached the word of God in the synagogues of the Jews: and they had also John to *their* minister.

REVISED STANDARD VERSION

ACTS 1   4 And while staying with them he charged them not to depart from Jerusalem, but to wait for the promise of the Father, which, he said, "you heard from me, 5 for John baptized with water, but before many days you shall be baptized with the Holy Spirit."

6 So when they had come together, they asked him, "Lord, will you at this time restore the kingdom to Israel?" 7 He said to them, "It is not for you to know times or seasons which the Father has fixed by his own authority. 8 But you shall receive power when the Holy Spirit has come upon you; and you shall be my witnesses in Jerusalem and in all Judea and Samaria and to the end of the earth."

2 When the day of Pentecost had come, they were all together in one place. 2 And suddenly a sound came from heaven like the rush of a mighty wind, and it filled all the house where they were sitting. 3 And there appeared to them tongues as of fire, distributed and resting on each one of them. 4 And they were all filled with the Holy Spirit and began to speak in other tongues, as the Spirit gave them utterance.

13 Now in the church at Antioch there were prophets and teachers, Barnabas, Simeon who was called Niger, Lucius of Cyrene, Mana-en a member of the court of Herod the tetrarch, and Saul. 2 While they were worshiping the Lord and fasting, the Holy Spirit said, "Set apart for me Barnabas and Saul for the work to which I have called them." 3 Then after fasting and praying they laid their hands on them and sent them off. 4 So, being sent out by the Holy Spirit, they went down to Seleucia; and from there they sailed to Cyprus. 5 When they arrived at Salamis, they proclaimed the word of God in the synagogues of the Jews. And they had John to assist them.

KEY VERSE: You shall receive power when the Holy Spirit has come upon you; and you shall be my witnesses in Jerusalem and in all Judea and Samaria and to the end of the earth. Acts 1:8.

HOME DAILY BIBLE READINGS

May	5.	M.	*Spirit Will Bring New Life.* Ezekiel 26:25–32.
May	6.	T.	*Spirit Will Bring a Peaceful Kingdom.* Isaiah 11:1–9.
May	7.	W.	*Spirit Will Bring Deliverance.* Zechariah 12:6–14.
May	8.	T.	*Spirit Given to Those Who Ask.* Luke 11:5–13.
May	9.	F.	*Spirit Given to Those Who Believe.* John 7:32–39.
May	10.	S.	*The Work of the Holy Spirit.* John 16:4–15.
May	11.	S.	*Awaiting the Spirit's Arrival.* Acts 1:1–11.

BACKGROUND

The Gospel accounts testify that God was present and acting in Jesus of Nazareth as nowhere else. Jesus' ministry was authorized and empowered by the Holy Spirit. The early disciples of Jesus also understood that Jesus was not only the bearer of the Spirit but also the giver of the Spirit. That is why the New Testament speaks of the Holy Spirit as the Spirit of Christ.

Various New Testament writers state this in different ways. Paul announces that Jesus Christ became the "life-giving Spirit" (1 Corinthians 15:45). John pictures the Risen Lord conferring His Spirit on His followers at Easter, and writes, "He breathed on them and said to them, 'Receive the Holy Spirit' " (John 20:22). In several ways, the New Testament authors try to say that the Risen Christ bestows on His followers the same Spirit, the same power and Presence of God, which He Himself had shown while on earth.

Luke, in particular, wanted to portray this fact. In his first volume, his account of Jesus' life, death, and Resurrection, Luke described "all that Jesus *began* to do and teach" (Acts 1:1). In his second volume, Luke told what Jesus *continues* to do and teach through His Spirit in the mission of the Church.

The disciples had not seen, heard, or touched the resurrected Lord since He was taken from them. They had waited. And prayed. Fifty days after Passover (*Pentecost* means "fiftieth") at the time the ancient Jewish feast of "harvest" (Exodus 23:16) or "first fruits" (Numbers 28:26) or "feast of weeks" (Deuteronomy 16:10) was held in the Temple to honor God's goodness as Lord of harvest, covenant renewal was also celebrated. An old tradition of the rabbis held that God's voice at Sinai was heard in seventy languages for all the nations, but only Israel heard. Luke remembered all the imagery of Pentecost. God's wind and fire shown at Creation, at Sinai, and through Jesus' life and ministry, touched the lives of Jesus' faithful followers at Pentecost. The Holy Spirit—God in action—gave them the authority and power to continue Jesus' ministry!

Pentecost is more than the birthday celebration of the Christian Church. Although the great event is part of our memory as God's people, The Holy Spirit is not the luxury bestowed on a few believers centuries ago in Jerusalem. God continues to fill us with the Spirit—when we ask and when we obey!

NOTES ON THE PRINTED TEXT

The Holy Spirit is the foundation of the Book of Acts. The coming of the Spirit is THE event in Acts. It is this event that is the key to the success of the Christian mission.

The disciples were certain that Jesus was alive. They had seen Him and talked with Him. They even risked their own safety to stay in Jerusalem because Jesus wanted them to stay in Jerusalem. *He charged them not to depart from Jerusalem.* However, since the disciples had missed the point of much of Jesus' teaching, they still nursed secretly the old ideas of the Messiah. They expected Jesus to lead a violent overthrow of the Romans and re-establish David's glorious kingdom. Jesus tried to dispel some of this confusion.

Wait for the promise of the Father. They had a promise from Jesus (*see* Luke

24:49). The promise of the Father was the Holy Spirit. Still, the disciples did not understand. Their conception of the Messiah was still at odds with the one Jesus presented. *Lord, will you at this time restore the kingdom to Israel?* The disciples literally pestered Jesus, asking repeatedly when He would make Israel the super-power of the Middle Eastern world. Jesus' answer was blunt. It was not their business but the Father's business. *It is not for you to know the times or seasons which the Father has fixed by his own authority.* Jesus makes it clear that it really was not a timetable the disciples needed but power. *You shall receive power when the Holy Spirit has come upon you.* Jesus assured the disciples that the Spirit would be their source of power. The Greek word for power is *dynamis* from which our English word *dynamo* comes. The disciples were to be energized, not by human power, but by the power of which Jesus spoke, the Holy Spirit. God Himself would empower them to witness *in Jerusalem and in all Judea and Samaria and to the end of the earth.* Significantly, the word translated into "witness" is exactly the same as our English word *martyr.* A witness is one who gives testimony by speaking, serving, and suffering.

God did not forget His promise. *When the day of Pentecost had begun they were all assembled in one place.* Pentecost was a Hebrew harvest festival cele-brated fifty days after the beginning of the barley harvest. It marked the comple-tion of the harvest. Obeying Jesus' command, the disciples had remained together in Jerusalem. *Suddenly a sound came from heaven like the rush of a mighty wind and filled the house where they were sitting.* The Energizer, the Empowerer, the Holy Spirit was given to them. Luke's verb form clearly states that the power was sent from a source outside of themselves. It came as a fulfillment of prophecy. *There appeared to them tongues as of fire ... resting on each of them.* Fire is a symbol of God's presence. *And they were all filled with the Holy Spirit, and began to speak ... as the Spirit gave them utterance.* The Holy Spirit empowered the disciples in a dramatic and symbolic way by enabling them to preach and witness persuasively to all the Jewish pilgrims from many lands who were in Jerusalem.

The Holy Spirit is the source of miraculous power, guidance, and administra-tive authority as Acts 13 illustrates. *While they were worshiping the Lord and fasting, the Holy Spirit said....* It was the Spirit who gave direction while the *prophets and teachers* were together. The early Christian Church experienced the leadership of the Spirit both corporately and individually. The Greek word for *worshiping* supplies the root for our English word *liturgy.* It means "work." Worshiping is work. Fasting means more than simply doing without food. Volun-tary discipline was also needed. Prayer, fasting, and worship were channels through which the Spirit led the early Church.

Set apart ... Barnabas and Saul for the work which I have called them. Through the Spirit, these two were set apart or separated for service and were ordained (the laying on of hands). The *Holy Spirit sent out* Barnabas and Saul on a mission with a job to do. They went to Seleucia, about sixteen miles from An-tioch. From Seleucia, they *sailed to Cyprus.* Cyprus had a large Jewish popula-tion that had settled there to work in the copper mines. Along with young John Mark, they proclaimed the word of God in the synagogues.

SUGGESTIONS TO TEACHERS

"My favorite hymn," the lady said, "is that one that has those lines: 'I think when I read that sweet story of old, when Jesus was here among men ... how I'd like to have been with him then.'" When a friend asked her why she would like to have been with Jesus back 2,000 years ago, she said, "Because nothing spiritual ever happens now."

The Holy Spirit did not disappear when Jesus was taken from His friends.

"Spiritual" things did not stop happening in the first century. The experience of the earlier believers in Jesus Christ was that the same Spirit which infused His life also infused their lives. Furthermore, they insisted that the Holy Spirit would continue to empower believers of every age to come!

This is the dynamically exciting news for you to share as teacher today!

1. *PROMISE OF HIS POWER.* Get your class to be aware of the promise in the opening chapter of Acts: Jesus assures His uncertain followers that they will be drenched ("baptized") with Holy Spirit (Acts 1:5). Furthermore, Jesus promises that they will receive power when the Spirit has come upon them. Point out to the class that the Greek word for power in Acts 1:8 is the word from which our words *dynamite* and *dynamic* are derived. Doesn't that suggest something about the way Christians can be today? How dynamically alive are those in your class?

2. *POWER OF HIS PROMISE.* Devote some of your lesson on Jesus' insistence that His followers will be empowered by the Holy Spirit to be His "witnesses in Jerusalem, Judea, Samaria, and the end of the earth" (Acts 1:8). Ask what it means to be "witnesses" to Jesus Christ in your community in these times. And what about "the end of the earth"? Have you talked about your church's missionary effort recently? You can get some up-to-date reports on the methods your denomination is using to witness overseas from your church magazine or your pastor. Remind your class that it carries out Christian witness by supporting your denomination's missionaries.

3. *PRESENTATION OF HIS PRESENCE.* Take plenty of lesson time to allow your class to understand the meaning of the Pentecost experience in the lives of class members. The second chapter of Acts describes the way whereby the Holy Spirit welds together disparate kinds of people. Furthermore, the Spirit enables those from a variety of backgrounds to communicate with each other. The key is that the Spirit focuses all these different and differing persons not on themselves or on their differences, but on Jesus Christ. They are able to make clear to one another that Jesus is Lord!

4. *PRESENCE OF HIS POWER.* The Acts 13:1–12 story of Elymas trying to buy the Holy Spirit is both an amusing account of a slick magician wanting to add another trick to his act and also a testimony to the power the Holy Spirit gave early Christians such as Paul. Do people around you and your class members sense the power in your lives? Have you asked the Spirit to give you His empowering Presence?

TOPIC FOR ADULTS
PROMISE AND POWER OF THE HOLY SPIRIT

God's Breath of Life. "Most of our fire company's personnel, nearly all of our rescue company's responders and all of our medical technicians are trained in CPR: Cardio-Pulmonary Resuscitation. It is a system of life support given by rescuers until medical personnel can take over. The goal is to maintain effective respiration and pulse in the victim. Each of the trained rescuers learns the *A-B-C* steps of effective CPR. These three basic steps are:

"*A*—Airway opened
"*B*—Breathing restored
"*C*—Circulation restored

"Steps *A* and *B* are nothing more than artificial respiration, but they are also the most important. The most important factor in CPR is getting enough oxygen into the victim's body. Without a sufficient supply of oxygen, the victim will die no matter how effective the chest compressions are in step *C*. The rescuer's breathing his very breath is the single most essential item in the process.

"Our lives are much the same. When we try to exist without God's Spirit, we die. We can choke and gasp our way through life without much heart, but we die without love and, most importantly, hope. To paraphrase Jesus' promise, 'I am going to give you the very breath of my life.'

"On Pentecost, God breathed new life into His disciples. He still breathes new life into His people, His church, and all those who believe in Him. He still restores each of us to a new, fresh life."—J. B. Barker.

Who Sustains the Church? "It is not we who can sustain the Church, nor was it our forefathers, nor will it be our descendants. It was and is and will be the One who says: 'I am with you always, even unto the end of the world.'

"For you and I were not alive thousands of years ago, but the Church was preserved without us, and it was done by the One (who is Jesus Christ). . . .

"Again we do not do it in our lifetime, for the Church is not upheld by us. For we could not resist the devil . . . and the sects and other wicked folk. For us the Church would perish before our very eyes and we with it (as we daily prove), were it not for that other man (Jesus Christ) who manifestly upholds the Church for us."—Martin Luther, *Works,* Weimer: Hermann Bölhous, 1914.

Still Waiting. An extra place is set this evening at Howth Castle in Ireland. It has been set each night since 1576. The empty dinner setting is for Grace O'Malley, who died 383 years ago. In 1559, Grace O'Malley had asked for hospitality at the Castle near Dublin but was rudely turned away. Stinging from the rebuff, Grace, a swashbuckling pirate leader, kidnapped the son of the owner of the castle. She sent word that she would release the boy only if the owner pledged perpetual hospitality for Grace O'Malley. The offer was accepted, the son was returned, and an extra dinner setting has been laid on at the castle dinner table ever since. Grace herself never returned, but a place is set for her ever since.

Some church people go through the motions of setting a place for the Holy Spirit in their lives without really expecting the reality of the Spirit ever to be known. They make worship a charade. Their service is formality. Like the perpetually empty place at Howth Castle, the Spirit's power is merely a quaint report from the distant past. The Spirit will never be with them, they think.

The promise of the Spirit, however, is that He continues to abide with believers. He empowers Christ's community today as surely as He energized that community at Pentecost! Expect great things from the Spirit. Attempt great things with the Spirit!

Questions for Pupils on the Next Lesson. 1. Does the Holy Spirit give gifts to *all* believers? 2. What special gift do you understand the Spirit has given to you? 3. Are the spiritual gifts of each person in your class the same? 4. Is the gift of the Spirit to each person needed by your church? 5. What are the gifts of the Spirit to be used for?

TOPIC FOR YOUTH
POWER TO SERVE

Power to Forgive. "On February 1, 1974, while serving a yoked parish (Athens-Sweetwater) in the state of Tennessee, I was surprised by an armed man who had entered my station wagon while I was paying a bill. I returned to my car, opened the door, and found myself staring into the business end of a .22-caliber revolver.

"After relieving me of what remained of my paycheck, I was ordered to drive to a lonely stretch of road where the drama was completed. I was assaulted with the firearm, receiving two gunshot wounds in my body. I, too, was aware of the Divine Presence, and did some very earnest praying as I drove to the place which was designated.

"My fierce response to the assault made on me caused the gunman to break free of my grip and flee from the scene. Somehow I drove myself to the Athens

Community Hospital, where my wounds were treated. I was permitted to go home twelve days later, though I still carried one of the bullets in my left thigh, just above the knee.

"My initial reaction to what happened was fear and dread of what could happen to me. This gave way to anger and resentment. If I had not felt such anger, I doubt that I would have grappled with the man as I did while receiving two bullets into my flesh. Quite frankly, for a time, I wanted to kill my assailant. In retrospect I am happy that I did not kill the man and that, although his bullet has left me a cripple, I am still alive.

"The bullets which tore my flesh did enough harm, but what really frightened me is what I allowed the experience to do to me. For at least a year after the experience I was never without a weapon and I hoped that I could run into the man again. It was God's presence that showed me what I had become and enabled me to climb up from the pit into which I had fallen.

"The certainty of that presence does not protect us from the irritational and criminal behavior of others. If we survive, it is what we do with ourselves and with our scars that tell us and others of the power of God's presence.

"I have forgiven my assailant, but I cannot forget the assault. I have to drag one of my legs because of what he did to me, and I remember him each time that I put the brace on my weakened leg. God's presence and protection sustained me through a terrible experience. I am stronger today for having gone through the fire, but believe me, I felt the fire and I hurt."—Charlie J. Johnson in a letter to *Presbyterian Outlook*, 512 W. Main St., Richmond, Va. March 7, 1983.

Trivia Freaks. Some persons seem to traffic in trifles. They store up bits of trivia such as the name of Rip Van Winkle's dog (Wolf) or Lawrence Welk's California license plate (A1ANA2). There is even a shelf full of books on sale offering such irrelevant tidbits of information as Walter Matthau's real name (Walter Matuschanskayasky) or what word Helen Keller attempted to say in "The Miracle Worker" (Water).

Why waste time and energy on such useless knowledge when you could realize you have power to serve others! The Holy Spirit strengthens and sends you to productive, adventurous living. Skip the minutiae of worrying over Matthau's real name. In Jesus' name, turn toward others and serve!

Meetings or Meeting? A girl in a high-school youth group recounted how she had been busy in her church choir, her youth fellowship, and her denomination's young people's group. She had been hurrying frantically from one gathering to the next. Finally, through the help of her pastor, she learned to pray and wait for the help of the Holy Spirit. Her tiredness and tension gave way to a sense of joy and peace. She later reported that she experienced new vigor to serve in Christ's name. Referring to her times of Bible reading and prayer as channels for the Spirit, she reports, "Before I knew only meetings. Now I know *meeting*, meeting in terms of spiritual presence and direction."

Questions for Pupils on the Next Lesson. 1. What gift has the Holy Spirit given you? 2. Does the Spirit give every Christian some gift? 3. Are some of the gifts of the Spirit more important than others? 4. What gift of the Spirit is to be coveted and shared by every Christian? 5. Why does the Holy Spirit give gifts to members of the Christian community?

LESSON XII—MAY 18

THE GIFTS OF THE HOLY SPIRIT

Background Scripture: 1 Corinthians 12; 13
Devotional Reading: 1 Corinthians 2:6–16

KING JAMES VERSION

1 CORINTHIANS 12   4 Now there are diversities of gifts, but the same Spirit.

5 And there are differences of administrations, but the same Lord.

6 And there are diversities of operations, but it is the same God which worketh all in all.

7 But the manifestation of the Spirit is given to every man to profit withal.

8 For to one is given by the Spirit the word of wisdom; to another the word of knowledge by the same Spirit;

9 To another faith by the same Spirit; to another the gifts of healing by the same Spirit;

10 To another the working of miracles; to another prophecy; to another discerning of spirits; to another *divers* kinds of tongues; to another the interpretation of tongues:

11 But all these worketh that one and the selfsame Spirit, dividing to every man severally as he will.

28 And God hath set some in the church, first apostles, secondarily prophets, thirdly teachers, after that miracles, then gifts of healings, helps, governments, diversities of tongues.

29 *Are* all apostles? *are* all prophets? *are* all teachers? *are* all workers of miracles?

30 Have all the gifts of healing? do all speak with tongues? do all interpret?

31 But covet earnestly the best gifts: and yet shew I unto you a more excellent way.

13   Though I speak with the tongues of men and of angels, and have not charity, I am become *as* sounding brass, or a tinkling cymbal.

2 And though I have *the gift of* prophecy, and understand all mysteries, and all knowledge; and though I have all faith, so that I could remove mountains, and have not charity, I am nothing.

3 And though I bestow all my goods to feed *the poor,* and though I give my body to be burned, and have not charity, it profiteth me nothing.

4 Charity suffereth long, *and* is kind; charity envieth not; charity vaunteth not itself, is not puffed up,

5 Doth not behave itself unseemly, seeketh not her own, is not easily provoked, thinketh no evil;

6 Rejoiceth not in iniquity, but rejoiceth in the truth;

7 Beareth all things, believeth all things, hopeth all things, endureth all things.

REVISED STANDARD VERSION

1 CORINTHIANS 12   4 Now there are varieties of gifts, but the same Spirit; 5 and there are varieties of service, but the same Lord; 6 and there are varieties of working, but it is the same God who inspires them all in every one. 7 To each is given the manifestation of the Spirit for the common good. 8 To one is given through the Spirit the utterance of wisdom, and to another the utterance of knowledge according to the same Spirit, 9 to another faith by the same Spirit, to another gifts of healing by the one Spirit, 10 to another the working of miracles, to another prophecy, to another the ability to distinguish between spirits, to another various kinds of tongues, to another the interpretation of tongues. 11 All these are inspired by one and the same Spirit, who apportions to each one individually as he wills.

28 And God has appointed in the church first apostles, second prophets, third teachers, then workers of miracles, then healers, helpers, administrators, speakers in various kinds of tongues. 29 Are all apostles? Are all prophets? Are all teachers? Do all work miracles? 30 Do all possess gifts of healing? Do all speak with tongues? Do all interpret? 31 But earnestly desire the higher gifts.

And I will show you a still more excellent way.

13   If I speak in the tongues of men and of angels, but have not love, I am a noisy gong or a clanging cymbal. 2 And if I have prophetic powers, and understand all mysteries and all knowledge, and if I have all faith, so as to remove mountains, but have not love, I am nothing. 3 If I give away all I have, and if I deliver my body to be burned, but have not love, I gain nothing.

4 Love is patient and kind; love is not jealous or boastful; 5 it is not arrogant or rude. Love does not insist on its own way; it is not irritable or resentful; 6 it does not rejoice at wrong, but rejoices in the right. 7 Love bears all things, believes all things, hopes all things, endures all things.

KEY VERSE: To each is given the manifestation of the Spirit for the common good. 1 Corinthians 12:7.

HOME DAILY BIBLE READINGS

May	12.	M.	*Gentiles Speak in Tongues.* Acts 10:44–48.
May	13.	T.	*Spirit Empowers the Church's Preaching.* 1 Corinthians 2:1–9.
May	14.	W.	*The Spirit Unites.* Ephesians 4:1–15.
May	15.	T.	*Appropriate Use of Our Gifts.* Romans 12:3–16.
May	16.	F.	*Spirit Reveals Hidden Nature of God.* 1 Corinthians 2:10–16.
May	17.	S.	*Gifts From the Holy Spirit.* 1 Corinthians 12:1–11.
May	18.	S.	*One Body With Many Parts.* 1 Corinthians 12:21–31.

BACKGROUND

The Corinthian congregation was Paul's "problem church." This unfortunate group seemed to be beset with a host of difficulties, including drunkenness and debauchery at the Lord's Supper, immorality by a church leader, disorder at worship, and, above all, dissension within the church.

One of the chief causes of this dissension within the Corinthian church was over whose spiritual gifts were most important. It seems that there was a "Holy Spirit" party within the congregation. The members of this faction spoke in tongues. There is, of course, nothing wrong in itself with speaking in tongues. However, these early charismatics in Corinth insisted that they were superior to other Christians who did not speak in tongues. In fact, they tried to lord it over everyone else, claiming that the Holy Spirit's gift of speaking in tongues was the only gift that mattered. They belittled all other spiritual gifts, thereby offending and alienating fellow Christians.

Paul dictated at least two letters, patiently trying to counsel the Corinthian believers. The biggest subject Paul discussed in the letter we call 1 Corinthians was the gifts of the Spirit. Paul made it clear that the Spirit gives gifts to all believers, not just to some. Furthermore, Paul insisted that the Spirit blesses believers with a variety of gifts. In fact, each believer receives a gift no other is given. Paul maintained that the gifts of the Spirit are intended for the good of the entire Christian community, not simply for the personal adornment of one paricular individual. Paul taught that the Church is endowed with many gifts, but there is only one Spirit. And that Spirit aids believers to come to maturity in Christ.

Most important, Paul pointed out that the greatest gift of the Holy Spirit is love. Love, Paul emphasized, is the guideline and motivator for the exercise of all spiritual gifts!

NOTES ON THE PRINTED TEXT

Paul's consideration of the divisions within the Corinthian church leads him to a lengthy section on spiritual gifts and how these gifts are exercised. *Now there are varieties of gifts but the same Spirit.* The Holy Spirit gives gifts to all believers. Paul is stating that the Spirit distributes or allots these divine gifts. All do not receive the same gifts because the Holy Spirit gives a variety of gifts. However, this same Spirit apportions these gifts which eliminates any reasons for divisions or feelings of superiority.

Paul uses repetition and variation in his terminology to emphasize this point. *There are varieties of service, but the same Lord.* There are various ministries and ways of serving, but it is the Lord who is honored by it all. *There are varieties of working, but it is the same God who inspires them all.* In this general statement, Paul writes that there are various activities which honor God. These activities are made possible by God who oversees them all. The point Paul is making is clear.

Christians differ not only physically, mentally, socially, and so on, but also in the gifts that are given to them. Therefore, Christians cannot expect uniformity. Unity lies in the Spirit who gives the gifts and the Lord who is served and oversees the work. The body of Christ is endowed with many gifts, but there is only one Spirit.

To each is given the manifestation of the Spirit for the common good. This is Paul's central point. Having argued against division in earlier chapters, Paul now emphasizes the unifying power of the Spirit. This power is to be used for the common good of all, not for personal or private advantage. The Holy Spirit works for the good of the community of believers called the Church.

Paul goes on to illustrate some of the gifts of the Spirit. *Through the Spirit* one is given *the utterance of wisdom.* Some have the ability to preach God's Word while others, through the *same Spirit,* can clearly explain with *knowledge* the truth of the faith. Still others, *through the same Spirit,* have the gift of *faith,* an unquestioning trust in God. Some individuals may even possess the *gifts of healing* or *the working of miracles* to demonstrate God's power. Other people have the ability to speak for God to people's consciences. By God's Spirit, they can move people to action or repentance through the gift of *prophecy.* In some cases, it is difficult to determine the Spirit's work from that of a demon's. Some church members are given the ability to *distinguish between Spirits.* Paul writes that some have the gift of tongues while others must interpret what is spoken. Paul summarizes his illustrations and at the same time subtly sermonizes. *All these* (gifts) *are inspired by one and the same Spirit, who apportions to each one individually as he wills.* The gifts come from God for everyone's advantage thus making spiritual pride unjustified. There should not be division caused by the gifts that various people possess.

God has appointed . . . apostles . . . prophets . . . teachers . . . workers of miracles, . . . healers, helpers, administrators, speakers in various kinds of tongues. Although these roles are individually performed, there is nothing that suggests that a person could not have more than one gift. However, Paul warns against any feelings of superiority. Some believers at Corinth believed that they might have every gift. Paul refutes this notion. He asks, *Are all apostles? Are all prophets?*

As good as the gifts of the Spirit (ones that Paul urges them *earnestly* to *desire*) are, he offers them something even better. *I will show you a still more excellent way.* Paul contrasts all the gifts of the Spirit with love. *If I speak in tongues, . . . but have not love . . . I am . . . noisy. And if I have prophetic powers, and understand all mysteries and knowledge, and if I have all faith, so as to remove mountains, but have not love, I am nothing.* Even if the believer gives all he possesses away for charitable works or he sacrifices his very body, if he has not done these things in love, he has not gained anything.

Having so vehemently described the worthlessness of the great spiritual gifts without love, Paul then describes what love is. *Love is patient.* Possessing love means the temper is not lost nor is there complaining about prolonged hardships. Love is *kind.* Love strives to ease pain and anxiety and wishes no one harm. *Love is not jealous or boastful.* Love means caring for others without being envious or boastful. Love is also *not arrogant or rude.* Love does not act in an unseemly manner. *Love does not insist on its own way.* Love does not seek its own advantage. *It is not irritable or resentful.* Love avoids flashes of anger. *It does not rejoice at wrong but . . . in the right.* Love desires justice and rejoices in goodness. *Love bears all things, believes all things, hopes all things, endures all things.* Love always believes the best about people. Love believes that God has a purpose for all His people. Love never ceases to hope. The greatest gift of the Holy Spirit is love. Love is the guideline and motivation for the exercise of all spiritual gifts. Through the aid of the Holy Spirit, believers come to full maturity in Christ.

SUGGESTIONS TO TEACHERS

Every Christian has charisma! Do you believe this?

Perhaps you don't understand the original meaning of the word *charisma*. In the Greek New Testament, *charisma* is the word for gift! In other words, every person who takes Jesus Christ seriously has been given some gift by the Spirit.

This is the basic message of 1 Corinthians 12 and 13. It is also the essential teaching of your lesson for this Sunday.

1. *BESTIRS BELIEVERS.* Open your lesson by asking what the people in your class understand about charisma. Many will say that having charisma means having charm or attractiveness. Tell the class what 1 Corinthians means by the term, and how 1 Corinthians states that the Holy Spirit prompts every believer to say that "Jesus is Lord" (1 Corinthians 12:3). In fact, the authenticity of a person's faith rests on whether the Spirit enables him or her to state unequivocally the Lordship of Jesus in his or her life. Do you and your people feel yourselves moved by the Spirit to put Jesus at the center of all of life as Lord?

2. *BESTOWS GIFTS ON EACH BELIEVER.* In this lesson, make sure that you get to the heart of 1 Corinthians 12, 13 in which it is stated that *every* believer is given some gift or charisma by the Holy Spirit. It would be helpful to those in your class to have each person's charisma pointed out, held up and affirmed. Make a special effort to see that no one in the class is overlooked when it comes to identifying the spiritual gifts given to your people.

3. *BESTOWS GIFTS FOR THE COMMON GOOD.* One Corinthians 12, you should remind your class, tells us that the Spirit grants gifts to each not to be hoarded nor to be considered a private blessing, but "for the common good" (1 Corinthians 12:7). Get that point across to those in your class. The various kinds of charisma which the Spirit has lavished on your people are for the good of community of the faith!

4. *BESTOWS A VARIETY OF GIFTS.* Refer to the list in 1 Corinthians 12, noting the variety of gifts given to the community of faith by the Spirit. Identify the variety of gifts among those in your class. Celebrate the fact that no person has a monopoly on gifts, and that each person has an indispensable gift as well as the gift that no one else has!

5. *BLESSES ALL WITH THE HIGHER GIFT.* Your class will need to learn that chapter 13 follows 1 Corinthians 12, and is not a literary composition on *love* in isolation from the rest of the Corinthian correspondence. The point is that *each* Christian must seek the Spirit's gift of the "higher charisma." Speaking in tongues, having prophetic powers, knowing Scripture and theology, having trust in God, being generous and willing to sacrifice—all these are fine gifts of the Spirit. But the greatest gift is love!

TOPIC FOR ADULTS
THE GIFTS OF THE HOLY SPIRIT

Even the Insignificant Strikes a Note! A friend of mine tells of an interesting relic which hangs in his study which illustrates the way every one is able to use his or her gift of the Holy Spirit. He points to an old iron ring, suspended from a rope. It's nearly ten inches across. It came off of an old sailing ship. "When I strike it with my ruler it gives off quite a tone, but I notice that even when I strike it with a long spear of grass it gives off quite a confident note," he states. "No matter how insignificant you may think you are, you can strike a note for Christ's cause!"

The Gift of Radiance. The great Quaker teacher, Rufus Jones, was a close friend of Baron Friedrich von Hugel, the noted English Catholic scholar. On parting after one meeting, von Hugel told Rufus Jones: "Before you go, I want to tell you of the four conditions of life which must be fulfilled before anyone can be canonized as a saint in my church." The four conditions he cited were loyalty to the Faith, heroism, endowments with powers beyond ordinary human capacities, and radiance. Rufus Jones recounted, "The old philosopher and mystic stood up in front of me, half a head taller than I was, and he raised his hands as high in the air as they would reach and said, 'They may possibly be wrong about those first three conditions, but they are gloriously right about the fourth condition—a saint must be *radiant*.' "

Von Hugel was correct. The Spirit enables those truly called by God to be radiant! Have you asked for this gift?

The Meaning of the Gift of Love. In his novel *Saint Francis*, Nikos Kazantzakis put these words in the mouth of Francis:

" 'What is love, my brothers?' he asked, opening his arms as though he wished to embrace us. 'What is love? It is not simply compassion, not simply kindness. In compassion there are two: the one who suffers and the one who feels compassion. In kindness there are two: the one who gives and the one who receives. But in love there is only one; the two join, unite, become inseparable. The "I" and the "you" vanish. To love means to lose oneself in the beloved.' "

Questions for Pupils on the Next Lesson. 1. What is meant by the phrase "works of the flesh" in Galatians 5? 2. What connection is there between the indwelling of the Holy Spirit and moral living? 3. Does the freedom of the Spirit mean you can do as you please? 4. Why do we have to be part of a faith community in order to grow in the Spirit? 5. Why do we need more than legalistic guidelines to live a Christian life?

TOPIC FOR YOUTH
USING GOD'S GIFTS

Air Sacs in the Lungs. A healthy person has air sacs in the lungs which enable him or her to breathe freely. If all the cells are open, the air passes into the lungs and provides life-giving oxygen to the body. Each air sac is needed. If some disease such as pneumonia infects the lungs, many cells are congested and unable to receive air. The remaining sacs must carry the burden of receiving air. They must inhale and exhale for the body. Just as sometimes a few breathing cells are enough to keep a person alive, so a few Spirit-filled persons are enough to keep the Church alive. However, all the sacs are necessary for a person to enjoy vigorous health. And all members must be able to receive the breath of the Spirit if the Church is to flourish and carry out Christ's ministry.

Gifts to Overcome. The noblest saints did not live in total seclusion on top of columns or hidden in caves. They practiced a skillful rhythm—a deliberate alternation between a life of devotion and a life of service. One of the best examples of this security is a letter written by a man named Cyprian to his friend, Donatus. Cyprian was born approximately A.D. 200—seventeen centuries ago. He wrote these words from Carthage in North Africa:

"This seems a cheerful world, Donatus, when I view it from this fair garden under the shadow of these vines. But if I climbed some great mountain and looked out over the wide lands, you know very well what I would see: brigands on the high roads, pirates on the seas, men murdered in the amphitheatres to please applauding crowds, under all roofs misery and selfishness. It is really a bad world, Donatus, an incredibly bad world. Yet in the midst of it, I have a found a *quiet* and a holy people. They have discovered a joy which is a thousand times better than any pleasure of this sinful life. They are despised and persecuted, but they care not; *They have overcome the world.* These people Donatus, are the Christians—and I am one of them."

Prophets for Profit Revealed. An Illinois minister describes the way a girl named Debbie was attracted for a time to the sensational claims of a miracle-talking revivalist who insisted he had all sorts of "gifts of the Spirit." Ken Edelman writes, "To Debbie, it appeared that these people had a faith head and shoulders taller than that of the Presbyterians. What seemed to attract Debbie was the power of a biblically rooted mysticism. Debbie was powerfully attracted by these visionary claims and she left their ranks when she saw some obviously false visions and claims.

"What is the name for this force that causes people to enter into less than the best in order to have excitement in faith? We need to begin to define the attraction. Is it hypnotism, meditation, mind control, trance, ecstasy, altered state of consciousness? Teresa of Avila in *The Interior Castle* says that 'ecstasy, rapture, and trance (or transport) are all the same in my opinion.'

"Teresa speaks of the experience, '. . . the soul was never so awake to the things of God. When the soul is in this suspension, the Lord likes to show it some secrets, things about heaven, and imaginative visions.' Such personal claims to direct revelation were carefully checked out by Teresa, but they are being wholesaled today without check."—Kenneth N. Edelman, *Monday Morning,* October 24, 1983.

Questions for Pupils on the Next Lesson. 1. How free are we as Christians to do what we want? 2. Does the Holy Spirit govern the sexual practices of a Christian? 3. Does a Christian live by a set of rules? 4. Why are we Christians responsible to minister to others? 5. How can you find help in your struggle against weakness?

LESSON XIII—MAY 25

THE FRUIT OF THE HOLY SPIRIT

Background Scripture: Galatians 5:13—6:10
Devotional Reading: Philippians 2:12–18

KING JAMES VERSION

GALATIANS 5 13 For, brethren, ye have been called unto liberty; only *use* not liberty for an occasion to the flesh, but by love serve one another.

14 For all the law is fulfilled in one word, *even* in this; Thou shalt love thy neighbour as thyself.

15 But if ye bite and devour one another, take heed that ye be not consumed one of another.

16 *This* I say then, Walk in the Spirit, and ye shall not fulfil the lust of the flesh.

17 For the flesh lusteth against the Spirit, and the Spirit against the flesh: and these are contrary the one to the other; so that ye cannot do the things that ye would.

18 But if ye be led of the Spirit, ye are not under the law.

19 Now the works of the flesh are manifest, which are *these*, Adultery, fornication, uncleanness, lasciviousness,

20 Idolatry, witchcraft, hatred, variance, emulations, wrath, strife, seditions, heresies,

21 Envyings, murders, drunkenness, revelings, and such like: of the which I tell you before, as I have also told *you* in time past, that they which do such things shall not inherit the kingdom of God.

22 But the fruit of the Spirit is love, joy, peace, longsuffering, gentleness, goodness, faith,

23 Meekness, temperance: against such there is no law.

24 And they that are Christ's have crucified the flesh with the affections and lusts.

25 If we live in the Spirit, let us also walk in the Spirit.

26 Let us not be desirous of vain glory, provoking one another, envying one another.

6 7 Be not deceived; God is not mocked: for whatsoever a man soweth, that shall he also reap.

8 For he that soweth to his flesh shall of the flesh reap corruption; but he that soweth to the Spirit shall of the Spirit reap life everlasting.

9 And let us not be weary in well doing: for in due season we shall reap, if we faint not.

10 As we have therefore opportunity, let us do good unto all *men*, especially unto them who are of the household of faith.

REVISED STANDARD VERSION

GALATIANS 5 13 For you were called to freedom, brethren; only do not use your freedom as an opportunity for the flesh, but through love be servants of one another. 14 For the whole law is fulfilled in one word, "You shall love your neighbor as yourself." 15 But if you bite and devour one another take heed that you are not consumed by one another.

16 But I say, walk by the Spirit, and do not gratify the desires of the flesh. 17 For the desires of the flesh are against the Spirit, and the desires of the Spirit are against the flesh; for these are opposed to each other, to prevent you from doing what you would. 18 But if you are led by the Spirit you are not under the law. 19 Now the works of the flesh are plain: immorality, impurity, licentiousness, 20 idolatry, sorcery, enmity, strife, jealousy, anger, selfishness, dissension, party spirit, 21 envy, drunkenness, carousing, and the like. I warn you, as I warned you before, that those who do such things shall not inherit the kingdom of God. 22 But the fruit of the Spirit is love, joy, peace, patience, kindness, goodness, faithfulness, 23 gentleness, self-control; against such there is no law. 24 And those who belong to Christ Jesus have crucified the flesh with its passions and desires.

25 If we live by the Spirit, let us also walk by the Spirit. 26 Let us have no self-conceit, no provoking of one another, no envy of one another.

6 7 Do not be deceived; God is not mocked, for whatever a man sows, that he will also reap. 8 For he who sows to his own flesh will from the flesh reap corruption; but he who sows to the Spirit will from the Spirit reap eternal life. 9 And let us not grow weary in well-doing, for in due season we shall reap, if we do not lose heart. 10 So then, as we have opportunity, let us do good to all men, and especially to those who are of the household of faith.

KEY VERSE: Walk by the Spirit, and do not gratify the desires of the flesh. Galatians 5:16.

HOME DAILY BIBLE READINGS

May	19.	M.	*Spirit Brings the New.* Joel 2:28–32.
May	20.	T.	*Life in the Spirit.* Romans 8:9–17.
May	21.	W.	*Spirit Intercedes for the Believer.* Romans 8:18–30.
May	22.	T.	*Spirit Helps Us Grow.* Romans 15:13–21.
May.	23.	F.	*Spirit Gives Us Concern for Others.* Romans 14:13–23.
May	24.	S.	*The Spirit and Human Nature.* Galatians 5:16–26.
May	25.	S.	*Bear One Another's Burdens.* Galatians 6:1–8.

BACKGROUND

How does a person become right with God? By keeping certain rules? Or by faith in Jesus Christ? Paul and all orthodox Christians insist that what matters is trust in God's grace through Jesus Christ, working through love.

In the Galatian churches (located in what is now central Turkey), certain Jewish Christians anxious to preserve Jewish customs had been unsettling recent converts. These "Judaizers," as they were called, demanded that true believers must be circumcised and observe the Law of Moses. Their ideas, needless to say, contradicted Paul's teachings about being saved by grace. Furthermore, these Judaizers' propaganda reduced the Gospel to a mere appendage to the old Temple traditions.

The Judaizers and their sympathizers replied that Paul was teaching people that "anything goes" and accused him of fostering immoral behavior in the name of "faith" and "Christian freedom."

Paul in the letter to the Galatians points out that we Christian believers are free to do as we please but are free to act responsibly and caringly for others. In other words, our faith in Jesus Christ means not license but love. And we cannot do what we like, throwing off moral restraints, because true freedom means living the life of the Spirit instead of existing in the bondage of selfishness.

The things we do when we are captured by our lower nature (which Paul calls "the flesh") are obvious, and Paul catalogues fifteen "works of the flesh" which are destructive. These fifteen range from sexual sins to sins of idolatry, from anger and dissension to drunkenness and carousing.

In contrast to these fifteen examples of the results of giving in to selfish, unregenerate human impulses, Paul calls Christians to live by the Spirit and says that the Spirit produces lovely virtues. He lists nine of these lovely virtues. He calls them the "fruits" of the Spirit, suggesting that they are the harvest or flowering of the indwelling Spirit of God in our lives. The nine lovely examples of the Spirit's power at work in us are all virtues associated with our ministering to others.

Check your own life. What seems to be harvested in your life? Works of the flesh or fruits of the Spirit?

NOTES ON THE PRINTED TEXT

Paul's converts in Galatia were in danger of losing their grip on the Gospel of grace which he had taught them. Certain men were teaching that in addition to faith in Jesus Christ, the new converts must accept circumcision and observe the Law of Moses. In great urgency Paul responds to these teachings. The last two chapters are an ethical section which claims that practice grows out of belief. Paul applies the Gospel in terms of liberty not in libertinism.

For you were called to freedom, brethren, Paul writes. He implies that Christians need no law to make them live in a right relationship with God or other people. This freedom is found in Christ who taught and demonstrated it in His works and words. Christ calls us to responsible freedom under the leadership of the Spirit.

Do not use your freedom as an opportunity for the flesh. Living in freedom does not allow the Christian to take liberties for there are still ethical standards to be followed. The believer is not totally free of all restraints. Paul cautions that freedom cannot be seized as an excuse for freedoms of the flesh such as sexual misconduct, idolatrous worship, and broken relationships (which Paul will develop later). Life in the Spirit is not a higher legalism but a responsible freedom exercised in love.

Christian freedom makes believers responsible to serve others. *Through love be servants of one another.* Believers are to be slaves of one another doing even the most menial of tasks for one another in love. As God did for His people, they must do for others and ultimately for Him. *For the whole law is fulfilled in one word, "You shall love your neighbor as yourself."* When believers love one another, the whole law is fulfilled and a unity is built on this love. *But if you bite and devour* (try and eat up or swallow) *take heed that you are not consumed by one another.* Bluntly, Paul cautions that mutual annihilation can only be the result if believers do not love.

I say, walk by the Spirit, and do not gratify the desires of the flesh. Paul links the dwelling of the Spirit with moral conduct. Paul's critics feared a repudiation of the Law would result in an orgy of wild living. So they urged, "Do these things and live." Paul says, "Walk in the Spirit, living and doing these things." *If you are led by the Spirit you are not under the law.* Life in the Spirit is governed by the law of love for neighbors. Paul conceived of liberty as a slavery to a new Master and to doing good. Christian liberty is not a license to do as people please. He draws a sharp contrast between the two ways of living. *The desires of the flesh are against the Spirit, and the desires of the Spirit are against the flesh; for these are opposed to each other to prevent you from doing what you would.*

Now the works of the flesh are plain. There is *immorality.* Works of the flesh are not hidden but are easily and blatantly seen. These works are done openly in utter defiance of God. All types of sexual immorality outside of the marriage vows is condemned. *Impurity* could be defined as anything that detracts from right Christian living. *Licentiousness* refers to sensual or lewd living. *Idolatry* can be defined as anything that draws one's true allegiance from God. *Sorcery* refers to acts involving drugs, the occult, or witchcraft. *Enmity* is the feeling of hatred between people and toward God. The outcome of people's enmity is *anger, strife* (fighting), *dissension* (small quarrels), or *party spirit* (the taking of sides). Desires of the heart are behind Paul's warnings of *jealousy* and *envy. Drunkenness* and *carousing* are also warned against as works of the flesh. Paul reminds the Galatians that *those who do such things shall not inherit the kingdom of God.*

Paul then lists the character traits of a responsible Christian who demonstrates the *fruit of the Spirit.* These people have *love.* The Greek word is *agape* which is characterized as a love that is unselfish and not a love that seeks its own gratification but is concerned with the welfare of others. It is not calculated but is freely given. These people also have *joy* which is more than mere common happiness. It is a graciousness and generosity that can be glad and forgiving even in persecution. They have *peace* which demands a harmonious world of right relationships between peoples. *Patience,* another trait they have, is best translated as a long tempered nature which knows no anger. Kindness and goodness share the same qualities. *Faithfulness* implies the acceptance and belief that is expressed both in worship and life. *Gentleness* denotes a meek, modest, graciousness, and *self-control* usually refers to the control of sexual desires. Paul uses it broadly to refer to all the "flesh works" he has inveighed against. *There is no law against the fruits of the Spirit.*

When a convert confesses Jesus as Lord, he changes. He puts aside his old sinful nature. He *crucified the flesh with the passions and desires.* Renouncing these old ways was the first step. Then, a believer's life was to reflect his commitment. *If we live by the Spirit, let us also walk by the Spirit.* Paul calls his followers to walk in step or fellowship with Christ their whole lives. However, this must be done with the recognition that there are differences between believers. *Have no self conceit, no provoking of one another, no envy of one another.*

Do not be deceived; for whatever a man sows that will he also reap. Christians who believed they could reap the fruit of the Spirit while performing works of the flesh (as defined in 5:19-21) were only deceiving themselves. *He who sows to his own flesh will from the flesh reap corruption; but he who sows to the Spirit will from the Spirit reap eternal life.* Believers cannot turn their noses up at God. *God is not mocked.* A new life is demanded of Christians. The reward of this new life is eternal life. Again, Paul urges the Galatians to *let us not grow weary in well-doing for in due season we shall reap, if we do not lose heart.* Members of the faith community have a responsibility to their sisters and brothers who are in need. *Let us do good to all men, and especially to those who are of the household of faith.*

SUGGESTIONS TO TEACHERS

A man in Tennessee insisting that, "I was led by the Holy Spirit" was arrested a few years ago for wife-beating and child-abuse. His defense consisted primarily of claiming that an emotional experience at a revival meeting meant that (1) he was filled with the Holy Spirit, and (2) he could do as he pleased because he was "Spirit-filled." The judge had other ideas.

In spite of this individual's assertions about the Holy Spirit's influence in his life, they are not consistent with the New Testament's teachings on the subject. Galatians 5:13—6:10, for example, offer a fine summary of the fruits of the Spirit in a person's life. And this summary describes more than an emotional experience. It stresses the way that the Spirit-led person will reflect Jesus Christ by his or her actions each day.

1. *WATCH YOUR FREEDOM!* Study the first verses in today's Scripture and what they say about freedom. Note how they speak about the way Christians are liberated from trying to save themselves by following rules. However (and this is crucial) Christians may not abuse that freedom. They are under the constraints of love! "Through love be servants of one another," the words state (Galatians 5:13). Let your class talk about this apparent paradox: We are free—free to care for others!

2. *WALK BY THE SPIRIT.* Have the class offer examples of what it means to "walk by the Spirit" from the experience of those in the class. Point out that the Spirit walks with believers.

3. *WITHSTAND THE WORLD!* Go over the catalogue of "works of the flesh" in Galatians 5:19-21. Have your class members remark on the way these are prevalent today. Comment on the pressures everyone feels to fall into practicing these "works of the flesh." Most of all, mention that the Spirit strengthens believers to withstand the temptation to conform to a sick society's lifestyle.

4. *WORK WITH SPIRIT'S FRUITS!* Spend considerable time in this lesson examining the Galatians' summary of "the fruits of the Spirit" (Galatians 5:22, 23). Consult a good commentary and note the notes on the printed text on the meaning of each of these words: *love, joy, peace, patience, kindness, goodness, faithfulness, gentleness, self-control.* Are these evident in the lives of those in your class? How can each member help the "fruit of the Spirit" to mature and ripen in the life of other class members?

5. *WEIGH YOUR RESPONSIBILITIES!* Move into the discussion in Gala-

tians 6:1–10 of how each Christian accepts responsibility for himself and for others. The Spirit-filled man or woman can live only to himself or herself. The spiritual person keeps a disciplined watch over his own life, because he knows his proneness to conceit. And the spiritual person patiently bears the burdens of others. Discuss why this is difficult in an age which emphasizes "doing your own thing" and asks, "Why get involved?"

TOPIC FOR ADULTS
THE FRUIT OF THE HOLY SPIRIT

Court Curbs "Church" With Sauna and Bar. The fruits of the Spirit always mean reflecting Jesus Christ. If a community calling itself by Christ's name fails to mirror the Lord, its claims to be inspired by the Holy Spirit are suspect. Recently, for instance, a man calling himself a minister in Wauconda, Illinois, insisted that he was as much led by the Spirit as anyone else and started his own church. "The Reverend" David Sholl organized the Universal Life Church in his home. Finally, Sholl who turned his house into a church, complete with sauna, indoor pool, and bar, was prohibited from charging for liquor or admission in 1983. The Unviersal Life Church, run by David Sholl, had drawn criticism from neighbors who likened the 10,000-square-foot mansion to Sodom and Gomorrah.

Judge William D. Block prohibited Mr. Sholl and his wife, Nancy, from charging for liquor or admission and has limited gatherings to fewer than fifty people. "This in effect closes the party operation permanently," said Margaret Mullen, an Assistant State's Attorney who argued that the church violated zoning, building code, and liquor license laws. Mr. Sholl became a minister by mail order in 1981 for a $30 fee.

Common Effort. The fruits of the Spirit come when we work together and pray together for the Spirit.

It is a united effort, a more-than-one discipline. It is what Martin Luther calls "common prayer"—a uniting prayer of seeking God together. Luther wrote very strongly about "common prayer." He wrote:

"The Christian Church has no greater power or work than such common prayer. This, the Evil Spirit knows well, and, therefore, he does all that he can to prevent such prayer. Gleefully he lets us go on building churches, making music, reading, singing, and multiplying ceremonies beyond all measure. This does not grieve him; nay, he helps us do it, that we may consider such things the very best. But if he noticed that we wished to practice this common prayer, even if it were under a straw roof, or in a pig-sty, he would indeed not endure it, but would fear such a pig-sty more than all the high, big churches, with their towers and bells, if such prayer be not in them. It is indeed not a question of the place in which we assemble but only of this unconquerable prayer, that we pray, and bring it before God as a truly common prayer."

What Kind of Fruit of the Spirit? Every minute, the world spends $1.3 million for military purposes. Every minute, thirty children die for want of food and inexpensive vaccines.

These are among the findings in a report issued on the world's military and social expenditures. It was prepared by Ruth Leger Sivard under the sponsorship of several private organizations, including the Arms Control Association and the Rockefeller Foundation.

"An arms race no country can afford crowds out social needs," she said in a summary.

Among the findings:

"The world's stockpile of nuclear weapons represents an explosive force over 5,000 times greater than all the munitions used in World War II.

"The cost of one nuclear submarine equals the annual education budget of twenty-three developing countries with 160 million school-age children.

"In a year when American farmers were paid to take nearly 100 million acres of cropland out of production, 450 million people in the world are starving."

Questions for Pupils on the Next Lesson. 1. When, where, and why did Jeremiah prophesy? 2. Have you ever felt inadequate to serve? 3. Do you think that God has a purpose for your life? 4. Why do so many people underestimate the potential for their lives? 5. Do you sometimes feel that your individual effort doesn't make much difference?

TOPIC FOR YOUTH
A WAY TO WALK

Invitation to Follow. In Copenhagen, Denmark, the great Protestant Cathedral holds a magnificent sculpture of Jesus Christ by Bertel Thorvaldsen. The statue is on the high altar and has a story behind it.

Thorvaldsen originally intended to depict Christ as a mighty authority figure. When he was preparing his clay model, the famous artist created a statue of Jesus triumphantly holding His arms high in an imperious pose. Thorvaldsen was delighted with the way he portrayed Jesus Christ as one like most other people think they want to be—stridently lording it over others. The sculptor went home, letting the clay harden overnight. He was startled when he entered his studio next morning. He found that the arms of the figure of Jesus which had been fashioned into such a pose of authority had sagged from the weight of the clay. Instead of the arrogant stance of human power, the arms had drooped into a position of gentle welcome. No longer did the statue seem to show a Christ who commanded anyone. The arms and hands seemed to have assumed a gesture of inviting. Thorvaldsen was crestfallen. His masterpiece seemed ruined. He felt angry and disappointed that the statue had not turned out as he had intended. But as he studied the transformed clay statue, Thorvaldsen the sculptor became transformed. He began to understand Jesus in a deeper way. The proud artist began to become a humble Christian. He saw Jesus as the person of compassion. He finally inscribed the words, "Come Unto Me" on the base of the completed statue.

Jesus invites. He does not command. Jesus stands humbly and pleadingly. He welcomes you to walk in His way, the way of gentle caring for others.

East End and West End Walk for Christ. "Do you not think our congregations are too much a kind of religious club, run for the benefit of its members? Well, it is very necessary that we should build up characters and hearts at which Christ can point and say, 'That is My case.' That takes some doing. And yet the Church is the body of Jesus Christ: we ought to be His feet running for Him, and His hands carrying for Him, every member doing its own part.

"I think if we had one hand in God's hand, and if the other hand were going out like Christ's own hand to heal hurt things, to save the lost, the folk that missed their way, in the West end because they think the world will satisfy them, and in the East end because they can make nothing of what life is all about, and they are losing their lives and their souls—if our one hand was in God's and the other was going out in a passion of unselfish sacrifice, would not the Spirit of God have come?"—Arthur J. Gossip, sermon, "The Marks of the Holy Spirit."

The Way to Walk. A young Scot once told the pastor, "I'm fed up with the church and Christianity. All I ever hear is 'Give, give, give.' " The pastor, Donald

Ross, fixed his steel blue eyes on the youth and in his soft, Inverness accent replied, "Well, can you think of a better definition of Christianity than that?"

Questions for Pupils on the Next Lesson. 1. Why did Jeremiah not want to be a prophet when God called him? 2. What were Jeremiah's excuses for not being a prophet for God? 3. Do you ever feel inadequate for what God expects of you? 4. What purpose do you sense that God has for your life? 5. How are you going to invest your time, energies, and talents for the rest of your life?

JUNE, JULY, AUGUST 1986

JEREMIAH, EZEKIEL, AND DANIEL

LESSON I—JUNE 1

GOD CALLS JEREMIAH TO PROPHESY

Background Scripture: Jeremiah 1
Devotional Reading: Psalms 139:1–6

KING JAMES VERSION

JEREMIAH 1 4 Then the word of the LORD came unto me, saying,

5 Before I formed thee in the belly I knew thee; and before thou camest forth out of the womb I sanctified thee, *and* I ordained thee a prophet unto the nations.

6 Then said I, Ah, Lord GOD! behold, I cannot speak: for I *am* a child.

7 But the LORD said unto me, Say not, I *am* a child: for thou shalt go to all that I shall send thee, and whatsoever I command thee thou shalt speak.

8 Be not afraid of their faces: for I *am* with thee to deliver thee, saith the LORD.

9 Then the LORD put forth his hand, and touched my mouth. And the LORD said unto me, Behold, I have put my words in thy mouth.

10 See, I have this day set thee over the nations and over the kingdoms, to root out, and to pull down, and to destroy, and to throw down, to build, and to plant.

13 And the word of the LORD came unto me the second time, saying, What seest thou? And I said, I see a seething pot; and the face thereof *is* toward the north.

14 Then the LORD said unto me, Out of the north an evil shall break forth upon all the inhabitants of the land.

17 Thou therefore gird up thy loins, and arise, and speak unto them all that I command thee: be not dismayed at their faces, lest I confound thee before them.

18 For, behold, I have made thee this day a defensed city, and an iron pillar, and brazen walls against the whole land, against the kings of Judah, against the princes thereof, against the priests thereof, and against the people of the land.

19 And they shall fight against thee; but they shall not prevail against thee; for I *am* with thee, saith the LORD, to deliver thee.

REVISED STANDARD VERSION

JEREMIAH 1 4 Now the word of the LORD came to me saying,

5 "Before I formed you in the womb I knew you,
and before you were born I consecrated you;
I appointed you a prophet to the nations."

6 Then I said, "Ah, Lord GOD! Behold, I do not know how to speak, for I am only a youth." 7 But the LORD said to me,
"Do not say, 'I am only a youth';
for to all to whom I send you you shall go,
and whatever I command you you shall speak.
8 Be not afraid of them,
for I am with you to deliver you, says the LORD."

9 Then the LORD put forth his hand and touched my mouth; and the LORD said to me,
"Behold, I have put my words in your mouth.
10 See, I have set you this day over nations and over kingdoms,
to pluck up and to break down,
to destroy and to overthrow,
to build and to plant."

13 The word of the LORD came to me a second time, saying, "What do you see?" And I said, "I see a boiling pot, facing away from the north." 14 Then the LORD said to me, "Out of the north evil shall break forth upon all the inhabitants of the land.

17 "But you, gird up your loins; arise, and say to them everything that I command you. Do not be dismayed by them, lest I dismay you before them. 18 And I, behold, I make you this day a fortified city, an iron pillar, and bronze walls, against the whole land, against the kings of Judah, its princes, its priests, and the people of the land. 19 They will fight against you; but they shall not prevail against you, for I am with you, says the LORD, to deliver you."

KEY VERSE: The Lord said to me, "Do not say, 'I am only a youth'; for to all to whom I send you you shall go, and whatever I command you you shall speak. Be not afraid of them, for I am with you to deliver you." Jeremiah 1:7, 8.

HOME DAILY BIBLE READINGS

May   26.   M.   *God's Call to Jeremiah.* Jeremiah 1:1–10.
May   27.   T.   *A Similar Call to Moses.* Exodus 2:23—3:6.
May   28.   W.   *The Divine Commission.* Exodus 3:7–12.
May   29.   T.   *God Reassures His Spokesman.* Exodus 3:13–20.
May   30.   F.   *God Gives His Message.* Exodus 3:10–17.
May   31.   S.   *Test of the True Prophet.* Deuteronomy 18:15–22.
June   1.   S.   *God's Assurance Is Given.* Jeremiah 1:11–19.

BACKGROUND

One of the earliest heretics in the Church was a man named Marcion. Marcion lived in the second century in a time when some Christians were still recoiling from the attempts of certain teachers to impose the Jewish Law on Christian believers. Around A.D. 140 Marcion put together one of the first versions of a Christian Bible. What disturbed many, however, was that Marcion omitted all the Old Testament from his Bible. Eventually the Church repudiated Marcion's idea of rejecting writings from the Jewish Scriptures.

From all practical purposes, however, many Christians are followers of old Marcion. Some, in fact, are probably in your class. These people haven't included the Old Testament writings in their own scriptural knowledge! This is one of the reasons this quarter of studies will address key Old Testament books. Specifically, you and your class will review Jeremiah, Ezekiel, and Daniel in the next fourteen lessons.

Today, you open with the first of six studies from the Prophet Jeremiah. This series appropriately is called "Jeremiah—God's Message for a Time of Turmoil." And what a time of turmoil it was!

The nation of Judah was overrun by the Babylonians in 597 B.C. In the decades preceding the fall of Judah, however, most of the nation's leaders seemed to exist in a dream world. Judah stubbornly clung to its illusions of being God's favorite and therefore invincible. Meanwhile, the proud leaders refused to show respect toward the Lord or to practice simple justice. Meanwhile, the Babylonian juggernaut was crushing kingdoms everywhere.

Jeremiah lived during the tumultuous period during the last days of his nation. He deeply loved his country and his countrymen. But he knew that he belonged to the Lord before he belonged to Judah. God's call frequently brought him turmoil within, as well as placing him in the midst of turmoil without. Some students have called Jeremiah the "Weeping Prophet." Turmoil such as Jeremiah experienced both inside and outside himself can't help but drive a person sensitive to God and others to tears! In fact, the test for any person claiming to be committed to the Lord is whether or not he or she has wept for fellow citizens!

NOTES ON THE PRINTED TEXT

Today begins a six week study of Jeremiah, a great prophet from a long and distinguished line of priests from Anathoth, a village northeast of Jerusalem (1:1). It was Jeremiah who had to speak for the Lord during the final days of his beloved nation, Judah. During the latter part of the seventh century and the early part of the sixth century B.C. (1:2, 3), he prophesied to Judah about Babylon.

Now the word of the Lord came to me. Jeremiah received a call. He had a strong sense that God had claimed his life and intended to use him. In fact, Jeremiah felt that God had consecrated him from his birth to be a prophet. *Before I formed you in the womb I knew you, and before you were born I consecrated you.* So strong was God's claim on his life that Jeremiah felt predestined to be the Lord's speaker. However, he was not appointed to be a prophet only to Judah but *to the nations.* The international perspective of God's call frightened Jeremiah.

Up to this point, God's call had been a spiritual experience for Jeremiah. Growing up in a priestly family and within the nation of Judah, he already had a sense of his responsibility. However, God suddenly was involving him in international affairs.

I do not know how to speak, for I am only a youth. Jeremiah objected to God's call. He pointed out that he was not an eloquent or compelling speaker. Furthermore, he pleaded that he was much too young. He was inadequate for the service God had in mind for him. Jeremiah offered excuses.

God did not accept any excuse. *Do not say 'I am only a youth.'* The Lord would not listen to Jeremiah's pleadings. The Lord announced, *To all to whom I send you, you shall go.* On whatever errand God required, Jeremiah would go. *Whatever I command you, you shall speak.* God insisted that Jeremiah would speak for Him.

Sensing Jeremiah's reluctance at obeying His commands, God reassured Jeremiah. *Be not afraid . . . for I am with you to deliver you.* Jeremiah would not go alone. God promised to be with Jeremiah always, especially as he faced strong opposition. *Then the Lord put forth his hand . . . touched my mouth and said. . . . "Behold, I have put my words in your mouth."* Jeremiah understood that God had given him the power to speak. God had placed His divine words in his mouth. God appointed Jeremiah to be His spokesperson. God would watch over his words (verse 12). Jeremiah was commissioned to be God's mouthpiece and overseer over the nations and kingdoms. He would have God's power and energy with him.

Prophets often received the Word of the Lord in a vision. Jeremiah envisions a *boiling pot, facing away from the north.* The two-handled cooking pot that symbolizes God's judgment is about to pour down from the north. *Out of the north evil shall break forth upon all the inhabitants of the land.*

Once again Jeremiah is encouraged to speak fearlessly. *But you, gird up your loins . . . and say to them everything that I command you.* God is commanding Jeremiah to make himself ready for work. God encourages Jeremiah not to lose his nerve, or He will make him the laughingstock of all those who oppose him. *Do not be dismayed by them, lest I dismay you before them.* God's strength will make Jeremiah strong. God will be his defense symbolized by a *fortified city, an iron pillar,* and *bronze walls.* His ministry will bring him into conflict with *the whole land. . . . the kings of Judah, its princes* (government officials), *its priests, and the people of the land* (the wealthy landowners). God does not promise Jeremiah an easy, conflict-free ministry, but He does promise him victory. *They will fight against you; but they shall not prevail against you, for I am with you . . . to deliver you.*

SUGGESTIONS TO TEACHERS

How does God call a person? Why does God call? What does a "call" mean?

These are a few of the many questions that arise any time any mention is made of God calling someone. The Bible considers God's call to a host of people—to Abraham, Moses, Gideon and the judges, to David and rulers, to Isaiah, Jeremiah, Ezekiel and the prophets, to the nation of Israel itself, to Jesus and His disciples, to Paul and to Christians.

Your lesson is not to look upon God's call as a bizarre event occurring to a few unusual souls in biblical times. Rather, this lesson is intended to help each person in your class to understand that God calls him or her to speak out for God in present-day times of turmoil. God's call to Jeremiah to prophesy can be understood in terms of the Lord's summons to every person in every age.

1. *CALLED IN CRISIS.* Jeremiah lived in a time of national and international turmoil. Many of his family and friends gave way to panic. The nation lurched toward ruin. Its leaders tried elaborate systems of political intrigue with other powers to stave off disaster. In such a setting, God called young Jeremiah to be His spokesman. This is the opportunity to emphasize to your class that the Lord does not wait for "perfect" times to issue a call. In fact, it usually is in a time of crisis for the community or country that God calls a man or woman!

2. *CONSECRATED AT CREATION.* Jeremiah senses that he has belonged to the Lord from the beginning of the world. So have others who have felt God has called them. And so should every believer today!

3. *CORRECTED IN COMPLAINTS.* Jeremiah, like nearly everyone who has been aware of God's whispers in their lives, protests that he is not worthy or able to respond to the Lord's call. Jeremiah whimpers that he is "only a youth" (1:7). What excuses have you and those in your class tried to pull on God? Take some time to share with each other some of the ways you all have tried to squirm away from God's call. You may find some of these attempts to evade God's call amusing!

4. *COMMISSIONED FOR COMMENTS.* God calls a person to communicate for Him. He promises, "I will put words in your mouth" (1:9). Remind your class members that when they realize that God has plans for them they may trust Him to guide them to ways of communicating for Him.

5. *CONVERSANT WITH THE CREATOR:* God intends to have a close relationship with all those whom He calls. In fact, He gives hints and visions of His intentions to Jeremiah in the form of visions of an almond rod in a boiling pot. These are not weird ramblings or hallucinations of a religious "nut." These are part of the conversation—often in the form of symbols and pictures—which God initiates with those He calls. Impress on your people the need to listen for God's attempts to converse through praying and Bible reading.

TOPIC FOR ADULTS
JEREMIAH: CALLED TO A DIFFICULT TASK

From the Heart. An American visitor tells of an interesting discovery he made in a quaint old church outside the town of Winchester, England. He was studying the old, carved oak lectern which held the Bible. It was a huge eagle, the usual symbol used for supporting the Bible. He noticed, however, that the eagle had the beak of a parrot, and on his head was carved a small heart. He asked the verger, who was showing him about, for an explanation of the parrot's beak and the little carved heart. "Well," said the verger, "This old eagle is a reminder to all who read the Holy Word to us, not to read it like a parrot, but from the heart!"

Jeremiah and all those called by God to difficult tasks realize that they speak the Word of God to others not as parrots but from the heart!

The Call to Ministry. "The call to ministry is a process that begins with God, not with us. It is our reaction to God's action. It is always a response to God's initiative. A call is not something we invent or manipulate or conjure up in our own minds. A call comes from beyond us, and it begins with God's love for us before we ever realize it. . . .

"We cannot predict what God wants us to do or where we shall be. We are not the ones who determine our lives. The pattern of God's will becomes clear to us only later in the perspective of God's grace. . . .

"God's call, however, can be a source of grave temptation. The history of the church is riddled with examples of people who were convinced of God's call and who wreaked havoc and devastation in the name of Jesus Christ. The temptation lies in the security and confidence of knowing the call of God and believing that all our responses are obedient to God's will. The danger lies in predicting our future, rather than surrendering it to God. God's call is not a blueprint for our lives, but a call to a pilgrimage in the wilderness, sustained by God's love and grace. . . .

"God does not abandon those who are called. The strength to fulfill our calling does not come from our own wits, genius, or dedication. Ministry is not a matter of pulling yourself up by your own bootstraps. It is surrendering to God and acknowledging that God's power will sustain us and strengthen us despite all our frailties and weaknesses. . . .

"What is our ministry? The Bible answers with stark clarity. Christian ministry is a call to sacrifice and service. . . . The difficulty is that service and self-sacrifice are themselves ambiguous and filled with temptations. . . . But what sustains us in our calling is not the quality or quantity of our response but the clear assurance that we are loved by God. We will never escape the ambiguities and confusions of mixing our own will with God's way, but we can take heart that through Christ we are forgiven."—John M. Mulder, in his opening address as president of Louisville Theological Seminary, 1982.

Body, Soul, and Brain. God's messengers have understood who they were. They have realized that God has called them to a difficult task. In spite of living in times of turmoil, they have been aware of their identity.

George Balanchine, the late great choreographer, had a sense of who he was as one who knew he was gifted in the world of dance. His entire life revolved around dancing. "I am a dancer, body, soul, and brain," he used to say.

We as people called by God, recognizing who we are as God's, can paraphrase Balanchine. "I am a Christian, body, soul, and brain," each of us can state!

Questions for Pupils on the Next Lesson. 1. With what human commitment did Jeremiah compare God's covenant? 2. What were Jeremiah's criticisms of his nation? 3. Why did Jeremiah say that false gods were like cisterns that could hold no water? 4. What were the priests like in Jeremiah's time?

TOPIC FOR YOUTH
CALLED TO SERVE

Love in the Mortar Joints. Millard Fuller knows the Lord has called him to serve the poor by providing houses.

Fuller is an author, lawyer, and former millionaire who gave up a successful business career to devote himself to doing something positive for the poor. That "something positive" is Habitat for Humanity, an organization that builds homes for low-income people in nineteen states in the United States and has sponsored projects in Central America, Latin America, and Africa.

Fuller's fundamental belief is simply stated: "People who are economically poor need capital, not charity. They need co-workers, not caseworkers. They need partners, people who will respect them and help them free themselves of the burdens they bear."

With this principle in mind, Fuller founded a network of housing groups in the United States and overseas, each operating on a non-profit, no-interest basis to establish simple but sturdy homes for the poor people.

With a small but dedicated team of staff members and volunteers, he has put together an operation that—translated into terms of bricks and mortar—parallels the parable of the loaves and fishes.

Habitat for Humanity projects accept no government funding. Instead, people at each project location pool their resources to form a "Fund for Humanity" made up of donations and no-interest loans. This fund provides the capital needed for construction. Volunteers are encouraged to help with the construction of each unit. The completed homes are purchased by needy families on a no-interest basis, with payments stretched over a twenty to twenty-five year period. These payments are "recycled" to build more homes.

As a home is built, the family that is to move in learns about the philosophy behind the movement and becomes imbued with its spirit of sharing. There is a dedication service when a home is completed, and the new owners are presented with a Bible as a momento of the occasion.

The whole process involves interpersonal relationships as well as the physical realities of home construction. Fuller says these homes have "love in the mortar joints."

Wanted It to Be an Ideal World. Norman Rockwell painted scenes which brought smiles of hope and remembrance to his viewers.

His nostalgic evocations of small town America had appeared on 321 *Saturday Evening Post* covers between 1916 and 1963 and helped three generations remember the way it was—or the way they wished it had been. His idealized paintings had made him perhaps America's best-known and best-loved artist.

"Maybe I grew up and found the world wasn't the perfectly pleasant place I had thought it to be," he said in 1960. "I unconsciously decided that if it wasn't an ideal world, it should be, and so painted only the ideal aspects of it, pictures in which there were no drunken fathers, or self-centered mothers, in which, on the contrary, there were only foxy grandpas who played baseball with the kids, and boys fished from logs and got up circuses in the backyard. If there were problems, they were humorous problems."

Rockwell's words have a ring to them which brings to mind the call of the prophets and the call of each of us by God. We must acknowledge that if it isn't an ideal world, it should be! We should portray the world as God means it to be and work to illustrate what it should look like! This is the task of every believer!

Called to Serve. Joe Delaney played professional football. He was a great running back. One day, in Louisiana in the summer of 1983, he saw two boys in a pond. Delaney heard the cries of the boys for help. He told a bystander, "I can't swim good, but I've got to save those kids." Joe Delaney plunged into the water to try to rescue the pair. Tragically, Joe drowned while attempting to bring the two boys to safety. His words, however, can be the motto of every Christian. Called to serve, each member of Christ's community must acknowledge the pleas for help from others and, in spite of limitations or excuses, respond by saying, "I've got to save those people."

Questions for Pupils on the Next Lesson. 1. Why does breaking your promises inevitably cause conflict with others and for yourself? 2. Does wrongdoing always harm you as well as others? 3. What did Jeremiah condemn in the nation in his times? 4. How had Israel, Judah, forsaken God? 5. What are examples of idolatry and social injustice in our society?

LESSON II—JUNE 8

THE WRONGS OF JEREMIAH'S NATION

Background Scripture: Jeremiah 2—6
Devotional Reading: Jeremiah 5:1-5

KING JAMES VERSION

JEREMIAH 2 Moreover the word of the LORD came to me, saying,

2 Go and cry in the ears of Jerusalem, saying, Thus saith the LORD; I remember thee, the kindness of thy youth, the love of thine espousals, when thou wentest after me in the wilderness, in a land *that was* not sown.

3 Israel *was* holiness unto the LORD, *and* the firstfruits of his increase: all that devour him shall offend; evil shall come upon them, saith the LORD.

7 And I brought you into a plentiful country, to eat the fruit thereof and the goodness thereof; but when ye entered, ye defiled my land, and made mine heritage an abomination.

8 The priests said not, Where *is* the LORD? and they that handle the law knew me not: the pastors also transgressed against me, and the prophets prophesied by Baal, and walked after *things that* do not profit.

11 Hath a nation changed *their* gods, which *are* yet no gods? but my people have changed their glory for *that which* doth not profit.

12 Be astonished, O ye heavens, at this, and be horribly afraid, be ye very desolate, saith the LORD.

13 For my people have committed two evils; they have forsaken me the fountain of living waters, *and* hewed them out cisterns, broken cisterns, that can hold no water.

REVISED STANDARD VERSION

JEREMIAH 2 The word of the LORD came to me, saying, 2 "Go and proclaim in the hearing of Jerusalem, Thus says the LORD,

I remember the devotion of your youth,
 your love as a bride,
how you followed me in the wilderness,
 in a land not sown.
3 Israel was holy to the LORD,
 the first fruits of his harvest.
All who ate of it became guilty; evil came
 upon them,
 says the LORD."

7 "And I brought you into a plentiful land
 to enjoy its fruits and its good things.
But when you came in you defiled my land,
 and made my heritge an abomination.
8 The priests did not say, 'Where is the
 LORD?'
Those who handle the law did not know
 me;
the rulers transgressed against me; the
 prophets prophesied by Baal, and went
 after things that do not profit.

11 Has a nation changed its gods, even
 though they are no gods?
But my people have changed their glory
 for that which does not profit.
12 Be appalled, O heavens, at this;
 be shocked, be utterly desolate,
 says the LORD,
13 for my people have committed two evils:
 they have forsaken me,
the fountain of living waters,
 and hewed out cisterns for themselves,
broken cisterns,
 that can hold no water."

KEY VERSE: "I brought you into a plentiful land to enjoy its fruits and its good things. But when you came in you defiled my land, and made my heritage an abomination." Jeremiah 2:7.

HOME DAILY BIBLE READINGS

June	2.	M.	*God Is Faithful to His People.* Jeremiah 2:1-8.
June	3.	T.	*Forsaking the Living Fountain.* Jeremiah 2:9-13.
June	4.	W.	*Consequences of Forsaking God.* Jeremiah 2:14-19.
June	5.	T.	*Conditions of Repentance.* Jeremiah 3:21—4:4.
June	6.	F.	*Results of God's Judgment.* Jeremiah 4:23-28.
June	7.	S.	*Judah's Foolish Stubbornness.* Jeremiah 5:20-25.
June	8.	S.	*No Substitute for Faithfulness.* Jeremiah 6:16-21.

BACKGROUND

What is a patriot? A person who does a lot of flag-waving? One who shouts slogans about his country being Number One and plasters love-it-or-leave-it stickers on both bumpers?

A lot of people in Judah in Jeremiah's time thought in these terms. They also resented anyone who did not agree. In fact, they accused any person raising any criticism of being unpatriotic. As the situation in Judah worsened, these superpatriots lashed out at those voicing moral concerns about the nation, denouncing the few dissenting voices as subversives.

Jeremiah was one of the few who would not go along with the jingoistic patriotism in the late seventh century B.C. Judah. Actually, Jeremiah loved his nation. The truth of the matter was that he cared more about his country than most others. He cared enough about Judah to dare to call attention to its wrongs. Jeremiah, in actuality, was more patriotic than all of the slogan shouters and flag-wavers.

What were the wrongs which Jeremiah protested so determinedly? Basically, Jeremiah remembered that his nation was covenanted with the Lord. To Jeremiah, that covenant relationship was like the marriage vow. Judah had promised to remain faithful to God, but had persisted in rejecting the Lord, thereby breaking the vow or the covenant. Jeremiah laid out the bill of particulars against his country and his fellow citizens. In blunt terms, he condemned the false worship, the idolatry and the social injustice of his time. He excoriated the religious establishment. Even the priests, he said, did not know the Lord. Coming from a man who was born into a priest's family and one of the bluebloods of the realm, these words aroused a furious reaction. But Jeremiah would not be silenced. He shouted that the very leaders who were supposed to instruct others in God's Law were not themselves listening to that Law.

No one minded prophets who denounced the sins of other nations. But when Jeremiah spoke out against Jerusalem and Judah's leaders, he was ordered to keep quiet, or face serious consequences. Jeremiah learned that love of country does not automatically mean honors and contentment. In fact, the kind of patriotism this prophet exemplified, like that of Jesus and Bonhoeffer and a legion of others, cost him dearly!

NOTES ON THE PRINTED TEXT

The Book of Jeremiah is a collection of oracles. These oracles were not long, well polished sermons, but brief, memorable, and to-the-point talks. Such an oracle was delivered to the ears of Jerusalem.

I remember the devotion of your youth, your love as a bride. The word translated as *devotion* most normally means faithfulness to the obligations of the covenant. Jeremiah compares the covenant vow with the marriage vow. He has in mind the covenant relationship between God and Israel, His bride. Speaking for God, the prophet remembers Israel's purity. She was devoted to God and protected by Him in the wilderness. *Israel was holy to the Lord.* To be holy is to be set apart. Israel had been chosen by God to belong to Him faithfully. She was to be *the first fruits of his harvest.* The first fruits were holy and could not be used for any profane purpose. They were consecrated to God. No one would eat them other than the priests, God's representatives. Like the fruits, Israel was formed to be holy, and yet Israel had become unclean. *All who ate of it became guilty; evil came upon them.* Israel had forgotten God's past favor. The original purity of her relationship with God, that of the bride loyal to her husband, has degenerated into infidelity, adultery, and harlotry. Israel has not maintained her purity. Israel has responded to God's goodness by failing to keep the covenant. *I brought you into a land to enjoy its fruits and its good things but when you came in you defiled my land and made my heritage an abomination.*

Jeremiah places the blame for the nation's wrongs on the leaders. *The priests . . . those who handle the law do not know God.* The priests are supposed to instruct people in God's Law, but they do not even know God. *The rulers transgressed against me.* Jeremiah claims that the rulers rebel against God. *The prophets prophesied by Baal.* The spiritual leaders have gone after useless things which are worthless. They prophesy by Baal. Jeremiah vehemently denounces this worship of the fertility god and the lascivious rites that accompany its worship. Moreover, he condemns false worship, idolatry, and social injustice. He asks, *Has a nation changed its gods, even though they are no gods?* The apostasy is total. Even the other countries do not exchange gods (which are not really gods at all, quips Jeremiah). Israel has been faithless. *My people have changed their glory for that which does not profit.* Jeremiah makes a play on words with Baal's name. Literally, he says that the people have left God for something useless. He summons the *heavens* to witness this appalling and shocking act.

My people have commited two evils. Jeremiah highlights two of the nation's wrongs. First, Israel has forsaken God, *the fountain of living waters,* for false gods. Secondly, he likens these false gods (or idols that have been hewn from stone) to *broken cisterns that can hold no water.* It is a vivid image to a water scarce people who must hew cisterns out of stone to store water. God is the living water as contrasted to stagnant, brackish water. Jeremiah asks why exchange the life-giving God for a polluted idol. Give to God all faithfulness and due that is His.

SUGGESTIONS TO TEACHERS

Some in your class may have the mistaken notion that Jeremiah and the Old Testament prophets were cranky faultfinders. Although at times they might have appeared cranky and although they usually catalogued all of their nation's faults, they were not doing so merely as social critics or editorial writers. Jeremiah, and the other genuine prophets, your class must understand, were first and foremost consecrated by God and sensitive to God's concerns. Their countrymen sometimes hated them for being curmudgeons, but Jeremiah and his kind knew they had to speak for the Lord.

Today's lesson introduces Jeremiah's bill of particulars against Jerusalem and Judah. You and your class will notice that Jeremiah indicts his nation a series of serious charges. Be sure to take note, however, that these are not the charges of a disgruntled malcontent but the cries of disappointment of a man who continued to love his country and his fellow citizens! This will open up a helpful lesson on how a Christian loves his country enough to work to correct its wrongs.

The background Scripture lists Jeremiah's bill of particulars against Judah, but it could also serve as God's indictment of every nation, including our own. Look carefully at the list of charges:

1. *INGRATITUDE.* Jeremiah states that Judah is guilty of apostasy. The nation has turned from its spiritual roots. It has forsaken the Lord. Using a magnificent image, Jeremiah says that Judah and its people have deserted the fountain of living waters for the stagnant stuff that will soon seep out altogether from a leaky cistern. Has our country seemed to have forgotten its heritage? Have we sought strength in "leaky cisterns" of military prowess and power instead of living up to our motto and pledge of allegiance that we are "under God"?

2. *IDOLATRY.* Jeremiah had blistering words for those who chased after phony gods. Before smiling, however, examine some of the causes and interests

which claim our time, our cash, our allegiance. Are not these our idols? Remind the class that *any* thing or *any* one which is placed ahead of the Lord is in effect an idol! Under that definition, even the church or job or patriotism or an ideology (including Communism and Capitalism) can become a "god."

3. *INFIDELITY.* Jeremiah in 4:30 uses particularly harsh phrases to describe his country. He portrays Judah painted up and decked out like a cheap whore. God's people have prostituted themselves. Deserting the Lord, they think they can attract other lovers to give them security and happiness. Jeremiah bluntly stated that whatever they sell themselves to will only despise them and try to destroy them. Consider with your class whether the Church, God's people today, remains faithful to its loving Lord. Or does it sometimes chase after enticing "lovers" such as success or headlines or power or money?

4. *INJUSTICE.* Leave lots of time to discuss the justice issues Jeremiah brings up. Look at each one: speaking lies, greed, ignoring the plight of the poor, permitting a widening gap between the haves and the have-nots, perpetuating a double standard of justice. Any similarities today?

TOPIC FOR ADULTS
A PEOPLE GONE ASTRAY

South Bronx Coverup. The South Bronx is a desolate wasteland of burned-out, abandoned buildings and rubble-strewn streets. Experiments by New York city authorities to change the South Bronx by using massive billboards with pleasant scenes and painting curtains, potted plants, and window shades on the plywood covering the broken windows are being tried. Several buildings now have the plywood in window openings covered with realistically-painted ruffled curtains and blooming flower pots. Discussions are continuing about erecting huge signboards painted with pictures of grassy knolls.

What would Jeremiah or the prophets say? Some contemporary prophets are saying that it is a sign of a people gone astray. They insist that the billboards are intended to keep commuters from seeing the squalor in the area. The spokesmen for the poor of the South Bronx say that they wish the money spent to paint scenes on the plywood boarding up windows could be spent to clear away the rubble and fulfill the promises made by two Presidents who visited the area.

How do we deal with the poor and needy of a nation? By keeping them hidden and isolated? By covering up the decaying mortar and ruined lives? By being indifferent and unresponsive to the pleas and dreams of those living behind the billboards and painted plywood windows?

God calls each society to beautify the lives of the poor and hopeless. To do otherwise is to be a people gone astray!

See It Feelingly. "There is general agreement in Washington these days about the 'interdependence' of the world, and endless talk about economics and statistics and the world balance of trade, and what to do about the consequences of world turmoil but very little about the causes of that turmoil.

"President Reagan talks a great deal about the gross national product and about religion, but very little about the sanctity of individual life—except when he's arguing against abortion.

" 'We are,' said Archibald MacLeish, 'the best informed people on earth. We are deluged with facts, but we have lost or are losing our human ability to feel them. . . . We know with the head now, by the facts, by the abstractions. We seem unable to know, as Shakespeare knew, who made King Lear cry out to blinded Gloucester on the heath: "You see how this world goes" and Gloucester answers: "I see it feelingly."

" 'Why we are thus impotent,' MacLeish added, 'I do not know. I know only

that this impotence exists and that it is dangerous: increasingly dangerous.' "—
James Reston, *N.Y. Times*, March 23, 1983. Copyright © 1983 by The New York
Times Company. Reprinted by permission.

Inevitable Collapse. The well-being of any nation depends upon the moral
strength of its people. When the people go astray from moral standards, collapse
is inevitable. This is what Jeremiah was trying to tell his people. This is what
prophets are trying to tell us.

Sometimes, little incidents occur which illustrate this truth. In Egypt, in one
recent year, sixty-five people have died because buildings collapsed of overbuild-
ing. Owners have contrived to skirt the regulations and add additional floors to
buildings. They have thereby been able to collect additional rents. Their greed,
however, has brought ruin—literally. They have put too much additional weight
on the structures. In Heliopoli, an affluent residential area filled with villas, for
example, one landlord illegally added on four floors to an apartment building.
Early one morning in 1983, it collapsed with a roar, killing him and injuring
twenty other people, including a Ministry of Tourism official and two of his children.

A people cannot flout God. Greed brings ruin! A nation goes astray when it ig-
nores moral principles!

Questions for Pupils on the Next Lesson. 1. What was the occasion of Jeremiah's Temple Sermon? 2. Why was Jeremiah arrested for preaching this sermon? 3. Why is genuine worship always related to ethical living? 4. Is worship
centered in a place or in a relationship? 5. In what do you place your trust most
frequently—culture, traditions, circumstances, or the Lord?

TOPIC FOR YOUTH
FOOLISH CHOICE

An eagle was perched on an ice block on the Niagara River. It enjoyed the
view, and paid no attention to the cries of other birds and animals that the great
cataract was ahead and that the floe was carrying him toward destruction.
Shrugging his mighty wings, the eagle said, "No fear, I can fly away." The eagle
continued to ignore the pleas of warning. "My great wings can carry me whenever I wish to rise, so why should I heed their words about the danger?" Finally,
the chunk of ice was rushed to the edge of the precipice of the mighty Falls. As
the huge floe teetered before tumbling over the great cascade, the eagle stretched
his wings. But he could not move. His claws had become frozen to the icecake. It
was too late.

Hope for Peace. "There is little chance of having genuine peace unless people
are treated justly and are convinced that they are being treated justly. But justice
does not come about as a casual accident. The interactions between people must
be governed. The dynamics within any social unit—from family to nation-
state—must be deliberately arranged and monitored in order to achieve communal well-being. Peace, therefore, depends upon how wisely and skillfully we
shape and nurture the life of the groups to which we belong! Doing this well depends upon being clear about what we intend to accomplish and how we will
overcome the obstacles that get in the way of social well-being."—*Peace Thinking in a Warring World*, Edward Leroy Long, Jr., The Westminster Press: Philadelphia, 1983.

Too Proud to Pray. "We have been the recipients of the choicest bounties of
heaven; we have been preserved these many years in peace and prosperity; we
have grown in numbers, wealth and power as no other nation has ever grown.

"But we have forgotten God. We have forgotten the gracious hand which preserved us in peace and multiplied and enriched and strengthened us. We have
vainly imagined, in the deceitfulness of our hearts, that all these blessings were

produced by some superior wisdom and virtue of our own. Intoxicated with un-
broken success, we have become too self-sufficient to feel the necessity of redeeming and preserving grace, too proud to pray to the God that made us."—
Abraham Lincoln. Thanksgiving Proclamation of 1863.

Questions for Pupils on the Next Lesson. 1. Why did Jeremiah preach his famous Temple Sermon? 2. Why did the authorities order Jeremiah thrown into
prison for preaching this sermon? 3. Should sermons ever criticize the government or its policies? 4. Should worship stick to so-called spiritual matters and not
mention society's problems? 5. Are there any "spiritual laws" which you take
seriously?

LESSON III—JUNE 15

JEREMIAH'S TEMPLE SERMON

Background Scripture: Jeremiah 7:1–15; 26
Devotional Reading: Jeremiah 26:1–6

KING JAMES VERSION

JEREMIAH 7 The word that came to Jeremiah from the LORD, saying,

2 Stand in the gate of the LORD's house, and proclaim there this word, and say, Hear the word of the LORD, all *ye of* Judah, that enter in at these gates to worship the LORD.

3 Thus saith the LORD of hosts, the God of Israel, Amend your ways and your doings, and I will cause you to dwell in this place.

4 Trust ye not in lying words, saying, The temple of the LORD, The temple of the LORD, The temple of the LORD, *are* these.

8 Behold, ye trust in lying words, that cannot profit.

9 Will ye steal, murder, and commit adultery, and swear falsely, and burn incense unto Baal, and walk after other gods whom ye know not;

10 And come and stand before me in this house, which is called by my name, and say, We are delivered to do all these abominations?

26 7 So the priests and the prophets and all the people heard Jeremiah speaking these words in the house of the LORD.

8 Now it came to pass, when Jeremiah had made an end of speaking all that the LORD had commanded *him* to speak unto all the people, that the priests and the prophets and all the people took him, saying, Thou shalt surely die.

9 Why hast thou prophesied in the name of the LORD, saying, This house shall be like Shiloh, and this city shall be desolate without an inhabitant? And all the people were gathered against Jeremiah in the house of the LORD.

12 Then spake Jeremiah unto all the princes and to all the people, saying, The LORD sent me to prophesy against this house and against this city all the words that ye have heard.

13 Therefore now amend your ways and your doings, and obey the voice of the LORD your God; and the LORD will repent him of the evil that he hath pronounced against you.

14 As for me, behold, I *am* in your hand: do with me as seemeth good and meet unto you.

REVISED STANDARD VERSION

JEREMIAH 7 The word that came to Jeremiah from the LORD: 2 "Stand in the gate of the LORD's house, and proclaim there this word, and say, Hear the word of the LORD, all you men of Judah who enter these gates to worship the LORD. 3 Thus says the LORD of hosts, the God of Israel, Amend your ways and your doings, and I will let you dwell in this place. 4 Do not trust in these deceptive words: 'This is the temple of the LORD, the temple of the LORD, the temple of the LORD.'

8 "Behold, you trust in deceptive words to no avail. 9 Will you steal, murder, commit adultery, swear falsely, burn incense to Baal, and go after other gods that you have not known, 10 and then come and stand before me in this house, which is called by my name, and say, 'We are delivered!'—only to go on doing all these abominations?"

26 7 The priests and the prophets and all the people heard Jeremiah speaking these words in the house of the LORD. 8 And when Jeremiah had finished speaking all that the LORD had commanded him to speak to all the people, then the priests and the prophets and all the people laid hold of him, saying, "You shall die! 9 Why have you prophesied in the name of the LORD, saying, 'This house shall be like Shiloh, and this city shall be desolate, without inhabitant'?" And all the people gathered about Jeremiah in the house of the LORD.

12 Then Jeremiah spoke to all the princes and all the people, saying, "The LORD sent me to prophesy against this house and this city all the words you have heard. 13 Now therefore amend your ways and your doings, and obey the voice of the LORD your God, and the LORD will repent of the evil which he has pronounced against you. 14 But as for me, behold, I am in your hands. Do with me as seems good and right to you."

KEY VERSE: *Amend your ways and your doings, and obey the voice of the Lord your God.* Jeremiah 26:13.

HOME DAILY BIBLE READINGS

June 9. M. *Jeremiah Speaks in the Temple.* Jeremiah 7:1–7.
June 10. T. *Deceptive Trust.* Jeremiah 7:8–15.

BACKGROUND

King Josiah had temporarily staved off the collapse of Judah for a few years by his energetic reform movement, culminating in the repair of the Temple in 619 B.C. and the discovery of the Book of Deuteronomy. But he died prematurely by recklessly jumping into battle when Neco, the Egyptian pharaoh, invaded northern Palestine.

The nation temporarily became a vassal state to Egypt. Neco removed Josiah's popular younger son and installed another son as ruler of Judah. Neco even assigned his handpicked Judean king a new name: Jehoiakim—to show how firmly under the pharaoh's thumb the monarch of Judah was.

The leaders of Judah, including the priests, lived with the illusion that everything was rosy. Never mind the Egyptian connection. After all, they had their own nation and weren't under the heel of the Babylonians who were menacing the Eastern world. These leaders turned a blind eye to the injustices and corruption which were grinding the poor and lower classes. They dutifully strutted into the great Jerusalem Temple on all the ceremonial occasions and went through the elaborate rituals. Reinforced by the statements of the priestly caste, they blithely stated that as long as they went through their Temple worship charade, the Lord would never let anything happen to Jerusalem.

When Jeremiah marched into the entrance of the magnificent Temple to deliver his famous sermon, Jehoiakim was just starting his infamous reign. What courage it must have taken! And what a price Jeremiah paid. He was arrested and imprisoned.

The burden of the sermon, however, was not so much against Jehoiakim personally as against the way he and the people of Judah had the mistaken notion that the bricks and stones of the great edifice would save Judah against the menace of the Babylonians. The rulers and people trusted in the inviolability of Judah simply because they kept up an elaborate pretense of worship in that Temple. Jeremiah told them what they did not want to hear. He preached that only the practice of justice, not faith in a physical building, would save Judah from Nebuchadnezzar and his hosts. Faithfulness to God, not religious ritual, saves a people!

NOTES ON THE PRINTED TEXT

God's call often plunged the prophets into opposition with the official Temple priests and prophets. Jeremiah sharply rejected the accepted belief of his day, that the Temple and the sacrifices carried out therein guaranteed protection and safety for the people. Jeremiah argues that faithfulness, not religious ritual, would save the people.

Following Josiah's death, his eldest son, Jehoiakim, was made king. During this period, the Lord instructed Jeremiah to *stand in the gate of the Lord's house.* Jeremiah stood in the Temple gate between the inner and outer courts, the traditional spot where prophets stood to speak to the people (*all men of Judah who enter these gates to worship the Lord*). As he stood there, he called for a radical change of attitude. *Amend your ways and your doings, and I will let you dwell in this place.* Ritual sacrifice, fasts, and worship were not what the Lord desired. If the people changed their behavior, God would permit them to dwell in the land.

Jeremiah scathingly attacked the supposition that the presence of the Temple protected the people. To believe in the *temple of the Lord* was to *trust in . . . deceptive words*. To believe that the Temple's presence was a good luck charm that protected them was nonsense.

Jeremiah preached that only the practice of justice, not faith in a physical building, would save Israel. The people would be delivered by keeping the Commandments. The people, however, were breaking nearly all of God's Commandments and were continuing in their *abominations. You steal, murder, commit adultery, swear falsely, burn incense to Baal, and go after other gods that you have not known.* The people were only deceiving themselves by believing that the Temple's presence guaranteed their safety. Jeremiah cried to them that they were trusting in a lie. They had to change their ways and amend their behavior. It was a call for repentance to *the priests and the prophets and all the peoples* who *heard Jeremiah speaking . . . in the house of the Lord.*

The audience was not receptive to the Word of the Lord. *The priests and the prophets and all the people laid hold of him* saying, *"You shall die!"* Jeremiah was arrested for his sermon against the people's mistaken reliance on the Temple. In the resulting trial, the priests and the prophets pushed for the death sentence, while the princes and the people supported him. Jeremiah was freed when certain elders reminded all those assembled of certain prophecies of Micah which were similar to Jeremiah's. The message of Micah, spoken nearly a century earlier, justified sparing Jeremiah's life. However, Jeremiah's trouble was not over yet.

SUGGESTIONS TO TEACHERS

Imagine for a moment that you have been invited to teach a Sunday-School lesson at Westminster Abbey in the presence of the Queen and the Royal Family, the Prime Minister and members of Parliament and the leaders in business, industry, the Church, the arts, education, and communications of Great Britain. How would you approach such an audience? Or suppose you are asked to speak at Washington's National Cathedral at a special service in which the President, members of Congress and Senators, the Supreme Court Justices, all leading bishops and heads of denominations, presidents of the Fortune 500 corporations, and heads of the most prestigious universities would be present, with your remarks carried live on CBS, ABC, and NBC? What would you say?

All right, so you probably won't have to face such audiences. But Jeremiah did! When he delivered his Temple Sermon that day in Jerusalem, he stood in awesome surroundings before an august gathering.

What did he say? A pleasing soufflé of piety and patriotism? Hardly, because his hearers denounced him to the king and had him arrested!

Your lesson should challenge those in your class to realize that they are sent by God into the world, calling everyone to "obey the voice of the Lord your God" (Jeremiah 26:13).

1. *PROCLAMATION FROM GOD.* Help your class members to be aware that there are occasions in the lives of all believers when they must respond to the Lord's summons to speak out and to stand up. In an age when all values are regarded as "relative" and human wisdom is exalted as "definitive," people need to hear the prophetic, "Thus says the Lord!"

2. *PASSION FOR GRACIOUSNESS.* Point out that God has a profound concern that His graciousness be shared in the world by everyone in society. He detests oppression and exploitation, especially of the poor and helpless. He will not even allow "religion" to replace responsibility for the hungry and weak.

3. *PLEA FOR GODLINESS.* Have your students examine Jeremiah 7:5, 6. In what ways is God calling us in our society, "Amend your ways and your doings"?

4. POLEMIC AGAINST GODLESSNESS. Would God ever allow America to be destroyed? Not a nice thought, but Jeremiah issued a stern warning to his nation that unless it changed its ways, it would perish. Ask if God would ever allow the Church to be destroyed? Remind the class that Jeremiah recalled to his hearers that the great shrine at Shiloh had been permitted by the Lord to be shattered by the Assyrians 150 years earlier! God wants faithfulness, not ritual, and does not act as the personal bodyguard for any country or community simply because they invoke His name!

TOPIC FOR ADULTS
FALSE WORSHIP CONDEMNED

True Worship. Seventy Wheaton College students gave up their Christmas break to help build a medical clinic and a school in Honduras. Students also got behind the $115,000 budget for the project. Thirty students went to the island of Roatan to help build the clinic, while forty went to Catacamas to work on the school, according to Missionary News Service in 1984. Here is true worship! These students, all evangelical Christians from the Illinois college, know that they must be committed both to serving the Lord and to serving fellow humans. Anything less than both of these cannot truly be called divine worship!

True Worship Means Peace and Justice. "We must not hesitate to address ourselves to the question of peace and to the possibility of total nuclear destruction. We must be clear. The nuclear arms race, the employment of God-given human talents and possibilities for the creation of ever more refined weapons of mass destruction, and the call to put our faith in these weapons so as to secure our peace is not simply a temporary madness, it is essentially sinful and contrary to the purpose of God for this world and for the people of His heart. . . . I remain convinced that the issue of peace as it faces us today lies at the very heart of the Gospel.

"But there is something else I must say about this. When the World Alliance of Reformed Churches met in Ottawa last August, we spent considerable time discussing a statement on peace. During the debate, a delegate from Africa made a remark that very poignantly raised some of the tensions surrounding this issue in the ecumenical movement today. He said: 'In this document the word *nuclear* is used a number of times, but I don't even see the word *hunger*. In my village the people will not understand the word *nuclear*, but they know everything about hunger and poverty.'

"What he was really talking about was the concern of many Christians in the Third World that the issue of peace will be separated from the issue of justice, making peace primarily a North Atlantic concern. This should not happen. . . . In the Bible peace and justice are never separated. Peace is never simply the absence of war, it is the active presence of justice. It has to do with human fulfillment, with liberation, with wholeness, with a meaningful life and well-being, not only for the individual, but for the community as a whole. . . .

"One cannot use the Gospel to escape from the demands of the Gospel. And one cannot use the issue of peace to escape from the unresolved issues of injustice, poverty, hunger and racism. If we do this we will make of our concern for peace an ideology of oppression which in the end will be used to justify injustice."—Allan Boesak, South Africa, Address at Vancouver, World Council of Churches, 1983.

Dangers of False Worship. We sometimes put comfort ahead of everything. When we do, we worship comfort. But we are in danger.

Hannibal, the great military leader of Carthage, defeated the Roman armies and advanced on Rome. When winter came, Hannibal decided to settle down at Capua with his troops and wait for pleasant spring weather. Hannibal and his men quickly discovered what a delightful and luxurious life Capua offered. The lovely city and its diversions did what the Roman legionnaires could not do. Capuan comforts turned the lean, tough North African troops into slack, luxury-loving layabouts. Spring came. Hannibal tried to rally his Carthaginians. They were no match this time against the Romans. Their worship of comfort had weakened them hopelessly, and they were easily routed.

Questions for Pupils on the Next Lesson. 1. Why did Jeremiah tell Baruch to read the scroll in the Temple instead of reading it himself? 2. What did King Jehoiakim do when he heard the words of Jeremiah's scroll? 3. Do you ever feel you have problems in reaching important goals in life? 4. How can you have the courage to pursue unpopular causes? 5. Have you ever had to stand up and take a stand that was unpopular?

TOPIC FOR YOUTH
FALSE SECURITY

Beer Company Blitz. Major beer companies are spending big money to try to convince you that you will feel more secure and grown-up by drinking.

They saturate televised sports programs with commercials equating drinking with youthful good life and fun-time U.S.A. In the trade, these are known as life-style commercials: You can't have life and you won't have style unless you and the gang are taking a long beer break.

During the football league playoffs, the nation's young are blitzed with beer commercials. The sports theme is stressed. As an ad last year for Miller Lite said, "Lite beer is like quarterbacks. We can't wait to knock 'em down."

The athletes may be playing games, but not the beer companies. In 1982 the combined ad budgets for the top ten beer advertisers was $501 million, a sum more than nine times the current $55-million budget of the National Institute of Alcoholism and Alcohol Abuse.

Don't let the beer ads blitz you. Only the Lord provides true security!

Royal Security. Most of us have the notion that if we have enough money and enough things we will be secure. Security, of course, can never come from possessions. Or, as one wag put it, "There is no security in securities"!

The Roman Emperors should have been the most secure persons alive if coins and comforts could bring security. They had almost unlimited resources and could indulge themselves in almost every whim. In one day, Caligula squandered the revenues of three provinces, amounting to almost a half million dollars. Nero once threw a banquet in which the imported roses alone cost him about $100,000. He never traveled with less than a thousand carriages, and had the mules shod with silver. Caligula languished at dinner parties in which costly pearls were dissolved in vinegar, then drunk. Vitellius, although emperor less than a year, spent the equivalent of twenty million dollars on food alone. All of these reckless spenders thought they were buying security and happiness. Yet, the study of their lives reveals they were the most insecure and unhappy persons imaginable!

God of the Earth, Sky, and Sea. In April 1963, the USS *Thresher* went down with 129 men aboard. During the tense period when it was not known if the crew was dead or alive, the wife of the skipper made the following statement: "I have confidence in my husband, in his knowledge and skill and in his sense of responsibility toward his men, and I pray for him and all the crew members. But even if the worst is true, God is still God of the earth, and the sky and the sea." What a powerful witness to the sovereignty of God!

But what if we were to universalize and generalize this statement, applying it to the greatest danger that has ever faced humanity? When we consider that the earth harbors 50,000 nuclear weapons equal to the explosive power of a million Hiroshimas, how then do we feel about the sovereignty of God?

Shortly after the development of the nuclear bomb, Reinhold Niebuhr stated that if these weapons were ever used against us, it would mean our physical annihilation; but if we ever used them against an enemy, it would mean our moral annihilation. Or, as Dwight D. Eisenhower said, "The problem in defense is how far you can go without destroying from within what you are trying to defend from without."

The irony is that if we were ever to use our absolute power to destroy, we would be committing not only genocide, but suicide. Although the defense of a nation may be a moral cause, as even Henry Kissinger has said, "It simply does not make much sense to defend one's way of life with a strategy which guarantees its destruction."

The nuclear doctrine of deterrence is based on a schizophrenic view of human nature—perfectionist in that there cannot be "one mistake," but also terribly cynical and suspicious, attributing such evil to our enemies that we would be willing to blow them from the face of the earth—and with them ourselves as well. The central theological question facing humanity today is whether we will believe in and be held captive by the claim of "nuclear demonology," that in death lies our hope for life.

Questions for Pupils on the Next Lesson. 1. Why didn't Jeremiah go in person to read his scroll in the Temple? 2. What was King Jehoiakim's reaction when he heard what Jeremiah had written? 3. What did the Lord promise would happen to Jehoiakim for disregarding Jeremiah's prophecy? 4. Have you ever had to take an unpopular stand? 5. How can you distinguish the "right voice" in the midst of all the voices tempting you to do wrong?

LESSON IV—JUNE 22

GOD'S WORD VERSUS THE KING

Background Scripture: Jeremiah 36
Devotional Reading: Jeremiah 17:5-10

KING JAMES VERSION

JEREMIAH 36 4 Then Jeremiah called Baruch the son of Neriah: and Baruch wrote from the mouth of Jeremiah all the words of the LORD, which he had spoken unto him, upon a roll of a book.

5 And Jeremiah commanded Baruch, saying, I *am* shut up; I cannot go into the house of the LORD:

6 Therefore go thou, and read in the roll, which thou hast written from my mouth, the words of the LORD in the ears of the people in the LORD's house upon the fasting day: and also thou shalt read them in the ears of all Judah that come out of their cities.

7 It may be they will present their supplication before the LORD, and will return every one from his evil way: for great *is* the anger and the fury that the LORD hath pronounced against this people.

8 And Baruch the son of Neriah did according to all that Jeremiah the prophet commanded him, reading in the book the words of the LORD in the LORD's house.

27 Then the word of the LORD came to Jeremiah, after that the king had burned the roll, and the words which Baruch wrote at the mouth of Jeremiah, saying,

28 Take thee again another roll, and write in it all the former words that were in the first roll, which Jehoiakim the king of Judah hath burned.

29 And thou shalt say to Jehoiakim king of Judah, Thus saith the LORD; Thou hast burned this roll, saying, Why hast thou written therein, saying, The king of Babylon shall certainly come and destroy this land, and shall cause to cease from thence man and beast?

30 Therefore thus saith the LORD of Jehoiakim king of Judah; He shall have none to sit upon the throne of David: and his dead body shall be cast out in the day to the heat, and in the night to the frost.

31 And I will punish him and his seed and his servants for their iniquity; and I will bring upon them, and upon the inhabitants of Jerusalem, and upon the men of Judah, all the evil that I have pronounced against them; but they hearkened not.

REVISED STANDARD VERSION

JEREMIAH 36 4 Then Jeremiah called Baruch the son of Neriah, and Baruch wrote upon a scroll at the dictation of Jeremiah all the words of the LORD which he had spoken to him.

5 And Jeremiah ordered Baruch, saying, "I am debarred from going to the house of the LORD; 6 so you are to go, and on a fast day in the hearing of all the people in the LORD's house you shall read the words of the LORD from the scroll which you have written at my dictation. You shall read them also in the hearing of all the men of Judah who come out of their cities. 7 It may be that their supplication will come before the LORD, and that every one will turn from his evil way, for great is the anger and wrath that the LORD has pronounced against this people."

8 And Baruch the son of Neriah did all that Jeremiah the prophet ordered him about reading from the scroll the words of the LORD in the LORD's house.

27 Now, after the king had burned the scroll with the words which Baruch wrote at Jeremiah's dictation, the word of the LORD came to Jeremiah: 28 "Take another scroll and write on it all the former words that were in the first scroll, which Jehoiakim the king of Judah has burned. 29 And concerning Jehoiakim king of Judah you shall say, 'Thus says the LORD, You have burned this scroll, saying, "Why have you written in it that the king of Babylon will certainly come and destroy this land, and will cut off from it man and beast?" 30 Therefore thus says the LORD concerning Jehoiakim king of Judah, He shall have none to sit upon the throne of David, and his dead body shall be cast out to the heat by day and the frost by night. 31 And I will punish him and his offspring and his servants for their iniquity; I will bring upon them, and upon the inhabitants of Jerusalem, and upon the men of Judah, all the evil that I have pronounced against them, but they would not hear.' "

KEY VERSE: *They will fight against you; but they shall not prevail against you, for I am with you, says the Lord, to deliver you.* Jeremiah 1:19.

HOME DAILY BIBLE READINGS

June 16. M.   *Jehoiakim Begins to Rule.* 2 Kings 23:34–37.
June 17. T.   *Doom Is Proclaimed.* Jeremiah 25:1–14.
June 18. W.   *God's Word Is Written.* Jeremiah 36:1–8.
June 19. T.   *Baruch Reads the Scroll.* Jeremiah 36:9–13.
June 20. F.   *Royalty Hears God's Word.* Jeremiah 36:14–18.
June 21. S.   *The Scroll Is Burned.* Jeremiah 36:19–26.
June 22. S.   *A Second Scroll Is Written.* Jeremiah 36:27–32.

BACKGROUND

From time to time, historians debate what American Presidents' faces would be chiselled on a Mount Rushmore for the four worst leaders the nation has ever suffered. Forget the American Presidents for the moment and apply the same process to Old Testament kings. Which would be candidates for the title of the worst rulers? Many would nominate King Jehoiakim.

We have already seen how he was placed in power by Pharaoh Neco, and therefore pro-Egyptian. He pursued a policy of aligning himself with Egypt against the threat of the mighty Babylonians. Jeremiah and a few other astute observers realized how short-sighted such an attitude was and tried to persuade Jehoiakim and the ruling establishment to rely on the Lord instead of clever but shaky alliances with unreliable human powers.

Jehoiakim's sins, however, included more than political ploys. He encouraged the popular heathen cults, including those that practiced such atrocities as child sacrifice. He ignored complaints about injustice in the realm. When he heard of anyone criticizing him, he had the dissident arrested and imprisoned. Jehoiakim even executed the Prophet Uriah. His cruelty and corruption hastened the decline of Judah.

Meanwhile, the Babylonian war machine continued to roll over neighboring states. The international political scene suddenly shifted when the Babylonian king, Nebuchadnezzar, defeated Egypt's Pharaoh Neco. Nebuchadnezzar made the king of Judah Babylon's puppet ruler.

Jeremiah pleaded the Lord's case to the authorities in Judah by dictating a scroll to his associate, Baruch, outlining dire warnings to the nation and its leaders. Jeremiah was barred from the Temple so he told Baruch to read the message from God on the scroll. The message made such a profound impression on the country's leaders in the Temple that day that they arranged to have it read to King Jehoiakim himself. Jehoiakim, however, refused to listen attentively to the words of Jeremiah's prophecy and contemptuously took a penknife to the columns of the scroll when the reader had finished reading, throwing the strips into the fire.

The Lord ordered Jeremiah to rewrite the prophecies on another scroll, and warned that Jehoiakim would be punished for rejecting His prophecy.

NOTES ON THE PRINTED TEXT

Today's lesson enables Christians to see where this book of the Bible originated. In the fourth year, Jehoiakim was king (605–604 B.C). We have this book because at God's command Jeremiah is to take a papyrus scroll and record all of his prophecies. This collection is to be shared with everyone in Judah in hopes that they will repent. The Lord is angry with His people.

Jeremiah called Baruch and Baruch wrote upon a scroll at the dictation of Jeremiah all the words of the Lord which he had spoken. Jeremiah commissioned Baruch to write the prophecies on a papyrus scroll. Baruch, the son of Neriah, came from a prominent and distinguished family. Well educated and a close friend of Jeremiah, he becomes Jeremiah's secretary.

A year later the document was finished. *Jeremiah ordered Baruch, saying, "I am debarred from going to the house of the Lord; so you are to go and . . . in the Lord's house . . . read the words of the Lord from the scroll.* Probably as a result of his Temple sermon, Jeremiah was not allowed in the Temple or to speak in the Temple, so Baruch is to read the scroll in the Temple for him.

It was a *fast day* (in all probability because of the fall of Ashkelon to the Babylonians). As a result of this fast, there was a large crowd in the Temple. Taking advantage of this situation, *Baruch . . . did all that Jeremiah the prophet ordered him.*

The scroll was read to the people and then to the officials and was finally brought to King Jehoiakim. Some officials were sympathetic, some fearful, and a few impressed. However, Jehoiakim refused to listen attentively to the words of Jeremiah's prophecy. He took his penknife and cut the scroll into pieces and burned it in his brazier. The king was unimpressed. No reforms were made and Jeremiah and Baruch were forced into hiding as marked men. What did happen was that Jehoiakim gave his allegiance to the Babylonians.

The Lord ordered Jeremiah to write the prophecies on another scroll. *"Take another scroll and write on it all the former words that were in the first scroll."* This time Jehoiakim and his newly offered allegiance to Babylon were singled out by Jeremiah. Jehoiakim questioned why the king of Babylon would come and destroy the land.

The second scroll was prepared. However, a fresh oracle was attached that concerned Jehoiakim's fate. The Lord said that Jehoiakim would be punished for rejecting the prophecy. *He shall have none to sit upon the throne of David, and his dead body shall be cast to the heat of the day and the frost by night.* Jeremiah knew that Jehoiakim's loyalties to Babylon were suspect so Jeremiah prophesied that the king's real loyalties lay with Egypt. The Babylonians would come again and seize Jerusalem, and Jehoiakim would be killed. Even his son Jehoiachin would not rule. Indeed, this did happen. The Babylonians came, and Jehoiakim was either assassinated or executed. Jehoiachin was deposed and taken to Babylon.

It is said the pen is mightier than the sword. In this instance, the pen was mightier than the penknife. Jehoiakim destroyed the book, but ultimately the Word, the living Word, triumphed!

SUGGESTIONS TO TEACHERS

Can you recall times when you would have preferred to have kept your mouth shut instead of speaking out for truth or justice? Or can you remember an occasion when you felt that discretion was the better part of valor, and later regretted your silence? Probably your class members can also think of such episodes when they should have taken a stand for the Lord.

Jeremiah was one of that valiant but tiny band of God's people who dared to stand and speak when it was not easy to do so. In fact, Jeremiah was commissioned to confront the king.

Using Jeremiah's experiences as a model, you will develop a lesson to help your people stand up to the powers and authorities of this world. Examining Jeremiah 36, work in the following points;

1. *GOD COMMANDS.* Jeremiah was ordered to carry out an unpleasant and unpopular assignment: to write a scroll listing the wrongs of the nation and issuing a warning of national doom. Point out to your people that frequently God's commands are not easy to accept! In fact, when the Lord calls a person to His service, He usually hands out risky assignments. Encourage your class members to

tell some of the times when they have been aware that God has ordered them to carry out responsibilities which they did not welcome or relish.

2. *GOD CONVICTS.* Tell the story of the dramatic confrontation between God's Word and King Jehoiakim. Let the feelings of fright and futility which God's people must have had come through. Remind your class of the way Jehoiakim threatened Jeremiah and Baruch. These details, however, all reveal how deeply King Jehoiakim resented God and God's Word. When we are convicted by God, our initial reaction often is to reject the message and the messenger. Resentment against God, however, does not nullify a sense of being convicted by Him!

3. *GOD COMFORTS.* In spite of opposition and setbacks to God's Word, God remains sovereign. And the Lord never deserts His faithful people, but stands with them. God comforted Jeremiah. He also told Jeremiah to go and write out His message on a new scroll. Although the king had shredded and burned the first scroll, God's Word would prevail!

4. *GOD CONDEMNS.* A nation which flaunts God's Word will ultimately perish! Jeremiah does not try to mute this message for King Jehoiakim or the royal henchmen. The ancient Word from the Lord still applies, however. Dire consequences result whenever any person in authority or any society willfully refuses to carry out basic justice and live in peace!

TOPIC FOR ADULTS
OVERCOMING OBSTACLES TO WITNESS

From Cross-Burner to Soul-Winner. God overcomes all obstacles so that there will be witness to His Word. King Jehoiakim could not silence Jeremiah. God continues to work in this world, often in surprising ways.

Look, for example, at the story of Tommy Rollins.

Tommy Rollins of Irving, Texas, former grand wizard of the White Knights of America, told "The 700 Club" audience that he lived in "constant terror, uncontrollable torment, twenty-four hours a day," yet he was skilled in the art of killing and always was heavily armed as the Klan's grand wizard. Today, a death warrant for Tommy Rollins has been signed in blood by an elite squad of the Klan and there have been three attempts on his life. But Rollins today is fearless, boldly proclaiming his new-found faith in Jesus Christ.

Rollins rose through the ranks to the top national executive of the White Knights of America in fourteen years, becoming the organization's chief hate monger. Rollins told of his life in the KKK and of his conversion experience in an interview in 1983 on "The 700 Club" TV show by black co-host Ben Kinchlow, ironically a former follower of Muslim Malcolm X and once bent on eradicating whites.

Rollins recounted his encounter with the Lord on Easter Sunday, 1983, in a church in Irving, Texas, where an intercessory prayer group had been praying specifically for Klan members. He has since moved from cross-burner to soul-winner, and has led hundreds of people to Jesus Christ.

"Seven months ago if someone had said I'd be sitting with Ben Kinchlow and saying the Klan is a Satanic cult, I'd have shot them dead," said Rollins.

Dimensions of Communion. "If the Bread of the Eucharist is the bread of eternal life, and if while breaking it we are becoming participants in the Eternal Feast of the Lamb of God's Kingdom, entering into communion with Christ and so with each other like brothers and sisters, it is only natural that we should take responsibility for fighting against hunger, poverty, illnesses and other manifestations of social injustice with regard to other people—who are all our brothers and sisters. . . .

"If the Church is one and is called to be a 'sign' of unity and renewal for the rest of humanity, and if we partake of the Chalice of peace, then it is a direct responsibility of every Christian and of all our churches to take part in peacemaking, to struggle against militarism, the arms race, all threats of war and nuclear annihilation, and to struggle for salvation of the sacred gift of life."—Vitaly Borovoi.

Call-In for Hope. Sometimes, the loudest and most insistent messages heard in the world are those about destruction and violence. The public hears little of hope. There are often obstacles to presenting God's message of hope. God, however, enables His servants to overcome these.

In November, 1983, ABC television presented the movie about nuclear war, *The Day After.* The picture vividly described the horrors of a nuclear attack on Kansas. Pat Robertson of the Christian Broadcasting Network wanted to buy network time for spots after the showing of *The Day After* to tell people to call a number for information on "The Ultimate Hope" so that they could learn that with the Lord "the situation isn't hopeless." ABC turned down the commercials on the grounds that its "policy does not allow advocacy spots during prime time." Although the Christian Broadcasting Network did not take a position on the issue of nuclear weapons, ABC continued to bar Robertson from purchasing special commercial spots for a message of God's hope. Nevertheless, Robertson persevered. He was finally able to buy two TV spots on other channels. These two thirty-second spots ran in forty-six television markets which covered about 25 percent of the homes with television sets in the United States. Over 12,000 people responded to these special messages of God's hope!

Questions for Pupils on the Next Lesson. 1. In what ways are the claims of the false prophet regarding hearing God's Word different from the claims of a true prophet? 2. How would you tell which was a false prophet or which was real? 3. How does a person know the intent of the mind of the Lord? 4. When were some of the times when you were misled by the words of others? 5. What criteria can you use for judging the truth of what others say?

TOPIC FOR YOUTH
SOUND A WARNING!

When the Absurd Sounds Reasonable. In some ways, King Jehoiakim understood God's message through Jeremiah very, very well. The King thought it was ridiculous. And he wanted no parts of this God or His Word. He sensed the threat the prophecy posed. He slashed the scroll.

We church folks seem to have lost the feeling of shock and awe over God's Word. William Willimon puts it well:

"One of the dangers of being in church as often as I am is that it all starts to make sense. You speak of the Christian faith so casually and effortlessly that you begin to think, 'Fine thing, this Christianity. Makes good sense.' If you are not careful, you'll find yourself believing all sorts of things in church that you wouldn't dare let anyone put over on you in the real world. That which people would choke on in everyday speech, they will swallow hook, line and sinker if it's in a sermon. That's a blessing for those of us who get paid to preach Christ crucified.

"And so Kierkegaard could say, 'Christianity has taken a giant step into the absurd,' and again 'remove from Christianity its ability to shock . . . and it is altogether destroyed. It then becomes a tiny, superficial thing, capable neither of inflicting deep wounds or of healing them.'

"It's when the absurd starts to sound reasonable that we should begin to worry. 'Blessed are the meek.' 'Thou shalt not kill.' 'Love your enemies,' 'Go, sell all you have and give to the poor.'

"Be honest now. Blessed are the meek? Try being meek tomorrow when you go to work and see how far you get. Meekness is fine for church, but in the real world. . . ? In the real world, the meek get to go home early with a pink slip and a pat on the back. Blessed are those who are peacemakers; they shall get done to them what they loathe to do to others. Blessed are the merciful; they shall get it done to them a second time. Blessed are those who are persecuted for righteousness' sake; they shall be called fanatics. . . .

"As Paul says, when you hear the gospel, not with Sunday morning ears but with Monday morning ears, it can sound foolish indeed—tragically foolish or comically foolish—depending on your point of view. For as urbane, worldly wise Gentiles, a crucified God strikes us as comic foolishness."—William H. Willimon, *On a Wild and Windy Mountain*, Nashville: Abingdon, 1984.

Sounding the Warning. "Nuclear war is the single most urgent problem facing the human family today. Even before it happens, the global armaments of large and small countries alike are preparing the world as a tinderbox for the final conflagration, depriving two-thirds of the world's children of food, adequate clothing and shelter. Seven hundred billion dollars are spent per year on the conventional and nuclear arms race, and the wealthy Western nations and the Soviet Union are peddlers of death and armaments to Third World countries. Unless we can break the cycle of corporate greed manifested by the role of armaments of death, the future of the planet is in gross jeopardy."—Helen Mary Caldicott.

Study in Contrasts. People complain about the cost to the government for subsidizing the school lunch program for low-income children. It costs about $1.20 per meal. At the same time, the United States subsidizes the top military officials at the Pentagon for meals in the amount of $14.00 per meal. What would Jeremiah and the prophets have had to say about this? What does the disparity in subsidies say about our values? What about the message of Scripture warning us to show concern for the poor and helpless?

Questions for Pupils on the Next Lesson. 1. How can you tell between the words of a false prophet and a true prophet? 2. What happens when a nation flouts God's Word? 3. Will evil deeds ever bring peace? 4. Have you ever been misled by someone's words which supposedly were based on God's will? 5. How can you judge whether someone is speaking the truth or not?

LESSON V—JUNE 29

GOD'S TESTS OF A TRUE PROPHET

Background Scripture: Jeremiah 23:9–40; 27; 28
Devotional Reading: Jeremiah 23:33–40

KING JAMES VERSION

JEREMIAH 23 16 Thus saith the LORD of hosts, Hearken not unto the words of the prophets that prophesy unto you; they make you vain: they speak a vision of their own heart, *and* not out of the mouth of the LORD.

17 They say still unto them that despise me, The LORD hath said, Ye shall have peace; and they say unto every one that walketh after the imagination of his own heart, No evil shall come upon you.

18 For who hath stood in the counsel of the LORD, and hath perceived and heard his word? who hath marked his word, and heard *it?*

21 I have not sent these prophets, yet they ran: I have not spoken to them, yet they prophesied.

22 But if they had stood in my counsel, and had caused my people to hear my words, then they should have turned them from their evil way, and from the evil of their doings.

28 5 Then the prophet Jeremiah said unto the prophet Hananiah in the presence of the priests, and in the presence of all the people that stood in the house of the LORD,

6 Even the prophet Jeremiah said, Amen: the LORD do so: the LORD perform thy words which thou hast prophesied, to bring again the vessels of the LORD's house, and all that is carried away captive, from Babylon into this place.

7 Nevertheless, hear thou now this word that I speak in thine ears, and in the ears of all the people;

8 The prophets that have been before me and before thee of old prophesied both against many countries, and against great kingdoms, of war, and of evil, and of pestilence.

9 The prophet which prophesieth of peace, when the word of the prophet shall come to pass, *then* shall the prophet be known, that the LORD hath truly sent him.

15 Then said the prophet Jeremiah unto Hananiah the prophet, Hear now, Hananiah; the LORD hath not sent thee; but thou makest this people to trust in a lie.

16 Therefore thus saith the LORD; Behold, I will cast thee from off the face of the earth: this year thou shalt die.

REVISED STANDARD VERSION

JEREMIAH 23 16 Thus says the LORD of hosts: "Do not listen to the words of the prophets who prophesy to you, filling you with vain hopes; they speak visions of their own minds, not from the mouth of the LORD. 17 They say continually to those who despise the word of the LORD, 'It shall be well with you'; and to everyone who stubbornly follows his own heart, they say, 'No evil shall come upon you.'"

18 For who among them has stood in the council of the LORD
   to perceive and to hear his word,
   or who has given heed to his word and listened?

21 "I did not send the prophets, yet they ran;
   I did not speak to them, yet they prophesied.

22 But if they had stood in my council,
   then they would have proclaimed my words to my people,
   and they would have turned them from their evil way,
   and from the evil of their doings."

28 5 Then the prophet Jeremiah spoke to Hananiah the prophet in the presence of the priests and all the people who were standing in the house of the LORD; 6 and the prophet Jeremiah said, "Amen! May the LORD do so; may the LORD make the words which you have prophesied come true, and bring back to this place from Babylon the vessels of the house of the LORD, and all the exiles. 7 Yet hear now this word which I speak in your hearing and in the hearing of all the people. 8 The prophets who preceded you and me from ancient times prophesied war, famine, and pestilence against many countries and great kingdoms. 9 As for the prophet who prophesies peace, when the word of that prophet comes to pass, then it will be known that the LORD has truly sent the prophet."

15 And Jeremiah the prophet said to the prophet Hananiah, "Listen, Hananiah, the LORD has not sent you, and you have made this people trust in a lie. 16 Therefore thus says the LORD: 'Behold, I will remove you from the face of the earth. This very year you shall die.'"

KEY VERSE: *Thus says the Lord of hosts:* "Do not listen to the words of the prophets who prophesy to you, filling you with vain hopes; they speak visions of their own minds, not from the mouth of the Lord." *Jeremiah 23:16.*

HOME DAILY BIBLE READINGS

June   23.   M.   *A Messiah Is Promised.* Jeremiah 23:1–8.
June   24.   T.   *False Prophets Condemned.* Jeremiah 23:9–15.
June   25.   W.   *Warning Against False Prophets.* Jeremiah 23:16–22.
June   26.   T.   *Prophets of Deceit.* Jeremiah 23:23–32.
June   27.   F.   *Reject False Prophets.* Jeremiah 27:16–22.
June   28.   S.   *Fulfillment Validates True Prophecy.* Jeremiah 28:10–17.
June   29.   S.   *A False Prophet Is Challenged.* Jeremiah 23:33–40.

BACKGROUND

It sometimes comes as a surprise to some to learn that there were false prophets as well as true prophets in the Bible. If it is disconcerting to you to learn this discomfiting fact, imagine what it must have been like to the people living in the midst of the claims of the true and false prophets!

The false prophet also claims to be speaking for God. Usually, he utters the same "religious" words. He often uses the kind of props popular with those purporting to speak for the Lord. The false prophet always gains an audience. And his words are well-received. He says what people want to hear, and therefore he receives good publicity and profuse compliments. When a person who insists he speaks for the Lord acts sincerely, prays piously, preaches forcibly, and rarely raises justice issues, he gets invited to the royal palace for dinner parties to offer the blessing. When such a spokesman for the Lord becomes popular, who can question his credentials? Most people assume that he is truly anointed by God.

In Jeremiah's time, a flock of such phony prophets had sprung up in Jerusalem. In actuality, they were merely yes-men to King Jehoiakim and his successor, Zedekiah. They gave divine blessing to the shoddy and shady activities of the Jerusalem upper crust.

Meanwhile, life in the royal capital was like a wild party on a sinking ship in which the revelers refused to heed the disaster calls. King Zedekiah, the last king of Judah, and his advisers were entering into silly, futile schemes with the Egyptians to oppose the Babylonians. Jeremiah, the true prophet, appeared one day wearing a yoke. It was a vivid way of advocating submission to Babylon because Zedekiah's plots to revolt would only bring a terrible end to the kingdom. False prophets led by Hananiah claimed confidently that they spoke for God and smashed Jeremiah's yoke. The false prophets, using the same religious vocabulary as Jeremiah, insisted that the Lord would never permit Babylon to destroy Jerusalem or conquer Judah, and assured King Zedekiah and all hearers that God would speedily smash Babylon. Jeremiah predicted death for Hananiah, and within two months the lying false prophet died!

The nation, meanwhile, teetered closer to its inevitable final day of doom.

NOTES ON THE PRINTED TEXT

The difference between Jeremiah and the false prophets was great. The two parties were at odds with one another. Jeremiah spoke of the evilness of the false prophets. According to Jeremiah, the false prophets walked in lies, committed adultery, and committed wickedness by strengthening the hands of the evildoers (*see* vs. 14). He urged the people not to listen to the words of these prophets. These men claimed to prophesy in God's name saying they had heard the Word of the Lord when they had not. *They speak visions of their own minds, not from the mouth of the Lord.* These men are *filling you with vain hopes.* The false prophets spoke of peace and prosperity rather than righteousness. These prophets claimed peace was coming while God was announcing judgment. They did nothing but delude individuals.

They say continually . . . "It shall be well with you"; and . . . "no evil shall come upon you." These statements were vain hopes. They offered soothing words instead of calling for repentance. Jeremiah reproved the false prophets for their assurance of well-being to those who flouted God's Word. If they were true prophets who *stood in the council of the Lord* to receive the Word of God, they would preach differently. True prophets knew that evil deeds could not bring peace. Had they perceived God's Word and *given heed to his word,* they would prophesy the truth. *But if they had stood in my counsel,* Jeremiah reiterates later, then they would have *proclaimed my words to my people.* True prophets have been in the council of the Lord and know the intent of the mind of the Lord. Again, the tone of Jeremiah's preaching returned to a need for repentance, especially amongst the false prophets. *They would have turned them from their evil way, and from their evil doings.*

Christians feel compelled to be peacemakers and attempt to stop conflicts. On the other hand, Jeremiah started conflicts. His preaching produced conflict with the false prophets, especially Hananiah. Hananiah confidently claimed that he spoke for God but Jeremiah did not. Using Jeremiah's vocabulary, he insisted that God would never permit Babylon to conquer Judah. Instead, God would smash the Babylonians.

Jeremiah countered with *Amen! May the Lord do so; may the Lord make the words which you have prophesied come true.* Acknowledging his own sympathy for Judah and his hope that Hananiah's prophecy would come to be, Jeremiah said, "May God confirm the truth of what you have said." Jeremiah was sincere. As a Jew, he honestly hoped that he could believe what Hananiah has said.

Jeremiah, however, insisted that prophetic tradition rested on his side. *The prophets who preceded me from ancient times prophesied war, famine, and pestilence against many countries and great kingdoms.* Jeremiah built the case that he was more in keeping with the prophetic tradition than Hananiah. Hananiah's prophecies contradicted the prophetic tradition. Jeremiah also noted that a prophet's ministry was validated when the prophecies came true. *As for the prophet who prophesies peace,* (as Hananiah did) *when the word of the prophet comes to pass, then it will be known that the Lord has truly sent the prophet.*

Jeremiah then reminded his hearers of the penalty of false prophecy (*see* Deuteronomy 18:20). The penalty was death. Jeremiah sentenced Hananiah. *Listen, Hananiah, the Lord has not sent you, and you have made this people trust in a lie. Therefore . . . the Lord will remove you from the face of the earth. This very year you shall die.* And he did die!

SUGGESTIONS TO TEACHERS

You and your class already sense that not everyone who claims to speak on God's authority is to be heeded. You and those listening to your lesson can recall instances of shady characters, screwballs, and charlatans who insisted that they were preaching and acting as the Lord's agents. False prophets are still with us. You may also have some misgivings about others who aren't as obviously "false." And you may be perplexed at times when clergymen or religious leaders, each presenting proper credentials and using religious words, come out on opposite sides of a moral issue. Who is right? How can you tell? What are the tests of a true prophet?

The Scripture describing Jeremiah's encounter with Hananiah offers helpful insights in sorting out the true from the false prophets.

1. *BROKEN HEART.* Jeremiah and true prophets ache for their people. They weep for the sins and hurts of society. Do those in your class have such a broken heart for our broken world?

2. *UNDER GOD'S INFLUENCE.* The true prophet senses that he is helplessly overcome by the burden of being God's person. Jeremiah even described his situation under the influence of the Lord in the way a drunk might state he is under the influence of alcohol. Do those in your class feel they are under God's authority in this way?

3. *CLEAR VIEW.* The true prophet, being under God's influence, usually sees more perceptively than others. The real prophet of God understands what's going on in the world more than others because he or she examines every event in the light of God's will. Do your class members perceive this?

4. *MORAL MINORITY.* God's true prophets are always lonely and few, always outnumbered and outshouted by the shrill know-it-all voices of the false prophets. God, however, never plays the "numbers game"; He never relies on majorities. He most often works through a despised minority.

5. *BURNED AND HAMMERED.* The tests of the true prophet also include "the pain test." That is, how much has he been forced to suffer for God? How much has he been hurt and burned and hammered by those opposing God's Word? Remind your class that being Christ's means accepting a share of His suffering for others.

6. *BURDEN OF THE LORD.* Jeremiah 23:33–40 describes the responsibility which must be accepted by a true prophet as "the burden of the Lord." Have your class members willingly picked up their share of these burdens?

7. *POLITICAL PARTICULARS.* A true prophet is deeply concerned about and involved in the life of the community and nation. Furthermore, the real prophet deals in specifics. He asks himself, "What would God have us understand what He thinks now?" The true prophet makes every effort to apply his faith to the current crises in his country.

TOPIC FOR ADULTS
GOD'S TESTS OF A TRUE PROPHET

Prophets for Profits. In 1984, William Drexler and members of his Life Science Church discovered again that holding a church charter and claiming to be a church does not prove that they are doing the Lord's work. Even the Internal Revenue Service questioned their assertions of being prophets and ministers.

Eighty-one persons who became "mail-order ministers" to avoid income taxes agreed to pay $1.5 million in back taxes, interest, and penalties, the Internal Revenue Service said. The IRS said that the eighty-one—all members of the Life Science Church—were among ninety-one church members who were under investigation as "illegal tax protesters." The remaining ten cases are pending. The church, founded by its self-styled archbishop, William Drexler, a former Minnesota lawyer, sold mail-order ministries to individuals, claiming that they could avoid federal income taxes by forming a church, taking a vow of poverty and donating all their assets to the church, the IRS said. It said that under the plan the church, which has its headquarters in San Diego, was to pay the personal expense of the "ministers."

Drexler was convicted in California in 1982 on twenty-six criminal tax violations, including conspiracy to help others evade tax. He was sentenced to five years in prison and five years probation and fined $50,000. According to testimony at his trial, he sold the church credentials for $560 to $4,000. Some of the protesters became disenchanted following Drexler's conviction and got accountants to help them solve their problems with the IRS.

The IRS says contributions to organizations operating exclusively for religious purposes are deductible under the law. But it says holding a church charter and claiming to be a church does not prove that an organization operates for religious purposes. The Tax Court has ruled in numerous cases that mail-order churches exist for the economic benefit of their founders and not exclusively for religious purposes.

Words and the Music. Mark Twain never seemed to forget the rough vocabulary which he picked up as a Mississippi river-boat captain. His speech in private was filled with profanity. His devoted wife tried many times to have him curb the use of swear words. Twain, however, continued as before. One day, his wife decided to try a different tack. When Twain came in the front door for dinner, she greeted him with a long line of vulgar expletives and profane speech. Twain listened impassively. When she finished, blushing for having used words she had never spoken before, the famous author smiled and said softly, "Honey, you have the words, but you don't have the music."

A false prophet only has the words. A true prophet has both the words of the Lord and the music, so to speak. The genuine prophet speaks with the authority and authenticity of a person who understands both the message and the mind of God. Such a person was Jeremiah!

True or False Prophets? In a gesture of despair and with a prediction that worse was yet to come, the editor of *The Bulletin of the Atomic Scientists* advanced the minute hand of their famous "doomsday clock" as a symbol of mankind's advance toward the nuclear abyss. The movement of the clock's hands as they appear on the face of each issue of the magazine symbolizes the editors' evaluation of the danger of nuclear warfare. The hands were fixed on December 23, 1983, at three minutes to midnight. They have been closer to midnight only once in the clock's thirty-seven-year history—in 1953, following the development of the hydrogen bomb by the United States and the Soviet Union. The one-minute advance was the first change since 1981, when the editors cited the development of nuclear weapons designed for fighting was, instead of deterring war, a dangerous step in promoting it.

However, opponents to arms control and advocates of additional nuclear build-up denounced the people who advanced the hands of the "doomsday clock." Some critics of *The Bulletin of Atomic Scientists* editors accused them of being Communist sympathizers, unpatriotic, and unrealistic.

Which do you think are the true prophets and which do you think are the false? Why? What might Jeremiah have said?

Questions for Pupils on the Next Lesson. 1. What did Jeremiah mean when he talked about a "remnant"? 2. What did Jeremiah mean when he discussed a new covenant? 3. What are the emphases of this new covenant? 4. Have you ever found yourself in an apparently hopeless situation? 5. Do you rely mostly on external authority or internal authority?

TOPIC FOR YOUTH
THE TEST

More Than Advice. Movie actress Rosalind Russell was once on a cruise. One day on the ship, she found herself sitting next to a man suffering from a nasty cold. After hearing him cough and sneeze, Ros Russell turned to him and gave him a long lecture on what to do about his cold. "You should go to bed early, drink lots of fluids, and take two aspirin. I'm sure you'll feel much better in the morning." The man looked at her blankly and said nothing. After a long silent period during which the man made no comment about her prescriptions, Miss Russell said, "Perhaps you don't recognize me. I am Rosalind Russell, and I make movies, in Hollywood, California." The man in the chair next to her said, "Yes, I know. My name is Dr. Charles Mayo, and I run a medical clinic in Rochester, Minnesota."

The false prophets were free with cheap advice and easy cures, but didn't seem to understand what was really ailing the nation. Like Rosalind Russell presuming to prescribe medical treatment without medical knowledge, the false prophets offered religious nostrums without knowing the Lord. Real physicians, like true prophets, understand more than the superficialities!

Whom Do You Heed? Are you critical of the claims of advertisers? Do you allow yourself to be manipulated by advertisements? Do you find yourself aware that advertisers are trying to persuade you but are not sure how to deal with it?

Dr. Marcia C. Linn, an educational psychologist at the University of California at Berkeley's Lawrence Hall of Science, has been conducting research on the problem of teenagers being misused by promoters of many products.

"Advertisers, it appears," said Linn, "succeed in defeating critical analysis of their potentially misleading messages."

Linn said she and her team decided to focus on teens and advertising because "this area seemed to cut across the spectrum the best. Adolescents see 20,000 advertisements each year. We thought that that was an area where they were going to reason well."

In short, the psychologist summarized, these teenagers are both aware and gullible when judging an advertisement. They may know what an ad says. They may even know that what the ad says may not be entirely true. But from that point on, they are often unable to translate their knowledge into practical action. She concluded that unless personal experience told them otherwise, teenagers tended to accept the claims of many advertisers—even while criticizing the tests and comparisons used in the ads.

False prophets are trying to lure you with their false promises. How do you listen?

The Test. There is an old story from the European Jewish tradition in which a follower comes up to a renowned leader. "Rabbi," says the disciple, "I love you." The old rabbi is not moved by the words, but looks intently at the follower and answers, "Do you know where I am hurting?"

"No," stammers the disciple.

"Then how can you love me if you do not know what gives me pain?"

The true prophet knows what gives pain and also loves!

Questions for Pupils on the Next Lesson. 1. Exactly what is Jeremiah talking about when he promises that God will raise up a remnant? 2. What is a covenant? 3. What are the terms of the "new covenant" discussed by Jeremiah? 4. What kind of value system have you adopted for yourself? 5. What motivates you the most, external authorities or an internal authority?

LESSON VI—JULY 6

HOPE FOR THE FUTURE

Background Scripture: Jeremiah 31
Devotional Reading: Jeremiah 30:18–22

KING JAMES VERSION

JEREMIAH 31 2 Thus saith the LORD, The people *which were* left of the sword found grace in the wilderness; *even* Israel, when I went to cause him to rest.

3 The LORD hath appeared of old unto me, *saying,* Yea, I have loved thee with an everlasting love: therefore with lovingkindness have I drawn thee.

4 Again I will build thee, and thou shalt be built, O virgin of Israel: thou shalt again be adorned with thy tabrets, and shalt go forth in the dances of them that make merry.

5 Thou shalt yet plant vines upon the mountains of Samaria: the planters shall plant, and shall eat *them* as common things.

6 For there shall be a day, *that* the watchmen upon the mount Ephraim shall cry, Arise ye, and let us go up to Zion unto the LORD our God.

31 Behold, the days come, saith the LORD, that I will make a new covenant with the house of Israel, and with the house of Judah:

32 Not according to the covenant that I made with their fathers, in the day *that* I took them by the hand to bring them out of the land of Egypt; which my covenant they brake, although I was an husband unto them, saith the LORD:

33 But this *shall be* the covenant that I will make with the house of Israel; After those days, saith the LORD, I will put my law in their inward parts, and write it in their hearts; and will be their God, and they shall be my people.

34 And they shall teach no more every man his neighbour, and every man his brother, saying, Know the LORD: for they shall all know me, from the least of them unto the greatest of them, saith the LORD: for I will forgive their iniquity, and I will remember their sin no more.

REVISED STANDARD VERSION

JEREMIAH 31 2 Thus says the LORD:
"The people who survived the sword
    found grace in the wilderness;
when Israel sought for rest,
3 the LORD appeared to him from afar.
I have loved you with an everlasting love;
    therefore I have continued my faithful-
        ness to you.
4 Again I will build you, and you shall be
        built,
    O virgin Israel!
Again you shall adorn yourself with tim-
        brels,
    and shall go forth in the dance of the mer-
        rymakers.
5 Again you shall plant vineyards upon the
        mountains of Samaria:
    the planters shall plant,
    and shall enjoy the fruit.
6 For there shall be a day when watchmen
        will call
    in the hill country of Ephraim:
    'Arise, and let us go up to Zion, to the LORD
        our God.'"
31 "Behold, the days are coming, says the LORD, when I will make a new covenant with the house of Israel and the house of Judah, 32 not like the covenant which I made with their fathers when I took them by the hand to bring them out of the land of Egypt, my covenant which they broke, though I was their husband, says the LORD. 33 But this is the covenant which I will make with the house of Israel after those days, says the LORD: I will put my law within them, and I will write it upon their hearts; and I will be their God, and they shall be my people. 34 And no longer shall each man teach his neighbor and each his brother, saying, 'Know the LORD,' for they shall all know me, from the least of them to the greatest, says the LORD; for I will forgive their iniquity, and I will remember their sin no more."

KEY VERSE: *I have loved you with an everlasting love; therefore I have continued my faithfulness to you.* Jeremiah 31:3.

HOME DAILY BIBLE READINGS

June	30.	M.	*Jeremiah Imprisoned.* Jeremiah 32:1–5.
July	1.	T.	*Jeremiah Buys a Field.* Jeremiah 32:6–16.
July	2.	W.	*Jeremiah's Prayer.* Jeremiah 32:16–25.
July	3.	T.	*The Promise of God.* Jeremiah 32:36–41.
July	4.	F.	*The Promise of Prosperity.* Jeremiah 32:42–44.
July	5.	S.	*The Promise of Restoration.* Jeremiah 33:1–9.
July	6.	S.	*Hope for the Future.* Jeremiah 33:12–18.

BACKGROUND

The future held no hope, as far as most citizens of Judah were concerned. The nation was doomed. For a long time, except for a few devout prophets, nearly everyone carried the illusion that the Lord would never permit anything disastrous to happen to the great Temple of Jerusalem or the people of Judah, His chosen agents on earth. Now the fury of the Babylonian armies under the ruthless Nebuchadnezzar was being unleashed against Jerusalem.

If only the leaders of Judah had not deluded themselves! They had foolishly allowed themselves to become involved in intrigues against the Babylonian overlords. Ever since Nebuchadnezzar had defeated Pharaoh Neco of Egypt at the pivotal battle of Carchemish in 605 B.C., the Babylonians had been in control. However, they did not interfere unduly with tiny Judah. If Judah's kings, Jehoiakim and Zedekiah, had not busied themselves so stupidly in conniving with the Egyptians against Nebuchadnezzar, the horrors of the Babylonian invasion probably would not have occurred.

Nebuchadnezzar besieged and captured Jerusalem. He carried off the cream of the population to captivity in Babylon. The Exile for the people of Judah began—the great catastrophe which most never expected could ever happen happened! In such turmoil, nearly all the people of Judah despaired of hope. Jerusalem was a smoking shambles. The Temple was a ravaged shell. Families were being separated. Thousands were being whipped in chains along a 600 mile forced march, knowing they would never again see their beloved homeland.

One of the handful of people of faith who could still speak hopefully of the future was Jeremiah. We don't know exactly what happened to Jeremiah or where he was living except that he was not among those carried off to exile in Babylon. But he wrote a letter to his countrymen in that distant land. He didn't write, "I told you so!" as he could have. After all, this prophet had been denounced, condemned, and imprisoned for his warnings—and his warnings had come true. Instead, this sensitive man of God wrote of the Lord's mercy. Speaking for God, he told his exiled friends and family hopeful words: "I have loved you with an everlasting love: therefore I have continued my faithfulness to you" (Jeremiah 31:3).

NOTES ON THE PRINTED TEXT

The word *homecoming* conjures up mental pictures of fall football games, tweed-suited queens, and parades. It also brings to mind a return, be it to an alma mater or to a family home or to a reunion. Jeremiah is talking about Israel's homecoming. Jeremiah has in mind a return home for the exiles. Through this lovely poem, Jeremiah reminds those that were left of the grace of the Lord.

Speaking for the Lord, Jeremiah says, *The people who survived the sword found grace in the wilderness when Israel sought for rest.* He reminds the people of the favor of God experienced by their ancestors in their wanderings during the Exodus. By God's action, these ancestors escaped the armies of Pharaoh. *The Lord appeared to him from afar.* Jeremiah recalls the Sinai experience when the Lord appeared to Moses, or Jeremiah has in mind the pillars of cloud and fire that went before Israel in the wilderness.

I have loved you with an everlasting love. Jeremiah declares God's everlasting love and care. *Therefore I have continued my faithfulness to you.* Love and faithfulness are seen as one and the same in this parallel statement. Jeremiah implies that God's grace is unending.

To prove this point, he offers promises of hope and comfort. Even though there has been terrible judgment made on the people through the exile, there will be a homecoming. *I will build you, and you shall be built, O virgin Israel.* Israel is personified as a virgin. As God's bride, she will be built securely once again. The

Lord promised to rebuild the cities from the remnant of God's chosen people. Again, the people *shall go forth in the dance of merrymakers.* There will be music of joy and happiness. Moreover, God promises to rebuild the lives of the people. *Once again you shall plant vineyards* and *the planters . . . shall enjoy the fruit.* With security restored, people will plant and enjoy the fruits of their labors. In the future, people will also be able to return to the Temple to worship. *Arise, and let us go up to Zion, to the Lord our God.*

Three little pieces follow the poem. The second, and best known piece, describes the restoration of all Israel through God's new covenant. *The days are coming . . . when I will make a new covenant with the house of Israel and the house of Judah.* A new covenant, *not like the covenant . . . made with their fathers* during the Exodus, is promised to God's people. *They broke* this original covenant. Though Israel was a virgin and expected to be faithful, she proved unfaithful to God whom Jeremiah likens to Israel's *husband.* However, the day is coming when God will forgive Israel's sins and offer a new covenant. Under this covenant, God's Law will be written, not on stone tablets, but in the hearts of God's people. *I will put my law within them, and I will write it upon their hearts.* This new covenant will emphasize a personal knowledge of God. *I will be their God, and they shall be my people.* In addition, *they shall know me, from the least of them to the greatest.*

Another feature of the new covenant will be the emphasis on the forgiveness of sins. *I will forgive their iniquity, and I will remember their sin no more.*

SUGGESTIONS TO TEACHERS

In the Prisoner-of-War stockades during the Vietnam War, some captured American servicemen endured terrible torture and deprivation—and survived. In other cases, prisoners suffered little—but died. Military authorities were baffled. Psychiatrists interviewed some of those who were finally freed. Among the findings: men who had a religious faith more often continued to cling to hope for the future, and this hope motivated them to live in spite of an apparently hopeless situation.

Such a disclosure should not surprise Christians such as you and those in your class. It merely reinforces what the Bible repeatedly states. In fact, the lesson for this Sunday from Jeremiah 31 puts it well.

Remember that there are probably some in your class who need this word of hope for the future. Bring them God's message for their lives that they may have new resolve to live.

1. *REMEMBRANCE AND REMNANT.* Jeremiah 31:2–4 is part of the prophet's letter in which he reminds his hearers of God's love for Israel. Do your people recall evidence of the Lord's love in their past lives? Have them offer examples. Remembering these reinforces hope for the future. Furthermore, Jeremiah's letter tells that God keeps a remnant of His people to continue His work. Help your class members to ponder the fact the Christian church members are a kind of divine remnant bringing hope in the midst of hopelessness in our culture.

2. *REDEMPTION AND REJOICING.* Through Jesus Christ, God has brought us release from the various forms of captivity which hold us. He freed the Jews from captivity in Babylon, and He restores us from exile from God! He offers each person a hope for the future! This means joy! Have your class enumerate some of the kinds of captivity and exile in which people today find themselves. Most of all, let the class realize the sense of release and joy which Christ our Deliverer brings!

3. *RETURN AND REPENTANCE.* Here is an opportunity to use the imagery

of the Exiles' promised return to illustrate the meaning of the Gospel. Do not forget the stress Jeremiah places on repentance (note carefully such verses as Jeremiah 31:19).

4. *RENEWAL AND RESPONSIBILITY.* Jeremiah announces that the time will come when a New Covenant will be given (31:31–34). Do your people realize that this promised New Covenant has been granted through Jesus Christ? But the New Covenant also means new responsibilities. The new law, coming as a result of the New Covenant, is written on the hearts of faithful believers. And it means that each person must "teach his neighbor and his brother, saying, 'Know the Lord' " (31:34).

TOPIC FOR ADULTS
HOPE FOR THE FUTURE

New Beginning Out of a Bad Situation. Jeremiah was able to see hope in the midst of disaster because of his knowledge of God. Persons of faith discover that God offers new beginnings in the midst of dismal situations.

When John Hawkins broke his ankle in a skiing accident a couple of years ago, friends commiserated with him on the unfortunate accident. Hawkins was incapacitated with a heavy, uncomfortable cast. There seemed to be little future for Hawkins for several months. The pressure in the cast grew painful, but worst of all was the itching. One day about a week after the accident, Hawkins chipped a hole in the cast with a hammer and chisel in a bid to relieve the pressure. While cleaning up the mess with a vacuum cleaner, Hawkins, on a whim, put the vacuum hose over the hole in the cast. "To my surprise," Hawkins said, "I could feel air being pulled through both ends of the cast." He found it very soothing.

Hawkins went to work with an architect friend, and together they designed a "cast ventilator," which is simply a flanged disc with air holes. The ventilator is designed to be inserted in a cast while it is being applied or plastered in later. More than one may be needed for a large cast. A vacuum hose can then be used to pull air or even talcum powder into the cast to relieve itching. Hawkin's company now is manufacturing and distributing the ventilators to doctors and hospitals across the country.

Just as John Hawkins could take a bad situation and use it for good, so God may take our hopeless situations and turn them into opportunities for new beginnings. With God, there is always a future!

True Patriot. Jeremiah was sometimes accused of being unpatriotic. In fact, he was arrested and imprisoned for pointing out the injustices his countrymen were permitting. However, Jeremiah tried to call the nation to be true to its heritage. In spite of the tribulations in the present, the prophet knew God had plans for the future. These are the marks of a true prophet! These are the signs of a real patriot!

In spite of cruel injustices, Martin Luther King, Jr., loved his native land and almost exactly twenty years ago dreamed his wonderous, prophetic dream on its behalf. That was an expression of patriotism.

In March 1980, Archbishop Oscar Romero of El Salvador was slain by an assassin's bullet. Not long before his death he said, "As a pastor I am obliged by divine command to give my life for those whom I love and that is for all Salvadorans, even for those who may assassinate me. If the threats should come to pass, I offer God from this very moment my blood for the redemption and resurrection of El Salvador." That was love of country.

Afraid of a Hinge-Tail Bingbuffer. "I wanted to show you a picture of a Hinge-Tail Bingbuffer this morning, but I couldn't find one. Maybe one of you could describe a Hinge-Tail Bingbuffer for us. You can't? Well, I'm not surprised. No one's seen one of those critters for nearly 100 years. They used to tell about them in Missouri, though.

"They used to say that a Hinge-Tail Bingbuffer was shaped something like a hippopotamus, only considerably larger with a tail some forty feet long. It was a very slow animal, we are told, because it had very short legs. Underneath its jaws it had a huge pouch. When it wanted to catch something to eat, it simply took a rock out of its pouch with its big tail, and used its tail like a slingshot and threw the rock and hit its victim. That is why it was called a Hinge-Tail Bingbuffer. At least that is what the folks in Missouri say.

"Personally, I doubt if there ever was such a thing as a Hinge-Tail Bingbuffer. I think someone's imagination got carried away with him. Imagination can do that sometimes—it can make us afraid of things that don't really exist.

"Has your imagination ever made you afraid? Perhaps your imagination has made you afraid of the dark. Or maybe at school, your imagination makes you think that other people won't like you, so you become very shy. Our imagination can do things like that to us. It can make us so afraid.

"God doesn't want us to be afraid. He tells people in the Bible time after time, 'Don't be afraid.' So the next time our imagination makes us afraid, let's say to ourselves, 'Aw, that's just a Hinge-Tail Bingbuffer. It can't hurt me.' Then let's ask God to take our fear away."—*Christian Communications Laboratory,* 7312 Badgett Rd., Knoxville, Tennessee, 37919.

Questions for Pupils on the Next Lesson. 1. Who was Ezekiel? Where did he live? Why did he write? 2. How would you describe Ezekiel's experience of God's presence? 3. Who were those in exile and why were they exiles? 4. Are you faced with a new role or a career change? 5. Why are we often hesitant to take a position opposed by others?

TOPIC FOR YOUTH
GOD'S EVERLASTING LOVE

Looking for the Wounded. During a part of the Vietnam War, an Army medic caused a lot of discussion by leaving the field hospital and going into areas where there had been casualties reported. He would look for those who might have been overlooked or who needed medical attention. Occasionally, this medic came across a badly wounded soldier and dragged him back to safety and the field hospital and was reprimanded because once in a while he brought back not only Americans but also Vietcong. One day, he was seen on a jungle path by an officer and asked what he was doing out there. "I'm looking for wounded," the medic replied; "That's my job."

God's everlasting love, Jeremiah knew, was like that medic's. He cared about all peoples. He sought out the wounded regardless of nationality or status. His everlasting love has been shown us through Jesus Christ.

Our task is to continue that seeking, caring ministry.

Recorded in the Book. If you've ever met Lowell Davis, he will be able to tell you your name has been recorded in a book. In fact, he has written down the name of every person he can recall he has ever met. Ever since Davis was three years old, he has carefully listed the names of those he meets. He now has 679 pages in a yellow binder with 3,487 names. He has them carefully catalogued chronologically and by towns in which he has lived. Each name also carries a short description of the person listed.

God's everlasting love is such that He remembers and knows each of us as special persons. He recalls us well, and cares for each as if we were the only one.

New Life With Father. Jimmy Korf is back with his father. He left home after a family quarrel over twenty years ago. He lived in vacant houses, elevator shafts, and Chicago subway tunnels. He got mixed up in the drug scene. Hospitalized for hallucinations, Jimmy Korf was released to a halfway house in February, 1981. He got into a fight there, and left for the street. He became a filthy derelict scrambling for food in garbage cans. By the spring of 1983, Jimmy was down to ninety pounds from trying to exist on moldy buns, lettuce scraps, and dirty chicken parts. He was grimy with dirt and had bugs in his hair and lice on his body. His clothes were ripped by dogs which fought with him for scraps of food. Jimmy had been beaten and assaulted by other street people. At this point, reporter Kirk Johnson wrote an article for the Chicago *Sun-Times* describing the city's street people. Jimmy was interviewed. His picture—a haunted young man peering from behind a metal fence—was published. Meanwhile, Jimmy Korf's father had been looking for his son for many years. The elder Korf decided to come from the family home in Minnesota to Chicago. He saw the article and recognized his son. Father and son were reunited. Korf, senior, took Jimmy back home to Hovland, Minnesota, where Jimmy has begun a new life.

God's love is everlasting. He cannot put us out of mind. He will go to any length to have us reunited in a loving relationship with Him. He wants us to know the joy and security of being with Him.

Have you been found by the Lord who comes to you in the person of Jesus Christ?

Questions for Pupils on the Next Lesson. 1. What does the Bible tell you about Ezekiel? 2. Why were his people in exile in Babylon? 3. Have you ever felt separated and alone and without hope? 4. Do you ever feel a sense of strength beyond yourself? 5. Are you sometimes tempted to rebel against authority?

LESSON VII—JULY 13

EZEKIEL'S CALLING

Background Scripture: Ezekiel 1—3
Devotional Reading: Ezekiel 3:16–21

KING JAMES VERSION

EZEKIEL 1 Now it came to pass in the thirtieth year, in the fourth *month,* in the fifth *day* of the month, as I *was* among the captives by the river of Chebar *that* the heavens were opened, and I saw visions of God.

2 And he said unto me, Son of man, stand upon thy feet, and I will speak unto thee.

2 And the spirit entered into me when he spake unto me, and set me upon my feet, that I heard him that spake unto me.

3 And he said unto me, Son of man, I send thee to the children of Israel, to a rebellious nation that hath rebelled against me: they and their fathers have transgressed against me, *even* unto this very day.

4 For *they are* impudent children and stiff-hearted. I do send thee unto them; and thou shalt say unto them, Thus saith the Lord GOD.

5 And they, whether they will hear, or whether they will forbear, (for they *are* a rebellious house,) yet shall know that there hath been a prophet among them.

6 And thou, son of man, be not afraid of them, neither be afraid of their words, though briers and thorns *be* with thee, and thou dost dwell among scorpions: be not afraid of their words, nor be dismayed at their looks, though they *be* a rebellious house.

7 And thou shalt speak my words unto them, whether they will hear, or whether they will forbear: for they *are* most rebellious.

8 But thou, son of man, hear what I say unto thee; Be not thou rebellious like that rebellious house: open thy mouth, and eat that I give thee.

9 And when I looked, behold, a hand *was* sent unto me; and, lo, a roll of a book *was* therein;

10 And he spread it before me; and it *was* written within and without; and *there was* written therein lamentations, and mourning, and woe.

3 MOREOVER he said unto me, Son of man, eat that thou findest; eat this roll, and go speak unto the house of Israel.

2 So I opened my mouth, and he caused me to eat that roll.

3 And he said unto me, Son of man, cause thy belly to eat, and fill thy bowels with this roll that I give thee. Then did I eat *it;* and it was in my mouth as honey for sweetness.

REVISED STANDARD VERSION

EZEKIEL 1 In the thirtieth year, in the fourth month, on the fifth day of the month, as I was among the exiles by the river Chebar, the heavens were opened, and I saw visions of God.

2 And he said to me, "Son of man, stand upon your feet, and I will speak with you." 2 And when he spoke to me, the Spirit entered into me and set me upon my feet; and I heard him speaking to me. 3 And he said to me, "Son of man, I send you to the people of Israel, to a nation of rebels, who have rebelled against me; they and their fathers have transgressed against me to this very day. 4 The people also are impudent and stubborn: I send you to them; and you shall say to them, 'Thus says the Lord GOD.' 5 And whether they hear or refuse to hear (for they are a rebellious house) they will know that there has been a prophet among them. 6 And you, son of man, be not afraid of them, nor be afraid of their words, though briers and thorns are with you and you sit upon scorpions; be not afraid of their words, nor be dismayed at their looks, for they are a rebellious house. 7 And you shall speak my words to them, whether they hear or refuse to hear; for they are a rebellious house.

8 "But you, son of man, hear what I say to you; be not rebellious like that rebellious house; open your mouth, and eat what I give you." 9 And when I looked, behold, a hand was stretched out to me, and, lo, a written scroll was in it; 10 and he spread it before me; and it had writing on the front and on the back, and there was written on it words of lamentation and mourning and woe.

3 And he said to me, "Son of man, eat what is offered to you; eat this scroll, and go, speak to the house of Israel." 2 So I opened my mouth, and he gave me the scroll to eat. 3 And he said to me, "Son of man, eat this scroll that I give you and fill your stomach with it." Then I ate it; and it was in my mouth as sweet as honey.

KEY VERSE: You shall speak my words to them, whether they hear or refuse to hear. Ezekiel 2:7.

HOME DAILY BIBLE READINGS

July	*7.*	*M.*	*Ezekiel Called by God. Ezekiel 1:1-3, 28—2:7.*
July	*8.*	*T.*	*Message to the Exiles. Ezekiel 3:4-11.*
July	*9.*	*W.*	*Promise of Restoration. Ezekiel 11:14-21.*
July	*10.*	*T.*	*"Turn and Live." Ezekiel 18:25-32.*
July	*11.*	*F.*	*"A New Heart." Ezekiel 36:22-32.*
July	*12.*	*S.*	*The Ruin Shall Be Rebuilt. Ezekiel 36:33-38.*
July	*13.*	*S.*	*Prayer for Cleansing. Psalms 51:10-13.*

BACKGROUND

Ezekiel lived during the tumultuous period immediately before the fall of Jerusalem and during the period of exile in Babylon which followed. His career therefore overlapped Jeremiah's. Ezekiel was in many ways Jeremiah's successor. His writings echo Jeremiah's. His ministry extended from 593 B.C. (*see* Ezekiel 1:2) to about 563 B.C.

Ezekiel was a priest by birth. However, his oracles or sermons make him one of the most compelling preachers of the Bible. Scholars tell us that his beautiful Hebrew prose and poetry set him apart as one of the finest literary figures in our Scriptures.

His very name reflects his powerful sense of mission, for Ezekiel in Hebrew means "God strengthens." And how the Hebrew people needed to remember that the Lord does strengthen! At the time Ezekiel lived, his fellow citizens of Judah were suffering the trauma of seeing Jerusalem captured and most of the leaders deported.

The Babylonians captured and destroyed the magnificent city and the Temple. After the Babylonian capture, many from Judah lost faith in God's power or presence. Some of those carried off as exiles to Babylon felt that the Lord had let them down, others believed that God dwelt only in Jerusalem and couldn't be concerned about exiles far away in Babylonia.

Ezekiel's major ministry was to these people in exile. Throughout the series of oracles or sermons, this strong voice emphasized the abiding presence of God even among displaced people hundreds of miles from the sacred city. This great prophet constantly stressed that God continued to have a role in the events of the day, assuring his hearers that the nations "will know that I am the Lord." This line, in fact, occurs so often throughout Ezekiel's writings that it almost becomes a refrain. At the same time, Ezekiel underlined the need for personal responsibility to God. He made it clear that each individual was required to live a life of integrity before the Lord. Both collectively and individually, God's people were to remember that they had to exhibit a holy quality.

Ezekiel himself wrote out of an intense sense of personal call by God to live a holy life. By *holy*, he did not mean a smug piety. Rather, Ezekiel meant that he belonged to God, and that he was set apart for God's service.

His call by the Lord essentially is a summons to holiness. Remember, as you read Ezekiel's account of his calling that you also have been set apart and belong to God!

NOTES ON THE PRINTED TEXT

As I was among the exiles by the river Chebar, the heavens were opened and I saw visions of God. Ezekiel was a temple priest who was carried in captivity to Babylon with the cream of Judah's leadership. Ezekiel ministered to this group of exiles living near the Tel Avib plain for a period of twenty-two years, from 592 B.C. through 570 B.C. The upheaval of the exile was the event that carried God's personal summons to Ezekiel. It served to introduce the vision in which Ezekiel received his call to be a prophet.

"Son of man, stand upon your feet, and I will speak with you." Ezekiel experienced a theophany (an appearance of God to man) and saw the glory of the Lord (1:4-28). Conscious of being in God's presence and deeply aware of his own unworthiness and sinfulness, Ezekiel had fallen to his face. The title *Son of Man* acknowledged all people's unworthiness, weakness, and mortality in the presence of God. Nonetheless, Ezekiel was literally commanded to stand at attention, for God had orders to issue to him.

Do not literalize Ezekiel's call by God. It is pointless to argue whether or not God's voice can be picked up on a tape recorder. The beauty of Ezekiel's experience is smudged by trying to externalize the internal. Ezekiel is conscious of God speaking to him. The Spirit has entered him, has picked him up, and has empowered him. The overwhelming point of Ezekiel's vision is that he was called by God and commissioned to be a prophet.

However, Ezekiel's commission is a hard one. *I send you to the people of Israel, to a nation of rebels, who have rebelled against me, . . . and their fathers have transgressed against me.* Ezekiel is commissioned to speak against the nation's sinfulness. The exiles are part of Israel and share in her guilt. God's complaints against His people are that they are *impudent and stubborn.* Ezekiel drives home the point of their rebellious nature against God. *They are a rebellious house,* He repeats four times. Therefore, God calls Ezekiel to take a stand against the people's rebellion.

He is not concerned about success or results. *Whether they hear or refuse to hear* is repeated twice. Implied is the fact that responsibility lies with the people. Only they can respond. Israel, God's chosen, has made her own choice to become a rebellious, and therefore a rejected, house.

Ezekiel is not to be *afraid* or *dismayed.* Ezekiel is not to foster any notions that the experience will be an easy one. With depressing straight-forwardness, God promises that there will be pain and conflict. *Briers, thorns,* and *scorpions* all indicate the potential pain that Ezekiel will encounter as he fulfills the Lord's calling to him.

However, Ezekiel must fulfill his mission. He must complete his job, for Ezekiel's ministry to the exiles will emphasize the abiding presence of God among the Israelites. *They will know that there has been a prophet among them.* Israel will recognize Ezekiel is a prophet and that God is with her. Unlike Israel, Ezekiel must be faithful to his calling.

Ezekiel is commanded to obey the Word that he hears and sees. Before him is an *outstretched hand* containing a scroll. Unlike most scrolls which have writing only on the smooth surface, this scroll has *writing on the front and on the back . . . words of lamentation and mourning and woe.* God commanded Ezekiel to *eat the scroll, and go, speak to the house of Israel.* Ezekiel fulfills the command and eats the scroll. The taste in his mouth is *as sweet as honey.* Once again, do not literalize the call. The symbol of eating the scroll and devouring God's Word signifies that Ezekiel has received God's Word and call. Ezekiel is not to simply swallow God's Word but to digest it and to assimilate it in his body. This will make him a true prophet.

SUGGESTIONS TO TEACHERS

Some people think that it sounds spooky and grow uncomfortable when they hear someone talk of being "called" by God. Especially when they encounter a person with a dramatic conversion story capped with a call, some folks feel uncomfortable.

Actually, every Christian has a "calling." Perhaps that calling may not be in the form of a startling supernatural phenomenon, but each person calling himself or herself a Christian has had some kind of an encounter with the Lord.

Your lesson for today is intended to help your class members to take a closer look at what it means to have a calling from God. You will use Ezekiel's calling as the basis for your class discussion.

1. *VISION.* The Latin words *mysterium tremendum* were used by the church leaders for centuries to describe the sense of awe which a person experienced before the majestic Lord. No one, of course, can program such an experience. Nor can words ever adequately portray it. But each person in your class has known some moments of deep reverence because of being aware of Another. Prompt each person to try to relate at least one such time in his or her life. If the class is too big, break it into two or more sections and have the people share both the occasion of such a vision and what it meant or still means.

2. *VOICE.* A calling may seem to have a voice literally speaking to one, or it may be a sense of the Spirit's summoning one. No two calls by God are exactly the same. Don't expect yours to be like the next person's. The essential thing is to stress that each one in your class, knowing something of Jesus Christ, must have some consciousness of belonging to Him. There might not have been a dramatic shout from the heavens for you or those in your class, but you must realize that in the person of Jesus, God has been summoning you to be His.

3. *VOCATION.* God's call always entails a task. He never calls to confer a status, but always calls a person to undertake a form of service. Here, you can introduce the topic of holiness and being holy. Remind the class members that *holy* does not mean becoming a prig or posing as a supersaint, but basically means recognizing that they are set apart for God's service.

4. *VIOLATORS.* Part of Ezekiel's difficult service was being called to speak candidly to his own people. However, the Lord warned that this people would be hard and rebellious. They would be unwilling to hear words from the Lord. Being called usually entails being out of step with contemporaries. Ezekiel quickly discovered his call put him at odds with most of his countrymen. You, likewise, will find that your calling seldom brings you popularity.

5. *VIEWER.* Ezekiel likened himself to a watchman. In olden times, the watchman stood on the city walls, scrutinizing the distant horizon for possible danger and sounding a warning. Ezekiel and the prophets knew their calling was to watch for signs from God and from society, and report these to their people. Today, Christ's Church is to be such a viewer. You and I, the Church, have this assignment. How faithful and how bold are we in our task of watching what God is doing and what the enemy is threatening to do?

TOPIC FOR ADULTS
EZEKIEL: MESSENGER TO A REBELLIOUS PEOPLE

Modern Messenger to Rebellious People. Some say that author Aleksandr Solzhenitsyn is a modern-day prophet. Solzhenitsyn, an exile from the Soviet Union now living in the United States, has been hailed as a pioneer in the renaissance of faith in Russia and atheistic nations. He is also renowned for his dire warnings to both Eastern and Western nations for their godless ways. The prize-winning writer assails the West for its materialism, spiritual vapidity, and timidity in the face of Communism. Recently the author said that Western secularism has been gaining force since the late Middle Ages and that this "gradual sapping of strength from within" is perhaps a more dangerous threat to faith than violent attack from outside, as under Communist rule.

"The entire twentieth century is being sucked into the vortex of atheism and self-destruction," the stern speaker warned his hushed audience. "We can only reach with determinination for the warm hand of God, which we have so rashly and self-confidently pushed away. There is nothing else to cling to in the landslide."

In the sweep of Solzhenitsyn's apocalyptic warnings, there is one note of optimism: "No matter how formidably Communism bristles with tanks and rockets, no matter what successes it attains in seizing the planet, it is doomed never to vanquish Christianity."

Solzhenitsyn's own sense of calling grew over the years. His first memory is of being hoisted above the heads of adults during an Orthodox service so that he could see what was happening. "Through a crowded church passed a number of men from the Cheka, the early form of security services, in their high, triangular caps, of course without taking their hats off as is the custom in any church. They tramped through all the way to the altar and began grabbing all the sacred vessels.

"As a youth, I was harassed and persecuted for my belief in God," said Solzhenitsyn, who resisted atheist indoctrination until age fifteen. In later years, "I considered myself as a Marxist, but deep inside me the attachment to the church, to the faith that I had always had as a child, lived on."

After military service in World War II, the author was arrested for writing letters criticizing Stalin and sentenced to hard labor in the Gulag. "I was eight years in camp and that, of course, induced a lot of thought. I met a great many Orthodox and had a lot of discussions with them. After that, I was mortally ill in camp, and, faced with that mortal illness, I found anew my faith."

Solzhenitsyn recalled, "I was being subjected to increasing pressure and harassment. At this time I experienced a feeling that I had support—supernatural support. I wrote of prayer in the consciousness of the various outcomes that could be called my fate: maybe this is the last moment. Maybe this is it." But it was only the beginning.

The Church as Messenger. W. E. Sangster, the late famous preacher in London, made a trip around the world before he died. When he returned, people asked him what impressed him the most. Dr. Sangster reported that he had seen no Atheists' Home for Orphans and no Agnostics' Hospital for the Poor. But everywhere he found the Christian Church at work caring for the needy and feeding the hungry.

The Church continues to exercise this prophetic mission. To a world rebelling against God, Christ's people speak and act on behalf of the God of justice and compassion.

Rejected but Persistent. The world frequently turns its back on its artists, prophets, and visionaries. Here are just a few examples from secular society.

An irate banker once ordered Alexander Graham Bell to remove "that toy" from his office.

"That toy" was the telephone.

A Hollywood producer scrawled a curt rejection note on a manuscript titled,"Gone With the Wind."

Henry Ford's largest original investor sold all his stock in 1906.

They told the young Albert Einstein he "showed no promise."

They decided *Star Wars* wouldn't be worth producing.

They told a new rock group, the Beatles, that "groups with guitars are on their way out!"

The prophets such as Jeremiah, Ezekiel, and Daniel also felt rejected. Society did not want to hear their message for God. Their calling impelled them to persist in speaking to the rebellious people around them.

There are times when you probably feel no one wants to hear your words or no one seems to appreciate your efforts for the Lord. Your calling, however, is to be faithful, not necessarily successful! Persevere. For God stands with you! The prophets discovered that they were never alone. With God, you are in the majority!

Questions for Pupils on the Next Lesson. 1. Why did some of those in exile blame God for their misery? 2. Is each person to be held accountable for everything he or she does? 3. What does it mean to repent? 4. Why do we vacillate when it comes to assuming responsibility for the consequences of our choices? 5. Have you ever doubted the value of your religious faith in the time of crisis?

TOPIC FOR YOUTH
CALLED TO TAKE A STAND

I Must Hold On. A few years ago, an American student was climbing in the French Alps. He decided to try to ascend the dangerous north face of the "Fool's Needle" in the Mont Blanc range. Somehow, he lost his footing and slipped. He managed to catch himself on a tiny ledge, where he dangled helplessly for several hours by clinging with his hands. Rescue workers finally reached him. His hands, however, were frozen. In the hospital later, he described the harrowing ordeal. He told reporters, "I repeated to myself over and over, 'I must hold on at any price.' "

Sometimes, in life, we are up against situations where it seems easier to let go. As Christians, however, we must hold on to our calling, our values, and our standards. We must cling tenaciously when we may be tempted to relax our grip on our faith. Ezekiel held on. So must we!

Courage to Take a Stand. It is risky to be a Christian. Faith calls for commitment. Some persons grow fainthearted and timid. They are like certain creative geniuses who lack the courage to stand with their ideas. Take the man named Roebuck who was an original partner of the great Sears Roebuck Company. His name was Alvah Curtis Roebuck, and he was an Indiana watch-repairman. In the 1880s, he teamed up with a freight agent named Richard Sears to sell watches by mail order. The business thrived. But Roebuck grew nervous with his partner's marketing techniques. Roebuck wasn't sure about Sears's ideas about advertising. In fact, Roebuck became so uneasy about the future of the company that he asked to sell out. He took $25,000 in 1895, relieved to sever his ties with Sears Roebuck and company. He never succeeded at anything again. In fact, in the 1929 crash, Roebuck went broke. He finally managed to be hired back by his old company at a low-level, low-paying position in the publicity department.

Ezekiel knew that his calling meant a bold and tenacious stand for the Lord. In spite of any uneasiness about the future he might have felt, he stood firmly and confidently as God's spokesman. He remembered that God had called him to take a stand!

Have you? Are you prepared to stand courageously because of your call?

Shoot Him to Stop Him. One day in the early days of professional football, the great halfback George Cafego was playing for the old Brooklyn Dodgers against the New York Giants. Cafego was running brilliantly. He carried the ball to within scoring position in a series of plays in which he ran each down just before the close of the first half. There was time for only one more play. The ball was snapped. Cafego took the ball and broke loose over left tackle. He knocked down one would-be tackler, then another. Cafego crashed forward. He was almost over the goal line when five giants jumped on him. He still kept moving, but just then the timekeeper's gun sounded, signalling the end of the half.

"Look at that!" one spectator shouted, "They had to shoot him to stop him!"

For a person with the commitment and determination of Ezekiel, it is almost a case of having to shoot him to stop him! Any person with a calling from God will push on toward the goal, regardless of the opposition!

Questions for Pupils on the Next Lesson. 1. Do you ever find yourself blaming God for your difficulties? 2. Do you sometimes try to put the blame on others, such as your family members or school friends or church members, when things don't go the way you want? 3. What leads you to think that God offers everyone the opportunity to start fresh? 4. Is life always fair? 5. Is living a moral life primarily not doing certain things?

LESSON VIII—JULY 20

PERSONAL RESPONSIBILITY

Background Scripture: Ezekiel 18
Devotional Reading: Ezekiel 18:14-20

KING JAMES VERSION	REVISED STANDARD VERSION

KING JAMES VERSION

EZEKIEL 18 The word of the LORD came unto me again, saying,

2 What mean ye, that ye use this proverb concerning the land of Israel saying, The fathers have eaten sour grapes, and the children's teeth are set on edge?

3 *As* I live, saith the Lord GOD, ye shall not have *occasion* any more to use this proverb in Israel.

4 Behold, all souls are mine; as the soul of the father, so also the soul of the son is mine: the soul that sinneth, it shall die.

5 But if a man be just, and do that which is lawful and right,

6 *And* hath not eaten upon the mountains, neither hath lifted up his eyes to the idols of the house of Israel, neither hath defiled his neighbour's wife, neither hath come near to a menstruous woman,

7 And hath not oppressed any, *but* hath restored to the debtor his pledge, hath spoiled none by violence, hath given his bread to the hungry, and hath covered the naked with a garment;

8 He *that* hath not given forth upon usury, neither hath taken any increase, *that* hath withdrawn his hand from iniquity, hath executed true judgment between man and man,

9 Hath walked in my statutes, and hath kept my judgments, to deal truly; he *is* just, he shall surely live, saith the Lord GOD.

10 If he beget a son *that* is a robber, a shedder of blood, and *that* doeth the like to *any* one of these *things*,

11 And that doeth not any of those *duties*, but even hath eaten upon the mountains, and defiled his neighbour's wife,

12 Hath oppressed the poor and needy, hath spoiled by violence, hath not restored the pledge, and hath lifted up his eyes to the idols, hath committed abomination,

13 Hath given forth upon usury, and hath taken increase: shall he then live? he shall not live: he hath done all these abominations; he shall surely die; his blood shall be upon him.

25 Yet ye say, The way of the Lord is not equal. Hear now, O house of Israel; Is not my way equal? are not your ways unequal?

30 Therefore I will judge you, O house of Israel, every one according to his ways, saith the Lord GOD. Repent, and turn *yourselves* from all your transgressions; so iniquity shall not be your ruin.

REVISED STANDARD VERSION

EZEKIEL 18 The word of the LORD came to me again: 2 "What do you mean by repeating this proverb concerning the land of Israel, 'The fathers have eaten sour grapes, and the children's teeth are set on edge'? 3 As I live, says the Lord GOD, this proverb shall no more be used by you in Israel. 4 Behold, all souls are mine; the soul of the father as well as the soul of the son is mine: the soul that sins shall die.

5 "If a man is righteous and does what is lawful and right—6 if he does not eat upon the mountains or lift up his eyes to the idols of the house of Israel, does not defile his neighbor's wife or approach a woman in her time of impurity, 7 does not oppress any one, but restores to the debtor his pledge, commits no robbery, gives his bread to the hungry and covers the naked with a garment, 8 does not lend at interest or take any increase, withholds his hand from iniquity, executes true justice between man and man, 9 walks in my statutes, and is careful to observe my ordinances—he is righteous, he shall surely live, says the Lord GOD.

10 "If he begets a son who is a robber, a shedder of blood, 11 who does none of these duties, but eats upon the mountains, defiles his neighbor's wife, 12 oppresses the poor and needy, commits robbery, does not restore the pledge, lifts up his eyes to the idols, commits abomination, 13 lends at interest, and takes increase; shall he then live? He shall not live. He has done all these abominable things; he shall surely die; his blood shall be upon himself.

25 "Yet you say, 'The way of the Lord is not just.' Hear now, O house of Israel: Is my way not just? Is it not your ways that are not just?

30 "Therefore I will judge you, O house of Israel, every one according to his ways, says the Lord GOD. Repent and turn from all your transgressions, lest iniquity be your ruin."

KEY VERSE: I have no pleasure in the death of any one, says the Lord GOD, so turn, and live. Ezekiel 18:32.

HOME DAILY BIBLE READINGS

July	14.	M.	*Who's to Blame?* Ezekiel 18:1–4, 19, 20.
July	15.	T.	*Accountable Before God.* Ezekiel 18:5–18.
July	16.	W.	*A Just and Forgiving God.* Ezekiel 18:21–29.
July	17.	T.	*Turn From Evil and Live.* Deuteronomy 30:15–20.
July	18.	F.	*Keeping God's Law.* Psalms 119:105–112.
July	19.	S.	*He Who Does God's Will.* Matthew 6:21–27.
July	20.	S.	*Thou Knowest Me, Lord.* Psalms 139:1–12.

BACKGROUND

The people, marched off to exile in Babylonia, began to play the "Blame Game." Unhappy over being uprooted and disillusioned over being defeated, they pointed fingers at others.

Some blamed God. They accused the Lord of failing to protect them. They bitterly assailed God for letting them down. Wasn't Jerusalem and the great Temple His earthly residence, and hadn't they looked after this magnificent place? Why had their God permitted them to suffer so when they had kept their end of the bargain with Him?

Others blamed their ancestors. These exiles quoted an ancient saying, "The parents ate sour grapes, but the children's teeth got the sour taste." Angry because of the misery of living in a foreign place, under the heel of the Babylonians, these former inhabitants of Judah accused their fathers and mothers and grandparents of causing the fall of Jerusalem and the exile. They whined that they were victims. They complained that it was not their fault that they should have to live in exile.

God knew that these exiles would never rally to carry out His work as long as they refused to accept personal responsibility and insisted on pitying themselves. The Lord sent His Prophet Ezekiel to the displaced Hebrews in Babylonia.

Ezekiel had a difficult assignment. He knew that his hearers would prefer to shift the blame for their hurt and unhappiness to others. Nevertheless, this prophet persisted with his message. He corrected the claim of the exiles that others, whether the Lord or their ancestors, were to blame for their misery. Furthermore, Ezekiel pointed out that God holds each person responsible for his or her own actions and consequences. Ezekiel assured his countrymen in Babylonia that the Lord is just in His treatment of persons. However, this messenger of God made it clear each one would have to accept personal responsibility for his or her own actions and for the life of the community. Against this motif of responsibility before a just God, Ezekiel reminded his hearers that God calls for each to repent.

NOTES ON THE PRINTED TEXT

"It ain't my fault. I'm a victim of circumstances," sarcastically quipped the youth to the arresting officer as he disclaimed any responsibility for the vandalism at the old school. The exiles' minds had similar attitudes. They felt they were suffering the consequences for the guilt of their fathers. Since they were victims of this circumstance, their attitude became, "Why try and live responsibly and righteously?" Ezekiel summarized their attitude with an old proverb: *"The fathers have eaten sour grapes, and the children's teeth are set on edge."* Unripe grapes, although more refreshing to the eater, leave a slightly bitter taste and a thin coating on the eater's teeth. Ezekiel's point is that anyone who eats these grapes must be prepared to put up with the aftereffects.

However, Ezekiel corrected the claim of the exiles that their ancestors and God were to blame. *This proverb shall no more be used by you.* The proverb will fall into disuse because of its falseness. *All souls are mine; the soul of the father as well as the soul of the son.* All people belong to God. It is God's right to do with His creations as He chooses. God judges each person in accordance with the life that he leads. *The soul that sins shall die.* Whoever sins shall be punished. Therefore, Ezekiel directly refutes the proverb.

Ezekiel continues to challenge the theory of guilt by inheritance by offering a hypothetical problem. He outlines the life of a *righteous* individual who *does what is lawful and right.* The man's characteristics are given. He avoids all moral and religious sin as defined particularly in Deuteronomy. The man does not eat sacrifices made *upon the mountains* or *lift up his eyes,* to seek help from idols. The righteous man *does not oppress anyone.* He gives back to the debtors their pledges made as collateral. He does not violently seize someone's property. He helps the needy. He is law-abiding in dealings of moneylending. In fact, throughout his life, the righteous man is careful to observe all the *statutes* and *ordinances* of the Lord. *He is righteous, he shall surely live.* The righteous man will be rewarded with the promise of full union with God.

Ezekiel sharply contrasts the righteous man's son with the righteous man. Unlike his father, the son is a robber and a murderer. He worships idols and oppresses the poor. He keeps none of the Lord's ordinances. *Shall he then live?* Ezekiel promises *he shall not live. He surely shall die.* Sin is not collective. Ezekiel points out that God holds each person responsible for his or her own actions and consequences. The soul that sins shall die and the soul that repents shall live.

You say, the way of the Lord is not just! The exiles feel that they are being unjustly treated (25–29). However, Ezekiel claims that what God desires is repentance and then righteous living. If a wicked man does this, then he shall live. *Therefore I will judge you, O house of Israel, every one according to his ways.* Every person is individually judged for his or her present actions. The exile, therefore, does not exemplify divine injustice but the exile's own wickedness. For God, Ezekiel affirms, is just in the treatment of all persons.

Ezekiel closes with a warning. God calls all persons to repent. *Repent and turn from all your transgressions, lest iniquity be your ruin.* God's grace is available, but His salvation is dependent on the repentance of the exiles. They must accept personal responsibility for their sins, change their attitude towards God, and live as God demands.

SUGGESTIONS TO TEACHERS

How many times have you heard, "Why did God let this happen to me?" Or, how often have you listened to someone claiming that all their problems arose because of something someone else did. It's an old ploy. "Shift the blame, then you won't have to accept responsibility," is the way it goes. But you know, of course, that God wants you to act as mature, responsible persons. And this is the point of today's lesson.

Ezekiel's ministry with the exiles in Babylonia provides the scriptural background for this lesson. But his words apply to each of us today.

1. *PREVIOUS PLOY.* The ancient "Blame Game" was played in the sixth century B.C. as well as in the twentieth century A.D. Take some time in your lesson to have your class members bring out the variations of putting the blame on another or others which they have tried. There will probably be some smiles of recognition as they relate instances when they accused God or parents or whomever for causing their troubles. Ezekiel, you will want to make clear, insisted that God holds each responsible. The ancient saying about the children's teeth being set on edge because the parents ate sour grapes has been reversed.

2. *PERSONAL PROBITY.* Before the Lord, each individual Christian must live a life of purity and personal morality. There is no goodness by proxy. Every believer stands constantly in the presence of God! Furthermore, each is held accountable. The kind of life for which each is accountable is one in which just dealings with others and mercy toward others is paramount.

3. *PROSPECTIVE PUNISHMENT.* Each is judged by the quality of his or her own life. Remind your people in your class that God does not punish a child for the sins of his parents. You may have some in your class who have the notion that they are paying for the wrongs committed by a father or mother or grandparent. Emphasize the knowledge you have through Jesus Christ of God's mercy toward all.

4. *PLEASANT POSSIBILITIES.* Ezekiel 18:21ff. stresses that there is not only room for repentance but hope for forgiveness. This great prophet showed tenderness as well as toughness because of his firsthand knowledge of God. Take some time in your lesson to talk together what it means to repent, and how each of us must repent and return to the Lord not just once but frequently.

5. *PUBLIC PLEA.* The great poet-preacher of the Exile pleads for a new heart and a new spirit on the part of his people. Don't we all daily need such a new heart and new spirit? Here is an opportune time to bring up the subject of personal daily devotions—a practice sadly neglected by most. Think together of ways in which your class people can receive new hearts and spirits.

TOPIC FOR ADULTS
PERSONAL RESPONSIBILITY

Rediscovering Joy. ". . . to live creatively is to struggle to be free. Yet to be free lays upon you and me the responsibility and the discipline that inhere in the freedom that comes to us. To accept that responsibility and that discipline creates a zone of joy in our existence. We then fulfill the chief end of our existence, which is to glorify God and to enjoy God's love and presence. Not to accept that disciplined responsibility is to lose our own sense of integrity and our awareness of fellowship with God.

"The end result of the freedom within responsible discipline is the rediscovery of a certain playfulness of being, a certain childlikeness—quite another thing than childishness. The latter has been put away in behalf of maturity. Yet that maturity, with all its awareness of finitude and limitation, has a playfulness that defies limits."—Wayne E. Oates, *The Struggle To Be Free: My Story and Your Story,* The Westminster Press: Philadelphia, 1983.

Shifting the Responsibility. A woman suffering from a severe depression was finally taken to a psychiatrist. After a few interviews, the doctor called in the woman's husband. "I want you to watch carefully what I do," the psychiatrist said. Leading the husband into the office where the woman was seated, the doctor walked over to the woman and gently kissed the woman on the cheek. The woman smiled.

The husband was elated. "Why, that's the first time my wife has smiled in three months!" he said.

"Now," replied the doctor, "You know what to do, don't you? You've got the idea?"

"Sure, Doc. I'll have her here every Tuesday afternoon so you can kiss her."

Sometimes we are as obtuse as that husband. We neglect to see the responsibilities which God lays on us, personally! We all have responsibilities to show kindness and extend mercy to those around us.

Sin Is When Life Freezes. "When I try to say how I see the world, I can't get away from an image that forces itself on me and won't let go: the Ice Age—this slow advance of a cold, a freezing process which we experience and try to forget. Ice Age in the schools, the factories, in those units formerly known as families. You don't have to be 'religious' or 'especially sensitive' to understand what I'm talking about. Sin—the absence of warmth, love, caring, trust.

"Marianne is an attractive young woman who owns her own home in the suburb where she lives with her two children. For her, 'sin' is a ridiculously old-fashioned word, connected with eating too many calories, illegal parking, or uncondoned behavior. You really can't take any of that seriously. Marianne feels guilty about her mother because she doesn't visit her often enough; occasionally she asks herself if she takes proper care of her children. But sin?

"Like so many people, she is superficially Christianized. In her youth, she was taught that sin means separation from God . . . an empty phrase, which has nothing to do with her life. She experiences this word *sin*, that is, being separated from God, most closely when she is depressed. She feels the Ice Age drawing near.

"When tradition says that sin is the destruction of our relationship to God, it doesn't mean individual 'sins,' but rather a general condition, the destruction of our capacity for relatedness. Everything becomes shadowy, unimportant; life loses its taste. Sin means being separated from the ground of life; it means having a disturbed relationship to ourselves, our neighbor, the creation and the human family.

"Coming of age means becoming capable of guilt. To understand what sin is, we need a standard by which we can measure false, unconscious, frozen life. We can begin to recognize and overcome sin only when we begin to use this standard; when we, related to one another, begin to learn to love. A voice calls, 'Turn around! Why do you want to die?' (*see* Ezekiel 18:31, 32)."—Dorothy Solle, *Christian Century*, September 15, 1982.

Questions for Pupils on the Next Lesson. 1. Does God judge nations as well as individuals? 2. What does God expect of every nation? What in particular do you think God expects of our nation? 3. In what ways had the leaders of Ezekiel's nation failed to live up to what God expected? 4. What are some modern forms of idolatry?

TOPIC FOR YOUTH
MY RESPONSIBILITY

A Matter of Personal Responsibility. What are some of the major cults? What are their characteristics? Why are they attractive to people, particularly young people? And what can the Church do in response and minister to people who are or have been involved with the cults?

These questions are discussed in a six-page study paper, "Lutheran Youth and Religious Cults," published by the American Lutheran Church in response to action of the ALC's 1982 general convention. Thumbnail sketches are given of five major cults: Unification Church, International Society for Krishna Consciousness, The Way International, Children of God, and Church of Scientology. Among the distinguishing marks of a cult, the paper says, are its tendency to stress the authority of the leader, its demand for rigid conformity of behavior, its exploitation of the recruit, and its use of some type of behavior modification. A cult generally implies that it has the corner on "special revelation" and often fronts as a commonly accepted group, the study paper says. Cults are said to be attractive to youth because they approach them at a critical time in their lives.

"In many cases the young person is at loose ends between the end of high school and the beginning of college or a career," the study paper says. "For many, this is the first time the young person has lived away from the parental home. For some, this time in life means the end of old friendships and the beginning of some new ones. With friends and the family gone, the cult becomes an inviting harbor in the middle of confusion." The paper argues that the best defense against having young people become involved with cults is a strong education program in the congregation that stresses the personal responsibility.

Noun or Verb? Buckminster Fuller was a noted inventor and philosopher. He is probably best remembered for designing the famous geodesic dome. He died in 1983. He once said something about himself which speaks to every Christian. He stated, "I am not a thing—a noun. I seem to be a verb, an evolutionary process— an integral function of the universe." "Bucky" Fuller essentially was reminding himself that he had responsibilities.

How do you see yourself? As a noun or as a verb? A "thing" or as an integral part of God's Creation, and therefore a responsible human being?

Children of Light or Children of Darkness. "President Reagan recently expressed interest in the biblical prophecy that seems to point to a future, final encounter between the forces of God and of Satan, a struggle known as Armageddon in the book of Revelation.

"In an article in *Christianity and Crisis,* Yehezkel Landau wrote about biblical prophecy and the present world turmoil. He is a lecturer on Judaism and Jewish-Christian relations and is active in the religious Zionist peace movement. He seems qualified to discuss Old Testament prophecy. Landau reported a telephone conversation between President Reagan and Thomas Dine of the American Israel Public Affairs Committee in which the President wondered if this generation would witness the Armageddon referred to in the Bible. He spoke about 'the times we're going through' as signs of events foretold long ago and which are expected to precede a global cataclysm before the end of the world.

"The President has named the Soviet Union as a major source of evil on Earth, implying that we of the free world are the people of God, we must be prepared to withstand the assaults of Satan incarnate—the final conflict between children of light and children of darkness. Now is the time to prepare for Armageddon by dusting off our Messianic complexes.

"Landau disagreed with an easy identification of ourselves as good guys destined to save the world. He wrote, 'Biblical psychology acknowledges the sinfulness of all human beings, including the prophets themselves. When we project evil onto our enemies and ignore our own sins, we are fueling the polarization which has bred countless wars and helped to make humanity an endangered species.' "—Joseph Mohr, *Call-Chronicle,* Saturday, January 7, 1984. Reprint from Call-Chronicle Newspapers, Allentown, Pa.

Questions for Pupils on the Next Lesson. 1. Does God hold nations responsible today for what they do? 2. Why was God so tough in judging the nation of Judah? 3. How had Judah's leaders misled the people? 4. What do you think Ezekiel and the prophets would criticize the most about our society? 5. What standards does God use when measuring our culture?

LESSON IX—JULY 27

GOD'S CHARGES AGAINST A CORRUPT SOCIETY

Background Scripture: Ezekiel 22
Devotional Reading: Ezekiel 33:30–33

KING JAMES VERSION

EZEKIEL 22 3 Then say thou, Thus saith the Lord GOD; The city sheddeth blood in the midst of it, that her time may come, and maketh idols against herself to defile herself.

4 Thou art become guilty in thy blood that thou hast shed; and hast defiled thyself in thine idols which thou hast made; and thou hast caused thy days to draw near, and art come *even* unto thy years: therefore have I made thee a reproach unto the heathen, and a mocking to all countries.

23 And the word of the LORD came unto me, saying,

24 Son of man, say unto her, Thou *art* the land that is not cleansed, nor rained upon in the day of indignation.

25 *There is* a conspiracy of her prophets in the midst thereof, like a roaring lion ravening the prey: they have devoured souls; they have taken the treasure and precious things; they have made her many widows in the midst thereof.

26 Her priests have violated my law, and have profaned mine holy things: they have put no difference between the holy and profane, neither have they shewed *difference* between the unclean and the clean, and have hid their eyes from my sabbaths, and I am profaned among them.

27 Her princes in the midst thereof *are* like wolves ravening the prey, to shed blood, *and* to destroy souls, to get dishonest gain.

28 And her prophets have daubed them with untempered *mortar,* seeing vanity, and divining lies unto them, saying, Thus saith the Lord GOD, when the LORD hath not spoken.

29 The people of the land have used oppression, and exercised robbery, and have vexed the poor and needy: yea, they have oppressed the stranger wrongfully.

30 And I sought for a man among them, that should make up the hedge, and stand in the gap before me for the land, that I should not destroy it: but I found none.

31 Therefore have I poured out mine indignation upon them; I have consumed them with the fire of my wrath: their own way have I recompensed upon their heads, saith the Lord GOD.

REVISED STANDARD VERSION

EZEKIEL 22 3 You shall say, Thus says the Lord GOD: A city that sheds blood in the midst of her, that her time may come, and that makes idols to defile herself! 4 You have become guilty by the blood which you have shed, and defiled by the idols which you have made; and you have brought your day near, the appointed time of your years has come. Therefore I have made you a reproach to the nations, and a mocking to all the countries.

23 And the word of the LORD came to me: 24 "Son of man, say to her, You are a land that is not cleansed, or rained upon in the day of indignation. 25 Her princes in the midst of her are like a roaring lion tearing the prey; they have devoured human lives; they have taken treasure and precious things; they have made many widows in the midst of her. 26 Her priests have done violence to my law and have profaned my holy things; they have made no distinction between the holy and the common, neither have they taught the difference between the unclean and the clean, and they have disregarded my sabbaths, so that I am profaned among them. 27 Her princes in the midst of her are like wolves tearing the prey, shedding blood, destroying lives to get dishonest gain. 28 And her prophets have daubed for them with whitewash, seeing false visions and divining lies for them, saying, 'Thus says the Lord GOD,' when the LORD has not spoken. 29 The people of the land have practiced extortion and committed robbery; they have oppressed the poor and needy, and have extorted from the sojourner without redress. 30 And I sought for a man among them who should build up the wall and stand in the breach before me for the land, that I should not destroy it; but I found none. 31 Therefore I have poured out my indignation upon them; I have consumed them with the fire of my wrath; their way have I requited upon their heads, says the Lord GOD."

KEY VERSE: *I sought for a man among them who should build up the wall and stand in the breach before me for the land, that I should not destroy it; but I found none.* Ezekiel 22:30.

HOME DAILY BIBLE READINGS

July 21. M. *Prophet to Displaced People.* Ezekiel 2:1–10.
July 22. T. *Israel's Watchman.* Ezekiel 4:1–13.
July 23. W. *A New Way to Communicate.* Ezekiel 36:25–31.
July 24. T. *The Watchman's Duty.* Ezekiel 33:1–9.
July 25. F. *The Stubbornness of Israel.* Ezekiel 3:4–15.
July 26. S. *The Outpouring of God's Spirit.* Joel 2:2–19, 27–29.
July 27. S. *Can Exiles Sing?* Psalms 137:1–6.

BACKGROUND

Like Jeremiah his contemporary, Ezekiel lived during the grim, tempestuous days of Judah's defeat and destruction. Like Jeremiah, Ezekiel realized that the nation's corruption would bring God's judgment. Both prophets knew that God is sovereign. Both announced that the collapse of Jerusalem was the inevitable day of reckoning before God. Ezekiel and Jeremiah undoubtedly knew each other, although neither mentioned the other, and the two preached that the sins of their rebellious fellow countrymen would have disastrous results. Both were vindicated in 586 B.C. when the Babylonians overran and demolished the great holy city. Jeremiah disappeared from sight. Ezekiel, however, continued to prophesy.

His writings in the Book of Ezekiel in our Old Testament are actually a collection of speeches. They are not always arranged in chronological order. The material in today's lesson, Ezekiel 22, like most of the first twenty-four chapters, was obviously one of the sermons spoken in Jerusalem before 586 B.C., although last week's lesson from Ezekiel 18 came from a message to the exiles after the fall of Jerusalem.

The sermon in chapter 22 blisters Jerusalem's leaders. When you read this section, you will notice that there are three sections. The first sixteen verses denounces the great capital as a city of blood. Ezekiel called it "the bloody city" partly because so many had shed blood while participating in heathen rites and partly because the leaders had acted so violently in oppressing the poor.

The second part of the sermon in chapter 22 extends from verse 17 through verse 22, and talks about God's smelting operation. This was a favorite figure with many prophets. As the Babylonian army advanced, the panic-stricken people fled from the countryside to Jerusalem. But the siege, Ezekiel stated, would be like the flame of a metalworker. God's refining fire would smelt out the impurities, except in the case of Jerusalem the mix was so bad that there would be no good metal left.

You will find the third portion of this oracle extending from Ezekiel 22:23–31. In this section, Ezekiel charges all the ruling groups with failing to act responsibly. He particularly denounces the priests, the nobles, and the prophets. As a member of the priestly caste, and therefore one of Jerusalem's bluebloods, Ezekiel felt keenly that his fellow leading citizens had ruined the nation by their corrupt, cruel ways.

NOTES ON THE PRINTED TEXT

Ezekiel's calls for repentance have been made, but God's charges against a corrupt society cannot be postponed any longer. God now pronounces judgment on the nation for its gross disobedience.

Jerusalem is indicted as a *city that sheds blood in the midst of her; . . . and makes idols to defile herself!* The bloody city is guilty of violent crimes (explained in verses 6–12) and is defiled by idolatry. The people have worshiped idols instead of God. So strong is God's charge that Ezekiel reiterates it for effect. *You have become guilty by the blood which you have shed and defiled by the idols you have made.* Judgment is coming, promises Ezekiel. *You have brought your day near, the appointed time of your years has come.* The judgment will be harsh. *I have made you a reproach to the nations, and a mocking to all countries.*

God not only charges Jerusalem but through Ezekiel God's charge is carried to all classes for their sins: princes, priests, nobles, and the people. There are no righteous people. The judgment that has come upon Jerusalem through its fall is a result of each class's failure. *You are a land that is not cleansed, or rained upon in the day of indignation.* The land will become a lifeless desert. The subsequent drought will be a judgment on all the people, for without moisture their survival is imperiled.

Her princes . . . are like a roaring lion tearing the prey; they have devoured human lives; they have taken treasure . . . they have made many widows. The nation's leaders have treated the people oppressively in order to get dishonest gain. Instead of upholding law and order, these leaders have resorted to murder and robbery to increase their wealth.

Her princes in the midst of her are like wolves tearing the prey, shedding blood, destroying lives to get dishonest gain. The nobles are like the leaders. They, too, are not models of morality.

And her prophets have daubed for them with whitewash, seeing false visions and divining lies. The nation's prophets have misled the people by claiming to speak for God when they have not even listened to God.

The people of the land have practiced extortion and committed robbery. Even the ordinary individual has oppressed the poor and the needy and deliberately mistreated the sojourner.

God looked for a righteous person among all those who should have been examples of righteousness, but He could not find even one! Therefore, He destroyed Judah. *I have poured out my indignation upon them; I have consumed them with the fire of my wrath.*

SUGGESTIONS TO TEACHERS

When we think of sin, we usually think of individual, personal wrongs. And this is proper. We are, each of us, guilty of individual, personal sins. But what about a nation? Is it accountable to God? Can a nation sin?

Many (perhaps most) rulers like to think that their nation is not to be considered sinful. They try to justify their nation's ways. They prefer not to believe that God judges nations as well as individuals. True, they may try to "use" God by invoking His name on special occasions. Every nation has its own form of civil religion. But few national leaders have ever faced up to the disobedience their nation practices before God.

1. *DECLARATION.* Ezekiel presents a complete catalogue of the evil in his land—including idolatry, immorality, cruelty, violence, and injustice. Sound familiar? You better believe it, and so had your people! Ezekiel calls such behavior "abominable deeds" and warns they will have disastrous effect. Put yourself in the role of the prophet in 1986 culture. What do you think God would have you say about this society?

2. *DISPERSAL.* Ezekiel states bluntly that a nation flaunting God so brazenly as Judah is doomed. He announces that her people will be deported. Think for a moment of these verses from Ezekiel 22 in terms of separation. Isn't separation the result of sin? Isn't separation from God, separation from each other (another word for loneliness and alienation) and separation from self the condition of so many persons? Or, look at the factionalism in our nation today. Isn't this simply a way we seem to be dispersed and separated? Our sin has calamitous results.

3. *DROSS.* Ezekiel warns of the refiner's fire. God always burns off the impurities in order to produce a purer substance. Can it be that some of the suf-

fering we experience as a nation may actually be the Lord's way of trying to purify and temper us?

4. *DESECRATION.* God was profaned by the priests and princes and prophets, according to Ezekiel. Furthermore, their self-seeking proved to be shortsighted. It brought national ruin as well as personal hardship. Ezekiel was particularly hard on the religious folk. What would he have to say to your congregation or your class, or to your denomination or the Protestant community, or to the Christian Church in North America in these days? How can your church be more faithful to its Lord?

TOPIC FOR ADULTS
GOD'S CHARGES AGAINST A CORRUPT SOCIETY

Prison Camp Parable. Langdon Gilkey, now a professor in a theological seminary in Chicago, was interned for three years in China during World War II.

There were 1,450 people in his camp, including men, women, and children; 200 of them were Americans. After two years of hunger on a frugal diet, suddenly in 1944 American Red Cross packages of food arrived, a fifty-pound package for each American. They contained powdered milk, butter, Spam, cheese, chocolate, sugar, coffee, dried prunes, and raisins—things a hungry internee had longed for and thought he would never see again. The Americans shared some of the food with others, but even then made it last for as long as four months.

In January of 1945, more American Red Cross food packages were delivered—this time 1,550 fifty-pound packages, with no instructions as to how they should be distributed. Most of the camp believed they would all get at least one package. Two days later the Japanese commandant posted a notice that the parcels would be distributed to all at 10 o'clock the next morning. Each of the 1,450 would get one package, and the 200 Americans would each get one-half package extra. It is impossible to describe the joy and excitement that gripped the camp that night. It was like every Christmas Eve of a lifetime rolled into one!

Next morning they lined up long before the time. But soon a guard posted a notice: "Due to protests from the American community, the parcels will not be distributed today as announced."

It was discovered that seven young Americans had demanded that all parcels be given only to Americans—7¾ packages (387 pounds) per person. The Japanese commandant had no instructions, so he referred the matter to Tokyo for decision. It would take ten days.

Gilkey relates that several of his American friends got together to confer about the matter. They could not believe that the seven really represented the opinion of the 200 Americans. Before calling a meeting, they decided to take a sampling. Gilkey interviewed three people. A small businessman from Chicago was the first. He replied, "These packages are mine because I'm an American, and I'm going to get every last one that's coming to me! I'm sorry for these other guys, sure. But why don't their own governments take care of them? No lousy foreigner is going to get what belongs to me!"

The next man was an American lawyer. He said, "With me, it's the legal principle that counts. This is American property . . . the rights of American property must be preserved and respected. We've got to be faithful executors, for the American donors who sent them to us."

The last man was a kindly, conservative American missionary. He replied, "I always look at things from a moral point of view. There is no virtue whatever in being forced to share. We Americans should be given the parcels, then each should be left to exercise his own moral judgment in deciding what to do with them." When asked how many parcels he thought each might share, he replied,

"At least two of them." Which of course meant 287 pounds of food for every American and sixteen pounds for every non-American.

The other men reported similar replies, and they gave up calling a meeting of the Americans.

Ten days later, Tokyo replied: Give every internee one package and return the 100 extra packages for distribution to other camps. Gilkey comments: "Even an enemy authority can mediate the divine justice in human affairs."

The story is a parable to what we face today. We must break the pattern of individual attitude and the voluntary system of distribution. This will be difficult—very difficult. We are the most powerful people in the world; our power is not shared with anyone or checked by anyone. This breeds pride and self-deception; we find it difficult to take our place as a nation in the world of nations and as Christians in the wider community.

How Divine Justice Weighs a Nation's Sins. In his acceptance speech for renomination on June 27, 1936, President Franklin Delano Roosevelt summarized his Administration's goals and accomplishments in ringing oratorical style:

"Governments can err, Presidents do make mistakes, but the immortal Dante tells us that Divine Justice weighs the sins of the cold-blooded and the sins of the warm-hearted on different scales. Better the occasional faults of a Government that lives in a spirit of charity than the consistent omissions of a Government frozen in the ice of its own indifference."

Prophetic Utterance? "Hunger is not an American word. It is a Bangladesh, Haitian, Cambodian word. Hunger is the swollen belly of an African baby. It is a famine. We look at it in Save the Children ads in magazines. Hunger is 41,000 deaths in the world every day due to chronic undernutrition and starvation.

"Americans see hunger as global, not national nor local. Forty-one thousand people may die of hunger every day, but none here. Obituary notices never cite hunger as the cause of death. Hunger is what middle and upper-class Americans feel when they diet, as promoted by the multibillion-dollar creative starvation industry.

"The hunger debate in America differs from the global one in still another way. Here the question is whether eating is a right or a privilege. For the past fifteen years, Congress ruled it a right. Programs like food stamps represented justice, not charity.

"They worked. In 1967, physicians from the Field Foundation went to impoverished areas and found 'Children in significant numbers who were hungry and sick, children for whom hunger is a daily fact of life.'

"Ten years later, the physicians returned to the Bronx, Appalachia, Mississippi, and Texas. One doctor said: 'It is not possible any more to find very easily the bloated bellies, the shriveled infants, the gross evidence of vitamin and protein deficiencies in children that we identified in the late 1960s.' Another doctor reported 'a striking decrease in the number of grossly visible signs of malnutrition.' The reason? 'Food stamps made the critical difference.'

"Government intervention had worked. A political solution had succeeded in solving the moral problem of how the nation's wealth was to be shared.

"Ronald Reagan rejected the government's successes. In his inaugural address he said: 'Government is not the solution to our problem ... government is the problem.' He has been obsessed with the idea. He once said that the social programs of the 1960s hurt the poor.

"A hungry person on television, yanked out of the soup line, couldn't have addressed in a few minutes of air time the obsessions of Reagan. He has an obsession of his own—the big one of eating."—Coleman McCarthy, "Hunger—Here, Elsewhere," Reprint from *Call-Chronicle Newspapers,* Allentown, Pa., October, 1983.

Questions for Pupils on the Next Lesson. 1. Why, according to Ezekiel, would

God bring the exiles back from Babylon? 2. What did Ezekiel say the conditions for the return from exile in Jerusalem would be? 3. Do you think that God has a future in store for you and your church? 4. Is it really possible to start life afresh when life seems to crumble around you? 5. How do you feel when you recall deeds in your past which you truly regret?

TOPIC FOR YOUTH
MEASURED BY GOD'S STANDARDS

Need for Standard Time. At noon on Sunday, November 18, 1883, most of the railroad stations, jewelers, courthouses, factories, and other timekeepers adjusted their clocks to four time zones in North America—Eastern, Central, Mountain, and Pacific. Until then, railroads had been coursing through at least fifty different regional time zones. And nearly every local community decreed when it thought what the correct time was. It caused hopeless confusion. Clocks in New York City, for example, were one minute and one second behind Albany, but ten minutes and twenty-seven seconds ahead of Baltimore. Finally, most communities agreed to the proposal of regional time belts, each fifteen degrees of longitude, or one hour, in width, on the appointed day in 1883. A year later, an international conference meeting in Washington, D.C., agreed to use Greenwich observatory's measurement of time as the prime meridian for the world's twenty-four time zones. Since that time, all clocks throughout the globe have been set by a common standard. But imagine how confusing it would be without such a standard!

Just as we set our watches and clocks by one basic measurement, whether we live in Seattle, San Antonio, Savannah, or Sauk Center, we must measure our lives by God's standard. We cannot imagine that we can do as we please when it comes to time, and we will have equally hopeless confusion within and without if we presume to ignore the Lord's measurings.

Keep the Shades Up. There is an old story of two men who were riding on a train through the outskirts of a large city. One of them reached over and pulled down the shade, saying, "I cannot stand to look at the sordid conditions of the slum area through which we are passing." His companion replied, "It may be there is nothing we can do at the moment about the conditions, but at least we can keep the shade up."—Charles L. Allen, *Perfect Peace,* Old Tappan, N.J.: Fleming H. Revell Company, 1979.

Mirrors or Windows. A Chinese story tells of a king who daily looked into a mirror. One day he replaced the mirror with a window. He saw starving children reaching into garbage cans; sick and maimed men and women and sufferings and wrongs he never knew existed. Maybe that's what we need—to replace our mirrors with windows.

Questions for Pupils on the Next Lesson. 1. Why did Ezekiel think that God would bring the exiles back to Jerusalem from Babylonia? 2. What did God want these people to be and to do when He returned them from exile? 3. Does God always help a person start afresh, or only sometimes? 4. Have you ever found that God has helped you to look to the future with hope after you have gone through a bad time?

LESSON X—AUGUST 3

RENEWAL OF GOD'S PEOPLE

Background Scripture: Ezekiel 36
Devotional Reading: Ezekiel 34:11–16

KING JAMES VERSION

EZEKIEL 36 22 Therefore say unto the house of Israel, Thus saith the Lord GOD; I do not *this* for your sakes, O house of Israel, but for mine holy name's sake, which ye have profaned among the heathen, whither ye went.

23 And I will sanctify my great name, which was profaned among the heathen, which ye have profaned in the midst of them; and the heathen shall know that I *am* the LORD, saith the Lord GOD, when I shall be sanctified in you before their eyes.

24 For I will take you from among the heathen, and gather you out of all countries, and will bring you into your own land.

25 Then will I sprinkle clean water upon you, and ye shall be clean: from all your filthiness, and from all your idols, will I cleanse you.

26 A new heart also will I give you, and a new spirit will I put within you: and I will take away the stony heart out of your flesh, and I will give you a heart of flesh.

27 And I will put my spirit within you, and cause you to walk in my statutes, and ye shall keep my judgments, and do *them.*

28 And ye shall dwell in the land that I gave to your fathers; and ye shall be my people, and I will be your God.

29 I will also save you from all your uncleannesses: and I will call for the corn, and will increase it, and lay no famine upon you.

30 And I will multiply the fruit of the tree, and the increase of the field, that ye shall receive no more reproach of famine among the heathen.

31 Then shall ye remember your own evil ways, and your doings that *were* not good, and shall loathe yourselves in your own sight for your iniquities and for your abominations.

32 Not for your sakes do I *this,* saith the Lord GOD, be it known unto you: be ashamed and confounded for your own ways, O house of Israel.

REVISED STANDARD VERSION

EZEKIEL 36 22 "Therefore say to the house of Israel, Thus says the Lord GOD: It is not for your sake, O house of Israel, that I am about to act, but for the sake of my holy name, which you have profaned among the nations to which you came. 23 And I will vindicate the holiness of my great name, which has been profaned among the nations, and which you have profaned among them; and the nations will know that I am the LORD, says the Lord GOD, when through you I vindicate my holiness before their eyes. 24 For I will take you from the nations, and gather you from all the countries, and bring you into your own land. 25 I will sprinkle clean water upon you, and you shall be clean from all your uncleannesses, and from all your idols I will cleanse you. 26 A new heart I will give you, and a new spirit I will put within you; and I will take out of your flesh the heart of stone and give you a heart of flesh. 27 And I will put my spirit within you, and cause you to walk in my statutes and be careful to observe my ordinances. 28 You shall dwell in the land which I gave to your fathers; and you shall be my people, and I will be your God. 29 And I will deliver you from all your uncleannesses; and I will summon the grain and make it abundant and lay no famine upon you. 30 I will make the fruit of the tree and the increase of the field abundant, that you may never again suffer the disgrace of famine among the nations. 31 Then you will remember your evil ways, and your deeds that were not good; and you will loathe yourselves for your iniquities and your abominable deeds. 32 It is not for your sake that I will act, says the Lord GOD; let that be known to you. Be ashamed and confounded for your ways, O house of Israel.

KEY VERSE: *A new heart will I give you, and a new spirit I will put within you; and I will take out of your flesh the heart of stone and give you a heart of flesh.* Ezekiel 36:26.

HOME DAILY BIBLE READINGS

BACKGROUND

Ezekiel, the priest who was also a prophet, was one of those deported to Babylonia after Nebuchadnezzar's conquest. He shared the hardships of the long forced march from Jerusalem to the Euphrates River. He ministered to the exiles in their hurt and anger.

Those deported to Babylonia resented being uprooted and banished to a strange, foreign land. Their defeat rankled deeply. Some quietly forsook their faith and allowed themselves to be absorbed by the Babylonian culture. What was the point of maintaining their religion and obeying the Lord? Others nursed their bitterness and wallowed in self-pity. Bolstered by Ezekiel, however, others organized temporary communities in Babylonia and tried to cling to their ancient faith. He encouraged the confused and depressed groups of exiles to continue to practice their prayers and keep the Law. Although the nation was dead, Ezekiel acknowledged, the Lord continued to be sovereign. The exiled Jerusalemites looked to Ezekiel as their spiritual advisor.

Although he had preached stern messages of doom before Jerusalem had fallen, chastising the nation's leaders for their stubborn disregard for the Lord and His ways, Ezekiel also had a tender side. We see this in chapter 36, the subject of today's lesson. He offered comfort. He held out hope. Although it was too late for repentance, he assured them that God would sustain them in the alien land. Furthermore, the priest-prophet stated that he was certain that God would bring them back to the land of their fathers and mothers and re-establish them as the new Israel.

Ezekiel taught that both the individual and the society must serve God. He preaches that God's people individually and corporately would have to act humbly and obediently when the Lord brought them back to Jerusalem. He knew human nature. And he knew God's nature. Ezekiel understood that God is good. True, Ezekiel understood that God judges. But the prophet of the exile also grasped that it is the goodness of God, not His judgment, which leads to repentance. In this insight, Ezekiel anticipates the Apostle Paul's writings in such places as Romans 2:4. The enjoyment of undeserved blessings makes people turn from their iniquities, not suffering, no matter how much it may be deserved.

NOTES ON THE PRINTED TEXT

After judgment comes renewal. Ezekiel outlines the basis of renewal to the exiles. *It is not for your sake . . . that I am about to act, but for the sake of my holy name.* Ezekiel bluntly tells Israel that God will restore His people not for their sake or for whatever they have done, but in order to restore His reputation. The exile that Israel is enduring is, in fact, a result of the attitudes of the people. They have not declared to others the true nature of God. God is acting to restore His *great name.* He will *vindicate* the holiness of that name. Because of the destruction of Israel, His holiness has been questioned by other nations. Now He is acting so that nations will recognize that He is the Lord. The chosen people will be restored for God's own sake, and their restoration will be a sign for all nations.

For I will take you from the nations, and gather you from all the countries, and bring you into your own land. God's judgment involved the scattering of the chosen people into various countries. Now God will gather the exiles and bring them back to the land.

I will sprinkle clean water upon you. Sprinkling with clean water is a symbol of cleansing. Israel will be cleansed, particularly from the defilement of idols. Cleansing is symbolic of divine pardon. God is forgiving His people for their sins.

A new heart I will give you, and a new spirit I will put within you. As God outwardly cleansed, so, too, will He inwardly renew His people. God will give the people a new heart and a new spirit. He replaces their *heart of stone* which represents their impulse to disobedience. The new spirit will enable Israel to be obedient, *to walk in my statues and be careful to observe my ordinances.*

By keeping His commandments, the exiles will again live in the promised land. *You shall dwell in the land which I gave to your fathers.* The renewal and restoration will be a result of God's action and not of the people's efforts. God reminds them that *I will deliver you from all your uncleanness.* Salvation comes from God alone!

In addition, God promises to abundantly bless the restored people. God *will summon the grain and make it grow abundant.* The fruit trees and fields will also bear abundantly so that Israel will never suffer the disgrace of famine.

Then you will remember your evil ways, . . . and you will loathe yourselves for your iniquities. The people of Israel were to learn to be ashamed and confounded for their disloyal ways. Ezekiel emphasizes this twice as he reminds them that God is not acting for them but Himself. It will not be an occasion for rejoicing but for humiliation and shame.

SUGGESTIONS TO TEACHERS

How many conferences have you attended on "Renewal?" How many books and pamphlets have you read on "renewing the Church"? How many sermons and addresses on the subject of renewal have you been subjected to? I confess that I have heard or read dozens of presentations on this topic. Some were like medicine; they dosed me with bad-tasting warnings. Some comments on renewal were like cotton candy; they were sugary fluff which seemed pleasant at the time but which didn't nourish. Perhaps you, as I, approach the subject of "renewal" with a mixture of wariness and weariness. If so, we both need to allow Ezekiel to speak to us. His words on the renewal of God's people are authentic and enduring. Before you begin planning this lesson, read chapter 36 from Ezekiel. You then can find some sense of being renewed yourself and will be better prepared to let the Holy Spirit use you as an agent of renewal in your class this Sunday.

1. *RETURN OF GOD'S SUFFERING NATION.* Ezekiel announces that God offers a future for His people. The prophet promises that God will lead the exiles back home. In spite of the disobedience of the past, Ezekiel insists that the Lord provides a new beginning. In your lesson this Sunday, stress the hope which God's people have. Let the class members relate conversations or examples they remember recently of how people they know don't think that there is any future. Also encourage those in your class to tell about times when they discovered God opened new vistas for them when they thought there was no hope.

2. *RECOGNITION OF GOD'S SOVEREIGNTY.* God is supreme. God is able. God is in control. God acts. God means to be taken seriously. "Not for your sake, O Israel, that I am about to act," the Lord states, "but for the sake of my holy name which you have profaned" (Ezekiel 36:22). God is determined that all nations as well as persons recognize that He is the Lord. You should have your students examine who or what our society holds to be sovereign. (Pleasure? Violence? Force of arms? National power? Buying power?) How are these others, given supreme status, trying to displace God as final authority?

3. *RENEWAL OF GOD'S SERVANT PEOPLE.* Devote sufficient time on

Ezekiel's words about a "new heart" and a "new spirit" which he says that the Lord will give His people (36:26). Remind your folks that this is God's doing, not something generated by a committee or program. In the person of Jesus Christ, through the power of the Holy Spirit, God has blessed each of us with new hearts and spirits, if we but realize the meaning of the Cross and the Resurrection! Furthermore, He gives His Church His own kind of heart transplant, so that the pulse of the Church may beat with Him!

4. *RESPONSIBILITY OF GOD'S SAVED REMNANT.* God renews us in order for us to serve! He does not merely allow us to return to Him and rebuild our lives for our own sakes, but for others! We are saved to be sent into the world for His sake!

TOPIC FOR ADULTS
GOD'S PROMISES OF RENEWAL

New Beginning With Jesu Swami. D. T. Niles told of a disaster to a village in India. Violent rains had melted most of the huts, and the whole village was a horrible expanse of mud. The pastor, who had come to comfort, wondered what to say. It seemed a mockery to tell the miserable people that God still cared for them. He went hesitantly to an old woman, who was huddled with her family by the ruin of their home, and said, "Amma! You all seem to be in much trouble here." "Yes, yes," she answered, "and but for Jesu Swami (the Lord Jesus), we should not be able to bear it."—D.T. Niles, *That They May Have Life.*

Reflections. "I feel strongly at the end of my life that nothing can happen to us in any circumstances that is not part of God's purpose for us. Therefore, we have nothing to fear except that we should rebel against His purpose, that we should fail to detect it and fail to establish some sort of relationship with Him and His divine will. On that basis, there can be no black despair, no throwing in of our hand. We can watch the institutions and social structures of our time collapse— and I think you who are young are fated to watch them collapse—and we can reckon with what seems like an irresistibly growing power of materialism and materialist societies.

"But that is not the end of the story. As Saint Augustine said when he received the news in Carthage that Rome had been sacked: 'Well, if that's happened, it's a great catastrophe, but we must never forget that the earthly cities that men build they destroy, but there is also a city of God which men didn't build and can't destroy.'"—Malcolm Muggeridge, "Christianity Today," *Quote*, December 15, 1982.

Sailing Away From It All. A church custodian from Newark, New Jersey, is fashioning scrap and debris from abandoned buildings into a modern-day ark, hoping to sail away from the blight that surrounds him to "live in peace" on the seas.

Kea Tawana has been working on the wood-frame vessel since August 1982. He says the 125-ton, four-masted ship, is 86 feet long and 18 feet wide. The ark will have four canvas sails and a diesel engine from an old truck. A gasoline-powered generator and transformer taken from an elevator shaft will provide electricity and light. About 90 percent of the ship, including the thick wooden hull and decks, comes from buildings that Tawana said he picked clean after wrecking crews left. There will be "no two of everything, just me and my three cats," he said with a smile, adding he plans to recruit a crew of six former merchant seamen—his former vocation—when launch time draws near. "Things have gotten so disgusting on land," Tawana said with a shake of his head. "There's no peace on land. I'm going to build a ship so I can live in peace on the great seas."

Mr. Tawana has the notion that things are so hopeless that even God has given up on the human race. He sees no future. He can find no hope for renewal. Therefore, he'll take his cats and six buddies and sail away from all that's disgusting.

But the Lord promises renewal! In spite of our discouragement with the world as it is, God brings new beginnings! We cannot build our arks and leave because God continues to make things new!

Questions for Pupils on the Next Lesson. 1. What was Ezekiel's vision of the restored Temple? 2. Do you have questions about the future of civilization, the Church, yourself, and the human race? 3. What has consoled you when you had deep feelings of failure? 4. How important is worship in your life? 5. Will God ever triumph completely over evil?

TOPIC FOR YOUTH
STARTING OVER

Freed After Thirty-One Years. A Chinese immigrant who was confined for thirty-one and a half years to a series of state mental hospitals, apparently because he could not speak English, gained his freedom in Chicago recently.

David Tom, fifty-four, and his attorney, Patrick Murphy, celebrated Tom's move out of the Illinois State Psychiatric Institute—one of at least four institutions where Tom has been confined.

Tom who was working as a dishwasher when he was first hospitalized for tuberculosis, was caught in a "Catch-22" situation. When Tom began acting strangely during treatment for tuberculosis and nobody could be found who understood his Chinese dialect, the state apparently decided he was psychotic and had to be institutionalized.

Murphy, who also is Cook County guardian, won Tom's freedom in a suit that alleged the state violated his rights by locking him up for thirty-one and a half years in institutions where nobody spoke his Chinese dialect.

Now Tom, a frail man who understands some basic English, lives at a community center for Indochinese refugees, where he is cared for by a couple running the center and receives English training.

Murphy said his happiness over winning the suit is tempered by the squalor and silence Tom endured.

You can imagine the joy and relief which David Tom must feel over being able to start over. But think of the way God offers *you* the opportunity of starting over after you have messed up your life and got yourself shut off from the Lord and others. Through Jesus Christ, God sets you free from the hopelessness you may feel. He brings new beginnings!

Exchange a Piano for the Church? Over in Glasgow, Scotland, a minister of a run-down congregation in a poor slum area, was once trying to scrounge a piano for his parish hall. He found an old instrument in a second-hand shop. Thinking he might work on the sympathies of the shopkeeper, he politely inquired, "Could I have the piano for the Church of Scotland?"

The dealer solemnly replied, "Seems like a fair exchange, sir; seems like a fair exchange."

The shopkeeper obviously had a low opinion of the Scottish Church, and expected little of it. Perhaps this is the way you feel. Undoubtedly, many of your friends wouldn't swap a decent guitar, let alone an old piano, for the Church! Remember the way Ezekiel and the scriptural writers promise that God continually starts over with His people! He surprises everyone by even starting over with church folks!

Couldn't Erase Those Moments. Robert A. Lewis was the co-pilot of the B-29 *Enola Gay* on its August 1945 mission to drop the atom bomb over Hiroshima.

He was a test pilot of the then-new B-29 bomber, and had been chosen because he was known to be cool under stress. However, when Lewis looked down to watch the blast from the atom bomb he dropped, he cried, "My God, what have we done!" Later, recalling that fateful day, he said. "If I live a hundred years, I'll never quite get those few minutes out of my mind."

We sometimes ask ourselves what we have done at various times in our lives. And we regret our actions and tell ourselves we can never forget what we did in a hundred years. But there is always a starting over with God. The story of the people of God is a record of astonishing fresh beginnings, thanks to the Lord!

Questions for Pupils on the Next Lesson. 1. Why was the Temple in Jerusalem so important to the people in exile in Babylonia? 2. What did Ezekiel promise the people about the Temple? 3. What exactly is worship to you? 4. Do you sometimes feel that you are alienated from others? From God? 5. When do you feel God is present?

LESSON XI—AUGUST 10

A VISION OF GOD'S GLORY

Background Scripture: Ezekiel 43:1–13; 47:1–12
Devotional Reading: Ezekiel 39:25–29

KING JAMES VERSION

EZEKIEL 43 2 And, behold, the glory of the God of Israel came from the way of the east: and his voice *was* like a noise of many waters: and the earth shined with his glory.

3 And *it was* according to the appearance of the vision which I saw, *even* according to the vision that I saw when I came to destroy the city: and the visions *were* like the vision that I saw by the river Chebar; and I fell upon my face.

4 And the glory of the LORD came into the house by the way of the gate whose prospect *is* toward the east.

5 So the spirit took me up, and brought me into the inner court; and, behold, the glory of the LORD filled the house.

6 And I heard *him* speaking unto me out of the house; and the man stood by me.

7 And he said unto me, Son of man, the place of my throne, and the place of the soles of my feet, where I will dwell in the midst of the children of Israel for ever, and my holy name, shall the house of Israel no more defile, *neither* they, nor their kings, by their whoredom, nor by the carcasses of their kings in their high places.

8 In their setting of their threshold by my thresholds, and their post by my posts, and the wall between me and them, they have even defiled my holy name by their abominations that they have committed: wherefore I have consumed them in mine anger.

9 Now let them put away their whoredom, and the carcasses of their kings, far from me, and I will dwell in the midst of them for ever.

10 Thou son of man, show the house to the house of Israel, that they may be ashamed of their iniquities: and let them measure the pattern.

11 And if they be ashamed of all that they have done, shew them the form of the house, and the fashion thereof, and the goings out thereof, and the comings in thereof, and all the forms thereof, and all the ordinances thereof, and all the forms thereof, and all the laws thereof: and write *it* in their sight, that they may keep the whole form thereof, and all the ordinances thereof, and do them.

12 This *is* the law of the house; Upon the top of the mountain the whole limit thereof round about *shall be* most holy. Behold, this *is* the law of the house.

REVISED STANDARD VERSION

EZEKIEL 43 2 And behold, the glory of the God of Israel came from the east; and the sound of his coming was like the sound of many waters; and the earth shone with his glory. 3 And the vision I saw was like the vision which I had seen when he came to destroy the city, and like the vision which I had seen by the river Chebar; and I fell upon my face. 4 As the glory of the LORD entered the temple by the gate facing east, 5 the Spirit lifted me up and brought me into the inner court; and behold, the glory of the LORD filled the temple.

6 While the man was standing beside me, I heard one speaking to me out of the temple; 7 and he said to me, "Son of man, this is the place of my throne and the place of the soles of my feet, where I will dwell in the midst of the people of Israel for ever. And the house of Israel shall no more defile my holy name, neither they, nor their kings, by their harlotry, and by the dead bodies of their kings, 8 by setting their threshold by my threshold and their doorposts beside my doorposts, with only a wall between me and them. They have defiled my holy name by their abominations which they have committed, so I have consumed them in my anger. 9 Now let them put away their idolatry and the dead bodies of their kings far from me, and I will dwell in their midst for ever.

10 "And you, son of man, describe to the house of Israel the temple and its appearance and plan, that they be ashamed of their iniquities. 11 And if they are ashamed of all that they have done, portray the temple, its arrangement, its exits and its entrances, and its whole form; and make known to them all its ordinances and all its laws; and write it down in their sight, so that they may observe and perform all its laws and all its ordinances. 12 This is the law of the temple: the whole territory round about upon the top of the mountain shall be most holy. Behold, this is the law of the temple.

KEY VERSE: I will dwell in their midst for ever. Ezekiel 43:9.

HOME DAILY BIBLE READINGS

Aug.   4. M.   *The Earth Is Filled With His Glory.* Isaiah 6:1–4.
Aug.   5. T.   *"Thou Art From Everlasting."* Psalms 93.
Aug.   6. W.   *"The Word of God."* Revelation 19:11–16.
Aug.   7. T.   *"The Earth Is the Lord's."* Psalms 8:1–9.
Aug.   8. F.   *Our God Is Forever.* Psalms 48:8–14.
Aug.   9. S.   *A Multitude Bowed Before the Throne.* Revelation 7:9–12.
Aug. 10. S.   *Perfection in Christ.* Colossians 1:19–28.

BACKGROUND

Some parts of the Book of Ezekiel sound strange. You have probably already come upon passages which describe visions which seem weird. The material in today's lesson from Ezekiel 43 and 47 may at first puzzle you.

Ezekiel, like other prophets, sometimes used symbolic language. It is his way of picturing an important truth about God and His people. The symbolic language has a rich meaning, but the reader must take the trouble to translate it.

You and I usually speak of *hearing* the truth. Ezekiel often finds it more comfortable to speak of *seeing* the truth. Therefore, the prophet records his visions. We should remember that it really doesn't make any difference whether truth is conveyed through the ears of faith or the eyes of faith. The main thing is to understand who God is and what He is doing.

Beginning with chapter 40 and continuing through chapter 48:35, Ezekiel shares his vision of the future Temple. At the time he gives this vision, he and his hearers were 600 miles from Jerusalem. Furthermore, the old Temple was a charred pile of rubble. It had been destroyed along with the rest of Jerusalem in 586 B.C. Ezekiel, however, offers God's people in exile a ground plan of the new Jerusalem, including details of the new Temple. These Temple details did not include a blueprint for the rebuilding of the structure but careful instructions to the priests and all worshipers. Ezekiel intended that the new Temple be arranged so that worship would remain pure. Most of all, Ezekiel wanted to motivate his people to return to their homeland, and center their lives on serving God obediently.

Ezekiel was the motivating spirit behind the Exiles' return. His vision of his people being a community centering its varied activities around worship, under God's direction, gave the exiles a direction and a program. Although Ezekiel did not live to accompany the people returning from Babylonia to Jerusalem in 536 B.C., and although the rebuilt Temple was only a pale reflection of the great abode in Ezekiel's vision, this great prophet pointed a group of defeated exiles to overcome defeat and catastrophe. He inspired them to start over! And he succeeded.

NOTES ON THE PRINTED TEXT

Earlier in his career as a prophet, Ezekiel had a vision that described God's departure. Immediately prior to this vision, God gave Ezekiel a vision of the restored Temple. Ezekiel describes to the people of Israel his vision of God's return to the new Temple. *The glory of the God of Israel came from the east; and the sound of his coming was like the sound of many waters; and the earth shone with his glory.* The glory which had departed from the east gate (11:23) now returns from the same direction. As when he was called *by the river Chebar,* Ezekiel is overcome by God's glorious presence. The roaring sounds and the splendid colors all overpower Ezekiel, and he is thrown down until after the Lord enters the

Temple. Then *the Spirit* lifts Ezekiel and brings him into God's glory in the *inner court.*

There, Ezekiel hears words addressed to him. *I heard one speaking to me out of the temple.* God announces that the Temple is His *dwelling place. This is the place of my throne and the place of the soles of my feet, where I will dwell in the midst of the people of Israel forever.* God will dwell forever in the midst of the faithful people. Archeologists have unearthed numerous reliefs that picture a king or king-god on a throne with a footstool. So Ezekiel uses this common reference to describe the throne room of God.

In the new Temple, no one will defile God's name. *Israel shall no more defile my holy name.* Neither Israel nor her king will defile God through idolatry (frequently referred to as *harlotry*). The presence of royal corpses in the Temple defiles it. The royal tombs defile the Temple by being constructed adjacent to the Temple and sharing a common wall: *their threshold by my threshold and their doorposts beside my doorposts, with a wall between me and them.* Reminding Israel that her exile was a direct result of God's anger, Ezekiel urges the Israelites to *put away their idolatry* and move the dead bodies of the kings outside of the city walls and away from the Temple.

Ezekiel is commanded to write down all the ordinances and laws so worship might be conducted properly by the house of Israel. In addition, the people of Israel were to learn to be *ashamed of their iniquities.* These were the laws of the Temple. The Temple was to be holy. The Temple of Ezekiel's vision will be used solely for the worship of God.

SUGGESTIONS TO TEACHERS

When you start to prepare this lesson, you will quickly discover that you are dealing with some unusual scriptural material. You are reading portions of some visions by Ezekiel. Don't dismiss these as the strange ramblings of a weird writer. You will have to decode them. They are in symbolic language. Once you have the code, you will find all of Ezekiel's prophecies to be God's special Word to you as well as to those in exile. The key to the code is Ezekiel's unwavering devotion to God and his zeal for God's glory.

In today's lesson, as a study of the Background and Notes will show you, Ezekiel's vision of a rebuilt Temple is a sermon in symbols. In spite of the hammer blows of history, Ezekiel inspires his hearers to move into the future with determination to live obediently before God. The description of the rebuilt Temple is a picture-language to move the returning exiles to carry on all their activities under God's direction.

You will begin to "see" Ezekiel's vision of a people of God centering all of their lives on obeying God. As a teacher, you can put your lesson together with this in mind that worship is the focus of everything. You and your class will be able to grow greatly when you realize Ezekiel's emphasis.

1. *DWELLING PLACE OF THE DEITY.* Ezekiel insisted that God's presence is particularly known in the midst of His people. Ask your class members where they think that God lives. In heaven, up "there" somewhere? God, of course, is not localized anywhere, and introduces evidence of His life everywhere. But the Lord chooses to make known His identity and purposes through the community life of an obedient people. In other words, He uses us, His chosen family, the Church. What a burden! But what a privilege!

2. *DEVOTION WITHOUT DEFILEMENT.* True worship is found not only in the Temple ceremonies but also in daily living. God wants not only respect in the acts of prayer and praise within the buildings set apart to His use but also through

acts of charity and justice within the structures and systems of national life. Worship means both personal devotion and corporate obedience. Discuss the ramification of this notion of worship.

4. *DELUGE IN THE DESERT.* The bizarre description of the stream flowing from the Temple is Ezekiel's vivid symbolism of cleansing and renewal from the Lord which flow out into a parched world. When God's people live responsibly before the Lord, the Spirit sends forth power which nourishes and changes the society around them! Is your church such a "spring" for the Lord's cleansing and nurturing?

TOPIC FOR ADULTS
A VISION OF GOD'S GLORY

Missed the Colors. Joseph Mallord William Turner, the nineteenth century landscape painter now honored as one of the first modern artists, completed his magnificent canvas *Grand Canal,* which now hangs in the Metropolitan Museum in New York. The painting attracted a crowd when it was first exhibited at a famous salon. One wealthy society dowager peered at the picture for a long time, then turned to Turner and sniffed, "Mr. Turner, I have been to Venice many times, and I have been on the Grand Canal many times. But let me tell you something. I have never seen the colors you see." Turner bowed slightly and replied, "Ah, Madame, don't you wish you could?"

The Prophet Ezekiel saw what others had missed. He had a vision of the beauty and design of his people worshiping and serving God again in Jerusalem.

Certain persons still "see" what others miss. Many Christians "see" a world in which nations live in peace, where the have-nots receive hope, and the hungry have food for tomorrow.

Meaning of Worship: Sent! Some Christians call the Lord's Supper the "Eucharist." But our Roman Catholic brothers and sisters even more frequently call it the "Mass." That title comes not from the beginning of the service, when Jesus gave thanks, but from the end, when disciples are dismissed. We are sent out on mission. Having been strengthened with heavenly food we pilgrims are sent now back onto the road. One church bulletin says, "The service begins when the worship has ended."

Vision of God's Glory in Toledo. Domenikos Theotokopolous was born on the island of Crete in 1541, but left to study painting in Venice. His career in Italy, however, languished, and he moved on to Spain. The young Greek artist became known simply as El Greco, "the Greek." He never was accepted by either the king or the Church—the two major sources of patronage in Spain at that time— and was constantly embroiled in litigation and criticism. "Experts" sneered at the way he elongated figures and faces and painted turbulent draperies and skies and clashed colors. Some said his distortions were the result of poor vision. Today, critics acclaim El Greco's works. His distortions came not from eyesight but from his insight! Religious leaders and poets speak of the mystical side of his art masterpieces. Intuition, not imitation, was the purpose of his art. El Greco's portraits of biblical figures and martyrs and his paintings of scenes from Scripture such as the Crucifixion or Pentecost seem to speak directly to viewers in every generation. They capture something of the essence of the glory of God in the human scene.

Ezekiel and the prophets were like that. Their masterpieces were their oracles or sermons which have been transcribed. Basically, they, like El Greco and the masters of religious painting, were attempting to portray their vision of God at work in the lives of men and women.

Questions for Pupils on the Next Lesson. 1. Why did the Babylonian king want to train four Jewish youths in Babylonian letters and skills? 2. How did Daniel manage to remain loyal to his faith and to the king? 3. What problems did Daniel encounter? 4. What part did discipline play in Daniel's actions?

TOPIC FOR YOUTH
LIVING IN GOD'S PRESENCE

Bigger Than All. In *Starling of the White House,* we read how Woodrow Wilson, the champion of the League of Nations, following his campaign in 1916 for a second term of office, was on the presidential yacht, the *Mayflower,* waiting the returns from the various states. While these were being received, Mr. Wilson finally went to sleep.

Later on that night Mr. Starling, who had been on the White House staff for many years, learned that Mr. Wilson had been re-elected. His comments are significant. "The boss had been re-elected and was in for a rough time. However unimportant, I was a member of the team. Suddenly I realised that I was a Wilson man; that I believed in the things for which he stood; that I would follow him wherever he led. Standing in the galley of the *Mayflower* in the darkness before the dawn of that November morning, I realised that the man on the boat stood for something bigger than myself, bigger than himself, bigger than America; he stood for the hope of the world."

Whether or not Woodrow Wilson merited such glowing epithets, it is certainly in that spirit that Christians ought to relate themselves to Jesus Christ, to someone bigger than themselves; someone bigger than any branch of the Church; bigger than the world itself—King of kings and Lord of lords, the champion of the family of nations, the hope of the world.

Typesetter's Error Inspired Mistake. A visitor to a city in the Northwest bought a newspaper on Saturday to look at the church announcements for the following day. He noticed one in particular. The typesetter obviously had transposed the line giving the church's location so that the morning sermon's topic read as follows: "11 A.M. 'I BELIEVE IN THE HOLY CATHOLIC CHURCH' AT SIXTH AVENUE AND ARGYLE STREET."

Some say this was an inspired error, because the Church as God's people is meant to live in His presence at the corner of Sixth and Argyle. We are intended to be aware of the Lord's nearness in our cities and towns, on the street corners and busy intersections. God's glory is not confined only to the distant heavens. We are given a vision of His glory in down-to-earth ways and in here-and-now locations.

Reminders Needed. Next year, the Lord Mayor of Oxford, England, will arrive with his city councillors in a gown and wig. He and his councillors will form a solemn procession outside New College. As Lord Mayors and councillors of Oxford have done every three years since 1382, when New College was built, they will check to see if a pledge is being carried out. They will proceed through a serene cloistered courtyard of the ancient New College to the city wall. There, they will examine the wall to make sure that the college continues to maintain the wall in good order. It seems that when the college was organized in the 1300s by the Bishop of Winchester, the city authorities permitted it to build against the city wall as long as the college properly looked after the city wall. From that time until the current date, the college has kept its word and the city authorities have come every three years to make certain of it.

Worship is maintaining the wall, and checking to see if promises are being kept. We live in the Lord's presence, and we assure God that we will be true to our word to build for Him in our lives. Sunday church services, in a sense, are welcoming the Lord for an official inspection of our lives.

Questions for Pupils on the Next Lesson. 1. What did the Babylonian king have in mind when he chose Daniel and his friends to stay in the royal court? 2. Why did Daniel find it difficult to carry out the king's orders? 3. How did Daniel resolve the conflict? 4. When was the last time you had to stand up for what you believed was right? 5. What place did discipline have in Daniel's life?

GOD HONORS FAITHFUL OBEDIENCE

Background Scripture: Daniel 1
Devotional Reading: Daniel 5:1–8

KING JAMES VERSION

DANIEL 1 3 And the king spake unto Ashpenaz the master of his eunuchs, that he should bring *certain* of the children of Israel, and of the king's seed, and of the princes;

4 Children in whom *was* no blemish, but well-favored, and skilful in all wisdom, and cunning in knowledge, and understanding science, and such as *had* ability in them to stand in the king's palace, and whom they might teach the learning and the tongue of the Chaldeans.

5 And the king appointed them a daily provision of the king's meat, and of the wine which he drank: so nourishing them three years, that at the end thereof they might stand before the king.

8 But Daniel purposed in his heart that he would not defile himself with the portion of the king's meat, nor with the wine which he drank: therefore he requested of the prince of the eunuchs that he might not defile himself.

9 Now God had brought Daniel into favour and tender love with the prince of the eunuchs.

10 And the prince of the eunuchs said unto Daniel, I fear my lord the king, who hath appointed your meat and your drink: for why should he see your faces worse liking than the children which *are* of your sort? then shall ye make *me* endanger my head to the king.

11 Then said Daniel to Melzar whom the prince of the eunuchs had set over Daniel, Hananiah, Mishael, and Azariah,

12 Prove thy servants, I beseech thee, ten days; and let them give us pulse to eat, and water to drink.

15 And at the end of ten days their countenances appeared fairer and fatter in flesh than all the children which did eat the portion of the king's meat.

16 Thus Melzar took away the portion of their meat, and the wine that they should drink; and gave them pulse.

17 As for these four children, God gave them knowledge and skill in all learning and wisdom: and Daniel had understanding in all visions and dreams.

REVISED STANDARD VERSION

DANIEL 1 3 Then the king commanded Ashpenaz, his chief eunuch, to bring some of the people of Israel, both of the royal family and of the nobility, 4 youths without blemish, handsome and skilfull in all wisdom, endowed with knowledge, understanding learning, and competent to serve in the king's palace, and to teach them the letters and language of the Chaldeans. 5 The king assigned them a daily portion of the rich food which the king ate, and of the wine which he drank. They were to be educated for three years, and at the end of that time they were to stand before the king.

8 But Daniel resolved that he would not defile himself with the king's rich food, or with the wine which he drank; therefore he asked the chief of the eunuchs to allow him not to defile himself. 9 And God gave Daniel favor and compassion in the sight of the chief of the eunuchs; 10 and the chief of the eunuchs said to Daniel, "I fear lest my lord the king, who appointed your food and your drink, should see that you were in poorer condition than the youths who are of your own age. So you would endanger my head with the king," 11 Then Daniel said to the steward whom the chief of the eunuchs had appointed over Daniel, Hananiah, Mishael, and Azariah; 12 "Test your servants for ten days; let us be given vegetables to eat and water to drink.

15 At the end of ten days it was seen that they were better in appearance and fatter in flesh than all the youths who ate the king's rich food. 16 So the steward took away their rich food and the wine they were to drink, and gave them vegetables.

17 As for these four youths, God gave learning and skill in all letters and wisdom; and Daniel had understanding in all visions and dreams.

KEY VERSE: *As for these four youths, God gave them learning and skill in all letters and wisdom.* Daniel 1:17.

HOME DAILY BIBLE READINGS

Aug. 11. M. *Faithfulness in Service.* 2 Timothy 4:1–8.
Aug. 12. T. *Endure All Things.* 2 Timothy 2:3–10.

BACKGROUND

Some Bible readers have had the mistaken notion that the Book of Daniel is mostly forecasts of dire events about to happen in our generation. These readers wrongly think prophecies are predictions. Therefore, Daniel has been elevated to major status by some Christians. In the Hebrew canon, however, Daniel is not even listed among the prophets. In fact, this book is placed among the Writings, following Esther and before Ezra, as one of the great books of stories of God's people. This indicates that the inspired people who put together the Old Testament clearly regarded the Book of Daniel not as prophecy but as a different form of literature. When we study this important book, we must keep this insight in mind.

The Book of Daniel contains six stories and four dream-visions. These stories and dream-visions are part of a type of writing called *Apocalyptic,* meaning an unveiling or revealing. Daniel and other apocalyptic writers used signs and symbols to interpret current history. These signs and symbols may seem strange to us, but were well understood by the readers in Daniel's time.

The author was a pious Jew living during the severe persecution by Antiochus Epiphanes, around 167 to 164 B.C. This was another terrible era for the Jewish people. Following Alexander the Great's death, his huge empire had been sliced up by various generals into smaller empires. Antiochus Epiphanes, the Syrian dictator of one of these mini-empires, treated the Jews oppressively. The author used the story of a faithful man of God named Daniel from an earlier era, the Babylonian exile, to sustain the faith of persecuted Jews in Antiochus Epiphanes's time. He saw the parallels between the temptations of Daniel and his companions four hundred years earlier and the temptations of God's people during the persecutions of the Syrian hosts.

Daniel and his friends were tempted to desert the Law and forsake their faith, but they stood fast. Finally, their persecutors were forced to acknowledge the power of the true God. God's people in any age may be forced to endure terrible personal and national trials and sorrows. But the Lord is sovereign. He ultimately cuts down the most oppressive dictators.

NOTES ON THE PRINTED TEXT

Daniel was a blueblood and an outstanding youth of Judah in the time of King Jehoiakim. When Judah collapsed under the Babylonian siege, the Babylonian king Nebuchadnezzar sought the most competent Jewish youths to train for his service. *The king commanded Ashpenaz ... to bring ... youth without blemish, handsome and skillful in all wisdom, endowed with knowledge, understanding learning, and competent to serve in the king's palace.* Nebuchadnezzar wanted the cream of the crop. He wanted the youth who were without physical defects, and who were good looking and intelligent. They were to be trained for the corps of court pages in the king's palace.

Ashpenaz, the *chief eunuch,* was *to teach them the letters and language of the Chaldeans.* Daniel and his fellow Judeans were to be indoctrinated in the language, customs, culture, and religion of the Babylonians. Their instruction was to last for the customary three years. Then they would be part of the civil service that stood *before the king.* During the training, they were to eat *a daily portion of the rich food which the king ate, and of the wine he drank.*

However, Daniel was determined to be loyal to his faith and sought a way to do this. *Daniel resolved that he would not defile himself* by eating the king's food. Eating food associated with idol worship or prepared in an incorrect manner or not allowed by Jewish Law would make him unclean. Ashpenaz was sympathetic to these scruples which he listened to in *favor* and *compassion*. Yet, he was also afraid for his life. He did not wish to endanger his head with the king. The eunuch was afraid that Daniel and his companions would be in poorer condition than the others if they did not eat as the king ordered. *I fear lest my lord the king . . . should see that you were in poorer condition than the youths who are of your own age.* Daniel suggested to the steward that a test be taken. *Test your servants for ten days; let us be given vegetables to eat and water to drink.*

Daniel's loyalty and observance of the rigid dietary laws and restrictions paid off. *At the end of ten days it was seen that they were better in appearance and fatter in flesh than all the youths who ate the king's rich food.* In spite of the poor fare, God honored their loyalty by making Daniel and his friends fitter than the other youths. So the steward allowed Daniel and his friends to serve their dietary regulations. They were not forced to eat the rich food and wine of the king. As a further reward for their faithful obedience, God *gave them learning and skill in all letters and wisdom.* They were given intellectual gifts as well as physical gifts. In addition, Daniel was given a special gift, an understanding of visions and dreams.

SUGGESTIONS TO TEACHERS

One stockbroker describes his life in his office "like existing in a snakepit." A woman calls her Monday-through-Friday week as a sales representative "a survival march." Many in your class, living in a competitive, secularized world, know the pressures and penalties on people trying to be faithful to God in the world. Obedience exacts a price.

Your lesson for this week addresses this subject. The first chapter of Daniel provides marvelous material for you to put together a good session on God honors those who trust and obey Him.

A good way to get the lesson off the ground would be to ask the people in the class to comment briefly on where it is hardest to be a Christian. You will quickly discover that many in your group know that it is truly difficult to live out their faith in the rough, tough world. Gossip, dirty tactics, dubious ethical practices, harassment, and other destructive occurrences are everyday fare for many. Some in your class, you will quickly observe, show real courage!

But the purpose of the lesson is not only to bring out the subtle persecution and hardships experienced by those in your class. It is primarily to help them to live faithfully and obediently as Christ's persons. Using Daniel, develop some of these ideas in your lesson.

1. *REMEMBERED.* Bring out the interesting details of the ways Daniel and his companions were pushed to forsake their faith and take on Babylonian ways. They had to dress, live, and think like Babylonians. They even were forced to take on Babylonian names. This subtle brainwashing was intended to have them forget their faith. But they remembered God! The pagan culture around us tries to make us over into its own likeness. Society exerts pressures to make us conform to the tastes, the goals, the values of the pagan world of power, wealth, and success. Behind these efforts is the intention of having us worship at other shrines. Tell your people to remember God! By daily devotions, disciplined living, and weekly worship.

2. *RECALLED.* Daniel recalled his heritage. He would not permit himself to let go of his Jewishness. It would have been easy and it would have been prudent

to have dropped his heritage. But he knew his identity rested on being God's person and part of God's community. Do your class members realize that their identity depends on their Christian heritage? Does the tradition of being part of Christ's community inform them about who they are and how they are to act?

3. *RESOLVED.* Daniel "resolved that he would not defile himself" (Daniel 1:8). He steeled himself to remain faithful. Even his diet reflected that resolve! Being God's person in the face of opposition calls for discipline. Be sure to get this point across in your class. Ask for examples of disciplined living from members of the class. Perhaps they may wish to draw up a discipline for themselves to be used on an experimental basis for a week, including such basics as times for prayer, study, rest, service to others, work, and family fun, and simplified lifestyle.

4. *RENEWED.* God gave Daniel and his friends learning and skill. God always stands by those who honor Him with lives of faithful obedience. Remind your class that God has made this promise through Jesus Christ.

TOPIC FOR ADULTS
DANIEL: A MAN OF COURAGEOUS CONVICTIONS

The Courage to Refuse to Go Along. Like Daniel, a man of courageous convictions, Paul Mulvey showed the courage of his convictions one night. Paul Mulvey is a professional hockey player. He is one of the best. He stands 6 feet 4 inches and weighs 230 pounds. By 1982 he was in his fourth season in the National Hockey League. Mulvey had moved from Washington to Pittsburgh to Los Angeles and had won a reputation as one who spent lots of time in the penalty box. But one night in January, 1982, in Vancouver, when the Los Angeles Kings were playing the Canucks, Paul Mulvey had the courage to take a stand. It happened when a fight broke out between two players on the ice. The Kings' coach, Don Perry, ordered Mulvey to get off the bench and join the battle. "And don't dance," shouted the coach. Mulvey knew what he meant, because dancing is when two players grab each other by their jerseys and slide around on the ice without hurting each other. Mulvey understood that he was to rush out and clobber others. The coach wanted him to be a goon. But Paul Mulvey said *no.* He had had enough of senseless violence on the rinks. And Paul Mulvey decided that was the night he would take a stand. It cost. Perry, the coach, was furious and dropped Mulvey from the team. Mulvey's protest won him support from many fans, coaches, writers, and players. But the National Hockey League's investigation merely resulted in a wrist-tapping six-game suspension for Perry. Paul Mulvey never has made it back to major league hockey after his demotion. But he knows his decision not to hit another that January night in Vancouver was right. It took courage. But many say that Mulvey's stand against senseless violence, hockey's biggest curse, has done more than anything to reshape the tainted sport.

Courage to Fail. "The fear of not succeeding is, for many people, the biggest obstacle in their way. It holds them back from trying anything at all. And for lack of trying, they never give themselves a chance of succeeding—the very thing that would cure them of their doubts. It is not, after all, such a terrible thing not to succeed straight away in some new undertaking. What is serious is to give up, to become stuck in a life that just gets emptier."—Paul Tournier, *Reflections: A Personal Guide for Life's Most Crucial Questions,* Philadelphia: Westminster Press, 1982.

Act of Bravery. Yale's William Lyon Phelps often recounted an episode which took place one day during World War I. "The trenches were filled on one side with Germans, and on the other side with Americans. The fire exchange intensified . . . separating them a very narrow no man's land. A young German soldier attempting to cross that no man's land has been shot, and has become entangled in the barbed wire. He cries out in great anguish, in pain; and he whimpers periodically.

"Between the shells all the Americans could hear him scream. When one American soldier could stand it no longer, he crawled out of the American trenches, and on his stomach crawled to that German soldier. When the Americans realized what he was doing, they stopped firing; the Germans continued. A German officer realized what he was doing, and he stopped his men from firing. Now there was a weird silence across no man's land. On his stomach, the American made his way to the German soldier, disentangled him. He then stood up with the German in his arms, walked straight to the German trenches and placed him in the waiting arms of his comrades. Doing so, he turned and started back to the American trenches.

"Suddenly there was a hand on his shoulder that spun him around. There stood a German officer who had won the Iron Cross, the highest German honor for bravery.

"He jerked it from his own uniform and placed it on the American, who walked back to the American trenches. When he was safely in the trenches, they resumed the insanity of war."

Questions for Pupils on the Next Lesson. 1. Why did the king Nebuchadnezzar order a huge golden image to be made? 2. Do you sometimes struggle to put together a value system? 3. When is it most difficult for you to remain loyal to the social, moral, and spiritual obligations of your faith? 4. When were some of the trying times in which God has helped you? 5. What are some examples of others which have inspired you to make right choices?

TOPIC FOR YOUTH
STAYING TRUE

Let's Dance. "A taxicab driver told this story to a friend of mine. One summer in a boys' camp where the cab driver serves as counselor, there was an eight-year-old by the name of Jim. He was small for his age and backward. He could not keep up with the other fellows on most games and sports. He could not tie knots as well, could not swim as far, could not row as fast. The others often teased him for being so little and so slow.

"Jim was not like most boys. When he was teased he did not get mad and fight. Instead he just chuckled with the rest, shrugged it off, and kept on trying to do better all the time.

"One day an interesting thing happened. A larger boy by the name of Pete—a kind of bully—came up to Jim and began razzing him about something. The eight-year-old just grinned and smiled back. That made the older fellow mad. He clenched his fists and got all ready to fight.

"What do you suppose Jim did then? He threw out his arms, grabbed the older boy's fists, and held on tightly. "So you want to dance," he said. "All right, let's dance." And with that he began dancing and jumping around, dragging Pete with him. It was all so funny to the other boys standing about that they burst out laughing. Finally even Pete had to grin and laugh at himself. Then it was all over.

"The campers had thought Jim was not very bright. Now they began to see that in getting along with others he was smarter than most of them.

"The biggest job for us in today's world is learning how to live with other people without getting mad and getting into fights. It is too bad that not all of us are as wise as Jim. If only nations were as bright as he! For Jim had learned the meaning of the verse: 'Do not be overcome by evil, but overcome evil with good.' "—Harold L. Lunger, *The Pulpit*, September, 1952 Copyright 1952 Christian Century Foundation.

Discipline of Staying True. Any opera buff knows that the singers must follow the director. Sometimes, a singer decides he will try to take over and run the show. The critic B. H. Haggin recalls a rehearsal where performer Leonard Warren once stepped forward and informed the great conductor Dimitri Mitropoulos that he had his own ideas about how to sing his aria and would expect Mitropoulos to conduct in accordance with his singing. Rudolf Bing, who ran the Metropolitan Opera, calmly stepped up and took out his watch. Turning to the baritone Warren, Bing announced he would give him three minutes to decide whether he would sing as Mitropoulos conducted the Verdi piece or not sing at all. Warren sang as Mitropoulos conducted the aria.

God honors faithful obedience. Sometimes, like obstreperous opera singers, we decide we know more than the Lord and we try to instruct Him on how to conduct the world. When we stay true to the Lord, however, we let Him direct. We follow. When we are obedient to His wishes, we perform to our fullest!

Act of Special Grace and Courtesy. Jesse Owens won four Olympic Gold Medals in track and field events in the 1936 Olympics in Berlin. Later, he told that he could never have done so without what he said was "an act of special grace and special courtesy" by a German athlete named Luz Long. Long encouraged Owens in the qualifying heats for the running broad jump when Owens had jumped short on his first try and fouled on his second. Jesse Owens took Luz's suggestion of making a mark well behind the takeoff point, qualified, and later in the finals, broke the Olympic record. His winning jump put Luz in second place. Hitler was furious. Determined to use the Berlin Games as an opportunity to prove his notion of the Aryan "master race," the Fuhrer refused to greet Jesse Owens or any other black winners. Luz Long, however, walked back down the runway and directly in front of Hitler's box put his arms around Owens! Hitler was outraged at Long, but Long stayed true to his principles and the traditions of great sportsmanship.

Questions for Pupils on the Next Lesson. 1. Why did Nebuchadnezzar want to be worshiped? 2. Why did Daniel refuse to follow the king's wishes? 3. How did the story of Daniel and Nebuchadnezzar finally turn out? 4. When do you feel the most severe pressure to deny your beliefs and values? 5. What helps you most to put together your system of beliefs and values?

LESSON XIII—AUGUST 24

GOD'S PRESENCE WITH THE FAITHFUL

Background Scripture: Daniel 3
Devotional Reading: Daniel 6:10–18

KING JAMES VERSION

DANIEL 3 14 Nebuchadnezzar spake and said unto them, *Is it* true, O Shadrach, Meshach, and Abednego? do not ye serve my gods, nor worship the golden image which I have set up?

15 Now if ye be ready that at what time ye hear the sound of the cornet, flute, harp, sackbut, psaltery, and dulcimer, and all kinds of music, ye fall down and worship the image which I have made; *well:* but if ye worship not, ye shall be cast the same hour into the midst of a burning fiery furnace; and who *is* that God that shall deliver you out of my hands?

16 Shadrach, Meshach, and Abednego, answered and said to the king, O Nebuchadnezzar, we *are* not careful to answer thee in this matter.

17 If it be *so*, our God whom we serve is able to deliver us from the burning fiery furnace, and he will deliver *us* out of thine hand, O king.

18 But if not, be it known unto thee, O king, that we will not serve thy gods, nor worship the golden image which thou hast set up.

23 And these three men, Shadrach, Meshach, and Abednego, fell down bound into the midst of the burning fiery furnace.

24 Then Nebuchadnezzar the king was astonished, and rose up in haste, *and* spake, and said unto his counselors, Did we not cast three men bound into the midst of the fire? They answered and said unto the king, True, O king.

25 He answered and said, Lo, I see four men loose, walking in the midst of the fire, and they have no hurt; and the form of the fourth is like the Son of God.

26 Then Nebuchadnezzar came near to the mouth of the burning fiery furnace, *and* spake, and said, Shadrach, Meshach, and Abednego, ye servants of the most high God, come forth, and come *hither*. Then Shadrach, Meshach, and Abednego, came forth of the midst of the fire.

REVISED STANDARD VERSION

DANIEL 3 14 Nebuchadnezzar said to them, "Is it true, O Shadrach, Meshach, and Abednego, that you do not serve my gods or worship the golden image which I have set up?

15 Now if you are ready when you hear the sound of the horn, pipe, lyre, trigon, harp, bagpipe, and every kind of music, to fall down and worship the image which I have made, well and good; but if you do not worship, you shall immediately be cast into a burning fiery furnace; and who is the god that will deliver you out of my hands?"

16 Shadrach, Meshach, and Abednego answered the king, "O Nebuchadnezzar, we have no need to answer you in this matter. 17 If it be so, our God whom we serve is able to deliver us from the burning fiery furance; and he will deliver us out of your hand, O king. 18 But if not, be it known to you, O king, that we will not serve your gods or worship the golden image which you have set up." 23 And these three men, Shadrach, Meshach, and Abednego, fell bound into the burning fiery furnace.

24 Then King Nebuchadinezzar was astonished and rose up in haste. He said to his counselors, "Did we not cast three men bound into the fire?" They answered the king, "True, O king." 25 He answered, "But I see four men loose, walking in the midst of the fire, and they are not hurt; and the appearance of the fourth is like a son of the gods."

26 Then Nebuchadnezzar came near to the door of the burning fiery furnace and said, "Shadrach, Meshach, and Abednego, servants of the Most High God, come forth, and come here!" Then Shadrach, Meshach, and Abednego came out from the fire.

KEY VERSE: Nebuchadnezzar said, "Blessed be the God of Shadrach, Meshach, and Abednego, who has sent his angel and delivered his servants, who trusted in him . . . and yielded up their bodies rather than serve and worship any god except their own God." Daniel 3:28

HOME DAILY BIBLE READINGS

Aug. 18. M. *He Is the Living God.* Daniel 6:25–28.
Aug. 19. T. *A Vision of God's Glory.* Acts 7:54–56.
Aug. 20. W. *The Lord Will Provide.* 1 Samuel 17:32–37.
Aug. 21. T. *The Lord Sent an Angel.* 2 Chronicles 32:20–23.
Aug. 22. F. *The Lord Is Thy Keeper.* Psalms 121:1–8.

Aug. 23. S. *The Secret Place*. Psalms 91:1–11.
Aug. 24. S. *Our Help in His Name*. Psalms 124:1–8.

BACKGROUND

The writer of the Book of Daniel wanted to help his hearers to stay faithful to the Lord in a period of harsh persecution. He chose Daniel as an example of a person who had remained true to God during a time of terrible testing for the Jews when Nebuchadnezzar, king of Babylon, tried to quash true worship.

Who was Daniel? His name means "God has judged" and this hero of the faith lived in a time when God judged the nation of Judah. The Babylonians conquered Daniel's nation, demolished Jerusalem, desecrated the Temple, and drove off the cream of the population, including Daniel and his companions, to exile. Daniel and his three friends were young men when they were forced to leave their homeland. Uprooted from their families, separated from the site of their religious roots, and subjected to the pressures of the most powerful ruler of those times, we would expect Daniel, Shadrach, Meshach, and Abednego, his companions, to be traumatized. Instead, this quartet of young Jewish men maintained an unwavering trust in God!

The four attracted the eye of King Nebuchadnezzar. They were picked out for special training. In spite of every pressure, they resisted all attempts to turn them away from God. They were deported Jews but they quickly distinguished themselves in the royal court.

Daniel, Shadrach, Meshach, and Abednego also stirred up the envy and dislike of other court officials. These officials grew enraged at seeing the king give honors to a group of foreign young men, and plotted to discredit Daniel's friends. The plot was cunningly simple: get the vain Nebuchadnezzar to agree to have a huge golden statue of himself and have a law passed compelling every person to bow down in worship before the image at stated times. Nebuchadnezzar agreed to the idea, and even approved the death penalty clause for anyone caught disobeying the law.

The trick worked. Shadrach, Meshach, and Abednego refused to forsake the faith of their parents by bowing before the idol. They were seized. In compliance with the royal decree, the three were hurled into a blazing furnace. While the distraught king watched, the three faithful young men were joined by a fourth, a divine being. The king knew that Shadrach's, Meshach's, and Abednego's God was among them and was powerful enough to save them.

You can imagine how this story of God's presence with this trio of faithful young men cheered those centuries later who were going through the fiery experience of persecution under Antiochus Epiphanes IV. Men and women by the thousands since that time have been inspired to remember that God is able!

NOTES ON THE PRINTED TEXT

Daniel and his friends did not live happily-ever-after following the food incident in last week's lesson. Immediately, the faith of three of Daniel's friends is under fire. King Nebuchadnezzar erects a huge ninety-foot image of gold. Messengers are dispatched summoning all court officials to a dedication festival. The customary music will be played prior to the real purpose of the ceremony which is to institute worship of and to this idol. The penalty for failing to worship the statue is exceptional and unusual—burning in a furnace. A huge furnace similar to a modern limekiln with a perpendicular shaft from the top and an opening at the bottom for the extracting of the fused lime is described.

However, Daniel's friends Shadrach, Meshach, and Abednego refuse to worship the idol. Certain jealous Chaldeans notice this and take advantage of the situation by pressing charges against them. The Chaldeans are jealous of the important positions the Jewish foreigners have received from the king and accuse these three of being disloyal traitors. The three are brought before a furious Nebuchadnezzar who has taken their refusal as a personal affront. He demands, *Is it true . . . that you do not serve my gods or worship the golden image?* Surprisingly, he gives the three a second chance to worship the idol. The three, however, stubbornly refuse to bow down before the golden image of the king's. The three boldly assert that *our God whom we serve is able to deliver us from the burning fiery furnace; and he will deliver us out of your hand.* They are confident that God will save them. Yet, at the same time, they recognize that He may for some good reason choose not to deliver them. So, they affirm, *Be it known . . . O king, that we will not serve your gods or worship the golden image.* Daniel's friends maintain their loyalty even in the face of death. They know that compromise could save their lives, but they choose death rather than compromise. They will be faithful to death and enjoy the reward of the faithful, or they will visibly see their faith justified in a miracle.

The furnace is heated (so hot, in fact, that it kills those assigned to the execution), and the three are cast into the fiery furnace. However, Nebuchadnezzar is shocked. In great excitement and alarm he says to his counselors, *I see four men loose, walking in the midst of the fire, and they are not hurt, and the appearance of the fourth is like a son of the gods.* The plain meaning of the author is that God is concerned about human needs and saves persons in their trying hours.

Nebuchadnezzar approaches the furnace door and calls the *servants of the Most High God* to come out. The astonished king recognizes the power of God in preserving the lives of the three Hebrew youths. Then he proclaims their religion to be acceptable within his kingdom, and he promotes them.

SUGGESTIONS TO TEACHERS

The story of Shadrach, Meshach, and Abednego is so powerfully compelling that you don't have to worry about generating discussion in this lesson! Let the story speak for itself.

The people in your class will discover that the Lord gives many lessons through this ancient, yet ever-new tale of three young men steadfastly trusting God. Here are a few ideas to get your class started.

1. *THE FOOLISHNESS OF THE FAITHLESS.* Point out the contrast between those trusting in the power of the Lord and those trusting in the power of a human. Those scorning God succumb to vanity. They imagine they are bigger than all others, even God! They worship themselves and want others to do the same. There are still plenty of Nebuchadnezzars strutting about. In fact, there is a streak of the Babylonian monarch within each of us! How silly to delude one's self and others by pretending to be so great and mighty! God is not mocked. He remains sovereign. All the Nebuchadnezzars of history have tumbled and fallen. The Lord remains!

2. *THE FANATICISM OF THE FAITHLESS.* When a person gets the mistaken notion about himself in relation to the Lord, he can quickly become destructive. Court officials, jealous of Shadrach, Meshach, and Abednego, allowed their envy to fester until they hatched a murderous plot. People sometimes seem surprised at the power and the prevalence of evil in the world. Christians who read their Bibles are not. They know the stories of malicious attempts to thwart God and those faithful to Him.

3. *THE FIRMNESS OF THE FAITHFUL.* Make certain that your class delves into the meaning of Daniel 3:17, 18, ". . . our God whom we serve is able to deliver us from the fiery furnace; and he will deliver us out of your hand, O king.

But if not, be it known to you, O king, that we will not serve your gods or worship the golden image which you have set up." What faith! Live or die, win or lose, these persons of faith are confident of God's ultimate victory. Are your people conscious that God is able? That God may be trusted, in spite of everything? And that God must be served, regardless?

4. *THE FURY OF THE FAITHLESS.* Remind the class that believing in the Lord is not like buying exemption from trials, temptations, or tribulations. We will continue to live in a cruel world. We must continually face people implacably opposed to God and determined to quash all goodness.

5. *THE FOURTH IN THE FURNACE.* God's presence continues with the faithful! He stands with us in the fires! Encourage those in the class to relate times in their own faith journeys when they were conscious of God's nearness in the midst of times when all seemed hopeless.

TOPIC FOR ADULTS
GOD'S PRESENCE WITH THE FAITHFUL

Alone, Yet Not Alone. The Lord presents Himself to those who remain faithful to Him. He bestows strength and hope when all human power is gone. The story of Shadrach, Meshach, and Abednego in the furnace discovering the Companion in the flames with them has been experienced by many.

Leif Hovelsen, the Norwegian Christian, lived in Norway during the dreadful days of the Nazi occupation in World War II. He worked to help the Jews and to overthrow the oppressors in his country. In 1944, an old school friend who had become a Nazi collaborator betrayed him to the German army authorities. Hovelsen was seized, placed in solitary confinement for months, taken out and cruelly tortured numerous times, and returned to his lonely cell. Miraculously, Hovelsen survived. He attributed his endurance to the Lord's presence with him in his pain and loneliness. At the end of the war, one day, Hovelsen was visiting a prison camp holding quislings who had sided with the Nazis. Hovelsen suddenly came across his betrayer. Memories of the tortures brought on by this man came back to Hovelsen. Leif Hovelsen struggled with the rage surging within him toward this man. In a sense, the worst fiery furnace experience was encountering the one-time friend whose betrayal had caused Hovelsen such horrors. However, the Lord also stood by Hovelsen in that time. He forgave the former schoolmate who had turned him in, and stood persistently with this man until that one-time traitor became converted to Jesus Christ!

Parable of the Clock. Corrie ten Boom in her helpful little book *Don't Wrestle, Just Nestle*—that title alone says a lot about coping with life—gives us one beautiful solution to our problem. She tells the old Dutch parable about the clock that had a nervous breakdown. "A certain little clock had just been finished by the maker, who put it on a shelf in the storeroom. Two older clocks were busy ticking away the noisy seconds next to the young clock.

" 'Well,' said one of the clocks to the newcomer, 'So you have started out in life. I am sorry for you. If you'll just think ahead and see how many ticks it takes to tick through one year, you will never make it. It would have been better had the maker never wound you up and set your pendulum swinging.'

" 'Dear me,' said the new clock. 'I never thought about how many ticks I have to tick in a year.'

" 'Well, you'd better think about it,' the old clock said.

"So the new clock began to count up the ticks. 'Each second requires 2 ticks, which means 120 ticks per minute,' he calculated. 'That's 172,800 ticks per day; 1,209,600 ticks per week for 52 weeks, which makes a total of 62,899,200 ticks per year. Horrors!' The clock immediately had a nervous breakdown and stopped ticking.

"The clock on the other side, who had kept silent during the conversation, now spoke up. 'You silly thing! Why do you listen to such words? That old grandfather clock has been unhappy for years. Nobody will buy him, and he just sits around the shop gathering dust. Since he is so unhappy, he tries to make everyone else unhappy, too.'

" 'But,' the new clock gasped, 'he's right. I've got to tick almost sixty-three million ticks in a year. And they told me I might have to stay on the job for more than one hundred years. Do you know how many ticks that is? That's six billion, two hundred million ticks. I'll never make it!'

" 'How many ticks do you have to tick at a time?' the wise old clock asked.

" 'Why, only one, I guess,' the new clock answered.

" 'There, now. That's not so hard, is it? Try it along with me. Tick, tock, tick, tock. See how easy it is? Just one tick at a time.'

"A light of understanding formed on the face of the clock, and he said, 'I believe I can do it. Here I go.' He began ticking away again.

" 'One more thing,' the wise old clock said. 'Don't ever think about the next tick until you have your last tick ticked.'

"I understand that was seventy-five years ago, and the clock is still ticking perfectly, one tick at a time."—Corrie ten Boom, *Don't Wrestle, Just Nestle*, Old Tappan, N.J.: Fleming H. Revell Company, 1978.

The King Who Endures! The poet Percy Bysshe Shelley once wrote a sonnet called "Ozymandias." In the verses of this poem, the person telling the story recounts meeting a traveler from Egypt who describes finding a statue in the desert west of the Nile. The statue actually was in pieces. All that remained were the chunks of the two legs and a piece of what was the head. On the pedestal, the traveler read the proud inscription:

> My name is Ozymandias, the king of kings.
> Look on my works, O ye mighty, and despair!

In his conceit, this powerful ruler imagined that he was greater than all others. He had the audacity to think that all others would stand in awe of his strength, his wealth, his accomplishments. Today, all that can be found of Ozymandias and his empire are a couple of shattered pieces of a carving of his likeness, lying forgotten in the drifting dunes of the desolate western desert.

The Nebuchadnezzars and the Ozymandiases, and a host of other supposedly "great" kings, have come and gone. Most are forgotten. A few have left a few broken chunks of stones. None are revered. Only one King continues to reign. Only Jesus Christ is loved and obeyed. Jesus and only Jesus can be accorded the title, "King of kings." And Jesus Christ continues to be present with His faithful subjects.

Questions for Pupils on the Next Lesson. 1. What did Daniel's vision or dream of the two beasts symbolize? 2. What was the purpose of Daniel's visions? 3. Do you believe that God has any influence on future events? 4. Do you think that the evil times you face will last forever? 5. What does the Bible say is the ultimate destiny of history?

TOPIC FOR YOUTH
GOD'S PRESENCE, OUR STRENGTH

Picture of Peace. Several years ago, a contest was held in which the contestants were asked to draw pictures depicting peace. There were many entries. Various artists tried to portray peace in an assortment of ways. The winner, however, was a startling scene of a tiny bird, sitting on its nest which was resting on a thin branch out over a raging, thundering cataract. The turbulent waters and the terrifying whirlpool of the deadly falls would have destroyed the bird or her young in a moment, but the nesting bird serenely sat tending her newly-hatched chicks. In the midst of chaos and destruction, they realized peace!

In the face of the death and tumult which threaten us, we may have the peace of knowing that the Lord is present. He is our strength!

An Old Plymouth Named "Hopeless." Jeffrey Souders was found sleeping in a loosely-constructed cardboard enclosure on the backseat of his broken-down green Plymouth, in Allentown, Pennsylvania, during the sub-zero temperatures of January, 1984. He tried to keep warm from the heat of a small kerosene lamp as he huddled under some tattered coats. Souders, thirty years old, had used the old car to travel to junk yards to pick used tires and sell them to tire shops for re-treading. He made just enough to keep him going. Then the old Plymouth developed carburetor trouble and electrical system problems. With the car not running, Souders couldn't eke out a living scrounging tires. Stranded with no place to live, his car became his home. He nicknamed the old Plymouth, "Hopeless." After a newspaper article told of Souders' plight, a young Vietnam veteran who didn't know Souders decided to help. He towed "Hopeless" to a garage and personally repaired the car's carburetor and electrical system, and then helped Jeffrey Souders get a job.

Perhaps you feel life has closed in on you and you think you must huddle in an existence you label "Hopeless." You are not forgotten, however. The Lord, The Friend, comes and offers His presence, His power, and His help.

Only a Cobbler. William Carey, revered as the father of the modern missionary movement, started off as a shoe repairman in a small shop in England. Undaunted by his lack of formal education or the rebuffs of government and church authorities, he went to India in 1793. He lost all of his equipment in the Hugli River. He lost his wife and all of his children from the diseases in the subcontinent. After painstaking labor over many years to produce a Sanskrit dictionary, he lost the entire effort in a fire which destroyed the printing shop. Nevertheless, Carey produced more than 200,000 Bibles and tracts in over forty languages and dialects in India. His Christian witness stimulated the formation of missionary societies and boards in nearly every Protestant denomination. Fame came late in life. Even then, Carey humbly pointed to Jesus Christ, and said that Christ's presence and Christ's power were what sustained him. "I was only a cobbler," the great Christian insisted to the end of his life.

Questions for Pupils on the Next Lesson. 1. How do you understand the strange vision of Daniel in which he said he dreamed of a ram and a goat? 2. Why are we so curious about the future? 3. Do you think God influences the future or is the future in the hands of "fate"? 4. Do you feel that the forces of evil are unconquerable? 5. Where do you think human history is heading?

LESSON XIV—AUGUST 31

GOD'S RULE WILL COME

Background Scripture: Daniel 7; 8
Devotional Reading: Daniel 9:14–19

KING JAMES VERSION

DANIEL 8 In the third year of the reign of king Belshazzar a vision appeared unto me, *even unto* me Daniel, after that which appeared unto me at the first.

15 And it came to pass, when I, *even* I Daniel, had seen the vision, and sought for the meaning, then, behold, there stood before me as the appearance of a man.

16 And I heard a man's voice between *the banks of* Ulai, which called, and said, Gabriel, make this *man* to understand the vision.

17 So he came near where I stood: and when he came, I was afraid, and fell upon my face: but he said unto me, Understand, O son of man: for at the time of the end *shall be* the vision.

18 Now as he was speaking with me, I was in a deep sleep on my face toward the ground: but he touched me, and set me upright.

19 And he said, Behold, I will make thee know what shall be in the last end of the indignation: for at the time appointed the end *shall be.*

20 The ram which thou sawest having *two* horns *are* the kings of Media and Persia.

21 And the rough goat *is* the king of Grecia: and the great horn that *is* between his eyes *is* the first king.

22 Now that being broken, whereas four stood up for it, four kingdoms shall stand up out of the nation, but not in his power.

23 And in the latter time of their kingdom, when the transgressors are come to the full, a king of fierce countenance, and understanding dark sentences, shall stand up.

24 And his power shall be mighty, but not by his own power: and he shall destroy wonderfully, and shall prosper, and practise, and shall destroy the mighty and the holy people.

25 And through his policy also he shall cause craft to prosper in his hand; and he shall magnify *himself* in his heart, and by peace shall destroy many: he shall also stand up against the Prince of princes; but he shall be broken without hand.

26 And the vision of the evening and the morning which was told *is* true: wherefore shut thou up the vision; for it *shall be* for many days.

REVISED STANDARD VERSION

DANIEL 8 In the third year of the reign of King Belshazzar a vision appeared to me, Daniel, after that which appeared to me at the first.

15 When I, Daniel, had seen the vision, I sought to understand it; and behold, there stood before me one having the appearance of a man. 16 And I heard a man's voice between the banks of the Ulai, and it called, "Gabriel, make this man understand the vision." 17 So he came near where I stood; and when he came, I was frightened and fell upon my face. But he said to me, "Understand, O son of man, that the vision is for the time of the end."

18 As he was speaking to me, I fell into a deep sleep with my face to the ground; but he touched me and set me on my feet. 19 He said, "Behold, I will make known to you what shall be at the latter end of the indignation; for it pertains to the appointed time of the end. 20 As for the ram which you saw with the two horns, these are the kings of Media and Persia. 21 And the he-goat is the king of Greece; and the great horn between his eye is the first king. 22 As for the horn that was broken, in place of which four others arose, four kingdoms shall arise from his nation, but not with his power. 23 And at the latter end of their rule, when the transgressors have reached their full measure, a king of bold countenance, one who understands riddles, shall arise. 24 His power shall be great, and he shall cause fearful destruction, and shall succeed in what he does, and destroy mighty men and the people of the saints. 25 By his cunning he shall make deceit prosper under his hand, and in his own mind he shall magnify himself. Without warning he shall destroy many; and he shall even rise up against the Prince of princes; but, by no human hand, he shall be broken. 26 The vision of the evenings and the mornings which has been told is true; but seal up the vision, for it pertains to many days hence."

KEY VERSE: His dominion is an everlasting dominion, which shall not pass away, and his kingdom one that shall not be destroyed. Daniel 7:14.

HOME DAILY BIBLE READINGS

Aug.	25.	M.	*He Will Not Fail Thee.* Deuteronomy 31:1-8.
Aug.	26.	T.	*I Am Alpha and Omega.* Revelation 1:4-8.
Aug.	27.	W.	*The Way, the Truth, and the Life.* John 14:1-6.
Aug.	28.	T.	*We Shall Reign Upon the Earth.* Revelation 5:1-10.
Aug.	29.	F.	*God Shall Wipe Away All Tears.* Revelation 21:1-7.
Aug.	30.	S.	*None Can Stay His Hand.* Daniel 4:19-37.
Aug.	31.	S.	*Handwriting on the Wall.* Daniel 5:5-31.

BACKGROUND

Four beasts, including a lion with eagle's wings, a four-headed leopard, a ten-horned animal with iron teeth, and a bear with three ribs in its mouth, emerging from the sea? Human eyes sprouting from a beast's horns, and mouths speaking profound statements? Huge rams fighting, with enormous horns growing out of broken horns? Chapters 7 and 8 of Daniel at first glance will seem to be so weird that you may be inclined to set them aside and go on to something else.

We have already mentioned earlier in this series on Daniel that this book must be understood as an example of Apocalyptic writings (from the Greek word for drawing aside a curtain or veil) which were written to unveil the future in order to show that God always triumphs. Daniel and other apocalyptic writings were "underground" literature, in that they appeared in times when the Jews were suffering under a brutal oppressor. They were "tracts for the times" for the faithful. However, they were written with wording which would not mean anything to government authorities in case they fell into the wrong hands. After all, if the author of Daniel wrote openly that God would destroy the kingdom of Antiochus Epiphanes who held Palestine at that time, the writer would have been arrested and probably executed and the copies of his writings destroyed! Therefore, if secret police would come across a copy of Daniel, they would not find it made any sense and ignore it. It would not sound like any kind of revolutionary writing, and the people caught reading it and the one who had written it would be dismissed as strange but harmless cranks.

The symbolism in these chapters is often so obscure that it is hard to decipher. Remember, however, that the original readers found it made sense and gave them courage to remain faithful. Keep in mind that the main point in Daniel 7 and 8 is to herald God's ultimate victory. Although God's people may find themselves being crushed under the heel of a cruel oppressor, God remembers and destroys those who try to destroy Him.

NOTES ON THE PRINTED TEXT

In the third year of the reign of King Belshazzar, Daniel had a vision. Son of the mighty Nebuchadnezzar, Belshazzar was the last king of Babylon before it fell to the Persians under Cyrus about 550 B.C. Daniel had a dream of two beasts (a ram and a he-goat), each a symbol for a specific nation of his time.

Confused and unsure of the meaning of the vision, Daniel is helped to understand the meaning of the vision by the angel Gabriel. However, at Gabriel's approach, Daniel is terrified and falls down on his face. (It might also be a sign of respect.) Gabriel tries to reassure Daniel by telling him that *the vision is for the time of the end.* The time of the end implies God's judgment is coming imminently. Whether he fainted or fell *into a deep sleep,* Gabriel arouses Daniel and makes him stand up.

Gabriel explains that he is about to tell Daniel what is going to happen at the *end of the indignation.* Through these visions, God is showing Daniel the things that are to come. The indignation refers to the period of God's anger with Israel. The period of His wrath is nearing its end. God's rule is coming!

As for the ram which you saw with the two horns, these are the kings of Media and Persia. Gabriel's interpretation is succinct. *The he-goat* (which earlier in the chapter was enraged and struck the ram breaking its two horns) *is the king of Greece; and the great horn between his eyes is the first king.* Alexander the Great and the Greeks' decisive victory over Darius and the Medes is symbolized in the victory of the goat over the ram. *As for the horn that was broken, in place of which four other arose, four kingdoms shall arise from his nation, but not with his power.* With Alexander's death, four smaller, weaker successor kingdoms arose, symbolized by the four horns. Only the Seleucid and Ptolemaic kingdoms are important. However, the interest is in the little horn that grew from one of the four horns (*see* 8:8–14). Gabriel moves directly to the *latter end of their rule* when a bold king will arise.

Antiochus Epiphanes is symbolized. Antiochus IV, like his Seleucid predecessors, has continued the policy of uniting the divergent peoples under his jurisdiction through a common culture built upon the Greek language, manners, and customs. He has taken the title Epiphanes ("God manifest") since he views himself as the incarnation of Zeus. Arrogantly, he interferes with Jewish religious customs. The Hebrew God, if He is acknowledged at all, is identified with Zeus. On the altar in the Temple, animals are sacrificed. The meat being burned is the flesh of swine. Jewish worship, fasts, sacrifices, practices, and the Sabbath are forbidden. The sacred writings are to be burned. Those who refuse are to be killed.

Antiochus Epiphanes is described as insolent and skilled in intrigue, double talk, double dealing, and treachery. Gabriel describes a king of *bold countenance, one who understands riddles, cunning,* and who makes *deceit proper. His power* and the *fearful destruction* caused by his armies during their conquest is great. The massacre at Jerusalem perhaps is what Gabriel had in mind as he mentions the destruction of the *people of the saints.* (Antiochus tricked Jerusalem into opening its gates by claiming his mission was a peaceful one. His soldiers then committed unspeakable acts of butchery and rapine.)

In his own mind he shall magnify himself. In his arrogance, Antiochus has overreached himself. The very title he assumed, "God manifest," indicates his arrogance.

Gabriel explains to Daniel that although God has used Antiochus to punish Israel, there is a limit to His indignation. Antiochus has overstepped his bounds. He has gone beyond the limits of wickedness. He has risen up against the *Prince of princes,* God Himself. Now, God Himself will break Antiochus.

Gabriel affirms that the vision is true, but it concerns a time yet to come, *many days hence.* Daniel is to seal up the vision and await its future fulfillment. History is firmly under the control of God. At the proper time He will fulfill all things.

SUGGESTIONS TO TEACHERS

Almost as soon as you start a lesson from Daniel 7, 8 or any other piece of apocalyptic literature, you will find someone trying to find in these writings a description of events in the modern world. You are perhaps familiar with the ways some television preachers or popular authors select passages from apocalyptic writers to attempt to prove that what was predicted is now about to come to pass. You may feel some apprehension about the times we are living in, and may also have some curiosity about the future. Most people do. But the first thing to be remembered in today's lesson material is that Daniel 7, 8 is not a crystal ball forecast of 1986 or any modern day. Don't try to twist the symbolic words in these chapters to make them fit some scheme of some one today who insists that Daniel is predicting events involving Russia, the United States, or the Middle East this year or next or any time soon. Rather, listen with the ears of faith. Use the Notes on the Printed Text and other commentary to help you decode the difficult wording. Above all, remember for whom the book was originally intended and why it was written. Then allow the Spirit to speak through these words to you and your class.

1. *SYMBOLS OF HOPE.* Remember that these strange dreams and visions are meant to be glimpses of God's activity in the world. As such, they are ways of announcing that the Lord still orders all human history. Perhaps some in your class may feel that events are beyond God's power. Remind them that God continues to reign.

2. *SIGHTING OF THE SAVIOR.* Daniel 7:13, 14 is a preview of the Messiah-Deliverer. As Christians, we realize that Jesus has fulfilled all the aspirations of Daniel, and, indeed, all the prophets.

3. *SOVEREIGN OF HISTORY.* Who runs this world, kings or Christ? Those in the age of Antiochus Epiphanes's empire might have been inclined to have said that the emperors did. But the writer of Daniel knew better. God remains Sovereign! However, we who claim we agree frequently do not reflect this fact in our daily lives. We worry. We try to find security in our possessions. Or we place personal success ahead of everything. Affirming God's sovereignty means exhibiting it in our choices each day.

4. *SUFFERING WITH PURPOSE.* The author of Daniel realized that even suffering may have a purpose with God. Allow plenty of time to talk together as a class how Christians may handle setbacks, persecution, and problems, especially when they are undeserved. Point to the Cross. With the Risen Lord, even our personal crosses may have a redemptive purpose.

TOPIC FOR ADULTS
GOD'S RULE WILL COME

Secret Messages of Victory. Murdo Ewen Macdonald, the Scottish minister, was with British parachute troops during World War II. Macdonald's unit was overrun after heavy losses in a raid, and he and the survivors were captured. He was sent to a Prisoner of War Camp deep inside the Third Reich. Macdonald and the other P.O.W.s were cut off from news of the outside world until one of the prisoners finally managed to build a small radio from scraps. The radio, of course, was forbidden, but a few men listened in secret each night for the B.B.C. news while the others watched for Nazi guards. They who heard the news carefully whispered the reports to fellow prisoners in the barracks. The problem, however, was to get the reports of the war to Allied prisoners across the barbed wire fence in the next part of the camp. Those hapless men had no radio, and therefore knew nothing about the progress of the war. German propaganda constantly beamed at the prisoners tried to have everyone believe that the Allies were ready to surrender. Most of the men in the compound were dispirited. Macdonald and his buddies knew that they could not talk out loud across the fence with men in the adjoining compound for fear of being overheard by the English-speaking Nazi guards, who would suspect a clandestine radio and search until they found it. How could they encourage those in the next compound by telling them the reports on the secret radio that the Allies were moving? Then someone remembered that Macdonald who was raised in the Hebrides spoke Gaelic, and sometimes chatted in his mother-tongue with a Gaelic-speaking Scottish prisoner across the wire. The guards, unable to understand Gaelic, dismissed the two as chatting harmlessly in a primitive gibberish. Macdonald began regularly sidling up to the barbed wire and conversing in Gaelic with his fellow Scot across the fence. The guards snickered and ignored them. Macdonald passed on the latest B.B.C. reports on the war in Gaelic, and the friend later translated these into English to his fellow prisoners.

This is something of what the Book of Daniel is. It is a strange language, with peculiar terms which may not at first make sense to us. But it was a secret way to avoid detection. Like Macdonald relaying the good news of ultimate victory, the Book of Daniel passes on the report of God's final triumph which will inevitably come!

Why Work to Make Things Better? Shortly after World War II, I met an elderly Aunt of mine who lived in the North of England. She was a widow, subsisting on a meager pension and living in a tiny cottage in a rural village. On the wall hung two small framed citations, stating that her two sons, my cousins, had been killed in action serving with the Durham Light Infantry in World War I, the war to end all wars. World War II was over, but the severe rationing continued. Coal was in short supply, rationed, and expensive. Tea, meat, sugar, and most foods, all clothing were all rationed. It was a bleak day in November when I called on her. Reflecting on the hardship she continued to experience, she sighed finally and said in her thick north-country accent, "Why work to make things better when the world stays just the same?"

Do you also feel this way and ask that question?

God has given us His promise that there is purpose to life. His rule will finally come. Through Jesus Christ's life, death, and Resurrection, we may be confident that ultimately His will prevails!

Without Dazzling. "God's love is not arbitrary power dazzling us with feats of magic. It is the spirit in which He takes upon Himself the burden of our human life in its joy and sorrow, its peace and anguish, its living and dying. The Resurrection of Jesus Christ means that God has created a new order of life in which everyone may share. Our whole being, past, present, and future, has been brought into a new relationship to God in which there is forgiveness, with the assurance that we share in the victory over everything that threatens community with one another and with Him."—Daniel Day Williams, *Christian Century*, February 3, 1954.

Questions for Pupils on the Next Lesson. 1. According to Genesis, did God create everything or only some parts of creation? 2. What does Genesis mean when it says that we humans are created in the "image" of God? 3. What responsibilities did God give humankind, according to Genesis 1:1—2:3. 4. How are we intended to regard the created universe—as good or evil? 5. What does Genesis tell us about our responsibilities to our environment?

TOPIC FOR YOUTH
EVIL'S DEFEAT

Snake in the Cellar. A small boa constrictor that escaped from a Tulsa high-school classroom more than a dozen years ago was soon forgotten, but teachers now believe the snake, grown to eight feet long, is living happily in the basement. George Sands, a biology teacher at Nathan Hale High School, said that a custodian was searching for a plumbing leak in a dark, damp utility tunnel when she noticed something wrapped around a steam pipe—an eight-foot snakeskin. "When she realized what it was, she like to . . . well, she made a very fast exit out of there," Sands said. The skin was pliable, the teacher said, and he believes it is fairly fresh. Sands, a teacher at Hale for twenty-three years, recalled that a student's pet boa constrictor escaped from a cage in the late 1960s. "We never did find the snake. It was a small one at the time," Sands said. "Apparently, it went down the plumbing through the floor and into the tunnels." Although boa constrictors are tropical, Sands said the steamy tunnel network of the school basement would be fine for the snake. The boa could survive with very little food, preying on mice, rats, and occasional frogs that find their way into the tunnels, he said. Sands said a snake could be expected to live a long time in such a suitable environment. Boa constrictors can reach lengths up to fifteen feet.

Just as that Tulsa High School has a boa lurking in its cellar, so there is evil lurking in the depths of our society. It may not be noticed, but it grows. While the snake in the steam tunnels may be relatively harmless, the evil in our culture is destructive. It wraps its coils around us in many ways. It can also ruin a nation, if left unchecked. The only hope is in the power of God, who has shown us through the Bible that He puts down evil! Turn to the Lord and be saved!

Despairing Genius. Roger Bacon (1214–1294) might have been a genius, but he also despaired at times of any hope for the future. He saw only evil around him. He wrote, "Never was so much ignorance. . . . Far more sins reign in these days than in any past age . . . boundless corruption . . . lechery . . . gluttony. . . . Yet we have baptism and the revelation of Christ . . . which men cannot really believe in or revere, or they would not allow themselves to be so corrupted. . . . Therefore many wise men believe that Antichrist is at hand, and the end of the world."

Sadly, the great thinker could not fathom the Good News that God has defeated evil and brings ultimate victory. Bacon failed to appreciate the message of the Bible.

Has the hope of the Scriptures permeated your thinking so that you see eventual victory for God and the forces of good?

Clue to the Mystery. "Yet a Christian theology of history is not an arbitrary construct. It 'makes sense' out of life and history.

"That the final clue to the mystery of the divine power is found in the suffering love of a man on the Cross is not a proposition which follows logically from the observable facts of history. But there are no observable facts of history which cannot be interpreted in its light. When so interpreted the confusions and catastrophes of history may become the source of the renewal of life."—Reinhold Niebuhr, *Faith and History,* New York: Scribner, 1949.

Questions for Pupils on the Next Lesson. 1. Why did God create the universe and us? 2. What does the writer of Genesis mean by saying that you have been created in the "image" of God? 3. What do the opening chapters of Genesis say to us about conserving and protecting the earth's natural resources? 4. Why must we Christians be concerned about the effects of nuclear war, pollution, and exploitation of the environment? 5. Is God still involved and concerned with this world?